The Reformation in England

The Reformation in England

The English Schism and Henry VIII, 1509-1547

by

G. Constant

Translated by the Rev. R. E. Scantlebury

HARPER TORCHBOOKS ❦ *The Cathedral Library*
Harper & Row, Publishers, New York

THE REFORMATION IN ENGLAND

Printed in the United States of America.

This book was originally published in French under the title *La Reforme en Angleterre* by Perrin et Cie., Paris, 1929-30. The English language translation by the Rev. R. E. Scantlebury, incorporating slight alterations and a new Appendix, was published in 1934 by Sheed & Ward, London. It is here reprinted by arrangement.

First HARPER TORCHBOOK edition published 1966 by Harper & Row, Publishers, Incorporated, 49 East 33rd Street, New York, N.Y. 10016.

CONTENTS

TRANSLATOR'S NOTE X

I. PRELIMINARIES AND CAUSES OF THE SCHISM . I
The spirit of nationalism and the weakening of papal
authority—Wiclif's attacks upon the Church—Bitter
criticisms by the Humanists—Feelings of the English people
towards the clergy—The members and mind of Parliament
at the time of the breach (1527-36)—The king and his
decisive influence.

II. HENRY VIII'S DIVORCE AND THE BREACH WITH
ROME 35
Henry VIII's marriage with Catherine of Aragon—Origin
of the divorce—The two phases—Fatal ending: the Primate
of England's sentence.

III. THE ROYAL SUPREMACY AND CONSUMMATION OF
THE SCHISM 91
The king "the supreme head of the Church of England":
history and consequences of this title—The schism, prepared
by a whole series of laws and furthered by the king's safe
position at home and abroad, is completed by the taking of
the oath to the "supreme head of the Church of England"—
Royal absolutism.

IV. SUPPRESSION OF THE MONASTERIES . . . 140
Causes of the suppression of the English monasteries—
Visitation of the monasteries (1535-36)—Dissolution of the
lesser monasteries; the Pilgrimage of Grace (1536-37)—
Surrender of the greater monasteries—Results of the
abolition of the religious houses.

V. THE CHAMPIONS OF CATHOLIC UNITY . . 200
Bishop Fisher—Chancellor Sir Thomas More—Cardinal
Reginald Pole.

CHAPTER		PAGE
VI.	THE ADVANCED PARTY IN THE SCHISM . .	285

Thomas Cromwell, Earl of Essex, the king's vicar-general—Thomas Cranmer, Archbishop of Canterbury — Their friends—Their share in the Reformation.

| VII. | THE MODERATE PARTY IN THE SCHISM . . | 341 |

The Henricians: Gardiner, Bishop of Winchester; Stokesley, Bishop of London; Bonner, Bishop of Hereford; Tunstall, Bishop of Durham—How they influenced the movement.

| VIII. | THE CHURCH OF ENGLAND'S DOGMA UNDER HENRY VIII . . . . | 391 |

Errors of certain historians—Orthodoxy and *autos-da-fe*—Attempts to unite the Churches of England and Germany: Conferences at Wittenberg (1536) and London (1538)—The First Confession or the Ten Articles of 1536—The Second Confession, "The Godly and Pious Institution of a Christian Man" (1537); the Thirteen Articles of 1538; the Six Articles (1539) — The Third Confession, "The Necessary Erudition of a Christian Man" (1543).

APPENDIX I: BIBLIOGRAPHY

A.	GENERAL BIBLIOGRAPHY	439
B.	BIBLIOGRAPHY, CHAPTER II	441
C.	BIBLIOGRAPHY, CHAPTER IV.	447
D.	BIBLIOGRAPHY, CHAPTER V	449
	(a) Cardinal John Fisher	449
	(b) Sir Thomas More	451
	(c) Cardinal Reginald Pole	455
E.	BIBLIOGRAPHY, CHAPTER VI	457
	(a) Thomas Cromwell	457
	(b) Thomas Cranmer	458
F.	BIBLIOGRAPHY, CHAPTER VII	459
G.	BIBLIOGRAPHY, CHAPTER VIII	461

APPENDIX II

COULD CLEMENT VII ANNUL HENRY VIII'S MARRIAGE? .	469

APPENDIX III

THOMAS MORE AND PAPAL AUTHORITY . . .	482
CHRONOLOGICAL TABLE OF EVENTS IN THE RELIGIOUS HISTORY OF HENRY VIII'S REIGN . . .	485
ADDENDA	490
INDEX	493

ABBREVIATIONS

L. and P.—Letters and Papers, foreign and domestic, of the reign of Henry VIII preserved in the Public Record Office, the British Museum, and elsewhere in England, 1509–1547, London, 1862–1910. See Bibliography A, pp. 440 and 464, n. 10.

Eng. Hist. Review.—English Historical Review.

Sp. Cal.—Spanish Calendar. See Bibliography A, pp. 440 and 464, n. 11.

Ven. Cal.—Venetian Calendar. See Bibliography A, pp. 440 and 464, n. 11.

Ana. Boll.—Analecta Bollandiana.

Fr. MS.—French MS., Dupuy, in the Bibliothèque Nationale, in Paris.

Transactions.—Transactions of the Royal Historical Society.

Ency. Brit.—Encyclopaedia Britannica.

Bibl. Nat.—Bibliothèque Nationale, Paris.

WORKS FREQUENTLY REFERRED TO IN THIS BOOK

ALBÈRI, *Relazione degli ambasciatori veneti.* Florence, 1839 *sq.*

ASCOLI, G., *La Grande-Bretagne devant l'opinion française*, etc., Paris, 1927. See Bibliography A, n. 23.

BAILY, THOMAS, English version of the Latin Life of Fisher, 1655. See Bibliography D, p. 450.

BECCADELLI, LUDOVICO, *Vita del cardinale Reginaldo Polo*, ed. Morandi. See Bibliography D (*d*), p. 455.

BÉMONT, CHARLES, French translation of Nicholas Harpsfield's Latin Chronicle on the Divorce, *Le premier divorce de Henri VIII.* See Bibliography B, p. 443.

BIRON, DOM A., O.S.B., *Un prince anglais cardinal legat au XVIᵉ siècle, Reginald Pole.* Paris, 1922. See Bibliography D (*d*), p. 457.

BLUNT, J. H., *The Reformation of the Church of England.* See Bibliography A, n. 23.

BOURRILLY, V. L., or BOURRILLY, V. L. and DE VAISSIÈRE, P., *Ambassades en Angleterre de Jean du Bellay*, Paris, 1905. See Bibliography A, n. 11, and B, p. 442.

BRIDGETT, T. E., C.SS.R., *Life of Blessed John Fisher*, London, 1888. See Bibliography D (*a*), p. 450.

BRIDGETT, T. E., *Life of Sir Thomas More*, London, 1891. See Bibliography D (*b*), p. 455.

BURNET, GILBERT, *History of the Reformation*, London, 1697–1715, Pocock's ed., Oxford, 1865. See Bibliography A, p. 462, n. 1; B, p. 444.

CARDWELL, E., Lloyd's *Formularies of Faith*, Oxford, 1856. See Bibliography G, p. 461.

CAVENDISH, *Memoirs of the Life of Cardinal Wolsey*, 1557, Singer's ed., 1827. See Bibliography B, p. 446.

CHACON-OLDOIN, *Vitae et res gestae Romanorum Pontificum et S.R.E. cardinalium*, Rome, 1677. See Bibliography D (*a*), p. 451.

COLLIER, *An Ecclesiastical History of Great Britain*, London, 1708. See Bibliography A, p. 463, n. 3.

COX, editor of Cranmer's *Works*, *The Remains of Cranmer*. See Bibliography E (*b*), p. 458.

CRAPELET, *Lettres de Henri VIII à Anne Boleyn*, 1835. See chap. II, n. 51.

DIXON, *History of the Church of England*, London, 1878–1902. See Bibliography A, n. 7.

DODD, *Church History of England*, Brussels, 1737. See Bibliography A, p. 463, n. 4.

DUSCHESNE, ANDRÉ, *Histoire d'Angleterre, d'Écosse, d'Irlande*, 1614.

EHSES, MGR. S., *Römische Dokumente*. See Bibliography B, p. 442.

ELLIS, *Original Letters*, Parker Society edition.

FISHER, *Political History of England*, Vol. V.

FOXE, *Acts and Monuments*, Strasbourg, 1554. See Bibliography A, p. 463, n. 5.

FRIEDENSBURG, *Nuntiaturberichte aus Deutschland*. See Bibliography A, n. 11.

FRIEDMANN, PAUL, *Anne Boleyn*, 1884. See Bibliography B, p. 445.

FROUDE, J. A., *The Reign of Henry VIII*, London, 1849. See Bibliography A, pp. 441 and 468, n. 28.

FULLER, *Church History of Britain*, 1655–56. Brewer's ed., 1845. See Bibliography A, p. 463, n. 2.

GAIRDNER, J., *History of the English Church in the Sixteenth Century*. See Bibliography A, pp. 439 and 464, n. 8.

GAIRDNER, J., *Lollardy and the Reformation in England*. See Bibliography A, n. 8.

GAIRDNER, J., *The Reign of Henry VIII*, London, 1884. See Bibliography A, n. 29.

GASQUET, CARDINAL, *Henry VIII and the English Monasteries*, London, 1888. See Bibliography C, p. 447.

GEE AND HARDY, *Documents Illustrative of English Church History*, London, 1896. See Bibliography A, n. 13.

GERDES, *Historia Reformationis*.

GOLDAST, *Monarchia S. Rom. Imperii*.

HALLETT's trans., *The Life and Illustrious Martyrdom of Thomas More*, a translation from Stapleton's *Tres Thomae*, see "Stapleton" below and Bibliography D (*b*), pp. 453–54.

HARDWICK, CHARLES, *A History of the Articles of the Church of England*, Cambridge, 1859. See Bibliography G, p. 461.

HERBERT, LORD, *Life and Reign of Henry VIII*, London, 1649. See Bibliography A, pp. 441 and 468, n. 26.

JANELLE, M. P., *Obedience in Church and State*, Cambridge Univ. Press., 1930. See Bibliography F, pp. 460–61.

JENKYNS, H., *The Remains of Thomas Cranmer*, Oxford, 1843. See Bibliography E (*b*), p. 458.

KAULEK, *Correspondance politique de MM. de Castillon et Marillac*. See Bibliography A, n. 11.

LE GRAND, JOACHIM, *Histoire du divorce de Henri VIII et de Catherine d'Aragon*, Paris, 1688. See Bibliography B, pp. 442–45.

LE LABOUREUR, *Mémoires de Michel de Castelnau*, Brussels, 1731. See Bibliography D (*b*), p. 451.

LEWIS' trans., see "Sander" below.

LINGARD, JOHN, *History of England*, London, 1819–30. See Bibliography A, p. 439.

LUMBY, ed. of *Utopia*, Rawson Lumby's edition of *Utopia*, Cambridge, 1908. See p. 17, n. 65.

MAITLAND, S. R., *Essays on Subjects connected with the Reformation in England*, 1849. See Bibliography F, p. 460.

MAKOWER, F., *Verfassung der Kirche von England*, 1894; Engl. Trans., *Constitutional History of the Church of England*, London, 1895.

MENTZ, G. D., *Die Wittenberger Artikel von 1525*, Leipzic, 1905. See Bibliography G, p. 462.

MERRIMAN, *Life and Letters of Thomas Cromwell*, Oxford, 1902. See Bibliography E (*a*), p. 458.

MULLER, J. A., *Stephen Gardiner and the Tudor Reaction*, London, 1926. See Bibliography A, n. 23 and F, p. 460.

PALLAVICINI, *Istoria del concilio di Trento*, Rome 1656–57. See Bibliography D (*d*), p. 455.

POCOCK, NICHOLAS, *Records of the Reformation*, Oxford, 1870. See Bibliography B, p. 442.

POLLARD, A. F., *Henry VIII*, London 1902.   See Bibliography A, pp. 441 and 468, n. 30.

POLLARD, A. F., *Wolsey*, 1929. See Bibliography B, p. 446.

POWER, MISS EILEEN, *Medieval English Nunneries*, Cambridge, 1922. See Bibliography C, p. 448.

QUIRINI, A. M., *Epistolae Reginaldi Poli*, Brescia, 1744–58. See Bibliography D (*d*), p. 455.

REYNER, *Apostolatus Benedictorum in Anglia*, Douai, 1626. See Bibliography C, p. 448.

ROPER, WILLIAM, *Life of Sir Thomas More*, Lumby's ed. of *Utopia*, Cambridge, 1908. See Bibliography D (*b*), p. 452.

RYMER, *Foedera, conventiones litterae et cujuscumque generis acta publica*, etc. See Bibliography A, n. 12.

SANDER, NICOLAS, *De origine et progressu schismati anglicani*, circa 1576. Lewis' trans., 1877. See Bibliography B, p. 443.

SAVINE, A., *English Monasteries on the Eve of the Dissolution*, Oxford, 1909. See Bibliography C, p. 448.

STAPLETON, *Tres Thomae*, English trans., by Mgr. P. Hallett, 1928. See Bibliography D (*b*), pp. 453–54.

STONE, MISS, *Renaissance and Reform*, London, 1904.

STRICKLAND, MISS AGNES, *Lives of the Queens of England*, ed. 1878. See Bibliography B, p. 445.

STRYPE, *Eccles. Mem.* (*Ecclesiastical Memorials*); *Mem. of Cranmer* (*Memorials of Thomas Cranmer*).   See Bibliography A, pp. 439 and 464, n. 6; E (*b*), p. 458.

THEINER, *Vetera Monumenta Hibernorum et Scotorum historiam illustrantia*.

TIRABOSCHI, GIROLOMO, S.J., *Storia della litteratura italiana*, Naples, 1777–86.

TURBA, *Venetianische Depeschen vom Kaiserhofe*, Vienna, 1889–95.

WILKINS, *Concilia magna Britanniae et Hiberniae*, London, 1737. See Bibliography A, n. 13.

WOOD, ANTHONY, *Athenae Oxonienses*.

WRIGHT, *Three Chapters of Letters relating to the Suppression of Monasteries*, Camden Soc. ed., 1843. See Bibliography C, p. 447.

TRANSLATOR'S NOTE

SLIGHT alterations have been made in this English version of *La Reforme en Angleterre* at the suggestion, or with the approbation, of the author.

The Notes, relegated to the end of the French edition, are given here as footnotes for the greater convenience of the reader. Several long notes which stood at the beginning of each chapter have been extracted and given as a Bibliography in Appendix I, whilst other notes, consisting chiefly of biographical details of various persons or quotations from English works, have been expunged and references to the French edition given for the sake of brevity. A second Appendix has been added which does not appear in the French edition. This is the translation of two articles written by the author in the *Revue d'Histoire Ecclesiastique*, Louvain University, Vol. xxviii, 1931, No. 3, and in *Mélanges Albert Dufourcq*, Paris (Plon), 1932. The author has taken advantage of this English version to make certain corrections in the original work and also to note the various volumes touching upon the period in question which have appeared since the publication of the French edition (1929-30).

References to French translations in the original edition have been altered here and the references to corresponding English translations substituted, wherever possible, e.g. Mgr. P. E. Hallett's translation of Stapleton is cited in lieu of Audin's, and Lewis's translation of Sander instead of the French one, save for certain passages not to be found in Lewis's translation.

In some instances I have been unable to trace the quotations in the English translations and have simply translated either the author's French citation or the original Latin work. Harpsfield is a case in point. Again, where references are given only to French works for certain statements made by ambassadors and others I have been obliged to translate those statements from the French.

The French edition of this work (published by Perrin et Cie., Paris) was awarded the *Prix Thérouanne* by the French Academy in 1931.

I am greatly indebted to the Rt. Rev. Mgr. J. Dey, D.S.O., Rector of Oscott College, for permission to use the College Library, to the Rev. A. G. McDonald for very kindly reading the proofs and making valuable suggestions, and to the Librarian and Staff of the Reading Public Library (Reference Dept.) for their unfailing courtesy and assistance in my researches.

R. E. S.

St. Swithun's,
Southsea.
December, 1933.

CHAPTER I

PRELIMINARIES AND CAUSES OF THE SCHISM

The spirit of nationalism and the weakening of papal authority—Wiclif's attacks upon the Church—Bitter criticisms by the Humanists—Feelings of the English people towards the clergy—The members and the mind of Parliament at the time of the breach (1527-1536)—The king and his decisive influence.

THE occasion of the English Schism is so patent and indisputable that many people scarcely trouble to look for the causes, while some even think that the occasion of it, Henry VIII's divorce, was in reality the cause. That is certainly a short, easy and simple solution, but truth is—generally —more complicated than that. In his *English Law and The Renaissance* Maitland admits that the history of the Reformation in England is complicated. To attribute everything to the king's despotism and the people's servility is an easy way of dealing with the subject, but it has the disadvantage of mistaking the effect for the cause. For it was precisely in his conflict with Rome that Henry's eyes were opened and he saw how far his power might be extended. "If the lion knew his own strength, hard were it for any man to rule him,"[1] said Thomas More to Cromwell, alluding to the king. But the lion was not yet aware that its claws had grown; and it experimented with them on the Church. We must then discover what it was that allowed the king to meddle with the Church and the Reformation to spring up and develop on English soil.

Henry VIII's Schism was but an episode in the eternal conflict between Church and State, and in England this conflict was not new. Who has not heard of the terrible struggles between Alexander III and Henry II in the twelfth,

[1] Roper's *Life of Sir Thomas More*, ed. Lumby of *Utopia*, Cambridge, 1908, p. xxxii.

and between Innocent III and John Lackland in the thirteenth century,[2] struggles which ended in humiliation for
the royal power? It would almost seem that the memory
of that humiliation had not been forgotten. "For his part,
Henry VIII meant to remedy it," wrote the imperial ambassador in 1533, "and repair the error of Kings Henry II
and John, who, by deceit, being in difficulties, had made
this realm and Ireland tributary."[3]

A few days before his death Warham, the Archbishop of
Canterbury, said that the king was beginning to follow in
the path of Henry II and that his policy resembled the
Clarendon Constitutions (1164).[4] Had he not already shown,
in 1515, his aversion to the Church's liberties and his desire

[2] F. W. Powicke's *Stephen Langton, Being the Ford Lectures delivered in the University of Oxford in Hilary Term, 1927* (Oxford, 1928) explains the struggle between John Lackland and Innocent III. Cf. Z. N. Brooke, *The English Church and the Papacy from the Conquest to the Reign of John*, 1931 (Birkbeck Lectures in Ecclesiastical History, 1929-1931).

[3] *L. and P.* VI, 235; VII, 94. See the surrender of the kingdom to the Holy See by King John in the reign of Innocent III, on May 15th, 1213, at Dover, and at London on October 3rd in the same year, in Gee and Hardy, *Documents Illustrative of English Church History*, No. XXV.

[4] Draft of a discourse which he drew up but was prevented by death from delivering, *L. and P.* V, 1247. Froude (*The Reign of Henry VIII*, chap. iv) also says that the first acts of the 1529 Parliament recall the Clarendon Constitutions and the famous quarrel between Becket and the Crown.

The Clarendon Constitutions violated ecclesiastical immunity to the advantage of the royal courts. The Archbishop of Canterbury, Thomas à Becket, opposed them in council, and then made his submission by compulsion, in order to prevent the massacre of the bishops; on his return to Canterbury he was sorry that he had given way, begged absolution from Pope Alexander, and kept up an opposition which drew down upon him the king's wrath, exile and martyrdom. But, after the murder, Henry II was obliged to abandon the principle laid down by the Clarendon Constitutions with regard to criminal churchmen and to admit their right to appeal to Rome. Cf. Z. N. Brooke, "The Effect of Becket's Murder on Papal Authority in England" (*Cambridge Hist. Journal*, II, No. 3, 1928); Miss A. Deley, "Papal Provision and Royal Rights of Patronage in the Early Fourteenth Century" (*Eng. Hist. Review*, October, 1928). The Clarendon Constitutions are in Gee and Hardy, No. XXIII.

For the conflict between the two powers, spiritual and temporal, especially in the time of Henry II and Edward I, see Pollard's *The Evolution of Parliament*, London, 1920, p. 194 *sq.*

Miss Leona G. Gabel ("Benefit of Clergy in England in the Later Middle Ages," *Northampton, Massachusetts, Smith College Studies in History*, Vol. XIV, 1928-1929) has studied the *privilegium fori*—which brought Henry II and Thomas à Becket into conflict—from the time of William the Conqueror down to the end of the fifteenth century. She mentions the Clarendon

to make the Church his servant? "We are King of England; and the King of England in times past never had any superior but God. . . . You interpret your decrees at your pleasure; but, as for me, I will never consent to your desire any more than my progenitors have done." From William the Conqueror to the death of Edward III, for three centuries the Crown and Parliament elaborated a long series of decrees and statutes tending to restrain papal jurisdiction in England; these were a source of inspiration at the time of the Schism.[5]

Henry VIII succeeded where Henry II failed because the sixteenth century was no longer the twelfth. The medieval ideal of unity, bringing the various parts of Christendom together in one body under a single temporal head and a single spiritual head,[6] had been succeeded by a national spirit, which is essentially separatist and has for effect division and partition. The spiritual unity was immediately weakened. Northern Europe broke up into independent national churches, which were proud of having shaken off what they termed the papal yoke. When the Church in England broke with Rome and the king made himself its supreme head very few voices were raised in protest.

Papal authority had suffered a gradual eclipse which deepened more and more during the captivity at Avignon and during the Great Schism in the West, a period of moral confusion and corruption. Richard II (1377-1399) and Henry IV (1399-1413) took advantage of this to deprive the papacy of a part of its temporal rights, and the primate of England (1414-1443), Chichele, did not hesitate, in 1427, to appeal to the council against a sentence pronounced upon him by Martin V.[7]

Constitutions as being in conformity with the customs of the realm as they existed in Henry I's time (p. 27).

[5] Cf. John Tracy Ellis, *Anti-Papal Legislation in Medieval England* (1066-1377), doctoral dissertation, Catholic University of America, Washington, 1930.

[6] See the excellent study on the theories in vogue from the tenth to the end of the twelfth century concerning the relations between the papacy and the empire, in R. W. Carlyle and A. J. Carlyle, *A History of Medieval Political Theory in the West*, London and Edinburgh, Vol. IV, 1922; Vol. V, 1928.

[7] Appeal to a General Council by Henry Chichele, Archbishop of Canterbury, on April 6th, 1427. Burnet, *History of the Reformation*, Vol. V,

Papal prestige was yet further weakened by the Renaissance disorders, and by the sixteenth century wars waged in Italy, in which the Popes had to take part on equal terms with petty temporal princes, exchanging the tiara for a helmet, like Julius II or, like Clement VII, casting themselves now into the emperor's arms, now into those of the King of France. In 1517 Pace, the Dean of St. Paul's, wrote a distressing account of the moral state of the Eternal City: *plane monstra, omni dedecore et infamia plena; omnis fides, omnis honestas, una cum religione a mundo abvolasse videntur.*[8] Ten years later, Rome was sacked by an unbridled and sacrilegious soldiery in the pay of the emperor,[9] the Pope was imprisoned in the Castle St. Angelo, and Charles V declared that it was a just judgment of God.[10] An ambassador of Charles V proposed to deprive the Pope of his temporal goods which, according to him, were the source of all the evil.[11] The question was asked whether "the King of France would not create a patriarch in his own realm and renounce the obedience due to the Holy See, and whether the King

p. 485; J. Gairdner, *Lollardy*, I, 136 *sqq.*; L. Spencer, *The Life of Chichele*, 1773; E. F. Jacob, *Two Lives of Archbishop Chichele, with an Appendix containing an early book list of All Souls College*, in *Ryland Library Bulletin*, Manchester, 1932.

For the Statute of Provisors of Edward III (1351) relating to the Pope's temporal rights over the kingdom (conferring of benefices, immunity of the clergy), see Burnet (*op. cit.*, ed. Pocock, Vol. IV, p. 182-187); and Stubbs (*Constitutional History*, II, 506, and III, 324) for the manner in which Richard II and Henry IV developed it. The second Statute of Provisors, passed in 1390 in Richard II's time, is in Gee and Hardy, No. XXXIX.

See G. J. Jordan, *The Inner History of the Great Schism of the West*, London, 1929; Berthem-Bontoux, *Sainte Françoise Romaine et son temps* (1384-1440), Paris, 1931.

[8] *L. and P.*, II, 5523. Richard Pace (1482-1536), secretary to Henry VIII in 1515, and Secretary of State the following year, was sent to Switzerland after Marignan, to Germany, to Ardres at the time of the Peace Treaty (1520), and to Venice (1521). Wood says that Pace was one of the lights of his century. Cf. Dodd, *Church History of England*, ed. 1737, I, 225. An American writer, Jervis Weg, has just published a book on him, *Richard Pace, A Tudor Diplomatist*, London, 1932, which, despite a few errors, is quite useful. See the reproaches against Rome by the Chancellor of Oxford, Thomas Gascoigne (†1458), in his *Loci e libro veritatum*, 13, 157 *sq.* Cf. J. Gairdner, *Lollardy*, I, 255, *sq.*

[9] See the Cardinal of Como's account in *Il sacco di Roma*, ed. Milanesi, p. 471.

[10] *Sp. Cal.*, III (1527-1529), p. 309.

[11] *Sp. Cal.*, III, 209, 210. Cf. *L. and P.*, IV, 3051, 3352.

of England and the other Christian princes would not follow this example."[12] Wolsey, together with four other cardinals, protested, in the name of England and France, against any act which the Pope might perform during his captivity. He claimed to have the powers of a kind of vicar-general for the two countries.[13] It was said that he was "going to France to separate the Churches of England and of France from that of Rome, not merely during the captivity of the Pope and to effect his liberation, but for a perpetual division,"[14] and some suggested to Charles V that, in order to avoid a schism,[15] he should depose Clement VII and offer the tiara to Wolsey.

The subjection of the papacy to the King of France had brought about the Great Schism; its dependency upon the emperor might have equally disastrous results. The distrust which had taken hold of men's minds in 1527 persisted in England throughout the reign of Clement VII, and was easily fed. When Charles V begged the Pope to forbid the English Parliament to discuss the divorce there were very few Englishmen who were not openly indignant.[16] More wounding still to national feeling was the summons issued

[12] *Il sacco di Roma*, edit. Milanesi, p. 517. Antonio Rodriguez Villa, *Memorias para la historia del asalto y saqueo di Roma en 1527 par el ejercito imperial, formados con documentos originales*, Madrid, 1875; by the same writer, *Italia desde la batalla de Pavia hasta el saqueo de Roma*, Madrid 1885 (Vol. I of *Curiosidades de la Historia de España*). There are also a few pages on the terrible *sacco* of May 6th, 1527, in Vol. I of *Die Schweizergarde in Rom und die Schweizer in papstlichen Diensten*, Lucerne, 1927.

[13] Letter from Wolsey and the four other cardinals to the Pope, Compiègne, September 16th, 1527, in Le Grand, *Histoire du divorce de Henri VIII et de Catherine d'Aragon*, III, pp. 4-13. Cf. Lewis, *Translation of Sander*, p. liii, lv. Cardinal Salviati considered it a step towards schism. He only signed the letter to gain time and to prevent the schism from breaking out immediately. (See his letter from Compiègne, September 18th, 1527. Ehses, *Römische Dokumente*, p. 250.)

[14] *L. and P.*, IV, 3291. The Queen-Mother, Louisa of Savoy, told Wolsey that the Christian princes ought to repudiate the papal authority as long as Clement remained in captivity; the cardinal replied that he would have put forward the same proposition, in his own name and in the name of the King of England, if she had not anticipated him. *L. and P.*, IV, 3247, 3263.

[15] *Sp. Cal.*, III, 273. See Creighton, *History of the Papacy from the Great Schism to the Sack of Rome*, 6 vols., 1901.

[16] *Sp. Cal.*, III, 979. *L. and P.*, VII, 193. Henry VIII, on several occasions, reproached the Pope for listening only to the emperor on the divorce business, and for depending upon him. Cf. chap. II.

to Henry to appear in Italy, a country dominated by the arms and influence of a foreign prince. "If his Grace" [the king], wrote Wolsey, "should come at any time to the Court of Rome, he would do the same with such a main and army royal as should be formidable to the Pope and to all Italy."[17] And, in 1532, Henry told Francis I that if he went to Rome the Pope would soon be sorry he had summoned him. The nation was inclined to distrust a jurisdiction which was said to be influenced by her enemies.

Moreover, with the passing of time, the bonds uniting England and Rome had weakened. For four centuries there had been no English Pope,[18] and the two setbacks Wolsey's hopes of the tiara had suffered, on the election of Adrian VI and Clement VII, made this exclusion more apparent.[19] It was indeed customary to have an English cardinal in the Sacred College, but what is one cardinal in a body of between fifty and sixty members? England's share of influence in the great Christian council had therefore greatly decreased. Then again, the all-powerful Wolsey had secured his nomination for life as the legate of the Holy See[20] (*Apostolicae Sedis*, Wolsey himself said, *non solum*

[17] *L. and P.*, IV, 5797. Wolsey's words were uttered a day or two before the news came that the cause had been cited to Rome.

[18] There was only one English Pope, Nicholas Breakspear, Adrian IV (1154-1159), who, moreover, had lived outside England from his youth. See Edith Almedingen's *The English Pope*, Foreword by Rev. C. C. Martindale, S.J., London, 1925.

[19] He tried to be elected when Leo X died (1521), by promising an important gift to the Sacred College (*L. and P.*, III, No. 1892; Burnet, *op. cit.*, ed. Pocock, Vol. V, p. 289). At the time of the Bruges Treaty (August 25th, 1521) Charles V had promised to uphold his candidature (*L. and P.*, III, 1868, 1876, 1884. Cf. Ranke, *Sämmtliche Werke*, Leipzic, 1878, Vol. XIV, p. 113; *Monumenta Hapsburgica*, Vol. II, Part I, p. 501; Le Grand, *op. cit.*, Vol. I, pp. 114, 141), but Charles caused his old tutor to be elected, Adrian VI. Before the Calais Conference, Francis I had promised him the votes of fourteen cardinals. The emperor also promised to support Wolsey, at the time of the conclave which elected Clement VII. But the letter which he wrote to that effect was stopped by Charles in Barcelona: a fact which Wolsey never forgot. Cf. Fisher, *The Political History of England*, Vol. VI, pp. 251 *sq.* Because he failed in his endeavours, Wolsey, says Roper (*Life of Sir Thomas More*), entertained a lively resentment against the emperor: "which was the beginninge of a lamentable tragedie" (the divorce of Catherine of Aragon).

[20] Leo X gave him this title in 1518; and Clement VII, a friend of England even before he was elected Pope, confirmed it for life when he was elected. See J. Galt, *The Life and Administration of Cardinal Wolsey*, London,

natus, sed etiam per universum Angliae regnum et alia loca illi adjacentia [Ireland] *de latere legatus*), an office which he held from 1518 to 1529, and by holding it exercised unlimited authority over the clergy. The Church in England had but one link with Rome[21]—its own legate; and when the one fell the other would fall too, as both Henry VIII and Anne Boleyn well knew.[22] The nation became accustomed to this mediate jurisdiction, which was the first step towards a national Church.[23] When, therefore, Henry VIII broke with Rome he was able to disguise the separation by giving to Cranmer the title of *legatus natus*, a title borne by the Archbishop of Canterbury in the twelfth century and one which, to the simple folk, might present the appearance of some vague bond between the Roman Church and the Church in England.

Finally, Rome's thunders were no longer able to shake the English nation. They had been used too frequently, especially in temporal matters, for Christian princes to have much fear of them. Charles V himself was scarcely moved

1812. Wolsey managed to give to this title, which was partly an honorary one, an active and permanent authority, and he succeeded in making the mission of *legatus a latere*, which in itself was a particular one and only for a limited time, a continuous and life-long office. The legate in France, Giovanni Salviati (1527-1529), compared Wolsey's excessive powers to those of the Pope: "Vicario universale del Papa per tutto . . . contanta potestà quanta ha S. Bne." (Salviati to F. Guicciardi, Compiègne, September 14th, 1527. Ehses, *op. cit.*, p. 249.) See Pollard's *Wolsey*.

[21] It is due to him, Campeggio wrote in 1528, that the Holy See maintains its rank and dignity (*L. and P.*, IV, 4898).

[22] *L. and P.*, IV, 5210, 5255, 5581, 5582. Cf. W. Busch, "Der Sturz des Cardinals Wolsey," in *Historisches Taschenbuch*, VIte Folge, Vol. IX, pp. 39-114; and below, chap. II.

[23] Ecclesiastical liberty and jurisdiction, until then allotted to various men, were now concentrated in the hands of Wolsey, who had at the same time all authority in the State; this union of the spiritual and civil powers was a precedent which Henry VIII was later to follow, in favour of the Crown. (Cf. Pollard, *The Evolution of Parliament*, pp. 211 *sq.*) The ambassador Falieri (Alberi, *Relazioni degli ambasciatori veneti*, Florence, 1839 *sq.*, Series I, Vol. III, p. 26) remarked that Wolsey, "of low extraction," held a real "papal power. He climbed so high that he held in his hands the king and the kingdom and disposed of everything in his own name, as though he were king and pope". The cardinal, and the king following his example, took great liberties with the Holy See, speaking or acting so unconstrainedly that the Pope had to complain more than once. Cf. Blunt, *The Reformation of the Church of England*, London, 1892-1896, Vol. I, pp. 239 *sq.*

by them.[24] The excommunication of Henry VIII passed almost unnoticed. "The king," wrote the imperial ambassador, "said that he took no account of it, but made as great cheer as ever . . . for if the Pope issued 10,000 excommunications, he would not care a straw for them."[25] And when the Holy See proposed to deprive Henry of his kingdom no one was willing to undertake the task. Although it concerned his aunt's honour, the emperor declined the offer. He would not even recall his ambassador from London, and was congratulated by his ministers because he had not to carry out the sentence against Henry.[26] The era of the crusades was over, and national jealousies and political and commercial rivalries had superseded all ideas of chivalry.[27] The helpless position of the Pope was clearly seen in the light of the apathy of the English and the political selfishness of other nations.

Feeling against the papacy and the Church was deep-rooted in England. In the fourteenth century William of Ockham (Surrey), a Franciscan theologian, had denied the popes' supremacy over kings, and had even questioned the divine origin of the primacy of the Holy See. His novel theology was to have its influence upon Luther.[28] About

---

[24] The censures incurred for the sacking of Rome were not taken away till the Treaty of Barcelona (1529). When Clement VII took Sicily and Naples from one of the emperor's vassals, the emperor said: " . . . which dealing may make me not take him as Pope, no, not for all the excommunications that he can make; for I stand under appellation to the next general council" (Lee and Ghinucci to Wolsey, April 17th, 1527, L. and P., IV, No. 3051).

[25] L. and P., V, 148 and VII, 469. An English archbishop in the fourteenth century had maintained that the Crown had the right to defy papal excommunication: Rotuli Parliamentorum, III, 304.

[26] L. and P., VII, 368. Cf. below, p. 114. He did not even wish to appear to disapprove of Henry's marriage with Anne Boleyn (L. and P., VI, 351).

[27] For details of all the above, see Gairdner's Lollardy, I, 243-328, Bk. I, chap. IV "The Eve of the Reformation"; and Bk. II, chap. I, "Forces at work in the Reformation before Queen Elizabeth." Cf. Maitland, English Law and the Renaissance, p. 11; Ph. Furlong, "The Renaissance and Individualism," in Cath. Hist. Review, Washington, 1930, XVI, pp. 317 sq.

[28] Super potestate Summi Pontificis octo quaestionum decisiones, Lyons, 1496 (Goldast, Monarchia S. Romani Imperii, II, 339-957), the third part of which, unfinished, treats de potestate papae, conciliorum et imperatoris. Cf. Disputatio super potestate praelatis Ecclesiae atque principibus terrarum commissa, in Goldast, op. cit., Vol. I, p. 13; Tractatus de jurisdictione imperatoris in causis

the same period an allegorical poem, which took the Pope
and clergy severely to task, was being circulated amongst
the peasants.[29] The Great Schism broke out in the West
in 1378. Wiclif, who was professor at Oxford,[30] seized this

matrimonialibus, ibid., p. 21; his *De imperatorum et pontificum potestate,*
hitherto unpublished, was re-edited in 1927 (Oxford) by C. K. Brampton
with useful annotations, but also with mistaken readings. Mr. Brampton
also re-edited Ockham's *Epistola ad Fratres Minores,* with Introduction and
Notes, in 1929.

William (†1347 or 1349), born at Ockham between 1270 and 1280, took
Louis IV of Bavaria's part against John XXII, and wrote numerous works
on that occasion. There is no monograph on William of Ockham, but the
following works may be consulted: Rinaldi, *Annales ecclesiastici;* Wadding,
Annales fratrum minorum; K. Müller, *Der Kampf Ludwigs des Bayern mit der
romischen Kurie,* Tübingen, 1879-1880, 2 vols.; Hurter, *Nomenclator literarius
Theologiae catholicae,* Innsbruck, 1903-1913, Vol. II, col. 525 *sq.* (according
to Hurter, the *Disputatio super potestate praelatis Ecclesiae atque principibus
commissa* was not written by Ockham); *Realencyklopädie* of Herzog-Hauck,
3rd ed.; Reg. Lane Poole, *Illustrations of the History of Medieval Thought and
Learning,* London, 1920 (this edition contains certain bibliographical
additions to that of 1884); Introduction and bibliography of T. Bruce
Birch, in his *De Sacramento altaris of William of Ockham,* Iowa, 1930. For
Ockham's influence upon Luther, see H. Boehmer, *Luther im Lichte der
neueren Forschung,* 1904, 5th ed., 1918. English translation by E. S. G.
Potter, *Luther and the Reformation in the Light of Modern Research,* London, 1931.
See also Nicolas Iung, *Un Franciscain, théologien du pouvoir pontifical au XIIIe
siècle: Alvara Pelayo évêque et pénitencier de Jean XXII,* Paris, 1931; and
especially Amann's article on "Occam," his life, works, vicissitudes of his
teachings, and the methodical bibliography in *Dictionnaire de théologie
catholique.*

[29] "The Vision of Piers Plowman" was its title.

[30] He was Rector of Lutterworth at the same time. He was made
Canon of Lincoln but never took possession of his canonical stall, neither
did he pay the annates. (Cf. H. S. Cronin's article in *Eng. Hist. Review,*
October, 1920.)

An abundant bibliography on Wiclif—of whom the best study has been
written by H. B. Workman (*John Wiclif: A study of the English medieval Church,*
Oxford, 1926, 2 vols.)—will be found in W. Cape's *History of the English
Church in the fourteenth and fifteenth centuries,* London, 1900; in Zibrt's *Biblio-
graphie ceské historie,* Prague, 1900-1911, Vol. II, pp. 1123 *sq.;* and in
Gross's *The Sources and Literature of English History,* London, New York,
Bombay, 1900. Cf. also G. Wolf, *Quellenkunde der deutschen Reformations
Geschichte,* Gotha, 1915-1916, Vol. I, pp. 189-199; Reginald Lane Poole,
op. cit. (n. 28) and his article in the *Encyl. Brit.* (he also edited the *Tractatus
de civili dominio,* and the *De dominio divino*); the long article in the *Realencyklo-
padie* (3rd ed.) by Loserth, who has made a great study of Wiclif; and that of
M. Uhlirz, which is important for the bibliography of Wiclif: *Die kirchen-
politischen Schriften Wiclifs (Mittheilungen des Inst. für osterreich. Geschichtsfor-
schung,* 1914-15). For his works, see W. Waddington Shirley *A catalogue of
the original Works of John Wiclif,* Oxford, 1865; F. D. Matthew, *The English
Works of John Wicliff,* London, 1880; Loserth, *Neuere Erscheinungen der
Wicliflitteratur,* in the *Historische Zeitschrift* of Sybel, Vol. XLI, 1916, No. 2;
the thirty-five volumes published by the *Wiclif Society,* founded in 1882 and

occasion to fight the rival popes, whom he dubbed impostors and members of the devil. He vilified papal authority. For him the Pope was anti-Christ[31]; he rejected the Pope's authority, saying that there was no need for it; Christ alone was necessary[32]; there was no such thing as the primacy of the Roman pontiff,[33] it was not of divine origin but merely the result of historical evolution[34]; the Pope's orders ought to be proved by the Bible; the Gospel was the only law, and the traditional authority of the Church was nothing.[35] Thus he destroys the principles upon which the hierarchy and the Church were based, and lays down in their stead those which John Huss and all the innovators of the sixteenth century afterwards adopted.[36]   He has consequently been

dissolved in 1926; the *Summa de Ente,* of which the various treatises have been or will be published by Dziewicki (1909, etc.) and S. Harrison Thomson (1930, etc.). The manuscripts are full of difficult abbreviations which have delayed publication of Wiclif's very numerous works. See S. Harrison Thomson's *Some latin works erroneously ascribed to Wyclif (Speculum,* July, 1928). For his influence on John Huss, cf. G. Constant's *Concession de la communion sous les deux espèces à l'Allemagne,* Paris, 1923, p. 16; and G. Wolf, *loc cit.*; Professor Frantisch Bednař of Prague: *The relations between the Lollards and the Hussites,* lesson given at King's College, October 28th, 1930.

[31] *Tractatus de blasphemia,* edited by Dziewicki, London, 1893. (The papacy, this book says, is the root of all blasphemy.) *Opus evangelicum* (1384), edited by Loserth, London, 1895, 4 vols.; *Dialogus sive speculum Ecclesiae militantis* (1382), edited by Pollard, London, 1896 (a stupid disputation against the Pope). Wiclif's pamphlets are particularly virulent: *De citationibus frivolis; De Christo et suo adversario antichristo; De dissensione paparum.* These pamphlets were published in London by Buddensieg, in 1883, in *J. Wicliff's polemical Works in Latin* (2 vols.). Moreover, there was no Pope after the death of Urban VI (1389); each nation had to follow its own laws, like the Greeks. (Wiclif's proposition condemned in London, in 1382, in Gee and Hardy, *op. cit.,* No. XXXVII.)

[32] *De civili dominio* (ed. R. L. Poole and Loserth, 1885–1905, Vol. I, p. 538): "Ecclesia catholica sit universitas praedestinatorum. Ex his colligi potest nullum papam cum cetu cardinalium citra Christum sit absolute necessarium capitaliter regere sanctam Ecclesiam."

[33] *Tractatus de officio regis* (ch. ix–xii), ed. A. W. Pollard and C. Sayle, London, 1887. In it Wiclif says that the emperor may depose the Pope at his pleasure.

[34] *De veritate sacrae Scripturae,* ed. R. Buddensieg, Leipzic, 1905.

[35] *De Ecclesia,* ed. Loserth, London, 1885. *De veritate sacrae Scripturae* already quoted.

[36] "The Reformation had its origin in England," says Macaulay, "and spread to Bohemia" (*History of England,* Vol. I, p. 43).

As regards justification, Wiclif said: "Fides est fundamentum justificationis hominis quoad Deum." Cf. Buddensieg's introduction to his edition, *De veritate sacrae Scripturae.*

For the dogma of the Eucharist and the Mass, in which transubstantiation

styled by Anglicans "the Morning Star of the Reformation," and it has been said that Cranmer taught his countrymen no error which was not already partly known to them.[37] Wiclif called for the secularization of Church property. According to him, the Church ought not to possess temporal goods,[38] and whoever took them away to purify the Church was performing a good work,[39] and the king, moreover, had unlimited rights over the Church's possessions as well as over the hierarchy.[40] These good counsels were not lost upon Henry VIII. He ordered search to be made at Oxford for the condemned articles of Wiclif so that he might learn what arguments he had used against the wealth of the clergy and the monks, and the reasons he had put forward for submitting the hierarchy to the royal power.[41]

Wiclif's disciples, joined to the Lollards, for whom they were soon mistaken, spread their master's teachings through the whole of England, and they were more powerful under Henry IV than heresy ever was in the time of Henry VIII.

and the corporal presence of Christ are denied, see *De Eucharistia tractatus major. Accedit tractatus de Eucharistia et poenitentia*, ed. J. Loserth, London, 1892; also the propositions condemned by the Convocation of Canterbury, in 1382, in Gee and Hardy, *op. cit.*, No. XXXVII. Transubstantiation, according to the Lollards, is idolatry, *ibid.*, No. XLI.

See also Wiclif's doctrine in his *Sermones* edited by Loserth, 1887–1890.

[37] Stevenson, *The truth about John Wicliff*, London, 1885, p. 187.

[38] *Dialogus sive speculum militantis Ecclesiae* (1382), ed. A. W. Pollard, 1886. *Supplementum trialogi sive de dotatione Ecclesiae* (1383).

[39] *Tractatus de civili dominio*, already mentioned. "That temporal lords can at their will take away temporal goods from ecclesiastics habitually sinful. That tithes are pure alms, and that the parishioners can withhold them for the sins of their curates, and confer them at pleasure on others." The 17th and 18th propositions condemned by the Convocation of Canterbury, in 1382 (Gee and Hardy, No. XXXVII).

[40] *Tractatus de officio regis; Tractatus de Ecclesia*, already quoted. Cf. H. Furstenau, *Johann von Wicliffs Lehren v. d. Einteilung der Kirche und v. d. Stellung der weltlichen Gewalt*, 1900. Oscar A. Marti, *Economic Causes of the Reformation in England*, London, 1929. Wiclif shows his ideas on the relations between Church and State in his *Complaint*, brought before Parliament in 1382. Hitherto only the English version of the *Complaint* has been known, but the Latin text was published in "The Speculum," January, 1932.

[41] *L. and P.*, IV, 6, 546. "There is little in the English Reformation," says A. F. Pollard (*England under Protector Somerset*, London, 1900, p. 106), "that was not anticipated by Wycliffe. Wycliffe had called upon the State to reform a corrupt Church, and the Tudors did but act upon his precept; he attacked Church property by his writings, they by the more practical method of appropriation."

In 1394 they presented to Parliament a small book which summarized their teachings: the priesthood, as it then appeared,
they said, was a Roman invention and not one of Christ's
institutions; ecclesiastical celibacy and vows of chastity for
women were a source of immorality; auricular confession
was the cause of many sins, and exalted the arrogance of
priests; the pretended miracle of the Mass was idolatry,
and the exorcisms and various blessings of the Church mere
charlatanry and necromancy; and Masses for the dead and
pious foundations for them were of no use and maintained a
race of idlers.[42] Their subversive theories of property made
them feared by the lords and by the king, who therefore
crushed them.[43]   Although they disappeared almost completely, their spirit persisted among a large proportion of
the population in a very simple form, viz. contempt for
tradition and established authority.[44] They belonged to the
lower class and were not *ex professo* teachers, and so comparatively few cases of heresy are to be found at the beginning
of the sixteenth century,[45] but these few cases (1516-1522)

[42] Episcopal documents for 1387 and 1389 mention the Lollard sect·
Cf. Loserth's article, previously quoted (n. 30) on the Lollards: *Wicliff und
der Wiclifismus;* J. Gairdner, *Lollardy and the Reformation in England: an
Historical Survey*, London, 1908–13, Vol. I. See their doctrine summarized in
the conclusions which they presented to the Parliament of 1394, in Foxe,
Acts and Monuments, ed. Pratt, Vol. III, pp. 203–207, where the date is
given as 1395; and in Gee and Hardy, *op. cit.*, No. XLI. G. R. Owst
(*Preaching in medieval England; an introduction to sermon manuscripts of the
period 1350–1450*, Cambridge, 1926) has made use of registers of episcopal
visitations and of sermon literature for details of the Lollards. To look upon
Lollardy as merely a political and social movement (*Revue d'Histoire de
l'Eglise de France*, April, 1931, p. 231) is to forget its origins and doctrines.

[43] Despite the contrary opinion of Oman (*The Great Revolt of 1381*,
Oxford, 1906), it is generally said that Wiclif's system with its social
tendencies ended in the rising of 1381, just as, later, Luther's resulted in the
Peasant War of 1525.

[44] For them, the sum total of truth was the Bible, not as interpreted by
reason (they despised it) but as revealed to men chosen by God, men He
knows as His own, or "known men" according to the expression of the
fifteenth century. This idea is still found among certain English sects.
Thence it follows that the hierarchy and the Church are useless. See
Buddensieg, *Wicliff und seine Zeit*, Halle, 1885; George Macaulay Trevelyan,
England in the Age of Wycliffe, London, 1889, republished in 1909, 1925, and
1929; Workman, *John Wyclif*, London, 1902 and 1926; J. Gairdner,
Lollardy, pp. 213 *sq.*; H. B. L. Manning, *The People's Faith in the Time of
Wycliff*, Cambridge, 1919.

[45] Moreover, all those who were accused made their abjuration. Cf.

reveal the spirit of Wiclif.[46] A synod was held in London
against the Lollards in 1511,[47] and five hundred of them were
arrested by the Bishop of London *circa* 1521.[48] On the Continent, since the beginning of the fifteenth century, the
English had been looked upon as heretics.[49]

Was it not Wiclif's theory on ecclesiastical property and
the immunity of the clergy that Henry VIII's subjects pretended to apply?[50] "The Lords intend," wrote du Bellay

Gairdner, *History of the English Church in the sixteenth century*, London, 1904,
p. 52; and the same writer's *Lollardy*, I, 273 *sq.*, 277 *sq.*

In this second work, Lollardy—with which the author is much less concerned than with the Reformation—occupies scarcely one half of the first
volume, whereas three and a half volumes deal with the Reformation from
Henry VIII's time up to Mary Tudor's marriage. Historians, more
conversant with the period of Wiclif and his disciples, have reproached
Gairdner for not having understood the extent and the force of the
movement, its persistence and its influence on the Reformation in England.
"He seems to us to fail to realise the moral force behind Lollardy, and unduly
to minimise its extent and its influence. The Lollards talked much that
was foolish, but they also taught much that most of us believe to-day"
(*The Spectator*, November 28th, 1908).

[46] They were accused of having said that the clergy were too wealthy
Some had favoured the Lollards and had had Wiclif's writings read.

[47] *L. and P.*, I, 4, 312.

[48] H. E. Jacobs, *The Lutheran Movement in England*, p. 3. Cf. *L. and P.*,
I, 1381.

In Henry VII's reign, from 1494 to 1505, one sees heretics forced to
make their abjuration (Pollard, *Henry VII, from contemporary sources*, Vol. III
[London, 1914], Nos. 70, 83), and excommunicated for having relapsed
(*ibid.*, No. 72), or burnt (*ibid.*, Nos. 73-89); and despite the religious
practices of the majority, a movement of dangerous opinions is noticeable
(*ibid.*, No. 60: Italian account), as well as doctrines which are new [1499]
(*ibid.*, No. 79) or else already herald the Reformation (*ibid.*, Nos. 71, 72
[1489 and 1509]). Cf. Fisher, *op. cit.*, pp. 137 *sq.* At the request of Archbishop Courtney, Richard II granted letters patent for the prosecution of
the Lollards to the ecclesiastical province of Canterbury in 1382, and to
that of York in 1384 (Gee and Hardy, *op. cit.*, No. XXXVIII). But the
first law against them, *de haeretico comburendo*, was passed by Parliament in
1401, in the second year of Henry IV's reign (*ibid.*, No. XLII, *Statutes of
the realm*, 2, Henry IV, c. 15). Re-enforced by Henry V in 1414, it was
suppressed by Henry VIII in 1534 and by Edward VI in 1547, and revived
under Mary Tudor by vote of Parliament on November 12th, 1554 (Gee
and Hardy, *op. cit.*, No. LXXV). Elizabeth again abrogated it by the
law of supremacy in April, 1559 (*ibid.*, No. LXXIX): which action was
confirmed by Charles II in 1678 (*Statutes of the realm*, 29 Charles, c. 9).

[49] *Ballade de la reprise de Paris* (1436), by a Picardian, *Revue des questions
historiques*, Vol. XVIII, p. 227, quoted by G. Ascoli in *La Grande-Bretagne
devant l'opinion française depuis la guerre de Cent ans jusqu'à la fin du XVIᵉ siècle*,
Paris, 1927, p. 48. As for the term "heretics," it is to be found in the
Complainte de bons Français of 1420, *ibid.*, *loc. cit.*

[50] In his Treatise *de Ecclesia* Wiclif declares that the sole source of all the

in 1529, "after Wolsey is dead or ruined, to impeach the
State of the Church and take all their goods; which it is
hardly needful for me to write in cipher, for they proclaim
it openly."[51] In that same year, at Easter, the legate
Campeggio reproached the king because Lutheran writings
were being circulated at Court advocating the confiscation
of ecclesiastical property and exhorting the civil powers to
bring the Church back to her primitive simplicity.[52] The
imperial ambassador, Chapuys, confessed that a law depriving
the clergy of certain revenues had been passed "to please
the people,"[53] whilst another man of conservative views,
John Husee, declared that if the Church were deprived of
her temporal possessions many people would rejoice and few
would be sorry.[54] Hatred of ecclesiastical immunities was
very strong too among the people. In 1515 a citizen of
London, who had been accused of heresy, was found hanged
in the episcopal prison. The bishop's chancellor was accused
of having put the man to death, and the bishop begged
Wolsey to see that the case was brought before the king's
council because he averred that there was not a single jury
in the whole of the town which would not condemn a cleric,
"be he as innocent as Abel; they be so maliciously set in
favorem hæriticæ pravitatis."[55]

There was no love for the clergy. Laymen were ill-disposed
towards them, Archbishop Morton remarked in Convocation

privileges and the immunity of the clergy was the king's favour. See the
repercussion upon the Reformation of Wiclif's economic theories in Oscar
A. Marti: *Economic Causes of the Reformation in England*, London, 1930.

[51] Campeggio to Salviati, April 3rd and 4th, 1521. Ehses, *Römische
Dokumente*, p. 76. *L. and P.*, IV, 6011.

[52] *L. and P.*, IV, 54. J. Gairdner observes that "Heresy, though publicly
dissolved, was really in great favour at Court during the period of Anne
Boleyn's ascendency. . . . The king, preparing for Anne's sake to throw
off the Pope, was encouraging all sorts of heresy" (*Lollardy*, I, 308, 387;
cf. *bid.*, 276, 277 *sq.*, 388 and chap. III, Bk. II: "The Church and Heretics
be ire the Act of Supremacy").

[53] *L. and P.*, VII, 114.

[54] John Husee to Lord Lisle, January 7th, 1534. *L. and P.*, VII, 24.

[55] Cf. Pollard, *Henry VII*, Vol. III, p. 247, n. 4. He was a London tailor
named Richard Hunne. Some said he committed suicide, others that he
had been killed. Wolsey instituted an inquiry and things calmed down
again. The Bishop of London's chancellor, Horsey, appeared before the
Attorney General, pleaded not guilty and was acquitted. Cf. Gairdner,
History, pp. 25-40, 41, 43, 48, 51, 52, and *Lollardy*, I, 278 *sq.*

in 1487, and advised preachers to abstain from censuring the abuses in their presence. Reginald Pole recorded that the layfolk were beginning to detest the priests.[56] The latter were blamed for refusing to bury people until they had received gifts for doing so, and for not administering the sacraments when they were asked.[57]

In 1512 James IV of Scotland complained to Henry that the English were ill-treating the Scotch commissioners as though they were "Pope's men."[58] More wrote to Erasmus, in 1516, saying that the *Epistolae obscurorum virorum* were in every hand and were popular everywhere,[59] and Heaven alone knows whether a more violent satire has ever been written against the clergy, the religious orders, and the Pope.[60] Luther himself called the author a clown.[61] In *The Obedience of a Christian Man* (1528), which Thomas More called the "Mad book of Obedience," William Tyndale scoffed at obedience to ecclesiastical authority and termed it "wily tyranny." He has naught but irony and sarcasm for bishops, prelates, and their judgeships: "O Peter, Peter, thou wast too long a fisher; thou wast never brought up at the Arches. . . . They are not content to reign over king and emperor and the whole earth, but challenge authority also in heaven and in hell." He accused the clergy, from the highest to the lowest ranks of the hierarchy, of violent avarice: "The parson sheareth, the vicar shareth, the parish priest polleth, the friar scrapeth, and the pardoner pareth; we lack but a butcher to pull off the skin." Discussing the subject of confession, he wrote: "This is their hold; thereby know they all secrets; thereby mock they all men, and all men's wives; and beguile knight and squire, lord and king, and betray all realms. The bishops with the Pope have a certain conspiration

---

[56] Pollard, *Henry VII*, Vol. III, p. 247, 249. *L. and P.*, V, Append. 10·
Strype, *Memorials of Archbishop Cranmer*, Append. I, ed. Oxford, 1848,
Vol. I, p. 318.   [57] *L. and P.*, I, 5725.
[58] *L. and P.*, I, 3320.
[59] *L. and P.*, II, 2492.
[60] Indulgences, relics, and the scholastic method were also ridiculed.
[61] Erasmus approved some of the letters, but blamed the work as a whole. *Opera* III (ed. Amsterdam, 1703), 1622, 1626. For these *Epistolae* see the French edition of this book, p. 304, n. 61. F. G. Stokes' edition of *Epistolae obscurorum virorum, the Latin text, with an English Rendering, Notes and an Historical Introduction*, 1909, with engraved frontispiece and one fascimile, may be consulted.

and secret treason against the whole world. . . . They have
with falsehood taken from all kings and emperors their right
and duties, which now they call their freedoms, liberties,
and privileges." All this was calculated not to displease
Henry VIII, who was about to lay hands on the clergy and
make them his servants. Accordingly, when he read *The
Practyse of Prelates* (1530), in which Tyndale attacked the
Roman hierarchy and counselled princes to free themselves
from Rome's "captivity" in which they were held, he was
heard to exclaim: "This book is for me and all kings to
read!"[61a]

The Humanists had set the fashion for these bitter criticisms
of current abuses. They wanted to reform the Church from
within. They intended to rid the Church of dross, not to
destroy her; but their efforts over-reached their object.
Unknowingly they prepared the way for the great religious
revolution of the sixteenth century.[62] By ridiculing the
scholastic methods they indirectly discredited the Church's
teaching. By demanding free criticism of the Scriptures they
opened the door to private judgment. Their sarcastic comments upon the exaggerated veneration of relics and images,
and upon the abuses connected with pilgrimages and
indulgences, led to the abolition of these practices, while
their attacks upon the clergy, who were more or less worthy
men, facilitated the overthrow of the ecclesiastical hierarchy.
In England, in Thomas More's house (1511), Erasmus wrote
his *Laus Stultitiae*,[63] in which monks, priests, popes, and
scholastic theologians were ridiculed by Folly dressed in her
cap and bells. His criticism of indulgences and the veneration
of relics and images was harsh and bitter; and the innovators

[61a] Tyndale, *Doctrinal Treatises*, Parker Soc. ed. 235 *sq.*, 281 *sq.*, *Narratives of the Reformation*, ed. Nichols, Camden Soc., 52 *sq.* Cf. J. Gairdner
Lollardy, I, 371 *sq.*

[62] For the Humanist movement, see the bibliography completed by the
author (G. Constant) in the 1922 edition, Vol. IV (p. 453 *sq.*) of the
Histoire Générale by Lavisse and Rembaud; Stone, *Renaissance and Reform*,
London, 1904.

[63] He came from Paris university to Oxford in 1498. There he made
the acquaintance of the king and of all the famous Humanists. He then
lived, until 1509, in France, Holland, and Italy; from the autumn of 1511
he taught Greek and Theology at Queen's College, Cambridge, for two
and a half years.

of the sixteenth century made good use of it.[64] The *Utopia* of Thomas More, who was to die for the faith, contains strange opinions on religion.[65] John Colet, a friend of More and Erasmus, professor at Oxford and afterwards Dean of St Paul's, spoke so strongly against the abuses that

[64] The first edition of *Moriae Encomium* or *Laus Stultitiae* was by Gilles Gourmont, Paris, June 1511. Cf. Renaudet, *Préréforme et Humanisme à Paris*, Paris, 1916, pp. 606–611.

Whilst Erasmus exaggerated the satirical side, he almost followed the method of the *Collectio de scandalis Ecclesiae*, by Gilbert de Tournai, O.F.M., at the end of the thirteenth century. (Cf. P. A. Stroick (a) *Verfassen und Quellen der Collectio de scandalis Ecclesiae*; (b) *Nova editio*, in Vols. XXIII and XXIV of the *Archivium Franciscanum Historicum*, 1930, 1931.) He defended himself against the interpretation given to his criticisms by the Reformers, and declared (*Epistola* 572, anno 1521) that he would not have written certain things, or else he would have chosen other words, if he had foreseen the religious revolution of his time. When the *Laus Stultitiae* appeared the whole of Europe was Catholic and Wittenberg alone knew Luther. Erasmus always asserted that he was orthodox, and Thomas More gave testimony to his orthodoxy. Cf. T. E. Bridgett, *Life of Thomas More*, pp. 85 *sq.*, 297 *sq.*; A. Meyer, *Étude critique sur les relations d'Erasme et de Luther*, Paris, 1909; Renaudet, *Erasme, sa vie et son œuvre jusqu'en 1517, d'après sa correspondance* (*Revue Historique*, 1912 and 1913); Imbart de la Tour, *Origines de la Réforme*, Vol. III (1914); P. Mestwerdt, *Die Anfänge des Erasmus*, Leipzic, 1917; R. H. Murray, *Erasmus and Luther: Their Attitude to Toleration*, London, 1920.

Allen began, in 1906, a new edition of the Letters of Erasmus (Vol. IV, 1922), with which may be classed a selection of the same Letters, translated into English and chronologically arranged by F. N. Nichols (London, 1901, etc., Vol. III [1517–18], 1918). The publication of the *Humanistenbriefe*, begun by Grauert, was resumed in 1922 with the dedicatory letters of Erasmus.

[65] In the kingdom of Utopia the priests, who are merely Moral professors, must be elected by secret vote, from the women as well as from the men. All the religious sects celebrate together the same worship in the same temple. See the end of the second book: *Of the religions in Utopia* (English translation by Ralph Robynson, according to Hearne's edition (1716), with notes by Rawson Lumby, Cambridge, 1908, pp. 143 *sq.*; cf. especially pp. 152, 153, 155–156). The political and social ideas of Utopia were very advanced for the age. See Bk. II: "Concernyng the best state of a commonwealthe, conteyninge the description of Utopia, with a large declaration of the politike governement, and all the good lawes and orders of the same ilande" (*ibid.*, pp. 67 *sq.*); particularly *Of the magistrates* (*ibid.*, pp. 76–78). The social order of the sixteenth century seems, according to *Utopia*, to be a permanent conspiracy of the rich against the poor (cf. *ibid.*, pp. 33, 35 *sq.*, 54, 55 *sq.*, 62, 95 *sq.*, 121 *sq.*, 162 *sq.*).

It must not be forgotten, however, that wit and humour play a large part in *Utopia*, and that we cannot therefore draw from this book the conclusions on More's religious sentiments—well known from other sources—which Seebohm drew in his *Oxford Reformers* [4th edition, London, 1893]. Cf. T. E. Bridgett, *Life of Blessed Thomas More*, pp. 102–107. And see below, chap. v, pp. 231 *sq.*

he was accused of heresy by his bishop.[66] He is depicted by Erasmus in the character of Gratianus Pullus, joking about relics and scandalizing their guardians by his indiscreet questions at Canterbury. The first public school in London was due to him, and it became a pattern for many colleges in which was developed that spirit of free criticism which facilitated the Reformation.[67] His sermon at the opening of the synod against the Lollards (1511) made a great stir. Instead of attacking the heretics he took the clergy to task for their abuses, which he said were the source of all heresy. He blamed the clerics for their ambition and covetousness and for the worldly amusements and secular occupations, to which they gave themselves up instead of attending to the duties of their office.[68]

Unfortunately the clergy in England laid themselves open to these criticisms.[69] The country clergy, who lived the life

[66] Prosecuted by FitzJames, the aged Bishop of London (†1522), he was declared innocent by the Archbishop of Canterbury, Warham.

For Colet, son of a Lord Mayor of London, see A. Wood, *Athenae Oxonienses*, I, 10 *sq.*; Dodd, *op. cit.*, I, 216 *sq.*; Th. Fuller, *The Life of Dean Colet*, 1635; Knight, *The Life of Dean Colet, Dean of St Paul's in the reign of K. Henry VII and Henry VIII and founder of St Paul's school*, London, 1724, German translation, Leipzic, 1735; Erasmus, *The Lives of J. Vitrier . . . and John Colet, translated by J. H. Lupton*, London, 1883; Lupton, *The influence of Dean Colet upon the Reformation of the English Church*, London, 1893 (Lupton, taking the matter used by Knight, and particularly the letters, has produced an important and very careful work in five volumes (1867–76); before he died he also drew up a *Life of Dean Colet*, 1887); Renaudet, *Préréforme et Humanisme*, pp. 386–389.

[67] He induced Erasmus to write several classical books for St Paul's School, of which the chief are: *De copia verborum et rerum* (1512); *De ratione studii et instituendi pueros Commentarii*. In addition to the works quoted (n. 66), on St Paul's School see R. B. Gardiner, *Register of St Paul's School*, 1884, which contains a valuable bibliography; Simpson, *Registrum statutorum ecclesiae cathedralis S. Pauli*, 1873, where the statutes drawn up by John Colet are to be found; Hartfelder, *Das Ideal einer Humanistenschule* (Colet's St Paul's school in London), Leipzic, 1892.

[68] The text of this sermon, published in 1511 and 1661, is to be found in Lupton's *Life of Dean Colet*, 1887.

Because Colet openly saw the abuses which had crept into the Church, suffered from them and fought against them, there is no reason to conclude, as F. Seebohm has tried to do (*Oxford Reformers of 1498, John Colet, Erasmus, Thomas More*, 4th ed., London, 1913), that he had leanings towards the reformed doctrine. "I consider the whole book [Seebohm's]," says T. E. Bridgett (*op. cit.*, p. xii), "to be fantastic and misleading, built up from conjectures and misunderstandings, and by false deductions."

[69] For the morals, worldliness, non-residence, and need of reform in the monasteries, see Pollard, *Henry VII*, Vol. III, Nos. 63, 65, 66, 67, 84

of the yeomen farmers, were ignorant and despised by the middle classes. Some fifty years before Henry VIII's time, Thomas Bourchier, the primate of England, had complained of these ignorant, non-resident, and sometimes irregular clerics, who by their carelessness countenanced breaches of the moral law amongst the people; and he had attempted to reform them. In 1535 Edward Lee, Archbishop of York, bewailed the fact that he had not twelve secular priests capable of preaching; that, with the exception of a few Dominicans, none of the religious were trained to preach; and that those who were appointed to the best benefices did not reside in them.[70] Thomas More regretted the lack of discretion in choosing clerics, and represented this as one of the chief abuses of the Church in England.[71] The higher clergy cared little about possessing the qualities necessary for their state. Since Henry VII's days a bishop had become a royal official drawing a pension from the Church's revenues; his cleverness had brought him to the king's notice, and he looked to the latter for preferment,[72] and continued to serve

[1484–1490]. Gascoigne mentions clerical concubinage in his *Loci e libro veritatum*, p. 35 *sq.*; J. Gairdner, *Lollardy*, I, 263 *sq.*, 268 *sq.*

A rather lively controversy on the subject of the moral and social position of the clergy in the fifteenth century, which might have conduced to the Reformation of the sixteenth century, arose in this country. Cardinal Gasquet published his *Eve of the Reformation* in 1900. G. G. Coulton in *More Roman Catholic History*, London, 1921 (*Medieval studies*, No. 15) tried to nullify the cardinal's thesis by laying stress, not on the hasty and interested reports of Thomas Cromwell's agents, but on the pastoral visitations. Beck answered him in *The Month* (August, 1921). Cf. *Revue Historique*, Vol. CXLI, p. 81. See chap. IV, n. 77.

[70] *L. and P.*, VII, 963. Father Bridgett (*Life of Bl. John Fisher*, pp. 327–328) comments thus on this quotation: "In these words lies perhaps the real reason of the quick spread of schism and heresy in England. Non-resident pastors and non-preaching clergy must have left the flock in the densest ignorance, and an easy prey to the wolf." Cf. article by G. Constant: *Le commencement de la restauration catholique en Angleterre par Marie Tudor* (1553), in Vol. CXII (1913) of the *Revue Historique*. Archbishop Bourchier's commission for the reform of the clergy in 1455 is to be found in Wilkins, III, 573, and in Gee and Hardy, No. XLV.

[71] T. E. Bridgett, *Life of Bl. Thomas More*, London, 1904, 3rd ed., pp. 34 *sq.* For the lack of culture and education amongst the clergy, see Pollard, *Henry VII*, Vol. III, No. 62.

[72] Thus, in 1511, the following had previously held other Sees: The Bishop of Bath and Wells that of Hereford; the Bishop of Chichester that of St. David's; the Bishop of Lincoln that of Lichfield; the Bishop of London those of Rochester and Chichester; the Bishop of Salisbury those

him at Court by undertaking either embassies or diplomatic missions. His own diocese never saw him, except when he was worn out, aged, or in disgrace. "Is it not shameful," wrote William Tyndale in 1528, "that no man should be found able to govern a worldly kingdom save bishops and prelates that have forsaken the world, and are taken out of the world and appointed to preach the kingdom of God?" In 1530 all the episcopal sees save four belonged to non-residents or royal officials.[73] The same could be said of half the deaneries and archdeaconries. All these men were better qualified to serve the State than the Church. All they desired from the latter was an income; they thought little of honouring her by their virtues. They were all ready for servitude, and so Henry VIII's task was simplified.[74] Despite his great qualities and his unquestionable superiority, their leader, Wolsey, cardinal and legate—the merchant's son raised to an insolent degree of fortune[75]—did not set them an example with his pomp,[76] arrogance,[77] love of riches,[78]

of Rochester and Hereford; and the Bishop of Winchester those of Exeter, Bath and Wells, and Durham.

Under Henry VIII Bath and Wells, Salisbury and Worcester were held by Italian prelates resident in Rome. Worcester did not have a resident diocesan for thirty-eight years (1497–1535). Cf. Creighton, "The Italian Bishops of Worcester," in *Historical Essays and Reviews*, London, 1902.

[73] The Sees with resident bishops were those of Salisbury, Hereford, Worcester and Llandaff. In the national synod of 1519 Fisher complained that he was always being called to court, and could not therefore remain in residence (*Ana. Boll.*, Vol. X, p. 258).

[74] Cf. Friedmann, *Anne Boleyn*, I, 136 *sq.*; F. A. Gasquet, *Henry VIII and the English Monasteries*, Vol. I, pp. 17 *sq.*

[75] It was in his will that Wolsey described himself as a merchant's son. Guizot calls him a butcher's son.

[76] The Venetian ambassador, Giustiniani, compared the sumptuousness of a banquet given by Wolsey to those of Cleopatra or Caligula, *L. and P.*, II, 407.

[77] When Giustiniani arrived in England Wolsey used to say: "His Majesty will do so and so." Subsequently, by degrees, he went on forgetting himself, and commenced saying: "*We* shall do so and so." In 1519 he had reached such a pitch that he said: "*I* shall do so and so" (*Ven. Cal.*, II, 1287). He "was the proudest prelate that ever breathed," a Venetian wrote (*ibid.*, III, 56). When, in 1521, he visited the emperor at Bruges, he treated him as his equal.

[78] As chancellor he had 5,000 ducats a year, according to Giustiniani. He was at once Archbishop of York and Bishop of Winchester; since 1523 he held the bishopric of Durham *in commendam*. Tournai had scarcely been conquered by England before he demanded that See *in commendam*, despite the recent prohibition of the Lateran Council (*L. and P.*, I, 5457).

or with his own neglect of his professional duties[79] or his behaviour in private life.[80]

The anti-clerical feeling of part of the population was reflected in Parliament, especially in the House of Commons,

When the alliance was made between the emperor and Francis I, Charles V had to promise to pay all that Wolsey would lose by the breach with France, that is £18,000 a year (*L. and P.*, II, 709, 2307; *Sp. Cal.*, II, 273, 600). He obtained pensions from the king, the emperor, and Francis I. When peace was signed in 1525, Francis I undertook to pay a pension to him as well as to Henry VIII, who received annually 300,000 French crowns. Wolsey was reproached for the manner in which he procured resources for his college at Oxford; and Henry VIII suspected him of having bought the exemption of certain monasteries for that purpose. The principal abbey in the kingdom, St Albans, was given to him as a reward for his services as Minister (*L. and P.*, III, No. 1759).

The ambassador Falieri wrote in 1531 (Albèri, *op. cit.*, 1st series, Vol. III p. 27)· "His income was 150,000 ducats, not to mention the gifts which His Right Reverend Lordship received from the English or from foreign princes, particularly from France, to which he was bound by very great friendship. His court was splendid, not only was it equal to, but it surpassed, that of the king." Cf. Pollard, *Wolsey*, 323 *sq*. Yet the numerous foundations which honourably perpetuate his memory must not be forgotten.

[79] He did not visit any of these three bishoprics, save York, whither he went the year of his death, after his disgrace; he was an "unpreaching prelate," and rarely said Mass.

[80] He cohabited with the daughter of a certain Lark, who obtained a prebend of St Stephen's (*L. and P.*, IV, introd., p. xlvi). He had two children by her, a son, Thomas Wynter, on whom were bestowed a deanery, four archdeaconries, five prebends, and a chancellorship, and who tried to obtain the bishopric of Durham (*L. and P.*, IV, Nos. 4824, 5581, 6026, 6075 (art. 27); Wood, *Athen. Oxon.*, ed. 1691, I, 54, 137, 577, 645, 673); and a daughter who became a nun (Ellis, *op. cit.*, II, 91 *sq*.). See Catherine of Aragon's reproaches against him in Le Grand, *op. cit.*, I, 140; cf. *ibid.*, 211.

For Wolsey's great qualities, the false judgments on him, and his efforts to reform the Church in England, see A. Wood, *Athenae Oxonienses*, 1691, I, 569, *sq*.; Blunt, *op. cit.*, Vol. I, pp. 42–99. Anthony Wood remarked that many historians, through contempt for his birth or envy of his order and hatred of his religion, had given unfavourable judgments on Wolsey, who, according to him, was incontestably the greatest churchman England ever had, and the most powerful cardinal of his time. A tradition had been created, he added, which everybody who spoke about Wolsey followed, and it was time for an accurate and faithful history to be written of the most eminent, the most disinterested, and the noblest ecclesiastic of his century. He lauded his cleverness in guiding a king so self-willed as Henry, his great intelligence, his schemes as large as his revenues, his inexhaustible generosity, and his love for splendid things which endowed England with imperishable monuments. Wolsey decreed a series of constitutions for his province of York; he recalled the Benedictines to the austerity of their primitive rule and planned a general visitation of the monasteries. Cf.

which was elected by the industrial and business classes, chafing, as usual, under the religious yoke and the ecclesiastical precepts.   Wolsey dissolved the 1515 Parliament because of its attacks upon the clergy and, save in 1523, when the financial distress obliged him to do so,[81] did not call a single Parliament together as long as he was in power, that is for nearly fifteen years.   The Parliament which assembled after his downfall (November 1529) was not less advanced in its ideas than its predecessor in 1515: "My lords," Bishop Fisher exclaimed in the House of Lords, "you see clearly what bills come hither from the Common House, and all is to the destruction of the Church.   For God's sake, see what a realm the kingdom of Bohemia was, and when the Church went down, then fell the glory of the kingdom.   Now, with the Commons is nothing but down with the Church!"[82]

Even before Parliament met, the legate Campeggio had appealed to the king to uphold ecclesiastical liberty, which was threatened, and to prevent the destruction of the Church. He knew well what was in the minds of the country's representatives.

Parliament detested the clergy's privileges and began to attack them.   John Taylor, who was a member both of Parliament and of Convocation, observed in 1515 that "in Convocation and in Parliament very dangerous dissensions

Taunton, *Thomas Wolsey, Legate and Reformer* (London, 1902). His activity in the diocese of Winchester, which he administered from 1529 to 1530, can be proved by consulting the *Registrum Thomae Wolsey, cardinalis ecclesiae Wintoniensis administratoris,* published in 1926 by Th. Madge and H. Chitty. See A. F. Pollard's *Wolsey,* Hilaire Belloc's *Wolsey,* and "Wolsey and the Great Seal" in the *Bulletin of the Institute of Hist. Research,* Nov. 1929. Cf. T. Corcoran, "Cardinal Wolsey, Educator," in *Studies,* March, 1931.

A. F. Pollard's last chapter in *Wolsey* gives a number of details concerning the cardinal's family, his relations with Miss Lark, and the place where he lived before he became archbishop and minister.

[81] Moreover, this Parliament refused to vote the slightest tax; and as England's greatness, in the eyes of Europe, rested upon its reputation for wealth (*L. and P.,* III, 1978), Wolsey's policy was singularly shaken. If, by not summoning Parliament, Wolsey deprived himself of the extraordinary taxes which that body would have voted him, he was at least making use of the regular revenues of the Crown. See the important note in Pollard's *Wolsey,* p. 130.

[82] "Entrai ne le cose . . . di questo parlamento, che si ha a fare, et li raccommandai molto la libertà ecclesiastica." Campeggio to J. Salviati, October 7th, 1529. Ehses, *Römische Dokumente,* p. 134.

arose between the clergy and the secular power on the subject of the Church's liberties."[83]

Parliament interfered in the administration of the sacraments and in ecclesiastical burials.[84] In 1512 it took the "privilege of the clergy" (which meant exemption from royal jurisdiction) from all clerics, not yet sub-deacons, who were accused of murder or felony.[85] The Abbot of Winchcombe protested against this law in the name of the Church's liberties, whereas Standish, guardian of the Franciscan convent in London, upheld and approved it. The secular peers demanded that the prelates should make the abbot withdraw his words.[86] As Standish had been summoned by the Convocation of 1515 to explain his conduct, the judges to whom he appealed declared that all who had taken proceedings against him were subject to the penalties of *praemunire*.[87] Pace says that he won favour with all the courtiers[88]; he became a favourite at Court and was soon made Bishop of St Asaph (1518).

Parliament had scarcely been recalled from the long rest to which Wolsey had relegated it before it resumed the work begun in the first years of Henry's reign. At that time the Duke of Norfolk wrote: "Notwithstanding the infinite clamours of the temporality here in parliament against the misuse of the spiritual jurisdiction, the king will stop all evil effects if the Pope does not handle him unkindly. This realm did never grudge the tenth part against the abuses of the Church at no parliament in my days as they do now."[89]

Fresh attacks were made upon the immunities of the clergy and upon the ecclesiastical courts. The latter were blamed for being so expensive, for their endless delays, and for the manner in which they condemned poor people either to abjure or else to burn at the stake, without allowing them

---

[83] *L. and P.*, II, 1312, original in Latin.

[84] *L. and P.*, II, 1315, cf. Vol. I, No. 5725, where a petition of the inhabitants of London bearing on this is mentioned.

[85] *Statutes of the Realm*, 4 Henry VIII, cap. II, p. 49.

[86] The bishops refused to obey this injunction.

[87] Law against those supposed to be infringing the sovereign's rights and prerogatives. See below, pp. 93 *sq.*, n. 7, chap. III.

[88] *L. and P.*, II, 4074.

[89] *L. and P.*, V, 831. Cf. *ibid.*, 898, 989, append. 28.

any witnesses.[90] The House of Commons complained that the clergy in Convocation issued precepts which were incompatible with the laws of the realm, that benefices were given to minors, that churchmen were taking up secular employment, and that there were too many festivals, especially in the autumn. They wanted to forbid monks to have anything to do with industry or business, and rectors and bishops' administrators to possess farms.[91] In 1532 they were doubtful about voting the suppression of the annates because they could not see any advantage in relieving the bishops of this tax.[92]

These ill-feelings, grievances, and jealousies against the clergy and their privileges had long been festering in the minds of a certain class of Englishmen.[93] To say that the Parliament which sat from 1529 to 1536 and which was responsible for the breach with Rome acted only under pressure from the king would be, to put it mildly, an exaggeration.[94] The Bills proposed in 1530 and 1531 were merely a repetition or a consequence of the recriminations

[90] Cf. *Eng. Hist. Review*, 1896, 1897; Maitland, *Canon Law in England*. For the liberties and jurisdiction of the English Church, see Pollard, *Henry VII*, Vol. III.

[91] A Supplication against the Ordinaries, of 1532. Gee and Hardy, No. XLVI. See below, chap. III.

[92] See the Italian account (Pollard, *Henry VII*, Vol. III, No. 191), which speaks of the Church's property in England at the beginning of the sixteenth century, and which states that the fortunes of the spiritual lords were much greater than those of the temporal lords.

[93] These grievances were not new. Ecclesiastical immunity and jurisdiction had been unceasingly envied and threatened by Parliament or the Crown and defended by the clergy. Cf. Pollard, *The Evolution of Parliament*, London, 1920, pp. 195 *sq.*, 204, 205 *sq.* The last edition, revised, appeared in 1926.

[94] They relieved the king of the loan contracted by Wolsey which amounted to £150,000 (*Statutes of the Realm* 21 Henry VIII, cap. xxiv, p. 315). John Petit opposed the project, and the king did not appear to bear him any ill-will for it (Nichols, *Narratives of the Reformation*, 1895, p. 25). At first the Commons refused the Bill, wishing to impose their own conditions. Finally they passed it. This Act is generally cited as a proof of parliamentary servility (Brewer, *L. and P.*, IV, Introd., p. dcxlvii, followed by J. Gairdner, *History*, p. 102); but the real effect is never indicated. If repayment of the royal debt had been exacted, a new tax must have been imposed and it would have touched more people than the loan itself had wronged. The burden lay upon those whom the king was soon to enrich with ecclesiastical spoils. In the time of the Tudors, the subsidies, the tithes and the fifteenths never went beyond fixed sums, despite the increase in public fortunes.

made in 1515. Why should Wolsey have dissolved and then ceased altogether to convoke Parliament, if it had been so easy to manage and if the anti-clerical prejudices were merely artificial?[95] Why were the Commons, at the time of the divorce, so ready and so willing to pass Bills for the subjection of the clergy, whereas they absolutely refused, with one exception, to vote for any fresh subsidies or taxes,[96] or expenditure on armaments?[97] Neither would they pass the Act on "Uses and Wills," for which the king had asked so often in order to make his feudal rights secure; yet the Lords had accepted it (1532) and there was nothing that the king desired more.[98] "The demand," Chapuys observed, "has been the occasion of strange words against the king and council. Nothing has been concluded."[99] "Henry," he wrote again, "has been trying to obtain from parliament the grant of a third of the feudal property of deceased lords, but as yet has got nothing."[100] More than one Bill presented by the government in 1534 was rejected or altered,[101] and the Parliament of 1545, which is supposed to have been the

[95] The first Parliament of the reign assembled in 1510; the second in February, 1512, and from November to December in that same year there was a second session (L. and P., I, 3502). The third Parliament held its first session January 23rd, 1514, its second February 5th, 1515, and its third November 12th in that same year (L. and P., I, 5616, 5725; II, 1130). This was the Parliament that Wolsey wanted to dissolve as quickly as possible. During the following fourteen years there was only one Parliament, that of 1523. These dates prove the antagonism that existed between the minister and Parliament and that Wolsey's fall would be the signal for Parliament's return.

[96] In 1532 they granted such a derisive sum that the king refused it (L. and P., V, 1046).

[97] In the January session, 1532.

[98] In Vol. V of L. and P., from page 805 onwards there are several requests made by the king.

The Act "of uses," after two defeats in Parliament, was passed in 1536, during the session in which the monasteries and their goods were suppressed; it was so unpopular, on account of the restrictions it laid upon the freedom of people in making their wills, that it had to be modified in 1540 by the "statute of wills." Many centuries were to elapse before the Crown found means to suppress its effects. See, in Fisher (op. cit., p. 378), the reasons for which this law was particularly hateful to the gentry.

[99] L. and P., V, 805.

[100] L. and P., V, 805. Cf. Joshua Williams, Principles of the Law of Real Property, 18th ed., 1896; Merriman, Life and Letters of Thomas Cromwell, Oxford, 1902, Vol. I, pp. 136 sq.

[101] L. and P., VII, 51. Lords' Journals, I, 71, 73, 80, 89. Pollard, The Evolution of Parliament, p. 336.

most servile of the whole of this reign, made great difficulties about accepting certain Bills, and passed others which the king had to veto.[102] If then Parliament threw out some of the king's proposals, may we not conclude that it could have rejected others, too, had it wished so to do?

Liberty of speech was enjoyed by all.[103] In the House of Lords the Bishops of St. Asaph and Bath attacked the speeches made by their episcopal brethren of Lincoln and London in favour of the divorce (1531), and a member of the House of Commons, Temse, did not hesitate to tell the king that he ought to take his wife back again (May 1532).[104] There was nothing the king would feel more than that. "There was great murmuring among them in the Chamber of the Commons," wrote Chapuys in 1531,[105] "where it was publicly said in the presence of some of the Privy Council that the king had burdened and oppressed the kingdom with more imposts and exactions than any three or four of his predecessors, and he ought to consider that the strength of the king lay in the affections of his people."

After Henry's death (1547) Bishop Gardiner regretfully recalled the days when men could speak freely in Parliament without having anything to fear.[106] In 1515 the clergy begged the king to grant them the same freedom in Convocation as was enjoyed in Parliament, where members might attack the laws of the country with impunity.[107]

---

[102] Secretary Petre's letter (L. and P., XX, 1030), quoted by Pollard, ibid., 336.

[103] Under Henry VIII the Speaker's recognised liberty of speech was extended to every member of Parliament. Cf. Lords' Journals, I, 167; Manning, Speakers, p. 192.

[104] L. and P., V, 989. Cf. Le Grand, op. cit., I, 223-224. The king had demanded money to fortify the borders against the Scots. Temse replied that the Scots could do nothing without the aid of foreigners; and in order not to attract foreigners, Henry ought to take back his wife, the aunt of the emperor, who would not allow the affront to go unpunished.

[105] L. and P., Vol. V, p. 171.

[106] He alludes to a speech he made in Henry VIII's reign "in the Parliament house, where was free speech without danger," L. and P., VI, 43.

[107] L. and P., II, 1314.

For the evolution and liberties of Parliament, see the work already mentioned, A. F. Pollard's The Evolution of Parliament. The Commons' Journals, which begin only in 1547, after Henry VIII's death, are lacking for a more precise study of the customs and institutions of the House of Commons. For these Journals in Tudor times, cf. J. E. Neale's article in Transactions of the Royal Hist. Society, 4th series, Vol. III, 1920. The Commons

The Bills laid before Parliament were carefully revised, and sometimes completely altered by the two Houses, as we can see by the rough drafts which have come down to us.[108] It was not therefore simply a case of writing them in the Statute Book. It cannot be said that because most of these Bills came from the government itself the two Houses were servile, for this was the ordinary mode of procedure, and it still obtains.[109] The theory that Parliament exists only to make its own laws was applied in England only when there was radical opposition between the legislative and executive powers. Certain Bills are to be found which were corrected by Cromwell[110] or by one of the king's clerks; but it does not follow that because nine-tenths of modern legislation is drawn up by parliamentary clerks that such legislation is against popular opinion.

Henry VIII possessed a real advantage in the fact that members of Parliament in the sixteenth century were representatives, and not delegates as at the present day. They had received no imperative mandate from the people,[111] and could therefore be more easily moved by exterior circumstances, such as a speech, or fear of the king, or other similar motives.

There was more freedom at the elections than has been

which, in 1604, thought that greater care should be taken of the verbatim reports of their deliberations, were completely disinterested in them at the beginning, and merely wondered, in 1571, that the Clerk of the House was obliged to write them out.

[108] Thus the rough drafts of the Treasons Bill of 1534, e.g., are materially different from the Act that was eventually passed.

[109] The comparison would even be in favour of the sixteenth century: the number of Bills rejected at that time is relatively greater than to-day; the fall of the Cabinet or the danger of dissolution was not then to be feared as a consequence.

[110] In the Record Office there are four rough drafts of the petition against the clergy in February, 1531, in which corrections by Cromwell are found (L. and P., V, 1016. Cf. Merriman, Life of Cromwell, Oxford, 1902, p. 104). After the discussion in Parliament the Commons agreed that all the seculars' grievances should be set down in writing and forwarded to the king; hence the rough drafts in the Record Office. The delegation, with the Speaker at its head, presented these complaints to Henry on March 18th, and demanded that he should consider the Commons' petition. This step has no meaning if it be said that the grievances existed only in the royal imagination and that the Bill was solely the king's own work. Cromwell's corrections do not necessarily represent Henry VIII's thoughtss

[111] They were accustomed, however, to give an account to the elector. of what they had done in the previous session. Cf. L. and P., III, Append. I.

asserted.[112] Thus the London elections of 1529 were carried out according to the laws laid down, *immensa communitate tunc praesente*.[113] The government was always careful not to alienate the liberty which the counties enjoyed,[114] and practically the only places where it could exercise any influence were the very limited number of royal boroughs[115]; no attempt was made to increase the number of these until after 1529.[116] It was not till later that the government systematically intervened in the elections.[117] This move was due to Thomas Cromwell, who wanted to make sure that he would have a majority; but he himself fell shortly afterwards.[118]   The purifying of the English Parliament was,

[112] Cf. *L. and P.*, Introd., p. dclx.

[113] *Narratives of the Reformation*, Nichols, pp. 295 *sq.* The basis of popular representation was restricted by the corporations, who had been sending their members to Parliament for over a century, or by the Lords, whose recommendation determined the choice of a candidate. (Cf. *L. and P.*, X, 816; XIV, 645. Foxe, *Acts and Monuments*, ed. Townsend, 1848–49, Vol. VI, p. 54. Hallam, *Constitutional History of England*, 1884, Vol. III, pp. 44–45.) Again it was only in so far as the latter desired to be agreeable to the Court that the elections could benefit the king; they could be against him; thus, in 1539, Cromwell's agents tried to get their candidate in against the candidate of the Bishop of Winchester (Stephen Gardiner).

[114] In 1547 the King's Council had recommended an official to the electors of Kent, and the sheriff was blamed for having exhibited the recommendation as an order, because, the Council said, it had never thought of taking from the county its freedom of election; they would simply have been very grateful if the electors had voted for the ministerial candidate (*Acts of the Privy Council*, ed. Dasent, 1547–50, pp. 516, 518, 519).

[115] However, outside these boroughs, certain royal nominations may be noted, in 1523 in Cumberland (*L. and P.*, III, 2931), and in 1534 at Worcester (*ibid.*, VII, 56).

[116] In 1529 there are only six more constituencies depending on the king than in 1477; this increase can be attributed only to the increase in the population, for it would have been useless to create such a small number of constituencies in order to make the Crown stronger in Parliament.

[117] In the by-elections of 1534, and especially in the general elections of 1536 and of 1539.

[118] See Cromwell's letter to the citizens of Canterbury on May 18th, 1536 (Merriman, *op. cit.*, Vol. II, p. 13), in which he demanded the annulment of an election and presented two candidates who were unanimously elected (*L. and P.*, X, 929). In the same year the rebels demanded the exclusion from Parliament of all the king's officials or pensioners (*L. and P.*, XI, 1149, 1182 [15], 1244, 1246).

To Cromwell also is due the Act of Parliament (1539) which gave force of law to the royal proclamations (31 Henry VIII, cap. 8. Cf. Kaulek, *Correspondance politique de MM. de Castillon et Marillac*, Paris, 1885, p. 211). A year later came his fall, and Gardiner, imbued with totally different ideas, became one of the most influential councillors. Consequently the majority of the proclamations (one hundred and twenty) from 1539 to the

generally speaking, the death agony of a dying government.[119]
Henry VIII had a greater influence in the House of Lords,
where he could create new peers, than in the House of
Commons. Most of the peers at the end of his reign owed
their existence to him[120]; for the Wars of the Roses had
long ago caused the disappearance of the lords who might
have resisted the Crown.[121]

The electors themselves, without the slightest intervention
of the Crown, constituted the House of Commons as the
king desired.[122] In the country districts, where the franchise
was given only to freeholders of property valued at forty

king's death, concerned things which are still embodied in royal proclamations to-day (such as the war with France in 1543), or the publication
of laws passed by Parliament. Henry VIII was therefore of opinion either
that the Act of 1539 gave him no new powers or else that it were better
not to use them. Somerset suppressed it as soon as he was Protector [1547]
(1 Edward VI, cap. 12). Cf. Steele, *Tudor and Stuart Parliaments*, Vol. I,
pp. 20 *sq.*; Pollard, *The Evolution of Parliament*, p. 266.

[119] The only Tudor Parliament which contained a great majority of
royal nominations was Northumberland's, on the eve of his fall (March,
1553). For the relations between Parliament and Henry VIII, Porritt's
work may be consulted: *Unreformed House of Commons*, 2 vols., 1903, and
the *Tudor Constitutional Documents, A.D. 1485-1603*, with historical commentaries, by J. R. Tanner, Cambridge, 1922.

[120] The number of temporal Peers had fallen, in 1523, to twenty-two,
which was quite abnormal (even when there were forty-four [1534], their
numbers were less than in 1454). The dissolution of the monasteries, and
the consequent suppression of twenty-five spiritual Peers, placed the laity
above the clergy; and when the king added six new bishops to the twenty-
one already created, the manner in which the episcopal elections were
carried out (see below, chap. III, p. 124, n. 156) secured for him in advance
the control of their votes. Cf. Pollard, *The Evolution of Parliament*, pp. 302 *sq.*

[121] The dukedoms of Norfolk, Suffolk, Somerset, Exeter, York and
Gloucester, and the earldoms of Revers, March, Rutland and Worcester
no longer existed in 1504; at the end of Henry VII's reign there was but
one duke, Buckingham, one marquis, Dorset, and half-a-dozen barons
(Daubeny, Cheyne, Dynham, Burgh, Darcy, Willoughby and Herbert
[Ch. Somerset]). Henry VIII said that at his accession there were but
"two noblemen worthy of the name" in the King's Council, Surrey [Thomas
Howard], in charge of the Treasury from 1501 to 1522, who became Duke
of Norfolk, and Shrewsbury [George Talbot], major-domo from 1502 to
1509. Cf. Pollard, *Henry VII*, Vol. III, p. 319 *sq.*

[122] For the Commons, see Pasquet's thesis: *Essai sur les origines de la
Chambre des Communes*, Paris, 1914; and J. E. Neale's article on the "Journals
of the House of Commons in Tudor Times," in the *Royal Hist. Society Trans.*,
3rd Series, Vol. XI, 1917. Miss McKisack's recent book (*The Parliamentary
Representation of the English Boroughs during the Middle Ages*, Oxford, first vol.
of a new Oxford Series), which deals with the formation of Parliament
in the fifteenth century and its transformation, helps us to understand what
it was at the beginning of the following century.

shillings,[123] parliamentary members were drawn from the gentry, and in the towns, where there were no longer any democratic pretensions, from the rich merchants.[124] Now these two classes were the strongest supporters the Tudors had, just as to-day they uphold the government and the Anglican Church. They upheld Henry VIII's policy as much as any royal officials would have done,[125] because the king and they had interests in common. To support Henry's secular politics was the only way to avoid civil war and the consequent harm it would do to public prosperity; and in matters of ecclesiastical policy both the gentry and the merchants agreed with the king that the clergy had too many privileges and too much wealth, and that in their own hands this wealth might be used to greater advantage. Hence Henry and his Parliament were perfectly in accord in their views. Brewer observes[126] that Parliament "faithfully reflected the king's wishes and his policy." Parliament and the king were close allies in their fight against all rival jurisdictions, and it was to the advantage of each party to increase the power of the other. The laws passed in the second half of this reign bear testimony to this. Their common interests produced harmony of action.[127]

[123] £30.

[124] The lower classes complained of the capitalist farmers, who bought up the farms, evicted the small farmers and converted the lands into pasturage, or of the wealthy merchants who monopolized the trade at the expense of their helpless rivals. Brinklow, *Complaynt of Roderik Mors*, Early English Text Society's edition, pp. 12, 13. Cf. Crowley's works edited by the same society; *The Sermons of Latimer*, Parker Society, 1844, p. 247.

[125] The complaint of Roderik Mors mentioned above said the constituencies made up in this way were "such as bear office in the country."

[126] *L. and P.*, IV, Introd., p. dcxlvii.

[127] "And further we be informed by our judges," said Henry VIII to the Commons (*L. and P.*, XVII, Part 4, 107; Holinshed, *Chronicles*, III, 956), "that we at no time stand so highly in our Estate Royal as in the time of Parliament, wherein we, as head and you as members, are conjoined and knit together in one body politic, so as whatever offence or injury (during that time) is offered to the meanest member of the House is to be judged as done against our person and the whole Court of Parliament." Henry did all he could to make Parliament greater and stronger: thanks to him, its privileges were confirmed and its members favoured, the sessions were lengthened and made more frequent and the constituencies enlarged, its political importance was exalted in the eyes of foreigners and its authority increased. And the malcontents scoffed at this "thirteenth article recently added to our creed," viz. that Parliament could not err (*L. and P.*, XXI, Part 2, 345). See chapter, "Growth of sovereignty in Parliament," in Pollard's *Evolution of Parliament*.

Dogma, in fact, did not have the same share in the Reformation in England as did justification by faith in Germany, or predestination in Switzerland. Englishmen are not lovers of abstract ideas. Not being logical like the French, nor mystics like the Germans, they do not enter into theological quarrels; they are more for questions of a practical nature. So the Reformation began in England, not with the proclamation of some theological novelty, but rather with the destroying of the clergy's privileges and confiscation of the Church's property. The Reformation in this country was brought about solely by a grievance of a practical order intimately bound up with a question of money. "At the beginning, the apostles left their fishing of fishes, and became fishers of men; and now we, which talk much of Christ and his holy word, have, I fear me, used a much contrary way, for we leave fishing for men, and fish again in the tempestuous seas of this world for gain and wicked mammon."[128]

All Henry had to do was to fan the passions of Parliament and thus secure an instrument by which he could dominate and govern.[129] There was no need to enslave it, he simply let it have the reins. He took good care not to dissolve Parliament, for in his hands it was another Ulysses' bow which he alone could bend.[130] On November 3rd, 1529, Parliament met at Westminster. It was not dissolved until the last link of the chain binding the Church in England to Rome had been severed, and the country had been plunged into that sixty years' conflict which ended only with the defeat of the invincible Armada. Parliament was aiming less

---

[128] Sir William Petre to Cecil, September 14th, 1551, in B. F. Tytler, *England under the reigns of Edward VI and Mary*, London, 1839, Vol. I, p. 427. William Petre had already been Secretary of State under Henry VIII. He was the first layman to preside over a Convocation in England when he came to that of 1536 as proxy for Th. Cromwell, vicar-general of the Supreme Head. Cf. Albèri, *op. cit.*, 1st Series, III, 25; J. Gairdner, *History*, p. 173; Pollard, *Henry VIII*, 378; Fisher, *op. cit.*, 391; J. Ford Laun, *Social Christianity in England*, translation, London, 1930.

[129] In order to conclude from the harmony which existed between Henry and his Parliament that the latter was servile, it would be necessary to prove that Parliament acted against its will. But nothing shows at all that it manifested any discontent over the Bills adopted, not even over that which later gave the royal decrees force of law (see above, n. 118).

[130] Under Henry VII Parliament's sessions had been short and far apart. Cf. Pollard, *Henry VII*, Vol. III p. 320.

at Rome than at the Church, whose privileges it hated and whose property it envied, but in striking at one it hit the other. In depriving the clergy of their independence and making them wholly subject to the king, it automatically removed them from papal jurisdiction.

The break with Rome was not, in fact, a spontaneous movement of the Church in England. It was not the rejection of a yoke which would have burdened it. In Convocation the Church adopted a purely defensive attitude. The clergy suggested no innovations; they would have been glad to be out of it all.[131] Resistance may possibly have been their only chance, but England no longer possessed a Thomas à Becket or a Winchelsey,[132] and the sole excuse their successor in the primatial see of Canterbury, Warham, could find for his compliance was the words of Holy Writ: *Ira principis mors est*[133]; and we shall see the sorry part the Convocations played.[134]

[131] The Pope being supreme head of the Church (*Rotuli Parliamentorum*, II, 172), the ecclesiastics were his natural allies against the encroachments of the civil power. The endless petitions of Parliament against the papacy all emanated from the Commons, the sole exception being Peter's Pence (*ibid.*, II, 290); they met with opposition from the higher clergy. The laity, and not the clergy, attacked the papal provisions and reservations of English bishoprics, as well as the *Annates* (or first-fruits on benefices). The Commons had protested against this last as early as 1373 and 1377 (*ibid.*, II, 320; III, 18); and in 1387 and 1413 they demanded that they should be paid to the king and not to the Pope (*ibid.*, III, 214): their demand was granted under Henry VIII. Cf. Pollard, *The Evolution of Parliament*, pp. 203 *sq.*, 212–13. For the *Rotuli Parliamentorum* preserved in the Exchequer, see Richardson and Sayles: "The early record of the English Parliament," in No. 18 (February, 1929) of the *Bulletin of the Institute of Hist. Research*.

[132] The Archbishop of Canterbury (1293–1313), Robert Winchelsey, energetically asserted that every English ecclesiastic was bound by a twofold allegiance, to the Pope and to the King, and that the former should come first. Cf. Pollard, *Evolution of Parliament*, pp. 134, 190, 211. The fourth part, which ends in 1301, of the *Registrum Roberti Winchelsey* was published in 1928 (London, Oxford University Press).

[133] "The Queen replied that they were fine councillors," wrote Chapuys to Charles V, June 6th, 1531 (*L. and P.*, V, 287), "for when she asked advice of the Archbishop of Canterbury he replied that he would not meddle in these affairs, saying frequently, *Ira principis mors est.*" Warham was one of Catherine of Aragon's councillors in the divorce affair. However, at the end of his life he protested against the religious legislation from 1529 to 1532. (*L. and P.*, V, 818. Cf. below, chap. III). One of the two portraits of Warham painted by Holbein is in the Louvre.

[134] Cf. chap. III. For Convocations, see the French edition of this book, p. 320, n. 138.

The Reformation in England, then, was wrought by agreement, by the combined action of Parliament and the king,[135] but Henry's was the larger share. It is true he did not create the factors of this religious revolution, but he used them with a coolness and calculation worthy of Machiavelli's *Prince*. He turned the needs of his people, their passions and grievances, and even their national spirit to his own advantage; everything had to fit in with his own plans. No matter how pressing Parliament might have been, the king could have decided in favour of the Church by ranging himself on her side. Before leaving England, Campeggio besought him to do so.[136]

In Henry IV's time the gentry and the temporal lords had also demanded the secularization of Church property, and Wiclif had called upon the civil powers to reform the Church. But the king upheld the Church then because he needed her help to make his crown secure, and so nothing was changed. Great revolutions depend upon a number of causes acting simultaneously, and often fail because one cause is defective. The defective cause in the Lancastrian period was the king himself. It was not so in the period with which we are concerned, not because Henry VIII had any leanings towards novelties—he maintained the orthodox teaching—not because Rome's yoke weighed him down— until then he had been perfectly in accord with the Holy See,[137] which had given him his title *Defensor fidei*[138]—but

---

[135] The abolition of the medieval liberties of the Magna Charta (1215), liberties which made the mass of the people subject to the will of a few barons or towns, was likewise due to the combined action of Parliament and the King, in Tudor times. See the chapter, "Parliament and Liberty," in Pollard's *The Evolution of Parliament*, pp. 173 *sq.*

[136] Campeggio to Salviati, Canterbury, October 7th, 1559. Ehses, *Römische Dokumente*, p. 134.

[137] The king, Wolsey wrote to S. de Gigliis in 1515, would be ready to endanger his person and his belongings to uphold the honour and the dignity of the Holy See. Indeed, when Clement VII was threatened by the emperor he came to his aid with effective assistance and subsidies (J. Fraikin, *Nonciatures de Clément VII*, Vol. I, pp. 153, 156, 204, 210, 226, 384; Vol. II, pp. 242, 248, 253-54, 256); and after Rome was taken by the Constable of Bourbon, Henry assured the Pope "that he was ready to endanger his own life to avenge the insult offered to Jesus Christ and His Church in the person of the Pope, and that he was sending Cardinal Wolsey to France in order to see, with Francis I, what could best be done to prevent the evils which threatened religion" (Henry VIII to Cardinal

because he wanted the Pope to divorce him from Catherine of Aragon. Clement VII's opposition threw Henry on the side which was hostile to the Church, and turned the tide in favour of schism. Hence the historical importance of Henry VIII's divorce is not that it was one of the causes in itself, but that by converting into enmity a former friendship it alienated from Rome the only power capable of keeping together the forces that were working against the Church and tending to rend it asunder.

Cibo. G. Russelli, *Delle lettere de Principi*, 1581, II, 74; Le Grand, *op. cit.*, Vol. I, p. 52; pp. 54 *sq.*).

In his *Adsertio septem sacramentorum*, Henry exalted the Pope's supremacy, and when More objected that difficulties of a political order with the Holy See might lead him to change his ideas, Henry replied: "Nay, that shall not be. We and all Christians are so much bound to the See of Rome that we cannot do it too much honour" (More's evidence in prison. Blunt, *op. cit.*, Vol. I, 246, according to Wordsworth, *Ecclesiastical Biography*, Vol. II, p. 169).

[138] He had received it from Leo X, October 11th, 1521, for his "Adsertio septem sacramentorum adversus M. Lutherum," completed in the May of that same year, a diamond from heaven, according to the Pope's expression, in which he refuted the doctrine of the "Babylonian Captivity" on the number of the sacraments. (Cf. L. O'Donovan, "Assertio septem sacramentorum," in the *Catholic University Bulletin*, 1906, pp. 342, 485.) Luther answered the *Adsertio* "very harshly," in July, 1522, purposely sparing the king, under whose name, he said, the sophists had written (1525). (Cf. Collier, *An Ecclesiastical History of Great Britain*, IX, 68, 72; W. Walther, *Heinrich VIII von England und Luther*, Leipzic, 1906; P. Smith, "Luther and Henry VIII," in the *Eng. Hist. Review*, Vol. XXV, 1910, pp. 656 *sq.*) The latest edition of the *Adsertio* is by the Rev. Louis O'Donovan, who also wrote an introduction to it, 1908 (New York). Luther's Latin answer to Henry VIII was translated into English for the first time by the Rev. E. S. Buchanan in 1928, *Luther's reply to King Henry VIII*, New York.

CHAPTER II

HENRY VIII'S DIVORCE AND THE BREACH WITH ROME

Henry VIII's marriage with Catherine of Aragon—Origin of the divorce—The two phases—Fatal ending : the primate of England's sentence.

IN the out-of-the-way village of Simancas in Castile, visitors to the castle are shown the marriage contract between Henry VIII and Catherine of Aragon.[1] Upon reflection, one cannot help feeling a certain emotion in beholding that parchment with its gold lettering and rich and delicate illuminations; the remote source, so to speak, of a religious revolution, the effects of which are still visible to-day. Catherine of Aragon's divorce, an old and complicated question upon which documents are by no means lacking, occasioned England's breach with the Roman Church.[2]

Catherine of Aragon was the daughter of Ferdinand and Isabella of Spain. She was only three years old when her first marriage was negotiated with Arthur, eldest son of King Henry VII of England. Henry VII was anxious to strengthen his own power by alliances with foreign nations. The negotiations between Ferdinand and himself were a lengthy matter, as neither of them was very scrupulous in his dealings, and

[1] For Simancas and its Archives, see a study by the author (G. Constant) in Vol. XCVI (1908) of the *Revue historique*, and J. Piernas Hurtado, "El Archivo de Simancas," in *Ateneo* (1906).

[2] We use here the traditional and consecrated term of "divorce," although it is not rigorously correct. In the eyes of the Pope and of the King of England during the negotiations which preceded Catherine's repudiation it was only a question of annulling the marriage. The Archbishop of Canterbury pronounced the annulment. This is the point of view adopted by Anglicans, who pretend that Henry and Catherine were never validly married. The Catholic view is that there was a divorce but not a legal one: hence the title given by the Catholic historian Harpsfield to his treatise (1519–1575), "The pretended divorce between Henry VIII and Catherine of Aragon" (Camden Society ed., 2nd series, Vol. XXI, 1878).

moreover in this marriage both men had only political ends
in view.[3]   Eventually, in November, 1501, Catherine, aged
sixteen, was married to the fourteen year old Arthur.   Five
and a half months later Arthur died (April 2nd, 1502).

What would happen to the dowry?   To Catherine herself
none paid any heed.   Ferdinand claimed the amount he had
already paid.[4]   Henry VII wanted the remainder, and even
entertained the absurd idea of marrying Catherine himself,
despite his advanced age.   Isabella protested[5]; and finally

---

[3] It was in order to ensure England's alliance against Charles VIII and
to recover Roussillon and Cerdagne that, in the Treaty of Medina del
Campo [March 27th, 1489] (*Sp. Cal.*, I, 34; Pollard, *Henry VII*, Vol. III,
No. 2. Cf. Gairdner's *Memorials of King Henry VII*, 1858, pp. 157 *sq.*),
Ferdinand promised his daughter Catherine, aged twenty-seven months,
to the Prince of Wales, aged eighteen months, and confirmed her right of
succession to the throne of Castile (articles 17–26). The agreement of
November 22nd, 1491 (Rymer, *Foedera*, XII, 462) stated that she would go
to England after her fourteenth year. When Henry VII gave his adherence
to the Holy League (July 18th, 1496), the essential provisions of the Treaty
of Medina del Campo concerning the alliance and the marriage were
renewed (*Sp. Cal.*, I, 158; Pollard, *op. cit.*, III, No. 9, Treaty of October 14th,
1496, confirmed by Henry VII July 8th, 1497, in Rymer, XII, 658). The
marriage *per verba de praesenti* was the occasion of difficulties between
England and Spain, and even amongst the different envoys of Isabella
(Pollard, *op cit.*, I, Nos. 132, 134); agreement was reached finally on May
19th, 1499 (*ibid.*, No. 140). The Treaty of Alliance of July 10th in that
same year was confirmed at Seville on January 20th, 1500 (Rymer, XII,
746; Pollard, *op. cit.*, III, No. 13). Cf. F. A. Mumby, *The Youth of Henry
VIII*, chap. 1, London, 1913.
   Ferdinand, to assure his daughter's peaceful possession of the throne,
demanded the Earl of Warwick's head, who had unwittingly been the
centre of several conspiracies from the time of Henry VII's accession to
the throne (*Sp. Cal.*, Vol. I, 249; *L. and P.* [Henry VIII], III, 1284; *L. and
P.* [Richard III and Henry VII], I, p. xxxiii, 113; Hall's *Chronicle*, ed.
Ellis, 1809, p. 491; *Transactions of the Royal Hist. Society*, new series,
Vol. XVIII, p. 187). He was executed on November 28th, 1499 (Pollard,
op. cit., I, No. 145; cf. No. 29). After her divorce Catherine of Aragon
attributed her misfortunes and calamities to this iniquitous execution
(Sander, *op. cit.*, French trans., 1587, f. 86).
   [4] He demanded that the 100,000 crowns which he had sent to England
should be returned to him, while for his daughter he claimed what had been
promised as a marriage-settlement, i.e. a third of the revenues of the
earldoms of Wales, Cornwall and Chester (Toledo, May 10th, 1502,
Sp. Cal., I, 317; Pollard, *Henry VII*, Vol. III, No. 14). Previously, in 1496,
calculating that the value of the crown, originally estimated at 4s. 2d.,
had changed since the Treaty of Medina del Campo (1489), he had tried
to reduce the dowry that had been promised at that time (Pollard, *ibid.*,
p. 34).
   [5] Henry VII had been a widower since 1503. But Isabella had immediately turned her thoughts to the new Prince of Wales, Henry. Scarcely
five weeks after Arthur's death she wrote to her ambassador, the Duke of

they came to an agreement. Catherine was to be given in marriage to Arthur's brother, the future Henry VIII; and the Pope was to be asked to dispense from the first degree of affinity, an impediment which Catherine had contracted by her previous marriage.[6]

Julius II's first reply was that this was a very serious matter, and at first sight, *prima facie*, he could not tell whether it was right for the Pope to grant a dispensation in such a case[7]; as a

Estrada (*Sp. Cal.*, I, 318; Pollard, *op. cit.*, III, No. 15), to negotiate this fresh marriage. This haste shown by the Catholic kings seems to indicate their great anxiety for the English alliance; and their demand for the dowry, on the same day (cf. previous note), seems to be a means of pressure for hastening a union which they desired more than any other. On various occasions Ferdinand showed his great delight in this alliance (Pollard, *op. cit.*, Vol. III, pp. 79, 81).

On the other hand, the Venetian ambassador Falieri wrote in 1531 (Albèri, *op. cit.*, 1st Series, Vol. III, p. 9): "As soon as Catherine was a widow she sought to return to the maternal nest, but her father-in-law opposed this, thinking to give her to his younger son, in order not to disburse what he had received from the dowry; and in the end the king's will triumphed."

[6] The Duke of Estrada had charge of the negotiations for Spain, and Warham, Chancellor and recently translated from London to Canterbury (†1532), the Bishop of Winchester, R. Fox (†1528) and the Master of the Rolls, William Barnes (Bishop of London, 1504–1505) for England. There is a rough draft of an agreement, drawn up in English, dated September 24th, 1502 (*Sp. Cal.*, I, 351). The final agreement, signed at Richmond, on June 23rd, 1503, was confirmed at Segovia by Ferdinand and Isabella, on September 30th (Rymer, *op. cit.*, XIII, pp. 76–86; summarized in the *Sp. Cal.*, I, 364, and in Pollard's *Henry VII*, Vol. III, No. 17). It inferred that the marriage was consummated (which was not believed in England on account of Arthur's youth and weakness; a few weeks later it was denied. *Sp. Cal.*, Vol. I, p. 370); consequently it was thought the agreement had been drawn up in Spain. (Cf. J. Gairdner, *History*, p. 8.) Catherine's right of succession to the crown of Castile was expressly maintained (art. 7), as in the Treaty of Medina del Campo (art. 24); and, in 1505, Ferdinand told the English ambassador (Pollard, *Henry VII*, Vol. III, p. 81) how pleased he was to know that Catherine was "as near to the crown of Aragon" as her sister Joan or Philip the Handsome. See the documents collected in F. A. Mumby's *The Youth of Henry VIII*, on Catherine's marriage with Henry, and on the position in which she found herself placed by the king's hesitations and by his son's, both before and after the dispensation.

[7] Adriano di Castello, Bishop of Bath, to Henry VII, Pocock, *Records of the Reformation*, Vol. I, p. 1. Ferdinand demanded the dispensation on August 23rd, 1503; Alexander VI had died on the 18th of that same month; Pius III, elected September 22nd and crowned October 8th, died ten days later, so that the matter fell to Julius II (elected November 1st, 1503). In January, 1504, Adriano di Castello and the Bishop of Worcester, Silvestro de Gigliis, complained that their entreaties had been until then ineffective (Pollard, *Henry VII*, I, No. 173), although a Bull of dispensation dated December 26th, 1503, is found in Rymer (*op. cit.*, Vol. XIII, p. 89).

matter of fact, a dispensation from the first degree in the collateral line was unknown until the fifteenth century.[8] It was only a year and a half later (November, 1504) that Julius granted this dispensation in the form of a Brief, in order to console Isabella upon her death-bed.[9]

A few months afterwards the dispensation was also sent to Henry VII in the form of a Bull.[10] The terms of the two documents, both ante-dated December 26th, 1503, were the same, save that the Bull, containing the adverb *forsan*, expressed a doubt about the consummation of the previous marriage.

It had been arranged that Catherine's marriage with the Prince of Wales should take place on the day the latter reached his fourteenth year: June 28th, 1505. But on the very eve of that date young Henry protested against a contract drawn up without his consent while he was a minor, and publicly declared that it was null and void.[11] This was Henry VII's answer to Ferdinand, who had not yet paid the dowry.[12]

The document sent to England in August, 1504 (Pollard, *op. cit.*, I, No. 170) appeared insufficient, since the Duke of Estrada impatiently awaited Sherborne's return to obtain the Bull applied for, which Sherborne did not bring back when he came in November (*Sp. Cal.*, I, 414). [Robert Sherborne, secretary to Henry VII in 1496, had been appointed by him Dean of St. Paul's (1499), and then Bishop of Chichester (1508), where he died at the age of ninety-six (1536).]

    [8] See Append. II, p. 476.

    [9] *Sp. Cal.*, I, 407, 409. But he demanded that the secret should be kept, and consequently complained because Ferdinand had sent a copy to England (*L. and P.*, I, 243). It is generally said that the dispensation was granted in a Brief; and during the trial of 1528–29 (see below, p. 64) a copy was produced, but of dubious authenticity (the Brief will be found in Burnet, IV, 61, and Dodd, I, 271); but, according to Silvestro de Gigliis (*loc. cit.*) it was a copy of a Bull that was sent by Ferdinand to Henry VII. Either the first dispensation was a Bull, or Silvestro de Gigliis is mistaken, or else, after the Brief, a Bull was sent to Spain (which appears to be less probable).

    [10] Julius II alluded to the dispensation for the first time in a letter to Henry VII in July, 1504. The Bull for England was given in the spring of 1505 and was entrusted to the Bishop of Worcester, Silvestro de Gigliis, who was returning to London. It is to be found in Rymer (*op. cit.*, Vol. XII p. 89), Burnet (ed. Pocock, V, 15), and Collier (ed. Lathbury, IX, 64).

    [11] *Sp. Cal.*, I, 435; Burnet, IV, 17; Collier, IX, p. 66.

    [12] "Henry, a very avaricious prince" (cf. Pollard, *Henry VII*, Vol. I, pp. 205 *sq.*; Vol. II, p. 4; Albèri, *op. cit.*, 1st Series, III, p. 8), writes Le Grand (*op. cit.*, I, 35) ". . . thought only of drawing as much as he could out of this new alliance; and thinking to intimidate Ferdinand or to induce him to give a sum of money, compelled his son to protest against his pretended marriage, but without dreaming of pushing things any further."

Moreover, events in Spain had opened up new political horizons for Henry VII, and he was no longer quite so anxious for an alliance with Spain.[13] Four years elapsed, and it was only after the death of Henry VII (April 21st, 1509) that Henry VIII decided to marry Catherine in order, as he said, to obey his father's last wishes.[14]

Certain members of the King's Council, particularly Richard Fox, Bishop of Winchester, and Warham, the Archbishop of Canterbury, scarcely approved of this marriage with a deceased brother's widow.[15] Ferdinand of Spain was obliged to write to the young king to remove his scruples of conscience. Still, at that time no one doubted the validity of the dispensation; and Warham himself married the royal couple on June 11th, 1509.[16]

The young king was nearing his eighteenth year. He had

According to the agreement of June 23rd, 1503 [art. 3 and 4] (see above, n. 6), Ferdinand had guaranteed to give 100,000 crowns, which had not been paid, out of the 200,000 promised at the time of Catherine's first marriage. Although he should have paid them ten days before or after the marriage (art. 4), he continually made excuses for not having been able to keep his promise (*Sp. Cal.*, I, 470, 484, 501–502, 508–509, 513–14, 529): which probably made Henry VII think that he could not, or would not, keep it afterwards. Catherine blamed her father for her own embarrassing position.

[13] For some time the English policy had been to seek the friendship of France as much as, if not more than, that of Spain, and Henry VII's adherence to the Holy League (1496) had scarcely been more than a nominal one. When Louis XII succeeded Charles VIII (1498) the treaties of alliance between the two kingdoms were renewed (Rymer, *op. cit.*, XII, 681, 684–85, 688–90, 736, 762); until his death Henry's sole care was to draw the pensions allowed him by France and to maintain between that country and Spain an advantageous rivalry. For his matrimonial and political schemes, see the French edition of this book, p. 333, n. 15. See Ch. Perrat's *Un livre d'heures de Marie, reine de France, et d'Henri VIII d'Angleterre*, published in *Documents manuscrits, typographiques, iconographiques*, Lyons, 1926.

[14] He wrote to Margaret of Savoy (*Sp. Cal.*, II, 3) saying that he did not wish to go against his father's orders, to which greater weight was added by the papal dispensation and the friendship contracted between the two families of England and Spain by the betrothal of his sister Mary to the Infante Charles, Catherine of Aragon's nephew.

[15] *L. and P.*, IV, 5574[6]. See the original document quoted in Lord Herbert's *Life and Reign of Henry VIII* (1649), reproduced by Kennett, *Complete History of England*, Vol. II, p. 113. For R. Fox, cf. E. C. Batten, *Life of Bishop Richard Fox, prefixed to the Register of R. Fox, while Bishop of Bath and Wells, A.D. 1492*, London, 1889, limited to one hundred copies.

[16] The ceremony took place at Greenwich nine weeks after the accession of the young king (*L. and P.*, IV, 5774), who was crowned at Westminster on June 24th.

won the hearts of all by his youth, beauty, love of sport, his precocious mind, his dignity and good manners.[17] "The king," wrote the Venetian ambassador about 1510, "is the handsomest potentate I ever set eyes on; above the usual height, with an extremely fine calf to his leg, his complexion very fair and bright, with auburn hair combed straight and short, in the French fashion, and a round face so very beautiful that it would become a pretty woman."[18] At the meeting on the Field of the Cloth of Gold (1520), the French themselves thought "the King of England a very handsome prince, 'honneste, hault, et droit,' in manner gentle and gracious."[19] "His features are angelic rather than beautiful," wrote the Venetian ambassador, Falieri, in 1531. "In him God has combined such physical and intellectual beauty that one cannot marvel too much at it. . . . Who would not be surprised to see such

[17] A prince "handsome and majestic in person, not destitute of judgment" (Sander, *op. cit.*, Lewis' trans., p. 5). For Henry VIII's youth, see F. A. Mumby, *op. cit.* For his character, see Dodd, *op. cit.*, ed. 1737, I, 125 *sq.*, and F. Chamberlin, *The Private Character of Henry VIII*, London, 1932. [In the Armoury Room, in the Tower of London, there are three suits of armour which belonged to Henry VIII at different periods, in his youth, at his marriage with Catherine (the Emperor Maximilian's gift), and in his declining years. The first gives some idea of the splendid proportions of his well-built body, and is in striking contrast to the third.—*Translator*.]

[18] *L. and P.*, II, 395. "The Lord King of England is so very pleasing and of such good-will that it is impossible to be more so," Margaret wrote to her nephew, Charles V, at the time of the interview, at Lille, between the Emperor Maximilian and Henry VIII (September, 1513) (A. Walther, *Die Anfänge Karls V*, Leipzic, 1911).

[19] *L. and P.*, III, 306. Another witness (*Ven. Cal.*, III, 80) adds that if Francis I was the taller of the two Henry outshone the other by the almost feminine charm of his countenance. "Le Roy [de France] et le Roy d'Angleterre montez sur chacun un cheval d'Espagne s'entre-aborderent . . . estans en la fleur de leurs aages, et estimez les deux plus beaux princes du monde, et autant adroits en toutes armes, tant à pied qu'à cheval" (*Mémoires de Martin du Bellay*, Paris, 1569, f. 15 and 16). A painting in Hampton Court shows Henry, Wolsey and Francis I on the Field of the Cloth of Gold with their brilliant retinue.

In the previous year (1519) Giustiniani (*Giustiniani's Despatches*, II, 312; *Ven. Cal.*, II, 1287; *L. and P.*, III, 402) had written about the King of England, saying that nature could not have been more generous towards him. He is "much handsomer than any sovereign in Christendom, a good deal handsomer than the King of France; very fair and well proportioned. On hearing that Francis I wore a beard, Henry allowed his own to grow. His beard was of a bright gold colour." Slim and vigorous, he did not suffer then from the obesity which, towards the end of his life, increased in a distressing manner, and of which the first alarming appearances are shown in Holbein's portraits.

singular beauty joined to a great physical aptitude for all
forms of manly exercise?"[20] Henry had no rival in the national
sports,[21] tennis,[22] hunting,[23] or boxing, nor in the more warlike exercises, with the bow and arrow, or in single combat,
wrestling, in joust or tournament; and this prowess assured
him a high place in the popular imagination. He was fond of
dancing, at which he was a past master,[24] and of music, and
the cares of State did not prevent him indulging in music
every day; surrounded by his minstrels, he would play the
lute, harpsichord and harp.[25] He even composed music, and
some of the favourite anthems in use in Anglican cathedrals
were written by him.[26] Art had always an attraction for him;
and Holbein found at Henry's Court the welcome and success

[20] Albèri, op. cit., 1st series, Vol. III, p. 10. The ambassador adds:
"If Nature has endowed him with so many singular gifts he, on his part,
omits nothing which will improve, preserve, and increase them, deeming
it monstrous for a prince not to fashion himself to the moral and intellectual
virtues. . . . He is kind, gracious, courteous, liberal, especially to men of
learning, whom he is always ready to help. . . . He appears religious
also, generally hearing two Masses a day, and on holy days High Mass
besides. He is very charitable, giving away ten thousand gold ducats
annually among orphans, widows and cripples."

[21] Cf. Ven. Cal., II, No. 1287; Sp. Cal., II, 44, 45. One of those who saw
him wrestling, on foot and mounted, with his brother-in-law, the Duke
of Suffolk, compared him to Achilles fighting against Hector. Yet he was
not such a good wrestler as Francis I. At the interview of the Field of the
Cloth of Gold, "le roy d'Angleterre print le roy de France au collet et lui
dist 'Mon frère, je veulx luytter à vous,' et luy donne ungne estrappe ou
deux. Et le roy de France, qui est fort et bon luytteur, lui donne ung tour
de Bretaigne et le jette par terre et lui donne ung merveilleux sault"
(Mémoires du marechal de Florange, ed. Goubaux and Lemoisne, Paris,
1913–24, Vol. I, p. 272). See the letter from Luis Carroz to Ferdinand,
May 29th, 1510, in Vol. II, Sp. Cal., and Mumby, op. cit., p. 142.

[22] "He is also fond of tennis," writes Giustiniani (Ven. Cal., II, p. 559),
"at which same it was the prettiest thing in the world to see him play." Cf.
Albert de Luze, La magnifique histoire du jeu de Paume, Paris, 1933.

[23] "He is extremely fond of hunting," Giustiniani adds (loc. cit.), "and
never takes his diversion without tiring eight or ten horses which he causes
to be stationed beforehand along the line of country he means to take."
Two months after his accession he wrote to Ferdinand the Catholic (Sp. Cal.,
II, 9) that he was amusing himself at hunting, hawking, and jousting.

[24] Cf. Pollard, Henry VIII, pp. 95, 239.

[25] L. and P., I, 4314; II, 4024. He brought from Venice the organist of
St. Mark's, Dionisio Memo (Ven. Cal., II, 780; L. and P., 2401, 3455).

[26] "O Lord, the Maker of all thyng," for example. Several pieces
composed by him are in the British Museum. Addit. MSS. 31, 922. See
Henry VIII, Songs, Ballads, and Instrumental Pieces, Oxford 1912 (Roxburghe
Club).

his own country had denied him. With his ambassadors, who loved to hear him talk so correctly, he delighted in speaking French, Latin, Italian and Spanish.[27] Erasmus, who saw him as a young man at Lord Mountjoy's, was surprised to find him so vivacious in mind; and Henry continued to improve and augment his intellectual qualities.[28] His accession was greeted with enthusiasm by all who were fond of letters.[29]

". . . There is this most invincible King," wrote Francesco Chieregato to Isabella d'Este in 1517, "whose acquirements and qualities are so many and excellent that I consider him to excel all who ever wore a crown; and blessed and happy may this country call itself in having as its lord so worthy and eminent a sovereign, whose sway is more bland and gentle than the greatest liberty under any other."[30]

At first the royal couple seemed to be happy. Catherine's confessor, Diego Fernandez, wrote that the king adored the

[27] Ven. Cal. II, p. 559. Albèri, op. cit., 1st Series, Vol. III, p. 11.

[28] Nichols, Epistles of Erasmus, I, 201. On this occasion Erasmus wrote a poem (printed in 1500 at the end of his Adages), followed by a letter in which he lauded the young Henry's application to study. A few years later (ibid., IV, 5412) he was astonished to find him writing with such elegance and penetration, and he spoke to Cochlaeus of the young prince's talents, who had written to him for the first time in Latin, January 17th, 1507; accordingly he had not the slightest doubt that he was the author of the Adsertio septem sacramentorum (cf. F. A. Mumby, op. cit., pp. 65 sq.). Henry had indeed taken to studying theology and the Scriptures as well as philosophy and letters (Albèri, op. cit., 1st series, Vol. III, p. 11), and Paolo Sarpi (followed by Lord Herbert in his Life of Henry VIII) alleges "that as he was the younger son, Henry had been destined by his father for the Archbishopric of Canterbury" (Istoria del concilio Tridentino, London, 1619, Bk. I, §19); but this is disputed by Burnet and Le Courayer, Sarpi's French translator (n. 78, Bk. I), but J. Gairdner (History, 78) practically admits it.

[29] Cf. Lord Mountjoy's letter to Erasmus in 1505 (Fisher, 158–159). See Henry VIII, Miscellaneous Writings, Gold Cockerel Press, 1924.

[30] Ven. Cal. II, No. 918. "This love for the king is universal with all who see him," wrote a Venetian (Ven. Cal. II, 336), "for his Highness does not seem a person of this world, but one descended from Heaven."

For the first years of Henry VIII's reign we have the account of a contemporary, Polydore Vergil (†1555), of Urbino, who had settled in England, as a collector of Peter's Pence, in 1502. But of the twenty-six volumes of his Anglica Historia devoted especially to the preceding reign, the last alone concerns the period with which we are dealing; moreover we must be on our guard against the author's judgments, for he was a bitter enemy of Wolsey, who had him thrown into prison. Vols. I to IV of Letters and Papers contain many documents about him. See the text of and commentary on "The Will of Polydore Vergil," by E. A. Witney and P. P. Cram, in Vol. VI, 1928, of the Transactions of the Royal Hist. Society, 4th Series. Cf. also Ed. Fueter, Geschichte der neueren Historiographie, Munich, 1911, pp. 163 sq.

queen, and she him. The first period, according to Catherine's own expression, was one continual festivity.[31] The winter evenings were spent in masquerades, comedies, games and rejoicing. On one such evening Henry made the acquaintance of Elizabeth Blount, Lord Mountjoy's sister, who became his paramour ten years after the marriage and who bore him a son, the Duke of Richmond.[32] Later on he had similar relations with Mary Boleyn, the famous Anne Boleyn's sister.[33] But nothing presaged a divorce. It was in 1527 that it was first noised abroad.

In 1514, however, a Venetian had written from Rome: "It is also said that the King of England intends to repudiate his present wife, the daughter of the King of Spain and his brother's widow, because he is unable to have children by her, and intends to marry a daughter of the French Duke of Bourbon. He means to annul his own marriage, and will obtain what he wants from the Pope, as France did with Pope Julius."[34]

[31] Her father, Ferdinand, had done all he could to make her acceptable to the people and pleasing to the Court. Although he had a special affection for her, he had sent her away at an early age so that she might receive an English education and retain nothing of the foreigner about her: he wanted her to be able to speak fluently the language of the country of her adoption, and recommended this to her and also questioned the English ambassador about it (Pollard, *Henry VII*, Vol. III, pp. 79 *sq*). In 1531 Falieri wrote (Albèri, *op. cit.*, 1st Series, Vol. III, p. 10) that she "has been in England thirty years . . . speaks Spanish, French, Flemish and English; more beloved than any queen that has ever reigned. . . ." Her confessor, Diego Fernandez, constantly told her "that she had to forget Spain and everything Spanish, in order to win the love of the king, of England, and of the English," for which advice the Spanish ambassadors, Fuensalida and Luis Carroz, did not forgive him. Cf. F. A. Mumby, *op. cit.*, pp. 103–116, 132 *sq.*, 137–41, 303 *sq.*

[32] *L. and P.*, II, 1461. Albèri, *op. cit.*, 1st Series, Vol. III, p. 10; W. S. Ch. Pemberton, *Elizabeth Blount and Henry VIII, with some account of her surrenderings*, London, 1913.

[33] Friedmann, *op. cit.*, Append. B., II, 322–27; Pollard, *Thomas Cranmer*, 35 and n. 1. For the Court in those times see H. B. Tree, *Henry VIII and His Court*, London, 1910.

It has been said that in 1528 the king had ten mistresses, because in a list of New Year presents mention is made of gifts for "thirty-three noble ladies" and "ten mistresses": but the word "mistress" had not then its present-day meaning, and stood for "gentlewoman" in opposition to the "noble ladies" previously mentioned. Cf. Taunton, *Wolsey*, 1902, p. 17.

[34] *Ven. Cal.*, II, 479. Cf. H. Belloc, *Wolsey*, n. H. Louis XII had obtained from Alexander VI (not Julius II) the annulment of his marriage with Louis XI's daughter, Jeanne de Valois, and had married Anne of Brittany (1499).

The first mention of a divorce had consequently nothing to do with Anne Boleyn, who was only seven years old at the time. In the letter just mentioned the idea is attributed to the king's desire for a male heir. He certainly was constantly preoccupied with the idea of securing for the English throne a succession which would maintain his own dynasty and preserve the country from another War of the Roses. Now, in 1514, Henry had no children. On February 18th, 1516, Princess Mary was born. He began to hope again : "We are both young," said the king; "if it was a daughter this time, by the grace of God the sons will follow."[35]   No sons, however, followed; the one that came into the world on November 10th, 1518, was still-born.[36]   In 1519, Henry made a vow that he would personally conduct a crusade against the Turks if a son were born to him.[37]   He was not satisfied with consulting English doctors, but brought others from Spain. All his efforts were unsuccessful. In 1525, Catherine of Aragon had reached her fortieth year and left Henry, who was but thirty-four, no hope of an undisputed succession.

At that period, indeed, the law forbidding women to reign existed almost *de facto* in England, so much so that the ambassador Falieri wrote in 1531 that "by English law females were excluded from the throne."[38]   Theoretically speaking, this was not true; but England's past history had created that impression. Only one woman had wanted to sit on the English throne, Matilda, and she had had exactly the same rights as Henry VIII's daughter, Mary. She was never crowned and her pretensions threw the country into a civil war which lasted nineteen years.[39]   Mary's marriage awakened

[35]   *Ven. Cal.*, II, No. 691. Louis XII's death (January, 1515) having ended the Anglo-French alliance, Henry had again assumed closer relations with Ferdinand and Spain, which was a sufficient reason for not following out his idea of 1514.

[36]   The previous one had not lived two months. Albèri (*op. cit.*, 1st Series, Vol. III, p. 10) holds that he reached the age of six months.

[37]   *L. and P.*, III, 432.

[38]   Albèri, *op. cit.*, 1st Series, Vol. III, p. 26.

[39]   In the fourteenth century the Duke of Lancaster, John of Gaunt, fourth son of Edward III, had maintained in Parliament (and it was the theory of the Lancasters; cf. Fortescue, *Governance of England*, pp. 352–55) that the crown could be handed down only in the male line, and that his son Henry IV (1399–1413) had a better claim to reign than Philippa, daughter of the Duke of Clarence, who was himself Edward III's third

other fears. If she married a subject, a situation would be
created similar to that which started the War of the Roses.
If she married one of the continental princes, there would be
a danger of the country coming under a foreign yoke; Spain
had acquired the Low Countries in that manner, and Austria
had also annexed Bohemia and Hungary in the same way.[40]

This question of succession made Henry suspicious at an
early stage.[41] The Duke of Buckingham had had hopes of the
crown; he paid for them with his life. He was accused of
treason in 1521, tried by his peers and beheaded. His crime
consisted in being a descendant of Edward III.[42]

The king's anxiety to secure the succession again showed

son. And Henry VII himself, who married Edward IV's daughter,
Elizabeth, only reigned by denying the women's right to reign.

James V of Scotland, by his mother Margaret, Henry VII's daughter,
was to Mary what Stephen, Henry I's nephew, had been to Matilda.
Accordingly as soon as his age allowed him (1532) he took the titles of
"Prince of England and Duke of York," a manifest derogation of Mary's
rights (L. and P., V, 609, 817); was that not sufficient to rekindle the Civil
War, which was barely extinguished?

In 1519 the ambassador Giustiniani named several pretenders to the
Crown: the Duke of Norfolk, who had married Edward IV's daughter
(1469–83); the Duke of Suffolk, married to Henry VIII's sister, Mary;
and the Duke of Buckingham, Edward Stafford, a descendant of Edward
III (1327–77) (Ven. Cal., II, 1287).

[40] Consequently when Catherine gave birth to a still-born son in 1518,
the people were of opinion that if this had happened two months before
Mary would not have been affianced to the French Dauphin. (For the
projects of marriage for the princess with the Dauphin or with Francis I
himself see Mémoires de du Bellay, ed. 1569, f. 243, 344; Le Grand, op. cit.,
Vol. I, pp. 48, 54, 55–56; Fraikin, Nonciatures de Clément VII, Vol. I (1906),
pp. 156, 186–87, 188, 196–97 sq., 200–201, 209, 219, 311–12, 321, 325, 326,
345–46, 347, 372, 391, Vol. II, pp. 248 sq., 265; Bourrilly and Vaissière,
Ambassades en Angleterre de Jean du Bellay, Vol. I, pp. xii, xiii, 456). "The
sole fear of the kingdom being that it might pass into the power of the
French through that marriage" (Ven. Cal., II, 1103).

[41] When William of Croy, Lord of Chièvres, proposed, in 1519, to give
his niece in marriage to Edward IV's grandson, the Earl of Devonshire,
Henry, alarmed, ordered Wolsey to find out if the emperor thought the
earl had a chance of succeeding to the English throne (L. and P., III, 386).

[42] L. and P., III, 1284, 1356. It is thought, the Venetian ambassador
wrote, that the Duke might easily succeed the king, if the latter died
without leaving a male heir (L. and P., I, 180, 233, 319). Through dynastic
jealousy, he had been excluded from all participation in political authority,
so also had his brother, the Earl of Wiltshire. Little satisfied with Tudor
government, he was still less satisfied under Wolsey, whose hostility—due,
according to Brewer (L. and P., III, p. lxvi), to one of Polydore Vergil's
calumnies—hastened his end (ibid., 1; cf. II, 3793). Cf. H. Belloc, Wolsey,
Notes C and D. Under Henry VII, the Earl of Warwick, Edward IV's
(1461–83) nephew, had also paid for his royal descent with his head (1499).

itself in the way in which he suddenly drew out of complete
obscurity the illegitimate son that Elizabeth Blount had
borne him. Two years before the divorce, in 1525, the king
and his Council were meditating a scheme to secure for him the
succession to the throne. Titles and offices were showered
upon him one after the other which left no doubt as to Henry's
designs concerning him,[43] and the English ambassadors were
ordered to negotiate a marriage with one of the emperor's
nieces.[44]

It seems difficult to doubt that this idea of succession
played a part in Henry VIII's divorce.[45] It was only natural

[43] He was made successively Duke of Richmond and Duke of Somerset,
titles equally significant; the former having been Henry VII's, and the
latter Henry VII's and Arthur's. In January 1527 he was spoken of
as King of Ireland (*Sp. Cal.*, III, 109; *L. and P.*, IV, 2988, 3028, 3140).
According to Falieri (Albèri, *op. cit.*, 1st Series, Vol. III, p. 10) the king,
whom he resembled, based great hopes upon him.

[44] She was the Queen of Portugal's daughter, already promised to the
Dauphin of France; if she retracted her promise, the English ambassadors
in Spain afterwards said, she would find "another Dauphin," for the duke
"may be easily by the king's means exalted to higher things" (*L. and P.*,
VI, 3051. See L. Vives' letter to Henry VIII in Stone's *History of Mary*,
London, 1901, pp. 39–40). When Mary was betrothed to the Dauphin
Charles V thought it was in order to leave the way to the throne free
for the Duke of Richmond (*Sp. Cal.*, III, 482). The law of succession
of 1536 gave the duke an additional hope in allowing the king to dispose
of the crown at his will, if Jane Seymour left him no male heir. But
Richmond died a few months later.

[45] This idea inspired the second reason alleged from the outset, before
the Roman Court, for the dissolution of the royal marriage: It is a question
of the welfare of the kingdom: the whole of the nobility and every single
subject, without exception, desire nothing more keenly than a male heir
to His Majesty for the permanent consolation, joy, peace and security
of the realm. So wise people think that God denies such a boon to the
error of a guilty marriage (Wolsey's first letter to Casale, December 5th,
1527, Burnet, *op. cit.*, Vol. IV, pp. 21 *sq.*; cf. *ibid.*, pp. 54 *sq*, 105 *sq*; *L. and P.*,
IV, No. 3913. See below, p. 79, the English nobles' petition to the Pope.).
The Pope, on his side, considered the want of a male heir a danger for the
English Church (Knight to Wolsey, Rome, January, 1528, *ibid.*, p. 34).
To resolve the difficulties of succession Campeggio proposed, in 1528, a
dispensation to allow Mary to marry the Duke of Richmond (*L. and P.*,
IV, 4881, 5072. Loemmer, *Monumenta Vaticana*, p. 29).
This idea of succession haunted Henry for a long while. In order to
legitimatize the son he was expecting he hastened his marriage with Anne
Boleyn as soon as he knew she was pregnant; and his loss of affection for
her was largely due to the fact that she did not give him the male heir he
expected (*L. and P.*, X, 199). Until Edward was born (1537) he presented
various laws on succession (1534 and 1536) which showed his fears; and as
that only son might possibly die, he had a final law passed which definitely
and minutely fixed his children's rights, and ensured their accession to the

that he should have thought that there would be no difficulty in obtaining this divorce, for he was a powerful prince whose two sisters had successfully tried the casuistry of nullity suits. [45a]

In addition, there were grievances of a domestic or political nature against Catherine. She was six years older than the king, sorrow had aged her, and her miscarriages deformed her; and, according to the brutal description of Francis I in 1519, she had already lost her charm. [46] Moreover, Catherine represented Spain, [47] and Henry had had scarcely anything but disappointment from that quarter. [48]

On the other hand, about 1527, Anne Boleyn had already gained the king's eyes and heart. Anne belonged to a family of wealthy London merchants, one of whom, Geoffrey, her great-grandfather, had been Lord Mayor. Her mother, Elizabeth Howard, daughter of the Earl of Surrey and Ormond, was a descendant of Edward I. Her father had taken advantage of the fact that the Howards had come into favour again when Henry VIII ascended the throne. In 1511, he was made a knight and governor of Norwich Castle, together with his brother-in-law, Sir Henry Wyatt.

throne against every rival. "After 1541, when Edward was four years old," Giacomo Soranzo relates (Albèri, *op. cit.*, 1st Series, Vol. III, p. 36), "the king desired to make his Will, and called Parliament together and had a law passed which gave him the liberty, in spite of all contrary laws, to make his daughters heiresses to the crown should his son die and leave no children: the laws of the realm indeed excluded illegitimate children." The nobility of the kingdom wrote to the Pope "begging him to give their prince some satisfaction for his marriage, bearing in mind the cruel wars which had lasted so long between the houses of York and Lancaster" (Cf. Le Grand, *op. cit.*, Vol. III, p. 201).

[45a] In order to marry Mary, Charles Brandon, Duke of Suffolk, had had his previous marriage annulled (1515); and Margaret, Queen of Scotland, obtained a divorce from her second husband, Angus (1527).

[46] *Ven. Cal.*, II, 1230. For her marriage, cf. Stone, *op. cit.*, p. 46.

[47] Ferdinand had even made use of her frequently as a political emissary; he accredited her to the English Court as ambassador.

[48] In 1514 Ferdinand had signed a truce with France, without informing him, in which the Emperor Maximilian soon joined, leaving Henry alone to face Louis XII. (Cf. *Ven. Cal.*, II, 479.) Furious at this betrayal by his father-in-law, Henry wreaked his resentment on Catherine so brutally as to cause, according to Peter Martyr (*L. and P.*, I, 5718), the premature birth of her fourth son (1514). Catherine's nephew, Charles V, had preferred Isabella of Portugal to Henry VIII's sister, despite his promises. And his victory at Pavia was useless for the king's plans, who wanted to take advantage of it in order to revive England's former rights over France; when he proposed to invade France, Charles replied that he had no money.

The following year he became ambassador to Margaret of Savoy, Regent of the Low Countries, and, in 1515, ambassador at the Court of Francis I. Later on, possibly on account of his daughter Mary's compliance with the king's desires, he received various donations, was made Viscount Rochford (1525) and then Earl of Wiltshire.[49] Anne was born in 1503, according to some, but according to others (and they are the majority), in 1507.[50] In 1519, she was at the French Court as maid of honour to Queen Claude, who is said to have taken the greatest pleasure in educating young girls of noble families.[51] On the eve of the breach between England and France (1522), she returned to Henry VIII's court.[52] They thought of marrying her to James Butler, one of the

[49] See notes 51-55, pp. 344-345, in the French edition of this book.

[50] Friedmann (*op. cit.*, Vols. I, 39; and II, Append. note A), who even speaks of 1502, gives at the most the first months of 1503. He bases his opinion largely upon one of Holbein's portraits, bearing the inscription, "1530, Aetatis 27.—Anna Regina." H. Belloc also shares this opinion (*Wolsey*, Note F). The others (Lingard, Froude, Brewer, Gairdner, who relies largely upon a marginal note in the Camden "History of Elizabeth," and Fisher) are for 1507; and according to Gairdner, Holbein's portrait represents Anne of Hungary, wife of Ferdinand I, who was actually born in 1503.

[51] According to Friedmann (*op. cit.*, II, Append. Note A), Anne accompanied Mary Tudor, Henry VIII's sister, to France when the latter went to marry Louis XII. According to those who place her birth in 1507, she accompanied her own sister, Mary Boleyn, who belonged to Mary Tudor's retinue. (Cf. J. Gairdner, "Mary and Anne Boleyn" in the *English Hist. Review*, VIII, pp. 53 *sq.*)
Francis I's (1514) wife, Queen Claude (1499-1524), had at times as many as three hundred young girls who received lessons from the best masters. The poem on Anne Boleyn's death, written by Lancelot de Carles, the Bishop of Tarbes' secretary in London, which was printed in 1545, and then by Crapelet (*Lettres de Henri VIII à Anne Boleyn*, Paris, 1835, pp. 168-214) and more accurately by G. Ascoli (*op. cit.*, pp. 231-273), has the following lines:

> . . . *Anne Boullant premierement sortit*
> *De ce pays, quand Marie en partit*
> *Pour s'en aller trouver le Roy en France* . .
> *Apres que fut Marie revenue*
> *En ce pays, elle fut retenue*
> *Par Claude qui Royne après succeda,*
> *Où tellement ses graces amenda*
> *Que ne l'eussiez oncques jugée Angloise*
> *En ses façons, mais naïfve Françoise.*

[52] *L. and P.*, III, 1994. Queen Claude died in 1524. And historians do not agree on the date of Anne Boleyn's return to England. Cf. Crapelet, *op. cit.*, p. 15, n. 2.

Irish chieftains.[53] Sir Henry Percy sought her hand,[54] but the poet Thomas Wyatt (who was also a suitor) relates that Anne said: "*Noli me tangere*, I belong to Caesar."[55] We do not know exactly when the king ousted these suitors. The first document in which Anne is mentioned is Henry's instructions for Rome addressed to his secretary, Knight (Autumn, 1527); the divorce proceedings had begun in the March of that same year.

The secret of Anne Boleyn's fascination over Henry remained an enigma for her contemporaries. "Madam Anne," a Venetian wrote,[56] "is not one of the handsomest women in the world; she is of middling stature, swarthy complexion, long neck, wide mouth, bosom not much raised, and in fact has nothing but the English king's great appetite, and her eyes, which are black and beautiful . . ." We get practically the same impression from her portrait in the National Portrait Gallery; she is the angular type of Anglo-Saxon. There was a slight defect on one of her nails; and she tried to hide it behind the other fingers. It was on account of this that Sander, in his *History of the Schism*, credited her with six fingers.[57] While she was in France she made the most of the

[53] Since J. Butler had pretensions to the earldom of Ormonde, it was thought that thus the quarrel between Butler and Boleyn would be ended.

[54] "This young lord," says Le Grand (*op. cit.*, Vol. I, pp. 42 *sq.*), "was one of the most notable in England, either by his possessions or by birth; for he was to be the Earl of Northumberland after his father's death, who was already very old." With other young nobles who were completing their education he formed part of Wolsey's household, and while the latter was dealing with State affairs he left him in the queen's room with the ladies of honour. It was there that the romance began which the king brutally interrupted by ordering Wolsey to break off the secret betrothal. The cardinal sent for the father, who called Percy a fool and a madman and threatened to disinherit him. Percy made his submission, and to remove all suspicion married shortly afterwards the daughter of George, Earl of Shrewsbury. Such was the origin of the hatred Anne conceived for Wolsey; at the same time she was sent away from the Court (cf. Burnet, I, 138; Dodd, I, 314).

[55] *Wyatt's Works*, ed. Nott, 1816, p. 143. In the summer of 1528 Henry wrote that for more than "ung anné" he had been "attaynte du dart d'amours" (Crapelet, *op. cit.*, p. 110).

[56] *Ven. Cal.*, IV, No. 824, p. 365.

[57] Sander (*op. cit.*, Lewis' trans., p. 25) scarcely flatters the portrait he gives of Anne: "Anne Boleyn was rather tall of stature, with black hair, and an oval face of a sallow complexion as if troubled with jaundice. She had a projecting tooth under the upper lip, and on her right hand six fingers. There was a large wen under her chin, and therefore to hide its

few rare gifts that Nature had given her: her very beautiful eyes, and her hair which she wore loose after the French fashion. Cranmer describes her as "sitting in her hair" when she was crowned; and the Venetian ambassador says she was covered in jewels and in her loose hair, *con li crini sparsi*, when she was made Marquis (*sic*) of Pembroke.[58] We do not know very much about her intellectual qualities, save that she spoke Italian and French, although she was not well acquainted with the spelling. From the French court she probably brought back certain airs and graces which contrasted with the staid English ways and roused Henry's interest.[59] No woman ever retained for so long such a fickle heart as the king's. Mindful of her sister Mary's example, who had received only slight gifts from the king, she made it known that she would accept nothing but a husband. She rejected Henry's dishonourable proposals, but made him feel great pleasure in his defeat and knew how to change his whims into an obstinate passion. She declared that she would be married only where queens were married and

ugliness she wore a high dress covering her throat. In this she was followed by the ladies of the Court, who also wore high dresses, having before been in the habit of leaving their necks and the upper portion of their persons uncovered."

Sander's assertion was reproduced in the *Dictionnaire des Sciences Médicales* (1813), where it was even said that she had six fingers on each hand, and other physical deformities were attributed to Anne. To these Sander, who looked upon the detested mother of Elizabeth as the cause of the schism and the woes of Catholics, added her moral deformity, of which he gives the chief features and details (*ibid.*, pp. 25-26) and against which Anglicans have always protested, and rightly too.

[58] Cranmer's letter to Archdeacon Hawkyns, in Strype, *Memorials of Cranmer*, Oxford, 1848, Vol. I, p. 327; *Cranmer's Works*, Parker Society ed. II, 245; *Ven. Cal.*, IV, 351; Sander, *op. cit.*, Lewis' trans., p. 25; Le Grand, *op. cit.*, I, p. 42.

[59] Lancelot de Carles' poem (Crapelet, *op. cit.*, p. 169; G. Ascoli, *op. cit.*, p. 243) describes Anne thus when she left the French Court:

> Oultre ces biens et graces tant exquises
> Qu'avoit en France heureusement acquises,
> S'elle estoit belle et de taille élégante
> Estoit des yeulx encor[es] plus attirante . . .
> Si tist que fut retournée en ces lieux,
> Elle employa la force de ses yeulx;
> Et son regard vint en si haut lieu mectre,
> Qu'en peu de temps elle pleut à son maistre.

Anne's French spelling may be judged by reading her letter to her father, written without assistance from anybody, in Ellis, *Orig. Letters*, 2nd Series, Vol. II, p. 10.

crowned. She played her game very skilfully—a crown was at stake—not only for a few months, but for nearly seven years. She yielded only when Henry was slipping downhill into schism with no hope of climbing back again, and only in order to hasten the conclusion of a scheme she had perseveringly worked out.[60]

At the time of the divorce, Henry pleaded scruples of conscience which he had not hitherto manifested. No king of England had ever married his brother's widow, no king of England had ever known such mortality in his family: five children all still-born or else dead almost immediately after birth.[61] Was it not a case of cause and effect? Scripture said (Lev. xx, 21) that "He who marrieth his brother's wife, doth an unlawful thing. . . . They shall be without children." Henry, who had an open wound in his leg during a great part of his life, and whose two sons, by different mothers, died of consumption before reaching the age of puberty, forgot to seek the cause of the evil in himself. He tried to make people believe that his scruples were shared by others. Three months after the Bishop of Tarbes had tried to negotiate the Dauphin's marriage with Henry VIII's daughter, Mary,[62] the king and Wolsey gave out that the Bishop of Tarbes had

[60] Cf. Crapelet, op. cit., p. 100 (letter IV); Chapuys' letter of October 1st, 1532, L. and P., V, No. 1377; Friedmann, op. cit., I, 45 sq.; Bémont, op. cit., pp. 47 and 100.

The few letters of Anne which have come down to us (Blunt, op. cit., I, 126, n. 9, published two which were addressed to Wolsey and taken from the Harleian Miscellany III) sufficiently show her eager impatience to oust the woman who had been wife and queen for more than twenty years.

[61] On January 31st, 1510, seven months after her marriage, Catherine gave birth to a still-born daughter (Sp. Cal., II, pp. xiv, 408), and on January 1st, 1511, to a son, the Prince of Wales, who lived only three days (Ven. Cal., II, 95, 96; L. and P., I, 1491, 1495; II, 4692), in September, 1513, to another still-born son (Ven. Cal., II, 239), and in June, 1514, to a third son, who died immediately after his baptism (L. and P., I, 5192). In 1517 she had miscarriages; and in 1518 her last child was still-born (November 10th).

[62] The betrothal of Princess Mary, born in February, 1516, to the Dauphin, born in July, 1518, was celebrated at Greenwich on October 15th, and in Paris on December 22nd, in that same year, 1518. Leland, Tunstall and Richard Pace commemorated the event in England in epigrams and speeches, while in France Templier hymned his Concordia Galliae et Britanniae, and the Italian Rinzio's account of the festival and his nuptial song were translated. Cf. Hauser, Sources de l'Histoire de France XVIe siècle, Vol. II, pp. 122 sq.; G. Ascoli, op. cit., p. 56.

voiced certain doubts regarding the legitimacy of the princess and the validity of Catherine's marriage. [63]

This was the starting-point of the famous divorce case. On May 17th, 1527, Wolsey, who was both a legate of the

[63] On November 7th, 1528, Henry VIII made known to the aldermen of London "*le scrupule de conscience ou de long temps il s'est trouvé de l'affaire susdit, qui terriblement luy a augmenté depuys qu'ung évesque françoys, grant personnaige et sçavant homme, signifiant monsieur de Tarbe, estant pour lors ambassadeur deczà, en avoit tenu en son conseil termes terriblement exprès.*" Jean du Bellay to Montmorency, November 17th, 1528. Bourrilly, *Ambassades en Angleterre*, etc., p. 464. Cf. Hall's *Chronicle*, ed. 1809, p. 754; *L. and P.*, IV, 5156; Cavendish, *Life of Wolsey*, ed. 1852, p. 151.

The few documents that we have on Grammont's embassy and the account of it by the French secretary Claude Dodieu say nothing about this statement, which is generally considered to-day to be a fiction invented at the time of the trial. (Cf. Gairdner, *Eng. Hist. Review*, XI, 675 *sq.*; A. Dreux, *Le premier divorce de Henri VIII et les relations entre la France et l'Angleterre de 1527 à 1534*, in *Positions des thèses de l'École de Chartes*, 1900, pp. 43 *sq.*; Ehses, *Die päpstliche Dekretale in dem Ehescheidungsprozesse Heinrichs VIII*, in *Historisches Jahrbuch*, 1888, pp. 611 *sq.*) For Grammont, see Lafforgue, *Histoire des évêques de Tarbes*, in *Rev. des Hautes-Pyrénées*, May, 1928.

According to Sander (Lewis' trans., p. 14) and Le Grand (*op. cit.*, Vol. I, pp. 49 *sq.*), who follows Polydore Vergil (*Liber*, XXVII, Ghent ed., 1557, Vol. II, pp. 1730 *sq.*), Wolsey—determined to "oppose the emperor with all his might" and becoming "a thorough partisan of the most Christian king"—was the author of these scruples, in order to marry Henry to Francis I's sister; according to this opinion he mentioned the matter first to the king's confessor, and then to the Bishop of Tarbes, who had come over to negotiate Mary Tudor's marriage with the Dauphin. Longland, "a simple and scrupulous man, who had more piety than knowledge, went then to the king with Wolsey and told that prince that everybody was scandalized at his marriage with Catherine, and that he believed himself bound in conscience, as his confessor, to warn him and to beg him to allow the question to be examined by some learned persons" (Le Grand, *loc. cit.* Cf. Roper, *Thomas More, Utopia*, ed. already quoted, pp. xix–xx; A. Wood, *op. cit.*, I, 58 *sq.*). And Sander (Lewis' trans., pp. 19–20) records the speech which Gabriel de Grammont, Bishop of Tarbes, is supposed to have delivered on the subject.

"As to the pretext for the divorce," wrote Nicolas Harpsfield (Bémont, *op. cit.*, pp. 47 *sq.*, 100), "he found it in a scruple which his disordered passion inspired: until then he had lived with Catherine for twenty years and had had children by her; he suddenly bethought himself that she had been his elder brother's, Arthur's, wife, and that consequently she had been legally unable to contract marriage with the deceased's brother; yet it was known that she had not had intercourse with him, a young man fourteen years old, and that moreover his father had carefully kept him from his wife's bed" (Cf. Stone, *op. cit.*, pp. 36 n. 3, 37). However that may be, the first motive brought forward, in the beginning, at the Roman Court, for the dissolution of the marriage was the royal scruple based on the nullity of the dispensation (see Wolsey's first letter to Casale, December 5th, 1527, in Burnet, Vol. IV, pp. 20 *sq.*; cf. Lemon, *State Papers*, pp. 23 *sq*).

Holy See and the Prime Minister, summoned Henry to appear before himself and Warham, the Archbishop of Canterbury, who seventeen years previously had been against Catherine's marriage.[64] The king's idea was for Wolsey to declare the dispensation for Henry's first marriage null and void, so that he could marry whomsoever he pleased, and for the Pope to confirm the legate's verdict. His brother-in-law, the Duke of Suffolk, had formerly adopted a similar method.[65]

There was only one drawback to this plan. The queen might deny the legate's jurisdiction and appeal to Rome, and

And Henry urged the same motive right to the end (see his letter to the Pope, July 13th, 1530, in Burnet, *op. cit.*, IV, 169).

Jean du Bellay would seem to have held the opinion attributed to the Bishop of Tarbes when he wrote, on November 1st, 1528 (Bourrilly and Vaissière, *op. cit.*, Vol. I, p. 437): "God has Himself delivered judgment." Wolsey insisted in order to get from him a favourable theological statement in writing, "begging me . . . to show that the present marriage is such that the Pope could not dispense . . . following purely and simply the Sacred Scriptures." Henry and the cardinal were so pleased with it that they begged du Bellay to send it to Francis I's mother so that she might obtain the opinion of some of the doctors of the Sorbonne (*ibid.*, Vol. I, pp. 454 *sq.* Cf. Le Grand, *op. cit.*, Vol. I, pp. 105 *sq.*).

On the contrary, "the English theologians and lawyers were not more favourable to Henry than were the other subjects. Not one of them wanted to write in favour of the divorce" (Le Grand, *op. cit.*, p. 105. Cf. Cavendish, *op. cit.*, ed. 1852, p. 119). The law of Deuteronomy, which was in fact later than that of Leviticus, prescribed that a man should marry his brother's widow in order "suscitare semen fratri suo." A reply from Richard Pace, Dean of St. Paul's, on Deuteronomy shows that already in 1526 the king was considering that question (*ibid.*, Vol. III, p. 1).

[64] *L. and P.*, IV, 3140. In April, 1527, Dr. Richard Wolman had repaired to Winchester to examine the case with the aged bishop, Richard Fox, who, it will be remembered, was not favourable to the marriage. And on May 17th, in the presence of Warham and Wolsey, he replied to the justification read by the king. It would be well to consult the important publication of P. S. and H. M. Allen, *Letters of Richard Fox, 1486–1527* (1929), for everything concerning the beginnings of Henry VIII's reign.

[65] *L. and P.*, IV, 5859. Cf. *ibid.*, 737. The Duke, breaking off his engagement with a certain Anne Browne, had married, after dispensation, Margaret Mortimer, who was a relation in the second degree of consanguinity. Later he maintained the nullity of this dispensation before the Archdeacon of London's officer, won his case, and married Anne Browne, and after her death took Henry VIII's sister, Mary, for his wife. On May 12th, 1528, Clement VII confirmed, by a Bull, the annulment of the first marriage and, under pain of censure, forbade that the other two marriages should be questioned. Henry thought he could proceed in the same manner. Wolsey would declare the insufficiency of the papal dispensation, and consequently the nullity of the marriage with Catherine, and the Pope would confirm this decision, after Henry had married whomever he pleased.

then nothing could be done.[66] Wolsey advised direct recourse
to the Pope, saying that sooner or later that must needs come.
At the same time it would be removing a great responsibility
from his own shoulders.[67] Wolsey thought, at this period,

[66] Cf. *L. and P.*, IV, 3311. This probably decided Henry to sound the
queen. He told her, after making her promise to keep it absolutely secret,
that some theologians and lawyers had shown him that in reality they
were not married. Catherine began to sob and swore that her union with
Arthur had not been consummated, a fact that rendered the dispensation
useless. Henry replied that at least there was the impediment of public
honesty, since in the eyes of the world she and Arthur had been married.
Wolsey used the same argument (see chap. x of Taunton's *Thomas Wolsey*).
    Meanwhile news was brought that Rome had been sacked (May 6th,
1527); the Pope was besieged in the Castle of St Angelo by the imperial
troops. "If the Pope be slain or taken it will hinder the king's affairs not a
little, which have been going on hitherto so well," wrote Wolsey on receiving
the news (*L. and P.*, IV, 3147). How indeed could it be hoped that in such
a situation Clement would confirm the decision against the emperor's
aunt? Wolsey then had the idea of getting the pontifical powers delegated
to himself for England and France (*L. and P.*, IV, No. 3400). "Pensa d'esser
legato in Inghilterra et Francia et comme dire Pontifice—Ha animo di
domendare al Papa che lo faccia suo vicario universale con summa potestà"
(Ehses, *Röm. Dokumente*, pp. 248, 250). "Desidera esser vicario universale
del Papa per tutto o almeno in Francia et Inghilterra" (*ibid.*, p. 268;
Le Grand, *op. cit.*, Vol. I, pp. 57, 59). The Cardinals Bourbon, Salviati,
J. de Lorraine, and A. du Prat, with Wolsey, wrote in fact to the Pope
(Le Grand, *op. cit.*, Vol. III, pp. 4–13) that, during his captivity, he might
delegate his powers to Wolsey in order to remove all suspicion that he was
acting under pressure from the emperor. At the same time the Kings of
France and England bound themselves, by secret treaty, to refuse to give
their consent to any Council as long as the Pope was a prisoner,
and to consider as null and void and not to allow the execution of "all
commandments, Bulls, letters, and Briefs given during the Pope's imprisonment, when they might be prejudicial to either of the two kings, or to the
Duke of York's legation" (Le Grand, *op. cit.*, Vol. I, p. 56).

[67] The divorce agreed so well with Wolsey's new policy that the Spanish
ambassadors and Charles V himself maintained that Wolsey was seeking
by this means to break off the imperial alliance with England, in order
to replace it by one with France. Hence their accusations against the
cardinal (*Sp. Cal.*, III, 193, 276, 300; *L. and P.*, IV, 3312). Cardinal
Giovanni Salviati, legate in France, calls him *inventore di questa causa*
(Ehses, *op. cit.*, Letter January 4th–6th, 1529). But the divorce was one of
those cases "in which the king was to be obeyed by everybody who thought
otherwise"; in his ministerial capacity Wolsey had to support the king,
even at a time when he was known to be most opposed to the marriage
with Anne Boleyn. "The affair displeases him very much, as far as I
gather," Campeggio wrote to Salviati on January 9th, 1529 (Ehses, *op. cit.*,
p. 69); "but your Lordship may rest assured that he dare not show it,
that he can do nothing, and that he is even forced to hide his feelings and
to pretend that he is very zealous in obtaining the king's desire." When the
cause was cited to Rome, the cardinal assumed all responsibility in order
to cover the king. "These words of Wolsey ['I am so from regretting
it, that if it had not been begun, I would have begun it now']," says Sander

that the king wanted to marry Renée, Louis XII's daughter, afterwards Duchess of Ferrara.[68] Knowing that the Boleyn party were very much against the cardinal, the king had not mentioned his secret intentions; and taking advantage of Wolsey's absence in France (July-September, 1527), he brought the business of the divorce before the Roman Court.[69]

(*op. cit.*, Lewis' trans., p. 74),"everybody understood, were meant for the king. Though he [Wolsey] certainly was the first who raised the question, yet, when he saw the king's passion for Anne Boleyn, the man who loved the glory of men more than the glory of God, was sorry for the counsel he had given, when it was no longer in his power to undo it" (cf. J. Gairdner in the *Eng. Hist. Review*, XI, 674). Therefore whatever be the part attributed to him at the beginning of this business by those who are most opposed to him, it must be recognized that he soon saw the seriousness of the case and the difficulty which at first was less suspected (cf. below, n. 69), and that he tried, as much as he could, to clear himself of the moral responsibility by submitting the question to Clement VII.

Wolsey was fatally caught in the wheels of the machinery: once the affair had been started, the more he tried to inspire Henry with disgust for his passionate desires, the more these grew in violence; and the less he succeeded, the more he urged the Pope to gratify the king. His embarrassment continued to increase, and finally changed to anxiety and fear, until the inevitable day when he fell from the king's graces. Cf. Le Grand, *op. cit.*, Vol. I, pp. 70, 80, 81, 82, 87, 88, 93, 96, 99–100, 111–112, 114, 119, 207 *sq.*, Vol. III, pp. 119, 235, 318 *sq.*, 327 *sq.*, 335. See some of his letters in Burnet, *op. cit.*, Vol. IV, pp. 19, 45, 46, 53, 59, 60, 63, 75, 79, 92, 102, 108, and in Lemon, *State Papers*, Vol. VII, pp. 18, 23–35, 50. See Note G in H. Belloc's *Wolsey*.

[68] Louis XII's daughter, Renée, Duchess of Chartres (1510–75), married Hercule d'Este, Duke of Ferrara, in 1528. Wolsey received instructions to sound Francis I on the divorce without, however, mentioning the sister-in-law's name. By error the Duchess of Alençon was mentioned later; she was married in the previous January. Wolsey is said to have insinuated the plan to Francis I's mother, at Compiègne, "in order to cause perpetual separation between the Houses of England and Burgundy" (J. du Bellay to Montmorency, July 30th and October 21st, 1528; Bourrilly, *op. cit.*, Vol. I, pp. 364 and 427; Le Grand, *op. cit.*, Vol. III, p. 166 (where he gives the date August 20th), and p. 186, cf. Vol. I, p. 58. See Rodocanachi, *Renée de France, duchesse de Ferrare*, pp. 26 *sq.*). Wolsey, whom Louisa of Savoy called "my good son and father" (Bourrilly, *op. cit.*, Vol. I, p. 248), and Francis I "very dear and great friend" (*ibid.*, pp. 250, 268, 417, 475), at the end of his career, did not cease to favour the alliance of England with France, at times to his own cost (cf. below, n. 128).

[69] Even this absence of Wolsey is supposed to have been brought about by Anne (Le Grand, *op. cit.*, Vol. I, p. 53, following Cavendish, ed., 1852, p. 74). Henry VIII indeed suspected that his marriage with Anne Boleyn would be little pleasing to the cardinal. Anne and her relations stood for the party which was not very favourable to the clergy, and which Wolsey had hitherto held in check by keeping them from Parliament. Her father, her cousins Sir William Fitzwilliam and Sir Francis Brian, and other near relatives were awaiting the first opportune moment to attack the cardinal and the Church. ". . . the lady [Anne Boleyn] and her father," wrote

His secretary, Knight, was given rather a strange errand.[70] He was told to ask for a dispensation for bigamy, in view of the services Henry had rendered the Church and the Holy See, and also to obtain a dispensation from the first degree of affinity, contracted by the king through his relations with Anne Boleyn's sister. Despite his absence, Wolsey got to hear of the first request and had little difficulty in convincing the king that he had exaggerated; was the book that he had written against Luther sufficient to obtain for him the right to have two wives? Knight, who had not yet reached Rome, was told to ask only for the dispensation for affinity.[71]

Chapuys (L. and P., V, 148, 850) ". . . are more Lutheran than Luther himself; . . . for he and his daughter are considered as true apostles of the new sect." The Duke of Norfolk, her uncle, was so hostile to the cardinal that hard words passed between them in the king's presence [May, 1527] (L. and P., VI, 1411). Consequently, the ambassadors, who had said that Wolsey was the author of the divorce, later received the impression that he was secretly against it (Sp. Cal., III, 432, 790; Ven. Cal., Vol. I, 1529. Cf. Le Grand, op. cit., I, 87.). And Cavendish (Life of Wolsey, ed. 1852, pp. 118 sq., 271 sq.) relates that he besought the king on his knees for hours to alter his plans, but without success (cf. above, nn. 63 and 67).

[70] On account of Wolsey's opposition to the Boleyn family, Henry chose his secretary instead of the three Italians whom Wolsey had advised him to choose: the Bishop of Worcester, Ghinucci, the nuncio Gambara, and Sir Gregory Casale, all conversant with the customs of the Roman Court. Girolamo Ghinucci, of Siena, auditor of the Apostolic Chamber, had been sent by Leo X as nuncio to England, where he received the bishopric of Worcester in 1522; for a short while he carried out the office of English ambassador to the Holy See, and then to Spain. In 1528 Henry asked for the red hat for him. He received it from Paul III in 1535 (Chacon-Oldoin, Vitae et res gestae R. Pontificum et cardinalium S.R.E., Rome, 1677, III, 569).

To save appearances, Knight had orders to take instructions from Wolsey, whom he saw at Compiègne (September 10th, 1527). For his mission see L. and P., IV, Nos. 3140, 3604, 3749, 3918, etc.

[71] Henry VIII to Knight, in Academy, XV, 239. Henry sent this letter (reprinted by Gairdner in the English Hist. Review, XI, 685) by John Barlow, chaplain to Anne Boleyn's father.

[J. Gairdner states in a note to Brewer's The Reign of Henry VIII (Vol. II, p. 223, n. 2): "He was not . . . the notorious William Barlow, afterwards bishop, but John Barlow, his brother."—Translator.]

Wolsey was not to know the contents. Barlow met Knight at Foligno. The latter got into Rome (which was occupied by the Imperialists) not without difficulty, and through Cardinal Pisani managed to pass the king's demand in to the Pope, besieged in the Castle St. Angelo. Clement VII expressed his gratitude to Henry for the steps taken to deliver him, and promised to do all he could in his favour when he was free (L. and P., No. 3638. Clement VII to Henry VIII, Orvieto, December 14th, 1527. Letter published by Molini in the Documenti di Storia Italiana, I, 280, and summarized by Ehses, op. cit., 10. Clement VII to Wolsey, same date, in

Wolsey then made him see that the divorce was the crux of the whole question, and that he ought to ask Clement VII to give Wolsey the power to decide the question, without any possibility of appeal to the Roman Court.[72] In this way he hoped to regain the royal favour which he felt that he was losing. His suggestions were carried out. The Pope submitted the case to an eminent Canonist, Cardinal Pucci, who exclaimed, when he had read the rough draft of the Bull drawn up in England, that the signing of it would be a perpetual dishonour for the Pope, for the king, and for Wolsey. It was modified so as to reserve to the Holy See the right to alter the decision; which was precisely what the king and his minister did not want.[73] Knight, not understanding the

Ehses, *op. cit.*, p. 10). Escaping a few days later from the Castle St Angelo, he arrived at Orvieto. There, after Knight had renewed his entreaties and after some unessential corrections (cf. Ehses, *Historisches Jahrbuch*, IX, 226, n. 3), he granted the Bull of dispensation from the impediment of affinity, should the first marriage be invalid [December 23rd, 1527]. Ehses, *Dokumente*, p. 14; Dodd, *op. cit.*, Part I, Bk. III, art. 3, "Records of the divorce." This letter had already been published by Lord Herbert, *op. cit.*, ed. 1706, p. 119. Cf. Knight's letters to the king and Wolsey, January 1st and 10th, 1528, in Burnet, IV, 37 and 40. The king's scruples were mentioned in them.

It seems that the demand for a dispensation for bigamy was known in Rome but remembered too late. See Gregory Casale's letter to the king, September 18th, 1530, in Collier, *op. cit.*, Vol. IX, p. 93.

[72] It is strange indeed that Henry VIII should ask for the dispensation before he had given his attention to the one thing that could make it of any use. His action served only to arouse the Imperialists. Possibly he had thought that the annulling of his marriage was an easy thing, bearing in mind the cases of Louis XII and the Duke of Suffolk (see above, nn. 34 and 65).

In case Wolsey should appear to be suspect of partiality, the Dean of the Rota, Stafileo, who was favourable to the king, was proposed (cf. Wolsey's letter to Casale, December 5th, 1527. Burnet, *op. cit.*, IV, 25 *sq.*, 30). Henry even thought of sending him to Rome as his own ambassador and also Francis I's (*L. and P.*, IV, Nos. 3400, 3765–67); and on January 5th, 1525 gave him a letter of credit to the Pope for the divorce business (Pocock, *Narratives of the Reformation*, I, 49).

Knight received the king's order on the way back (December, 1527). He returned to Orvieto, and accompanied by the royal agent Gregory Casale and the nuncio Gambara, recalled to Italy, he presented his new demand to the Pope, and emphasized the king's devotedness to the Holy See and the necessity of avoiding in the realm a succession which was rendered debatable by a doubtful dispensation of marriage.

[73] Knight to Wolsey, January 1st, 1528 (Burnet, *op. cit.*, Vol. IV, 34–39). This document no longer exists. It was probably a mandate to Wolsey and perhaps to Stafileo to examine the alleged defects in the Bull granted by Julius II; if power was given to pronounce on the validity of the marriage

extent of this modification, set out for England, delighted
with the success of his errand. But when Wolsey had the Bull
in his hands he declared that it "was as good as none at all."[74]

What they wanted, in fact, was that the case should be
tried in England and an irrevocable decision given, so as to
prevent Charles V from intervening at Rome in favour of his
aunt. During the whole of these divorce proceedings everything tends in the same direction, for the king and his minister
were continually haunted by fear that the emperor would
bring pressure to bear upon the Pope.[75]

Knight's failure benefited Wolsey, for the king placed the
whole business entirely in his hands; and the cardinal, knowing
that his credit with the king depended upon it, left no stone
unturned to bring it to a successful issue.[76]

He sent to the Pope two uncommonly clever and talented
men, who afterwards received mitres for their services, his
secretary, Stephen Gardiner, the best Canonist in England,
and Edward Foxe, who, in 1536, was told to try and effect a
rapprochement with the German Protestants.[77] With the

the clause making the decision irrevocable was at least removed, as Ehses
remarks. The Pope still hesitated to send the Bull; he promised to send
it when the French army, under the orders of Lautrec, approached Orvieto
(cf. *L. and P.*, IV, Nos. 3751, 4120).

[74] *L. and P.*, IV, 3913. Knight's letters had at first pleased Wolsey
(*ibid.*, No. 3851), but in April (1528) he writes from Poissy begging
the king's pardon for the failure of his mission (*L. and P.*, IV, No. 4185.
Cf. Bourrilly, *op. cit.*, I, 143).

[75] Cf. below, nn. 85 and 92; and Burnet, *op. cit.*, Vol. IV, pp. 74, 80, 94,
109, 115, 118 *sq.*, 122 *sq.*

Already every precaution had been taken to prevent Catherine com-
municating with her nephew; and the messenger whom she had sent to
claim his protection had been arrested (August, 1527). In spite of that
Mendoza got wind of the business; and on July 29th the emperor sent the
Cardinal Quiñones to Rome to act on behalf of the queen and to persuade
the Pope to take from Wolsey his powers as legate (*Sp. Cal.*, III, 193,
276, 300; *L. and P.*, IV, 3312). Clement VII told Knight that during his
captivity he had been urged not to do anything with regard to the royal
divorce (*Eng. Hist. Review*, XI, 690).

[76] He had already changed his tactics: fearing that his partiality would
be objected to if he alone pronounced the decision, he wanted to give it
indisputable authority by having it pronounced by a legate of the Pope.
Knight had left Orvieto; and it was Casale who received the fresh instructions. But the Curia tried to evade all responsibility. The Cardinals Pucci
and Simonetta proposed, according to Casale, a combination, which added
nothing either to his powers as legate or to the value of the dispensation
(cf. Ehses, *Dokumente*, pp. 23, 48; *L. and P.*, IV, No. 3082).

[77] J. du Bellay to Montmorency, February 6th, 1528, in Bourrilly, I,

shrewdness and cunning of a diplomat Gardiner combined a
lawyer's adroitness and debating powers. By blending extreme
cleverness with extreme audacity he was able to get the best
possible result out of instructions which were very difficult
indeed to carry out.[78]

It was shortly after Rome had been sacked.[79] Clement,
who had taken refuge in the Castle St Angelo, was at Orvieto,
forsaken and in want. The English envoys "spake roundly
unto him," as they themselves admitted. Gardiner scarcely
troubled to veil his threats. After a month of daily conferences,
in which the discussion lasted three or four hours without
interruption,[80] a first Bull was obtained. Cardinals Campeggio
and Wolsey were delegated to pass sentence without publicity
or the usual forms of justice. None could deny their verdict
or appeal from it. Finally, each of the delegates had the right
to act alone, if the other no longer wished to do so.[81]

143; Wolsey to Clement VII, February 10th, 1528, and to Gregory Casale,
February 12th, 1528, in Burnet, IV, 15, and Lemon, *State Papers*, VII, 50,
to accredit Gardiner and Foxe. For the way they acted on the Pope, see
J. A. Muller, *Stephen Gardiner*, chap. IV, London, 1926.

[78] The different proposals suggested by the instructions (*L. and P.*, IV,
No. 3913, cf. Bourrilly, *op. cit.*, I, 151 *sq.*, 156) were less and less difficult
to grant. Wolsey knew with certainty that the king would not go back
on his resolution, whether the Pope favoured it or opposed it; and so
he made it clearly understood, saying that was the time for Clement to
show his gratitude to Henry, and trying to dissipate the bad impressions
of Anne Boleyn which the Imperialists might have given him.

[79] Cf. P. Balan, *Monumenta Saec. XVI historiam illustrantia, Vol. I: Clementis
VII epistolae per Sadoletum scriptae, 1524–28*, Innsbruck, 1885.

[80] One day Gardiner remained with Simonetta from seven in the
morning until night fell. He has left us, in his dispatches to Wolsey and to
the king, an account of those conferences written in a glowing style calculated to bring out the force of his own arguments. But a memorandum of
Cardinal Pucci (Ehses, *op. cit.*, pp. 22 *sq.*), the simplicity of which forms a
contrast to Gardiner's reports, proves that the Roman Canonists had
answers equally as good.

[81] "Vobis conjunctim et, altero vestrum nolente aut impedito, divisim."
This last clause had been the subject of a lively discussion: it had even
been taken out of the last draft of the Bull, and Gardiner had obtained its
re-insertion only by stating that the Holy See would be ruined, since it was
alienating the only prince who was really its friend; Clement VII was
extremely excited (*L. and P.*, IV, p. 181).
The Bull granted by Clement VII on April 13th, 1528 and renewed in
the June of the same year has been published by Rymer, *op. cit.*, XIV, 237;
Collier, IX, 75; Dodd, Part I, Bk. 3, art. 3, "Records of the divorce"; and
Ehses, No. 24. Gardiner, in his letter of May 4th (Burnet, IV, 23; cf.
Brian's letter of the next day, *State Papers*, VII, 169), relates how the Pope
was trying to evade the English demands.

In order to make the decision irrevocable, Wolsey also demanded, quite secretly and so that no human eye should see it, a Decretal Bull establishing the law in this particular case, and stating that certain defects (the very ones which were said to vitiate Julius II's dispensation) rendered any Bull of dispensation null and void. Thus there could be no reversing the verdict, which had merely to establish the fact. Wolsey had given the gist of it, asserting that the Holy See's authority in England as well as his own life depended upon it. Clement gave way and granted the Decretal; but left the final decision to the legates' consciences (July 1528).[82] At the same time he adopted certain precautions so as to restrict the practical effect of this document. It was a secret one. Campeggio was to show it only to the king and Wolsey. He could not use it in the trial. During the proceedings Wolsey unsuccessfully begged the Pope to allow him to show it to some of the Council.[83]

On July 25th, Campeggio, released from governing Rome, embarked at Corneto for France. He did not reach England till the beginning of October. He was a distinguished Canonist, supple in character, and was also Bishop of Salisbury. The King's generosity had supplied him with his new palace; and so Henry relied upon him to give the desired ending to the proceedings.[84]

[82] The autograph promise not to revoke the Bull and to confirm the cardinals' decision (published from Lord Herbert, by Burnet, VI, 26; Ehses, p. 30) was conceded on July 23rd, despite the imperial ambassador's protest against Wolsey's and Campeggio's delegation; the protest was published in the *Eng. Hist. Review*, 1897, Vol. XII, p. 111. Henry was haunted by fear of an appeal being made to the Pope or his successor which might invalidate his second marriage, and so compromise the succession to the throne, and the peace of the realm (cf. Ehses, p. 25).

"Mihi certe molestissimum est futurum vivere diutius, ob innumera mala quae inde subsecutura videntur . . . ; vereor ne . . . [apostolicae] sedis contemptus in dies excresceret, hoc praesertim tempore admodum periculoso," wrote Wolsey, in the letter to Casale (Burnet, IV, 55 *sq.*), in which he insisted on the necessity of the decretal Bull. It was through fear of the Imperialists who would not have failed to set themselves against it that he demanded such an absolute secret (*ibid.*, p. 60). The model for this Bull had been drawn up by him in England; it may be found in Burnet, IV, 48; and Collier, IX, 77.

[83] Campeggio was faithful to the conditions laid down (Ehses, p. 55). See Wolsey's and his agents' solicitations in Rome to get the Pope (who became angry and refused) to allow them to show the decretal Bull, with the greatest secrecy, to some of the royal counsellors, in Burnet, IV, 63 *sq.*

[84] Cf. Burnet, I, 100. Campeggio was deprived of his bishopric, at the

Campeggio received fresh instructions from the Pope en route. Troubled by the success of the imperial arms in Italy and rightly anxious not to appear to favour Charles V's adversary Henry, the Pope ordered the legate to delay the decision. He was to prolong the business as much as possible, and to content himself with re-establishing mutual affection between the king and queen.[85]

Campeggio promised the Pope not to give judgment, but asked for faculties to examine the case. The English people, he said, "would think I had come to hoodwink them, and might resent it. You know how much that would involve."[86]

So while Henry, more infatuated with Anne than ever, promised himself a prompt solution,[87] in reality it was more remote than before. The Pope "being a man of such a nature," Gardiner wrote to the king, "as he never resolveth any thing, but by some violent affection compelled thereunto . . . there shall every day rise new devices, and none take effect, but

same time as another Italian, Ghinucci, Bishop of Worcester, by an Act of Parliament in 1534 (*Statutes of the Realm*, 25 Henry VIII, c. 5; and Burnet, IV, 192).

[85] Dispatch from Sanga, papal secretary, September 11th, 1528 (*L. and P.*, IV, 4721; cf. *ibid.*, 4736–37). Clement VII had formed no opinion either for or against Henry, whose case he had not been able sufficiently to study. He probably wanted to recall to Rome a case which he had only after much hesitation allowed to be judged elsewhere. He himself wrote to the emperor that he would do nothing to the detriment of Catherine and that Campeggio had gone to England only to urge Henry to do his duty, and that the process would be cited before the Roman Court (*Sp. Cal.*, III, 779).

To prevent, in general, the emperor from having any influence over Clement VII, the idea of establishing a guard of French and English soldiers in Rome was conceived (*L. and P.*, IV, 5179). At the same time as they promised to restore to the Pope Ravenna and Cervia, which were held by the Venetians and which Clement was persistently claiming (cf. *L. and P.*, IV, 5447; Bourrilly, *op. cit.*, pp. 385, 393, 403, 417, 424, 425, 427, 438, 460, 482–83, 488, 494, 506, 520, 521), they made known to him the plan for a formidable coalition of the Italian States, of France, and of England against Charles V.

[86] *L. and P.*, IV, 4736. See a similar letter from Wolsey to the Pope, in Burnet, IV, 110.

[87] He wrote to Anne Boleyn that he could not help expressing to her his joy at seeing the day approach when the legates could begin the proceedings. *Love Letters of Henry VIII* (the last edition was in 1907), English eds., 1720, 1745, 1813, No. VI; cf. Nos. XI, XVIII; French ed. by Crapelet, pp. 117, 126, 140; cf. pp. 148, 149, 151. [Cf. Brewer's *Reign of Henry VIII*, II, p. 294, n. 1.—*Translator.*]

For these letters, and the "sweating sickness" which occasioned them, see the French edition of this book, pp. 360 *sq.*, and 773.

long delays, and wasted time." Rome's policy was delay. It was hoped that Henry's passion for Anne would die in time as all its predecessors had done, and that he himself would then give up the divorce.[88] The delay lasted several years, but ended in a catastrophe.

Neither Wolsey nor Henry wanted to lose any time. When Wolsey saw Campeggio's state of mind, he warned him that "if the king's desire was not complied with, fortified and justified as it was by the reasons, writings and counsels of many learned men who feared God, total ruin would specially ensue of the kingdom, of himself (Wolsey), and of the Church's influence." "Beware," he added, "lest, in like manner as the greater part of Germany, owing to the harshness and severity of a certain cardinal, has become estranged from the Apostolic See and the Faith, it should be said that another cardinal has given the same occasion to England with the same result." "He often impresses upon me (Campeggio) that, if this divorce be not granted, the authority of the See Apostolic in this kingdom will be at an end." Wolsey continually insisted upon the imminent peril of schism if the king were displeased.[89]

When, in accordance with his instructions, Campeggio tried to dissuade Henry from his purpose, the latter quite openly replied that he only wanted them to say whether his marriage was valid or not. He wanted nothing else, because he was certain that it was invalid. "And I believe," the legate

[88] Gardiner's letter to Henry VIII is dated April 21st, 1529. Burnet, V, 448. Cf. Brian's letter of the same day, in Lemon, *State Papers*, VII, 166. Clement VII, "*soit qu'il craignît d'offenser l'empereur, soit qu'il voulüt ménager le Roy d'Angleterre, ne pouvoit pas prendre d'autre party que celui qu'il prît, qui étoit de faire durer ce procés*. . . . *A la vérité, le pape espérant toujours que le tems pourroit guérir le Roy de sa passion avait sur tout recommandé à Campége de prolonger cette affaire le plus qu'il pourroit*" (Le Grand, *op. cit.*, Vol. I, pp. 91, 107). "*Plus de temps il s'écoule en cette affaire*," Giovanni Salviati wrote to J. Salviati on December 14th, 1528 (Ehses, 260), *plus cela convient à Sa Sainteté qui peut mieux délibérer et connaître le parti à suivre*." "*Je sais que l'idée de Sa Béatitude est qu'on ne porte pas de sentence, que je fasse durer l'affaire le plus qu'il se peut*" (Campeggio to J. Salviati, June 21st, 1529; Ehses, *op. cit.*, No. 49).

[89] Wolsey's words to Campeggio, quoted here, are taken from a letter from Campeggio to J. Salviati, London, October 26th, 1528 (Ehses, No. 31). [Cf. also Brewer, *Henry VIII*, II, 297 sq.—*Translator.*] As for the insistence of Wolsey and his agents in Rome on the imminence of a schism if the Pope alienated the king, see their letters in Burnet, IV, 55, 56, 74, 79 sq., 97, 106 sq.

added, "that if an angel descended from Heaven, he would not be able to persuade his Majesty to the contrary . . . I believe in this case he knows more than any great theologian and jurist."[90] Henry even wrote a book and Gardiner took the manuscript to Rome. It was printed some time later.[91] From the king nothing could be expected. Already he was insinuating that Clement was on the emperor's side and was no longer neutral in the matter.[92]

Campeggio was caught between Rome ordering a delay and the king and Wolsey who would not hear of one. In desperation he turned to Catherine. He wanted her to take religious vows. This was the second point in his instructions. If the queen entered the cloister, she would keep her dowry estates, her title of Princess, and the direction of her daughter, who would be sure of the succession. All she would lose would be the king's favour, and for a long time already he had abandoned her and would never return to her. If she refused she would lay herself open to a decision which would deprive her of her honour, reputation, and dowry, and cause her innumerable worries and enmities. She had only to follow the example of the Queen of France, Jeanne de Valois. After living with Louis XII for twenty-two years, Jeanne had withdrawn into a convent just a few years before this period, and her memory was greatly honoured by her former subjects.[93]

[90] Campeggio's letter, already quoted, October 26th, 1528. *"Suivant religieusement ses instructions, il [Campeggio] commença à exhorter le roy de la part du pape, de ne point songer à quitter sa femme. Il représenta le tort qu'il allait faire à sa réputation, les malheurs qui en pourraient arriver à la chrétienté, les guerres qu'il faudrait soutenir, le peu de secours qu'il devoit attendre de la France, qui par son imprudence, venoit de perdre le seul homme qui pouvoit soutenir son credit en Italie. Toutes ces raisons ne furent point capables de toucher Henry"* (Le Grand, *op. cit.,* Vol. I, p. 101).

[91] Gardiner and Foxe gave it to the Pope (Strype, *Eccles. Mem.,* 72, 75). The king had it printed in 1530, together with the decisions of the universities obtained in his favour (Burnet, I, 166, n.). In Burnet (IV, 76-79), under the date May 21st, 1529, may be found a summary of the reasons for the royal divorce and a refutation of the objections that might be made against it.

[92] Ehses, No. 31. The fear of imperial intervention dominated the whole of the divorce (cf. Burnet, IV, 74, 80, 94 *sq.,* 109 *sq.,* 115 *sq.,* 118-25; see also above, nn. 75 and 85).

[93] Campeggio to Salviati, June 21st (Ehses, No. 49). Campeggio had advised writing to the emperor so that the latter might persuade Catherine to enter religion (Ehses, p. 57; cf. Burnet, II, 108 *sq.*), and Henry had thought of setting the queen an example, provided the Pope released him

With proper Spanish pride and obstinacy Catherine would not listen to these fine counsels. After mature deliberation, she replied (October 24th-26th) that she would not take the vow of chastity. She wished to live and die in the married state to which God had called her; and neither the prospect of a kingdom nor of greater sufferings could shake her resolution, even if they hacked her to pieces.[94] Nothing could move her, neither the thought of the country's or of the king's peace, nor the pleadings of the two cardinals and her counsellors; and vainly did Wolsey cast himself on his knees before her.[95]

Campeggio saw himself obliged to undertake the proceedings,[96] when suddenly an unexpected occasion for postponing them cropped up. There existed in Spain, unbeknown to Henry, Wolsey, or Clement VII, a dispensation in the form of a Brief granted prior to the Bull. Julius II had despatched it to Isabella on her death-bed. No doubt about the consummation of the marriage with Arthur was expressed in it.[97] The dispensation under this heading existed therefore in its entirety, and there was no need for Catherine to swear that she had been Arthur's wife only in name.[98] Catherine obtained at once from the vow which concerned him (*L. and P.*, IV, pp. 2157, 2161).

For the annulment of Jeanne de Valois' marriage, see the French edition of this book, p. 364, n. 100.

[94] Campeggio to Salviati, October 26th, 1528 (Ehses, *op. cit.*, No. 31). It was then that the queen asserted that her marriage with Arthur had not been consummated (*ibid*, p. 59; see Note K, H. Belloc's *Wolsey*).

[95] Campeggio to Salviati, October 28th, 1528 (Ehses, No. 32).

[96] Campeggio was being importuned on all sides (Ehses, pp. 50, 51, 57). "Questo re persevera piu che mai nel suo desiderio di volere questa per moglie. . . . El Rev. Eboracense è sforzato di mostrarsi fervente in procurare il desiderio del re" (Campeggio, January 9th, 1529; Ehses, p. 69). [Cf. also Brewer, *Reign of Henry VIII*, Vol. II, pp. 480 *sq.*—*Translator*.]

Campeggio, frightened of his responsibility, advised that the cause should be cited to Rome (Ehses, p. 60); and he sought to bring Wolsey round to that idea (*ibid.*, pp. 69, 71; letter dated January 9th, 1529) [cf. also Brewer, *loc. cit.*, p. 480.—*Translator*], by displaying the imperial "bogey" before him (*ibid.*, p. 69).

[97] It did not contain the adverb *forsan*, as did the Bull addressed to Henry VII (cf. Busch, *England under the Tudors*, chap. VI, No. 3).

[98] There are indeed two stages in the divorce proceedings: in the first, an attempt was made to prove that the dispensation for affinity was null and void, because Julius II thought he was giving a dispensation for a non-consummated marriage, whereas it had been really consummated (cf. below, n. 155). Later, as we shall see, it was not the validity of the dispensation that was attacked, but the very *right* of the Pope to dispense

a copy of the Brief through the Spanish ambassador and gave it to Campeggio. Henry did all he could to get the original. Catherine was subjected to pressure. She was made to write to the emperor saying that the Brief was necessary for her honour and for the legitimacy of her daughter. But on arriving in Spain, her messenger informed the emperor that his aunt's intention was exactly the opposite. The king then sent envoy after envoy to Rome[99] demanding that Clement should either declare the Brief to be false or else imperatively, *imperioso modo*, ask the emperor for it.[100] Meanwhile Ghinucci and Lee, the English ambassadors in Spain, examined the Brief and stated that it was not authentic,[101] though most modern historians believe that it was.[102]

The new direction suddenly given to the divorce business made the king and Wolsey drop the Brief question and try to hasten the legates' verdict. Gardiner had sent a special messenger to Henry in May warning him that the cause was about to be cited before the Roman Court.[103] Deprived of

in the case of an impediment *juris divini* (and such was the impediment in a marriage with a sister-in-law).

[99] See these envoys' names in Ehses, No. 45.

[100] *L. and P.*, IV, No. 4978. The Pope refused to pronounce the Brief false without seeing it and without hearing the parties: yet he promised to ask the emperor for it without, however, ordering it to be given up (*ibid.*, IV, No. 5529). The English envoys were so importunate and arrogant that the Pope, who was just recovering from an illness, had a serious relapse (*ibid.*, IV, No. 5534). Wolsey, who was concerned about the succession (Burnet, IV, 75; Dodd, I, 309), warned the English envoys to see that the tiara did not fall to one of the king's adversaries.

[101] *L. and P.*, IV. 5376-77, 5470-71, 5486-87. Wolsey deemed it false, because its author, in order to date it the same day as the Bull addressed to Henry VII, had followed the year of the Incarnation as for the Bulls, whereas for the Briefs the year of the Nativity was always used (cf. Burnet, Vol. IV, 101).

[102] The original was found at Vienna. Cf. Busch, *England under the Tudors*, appendix and chap. XI; Friedmann, *Anne Boleyn*, I, 92, II, Appendix C; Lord Acton, in the *Quarterly Review*, Vol. CXLIII, pp. 1-51. For this affair of the Brief see J. Gairdner, in the *English Hist. Review*, XII, 237-48; H. Belloc, *Wolsey*, Note J. As for this Brief, of which the copy sent from Spain to England has been published by Burnet (IV, 61) and Collier (IX, 82, cf. above, n. 9), Wolsey and Campeggio asked the Pope to pronounce it null and void, which would have simplified very much the proceedings (Burnet, IV, 92, 102). Clement VII replied that he could not declare the Brief false without hearing both parties (*L. and P.*, IV No. 5474).

[103] Henry VIII to Gardiner and Brian, April 6th, 1529; Wolsey to the same, May 21st, 1529, in Burnet, IV, 108 and 115. The English ambassador's dispatch announcing this news, which took ten days to reach London,

all friendly aid, visited by people who blamed her for her conduct, and subjected to pressure, Catherine had indeed managed to write to the Pope; and he had been touched by her letter.[104] At the same time the emperor had taken up his aunt's cause and had given her his own ambassadors for proctors.[105] There was therefore no time to be lost. A favourable judgment had to be obtained from the legates before the cause was cited to Rome.

On the other hand, Campeggio could no longer find excuse for delay. "I know well that His Holiness does not wish us to pass judgment," he wrote to Rome, "and that he wants me to prolong the business as long as possible. But they will no longer grant me any of the delays I ask for, unless they are evidently required by the cause. . . . It would be no use my saying that I will not or cannot give a decision, because the Bull provides for that case by allowing the second legate to give one by himself."[106]

On May 30th, 1529, permission was given to Campeggio and Wolsey, under the great seal, to proceed with their papal delegation. On the 31st, despite their desire "to avoid reefs and quicksands," the legates' court was opened in Blackfriars Hall, London.[107] The king and queen were summoned

seems to have been lost (Ehses, p. 98, n. 1). Gardiner had been sent back to Rome with Sir Francis Brian on January 20th, 1529 (Bourrilly, I, 539, 543; Le Grand, III, 282, 295). His first letter to the king is dated March 3rd (Lemon, *State Papers*, Vol. VII, p. 152; cf. the instructions brought to him by Bennet, *ibid.*, p. 171). He was to leave Rome, and Brian also, at the end of May; on the 31st of that month Clement VII handed them an autograph letter for the king, expressing his regret at being unable to do more to please him (Burnet, IV, 114). Cf. chap. v of J. A. Muller's *Stephen Gardiner*.—At the beginning of the same month, or at the end of April, Gardiner had had to debate the question of the appeal, in open consistory, against Mai, the imperial ambassador, who was striving to bring the cause before the Roman Court. As a man of experience and a faithful servant, he upheld the king (Lemon, *State Papers*, VII, 160; *L. and P.*, IV, 5417, 5440, 5529).

[104] *Sp. Cal.*, Vol. III, Part II, 971, 974.

[105] *L. and P.*, IV, Nos. 5518, 5576. At the same time the emperor protested against the procedure followed in England (*L. and P.*, IV, No. 5529). Mai, his ambassador in Rome, had already taken the matter in hand (cf. above, n. 103).

[106] Ehses, No. 49. Cf. J. du Bellay to Montmorency, January 25th, 1529; Bourrilly, *op. cit.*, p. 540.

[107] Campeggio to Salviati, June 4th, 1529 (Ehses, No. 46). The description of the first session, the appearance of the room, the enumeration of the people present and their words have been preserved for us by Cavendish,

to appear on June 18th.[108] Henry was represented by a proctor. Catherine appeared personally to protest against the competency of the tribunal. She appealed to Rome and would not accept the judges on account of their partiality. Her protest was taken down in writing.[109] The legates rejected it on June 21st. They relied upon the Bull delegating them and declared themselves competent judges.[110] The queen then threw herself at the king's knees. Twice did he raise her up. She begged him to think of her own and her daughter's honour and of the House of Spain, and to allow her to send messengers to Rome. Henry had already declared that he sought only justice and the relief of his conscience. He granted the queen's request, but added that it was unreasonable on account of the emperor's power with the Curia.[111] Catherine departed after making a formal appeal to the Holy See. The king was anxious to dispel the painful impression of this scene: "She is, my lords," said he, "as true, as obedient, and as conformable a wife as I could in my phantasy wish or desire. She hath all the virtuous qualities that ought to be

---

Wolsey's gentleman-usher, who had always eyes and ears well open to retain all that he witnessed (*Life of Wolsey*, ed. 1852, pp. 125, 146). Gardiner was the chief secretary.

The sentence "ut hos scopulos et has syrtes evitemus" is taken from Wolsey's letters to his agents at the Roman Court (Burnet, IV, 107).

[108] Ehses, *op. cit.*, pp. 103, 104.

[109] She reproached Wolsey for his pride and ambition, and accused him of satisfying, by this trial, his resentment against the emperor, who had not allowed him to assume the tiara. See her speech in Dodd, *op. cit.*, Part I, Bk. 3, art. 3, "Records of the divorce."

On June 15th she had been to Campeggio to ask him if the cause had been cited to Rome, and how if the case were pending it could be proceeded with in England. The legate had replied that the cause was not pending in the Roman court; but that His Holiness had charged two delegates to examine the suit, and that he would not have it cited before himself without great consideration. Catherine complained that the counsellors given to her by Henry had more in view the king's wishes than her own needs. Campeggio advised her to have confidence in him and to rest assured that the legates would never go against justice and reason (Campeggio to Salviati, June 16th, 1529, Ehses, No. 47).

[110] "Omni recusatione et appellatione remotis" (Campeggio to Salviati, June 21st, 1529, Ehses, p. 109).

[111] Campeggio to Salviati, June 21st, 1529, Ehses, Nos. 48 and 49. Wolsey begged Campeggio to beseech His Holiness not to cite the cause to Rome, and warned him that the king would also send to Rome (Ehses, p. 109). The queen's words are recorded by Cavendish, *Life of Wolsey*, ed. 1852, pp. 129 *sq.*

in a woman of her dignity, or in any other of baser estate."[112]

The figure of this noble queen, crowned with a halo of conjugal fidelity and proudly courageous, is one of the most pathetic in England's history. Her name was never tarnished by the slightest breath of scandal.[113] Her unhappiness as well as the justice of her cause had won for her the sympathies of the people, especially of the women. One day she was passing through the gallery leading from Bridewell Palace to Blackfriars Convent when the crowd caught sight of her and loudly cheered her.[114] The king was displeased and gave orders that henceforth none should loiter there.[115] When Campeggio landed in England the people lampooned him and gave him a very bad reception, thinking that he was come for the proceedings against the queen.[116] On the other hand, popular feeling had flared up against Anne. About the month of August, 1532, it was rumoured in France that a band of men and women, all disguised as women, had attempted to lay hold of her and that she had had great difficulty in escaping. When the prior of the Augustinians prayed for Anne as the queen (Easter 1533), at St. Paul's Cross, nearly the whole of the congregation left the church by way of protest.[117] According to Aleandre, More, Fitzwilliam, the

[112] *L. and P.*, IV, Introd., p. cccclxxv. Cf. Cavendish, ed. 1852, pp. 131 *sq.*

[113] See Sander's description of Catherine (Lewis' trans., p. 7). Luis Vives had a great influence upon her moral life. Cf. Stone, *op. cit.*, pp. 39-40.

[114] "The queen is so much loved, so much respected that already the people are beginning to murmur, and there is no doubt that, if a leader of a party arose, the English nation, which is prone to novelties and changes, would take up arms for her, especially if he had the sense to marry the princess Mary." Report of the ambassador Falieri, 1531 (Albèri, III, 26; cf. *ibid.*, p. 10).

[115] It was then he made the speech, at the Bridewell, to the Lord Mayor and aldermen, which we have already mentioned (Sunday, November 8th, 1528). Dodd, *op. cit.*, Part I, Bk. 3, art. 3, gives the whole of it.

[116] Giovanni Salviati, legate in France, to Jacob Salviati, October 13th, 1528. Ehses, *op. cit.*, p. 259. Cf. Vourrilly, 411 *sq.*, 481 *sq.*; Le Grand, III, 169, 232; J. Gairdner, *History*, 119.

[117] A severe and threatening message, addressed by Henry on the following Sunday to the Lord Mayor and transmitted to the corporations by the latter, imposed silence on the people (Friedmann, *op. cit.*, I, 200; Chapuys to Charles V, April 27th, 1533; *L. and P.*, VII, No. 39). The day Anne was crowned the merchants of the Steelyard, one of the quarters of London, received orders to erect a triumphal arch; but they did it with such bad grace that they placed Catherine's arms at the top, the king's arms underneath, and in the last place Anne Boleyn's coat of arms. For Anne's unpopularity see Friedmann, *op. cit.*, II, 127 *sq.*

comptroller Guildford and many other noblemen were hostile
to the scheming "Night Crow" at Court. They did not like
her ways and wished to see her humiliated.[118]

Catherine did not appear again before the legatine Court
and was declared contumacious. This naturally favoured
the king's cause.[119] The queen's chief defender was Bishop
Fisher, one of her counsellors. He made a vigorous speech
declaring that he had studied the case for two years and was
persuaded that the royal marriage was valid. He professed
himself ready, like St John the Baptist, to lay down his life
in defence of its indissolubility.[120]

After the queen's appeal, Henry and Wolsey hurried the
proceedings, fearing lest the cause should be cited before the
Roman Court.[121] "We are going ahead very quickly," wrote
Campeggio, "at more than a trot, so that judgment is expected
within a week. Although there is much to do, writing, cita-

[118] Aleandre to Sanga, April 17th, 1532 (Ehses, No. 126). Wolsey,
according to Cavendish, called Anne a "Night Crow."

[119] Cf. Sander, op. cit., Lewis' trans., p. 54.

[120] Ehses, Nos. 53 and 54; L. and P., IV, Introd., p. ccclxxix. See
below, chap. v, pp. 204 sq. Sander, op. cit., Lewis' trans., pp. 66 sq.
Besides Fisher, Catherine had H. Standish, Bishop of St Asaph, for
counsellor (cf. A. Wood, op. cit., ed. 1691, 1, 36, 46, 47; Cavendish, ed.
1852, p. 127). Four theologians upheld the queen's cause, and two of them,
Abel and Powell, wrote a treatise De non dissolvendo Henrici regis cum Catherina
matrimonio. In the Cambridge University Library there is a tract by
Fisher (MS. 1315) divided up into six "axiomas": "Constet . . . Regem
Henricum 7um, etc." Therein the bishop shows "that the Pope had full
power to grant a dispensation for Henry VIII's first marriage with the
wife of his deceased brother, and that consequently the marriage was to be
considered as valid." Gardiner replied to this, and his reply will be found
in L. and P., IV, Part III (No. 5729), where it is erroneously attributed to
Wriothesley. Cf. M. P. Janelle, Obedience in Church and State, Cambridge,
1930, xvii sq.

[121] When Gardiner came back from his second mission (June, 1529),
he was afraid lest "the Pope should revoke his commission" and cite the
suit before his own tribunal (Le Grand, III, 330, 333 sq. Cf. Ehses, pp. 103,
109, 112; Burnet, op. cit., IV, pp. 118, 122). As early as April and May
the king and Wolsey were troubled lest the trial should be cited before the
Roman Court, and they attempted to prevent this (ibid., pp. 108 and 115).
As for Campeggio, he remained impartial until the end, desiring only
to be enlightened and to solve the question according to Canon Law,
without prejudice: "When I shall know positively that the king is in the
wrong," he wrote in cipher to Rome, "I shall be found ready to give
sentence against him fearlessly, even were I certain to suffer death that
moment; and of this do not doubt. But that His Holiness should be
convinced . . . that the thing cannot end otherwise . . ." (Ehses, No. 49
[Brewer's Henry VIII, II, p. 491.—Translator]).

tions, and processes, yet there is such insistence that we have not a moment to breathe." He did try a diplomatic illness. But while he was in bed with the gout, fifteen doctors, armed with enormous volumes, were shouting and gesticulating, and they decided that the process was a judicial one and that nothing else could or ought to be done.[122]

A definite judgment was expected on July 23rd.[123] The king came to assist that day with the chief members of his Court. Campeggio rose . . . and declared that it was vacation time, and that according to the Roman custom the tribunal was adjourned until October 1st.[124] "By the Mass!" exclaimed the Duke of Suffolk, striking the table with his fist, "now I see that the old-said saw is true, that there was never legate nor cardinal that did good in England."

To which Wolsey coldly replied: "Sir, of all men within this realme, ye have least cause to dispraise cardinalls; for, if I, poore cardinall had not bine, you should have had at this present no head upon your shoulders. . . . Therefore put your hasty malice and despight away, and consider that we be but commissioners for a time, and cannot, ne may not, by virtue of our commission procede to judgement, without the knowledge and consent of our authority and licence of him obtained, which is the pope . . ."[125]

Seven days before the legatine Court was prorogued, Clement VII had signed the citation of the cause before the Roman Court, upon the unanimous advice of the referendaries of the Rota. The legatine Court was dissolved, and the matter postponed until Christmas.[126]

[122] Campeggio to Salviati, June 21st, 1529 (Ehses, p. 108). For the development of the suit and the various points treated in it, see Sander, *op. cit.*, Lewis' trans., pp. 56 *sq.*

[123] *L. and P.*, IV, 5789.

[124] Cf. *L. and P.*, IV, 6452; Cavendish, ed. 1852, pp. 140 *sq.*; and Dodd, *op. cit.*, Part I, Bk. 3, art. 3, give the speech in which Campeggio adjourned the legates' Court.

[125] Cavendish, ed. 1852, pp. 144 *sq.* Wolsey had already blamed Anne Boleyn's father for having "put any such fantasy into the king's head, whereby you doe trouble all the realme; and at length get you shall small thankes for your laboures, both of God and the world" (*ibid.*, p. 137).

[126] Theiner, *Monumenta*, 564, 566; Ehses, No. 64. On July 8th Clement VII had written his decision to Wolsey (Ehses, No. 55), saying that hitherto he had gone beyond the limits of condescension in giving way to the English envoy's demands, but that now, in order not to give scandal to Christendom, he wanted to give an impartial judgment with, however,

Wolsey had often warned Clement that any setback in this matter of the divorce would be the signal for his own downfall.[127] He had spoken the truth. His influence had been undermined for some time past. The subjects were dissatisfied with his policy, which had emptied the treasury and achieved a result more brilliant than solid. The king, too, instead of allowing his minister to be cardinal and "king," as before, now wished to rule by himself.[128] Wolsey's wealth, greater by far than his own, at once offended and tempted him. The

due regard for the king's desire as far as possible. On July 19th he announced to the king that the queen's appeal to the Roman Court had been accepted, on the advice of all the auditors and referendaries of the *Segnatura* (Ehses, No. 58). In another letter of the same day (Rinaldi, *Annales eccles., ad ann., 1529*, no. 92), he begged the king to bow to necessity and to preserve his friendship with him, remembering that he resisted the just and urgent entreaties of the Imperialists, as long as it was possible; and he charged Wolsey to use his influence with the king for the good of the Church (Burnet, IV, 125). Gardiner had objected that in the king's eyes Rome was no more trustworthy than England was in the eyes of the queen. To remove this suspicion Clement admitted the appeal to the Roman Court a few days before he signed the Treaty of Barcelona, which sealed the reconciliation of the Pope and the emperor (cf. *Sp. Cal.*, IV, 117, 156, 161; *L. and P.*, IV, 72, 5779).

The Pope was anxious to preserve the king's friendship: he wrote to him to soften the blow and gave him gleams of hope (August 29th, September 4th, October 6th, 1529; Theiner, pp. 564, 566; Ehses, Nos. 64, 71); and he insisted that Wolsey should do all he could to keep the king obedient to the Church. But Henry complained to the Pope because the cause had been cited before the Roman Court (Theiner, p. 564, No. 1003).

[127] Cf. Ehses, p. 48; Theiner, p. 571; Burnet, IV, pp. 55 *sq.*

[128] Henry indeed never brooked a rival in anything in which he excelled; he was nearing his fortieth year: the physical exercises and amusements of his youth had given place to the subtle business of politics. Wolsey was no longer the "king" as in 1519: "We have to deal with the cardinal," Fox wrote at that time, "who is not cardinal but king" (*L. and P.*, II, 3558; cf. *Ven. Cal.*, II, 671, 875, 894). Henry, as du Bellay observes, had now taken charge of everything (*L. and P.*, IV, 5983; cf. *ibid.*, 3992).

For the discontent caused by Wolsey's policy, see *Cambridge Modern History*, p. 429; Pollard, *Henry VIII*, p. 223; *L. and P.*, IV, 4993.

Wolsey confided in du Bellay that he would retire from the government and consecrate the rest of his days to God as soon as the king's marriage had taken place and the friendship between France and England was assured, "of which he hoped to be the solid and stable pillar as long as he lived." "He came and told me . . . that he had to be very careful and adroit in all he did; for there were people watching him so closely that on the slightest occasion in the world for calumniating his acts and showing that he was too much in favour of our party and forgetful of his master's good and profit, they would be down on him. . . . I am of opinion that he does not know too well where he is, however much he may dissimulate" (du Bellay to Montmorency, July 30th, 1528; Bourrilly, pp. 360-61; Le Grand, *op. cit.*, I, pp. 157, 160, 164).

Boleyn party and their set seized the opportunity to overthrow
the man who had ruled England for sixteen years. They
made use of Anne's influence, who herself suspected the
cardinal of obstructing her marriage.[129]

On October 4th, 1529, du Bellay wrote:[130] "I see plainly
that the cardinal will be completely finished through this
Parliament." Henry anticipated Parliament. Campeggio
had scarcely left London[131] before a Bill of *praemunire* was
issued against Wolsey (October 9th).[132] The Dukes of Norfolk
and Suffolk took the great seal away from him on October 17th.
On October 22nd, in order to evade his enemies, the Cardinal
abased himself and confessed that he was guilty of violating
the *praemunire* statute, although he had never acted without
the king's consent.[133] He gave all his personal possessions

[129] Together with her father, Rochford; her uncle, the Duke of Norfolk;
and the Duke of Suffolk, she was plotting Wolsey's downfall, and she did
him much harm with the king (Cavendish, ed. 1852, pp. 152 *sq.*). From
Rome her cousin, Francis Brian, blamed the cardinal for leading the
king to think that the divorce would be an easy matter (*L. and P.*, IV,
No. 5519; cf. Gairdner, *History*, p. 96). On January 25th, 1529, du Bellay
wrote to Montmorency on the divorce (Bourrilly, *op. cit.*, I, 543; Le Grand,
op. cit., III, p. 295): "And be convinced, My Lord, that His Lordship the
legate is greatly troubled, for the matter is so far forward that, if it does not
succeed, the king, his master, will lay the blame on him, and even if it
succeed, he still sees that he will have to deal with a strong party. . . .
The Duke of Norfolk and his lot are already indulging in big talk."
See Shakespeare, *Henry VIII*, Act IV, Sc. 2.

[130] Le Grand, III, pp, 363–64.

[131] Until then Henry hid his feelings; he waited till the departure of
Campeggio, whom he received very affably when he was leaving (Ehses,
No. 72). But "Campeggio was stopped on his journey by the agents of the
royal treasury, who wanted to see that he was not carrying away any silver
other than his own" (N. Harpsfield's account, in Ch. Bémont, *op. cit.*,
pp. 50, 102). Sander (*op, cit.*, Lewis' trans., pp. 73–74) says that the
cardinal's baggage was searched by order of the king. "That search was
made chiefly for the purpose of seizing any letters of Wolsey's; none,
however, were found."

[132] *Praemunire*, a corruption of the Latin verb *praemonere*, was the first
word of the warrant of accusation against anyone who violated the laws
designed to prevent the encroachments of ecclesiastical jurisdiction on
civil jurisdiction. Wolsey was accused of having violated those laws by
impairing the rights of the crown and of the episcopacy in exercising his
functions as legate. It was a legal accusation, since the English laws forbade
it, but it was unjust because he had never acted without the king's authorization (cf. chap. III, n. 7). The whole of this business, which greatly
concerns the history of English institutions, is clearly set forth in Pollard's
Wolsey (pp. 242-52).

[133] *L. and P.*, IV., 6017; Dodd, *op. cit.*, ed. 1737, I, 310. This touching
letter is not lacking in dignity.

and part of his benefices to Henry, and settled pensions upon Anne's relations from the revenues of his See at Winchester.[134]

Wolsey fell a victim to "the Nemesis of Power." He had no one on his side. Some accused him of being too much in favour of the divorce, and others blamed him for not obtaining it.[135] The chancellor's successor, Thomas More, spoke very harshly of Wolsey in his speech at the opening of Parliament. He likened him to a scabby sheep, and said that he had made use of the power and favour given him by the people's shepherd to deceive the people, and had therefore been punished as an example to others.[136] The lords passed a Bill of attainder. It would also have passed in the Commons, had not Cromwell rejected it at the instigation of the king. Henry did not want them to go to extremes.[137]

The cardinal's enemies, particularly Norfolk then very influential in the King's Council, were afraid lest Wolsey should regain his former influence.[138] They got the king to relegate him to his See of York. Wolsey was to keep that archbishopric, a thousand marks from his Winchester diocese, and possessions to the value of £70,000, and to surrender York Palace, London (now Whitehall), to the king. The cardinal had lost all ambition and willingly obeyed. He spent the summer of 1530 not far from Lincoln, at Southwell.[139]

[134] L. and P., IV, 6017 and 6115. Cf. Sander, op. cit., Lewis' trans., p. 145. The king had begged him "to make him a gift" of part of his benefices (Collier, IX, 83): a request which, coming from those lips, was an order. See Wolsey's letter to the king, the "Memorandum of the Surrender," October 25th, 1529, and Chapuys' letter to the emperor, on the same day, in L. and P., IV, Nos. 6024, 6025, 6026.

[135] "Metuabatur ab omnibus, amabatur a paucis, ne dicam a nemine," Erasmus wrote of Wolsey (Letter MCLI of the Epistolae).

[136] Hall, Chronicle, p. 764; cf. Froude, The Reign of Henry VIII, chap. III.

[137] Chapuys wrote, on February 6th, 1530 (L. and P., IV, 6199; cf. 6050) that the king did not wish Parliament to judge the cardinal's case lest he should be unable to pardon him. The "articuli pardonationis Rmi Patris Thomae cardinalis" are dated February 12th, 1530 (Collier, IX, 83).

Thomas Cromwell remained attached to his former master until the end. Only in him and in Gardiner did Wolsey, abandoned by everybody, retain a certain confidence: in his distress, and to obtain what he needed, he applied to them (Ellis, Orig. Letters, 1st Series, II, 1–16).

[138] Anne and her relations rejoiced at Wolsey's death. Friedmann, op. cit., I, 127.

[139] At Southwell, to his great sorrow, Wolsey learnt that the king had resolved to suppress his college at Ipswich. The building of the one at Oxford was so far advanced that it was afterwards finished, though on a

He was to be at York on November 7th, and everything had been prepared for his reception, but he was arrested for treason on the 4th. His Italian doctor, Agostini, who had been bought by Norfolk, accused him of having asked Francis I to intercede with Henry in his favour,[140] of having sought the emperor's mediation, and of having asked the Pope to excommunicate Henry. Ill and broken in spirit,[141] Wolsey made his way slowly, by short stages, towards London. He was to be taken to the Tower. A more gentle end was in store for him. "I am come hither to leave my bones among you," he said to the monks on entering Leicester Abbey. There he died at 8 o'clock on November 29th, 1530. "If I had served my God as diligently as I have done the king," he murmured shortly before his death, "He would not have given me over in my grey hairs; Howbeit this is the just reward I must receive. . . ."

"That which in twenty yeares with great travaile and study he obtained," says Cavendish, "was in one yeare and less, with grete care and sorrowe lost and consumed!—O madness! O, fond desire! O, foolish hope! O, greedy desire of vaine hounors, dignities and riches! Oh what unconstant hope and trust is it in the false fayned countenaunce and promise of fortune!"[142]

more modest scale. This college, on the death of Wolsey, was ca, ed "King Henry VIII's College." To-day it is known as Christ Churchthell most beautiful in Oxford.

York (or Whitehall) Palace, with its two thousand rooms, has been reconstituted and is described in Vol. XIII of *Survey of London*, 1930. There is also a reproduction of the picture showing Wolsey, dispossessed by the king, standing in the midst of tables loaded with materials, cups, and valuable books whilst his stewards are making an inventory of the riches which will soon be his no longer.

[140] The import of his conversations with the French ambassador had been very much exaggerated (cf. *L. and P.*, IV, 6018, 6199, 6273, 6738). He was also reproached for having communicated with the imperial ambassador, Chapuys.

[141] He had already written several times to Gardiner (Ellis, *op. cit.*, 1st Series, II, pp. 7–13) that he was very ill "cum prostratione appetitus et continuo insompnus," and that he could not live long.

[142] Cavendish, ed. 1852, p. 271. Cf. N. Harpsfield in Bémont, *op. cit.*, pp. 51 and 103.

Henry VIII confiscated the sumptuous tomb of Wolsey, erected by Pietro Torrigiano in the Wolsey Chapel (St George's Chapel, Windsor); with the idea of appropriating it to himself, he had the recumbent statue of the cardinal, with his feet upon a griffin, taken away; Bernardo da Rovezzano transformed it and took away its charm when he tried to embellish it still more (cf. André Michel, *Histoire de l'Art*, V, 370 *sq.*).

As he had predicted, Wolsey's fall involved the overthrow of the Church in England.[143] Until then the king had done all he could to get his marriage annulled by the Pope. Thenceforward he began to take steps which led him to decide the case without the Pope and, as it were, by his own authority.[144] "They are planning to call Parliament together this winter," du Bellay wrote on August 23rd, 1529, "and to act by their own authority if the Pope does not do them justice in this business of the divorce."[145]

The first phase of the divorce was over, and the second was beginning. A few days after the closing of the legatine Court (July 23rd, 1529), Henry was hunting at Waltham. Fox and Gardiner, his chaplain and his secretary respectively, were staying with the Cressys, where Cranmer, the future Archbishop of Canterbury, was tutor. At table, conversation turned upon the divorce. Cranmer suggested that the quickest method would be to obtain the opinion of all the great theological universities, at home and abroad. Fox and Gardiner mentioned it to the king.[146] Henry liked the idea.[147] Univer-

---

[143] Burnet, IV, 67. Wolsey had often repeated to Campeggio "si hoc non fiat, actum esse de auctoritate Sedis Apostolicae in hoc regno" (Ehses, p. 50; cf. *L. and P.*, IV, 4897; Ehses, p. 69).

[144] Amongst those who suggested these steps to the king, besides Anne's relations, were Thomas Cromwell, who had been in Wolsey's service, and Thomas Cranmer (*Cranmer's Works*, Parker Society ed., 1844–46, II, 327; *L. and P.*, II, 303). As early as November, 1529, Cromwell, according to some, had already inspired Henry with the idea of abolishing papal jurisdiction in England (cf. J. Gairdner, *History*, 101).

[145] Le Grand, *op. cit.*, III, p. 342.

[146] Strype, *Memorials of Cranmer*, ed. 1848, I, 6 *sq. Narratives of the Reformation*, p. 241. Dean Hook, *Lives of the Archbishops of Canterbury*, VI, 439. In 1527, before recourse was made to Rome, R. Wakefield, the Hebraist, who was rewarded by being made Professor of Hebrew at Oxford, had suggested the same idea, according to a letter published in Henry VIII's time (Blunt, *op. cit.*, I, 130), and according to Cavendish (ed. 1852, pp. 111 *sq.*) the bishops consulted by Wolsey at the commencement of this business had given this advice. In June, 1529, Gregory Casale, in Rome, put forward as a threat the opinions of many learned men in France and in England who were advising the king to disregard the Pope's authority (*L. and P.* (1529), No. 5641).

[147] A few days later (August 23rd) the king and Wolsey spoke about it to du Bellay, showing "a strong desire that I should go round, in order secretly to make known, through the most learned in the realm, the question of the divorce, in which they are as strongly rooted as ever, and to discuss it with them, making known to them the reasons of the opposing party and to draw from them some good advice and reasons" (Le Grand, *op. cit.*, III, p. 339, 355).

sities in those days were not only educational establishments, they were a kind of tribunal for scientific questions; and they were to be "the scattered council" whose opinion would prevail over that of the Pope. Two months later Stokesley left for France and Croke for Italy.[148] In 1530 Gardiner and Fox succeeded in obtaining a favourable opinion from Oxford (April 8th) and Cambridge (March 9th) universities. English agents travelled through France and Italy for the same purpose. One of the king's relations, the young scholar Reginald Pole, was commissioned to ask the Sorbonne's opinion.[149]

The Greek scholar, Richard Croke, was sent to search the Italian libraries and to secure the support of the most famous doctors in Italy. Stokesley, afterwards Bishop of London, was despatched especially to the university at Bologna.[150] Ghinucci, the Bishop of Worcester, was said to have received full powers to buy over the Italians.[151] Francis I was expected

---

[148] *L. and P.*, IV, 2684. At the same time a series of delays was obtained from Rome for the trial of the cause (Ehses, p. 158 and Nos. 83, 84).

[149] For the way in which R. Pole acted see chap. v, pp. 261 *sq.*

At Cambridge, where they had formerly studied, Gardiner and Fox came to an understanding with the vice-chancellor to exclude one or two adversaries from the council of the university (cf. Burnet, IV, 130; VI, 28–36). At Oxford a few threats from the king caused a decree to be issued in conformity with his wishes, on April 4th (Burnet, VI, 36–41). This decree is to be found in Collier, IX, 85. Public opinion had been prepared by the book which Cranmer wrote at the request of Anne Boleyn's father (cf. Pollard, *Thomas Cranmer*, p. 42; Le Grand, pp. 170–174).

[150] He visited Ghiberti and Caraffa, afterwards Paul IV (Ehses, p. 267). See his letter from Venice, July 1st, 1530, for the opinion of the theologians he had consulted, and for the decision obtained from the university of Padua, in Burnet, IV, 134. At Venice he was rejoined by Cranmer, who was accompanying the Earl of Wiltshire, Anne Boleyn's father, Stokesley, and the future Archbishop of York in their embassy to the Pope and the emperor at Bologna.

The decision of Bologna university is dated June 10th, 1530.

[151] Cf. Friedmann, *op. cit.*, I, 115; *Ven. Cal.*, IV, 1251. "Non desunt qui asserant magnam pecuniae quantitatem in Italiam a te transmissam ad alliciendos, quin potius corrumpendos scribentes, quod tamen nobis nullo modo persuadere possumus" (Ehses, No. 96).

In May, 1532 Henry VIII, already much at variance with Rome, took the trouble to write to the sacred college to obtain the red hat for Ghinucci: "We have set our heart very much on this, and we recommend him very earnestly indeed to your Eminences" (Collier, IX, 101). For R. Croke, tutor to the Duke of Richmond, see Wood, I, 85 *sq.*

to give his support in France.[152]   The universities of Paris
(July 2nd, 1530), Orleans (April 5th, 1530), Angers (May 7th,
1530), Toulouse (October 1st, 1530), Ferrara, Pavia, and
Padua (July 1st, 1530), not to mention the individual opinions
of a few doctors, decided in Henry's favour.[153]   "So far as those
published by the king are concerned," wrote an Anglican,
"they are little better than sonorous echoes of his strongly
declared pre-judgment of his own case."[154]

Until then the dispensation granted by Julius II had been
attacked only for the canonical defects which would have
made it invalid.[155]   Thenceforward, without neglecting that
point, they sought to prove that the Pope had no power to
dispense in the case of a marriage with a deceased brother's
widow. A new school relying upon the two texts in Leviticus
(xviii, 16; xx, 21) maintained that this prohibition of marriage

[152] Cf. *L. and P.*, IV, 2903.
[153] Ehses, p. 181., *L. and P.*, IV, 6332, 6448, 6491, 6632, 6636. Dodd, *op.
cit.*, Part 1, Bk. 3, art 3, ed. 1737, pp. 281–86. *The determinations of the most
amous and most excellent Universities*, the work of Edward Foxe, afterwards
Bishop of Hereford, written in collaboration with the Bishop of London,
Stokesley, and Nicolas de Burgo, was altered and augmented by
Cranmer who published it in London in 1531. A summary of it, albeit in an
order different from the original, is in Rymer, XIV, 390 *sq.*; Burnet, IV,
136 *sq.*
   See the manner in which the decision of the French universities was
obtained in Le Grand, *op. cit.*, I, pp. 175–86; III, 507. For this confused
intrigue in the Sorbonne over the divorce, consult Book II of the thesis:
Guillaume du Bellay, seigneur de Langey, 1491–1543, Paris, 1904, by W. L.
Bourrilly, where all the references to be desired will be found.
   Henry "could find none in the whole of Germany to write in his favour.
The Lutherans were even more resolute than the Catholics on this occasion"
(Le Grand, I, 187; cf. *ibid.*, 189–201).
   Anglicans themselves do not attach any importance to the universities'
decision, which was obtained, as they acknowledge, by means less than
honest.
[154] Blunt, *op. cit.*, I, p. 174.
[155] The power to dispense was not at all doubted then in the case in
question: the arguments for the annulment of the marriage were based
only on canonical defects which would render the dispensation null and
void, and surreptitious. One of the chief arguments was the king's protestation on the eve of the day when the marriage should have taken
place. It was a question of knowing whether it annulled the dispensation,
"quia tunc nulli dubium quod matrimonium inde secutum fuit et est
nullum." For that reason the English ambassadors earnestly asked for a
decretal stating that in law a dispensation can be renounced or disavowed,
and is rendered null and void by the disavowal (Ehses, No. 19; Bourrilly,
I, 141 and 142). The objection was indeed made that since the queen had
not disavowed the marriage, the dispensation was revalidated by the
subsequent contract (Bourrilly, I, 141).

with a brother's widow was a divine law, and no power on earth could dispense from it.[156]

Henry took advantage of the favourable opinions which came to him from the universities to make a final attempt to move Rome. Writing to Clement VII, he set against the opinion of a few men around the Pope, that of the universities of England, France, and Italy, as well as of learned men of repute. Against the papal dispensation he put forward the divine law which allowed no dispensation. He protested that "no princes heretofore have more highly esteemed, nor honoured the see apostolic

[156] Ehses, p. 239. According to this school, the text of Deuteronomy which counselled a man whose brother had died childless to marry his sister-in-law expressed a dispensation *juris divini* and not *juris humani*, which applied only to the Old Law, like the divorce granted to the Hebrews under certain circumstances *ad duritiam cordis*. In December, 1527, in his first letter to his agent at the Roman Court (Burnet, IV, 21), Wolsey said: "A variis multisque ex his doctoribus asseritur quod papa non potest dispensare in primo gradu affinitatis tanquam ex jure divino, moraliter, naturaliterque prohibito." When things were beginning to lock bad for him in the Curia, Henry VIII wrote to Gardiner and Brian (April 6th, 1529 (Burnet, IV, p. 117): "And by your next letters we will that ye advertise us what advocates ye have on our part, with their names and qualities; finding the means also, if it be possible, to retain some notable and excellent divine, a frere, or other that may, can, or will firmly stick to our causes, in leaning to that, *quod pontifex ex jure divino non potest dispensare*." The adversaries gave numerous reasons in answer to this. (See in Ehses, p. 240, the opinion of Felix de Prato, an Augustinian hermit who, being a converted Jew, was admirably acquainted with the Hebrew text of the Bible.)

On several occasions and for long hours at a time, the king himself discussed the question *An papa possit dispensare cum jure divino*, etc., with the chancellor of Cambridge, whom he summoned to Windsor. (See the latter's letter in Blunt, I, 168–169.) And when he had obtained what he desired from this university he thrice demanded that Oxford—where he called those who opposed him the rebellious youths—should assert, as Cambridge had done, "prohibitionem esse divini et naturalis juris ne frater uxorem fratris etiam mortui sine liberis ducat uxorem" (*ibid.*, I, 170 *sq.*).

In October, 1529 Clement VII had been moved by the opinion of this new school; and he wrote to Henry VIII that it was contradicted by a decision of one of his predecessors (he mentioned Innocent IV instead of Innocent III; cf. Rinaldi, *ad ann. 1212*, No. 38; *1243*, Nos. 33–34; *1245*, No. 91; Voigt, *Gesch. Preussens*, II, 615) who asserted that it was by positive law that a man was forbidden to marry his brother's widow and that therefore such a case was subject to the Pope's right to dispense (Clement VII to Henry VIII, October 7th, 1529. Theiner, *op. cit.*, p. 556, No. 1008). The interpretation of divine law, he added, belongs to the Pope: "Quia causa hujusmodi in qua de interpretatione juris divini et potestate S^{mi} Pontificis tractatur ad nos procul dubio pertinere dignoscitur" (Ehses, p. 174). He himself asked Felix de Prato for advice, as well as several other theologians (Ehses, pp. 180, 240. Cf. p. 80 and n. 165).

than we have," and concluded in these terms: "And God is the truth to whom we are bound to obey rather than to men." In this letter the reproaches and invectives designed to force the Pope's hand are an omen of the coming schism. Even if it were not delivered to the Pope, as is believed, yet it sufficiently indicates the direction the divorce question had taken as well as the path the king was definitely following.[157]

In June (1530) the king called his noblemen together in London and got them to sign a petition to Clement VII. In it they asked the Pope to decide in favour of a cause which the most famous universities considered to be just. Moreover, by ensuring the succession to the throne the danger of civil war would be averted. If the Pope refused, it would mean that the country was forsaken and would be obliged to seek means of obtaining justice elsewhere, and, if necessary, to have recourse to "extreme remedies, which are always rather harsh."[158] This petition was sent to the dukes, marquises, earls, barons, bishops, abbòts, members of Parliament, and lawyers, and was covered in signatures. The first on the list is Wolsey's, then at Southwell, followed by that of Warham, Archbishop of Canterbury. It was sent to Rome on July 13th. The Pope replied on September 27th, in an evasive but dignified tone. It would be harmful for the king's conscience as well as the Pope's to give a premature decision which would also break the law. He complained of the threat made at the end of the petition: "We pardon your transport of impatience, exhorting you, with a fatherly affection, to keep your temper: and we hope your prudence and piety will prevail upon you, to make no resolutions but what are wise. But if a patient will be ungovernable, and will embrace no advice but what is destructive, the physician ought not to be blamed."[159]

Clement VII's position at this period is clear. On the one hand, after consulting the best Canonists, such as Simonetta,

[157] Burnet, IV, 169–174. This letter, undated, in Burnet, was written on July 13th, 1530 (cf. Ehses, p. 154).
[158] Herbert, op. cit., p. 141; Rymer, Foedera, XIV, 405; Collier, IX, 86–89; Pocock, I, 429; Blunt, I, 156. It seems indeed that one of the extreme remedies mentioned was a General Council to which Henry should appeal. (Cf. Propositions submitted to the Council in December, 1533, in Collier, IX, 134.)
[159] Collier, IX, 89–93; Dodd, ed. 1737, I, 290.

Cardinal Cajetan and Aleandre, he had a bad opinion of the king's cause.[160] And since on the other, he was inclined to listen to Catherine, who pleaded that the venue was suspect he did not wish the case to be tried in the country of the opposing party, especially as that party was a very powerful king. But he had no desire to do anything hastily. Whilst Charles V was continually urging him to bring the trial to an end, and complaining of the delays prejudicial to his aunt,[161] the Pope continued to hope that time itself would solve the problem.[162] He knew that judgment could be given at any time, but that but once given it could not be recalled.[163]

He contented himself with preventing Henry from deciding in his own country a case that was pending before the Roman Court. Hence the first admonition of March 7th, 1530, forbidding the king under pain of excommunication to contract a fresh marriage before the cause had been concluded.[164] Hence also the second admonition of January 5th, 1531, forbidding Parliament, the universities, the law-courts, and

---

[160] Cajetan's opinion of March 13th, 1530 is in part in Rinaldi, *ad ann 1530*, Nos. 193-201. Consulted afresh, and by Henry VIII himself, the cardinal replied in the same way (*ibid.*, *ad ann. 1534*, Nos. 1 and 2; cf Burnet, I, 104; III 57).

Aleandre's opinion, which is to be found in the Vatican archives (*Arma. XI*, 38, fols. 173-194) seems to emanate less from him than from somebody in his service, as the Latin text shows.

[161] "S. Mtà non solum aegre sed aegerimme tulit hoc et che gli pare sia in sugillatione honoris sui et in desperatione della regina" (Ehses, No. 84). The emperor did not cease to insist, either directly or through his ambassadors, in 1530, 1531 and 1532 (*ibid.*, Nos. 83, 93, 110, 114, 116, 128, 140, 197, 199; cf. Account of Nicholò Tiepolo, ambassador to Charles V, 1532, Albèri, Series 1, Vol. I, pp. 83-84). Ferdinand, afterwards emperor, joined his supplications to those of Charles V (Theiner, *op. cit.*, No. 1037, p. 603; cf. No. 1041, p. 605. Friedensberg, *Nuntiaturberichte aus Deutschland, 1533-59*, Vol. I, pp. 85, 107, 214).

[162] Aleandre to Sanga and to J. Salviati, Brussels, November 14th and 19th, 1531. Ehses, No. 114.

[163] "Dio sa che . . . sempre si potea far sententia, ma poi fatta se nascerà scandalo, non si puo cosî remediare" (Aleandre to Sanga, November 14th 1531. Ehses, No. 114. Cf. *ibid.*, No. 100). Therefore he charged Campeggio and Aleandre to show the emperor the inconveniences resulting from too hasty a decision, and to make him wait patiently (Ehses, Nos. 93, 100, 102, 103, 114); and he granted the king delay after delay (Ehses, pp. 158, 192, 193, 207, 209, Nos. 76 and 92).

[164] Brief of March 7th, 1530 (Le Grand, III, 446-53; Dodd, Part 1, Bk. 3, art. 3; *L. and P.*, IV, 6256). Henry was to take Catherine back as long as the case was undecided.

the Archbishop of Canterbury to interfere in this question.[165]
The nuncio had written that the king thought of having the
case decided in England.[166]

Convinced indeed that his case would be lost in the Roman
Court, Henry endeavoured to have it brought back to his
own country for trial. Having failed in his overtures to the
emperor and also in imploring Catherine to revoke her
appeal, the king attempted to prove that his citation before
the Roman Court was null and void.[167] His agents at the
Pope's Court maintained that it was contrary to the privileges
of the realm. The universities of Paris (August 19th, 1531)
and Orleans (June 22nd, 1531) declared it to be of no effect.[168]

[165] Le Grand, III, 531–40. Rinaldi, *ad ann. 1531*, Nos. 78 and 80.
Pocock, II, 109. *L. and P.*, V, 27. In the consistory of December 23rd,
1530 (Ehses, p. 206) the Archbishop of Canterbury was forbidden to take
cognizance of the case. The universities had already given their opinion.
  On May 21st, 1530 Clement VII had forbidden all ecclesiastical judges,
doctors, barristers and lawyers to take part in the divorce suit either by
word or in writing, under pain of excommunication (Theiner, *op. cit.*,
No. 1017. *L. and P.*, IV, No. 6279). But on the protestation of the English
envoys (Ehses, No. 82), he declared in a new Brief of the following August
4th (Theiner, No. 1018) that this prohibition affected only those who pronounced on the suit, after being won by favours or money (cf. Ehses,
p. 172). It was not until January, 1531 that a Bull forbade the universities
to give any decision on the divorce. Dodd, *op. cit.*, Part 1, Bk. 3, art. 3.
  These Bulls or Briefs were not published at all in England. The Parliament of 1530 (September 12th), in virtue of the Statutes of Provisors, had
forbidden publication (*L. and P.*, IV, 6615; V, 45); and Norfolk reminded
the nuncio of the penalties for the importation of Bulls without the king's
consent.
  The papal prohibitions were always meant to prevent Henry VIII from
marrying again, and they followed rather than preceded any attempt of
the king to do without Rome.
[166] Ehses, No. 92.
[167] At first he tried to win the emperor; and with this end in view,
when the latter was crowned by Clement VII at Bologna (March, 1530),
Henry sent an embassy to him composed of Drs. Edward Lee, John
Stokesley, Edward Carne, Cranmer, and the Earl of Wiltshire, Anne
Boleyn's father; but this embassy was unsuccessful. (Cf. Friedmann,
op. cit., I, 105 *sq.* For the interview at Bologna, see Ehses' article in the
Römische Quartalschrift, 1891, pp. 299 *sq.*)
  Then he tried to make Catherine waver when the trial was about to
begin. On May 31st, 1531 a deputation of lords, bishops and doctors
(Cromwell was one of them) made known to the queen the king's great
displeasure at being cited before the Roman Court—it was inconsistent with
his rank and dignity—and begged her to withdraw her complaint. But she
was adamant. From that moment the king, who had been seeing her every
three days, did not wish to see her any more, which was a triumph for
Anne Boleyn. (Cf. Friedmann, *op. cit.*, I, 149 *sq.*)
[168] Rymer, *Foedera*, XIV, 416 *sq.* Froude, chap. v: "Marriage of

Armed with this declaration, the king insisted with the nuncio and the Pope that the case should be sent back to England and tried by the Archbishop of Canterbury or by his chapter. As the queen had done, he also pleaded that the venue was suspect, and added that any judgment given outside the realm would be against the laws of the country and Parliament would oppose it.[169]

Burgio, the nuncio, thought of choosing a neutral venue, some town not under the imperial influence. Cambrai was mentioned, but neither Catherine nor the emperor would hear of it.[170] Taking advantage of the universities' decision, the king then arrogantly demanded that the case should be tried in his own kingdom; and this time he openly threatened to withdraw from the papal jurisdiction (December 28th, 1531).[171]

He had already placed himself in a position to carry out his threats, by gradually assuming control of the Church. The year 1532 was spent in restricting Rome's authority. With the help of the anti-clerical tendencies in Parliament and the prelates' compliance in Convocation, he had a whole series of laws passed subjecting the Church to the State and slowly detaching it from Rome.[172] Still his agents in Rome, William Bennet, Edward Carne, Edmund Bonner, Ghinucci and Gregory Casale, continued to hold their position on judicial ground, and to contest step by step the claims of the opposing party. From March to July, 1532, i.e. until the Roman tribunals rose for vacation, they tried to get an excusation admitted for the king, and to prevent him from being obliged to appear by proxy.[173] As for the Pope, despite

---

Henry and Boleyn" (*The Reign of Henry VIII*) gives two letters (*a*) from Francis I to the Pope (January 10th, 1532) and (*b*) from Cardinal Lorraine to a cardinal residing in Rome (January 8th, 1532)—both taken from the *Bibliothèque nationale*—in which both Francis I and Lorraine insist on the cause being tried in England and not in Rome, according to the king's wishes.

[169] Cf. Ehses, Nos. 92 and 100; *L. and P.*, VI, No. 102.

[170] Ehses, Nos. 97, 102, 103.

[171] Theiner, II, 599, No. 1031; *Pocock*, II, 148.

[172] See chap. III. In 1531 the ambassador Falieri (Albèri, *op. cit.*, Series 1, Vol. III, pp. 25, 26) wrote that the king was on fairly bad terms with the Pope because he had been unable to obtain the divorce, and that already separation from the Roman Church was openly mentioned.

[173] See their letters in Burnet, IV, 174–89; and Lemon, *State Papers*

the urgent entreaties of the emperor, he continued to postpone judgment.[174]

The decisive moment was at hand. The Pope and Charles V were to meet in the month of December, 1532, and the Imperialists hoped this would mean the end of the trial. As an offset to this, Henry VIII and Francis I met at Boulogne in the October of that same year. Anne Boleyn accompanied the king. She was presented to Francis, who made very fine promises to her, and was alleged to have advised Henry to marry her, promising that he would not abandon Henry should the latter be excommunicated: the two kings would appeal to a council if the King of England were made to appear in Rome.[175] Catherine and Henry had not been seeing each other since July 14th in the previous year; they never met again.[176]

Anne was more powerful than ever. She had yielded to the king's desires, probably in order to hasten a solution which had been postponed for seven years. In return she was created Marquis (sic) of Pembroke (September 1st, 1532).[177]

VII, pp. 352, 362; and one of the king's letters, ibid., p. 350. Cf. Mémoires de du Bellay, ed. 1569, 99–101.

[174] Ehses, Nos. 124, 126, 127, 128. Henry VIII, on his side, in order not to be declared contumacious, had sent an excusator to Rome, Dr. Carne, who for two years asserted that the king's powers were sufficient. It was on this occasion that the king wrote his last letter to the Pope (February 28th, 1532, ibid., No. 123); he complained that Dr Carne had not been accepted as his excusator, and begged Clement to settle the case in his favour.

[175] Account of the interview at Boulogne in Camusat, Meslanges historiques 1390–1580, Troyes, 1619, Vol. II. Cf. Hamy, Entrevue de François Ier avec Henri VIII à Boulogne, 1532, Paris, 1898; L. and P., V, 1541; VI, 230, 259; Friedmann, I, 171 sq. Francis I's sister, Marguerite of Navarre, refused to attend the interview because she did not wish to meet Anne Boleyn, and her refusal annoyed Anne very much. Cf. Friedmann, I, 166 sq.; L. and P., V, No. 1377; and L. E. Marcel, Le Cardinal de Givry, 1926, pp. 245 sq.

[176] Hitherto, although de facto separated for six or seven years, they had lived under the same roof. In June, 1531 Henry had tried, but in vain, to get Catherine to withdraw her appeal by sending some of the lords of the Council to her, who showed her the decision of the universities. On July 14th he hastily left Windsor; and Catherine withdrew to More, in Hertfordshire, to a castle belonging to the Archbishops of York; and then to Ampthill, in Bedfordshire, where the king had a manor; there she was destined to pass the greater part of the time that she still had to live.

[177] Marquis, and not Marchioness of Pembroke (L. and P., V, pp. 522

A few months later (January, 1533) she was pregnant. The child Henry desired so ardently for the succession had to be made legitimate at all costs. In great secrecy the king was married to Anne.[178] All that remained to be done was to have the child publicly acknowledged as legitimate and the previous one illegitimate. They could no longer hope for anything from the Pope. After his meeting with the emperor and Anne's visit to Boulogne, Clement VII had sent Henry a third admonition (November 15th, 1532) ordering him to leave Anne and to take Catherine back again.[179] Even if Rome did show opposition, there was still Canterbury, the primatial see of the Church of England.[180] It would suffice to have the court of that diocese recognized as the supreme tribunal for English ecclesiastical causes. Even then it would be necessary to have an archbishop who could be relied upon.

585; cf. Pollard, *Henry VIII*, p. 294). She received an endowment of £1,000 and jewels taken from the queen's casket. *L. and P.*, V, p. 585. Cf. Friedmann, I, 162 *sq*; H. Belloc, *Wolsey*, Note J.

[178] It is not known who married them. It has been said that Roland Lee, afterwards Bishop of Lichfield, officiated (cf. Blunt, I, 182; Gairdner, *Lollardy*, I, 452). Chapuys wrote, in a letter of January 28th, 1535 (*L. and P.*, Henry VIII, 1535, No. 121) that George Browne, "an Augustinian friar, has been appointed by the king general of the Mendicant Orders, in reward for having married the king and the lady [Anne Boleyn]." Cranmer always denied that it was he and said that he only heard about it a fortnight afterwards (*Cranmer's Works*, II, 246. Cf. Ellis, *Original Letters*, 1st Series, II, pp. 33–34; Pollard, *Thomas Cranmer*, p. 60, n. 1). Hall and Holinshed, to save Anne's honour, antedated the marriage, making it November 14th, 1532.

For Anne Boleyn's marriage, see Friedmann, Vol. I, chap. v.

[179] Brief of December 23rd, 1532. Le Grand, III, 588; Dodd, ed. 1737, I, 288; Pocock, II, 378. See Charles V's letter to his sister Mary in Lanz, *Korrespondenz Karls V*, Vol. II, p. 22, and Henry VIII's declaration when the Brief was announced, in *L. and P.*, VII, 421.

The nuncio informed Henry that the Brief would not be published if he consented to the suit being continued in the Roman Court, and to avoid all scandal during that time. On the king's refusal it was dated December 23rd, and proclaimed in Rome and in the Low Countries.

[180] Henry had long had this in mind, since Salviati wrote to Campeggio on October 21st, 1530 (Ehses, No. 92) saying that the king distrusted the Rota's judgment and would like the cause to be submitted to the Archbishop of Canterbury, or to his own council. So in the consistory of December 23rd, 1530 (Ehses, p. 206) the queen's proctors insisted "ut inhiberetur specialiter per breve S^{is} S. primati archiepiscopo Cantuariensi ipsius regni Angliae quod nullo facto se immisceret dictae causae"; and the Brief of the following January 10th (Le Grand, III, 536) indeed forbade the Archbishop of Canterbury to take cognizance of the case. Cf. p. 80 and n. 165.

And in this Henry was admirably assisted by Fate. Warham, whose conscience had begun to revolt against the king's oppressive measures—Cromwell had spoken of having him hanged twice as high as any other—had just died (August, 1532).[181] Cranmer was the man to succeed him, for Cranmer had first suggested that Henry should approach the universities and had also written a book in favour of the divorce. As quickly as possible Henry recalled him from his embassy at the emperor's court. But would the Pope consent to his nomination as archbishop? Everybody knew that Cranmer favoured the divorce.[182] Moreover, he was secretly married to the niece of Osiander, the famous German Lutheran. But while Clement was resolute so far as the question of the divorce was concerned, he was anxious to avoid further difficulties, and so the Bulls were granted (February 21st, 1533).[183]

The king was now sure of obtaining a favourable decision. All that remained to be done was to make it irrevocable. A law was immediately (March, 1533) laid before Parliament forbidding all appeals to the Roman Court. Henry main-

[181] *L. and P.*, V, Nos. 818, 1247. On account of his half-hearted resistance, Warham was accused of treason for having consecrated in former years the Bishop of St Asaph before presenting the Bulls to the kings In defence he made a distinction between the spiritual and the temporal power and between the rights conferred by each of them. For Warham'; last days, see Harpsfield's account in Ch. Bémont, *op. cit.*, pp. 53 *sq.*, 105 *sq.* and Wood, *op. cit.*, 1691, I, 572.

[182] He had accompanied Anne Boleyn's father to Italy, and in his book he maintained that by divine law none could marry his own brother's widow, and that the Pope could not dispense from such an impediment (Strype, *Memorials of Cranmer*, ed. 1848, I, 17). This book on the divorce, containing ninety-one pages in 4to, has twelve articles followed by a development of the arguments. The original copy offered by Cranmer to the king is in the British Museum (Cotton, Vesp. B.V.); and Burnet (IV, 146) has given a statement of the articles.

Chapuys had endeavoured to delay the Bulls for Cranmer's appointment, for Cranmer, said Chapuys, had asserted that he would defend the king's right to marry Anne even if it meant going to the stake (*L. and P.*, VI, 142, 180).

[183] He even gave up his right to 10,000 marks for sending the Bulls, lest the king should apply the law of 1532 on the Annates.

He had already conceded the bishoprics of Winchester and York to Gardiner and Lee, who had taken such an active part in the matter of the divorce, and also a benefice to one of the Duke of Norfolk's nephews, who was four or five years old (Ehses, No. 101).

For all these things see Dean Hook, *The Lives of the Archbishops of Canterbury*, Vol. II, pp. 458–61.

tained that the General Councils had decreed that every suit was to be tried in its place of origin.[184] The step was a serious one, for it withdrew the country from papal jurisdiction. The Commons were afraid of it, not from any religious principles, but because they feared an interdict which would destroy all trade with the Low Countries. "As yet," wrote the imperial ambassador, "the secular deputies of the Commons have refused to consent to the king's demands against the authority of the Pope, and have even strongly resisted them, alleging several reasons, among which it has been well considered . . . it would only interrupt their traffic in wool."[185] It took three weeks to convince them that trading between the two countries was more necessary to the Flemish than to the English, and that an interdict would consequently remain an ineffective threat. Eventually the Statute of Appeals passed so easily that everybody was surprised.[186]

Moreover, the opposition was disconcerted. The delays of the Holy See in the divorce question, and the ready way in which Cranmer's nomination had been confirmed had combined to break it up. "Many," said Chapuys, "think there is some secret intelligence between the king and the Pope"; and the king did all he could to foster and spread this idea.[187] To the nuncio he was all kindness, and very gracious in his speech.[188] When Parliament was opened (February, 1533) he made the nuncio accompany him, to show that he was keeping on good terms with Rome.[189]

Convocation, at the king's mercy, passed two propositions favourable to the divorce, on March 26th.[190] The first (concerning the law) ruled that the Pope had no right to dispense from the impediment existing between a man and his deceased

---

[184] *L. and P.*, VI, 1489.

[185] *L. and P.*, VI, 296.

[186] *L. and P.*, XII; II, 952.

[187] *L. and P.*, VI, 89, 142.

[188] Cf. *L. and P.*, V, 1579; VI, 296.

[189] *L. and P.*, VI, 142, 160.

[190] The one hundred and nineteen ecclesiastics present represented more than two hundred others by delegation: this fact enabled the names of men reputed hostile to the divorce, such as the Bishops of Norwich and Chichester, to be included amongst the majority. The minutes are in Pocock, *Records*, No. CCCXXVI. Cf. Friedmann, *op. cit.*, I, 197 *sq.*

brother's widow. The second (concerning the fact) decided that the marriage between Catherine and Arthur had been consummated.[191] The conclusion was evident, and Cranmer was the man who drew it.

On April 11th, acting upon secret orders, he humbly asked the king—in terms considered abject by Anglicans[192]—to allow him to try "your Grace's cause of matrimony . . . through all Christianity divulgated, and in the mouths of the rude and ignorant common people of this your Grace's realm so talked of."[193] Henry replied that he was pleased to grant the request of "the most principal minister of our spiritual jurisdiction within this realm," and begged him—which was a bold lie[194]—not to be guided by any human consideration but to "make an end according to the will and pleasure of Almighty God, in our said great cause of matrimony which hath so long depended . . . undetermined, to our great and grievous inquietness, and burthen of our conscience." The Archbishop's Court was opened at Dunstable, where Catherine was living, on May 10th.[195] She refused both to acknowledge Cranmer's authority in a cause then pending before the Roman Curia, and to renounce her title of queen, even at the sacrifice of her possessions and her life. She entrusted herself solely to the decision of Christ's Vicar.[196] On the 23rd the

[191] *L. and P.*, VI, 276, 311, 317, 491.

[192] Blunt, *op. cit.*, p. 184 and n. 8. The text is in Vol. I (p. 390) of *L. and P.* Cranmer submitted two petitions to the king, who chose the one which was more humiliating for the archbishop.

[193] *Cranmer's Works*, II, 237. [Belloc, *Cranmer*, 100.—*Translator.*]

The nuncio Burgio, fearing complications, had not dared to make known to Cranmer the Brief of January 5th, 1531, which forbade, under pain of excommunication, any one, and especially the Archbishop of Canterbury, to pronounce a judgment on the case at issue. Chapuys to Charles V, May 10th, 1533. Cf. Friedmann, *op. cit.*, I, 203 *sq.*

In answer to the objection that the case could not be debated while it was pending in the Curia, Stokesley read the Brief of August 4th, 1530 (Theiner, *op. cit.*, No. 1017) which forbade only those who had been won by favours or money to discuss the case, but he did not add that the Brief of January 5th, 1531 (Le Grand, *op. cit.*, III, 351) forbade all English subjects, ecclesiastics or laymen, to meddle in the question; and he boldly concluded: "Summus Pontifex voluit unumquemque declarare mentem suam et opiniones suas in dicta causa libere et impune." Cf. Friedmann, *op. cit.*, I, 196.

[194] Blunt, *op. cit.*, I, 185. Henry VIII's letter to Cranmer, April, 1533 is in Collier, IX, 103.

[195] More correctly, she was at Ampthill, four miles from Dunstable.

[196] She declared that Cranmer was but a "shadow" and his tribunal a

archbishop gave judgment in accordance with Convocation's decision of the previous March. The king's first marriage was null and void, because the Pope had no power to dispense in Catherine's case, the impediment being of divine law: "decernimus et declaramus ipsum pretensum matrimonium . . . divino jure prohibente contractum et consummatum nullius valoris aut momenti esse."[197] Mary, however, was not illegitimate, her parents having been in good faith.[198]

Five days later, after a secret investigation, Cranmer declared that Henry and Anne Boleyn were legally married. And the new queen was solemnly crowned in Westminster Abbey on June 1st.[199] Three months afterwards (September 7th) Greenwich saw the birth of Elizabeth, the future Queen of England who was to complete the work begun by Henry VIII.[200]

"mockery," and she was of opinion, and not without reason, that the Archbishop's only aim and commission was to give a legal form to the intentions of the king, who was "a party in the case." See the reports of the Archbishop of York, Edward Lee, and of the Bishop of Durham, Tunstall, in Collier, IX, 105.

[197] The text of Cranmer's judgment, published by Lord Herbert (*op. cit.*, 375), Rymer (XIV, 468), Burnet (IV, 189), was reproduced by Froude (*op. cit.*, chap. v).

In a letter to Archdeacon Hawkyns, who had succeeded him as ambassador to the emperor, and who died in 1534, Cranmer relates the way in which he proceeded against Catherine. Strype, *Memorials of Cranmer*, I, 325 *sq*; Ellis, II, 36 *sq*. See *L. and P.*, II, 241, 244; VI, 332, 469, 470, 525; *Diario di Sanuto*, Vol. LVII; Stone, *op. cit.*, pp. 47, 55.

Some weeks later the lords of the Council handed Cranmer's judgment to the queen. She protested against the title of princess, which she struck out with her pen (the original, published in *L. and P.*, I, 397 and 402, is in the British Museum, Cotton MS., Otho X, fol. 99), saying that queen she was and queen she would remain as long as the Pope had decided nothing against her; she said she knew she had been a faithful wife to the king . . . and that the Archbishop of Canterbury was not an impartial judge in the case.

[198] *L. and P.*, VII, 94

[199] Letter mentioned, from Cranmer to Archdeacon Hawkyns, in which he tells of the coronation. The description of the ceremony will be found in Camusat (*Meslanges historiques*, 2nd Series, pp. 17 *sq*.), whom Le Grand follows (I, 260 *sq*.), and in Pollard, *Tudor Tracts*, 1903, pp. 10–28; *L. and P.*, VI, 561, 563, 584, 601. See chap. vi in Friedmann, *op. cit.*, I, 200–228.

"Three short years have yet to pass, and again, on a summer's morning, Queen Anne Boleyn will leave the Tower of London—not radiant then with beauty on a gay errand of coronation, but a poor wandering ghost, on a sad tragic errand, from which she will never more return" (Froude, *History of England*, ed. 1867, I, pp. 464–65).

[200] *L. and P.* VI, 1089, 1111. Cf. Sander, *op. cit.*, Lewis, trans., p. 110

Henry's second marriage, Cranmer's judgment, and Anne's coronation were a bold and flagrant challenge to the Holy See and open contempt for papal authority. The Pope could not do less than place the king outside the Church's pale. Accordingly, on July 11th, 1533, at the request of the emperor and the queen, Henry was excommunicated and his marriage with Anne declared invalid.[201] Still the final clause showed Clement's forbearance. The penalty was held over until September, and would take effect only if Henry had not separated from Anne by that time.[202] It was a remnant of hope.

That hope was merely an illusion. The contrary decisions of the Pope and the English primate were expressions of two adverse jurisdictions. In the face of the old Roman Church from which Henry had received his title of *Defender of the Faith* there arose a new Church which depended solely upon the king. In spite of Francis I's efforts, in 1534, to re-unite England and Rome,[203] the breach was real and final. At the end of 1533 the position was hopeless. Henry was excommunicated and the English Church was completely subjected

F. A. Mumby, *The Girlhood of Queen Elizabeth: a Narrative in Contemporary Letters*, London, 1909, pp. 2 *sq*. The first letter taken from the *Harleian MSS.* which Mumby gives is from Anne Boleyn to Lord Cobham, September 7th, 1533, announcing the birth of a princess. Cranmer, who gives her birth as September 13th or 14th, was her godfather. Strype, *Memorials of Cranmer*, ed. 1848, I, 337.

[201] Diary of Blaise de Cesena, in Ehses, p. 228.

[202] Ehses, No. 125. The marriage with Catherine was not declared valid by the Bull; the cause was still pending before the tribunal of the Rota. Henry was excommunicated for having contracted a second marriage while the trial of the first was still pending before the Roman Court (Ehses, p. 287). Sander was the first to publish this Bull (*op. cit.*, Lewis' trans., pp. 102–103), and he took it for a definite judgment. Rinaldi followed him, and for that reason placed it in 1534 (No. 4). Pocock also, *Records*, II, 677. The definite decision declaring Catherine's marriage with Henry VIII valid is dated March 23rd, 1534, and is in Dodd (ed. 1737, I, 294), in Foxe (*Acts and Monuments*, ed. Pratt, V, p. 657), and in Laemmer (*Meletematum Rom. mantissa*, 203).

When Francis I requested, through Cardinal Tournon, that the Pope should again "prolong the said suspension of censures for the whole of October," Clement VII expressed "the hope that he had that, through your prudence and good offices at the coming interview, the said business in England should shape well, which His Holiness, Sire, says is one of the things he most desires in the world, together with God's honour and your satisfaction" (Nicolas Raince, secretary of the Roman embassy, to Francis I, September 26th, 1533. Le Grand, III, 570 *sq*.).

[203] See next chapter.

to him. Soon afterwards he constituted himself its supreme head and took the Pope's place.[204]

With a selfish principle for starting-point Henry had ended in schism. The obstacles he met in pursuing his divorce brought about his conflict with Rome. Then, generalizing from a particular case, after attacking a marriage dispensation he attacked the papal power of dispensing itself, and finished by a general onslaught on all papal prerogatives. At the beginning he had no idea of breaking with Rome, or of reforming the Church in England. In his *Apologia ad Carolum Quintum* Pole tells us that at the time of Cardinal Wolsey's fall Henry was affected by the difficulties his plan had raised and altogether upset by the whole business, and that he regretted this divorce which he had thought could be obtained so easily from Rome, and did not wish to hear it mentioned. He says that this crisis lasted three days, but that Cromwell overcame his scruples, as well as those of Parliament, and dragged them into their fatal revolt. This was the remote consequence—unheeded at first—of a royal whim.

[204] See next chapter.

The Venetian ambassador, Daniel Barbaro, wrote in 1551 (Albèri, *op. cit.*, II, 243 *sq.*): "Henry, despising the Pope's authority, obtained a divorce and immediately married Anne Boleyn, a lady at court, with whom he was smitten. . . . His anger against the Pope, on account of the judgment given against him in the divorce suit, and the bad counsels of Lord Cromwell who was then in great favour, drove him to have himself declared by Parliament supreme head of the Church. All the disorders which followed, and still follow, are all a punishment of the first sin."

CHAPTER III

THE ROYAL SUPREMACY AND CONSUMMATION OF THE SCHISM

The King "the supreme head of the Church of England": history and consequences of this title.—The schism, prepared by a whole series of laws and furthered by the King's safe position at home and abroad, is completed by the taking of the oath to the "supreme head of the Church of England"—Royal absolutism.

AFTER waiting for seven years Henry had cut the Gordian knot of the divorce by transferring the case, on his own authority, to the spiritual jurisdiction of this country. This was the first act of that royal supremacy which, by making him "supreme head of the Church of England," had given him full control of all religious authority in his own realm. That supremacy was fraught with enormous consequences. It completed the English schism by breaking every link with Rome. In its name Henry VIII's successors overthrew the old religion and planted the Protestant Reformation in English soil. In what circumstances did the king have this title assigned to himself?

After Wolsey's fall Parliament—set aside by the cardinal on account of its anti-clerical tendencies since 1515—met in Blackfriars Hall, London, on November 3rd, 1529. The Church, du Bellay wrote, was terribly alarmed[1]; and not without reason. Parliament sat time after time in order to pass laws designed to coerce the Pope and force his hand in the divorce question. The Church's privileges and the prerogatives of the papacy disappeared one after the other, until not one stone was left standing upon another of the stately structure of Church liberties and of papal authority in England.[2]

[1] "It is not as yet known who is to have the seal. I verily believe that the priests will not touch it any more, and that in this Parliament they will have terrible alarms" (J. du Bellay to Montmorency, October 22nd, 1529; Le Grand, III, 378).

[2] Cf. Pollard, *Henry VIII*, p. 277; Froude, chap. III: "The Parliament

The Commons resumed the projected Bills of 1515 and enacted a whole series of laws which betokened a formidable interference of the civil power in Church matters.[3] Fisher exclaimed that the Church was in peril.[4] Henry could rely upon the Commons to help him reduce the Church to subjection.[5] His determination to obtain the divorce and his desire to have the case taken out of Rome's hands, brought to this country, and decided here in his favour, gradually drew him into a struggle, the issue of which was bound to be fatal. While this struggle lasted he was afraid lest the clergy should evade him and obey the Pope, and so he made them dependent solely upon himself.

In 1530 the scheme was ready. Writing from London, in December, 1530, a Florentine said that the constant preoccupation of the moment was to make preparations so as to do without the Pope in everything.[6] The *Praemunire* Statute

of 1529"; Fisher, chap. xi, in Vol. VII of the *Political History of England:* "The Reformation Parliament."

[3] These Bills limited the Bishops' fees, forbade, save in certain cases, pluralities, decreed penalties for non-residence, and prohibited clerics from acquiring tanhouses and breweries (*L. and P.*, IV, No. 6083). The Upper House with the help of the ecclesiastical lords, threw out these proposed Bills. Henry VIII then proposed to refer these matters to a delegation composed of sixteen members, i.e. eight from each House. The Lords deputed four ecclesiastical and four secular peers; the latter sided with the Commons and the Bills were passed (December, 1529). *Statutes of the Realm*, 21 Henry VIII, cap. iv, v, vi, xiii. Cf. Stubbs, *Lectures on Medieval and Modern History*, 1887, p. 317.

[4] The Commons were offended and complained to the king, and the bishop had to explain what he meant.

[5] Until he had the decision of the universities upholding the divorce in his hands, he was above all preoccupied in preventing any decision by the Roman Court. He asked for delay after delay (see pp. 76 *sq.*, nn. 148 and 167 of Chap. II). To obtain them he promised to make no innovations in his kingdom. So, in 1530, Parliament passed no laws on ecclesiastical matters; but on September 12th, foreseeing the Bulls which threatened Henry, it forbade the publication of anything that was contrary to the king's plans. *L. and P.*, IV, 6615; V, 45.

[6] Cromwell wrote to Wolsey on October 21st, 1530 (by this time Clement VII had refused the petition from the nobles of the realm. Cf. p. 79): "The parliament ys prorogyd [until the] vi daye of January. The prelatts shall not appere [in the] *praemunire*. Ther ys another way devysyd in [place thereof] as your Grace shall farther know" (*L. and P.*, IV, No. 6699). They came back, as we shall see, to the first idea of the *praemunire*. When Parliament opened in November, 1529 Henry VIII had granted a general pardon to all his subjects, but offences against the statute of *praemunire* were not included in this (*Statutes of the Realm*, 21 Henry VIII, cap. i).

More than once Henry had threatened the Pope with separation:

was used. It was an old law, practically obsolete.[7] The clergy had protested against it when Parliament passed it [8] and, according to Chapuys, no one was able to fathom it: "it rests only on the imagination of the king, who comments and amplifies it at pleasure, connecting with it any case he chooses."[9] The

"La charge du Dr. Stephen [Gardiner] est entre aultres choses de dire à nostre Sainct-Père que, s'il ne faict procèder le cardinal Campège à ce divorce et s'en dépescher, le roy d'Angleterre se lèvera de son obéyssance, et qu'il le tienne pour tout certain" (J. du Bellay, January 25th, 1529; Bourrilly, I, 543; Le Grand, III, 295).

[7] This law of Edward III (1353), which among other things declared an appeal to the Pope against the king to be treason, had been confirmed by Richard II (1393). Martin V, immediately after the Great Schism, energetically protested against it and against the *Statute of Provisors* (cf. chap. I, n. 7), of which it was merely a corollary, and called upon the Archbishop of Canterbury, H. Chichele, the minor king, Henry IV, and Parliament (1426) (see these three letters in Burnet, IV, 148–58, and the two last in Wilkins, III, 479, who also has others on the same subject, *ibid.*, p. 480 *sq.*, also Dodd, *op. cit.*, I, 267) to revoke it, under threat of the gravest penalties; if it was not repealed, it fell nevertheless into desuetude, and does not appear ever to have had great effect. (Cf. Burnet, I, 182–90. It is to be found in Gee and Hardy, *op. cit.*, Nos. XXXV and XL, together with the second Statute of Provisors of 1390, No. XXXIX; Dodd, I, 259–67, gives a lot of documents relating to the *Praemunire* and the *Statute of Provisors*.) To protect themselves against it the clergy had requested Henry shortly before (1529) to make Parliament define its limits, so that they might not unwittingly break it. (Collier, IX, 117. See also the "Statutum contra adnullatores judiciorum curiae regis," 27 Edward III cap. i.)

Contradictory estimates of the law itself and its scope have been made. Although it did not create a new legislation or a new procedure in the relations between England and the Holy See, yet it placed formidable weapons at the service of the crown, especially by the modifications made in the text itself in the course of time. Stephen Gardiner, Bishop of Winchester, who was a lawyer, declared in a letter to Somerset on October 14th, 1547 (Foxe, ed. Pratt, VI, 43: cf. J. A. Muller, *Stephen Gardiner*, p. 53) that his reason had never been able to admit the justice of the sentence against Wolsey in virtue of the *Praemunire*, although it was in conformity with the laws of the realm. Cf. the article by W. Th. Waugh on the great statute of *Praemunire* in the *Eng. Hist. Review*, April, 1922; Froude, *op. cit.*, chap. IV.

[8] The clergy had protested by the voices of the Archbishops of Canterbury and York representing the two ecclesiastical provinces of England (*Rotuli Parliamentorum*, III, 264). And by the oath which the primate of England gave to the Pope he recognized that the statute of *praemunire* was worthless (Pollard, *Henry VII*, No. 44): "Et si talia a quibuscumque procurari novero vel tractari impediam hoc pro posse et quantocumque potero, commode significabo eidem domino nostro . . . regulas sanctorum patrum . . . observabo et faciam ab aliis observari." "Papatum Romanum et regalia S. Petri adjutor eis ero, ad retinendum et defendendum, salvo meo ordine contra omnem hominem." (Oath taken by Cranmer at his consecration. Strype, *Memorials of Cranmer*, ed. 1848, I, 331.)

[9] Cf. *Sp. Cal.*, IV, Part II, No. 635.

entire body of the English clergy was accused of having
accepted as legitimate Wolsey's authority as papal legate.[10]
We have already seen[11] that Wolsey confessed to having
broken this statute in order to escape from his enemies by this
voluntary humiliation. From this avowal it followed that his
jurisdiction as legate was an illegal one, and that the clergy
were also guilty because they had submitted to it. This was
indeed unjust because Wolsey had never used his powers
except with the approbation of the king; but it was legal.
To blame the king for his own acts was unconstitutional; his
subjects had to pay the penalty for those acts.

Five days after the opening of Parliament, Convocation
met in Westminster Abbey (January 21st, 1531). The indictment was made known to the clergy. At first they thought it
was merely a trick to get a larger "gracious gift" than usual
out of them; Henry needed money.[12] £40,000 were offered
(January 24th) and then £100,000,[13] though they purposely
refrained from mentioning the reason for this extortion, viz.
the infringement of the *Praemunire* Statute.[14] This immense
sum, which would involve the sale of chalices and reliquaries,
was refused, and Convocation was greatly bewildered. On
February 7th the clergy were informed that Henry would
accept it only if certain clauses were inserted in the preamble,
and one of these specified the king's pardon for transgression
of the *Praemunire* Statute. The first two were the most serious
of all: the king was to be recognized as "Protector and
Supreme Head of the English Church and Clergy"; the
second insinuated that he had the care of his subjects' souls
committed to him.[15]

[10] According to Holinshed (*Chronicles*, p. 766) it was on December 30th
that the King's Council declared all the clergy in England were in a
praemunire. A few days later (January 5th, 1531) Clement VII forbade,
under the most severe penalties, the universities, and every cleric or layman
in England, to interfere in the divorce suit. (Le Grand, III, 531 *sq.*)

[11] See above, p. 72.

[12] He pretended that the clergy would have to pay for the war, if it
resulted from the Pope's refusal to grant the divorce. (*L. and P.*, VI, 1381
[3].)

[13] £100,044 8s. 4d., to be precise.

[14] This gift was said to have been made in consideration of the king's
great services to the Church in opposing the heretics. The clergy thanked
the king for resisting the hypocritical agitations against ecclesiastical
property which might have compromised the peace of the realm.

[15] Wilkins, III, 725. Cf. Gairdner, *History*, p. 108. Another clause

This was nothing less than an encroachment upon spiritual matters by the civil powers, seizure of the Church by the king, and loss of ecclesiastical liberties; schism was threatening. It was one of the gravest and most solemn moments in history. Upon it the religious future of England might depend. Infringement of the *Praemunire* Statute was punishable by confiscation and imprisonment. But to refuse to yield to the king's wishes would mean the total destruction of his plans. What would the bishops do? Prompted by the imperial ambassador, the nuncio attended Convocation in order to persuade them to resist. They were terrified at the sight of him. Fearing that the king would make them pay for this attack upon the constitution, they besought the nuncio to leave them immediately and silenced him.[16]

Three sessions were spent in discussing the title *Supremum caput Ecclesiae*.[17] The king's pardon depended upon the voting of this title. Anne Boleyn's brother, Viscount Rochford, informed the prelates, on behalf of the king, that they might add *post Deum* after *Supremum caput*. But this addition altered nothing, it even made matters worse. Since the Pope alone was in question, the words *post Deum* abolished his authority more explicitly. Several Latin pamphlets against papal authority were published and distributed at this same period. On February 11th Warham, the Archbishop of Canterbury, suggested this formula: "We recognize his majesty as the singular protector, the only and supreme lord, and so far

(the third) aimed at the legislative power which was taken from the clergy in 1532: "Privilegia et libertates ejusdem (Ecclesiae) quae regali suae potestati et legibus regni sui non detrahant, confirmando defendit."

[16] ". . . It was agreed between the Nuncio and me that he should go to the said ecclesiastics in their congregation and recommend them to support the immunity of the Church, and to inform themselves about the queen's affair, showing them the letters which the Pope has written to them thereupon and offering to intercede for them with the king about the gift with which he wishes to charge them. On coming into the congregation they were all utterly astonished and scandalised, and, without allowing him to open his mouth, they begged him to leave them in peace, for they had not the king's leave to speak with him." *L. and P.*, V, 62. Stubbs (*Lectures on Medieval and Modern History*, p. 318) is mistaken then when he represents the nuncio as acting in the king's name and the clergy as resisting him.

[17] Hall (*Chronicle*, p. 774) insinuates that Convocation spontaneously offered this title to the king in its petition for pardon: this is contrary to the official version recorded by Wilkins.

as the law of Christ permits, even the supreme head."[18] All were silent. "Whoever is silent," said the archbishop, "seems to consent." "Then we are all silent," one voice replied. Thus did the clergy pass the first measure subjecting the Church to the king.[19]

There was indeed the restrictive clause *quantum per Dei legem licet*, but as Chapuys observed, it meant nothing, "for henceforward no one will dare dispute with his lord and master" as to the extent of that reservation.[20] "The point," he added, "which, as I have said before, has lately been discussed, and will, if carried out, be very injurious to the Pope's authority, is this: that under the penalty of the said writ of 'praemunire' the English clergy have been induced and compelled to declare, constitute, and accept the king as the chief and principal head of the whole Anglican Church, which amounts almost to making him Pope in England."[21]

The Church had yielded almost without a struggle. Henry saw clearly that if there was to be any opposition it would

[18] "Ecclesiae et cleri anglicani cujus singularem protectorem, unicum et supremum dominum, et quantum per Christi legem licet, etiam supremum caput, ipsius majestatem recognoscimus." Wilkins, *Concilia*, III, 275. According to Wilkins, this was Warham's formula.
For the pamphlets against the Pope's authority, see *L. and P.*, V, 7, 9; VI, 416.

[19] For this Convocation of 1531, see Wilkins, *Concilia*, III, 724-26, or Atterbury, *Rights, Powers and Privileges of an English Convocation*, 2nd ed., 1701, appendices iv-vi; *Statutes of the Realm*, 22 Henry VIII, cap. xvi, pp. 335 *sq.*; *Life of Fisher*, Van Ortroy, *Ana. Boll.*, 351 *sq.*; Sir Lewis Dibdin, *Establishment in England*, London, 1932.

[20] *Sp. Cal.*, IV, Part II, No. 635. Friedmann (*Anne Boleyn*, I, 142) followed by Merriman (*Life and Letters of Cromwell*, I, 95) gives to Chapuys' letter quite a contrary meaning. This clause, according to the ambassador, took all real value from the act; but Friedmann omits Chapuys' text. This is the text: "That is exactly as though the clergy had made no reservation, for henceforth none will dare to dispute the extent of that reservation with the king."

[21] Letter quoted from the *Sp. Cal.* of the previous note. He also wrote about "this new papacy made here" (*L. and P.*, V, 112). "There is news from England," the ambassador Muxetula wrote from Rome, "that the king has altogether renounced obedience to the Pope. . . . The Pope thinks it will be necessary to recall his nuncio." Probably, as Father Bridgett remarks, the clergy did not then perceive the full force of their act, nor that they were opening up the path down which Henry was to drag them four years later.
One of Edward II's statutes, of November 24th, 1319, set forth a principle which, interpreted by a Cromwell or a Henry VIII, could lead to the oppression of the clergy: "Non debet dici tendere in praejudicium ecclesiasticae libertatis quod pro rege et re publica necessarium invenitur."

not come from that quarter. The prelates, too, were beginning to feel the importance of their act. "The clergy," wrote Chapuys, "are more conscious every day of the great error they committed in acknowledging the king as sovereign of the Church." In the House of Lords the spiritual peers made some efforts to secure the rejection of what they had conceded in Convocation; and a member of the Privy Council made a vigorous protest.[22] The northern clergy, in Convocation at York, voted the sum of £18,840[23] to redeem their transgression of the *Praemunire* Statute, and recognized the king's title of "supreme head of the Church of England" after listening to a respectful protest by Tunstall, the new Bishop of Durham.[24] In May a certain number of the northern and southern clergy signed a protest. "Four days ago," wrote Chapuys to Charles V, "the clergy of York and Durham sent to the king a strong protestation against the supremacy which he pretends to have over them. The province of Canterbury have done the same, of which I send a copy to Granvella. The king is greatly displeased."[25] Henry may have been greatly displeased, but what did these futile protests matter to him?[26] He had obtained the title which subjected the Church to himself, and it had been formally recognized by Convocations in the north and south. What he wanted to

[22] *L. and P.*, V, 124.
One of the members of the Privy Council pointed out to the king that already "in this business of your divorce and second marriage . . . you would make use of your own or the Pope's authority," and that now in assuming the spiritual supremacy he was making "a dangerous innovation." "Is not the Pope the *communis pater* in the Christian world, and arbiter of their differences?" Dodd, *op. cit.*, Part I, Bk. 3, art. 4: "Records of the supremacy."

[23] £18,840 0 10d., to be precise.

[24] Wilkins, *Concilia*, III, 762. The king thought he ought to answer Tunstall's arguments by letter. He protested that he had no desire to interfere with the priestly functions, and he cited Fisher's compliance. (Wilkins, *Concilia*, III, 762.) Tunstall who, since Wolsey's death, was, besides Kyte, the Bishop of Carlisle, the only bishop in the north, insisted on the ambiguity of the clause *quantum per Christi legem licet*.

[25] Chapuys to Charles V, May 22nd, 1531. Text quoted by Friedmann, according to the archives of Vienna (*Anne Boleyn*, I, 142, n. 2).

[26] Many disapproved of the step taken only for fear of complications. "Many there are," wrote Chapuys, "who dislike this measure, not so much out of zeal for religion and its ministers as for the scandal that may arise therefrom, imagining that the Pope declare this king schismatic and deprive him of his kingdom which is a tributary of the Apostolic See" (*Sp. Cal.*, IV, Part II, No. 641).

do was not, as he assured them all, to interfere in the priestly functions, but to be able, if need arose, to suppress papal jurisdiction in England. [27]

The title of "supreme head of the Church of England," however, remained merely a threat for several years, a means of bringing pressure to bear on the Pope. Henry assured the nuncio that he was not striving to diminish the Pope's authority, "provided he [the Pope] give me no cause to act differently," in other words, provided he decided the question of the divorce in his favour. The remainder of 1531 passed without any fresh attack. [28] But in Rome the cause was proceeding, and Clement did not seem disposed to give way. [29] Henry showed his displeasure by writing to the Pope on December 28th, 1531. The letter was full of reproaches and threats. He accused the Pope of being dependent upon the emperor, and threatened to withdraw from his jurisdiction. [30] A few days later he struck a fresh blow.

Parliament met on January 15th, 1532, and was called upon to examine a Bill for the abolishment of the annates, or first fruits. [31] The annates were a payment made to the Holy See by newly elected bishops on their appointment. It practically amounted to a year's income, *annalia annates*. Rome received a good deal of its income from this

[27] When the priest, Dr. Crome, had been condemned for denying the papal supremacy, he saved him from the stake. "That ought not to be entered among the heresies," he said, "for it was quite true and certain." Crome had appealed from his archbishop (Canterbury) to the king himself (*L. and P.*, V, 129, 148). A preacher having alluded in his presence to the story of Constantine refusing to judge a dispute between two bishops because it was not within the province of a secular prince, "the king . . . ost patience . . . and told him . . . not to tell such falsehoods." The preacher respectfully pointed out to him that it was the truth. Then "the king turned his back and went away displeased" (*L. and P.*, V, No. 216).

[28] Parliament passed certain acts which limited the abuses of the right of sanctuary: those guilty of felony were deprived of this right. The king himself recommended this act to the Houses, and moreover it was not directed against the Church. *Statutes of the Realm*, 21 Henry VIII, cap. xiv. Cf. Dixon, *History of the Church of England*, I, 73.

[29] *Acta consistorialia* and *Diarium Blasii de Cesena*, in Ehses, 207 *sq.*, 255 *sq.*

[30] Theiner, *Vetera Monumenta Hibernorum et Scotorum historiam illustrantia*, Rome, 1864, No. 1031. Pocock, *Records of the Reformation*, II, 148.

[31] The text, as it was passed, can be found in *Statutes of the Realm*, 23 Henry VIII, cap. xxxiii; Burnet, IV, 162; and Gee and Hardy, No. XLIX.

source, and Henry knew well that the blow would be felt. The Bill was passed by the House of Lords, but stopped by the Commons. Not that the latter had any love for the clergy, but simply because they hated the clergy's privileges and saw no reason why this financial burden should be lifted from the bishops' shoulders.[32] Cromwell wrote to Gardiner saying that he did not know what would happen to the proposed Bill.[33] In both Houses Henry made the members vote in his presence. In the Commons he resorted to a very rare mode of procedure, viz. a division: the "ayes" lined up on one side of the hall and the "noes" on the other.[34] In this way the Act of the Annates was passed.

There was one clause that facilitated the passage of the Bill, and it also placed a new weapon against Rome in Henry's hands. The application of the law was left to the king's good pleasure. "The king," wrote the French envoy, "has been very cunning for he has caused the nobles and people to remit all to his will, so that the Pope may know that if he does nothing for him he has the means of punishing him."[35] Henry told the nuncio that he had had nothing to do with this law, that it was entirely the work of the House of Commons.[36] He also ordered his agents in the Curia to say that he had silenced Parliament and had made the members leave the question of annates to himself.[37]

The Commons had shown no enthusiasm when Rome was directly attacked, but they certainly did when it came to

[32] It has been erroneously pretended that this Bill was inspired by the clergy, who reluctantly put up with this tax. Dixon (I, 113) made this mistake through Strype. Strype indeed printed a petition, which Parliament had intended to adopt as a law, with the erroneous heading "An address from the Convocation to the king for an Act to take away Annates." The error was repeated by Blunt (I, 250–53). In the document the case is foreseen "in which, for this reason, the Pope would bring a suit against the kingdom," and advice is given to break away from the Holy See after the example of the King of France in the time of Benedict XIII.

[33] L. and P., V, 723.

[34] L. and P., V, 898.

[35] L. and P., V, 150. This letter is dated March 23rd, 1532, and not March 23rd, 1531. Gilles de la Pommeraye arrived in England only at the end of 1531. Cf. L. and P., VII, 360.

[36] "The king sent to tell the nuncio," Chapuys wrote on February 28th, 1532, "that these measures were not taken by his consent, but were moved by the people who hated the Pope marvellously" (L. and P., V, No. 832).

[37] L. and P., V, 886.

depriving the Church of one of her most ancient privileges: the right to legislate in Convocation.[38] At the beginning of the session (January, 1532), prompted by the Court, they presented a long petition setting out all their old grievances against the clergy. They complained of the ecclesiastical courts,[39] trials for heresy,[40] the clergy's excessive fees, and the great number of feast-days. They demanded that Convocation should not be allowed to draw up constitutions without the consent of the king and the laity. The latter, they said, were subject "in body and in their possessions," under pain of censure, to laws which were not even promulgated in English. They argued that this impaired the royal prerogative, as well as the peace and well-being of the subjects. If such a state of affairs were remedied, their compassionate lord would win the gratitude of their hearts and eternal happiness.

Convocation had the same right to legislate in spiritual matters as Parliament had in temporal affairs.[41] The Commons' petition, called "A Supplication against the Ordinaries," was sent to Convocation at Westminster and read by Warham on April 12th. He demanded that a prompt reply should be given.[42] This reply, refuting the Commons'

[38] For the four drafts in which corrections by Cromwell are found, see chap. I, p. 27, and n. 110. If the grievances came from the king alone, no reason can be seen why he should not have applied directly to Convocation without the intervention of the Commons, as was the rule and as he had done in 1531 for the declaration of his title. At all events, the Commons were of the same opinion as Henry, since they presented the petition against the Ordinaries, instead of resisting as they had done in the question of the annates.

[39] Their endless delays were blamed. Moreover, the Court of Arches, recently altered by Warham, was placed entirely in the hands of ten proctors, so that defendants were unable to have impartial counsel. At times poor people were brought before the Ordinaries *ex officio*, by pure malice or whim on the part of the apparitors, and they then had to pay the costs which were not refunded to them, even when they were declared innocent. Cf. Gairdner, *History*, p. 113 *sq.*

[40] Those who were in easy circumstances, the commercial classes, had long been seeking to limit the powers of ecclesiastics in matters of heresy. At that very time (1532) public opinion had been aroused by an act of Parker, vicar-general to the Bishop of Worcester, who had caused the body of a squire in the County of Gloucester to be exhumed from a Catholic cemetery and burnt at the stake because of heresies found in his will (*L. and P.*, VI, No. 40). Parliament took the matter up and fined Parker £300.

[41] See the French ed. of this book, chap. I, n. 138.

[42] Text of this petition in Gee and Hardy, No. XLVI; *L. and P.*, V,

complaints one by one, in detail and at length, was partly drawn up by the lawyer Gardiner, not long appointed to the see of Winchester (October, 1531),[43] and it received the unanimous approbation of the Upper House on April 15th, and of the Lower House on the 19th. It proved that the Church's power of legislating was based upon the Scriptures and determined by the Church; that the use of this power, which in no wise interfered with the laws of the realm, could not possibly depend upon the good will of the king, whose prerogative was untouched by it. Yet if Henry wished to express his opinion on any particular point the clergy would do their utmost, so far as their duty allowed them, to please him.[44]

The Ordinaries' reply was presented to the king. On April 30th he handed it to the Speaker and a delegation from the House of Commons, maliciously observing: "We think this answer will smally please you, for it seemeth to us very slender. You be a great sort of wise men: I doubt not but you will look circumspectly in the matter, and we will be indifferent between you."[45] The Commons were thus encouraged in their attack upon the Church.

Convocation, knowing that the king was dissatisfied with their first answer, drew up another. The prelates maintained their point of view, and said that, in virtue of their spiritual jurisdiction, they had the right to make laws without the

No. 1016 [1-4]; Froude, I, 208, under the date November 5th, 1529; and Blunt, I, 212-220. Cf. Hall, *Chronicle*, ed. 1809, p. 784. The Record Office has four drafts of this supplication, three of which were corrected by Cromwell. Merriman gives the first, *Life and Letters of Cromwell*, I, 104-111; it bears the title: "A boke against the clergy for taking excessyve Fees." This is good proof that the petition, as we have said, was presented at the instigation of the court from which it emanated, Cromwell being one of the Privy Council since 1531.

[43] Ehses, Nos. 108, 109.

[44] Each grievance of the Commons was answered *seriatim*: See this answer, more than 26 pages in 12mo, in Wilkins, III, 750, where there is more than one omission; in *L. and P.*, V, 1016 [5]; Gee and Hardy, No. XLII; Froude, *Henry VIII*, chap. III.

[45] Cf. Gairdner, *History*, 118. On this occasion the king replied to Temse's attack, who had told him to take back his wife (cf. p. 26). He had been very much surprised that in the Commons they had dared to speak of his relations with the queen; he had acted only from motives of conscience, and according to the advice of doctors of the universities; being now forty-one years old, he was no longer at an age when passion inspired his actions.

approbation of the temporal power, and added that Christian princes had always recognized this right, Henry himself particularly, in his book against Luther. Nevertheless taking the king's wisdom, knowledge, and perfection into account, they were prepared, "during your highness' natural life," not to legislate without the royal consent in matters unconnected with faith, and to suppress all former laws which did not bear upon matters of faith or the correction of sin.[46] That was their first concession; but it was not enough for the king.[47]

On May 11th the king sent for the Speaker and a deputation from the Commons to inform them of his discovery that the clergy owed him only half allegiance, "for," he added, "all the prelates at their consecration make an oath to the Pope clean contrary to the oath they make to us so that they seem his subjects and not ours."[48] Henry knew very well that the two oaths were not incompatible. The oath which the bishops gave the king bound them not to accept anything from Rome which might be harmful to their sovereign, whose loyal subjects they had sworn to remain. But this declaration revealed to all that Henry's plan was developing more and more along definite lines, that his object was the suppression of papal authority in order to leave a clear field for his own It was up to the clergy to grasp this fact.

On May 10th Convocation had received a kind of ultimatum completely abolishing their right to make laws. It consisted of three articles: (1) Thenceforward no new canons, constitutions provincial, or ordinances provincial or synodal were to be enacted without the royal licence. (2) All existing laws would be revised by a commission of sixteen members of Parliament and sixteen ecclesiastics, all chosen by the king; and every law considered by the majority to be against the laws of God or of the realm would be abrogated. (3) The

[46] Wilkins, *Concilia*, III, 753; *L. and P.*, V, 1018.

[47] He showed his displeasure to Gardiner who had inspired that reply The bishop answered in a respectful but faintly ironic letter, saying that being but little learned in theology, he hoped he was not making a mistake in following a number of grave authorities, including the king himself in his book against Luther.

[48] According to Foxe, in his *History concerning the Life . . . of Lord Thomas Cromwell* (*op. cit.*, ed. Pratt, V, 367), Cromwell gave the king this idea. Cf. Dixon, I, 104 n.

constitutions upheld by the majority would receive the royal assent and continue to be in force.[49]

These articles were discussed for several days, from May 10th to the 15th, and various schemes thought out.[50] On the 15th, in order to cut their resistance short, the king notified Convocation that it was adjourned until November 5th, on account of the plague, but that before they adjourned he required an answer to his three articles.[51] That same evening all the members of the clergy, with the exception of Clerk, Bishop of Bath, adopted the articles.[52] They hinted, in the preface, that their submission was a personal one, made out of confidence in the king's "excellent wisdom, princely goodness, and fervent zeal to the promotion of God's honour and Christian religion, and also in your learning, far exceeding in our judgment the learning of all other kings and princes that we have read of." Thus did the prelates cherish a vain hope that in subsequent reigns they would regain their liberty.[53] This famous document, known as the Submission of the Clergy, was a fresh surrender.[54] As an independent body

[49] Collier, IX, 97, with some verbal differences which come from the Cotton MS., whence the author has taken his text; Wake, *State of the Church*, 477; *L. and P.*, V, 1023, II.

[50] The MS. Cleopatra F.I. in the Cotton collection at the British Museum contains three drafts of compromises submitted by Convocation. Atterbury published and discussed them in his *Rights, Powers and Privileges of an English Convocation*, pp. 534 *sq.* Cf. Burnet, VI, 50; Dixon, I, 106 n.

[51] The question of the oath was postponed.

[52] Wilkins, III, 749. Cf. Dixon, I, 106. Standish, Bishop of St. Asaph, proposed to add: "provided that the king allow those constitutions which are not contrary to the law of God or of the realm to be put in execution as before." The Bishop of Lincoln, Longland, added this condition: "so that the king permit the other constitutions which have been made to be executed by the Ordinaries until the matter be examined." The Bishop of London said: "so that the said schedule be not against the law of God, nor contrary to the General Councils."

[53] That was the meaning of the second answer of the Ordinaries. The Parliament of the next year, in adopting the act of the clergy, added or took away certain words which made the submission of the clergy still more absolute. Cf. Atterbury, *op. cit.*, p. 83; Sir Lewis Dibden, *op. cit.*

[54] The document is entitled: "Instrumentum super submissione clericorum Domino Rege quoad celebrationem conciliorum provincialium." It will be found in Wilkins, III, 754; *L. and P.*, V, No. 1023; Collier, IX, 98, where the English text is preceded and followed by an attestation in Latin; Blunt, I, 227-29; Gee and Hardy, No. XLVIII, where the verbal differences between the king's rough draft and the definite act are indicated (the chief is the addition of the word *new* canons, *new* ordinances to the adopted text).

the clergy no longer existed. On May 13th Chapuys wrote: 'Churchmen will be of less account than shoemakers, who have the power of assembling[55] and making their own statutes."[56]

In the House of Lords the bishops, with the help of Gardiner and Thomas More,[57] rejected the concessions the Church had made to the king. It was not till the following year (March 30th) that they were passed by Parliament.[58] On May 14th Parliament was prorogued. Two days later More resigned the Chancellorship,[59] and Gardiner retired in disgrace to his see at Winchester. Three months afterwards Warham died, having previously lodged a protest, through notaries, against any law, past or future, derogatory to the Church's powers, or tending to diminish the prerogatives and liberties of the metropolitan and primatial Church of Canterbury.[60]

It needed but little now to enslave the Church completely to the king; very slender indeed were its links with Rome. The next year (1533) was the decisive one. Henry's marriage with Anne Boleyn, the Act against appeals,[61] Anne's coronation, the two conflicting judgments of Cranmer and the Pope, and the king's excommunication had all caused a real

[55] The clergy engaged not to meet together without a positive order from the king. "Sequens sessio (May 15th) submissionem clericorum domino Reg; absque ulla limitatione vel reservatione, quoad celebrationem conciliorum provincialium, obtulit ac assensum majoris partis Convocationis obtinuit." *Reg. Convocationis* (Wilkins, *Concilia*, III, 749).

[56] "The bishops whom Christ destined to direct the Church acquired by his blood," wrote Harpsfield (Bémont, *op. cit.*, pp. 70 *sq.*), "abandoned the government of the Church to the king. . . . The king thus possessed all the powers, he was armed with two swords."

[57] *L. and P.*, V, 1013.

[58] *Lords' Journal*, 25 Henry VIII, cap. 20. Wake, *State of the Church*, p. 479.

[59] His place was taken by Audeley, Speaker of the Commons, who remained Chancellor until his death in 1544. Audeley received this title only in 1533; in 1532, he was Keeper of the Great Seal.

[60] Cf. Hook, *Life of the Archbishops*. Warham's protest is in Burnet, VI, 54, in Wilkins, III, 746, and has been reproduced by Froude at the end o chap. IV.

[61] This law, which forbade an appeal to the Roman Court, made every judgment given by the ecclesiastical tribunals in England a definite one. By this means Henry VIII had had his first marriage with Catherine of Aragon definitely declared null and void, and his second with Anne Boleyn valid.

breach between Rome and England. Henry no longer troubled to disguise the fact. The laws, of which the execution had been left to Henry by Parliament, were brought into operation. On July 9th he confirmed the 1532 Act of the Annates by letters-patent.[62] At the same time he recalled his ambassadors from Rome and drew up an appeal to the Council against the Pope.[63]

Clement VII was dismayed at this breach, which he had tried to stave off by using every possible delay. He could not see eye to eye with the Imperialists, who tried to persuade him that England was not a very profitable isle, and that he would be amply compensated for its loss by the fidelity of Spain and the emperor's other dominions.[64] Francis I, for his part, was afraid of a schism which might complicate the political situation by causing war between Charles V and Henry, France's ally. Consequently Clement and Francis, who met at Marseilles in November, 1533,[65] did all they could to bring England back into obedience to the Holy See.[66] But where the divorce was concerned Henry would not hear of concessions; he simply wanted them to acknowledge that it was legitimate. On the other hand, the Pope could not and would not reverse the decision of July 11th, 1533, declaring Henry's marriage with Anne Boleyn invalid; he

[62] *L. and P.*, VI, 793.

[63] *L. and P.*, VI, 721, 979, 980, 998.

[64] *L. and P.*, VI, 997.

[65] The Pope landed near Marseilles, on October 11th; the next day he made a solemn entry into the town. Secretary Berthereau to J. de Dinteville, October 15th, 1533. *Bibliothèque Nationale*, Dupuy MS., I, 547, f. 273.

[66] Carnesecchi, in his letter to Vergerio of February 14th, 1534 (Friedensburg, *Nuntiaturberichte aus Deutschland*, I, 180), said that one of the chief aims of the Pope in the interview had been to bring Henry back through the medium of Francis I, whose friendship for the King of England was known to him. For the interview at Marseilles, see J. du Bellay's account (*Bibliothèque Nat.*) Dupuy MS. XXXIII, fol. 52; Friedmann, *op. cit.*, Vol. I, 247-56. Carnesecchi in his letter to Vergerio of February 14th, 1534 (Friedensburg, *op. cit.*, pp. 177-81), gives the reasons for the interview, to dispel the emperor's suspicions. Cf. *Mémoires de du Bellay*, ed. 1569, fol. 111 *sq.*; 117 *sq.*; Ehses, 272-77. For Francis I's efforts to prevent the breach between England and the Holy See, see Varillas, *Histoire de François Ier*, ed. 1689, II, 220-32; L. Bourrilly, *L'intervention de la France dans l'affaire du divorce à propos de travaux récents*, in the *Revue d'histoire moderne et contemporaine*, Vol. I, 1899.

made this clear to Francis I immediately they met. Every attempt to reconcile matters was therefore useless.[67]

Meanwhile a proposal was made to the king to have the cause examined afresh at Avignon by two legates, a Frenchman and another chosen by the Pope, on condition that Henry accepted the Holy See's authority and promised to abide by the final decision. And as Gardiner, who had been appointed ambassador to Francis I a little while before, averred that he had no power to accept a compromise, the King of France induced him to ask Henry to give him the power of proctor.[68] Henry refused. Why Avignon? Formerly Cambrai had been suggested to him, and that was a more suitable and safer town for him. And why this proxy? Francis I had himself several times promised to be the king's proxy.[69] He concluded with the words: "Item to provoke as may be the general council, which will more fear the Pope than all other things."[70] Dr. Bonner, who accompanied Gardiner, undertook to carry out these instructions. On November 7th, with Girolamo Penizzoni for witness, he gained admittance to the Pope and told him of Henry's appeal to the General Council. Incensed, Clement VII interrupted him, and as Francis I happened to enter at that moment the Pope complained to him very violently of this lack of respect. He even tried to make Francis break off his English alliance. "Being your guest," said Clement in effect, "I allow people to enter without insisting on all the formalities which are used at Rome. These men, relying on this, have come in without asking the permission of anybody, and have just done that which at Rome would entail capital punishment. I have

[67] Gardiner, who followed the French Court, warned Henry that there was no hope of an understanding. Gardiner, Brian and Wallop to Lord Lisle, October 17th, 1533. *L. and P.*, VI, p. 526.

[68] Francis I's instructions to J. du Bellay in Le Grand, III, 571-88; du Bellay's account, Dupuy MS. XXXIII, f. 62. Gardiner, who left England on September 3rd (Friedmann, *Anne Boleyn*, I, 227) had only received general and indeterminate instructions (J. du Bellay's account, *ibid.*, f. 54).

[69] A bitter criticism followed of Francis I's dealings with Henry VIII.

[70] Instructions to the ambassadors. *L. and P.*, VI, 333. The messenger who carried them left London on November 1st and arrived in Marseilles on the 6th. A copy of the appeal to the council had been sent to Bonner on August 18th. Henry VIII to Bonner, in Pocock, *Records*, App. No. XXXV; and Strype, *Memorials of Cranmer*, ed. 1848, I, 329; cf. *ibid.*, p. 37.

shown myself ready to do all that I can, but the King of England has acted in a totally different manner. You ought, therefore, to forsake his alliance and to unite with the Holy See against him."[71] Clement rejected Henry's appeal as illegal, on November 11th, and sailed for Italy on the 12th.

The King of France rebuked the English for their conduct. "You will have me do for you," said he, " . . . and as fast as I study to win the Pope, ye study to lose him."[72] He asserted that had he known beforehand that the Pope was to be intimidated, he would have stopped it. "Your king," he had already said,[73] "thinks himself a wise man, but he is simply a fool. He is working in the interest of the queen, for by this appeal he admits that he knows of the sentence of July 11th and nevertheless disregards it. Let him know that if, in consequence of his behaviour, he is excommunicated, I have declared and declare that I shall not assist him against the Pope."

But, unlike Francis I, Henry had no desire to soothe and win the Pope over. His Council arranged for it to be preached from the pulpit and set forth everywhere that the Pope was inferior to a Council; that until then the authority he had exercised within this realm, by the sufferance of its princes, was a usurping of the council's power, and that thenceforward no papal censure could take effect since appeal had been made to the council (December, 1533).[74] Henry himself at this time knew that the breach with Rome could not be remedied. He admitted to the French ambassador that he was determined on it, and added that it would not make him

---

[71] Du Bellay's account quoted by Friedmann (*op. cit.*, I, 253 *sq.*). Francis I made it understood that he wanted Calais as the price of his breach; Clement VII agreed, but the Imperialists were not of the same mind.

Bonner related the scene of his interview with the Pope, in his letter to the king dated November 13th, 1533 (Marseilles). Burnet, VI, 56-98.

[72] The English ambassadors to Henry VIII, Marseilles, November, 1533. *L. and P.*, VI, p. 571.

[73] Cifuentes to Charles V, November 9th, 1533. British Museum, Add. MSS. 28, 586, f. 62. Cf. Friedmann, I, 253.

[74] Propositions submitted to the council and the council's decisions upon them, December 2nd, 1533, in Collier, IX, 134-36. Declaration of the superiority of a council over the Pope and of the right of each prince to appeal to a general council, to obtain justice in spiritual matters, and to have recourse to the sword for temporal affairs. *Ibid.*, IX, p. 141.

less of a good Christian, for he would arrange for the word
of God to be preached in lieu of the canons and papal
decrees.[75] "And moreover," wrote Castillon on November
17th, "he is resolved to place himself and his country entirely
beyond obedience to the Pope, desiring to have God's holy
word preached throughout the country . . . ; he is quite
determined, and most of the lords around him and in the
land are also inclined that way."[76] And a few months later
after a definite decision had been given by Rome, Henry
wrote to his ambassador at the French Court: "Ye shall
assure our said good brother upon our honour that in case
he had given sentence with us we would have laboured as
diligently and as studiously for his reformation as we will
now."[77]

Consequently when Francis I made another attempt after
the meeting at Marseilles it was useless. The Bishop of Paris,
du Bellay, came to London, on December 17th, 1533, for a
final endeavour.[78] The only promise he could obtain was that
Henry would not complete the destruction of papal authority
in England, if the Pope declared Catherine's marriage null
and Anne's valid, before Easter.[79] Du Bellay fastened on to
this last hope. He hastened to Rome, and arrived there on
February 2nd, 1534. He described the dangers of schism
to the Pope and to the cardinals in consistory,[80] asked that

[75] *L. and P.*, VI, 1435, 1479.

[76] Castillon to J. du Bellay, November 17th, 1533. *Bibliothèque Nat.*,
Dupuy MS. XXXIII, f. 18. Cf. Henry VIII to his ambassador in France,
Wallop, December 1st, 1533, *L. and P.*, VII, 524.

[77] Henry VIII's instructions to Sir John Wallop, April, 1534. Cf.
Friedmann, *Anne Boleyn*, I, 308.

[78] His mission was also to justify Francis I, whom Henry did not cease
to accuse of bad faith since the interview at Marseilles (Castillon to du
Bellay, November 17th, 1533; *Bib. Nat.*, Dupuy MS. XXXIII, f. 19;
J. du Bellay's instructions for London; Le Grand, III, 571 *sq.*). When
Henry was about to repeat his invectives against the King of France, du
Bellay silenced him by threatening immediate war. Du Bellay's account
(Dupuy MS. XXXIII, f. 61).

[79] Castillon to Francis I, March 16th, 1534. *Bib. Nat.*, French MS.
5499, f. 197. Cf. *L. and P.*, XII, 171 and 952.

[80] J. du Bellay and C. Denonville to Francis I, February 8th, 1534.
Bib. Nat., French MS., 5499, f. 189. "The Bishop of Paris," Carnesecchi
records, February 14th, 1533 (Friedensburg, *Nuntiaturberichte*, I, 180),
"says in short that the king, more obstinate than ever, is resolved to break
with the Apostolic See, that he is making up to the Lutherans, and,
in order better to prepare for the war which might happen, is making

the cause should be judged at Cambrai, received promises
from the Pope,[81] and wrote both to Francis I and to Castillon,
telling the former his hopes[82] and asking the latter to obtain
a fresh delay from Henry.[83]

But Clement, irritated by Henry's appeal to the council
and aware of everything that was being done against his
authority in England,[84] had made up his mind to end this
trial, which had been pending in the Roman Court for more
than four years. "I wish to put an end to this trial," he had
remarked to Cifuentes two days after he returned from
Marseilles.[85] When du Bellay arrived Simonetta's report
was ready, and the Pope had sought Charles V's aid in
carrying out the decree.[86] On March 23rd, 1534, whilst du
Bellay was full of hope, the final decision pronouncing the
validity of the marriage between Henry and Catherine was

peace with the King of Scotland. . . .   The above-mentioned Bishop of
Paris relates many facts which show the king's bad intentions and very
bad dispositions towards His Holiness and the Holy See. . . .   Things
could not be worse or more desperate." J. du Bellay's brother says in his
Mémoires (ed. 1569, f. 133): *"Ledit evesque de Paris, arrivé qu'il fut, trouva le
roy d'Angleterre en grande colere contre le pape et tout le sainct siege apostolique. . . .
Mais après plusieurs remonstrances qui luy furent faictes par ledit evesque de Paris
se condescendit que là ou ledit sainct père voudroit superseder en sadite sentence . . .
il supersederoit aussi l'execution qu'il avoit deliberé de faire, qui estoit de se separer
du tout de l'obeissance romaine."* Rabelais, who was a friend of the Bishop of
Paris, accompanied him on this journey.

[81] He had already ordered everything to be prepared for the court at
Cambrai. J. du Bellay and Denonville to Francis I, February 8th, 1534
(*loc. cit.*), and to Castillon, February 22nd, 1534. *Bib. Nat.*, Fr. MS. 5499,
f. 191.

[82] Letter quoted, of February 8th, 1534. Cf. J. du Bellay to Montmorency, February 8th, 1534. *Bib. Nat.*, Fr. MS. 5499, f. 189.

[83] *Bib. Nat.*, Fr. MS., 5499, f. 199.

[84] Carnesecchi to Vergerio, February 24th, 1534. Friedensburg, *op. cit.*,
I, 180.

[85] Cifuentes to Charles V, December 13th, 1533.

[86] Dr. Ortiz to Charles V, February 25th, 1534. British Museum, Add.
MS. 28, 586, f. 124. Clement thought it would be very detrimental to
the Holy See to pass a sentence which would not be carried out. "The
reason His Holiness wants to be sure that the sentence will be executed is
none other than a zeal for the honour of justice and of the authority of the
Apostolic See, which would receive too grave an injury if a sentence of such
importance remained ineffectual." (Carnesecchi, Clement VII's secretary,
to Vergerio, February 14th, 1534. Friedensburg, I, 180-81. See Charles
V's instructions, May, 1533, in Weiss, *Papiers d'État de Granvelle*, Vol. II
33; the letter from Carne and Revetta to Henry VIII, April 7th, 1534.
L. and P., VII, 554; *Mémoires de du Bellay*, ed. 1569, f. 111.) Vergerio
insists with Ferdinand that the emperor should carry out the sentence
(Friedensburg, I, 214-15).

solemnly given in consistory, with the unanimous assent of
the cardinals present.[87] This time everything was settled,
and completely settled. Negotiations and conferences were
no longer of any use. It meant either submission to or separation from Rome.[88]

Henry was prepared. In case the French alliance failed
him—and there was little likelihood of that, on account of the
rivalry between Charles V and Francis I—he was negotiating
with the German princes of the Smalcaldic League.[89] In the
country itself everything was prepared for the organization
of the schism. More than ever Parliament was ready to
maintain his policy. Several opportunities for changing the
members had recently occurred. In the autumn of 1533
Cromwell had taken advantage of vacancies created by
death or other causes to fill four seats at "the king's pleasure."[90]
This was the first interference of the Crown in the elections.

[87] *Diarium Blasii de Cesena*, in Ehses, p. 228. J. Korzeniowski, *Excerpta
ex manu scriptis Archivi Consistorialis*, p. 51. At the beginning of the session
Cardinal Trivulzio, a friend of France, had proposed that judgment
should be postponed; he was supported only by Pisani and Ridolfi (J.
du Bellay and Denonville to Francis I, March 23rd and 24th, 1534. *Bib.
Nat.*, Fr. MS. 5499, f. 199 and 201). The eight French cardinals were
absent from Rome (cf. Friedmann, *op. cit.*, I, 302-308). The cardinals
assured J. du Bellay that this decision, which was maintained in the
consistory of July 31st, was not to be made public until its execution by
Charles V was certain (Friedmann, *op. cit.*, II, 1).

[88] Dr. Carne, the king's *excusator*, protested from Bologna, on April 14th,
against the decision of March 23rd (Theiner, *op. cit.*, p. 604 and No. 1040).

After Catherine of Aragon's death (January, 1536) J. du Bellay made a
final attempt to prevent Henry VIII's deposition by applying to Paul III,
but Francis I showed no interest in the matter (Friedmann, *op. cit.*, II,
203-14); and a few futile efforts were made to secure a rapprochement
between England and the Holy See (*ibid.*, pp. 209, 212-14).

[89] Particularly with the Elector of Saxony and the Landgrave of Hesse
(Friedensburg, *Nuntiaturberichte*, I, 180. Dispatches from the English
agents in Germany, Vaughan and Mundt, in *L. and P.*, VII, 499, 501,
536). Negotiations began in 1533. Stephen Vaughan was sent to Germany
to make an alliance with the Elector of Saxony, the Landgrave of Hesse,
and the Duke of Brunswick-Luneburg, whilst Christopher Mundt, an agent
of German nationality, was sent for the same purpose to Bavaria, where
the dukes, albeit Catholics, were enemies of the Hapsburgs. Cf. Friedmann,
op. cit., I, 226. See below, chap. VIII, n. 18.

To Luther, in 1535, Henry sent Robert Barnes, who was afterwards
burnt as a heretic (1540). Friedensburg, *Nuntiaturberichte*, I, 542. Cf. W.
Walther, *Heinrich VIII von England und Luther*, Leipzic, 1908; and P. Smith
in the *Eng. Hist. Review*, Vol. XXV.

[90] *L. and P.*, VI, 1382; VII, 56.

In that same year several abbots died or were forced to resign. Their places were filled by the royal commissioners.[91] Moreover, since Wolsey's fall the king had had occasion to appoint bishops to the sees of York, London, Winchester, Durham and Canterbury. In 1533 four other sees fell vacant: Bangor, Ely, Coventry and Lichfield, and an Act of Parliament deprived Campeggio and Ghinucci of their episcopal sees because they were foreigners and non-residents.[92] The Bishops of Norwich and Chichester were both over ninety,[93] and the Bishop of Llandaff, Catherine's confessor, was a Spaniard who could not speak a word of English. Amongst all the prelates Fisher alone had the courage to offer effective resistance to the laws against the Church.

Almost as soon as Parliament assembled (January 15th, 1534) measures were discussed to complete the schism. The opposition in both Houses was so feeble that Chapuys prophesied that the little papal authority remaining would easily be abolished.[94] The second Act of Appeals was passed first. By this the Submission of the Clergy, rejected two years previously by the Lords, became law.[95] Thenceforward the Church could not legislate without the king's assent, and Henry was to appoint a commission to reform the Church's constitutions.[96] Appeal was allowed from the archiepiscopal Court of Canterbury to the royal chancellor.   Abbeys and

[91] Yet it cannot be definitely said whether it was to purify the Upper House, or to prepare for the dissolution of the monasteries. At this period it was said that Cromwell, the author of the dissolution, "rules everything."

[92] *L. and P.*, VII, 48, 54, 634.

[93] *L. and P.*, VII, 171.

[94] *L. and P.*, VII, 171; cf. XII, Part II, 952.

[95] The first law was passed in February, 1533, and was entitled: "Act for the restraint of Appeals" (24 Henry VIII, cap. 12; Gee and Hardy, No. L). It was laid down, in the preamble, that England is an independent empire, wherein the highest source of justice here below is none other than the king. Abolished by Mary Tudor in 1554, it was re-established by Elizabeth at the beginning of her reign (1 Elizabeth, cap. 1; Gee and Hardy, No. LXXIX), by the Act of Supremacy, 1553; since then it has never ceased to be in force. Cf. Blunt, I, 257-62.

[96] This commission, which was mooted in Henry VIII's time (cf. Cranmer's letter to the king, January 24th, 1545, Burnet, VI, 353), was not appointed till 1551 (see Pollard, *Cranmer*, pp. 280-84). In practice, until this time, the Church was without laws, although before Henry's death Cranmer had drawn up a partial rough draft called *Reformatio legum ecclesiasticarum*.

other religious houses depending directly upon Rome were also placed under the chancellor's jurisdiction.[97]

A new law on the annates, called at first "Law concerning the consecration of bishops,"[98] definitely abolished the payment of annates to Rome,[99] and decided how bishops were to be nominated in the future.[100] The king would give the *congé d'élire* to the chapters,[101] and indicate his own choice of candidate. If after twelve days no one had been elected the king would appoint a bishop by letters-patent.[102]

A third law forbade the payment of Peter's Pence and other dues to the Roman Curia.[103] All dispensations were to

[97] *Statutes of the Realm*, 25 Henry VIII, cap. 19; Gee and Hardy, No. LI. This law of 1534 on the submission of the clergy and on the appeals was revoked by Mary Tudor before the end of 1554 (*ibid.*, No. LXXVI), and re-established by Elizabeth in 1559 (*ibid.*, No. LXXIX).

[98] The first was dated 1532 (see above, n. 31) and the application of it was entrusted to the king. This time the proposed law was thrown out by the Lords on February 27th, and submitted again in an amended state and passed on March 16th.

[99] *L. and P.*, VI, 793. Henry VIII signed and confirmed this law on July 9th, 1534 (Burnet, IV, 168; Collier, IX, 97).
The *Valor ecclesiasticus*, the valuation of all the benefices in England, was established by the government when the annates definitely ceased to be paid to Rome (cf. chap. iv).

[100] In the previous laws Henry had already demanded legislation on this point. At the time of he first law on the annates (1532) the king proposed, wrote Chapuys, that the right of nomination, which certainly belonged to the Apostolic See, should be suppressed (letter of February 28th, 1532, *L. and P.*, VI, No. 832). The Parliament of 1533, voting on the appeals, also discussed the ratifying of bishops' appointments without having recourse to Rome. See Blunt, I, 262 *sq.*: "Abolition of papal authority in the appointment of bishops."

[101] Rymer, *Foedera*, VI, Part II, p. 192. The former *congé d'élire* (cf. Pollard, *Henry VII*, No. 46, following Rymer) left freedom of election to the chapters. Henceforth it was no longer so. Cf. below, n. 156.

[102] *Statutes of the Realm*, 25 Henry VIII, cap. 20. Gee and Hardy, No. LII. This law of 1534 concerned then ecclesiastical appointments, the definite suppression of the annates, the election of bishops, and the letters-missive. The part relating to episcopal elections was abolished in the first year of the reign of Edward VI, who replaced them by direct appointment by the Crown; but this prerogative was revoked by Mary Tudor in the first Act of Repeal of 1553 (Gee and Hardy, No. LXXIII).

[103] "The English kings and the Danish kings who reigned in England, bound themselves to pay a certain alms every year to the Church of St Peter of Rome, which from that reason was called *Denarius Petri*. In later times the bishops . . . entered into composition with the Apostolic chamber to pay a certain sum at once to some person who should reside in England for the purpose, on behalf of the Holy See, which agent goes by

be obtained from the Archbishop of Canterbury. At the same time it was asserted that neither the king nor the country had any desire to forsake the articles of faith which Christendom professed.[104]

The papacy was definitely banished from the realm by this series of acts. The Pope, who was to be known only as the "Bishop of Rome," was no more than any other foreign bishop, and he had no authority in England.[105] Some of his powers were transferred to the Archbishop of Canterbury,[106] whose title was changed from *Apostolicae Sedis legatus* to *Metropolitanus*.[107] A new law on heresy decreed that words or acts against the Pope or his decrees would no longer be considered heretical.

When the news of the papal sentence of March 23rd arrived in England Henry had ratified all these acts (March 30th, 1534) with the exception of the one concerning Peter's Pence; this was ratified later. The schism had therefore taken definite shape before Rome had spoken. It was not due, as Burnet says it was in his *History of the Reformation*, to the haste of the imperialist cardinals, who refused to wait a few days for a

the name of Apostolic collector." Italian account in Henry VII's time (Pollard, *Henry VII*, III, No. 35). Cf. Falieri's account in Albèri, III, 16 *sq*.

In 1575 the Spanish nuncio Ormanetto, who had followed Reginald Pole to England as secretary (1554–57) and was there appointed collector for the Apostolic Camera, said that Peter's Pence in this realm brought in 700 or 800 golden crowns. Cf. Carini, *Monsignor Niccolò Ormaneto Veronese, vescovo di Padova, nunzio apostolico alla corte di Filippo II re di Spagna, 1572–77*, Rome, 1894, p. 137.

[104] This law of 1534, forbidding Peter's Pence, together with all papal dispensations, is a very long one (more than twenty-one pages in Gee and Hardy). It was read in the Upper House on March 13th, 14th and 19th, and on the 20th in the Commons; it was passed on the 30th. It was drawn up in the form of a petition to the king against the usurpations of the Holy See. It enumerates the taxes of every kind which the Pope received from England (*Statutes of the Realm*, 25 Henry VIII, cap. 21, Gee and Hardy, No. LIII). Mary Tudor abrogated it in the first year of her reign (1554), and in 1559 Elizabeth re-established it (Gee and Hardy, Nos. LXXVI and LXXIX).

[105] Already at the end of 1533 the king's council no longer allowed preaching at St Paul's Cross, unless a promise were made to declare from the pulpit that the Pope had no more authority than a foreign bishop. The four religious orders in London received a similar command.

[106] Such as the power to dispense. See in Blunt, I, 268–71 the article: "Spiritual jurisdiction from the Pope to the Archbishop of Canterbury."

[107] *L. and P.*, VII, 1555. Cf. Strype, *Memorials of Cranmer* ed. 1848, p. 69.

courier's return.[108] All hope of reconciliation was futile, and the breach had taken effect since the end of 1533.

Henry's political education was now complete. The events of the last five years had opened his eyes and shown him that he was master in his own house. Formerly, when the nuncio had hinted at the excommunication which threatened him, the king had replied that the Pope could do as he pleased, but that in his own kingdom he, Henry, would do just as he wished.[109] He had long summed up the cost and risks of schism, and had long been convinced that his position was safe at home and abroad.

From abroad he had nothing to fear. The emperor was desperately anxious for peace and would not take any steps against Henry. He dared not even openly blame the king's marriage with Anne,[110] and he persuaded Catherine not to leave England.[111] In the imperial Council of May 31st, 1533, the question of war was discussed as a means of preventing the royal divorce.[112] They came to the conclusion that war would endanger the whole of Europe, and especially Charles V's dominions. Moreover, the King of England had not adopted violent measures with Catherine nor given Charles any pretext for breaking the Cambrai treaty. They might possibly expedite the papal sentence, but without any interdict upon England, for "the publication of censures would disturb intercourse with Spain and Flanders. If,

[108] Burnet (III, 182–83) follows J. du Bellay's brother (*Mémoires de du Bellay*, ed. 1569, f. 134. Cf. *L. and P.*, VII, App. Nos. 8, 12, 13; Paolo Sarpi, *Istoria del concilio Tridentino*, French trans. by Le Courayer, ed. Basle, 1738, I, 129). Friedmann (*op. cit.*, I, 305) shows that J. du Bellay did not always speak the truth and, for diplomacy's sake, exaggerated the chances of keeping the King of England in union with the Church.

[109] *L. and P.*, V, 287.

[110] *L. and P.*, VI, 351. To the letter written in a sufficiently humble spirit trying to justify the king's marriage, Charles V replied in ambiguous terms (see the speech on the same subject by the English ambassador to the emperor, in Dodd, ed. 1737, 292). While he said he would provide for Catherine and her daughter, whose rights had been violated, he gave an assurance that he wished to remain on friendly terms with Henry. If he ever thought of taking up arms in his cousin's cause (which is very doubtful), he waited so long that Catherine's death robbed him of the motive for doing so.

[111] *L. and P.*, VI, 863.

[112] *L. and P.*, VI, 568.

therefore, an interdict be resorted to, it should be limited to one diocese, or to the place where the king dwells."[113] They could exhort the Pope to depose Henry. That would prepare the way to the throne for Mary, and secure a preponderance of Spanish influence in England.[114] But execution of the sentence must be entrusted not to the emperor,[115] but to James V of Scotland or to the Irish.[116]

Charles V feared Francis I. An attack upon Henry would throw the king into the arms of the King of France and provoke them both to united action against Flanders, and possibly even in Germany, where the Kings of England and France were already intriguing with the Lutherans. Francis I was believed to be plotting an attack against the empire with the Turks, and the corsair Barbarossa was menacing the Mediterranean coasts. The Venetian ambassador to Charles V observed that the emperor would never have consented to

[113] *L. and P.*, VI, 570.

[114] This control over England was one of the chief aims of the Hapsburgs' policy (cf. *L. and P.*, I, 4833). By leaving England Catherine would have prejudiced Mary's rights to the crown. After Catherine's death, Charles tried to gain the favour of Anne and of the king in order better to safeguard Mary's rights (Friedmann, *op. cit.*, II, 217 *sq.*).

[115] In January, 1534 the imperial ambassador in Rome denied that the emperor had offered the Pope his assistance to carry out the sentence. *L. and P.*, VII, 96. Cf. the emperor's instructions to his ambassadors to the Holy See, May 1533, in Weiss, *Papiers d'État de Granvelle*, II, 33.

[116] But James V, to whom now both the emperor and the Pope were paying court (*L. and P.*, V, 609, 807), knew very well that a Scotch invasion would have united the whole of England against him. Charles V afterwards became convinced of this and moderated Chapuys' zeal, who was urging Scotland to make war: he saw that it would be more disastrous for him than for Henry VIII. True, in 1544, Henry was at war with Scotland, but he himself had broken the peace, after making an alliance with the emperor, in order to ruin French influence in Scottish affairs. He had tried from the beginning to combat that influence in preventing Mary of Lorraine's marriage with James V of Scotland [1513–42] (Kaulek, *op. cit.*, pp. 5, 10, 12, 13, 15, 17, 19, 48, 51, 52), or to counterbalance it by himself marrying a princess of Guise (*ibid.*, 51, 64, 68, 69, 71, 73, 75, 80 *sq.*).

As for the Irish, whom the emperor tried to stir up against England (cf. *L. and P.*, VII, 342, 353), they did not lend themselves to this scheme; and the partial revolt of Thomas Fitzgerald, son of the Earl of Kildare (Lord Deputy of Ireland), in 1534, was due to a personal motive rather than to a reason of general interest. Owing to a false report Fitzgerald thought that they had condemned to death his father, who had been summoned to London to explain his conduct in allowing the royal artillery to be used in his own castles (1533–34). See Froude, chap. VIII, "The Irish Rebellion."

be at variance with the King of England, because he feared lest the latter should ally himself with the King of France.[117]

If Francis could have been weaned from the English alliance things would have taken quite a different turn. But the emperor was niggardly. At the meeting at Marseilles Clement had told the emperor to give Calais to the King of France.[118] But Charles thought Calais was better as it was (i.e. in Henry's hands) for the security of Flanders.[119] The Pope then hinted that he should give Milan, but the emperor would rather have sacrificed a dozen aunts than see the duchy in French hands.[120] Political considerations stifled all family interests in Charles V. "Although the emperor", he once said when speaking of Catherine's divorce, "is related to the queen, that is a private matter; what concerns the public interest must be considered"; and these considerations, as he admitted a year later, "obliged him to reconcile himself with Henry".[121]

[117] Report of Alvise Mocenigo, in Fiedler, 1548, *Fontes rerum austriacarum*, XXX, 165. In June 1534, Philip of Hesse, encouraged by France, severed himself from the Hapsburgs' protectorship. Henry VIII had started relations with Luebeck, Hamburg, and Denmark, the crown of which country had been offered to him. *L. and P.*, VII, 737, 871, 957–58; VIII, *passim*. Cf. C. F. Wurm, *Die politischen Beziehungen Heinrichs VIII zu M. Meyer und J. Wullenwever*, Hamburg, 1852; Stern, *Heinrich VIII und das Schmalkaldische Bund*, Göttingen, 1870.

In proportion as he lost hope of seeing the Pope withdraw rom the emperor, Francis I drew nearer to England and the Lutherans (Friedensburg, *Nuntiaturberichte*, I, 242, n. 2).

Even after Francis I's death, Charles V did not cease to envy and to fear France, whose power he especially sought to diminish. Alvise Mocenigo's report mentioned above, 1548. See W. Bradford, *Correspondence of the Emperor Charles V and his ambassadors of the courts of England and France from the original letters in the imperial archives at Vienna*, London, 1850.

[118] Francis I and his two chief ministers, the grand master and the admiral, would have given up Henry VIII's alliance for Calais. Cf. Friedmann, *Anne Boleyn*, I, 256.

[119] *L. and P.*, VI, 774.

[120] The emperor thought that with Milan in French hands the kingdoms of Naples and Sicily would no longer have been safe. Alvise Mocenigo's Report. Fiedler, *op. cit.*, XXX, 163.

[121] *L. and P.*, VII, 229. "He was so little anxious as to how his three sisters fared," the nuncio in France wrote in March, 1528, "that it is difficult to believe his aunt's interests would be dearer to him than theirs To-day necessity or fear, and not affection or relationship, make Christian princes friends or enemies" (Ehses, 255 *sq.*). After Catherine's death Charles made offers to Henry VIII to ensure his co-operation against Francis I and the Turks, and "that he [Charles V] would be a mean to have a reconciliation between us and the Bishop of Rome" (*State Papers*, VII, p. 683; Burnet, VI, 168).

For his own part Francis I did not think lightly of the English alliance.[122] His memories of the disastrous results which ensued from the union between Henry and Charles from 1521 to 1525 were still too vivid for him to provoke another such union.[123]   Francis respected Henry VIII because he feared that the latter might take Catherine back and form an alliance with the emperor.[124]   This desire to have Henry on his side and to keep all imperial influence away from the English throne must have played a large part,

[122] At his accession Henry VIII was considered, in the eyes of diplomatists, as an enemy of France (*Diario di Mario Sanuto*, VIII, 219). Maximilian, his daughter Margaret, and Charles V neglected nothing in order to bring him into an alliance with them. Cf. A. Walther, *Die Anfänge Karls V*, Leipzic, 1911, pp. 91 *sq.*

[123] The Earl of Surrey, Lord High Admiral of England, landed in France, burnt Morlaix in July, 1522, and in September sacked a number of towns in Picardy. In 1523 the Duke of Suffolk with a fresh invading army, prevented Francis I from leading a personal expedition into Italy; he devastated Picardy; and his march upon Paris was already a topic of conversation.   In 1524 negotiations were on foot for a combined attack of the emperor and the King of England; shortly afterwards the disastrous battle of Pavia took place (1525).

[124] *L. and P.*, VI, 1572. J. du Bellay's account (*Bib. Nat.*, Dupuy MS. XXXIII, f. 60): "*Il estoyt eschappé au roy dangleterre de dire a quelqung que la où le roy son frère luy fauldroyt au pis aller, il seroit toujours quicte pour reprendre sa femme au contentement de lempereur, entretenant lautre pour sa mye.*"

"The emperor's resentment against Francis I and Henry VIII," the ambassador to France, Marino Giustiniani, remarked in 1535 (Albèri, I, 168–69), "brings the two kings together and makes them friends." Cf. Trésal, *Les responsabilités de la France dans le schisme anglican* (*Revue des Questions Historiques*, 1906), in which the dangerous position of France from a political point of view is not sufficiently taken into account.

Francis I feared the emperor and did all he could to preserve the friendship of his "very dear brother, cousin, confederate, good fellow, and perpetual ally," as he called him (Bourrilly, *op. cit.*, I, 250, 312, 369, 373, 475). For the same reason, Henry endeavoured to convince Francis that he could not have a more loyal or a more sure alliance than Henry's (Kaulek, *op. cit.*, p. 51; cf. p. 50); he watched him with a suspicious eye (cf. Friedmann, II, 6–7, 101), "fearing lest the king, the emperor, and the Pope should join forces against him to drive him out of his kingdom" (Kaulek, *op. cit.*, p. 89): a truce (*ibid.*, pp. 31, 35, 37 *sq.*, 39, 46, 47, 51, 61 *sq.*, 64, 67 *sq.*, 72; cf. Albèri, *op. cit.*, 1st Series, II, pp. 75 *sq.*), or the simple news of a rapprochement between France and the empire (Kaulek, *op. cit.*, pp. 9, 13 *sq.*, 22, 24 *sq.*, 41 *sq.*, 73, 78–79, 80) arouses his "discontent" and gives him a "head-ache."   And so, according to circumstances, he approaches or withdraws from Francis (*ibid.*, pp. 27 *sq.*, 40–41, 49 *sq.*, 51–54, 58, 67, 71, 73, 76, 77 and *passim*) in order to keep him in a state of dependency; more than once he tried to detach Francis from the Pope "towards whom his said brother should conduct himself quite otherwise," and to drag him "out of subjection to Rome" (Le Laboureur, *Mémoires de Michel de Castelnau*, Brussels, 1731, I 411).

after Clement's death, in making Francis admit the invalidity of Catherine's marriage and the illegitimacy of her daughter, much to the benefit of Anne Boleyn and Elizabeth. This incurable jealousy between Francis and Charles was the best safeguard the King of England had for his security abroad.[125]

At home, his strength also lay in the lack of union among his domestic enemies, for enemies he certainly had. Fisher and the young Marquis of Exeter, a possible claimant to the throne, advised the emperor to land in England.[126] Certain lords, Abergavenny and Darcy amongst others, were beginning to murmur. Many people were lending an ear to the prophecies of the "Holy Maid of Kent," who said that Henry had only a year to live.[127] And Chapuys wrote to the emperor: "You cannot imagine the great desire of all this people that your Majesty should send men here. Every day I have been applied to about it by Englishmen of rank, wit, and learning, who give me to understand that the last king, Richard, was never so much hated by his people as this king."[128] There were always malcontents under the Tudors, but they were never able to unite their forces to take common action.[129] The surviving members of the old nobility detested the new government's methods, and the poorer folk were murmuring against their bad treatment at the hands of the landowners. But there was between these two groups of mal-

---

[125] Francis I's acknowledgment of Anne Boleyn's marriage in Burnet VI, 122; Collier, IX, 136. Cf. Dodd, Tierney's ed., App. p. 411. For the rivalry between the emperor and Francis I, see Mignet, *Rivalité de François Ier et de Charles-Quint*, Paris, 1875; A. C. P. Haggar, *Two great rivals and the women who influenced them*, London, 1910; Charles V's instructions to his son Philip, January 15th, 1548, in *Sp. Cal.*, IX, 536 *sq.*, 543.

[126] *L. and P.*, VI, 416. The Marquis of Exeter, removed from the court in 1531 (cf. Friedmann, *op. cit.*, II, 58), said he was ready to shed the last drop of his blood in Catherine's cause, as Chapuys wrote to Charles V on February 25th, 1535. See chap. xv in Froude: "The Exeter conspiracy," and Friedmann, Vol. II, chap. xi, for the malcontents.

[127] *L. and P.*, VI, 1419, 1445, 1464, 1467, 1468. *Transactions of the Royal Hist. Society*, New Series, Vol. XVIII.

[128] *L. and P.*, VI, 508; VII, 121. Ortiz, the imperial ambassador in Rome, was convinced that England would rise in a body. For his defence Henry had but one castle in London and about a hundred bodyguards (*L. and P.*, VI, App. 7).

[129] According to Pollard (*Henry VIII*, p. 413) the people's discontent existed chiefly in the imagination of the enemies of the king, whom the people did not seriously think of overthrowing.

contents no bond which could band their scattered forces together. Besides, there was a natural offset to each of these groups. The old nobility, decimated in the Wars of the Roses, was faced with the new aristocracy, full of quite opposite ideas and pretensions. The poorer classes were met by the rich commercial class, who feared the people below them and had no grievance against Henry. A policy involving spoliation of Church property would, therefore, certainly bring both the newly-created nobles and the merchants to the king's side.

The only thing that might have kept them aloof was the fear of war and the interruption of trade with Flanders. When the alliance between England and France had resulted in a declaration of war against the emperor, in 1528, a storm of protests and murmurings arose throughout the country.[130] Du Bellay wrote, speaking of Wolsey: "You may be sure that he is playing a terrible game, for I think he is the only Englishman who desires a war with Flanders."[131] The drapers of Kent discussed a plan for making Wolsey a prisoner and casting him adrift in a leaking boat.[132] Those of Wiltshire were said to be on the point of revolting, and in Norfolk the employers had to dismiss their workmen.[133] Hostilities did not take place. An agreement between Henry and Charles, which assured the English trade with Flanders,[134] was followed by a truce, and then by the treaty of Cambrai.[135] The Commons at first opposed the Act of Appeals (1533) because they were afraid of an interdict which would ruin their trade with Flanders.[136] They feared especially that much harm would be done to the woollen trade, on which

[130] *L. and P.*, IV, 4, 564. *Sp. Cal.*, III, 729.

[131] J. du Bellay to Montmorency, February 16th, 1528. Bourrilly, *op. cit.*, I, 158. Le Grand, *op. cit.*, I, 81. Nothing could have been more unpopular. Cf. Pollard, *Henry VII*, III, pp. 121 *sq.*; Bourrilly, *op. cit.*, I, pp. xiv, xvi, xvii, xviii, xix, xxii, xxv, xxx, xxxi, 162, 166, 359 *sq.*; Le Grand, *op. cit.*, I, pp. 76; III, pp. 85 *sq.*

[132] *L. and P.*, IV, 4310.

[133] *L. and P.*, IV, 4012, 4040, 4043, 4044, 4239.

[134] *L. and P.*, IV, 4147.

[135] *L. and P.*, IV, 4376.

[136] *L. and P.*, VI, 296. Reginald Pole had already shown the king how dangerous it would be to alienate the emperor in the divorce suit, who by interrupting business relations with Flanders and Spain could cause harm and ruin to the kingdom. Strype, *Memorials of Cranmer*, ed. 1848, Append. I, 319, and cf. p. 15.

half the country subsisted.[137]   The hesitation they showed
from time to time in following Henry in the path of schism
had no higher motive.[138]   That was why "the king," as
Chapuys wrote to Charles V, "persuades the people that it is
not in the power of your Majesty to do so [i.e. forbid intercourse with Flanders]."[139]   In 1533 the king was even able
to give his subjects an object lesson.   Following a dispute
between himself and the merchants, he closed the Calais
market.[140]   This caused great distress in Flanders, and the
Regent sent post haste to Henry to inform him that the closing
of the market was an infraction of the commercial treaties.[141]
It was easy then for the king to point out that the Flemish
could do nothing without England's trade, since that incident
lasting three months had caused such an outcry on the
Continent.   Moreover, it had been arranged that if the
breach with the Pope took place, the king's appeal to the
General Council was to be placarded throughout Flanders,
"that the injustice of the Bishop of Rome may thereby appear
to all the world."[142]

Henry had reason then to think himself safe.   Besides, as
Chapuys remarked, he was very carefully watching his
people to see how far he could go, and when he had to stop.[143]
No precaution for his personal safety and that of the realm
was omitted.   The royal fleet was augmented, armaments
made perfect, and the fortifications of Calais and of the
Scotch borders raised or remade.

[137] *L. and P.*, VI, 1528.
[138] "Many there are," Chapuys wrote on February 21st, 1532, "who
dislike this measure (the title of supreme head of the Church) not so much
out of zeal for religion and its ministers as for the scandal that may arise
therefrom, imagining that the Pope declare this king schismatic and deprive
him of his kingdom." Letter (*Sp. Cal.*, IV, Part II, No. 641). In 1538
Castillon wrote (Kaulek, *op. cit.*, 41) that the best means of bringing Henry
to reason was to prevent business relations with Flanders by putting an
interdict upon all who dealt with England.
[139] *L. and P.*, VI, 1460.
[140] *L. and P.*, VI, 1510, 1523, 1571.
[141] Henry replied that it was a question of a dispute between himself
and the merchants and that it did not touch the treaties in any way.
[142] *L. and P.*, VI, 568; Burnet, VI, 103; and Collier, IX, 135, where
will be found the propositions laid before the king's council for an appeal
by the king to the General Council.   In the original there are some autograph notes of Henry VIII in the margin.
[143] *L. and P.*, VI, 351.

Convinced that he was safeguarded at home and abroad, Henry put the finishing touch to the schism. During the March session, 1534, Parliament had passed a law ensuring succession to the throne to Anne Boleyn's children.[144] In this law it was stated that the king's first marriage was against the law of God,[145] and that all who disputed the second by word of mouth or in writing, in publications and so forth, were guilty of treason.[146] All who had attained the legal age had to take this oath. The members of both Houses set the example on March 30th.[147] In November of that same year, Parliament strengthened the Act of Succession by making the terms of the oath more precise, and by stating that an affidavit of refusal signed by two commissioners sufficed; that affidavit was equal to a formal indictment.[148]

In that same November session the annates and the tithes were transferred from the Pope to the king.[149] Twenty-six sees

[144] This was a constitutional novelty. This law of succession, the second in the history of England (*Statutes of the realm*, 7 Henry IV, cap. 2), is the first of this reign (25 Henry VIII, cap. 22; Gee and Hardy, *op. cit.*, No. LIV); there were others under Henry, according to the fortunes of his marriages.

[145] Apropos of this the list of prohibited degrees for marriage was drawn up. Cf. *Statutes of the realm*, 32 Henry VIII, cap. 38.

[146] Those who opposed him by word of mouth were also subject to a penalty. According to the government's proposition, which was modified by the Commons, words as well as acts made one guilty of treason (*L. and P.*, VII, 51).

[147] The form of this oath was fixed, not by Parliament, but by letters-patent on March 30th, 1534 (*Lords' Journal*, p. 82).

[148] Previously the testimony of twelve jurymen had been necessary (Gee and Hardy, No. LVI). This second *Act of Succession*, which interpreted the first by the formula of an oath in favour of the children of Anne Boleyn and the king, was abrogated after the queen's condemnation two years later (*Statutes of the realm*, 28 Henry VIII, cap. 7).

[149] *Statutes of the realm*, 26 Henry VIII, cap. 11. In this session, from February to April, Parliament made the charges upon the clergy lighter by declaring that they would not have to pay tithes the year they paid the annates.

"*Cromwell me parla fort avant de la prospérité de sondit Maistre, grande obeissance, pouvoir de deniers contans, repos et pacification en son royaume, qu'il a augmenté de revenu de plus de cinq mille escus chaque an, car depuis vostre partement ledit Parlement et Estats dudit royaume luy ont accordé les dixmes ordinaires, outre lesquelles il prendra cette année tous les annates des eveschez, abbayes et autres benefices de ses pays. . . . Et (ledit Roy) déclara que si le Roy son frère venoit à faire de mesme qu'il accroistroit son Royayme de plus de deux millions*" (Palamedes Gontier to Admiral Chabot, February 5th, 1535, in Le Laboureur, *op. cit.*, I, 409, 411).

The question of transferring the tithes and annates to the king had already been mooted in the law on the annates (1532). "The king has

of suffragan bishops were created by law, probably to replace
the abbots or bishops *in partibus infidelium* whom the Pope used
to delegate to assist the Ordinaries.[150]

Finally the title of "the only supreme head in earth of the
Church of England," rejected two years previously by the
Lords, was conferred upon Henry by a vote of both Houses,
and became law. The Convocations of York and Westminster,
which had recognized this title in 1532, were alluded to, but
no mention was made of the restrictive clause *quantum per
legem Christi licet*.[151]   As supreme head, the king was given
by this law "full power and authority, from time to time,
to visit, repress, redress, reform, order, correct, restrain, and
amend all such errors, heresies, abuses, offences, contempts,
and enormities, whatsoever they be, which by any manner of
spiritual authority or jurisdiction ought to be or may lawfully
be reformed, repressed, ordered, redressed, corrected, restrained, or amended, most to the pleasure of Almighty God,
the increase of virtue in Christ's religion, or for the conserva-
tion of the peace, unity, and tranquillity of this realm, any
usage, custom, foreign laws, foreign authority, prescription,
or any other thing or things to the contrary hereof notwithstanding."[152]   The royal supremacy, which had taken five

proposed to Parliament," Chapuys wrote on February 28th, 1532, "to
withdraw the annates paid to the Pope for vacant benefices and have them
paid to him as sovereign of the ecclesiastics in his kingdom" (*L. and P.*, V,
No. 832).

[150] *Statutes of the realm*, 26 Henry VIII, cap. 14; Gee and Hardy, No.
LIX.   This law on the "Suffragan Bishops," of November, 1534, was
abolished by Mary Tudor in 1554, and re-established by Elizabeth in 1559
(Gee and Hardy, Nos. LXXVI and LXXIX).

In the Act the twenty-six sees in which the suffragans were to reside
are mentioned: Thetford, Ipswich, Colchester, Dover, Guildford, Southampton, Taunton, Shaftesbury, Molton, Marlborough, Bedford, Leicester,
Gloucester, Shrewsbury, Bristol, Penrith, Bridgewater, Nottingham,
Grantham, Hull, Huntingdon, Cambridge, Perth, Berwick, St Germain's
and the Isle of Wight (Burnet, IV, 206).   This new organization remained
theoretical until 1546.

[151] "This important limitation clause," says Blunt (*op. cit.*, I, 231, n. 1),
"was dishonestly ignored."

[152] *Statutes of the realm*, 26 Henry VIII, cap. 1; Collier, IV, 248; Gee
and Hardy, No. LV.   This "Supremacy Act" of November, 1534 was
abrogated by Mary Tudor in 1554, by the second "Act of repeal" (Gee
and Hardy, No. LXXVI); and the abrogation was maintained and
confirmed by Elizabeth in the first year of her reign (*ibid.*, No. LXXIX).
The title of Supreme Head of the Church was incorporated in the royal
titles by letters-patent of January 15th, 1535 (Rymer, XIV, 549; *L. and P.*,
VIII, 52).

years and a whole series of laws to bring into being, was now an accomplished fact.

Henry, in the words of Chapuys, was Pope in England, but only from the point of view of jurisdiction. He never claimed Orders, which would have given him the right to administer the Sacraments, although Cranmer once maintained, when discussing the question with other prelates, that princes could create bishops.[153] Henry, of his own authority, chose the channels through which spiritual benefits reach the soul, but never pretended to be one of those channels. Albeit more than one churchman objected that Christ had entrusted the government of the Church to the Apostles and their successors, when he invested them with a mission independent of the State, yet the lawyers did not fail subsequently to draw conclusions from the principle laid down by the Act of Supremacy and by all that corroborated it, "although the power of the keys be not exercised by the king himself, it derives from him." Consequently "all spiritual jurisdiction formerly exercised in England and Ireland emanates henceforward from the Crown; every subject possessing spiritual jurisdiction in the said countries, holds it *from* the king, and exercises it *through* and dependently *upon* the king."[154] Had not Henry expressly delegated his powers of jurisdiction to the bishops because he and his vicar-general were unable to exercise them all in person? When, in 1533,

[153] Burnet, IV, 481–87; Strype, *Memorials of Cranmer*, ed. 1848, I, 430 n.; cf. *L. and P.*, VII, 1384. Henry even made this remark in one passage: "Since you confess that the apostles did occupate the one part, which you now confess belongeth to princes, how can you prove that ordering is only committed to you bishops?" Dixon concludes (II, 311) from this note written in the royal hand that the king was not far from believing that he possessed the power of Holy Orders; Harpsfield is also of the same opinion (Bémont, *op. cit.*, pp. 71 and 116).

Yet a document which emanated from the government when the Act of Supremacy was being debated in Parliament expressly declared, in order to explain its scope, that by his title of Supreme Head of the Church the king had no intention of assuming any of the spiritual powers given by the Gospel to the ministers of religion. (This document was printed by Froude, *op. cit.*, chap. IX.) Henry VIII always denied all claim to this power. Cf. F. Makower, *Verfassung der Kirche von England*, German ed., p. 265, English ed., p. 255. Richter, *Kirchenrecht*, §91.

[154] See a treatise by a learned lawyer in Charles I's time: "A discourse concerning his Majesty's supreme power ecclesiastical established by the laws of this kingdom, at this present time in their fulle force and vigour," with Collier's objections, in Collier, *op. cit.*, IV, 155–57 and 250–63.

he yielded to Cranmer's judgment on the divorce, it was only after declaring that his own pre-eminent power and supreme authority were unprejudiced thereby, since he had no "superior but God" and the archbishop was "principal minister of our spiritual jurisdiction" only because he was called to that office by God and by the king.[154a]

Hitherto the Church had had two masters, the Pope as spiritual, and the king as temporal, head. Now there was only one, the king, who had taken the Pope's rôle upon himself. The law stated that henceforward "the king . . . shall have and enjoy annexed and united to the imperial crown of this realm . . . all honours, dignities, immunities, profits and commodities to the said dignity of supreme head of the said Church belonging and appertaining." Henry assigned to himself all the dues formerly paid to the Holy See. The legislative power of the Sovereign Pontiff or of Convocation was transferred to the king.[155] The election of bishops became purely a royal affair.[156] The King's Chancery was substituted for Rome as the court of final appeal in all ecclesiastical cases; the primatial Court of Canterbury had been the court of final appeal only for one year.[157] The Church in England received none of the authority taken from Rome;

[154a] L. and P., VI, 332; Collier, IX, 103.

[155] The Pilgrimage of Grace demanded that the liberties granted by the Magna Charta and "in use six or seven years ago" should be restored to the Church; it also claimed for Convocation the right to deal with spiritual matters.

[156] The king gave the Congé d'élire to the chapters it is true, but accompanying it was a "letter-missive," in which was designated the one to be elected under pain of incurring the penalties of praemunire (confiscation of goods and perpetual imprisonment). The servile submission of the chapters proved that the first clause of the Magna Charta which ensured freedom of election for them had been abolished (cf. Pollard, The Evolution of Parliament, 169 sq., 187 sq.). Edward VI even suppressed the congé d'élire because it restricted the royal power too much. Mary abolished Edward's statute, and Elizabeth did not re-establish it, so that the episcopal appointments were afterwards made as in Henry VIII's time (cf. Hardwick, A History of the Christian Church, London, 1886, pp. 333 sq.).

[157] This function had been given to it on the occasion of the divorce, as we have already seen. At the end of one year, too, the title of Apostolicae Sedis legatus was taken from Cranmer, who by a strange anomaly had been exercising, under that title, a jurisdiction the source of which was no longer recognized (Strype, Memorials of Cranmer, ed. 1848, I, 69 sq., 366 sq.). In May, 1535 he gave up the title of totius Angliae primas which, according to Gardiner and Cromwell, derogated from the authority and sovereign power of the supreme head of the Church (ibid., I, 68 sq., and App. XIV).

it was not more autonomous than before.[158] Everything was
concentrated in the king's hands. He began to speak of
"my Church"[159] and "our spiritual jurisdiction,"[160] and
delegated this jurisdiction to the bishops for his kingdom, as
though he held it directly from God.[161] There was a *translatio
imperii* and not *imperium in imperio*.[162] Henry, Chapuys wrote,
said "that he was at once king, emperor (and if I recollect
right) Pope also in his dominions."[163] The Church in

[158] The Anglican clergy almost regret their former liberty and blame
Henry for his spiritual supremacy. Dixon (*op. cit.*, I, 444) calls it "foolish
and needless," and Blunt (*op. cit.*, I, 231, 237) an "illegal tyranny." The
Oxford Movement tried to establish the limits of the royal supremacy so
as to prevent abuses on the part of the temporal powers (E. B. Pusey,
*The royal supremacy not an arbitrary authority but limited by the Church of which
kings are members*, Oxford, 1850). Churchmen under Elizabeth discovered
that it was contrary to the Scriptures to obey a woman in spiritual matters,
and so did all they could to limit the queen's supremacy when they defined
it (cf. Blunt, I, 234 *sq.*). See *Dyvers articles which have been a special cause of
the division that is betwyxt the spiritualitie and temporalitie in this realm*, undated
(sixteenth century). Cf. Hardwick, *op. cit.*, 176 and n. 4; 177 and n. 1,
330 and 331; Makower, *op. cit.*, pp. 265, 304, 504 (the 1604 canons);
J. P. Whitney, *The Episcopate and the Reformation*, London, 1917. In 1689
(1 William and Mary, cap. 8) all that Parliament retained of the old
formula was the repudiation of papal authority. In 1535 Gardiner had
already questioned the effect the royal supremacy would have upon the
apostolic succession, maintaining that bishops held their powers from God.
Archbishop Bancroft was accused by the Puritans, in Elizabeth's time, of
asserting the divine right of bishops against the queen's supremacy (cf.
R. G. Usher, *The supposed origin of the doctrine of the divine right of Bishops*, in
Mélanges Bémont, Paris, 1913, p. 541 *sq.*)
In foreign countries the title of "supreme head of the Church" was
ridiculed (Merriman, *Life and Letters of Thomas Cromwell*, Oxford, 1902, I,
242); even the Lutherans would not recognize it (Pollard, *Cranmer*
p. 144; cf. Makower, *op. cit.*, German ed., p. 72).

[159] *Cranmer's Works*, II, 268.

[160] *L. and P.*, VI, 332.

[161] "Quandoquidem omnis jurisdicendi auctoritas, atque etiam jurisdictio
omnimoda, tam illa quae ecclesiastica dicitur quam saecularis, a regia
potestate velut a supremo capite et omnium infra regnum nostrum magis-
tratuum fonte et scaturigine primitus emanavit sane, illos qui jurisdictionem
hujusmodi antehac non nisi precario fungebantur, beneficium hujusmodi
sic eis ex liberalitate regia indultum, gratis animis agnoscere . . . con-
venit." *Licencia regia concessa domino episcopo* [Bonner] *ad exercendum jurisdictionem episcopalem* (November 12th, 1539), in Burnet, IV, 410. A law of
1545 declared that "Archbishops and other ecclesiastical persons had not
manner of jurisdiction ecclesiastical, but *by*, under and *from* his royal
Majesty" (*Statutes of the realm*, 37 Henry VIII).

[162] *L. and P.*, XIV, Part II, p. 141.

[163] July 31st, 1531. *L. and P.*, V, 361. Cf. J. Bekinson's work, *De supremo
et absoluto regis imperio*, London, 1546; and the anonymous book published

England became a "body politic," to use Cromwell's expression.[164]   It was nationalized.   Shorn of its pristine characteristic of universality, it ceased to be a branch of the Catholic Church *in* England and became the Church *of* England.[165] The Act of Supremacy was in reality a revolution,[166] in which the Crown alone gained and the Church lost.

Up to a certain point, the "supreme head of the Church" settled her doctrines.   It is true he consultrd the assembled bishops and asked their advice, but he always carefully revised and annotated their resolutions, and eventually his own opinion prevailed, so that at the end of his reign the words "the king's doctrine" were usually employed to signify orthodox teaching.   His title of Defender of the Faith was applied literally.   But this doctrinal authority invested in the civil powers did not suit the ideas of those days.   It was contrary to the tenets both of Catholics and of Protestants;

between 1520 and 1550: *Disputatio inter clericum et militem super potestate praelatis Ecclesiae atque principibus terrarum commissa, sub forma dialogi.* A lawyer of the thirteenth century, Bracton, had already maintained (Bk. I, chap. viii) that: "Rex est vicarius et minister Dei in terra: omnis quidem sub eo est et ipse sub nullo, ni tantum sub Deo . . . sub Deo et sub lege, quia lex facit regem . . . Dei vicarius tam in spiritualibus quam in temporalibus."

The King of France, Charles VI, indeed styled himself *non immerito Dei vicarius,* but he added *quoad jurisdictionem temporalem* (Decree of August 14th, 1385, in Pierre Dupuys' *Preuves des libertez de l'Eglise gallicane,* 2nd ed., 1651, I, 270 *sq.* Cf. G. Dodu's *Les idées de Charles V en matière de gouvernement* in *Revue des Questions historiques,* 1929, p. 42 *sq.*). "The maxim *rex est vicarius Dei,*" remarks Sir Lewis Dibdin (*Establishment in England,* London, 1932), "is centuries older than Henry VIII."   There is not the least doubt that ecclesiastical acceptance of the Royal Supremacy was eased by the fact that the king was himself a semi-ecclesiastical person: he is still—alone of laymen—anointed at his coronation.

[164] This expression is found in a draft of the Bill for the *Submission of the clergy* (*L. and P.,* V, 721).

[165] The Anglican Church still styled itself Catholic and Apostolic, but not Roman. "Ista est ecclesia nostra catholica, apostolica, cum qua nec pontifex Romanus, nec quivis aliquis praelatus aut pontifex habet quicquam agere praeterquam in suas dioceses." Autograph note of Henry VIII on the definition of the Church (Burnet, *op. cit.,* IV, 408; Strype, *Eccl. Memorials,* I, art. II, No. CXII).

[166] Pollard, *The Evolution of Parliament,* 214, 277. This is also the opinion of J. Brewer (Introduction to *L. and P.,* I, 107) and of J. Gairdner (*ibid.,* VIII, I). Pollard adds that it was an unconstitutional Act, but "Parliament became so closely identified with the constitution that nothing done by Parliament was regarded as unconstitutional."

and the followers of the two religions were persecuted.[167]
Consequently it could last only as long as the ruler was
strong enough to balance the two opposing forces and as
long as this idea of the State being represented by the king
prevailed over every other consideration.

Was the king's supremacy limited by the common laws of
the realm in the same way as his temporal sovereignty?
Bishop Gardiner put this question to the Protector Somerset
after Henry's death (1547).[168] The chancellor, Audeley,
replied that the supremacy could not be in opposition to the
Acts of Parliament, but that in the ecclesiastical sphere there
was no limit to the king's authority. Henry was, in fact, an
absolute monarch in the Church and a constitutional monarch
in the State. He needed the assistance of Parliament to
reform the State, but he could reform the Church by his
own authority. Thus was the Reformation brought about,
the civil powers commanded and the clergy obeyed.[169]

In his *De Unitate Ecclesiae*, Reginald Pole violently attacked the title
which had been assumed by the king, who had superseded the Pope and
had confused the royal with the priestly functions, a thing no Christian
king had dared to do.

Foreigners, even the simple layfolk, were scandalized at this novelty.
"*Ils (les evesques) permectent à leur roy, en loy divine, de pouvoir plus interpréter,
augmenter, oster et faire que les appostres ny leurs vicaires et successeurs osairent
oncques entreprendre; . . . et luy veulent attribuer non pas seulement obéissance de
roy . . . mais en faire une vraye statue pour ydolâtres*" (Marillac to the Constable
of France, Montmorency, August 6th, 1540, Kaulek, *op. cit.*, p. 211).

[167] See p. 394. *Certainement le spectacle fut merveilleux de veoir mourir en
mesme jour et heure ceulx qui adhéroient aux deux partys contraires, et fut aussi
scandaleux pour les deux parts qui par là prétendaient avoir esté offensées*" (Marillac
to Francis I, August 6th, 1540, Kaulek, *op. cit.*, pp. 208–209. Cf. Macaulay,
I, 55).

[168] Gardiner to Somerset, October 14th, 1547. Foxe, VI, 42.

[169] In the main this was only the application and consequence of the
theories of Frederick II and Pierre de la Vigne (cf. Huillard-Bréholles, *Vie et
correspondance de Pierre de la Vigne*, 1865), Philip the Fair and Peter Dubois,
Louis of Bavaria and Marsilius of Padua, who had maintained the
supremacy of the temporal power over the spiritual (cf. Pollard, *The
Evolution of Parliament*, 222; F. Battaglia, "Marsilio e la filosofia politica
del medio evo," *Studi filosofici diretti da G. Gentile*, 2nd Series, Vol. IV,
Florence, 1928; W. J. Brandt, "Pierre Dubois, Modern or Medieval,"
American Hist. Review, 1930, pp. 507–21). So it is not surprising that Thomas
Cromwell, who found therein support for his theories, gave financial
assistance for the printing of Marsilius' *Defensor pacis* (1534), and that his
friends recommended the reading of it to the London Carthusians and to
Cardinal Pole (*L. and P.*, VII, 423; VIII, 1556; IX, 523). Previté-Orton
has recently published an edition of it (Cambridge Univ. Press). Dino
Bigongiari has made quite a number of corrections in this text, in *Speculum*,

Henry VIII's ecclesiastical prerogative was a personal and not a parliamentary one. Both he and his daughter Elizabeth stoutly refused to share it with Parliament.[170] Parliament and Convocation were two co-ordinate legislative bodies, independent of each other, but both subject to the sovereign. Such was the Tudor system, but it did not survive them. When the monarch was no longer able to bear the two temporal and spiritual sceptres together Parliament took possession of the former and attempted to seize the latter. Convocation tried to wrest the spiritual sceptre from its grasp, but was unable to claim sole possession of it. Between these two bodies the ecclesiastical supremacy became escheat, and their rival claims produced a situation bordering on anarchy.[170a]

The king had been proclaimed "supreme head of the Church of England" by Convocation and by Parliament. It only remained to obtain universal recognition of this title by the nation and to drive all traces of the papacy from the country. The two years 1534 and 1535 were devoted to this

January, 1932, "Notes on the Text of the *Defensor Pacis* of Marsilius of Padua."

[170] The Crown alone being "the supreme head of the Church," alone has the right to exercise jurisdiction. "You bishops," said Chancellor Audeley to Gardiner (letter already quoted from Gardiner to Somerset, Foxe, *op. cit.*, VI, 43), "would enter in with the king, and by means of his supremacy order the laity as ye listed." For the exercise of this ecclesiastical sovereignty force of law was given to the royal decrees (1539 Act, suppressed by Somerset in 1547). Cf. Pollard, *The Evolution of Parliament*, pp. 214, 268.

[170a] Recently the Anglican Church has attempted to throw off the guardianship of Parliament. The "Enabling Act" of 1919 ("Church of England Assembly Act") and other supplementary Acts (1919–23) have transferred the discussion of religious questions from Parliament to the Church Assembly, which consists of an Upper House or House of Bishops and two Lower Houses (House of Clergy and House of Laity). Parliament has, however, retained a sort of overseer's right, which gives it the last word on any question. A parliamentary committee, the Ecclesiastical Committee, examines any Bill passed by the Church Assembly, brings it before Parliament, sees to the voting on it and obtains the Royal Assent. Every Bill presented to Parliament from 1920 to 1927 was approved without any discussion, and the Church of England, seeing in this parliamentary endorsement a mere legal formality, began to think she had won back her legislative freedom. But the rejection of the New Prayer Book by the House of Commons (December 15th, 1927) proved that she was under a delusion.

purpose. Yet in his book against Luther Henry had stigmatized all who tried to set the people against the chief bishop,
Christians against the Vicar of Christ. He compared them to
a man setting children against their parents, and said that
to urge rebellion against the head was the sin of witchcraft,
and to consent to such a rebellion the sin of idolatry.

All subjects, of either sex, who had "arrived at full age" were
required to swear to the Act of Succession already mentioned.
This act implied a denial of papal authority, since it recognized the validity of the marriage between Henry and Anne
Boleyn. The wording of the oath showed that it was a blow
aimed at the Pope, for the people swore faith, fidelity and
obedience only to the king's majesty, and not to any foreign
authority.[171] Since the Treason Act of November, 1534, it
was a crime of high treason to call the king schismatic.[172]
A commission consisting of Cranmer, the chancellor Audeley,
and Suffolk sat in Lambeth Palace to receive the oath.
Laymen and churchmen passed before them in turn and
took the oath, with the exception of Fisher and Thomas
More.[173] There were possibly some who made certain
restrictions, like More's daughter, who added, "as far as it
would stand with the law of God,"[174] or else tacitly distinguished between the temporal and spiritual dominion. When
the priest John Rugg—who was put to death for denying the
royal supremacy—was asked how his conscience allowed him
to take the oath at first, he replied that mentally he had
added the condition that he would accept the king as supreme
head in temporal, but not in spiritual, matters.

[171] Oath taken by Parliament in March, 1534. The oath formulated in
November of the same year by the second law of succession is still more
explicit (Gee and Hardy, No. LVI).

[172] *Statutes of the realm*, 26 Henry VIII, cap. 13; Gee and Hardy, No.
LVII. This law lasted until 1863.

[173] More has described the scene of the taking of the oath by the clergy
at Lambeth. Cf. chap. v. For Lambeth Palace see W. Jenkinson, *The
Royal and Bishops' Palaces in old London*, 1921; also Mrs. D. Gardiner's *Lambeth
Palace*, 1930, with Introduction by the late Archbishop Davidson, at whose
request it was written. For the royal supremacy and the submission of the
kingdom to this supremacy, see Bridgett, *Fisher*, chap. xiv.

[174] "Sic demum in verba regis juravimus sub conditione tamen quatenus
licitum esset," records Chauncy (*Historia aliquot martyrum*, ed. Doreau,
1888, p. 91), one of the Carthusians, from whom only a conditional oath
could be obtained.

On March 31st the southern Convocation declared, by thirty-four votes to four (and one doubtful vote)—and the northern Convocation followed its lead with a unanimous declaration on May 5th—that, according to the Scriptures, the Bishop of Rome had no more power in England than any other foreign prince, and no more jurisdiction than any other foreign bishop.[175] The universities of Cambridge (May 2nd) and Oxford (June 27th) made similar pronouncements,[176] and on June 9th a proclamation by the king abolished the "Pope's usurped power." Cranmer visited his province and obtained the signatures of his clergy to a form in which they declared "that the Bishop of Rome . . . had no greater jurisdiction given him by God in this kingdom of England than any other foreign bishop." Commissioners went through the northern and southern parts of the country receiving the oath from churchmen and meeting with no difficulty.[177]

[175] Cranmer had asked the assembly: (1) According to Holy Scripture, has the Pope more power in England than any other bishop? (2) Is there any teaching in the Scriptures on the relations between Rome and England?—The voting of the Convocations of Canterbury and York may be found in Wilkins, III, pp. 769, 782, and in Gee and Hardy, No. LVIII; of York alone in Burnet, VI, p. 77, and Collier, IX, 108. Cf. Blunt, I, 275.

By the oath of obedience to the Pope taken upon appointment or the reception of the pallium (Pollard, *Henry VII*, III, No. 44) every archbishop bound himself "ad retinendum et defendendum papatum Romanum contra omnem hominem."

[176] Rymer, *Foedera*, VI, Part II, p. 195. Burnet, VI, 78; Collier, IX, 110; Dodd, ed. 1737, pp. 298 *sq*. See also, in Collier IX, 112 and 115, the letters from Cambridge university, October 12th, and from Oxford university, November 12th, congratulating Henry upon having abolished papal supremacy and the superstition which resulted from it. Cf. Blunt, I, 274 *sq*. For those who resisted the Reformation at Cambridge, see L. K. Patterson's "The Reformation at Cambridge," *Cath. Hist. Review*, 1930, pp. 51–63.

[177] At the Exchequer the adhesions of thirty dioceses are preserved (cf. Blunt, I, 275). Burnet (VI, 81–85) published, according to the registers of the Worcester Chapter, the adhesion and the oath of that Chapter and its Dean "et in quali aestimatione habebimus episcopum Romanum." Rymer (*Foedera*, XIV, pp. 495–527) gives the *Juramenta* and *Fidelitates* of one hundred and sixty-four ecclesiastical foundations of all kinds, which were signed without protest, with the exception of Balliol College: "ista protestatione praehabita quod nos nihil agere intendimus contra legem divinam, nec contra orthodoxae fidei normam, nec contra sacrosanctae Matris Ecclesiae catholicae doctrinam."

At this period Henry, together with Cromwell, boasted that he had obtained "an increase of revenue, the union and obedience of his realm, ease and peace of conscience . . . having placed and thrown himself entirely out of submission to Rome" (Palamades Gontier to Admiral Chabot, February 5th, 1535; Le Laboureur, *op. cit.*, I, 411).

"I am ashamed to say," wrote Harpsfield, "how easily many people consented to take the oath, despite the protests of their conscience. *Sed quo non impellit timidam et inernem multitudinem armata regum potentia?*"[178]

The oath required from the religious orders was still more explicit. Having acknowledged the chaste and holy marriage between Henry and Anne, they had to swear and promise to preach that the king alone was the supreme head of the Church of England, and "that the Bishop of Rome, who in his Bulls, usurps the name of Pope, and arrogates to himself the principality of Supreme Pontiff, has no greater jurisdiction given him by God in this realm of England than the English bishops in their own dioceses"; that they renounced for ever his laws and his decrees, and would recognize only those laid down by Parliament and ratified by the king.[179] Perhaps it was hoped that this intolerable oath would furnish a pretext for the suppression of the religious houses. All such hopes were vain. If the religious orders were looked upon as the permanent army of the papacy, no army ever surrendered more easily. Two monks undertook the task of visiting the English monasteries to receive the oath, which had to bear the monastery seal and the autograph signature of each monk. They were George Browne, Augustinian prior, and Hilsey, Dominican provincial,[180] and the latter wrote from Exeter, on June 21st, that "he had not met many who have refused the oath of obedience."[181]

Yet there were three religious orders which offered a splendid resistance.[182]

[178] Ch. Bémont, *op. cit.*, 6. Cf. Van Ortroy, *Ana. Boll.*, XII, 131.

[179] *L. and P.*, VII, p. 236; Rymer, *Foedera*, XIV, 489; Burnet, IV, 202; Gerdes, *Historia Reformationis*, IV (145). In this document, a specimen of abjuration of papal authority signed by the superiors of six religious houses, May 5th, 1534, each religious adds, after his name: "Non coactus, sed sponte subscribo." The royal injunctions for the visitation of the monasteries indeed prescribed that each abbot, prior, and religious was to sign the oath *manu propria*, and it had to bear the seal of the community.

[180] The prior of the Dominicans at Canterbury, however, resisted Cranmer, who complained to the king. *Memorials of Cranmer*, ed. 1848, pp. 64-67, and App. XIII.

[181] H. A. L. Fisher, *op. cit.*, p. 343, and Bridgett, *Life of Bl. John Fisher*, p. 312, who quote *L. and P.*, VII, 869.

[182] See chap. IX in Froude, "The Catholic Martyrs." J. Spillman's work (*Die englischen Martyrer unter Heinrich VIII*, Freiburg, 1887, chaps. VI and x) is not critical enough, according to O. Meyer (*England und die*

The Franciscan Friars of the strict Observance—to whom the most famous preachers of the day belonged, such as Elstow, Peto, and Forest[183] (all three openly against the divorce)—had seven houses, one of which was at Greenwich. Here the king used to attend the services, and here also Elizabeth had been recently baptized.[184] The religious in

katholische Kirche unter Elisabeth, Rome, 1911, p. 2, n. 1); but Dom Bede Camm, O.S.B., in collaboration with several historians, has published *The lives of the English martyrs declared blessed by Pope Leo XIII*, London, 1914, the first volume of which concerns the *Martyrs under King Henry VIII* (1535-45).

[183] Stowe relates in his chronicle how Peto, "another Micheas," preaching before Henry, at the Grey Friars' Convent at Greenwich, on the story of Achab, clearly alluded to the king's "illegitimate marriage," and to those who, driven like "the four hundred prophets of Israel, by a lying spirit, sought to deceive him." Henry pretended not to understand. But on the following Sunday (May 8th, 1534) [Card. Gasquet remarks that Stowe gives the date as May 28th, and adds that probably both dates are wrong, as neither the 8th nor the 28th was a Sunday in any year about this time, but that May 18th was a Sunday in 1533 (*Henry VIII and the English Monasteries*, I, 161, n. 1).—*Translator*] one of his chaplains, Richard Curwen, preached in the same place and called the provincial Peto, who had been summoned to Canterbury and so was obliged to be absent, "dog, slanderer, rebel and traitor." "I speak to thee, Peto, who makest thyself Micheas, that thou mayest speak evil of kings, but now thou art not to be found, being fled for fear and shame, as being unable to answer my arguments." Elstow, the warden of the convent, cried out with a bold voice: "Good sir, you know that father Peto is . . . not fled for fear of you, for to-morrow he will return again. In the meantime I am here as another Micheas, and will lay down my life to prove all those things true which he hath taught out of the holy scripture. . . . Even unto thee, Curwin, I speak, who art one of the four hundred prophets into whom the spirit of lying is entered." Elstow and Peto were brought before the Council and sharply reprimanded by the Lords, one of whom [the Earl of Essex] told them "that they had deserved to be put into a sack and cast into the Thames." To which Elstow replied: "With thanks to God we know the way to heaven to be as ready by water as by land." [Cf. Card. Gasquet, *Henry VIII and the English Monasteries*, I, 160-161; J. Gairdner, *History of the English Church*, p. 118 *sq.*—*Translator*.]

Peto, who had to take refuge on the Continent till the accession of Mary Tudor, was created cardinal by Paul IV on June 14th, 1557 and died shortly afterwards. For Peto, cf. Dodd, ed. 1737, I, 480. J. Forest was condemned to be hanged and at the same time burnt alive, after a cruel captivity of two years amongst thieves and criminals. Catherine of Aragon, whose confessor he had been, wrote a very touching letter to him in prison, to which he replied. Sander (*op. cit.*, French ed., 1587, fol. 84-85 v [? missing in Lewis' trans.—*Translator*]) published these letters. Forest died two years after Catherine.

[184] This house had been founded by Henry VII (December 14th, 1485, Pollard, *Henry VII*, III, No. 190) who, like Henry VIII at the beginning of his reign, showed great favour to the Franciscans. For the Franciscans in England, see Parkinson, *Collectanea Anglo-Minorotica, or Collection of the*

this house were visited by Bedyll, archdeacon of London, and Roland Lee, Bishop of Lichfield, and they refused to take the oath. The whole order was attainted. The seven houses they possessed in England were closed and given to the Augustinians.[185] Of the two hundred monks living in these houses the most obstinate were sent to the Tower, and the remainder to the unreformed Franciscans, where they were loaded with chains by the king's order. Fifty died in prison, and many left for Scotland and France.[186] These monks were the first to be driven out by Henry, and they were the first to return in Mary Tudor's time.[187]

The Bridgettines of Sion Abbey were less resolute in their opposition to the schismatical laws. Cromwell visited them, secured the adhesion of the majority and dispersed the rest.

The most noteworthy resistance was that of the London Charterhouse. In 1534 the prior, John Houghton, and the procurator, Humphrey Middlemore, after having been sent to the Tower, took the conditional oath "quantum per legem Dei licet," with the rest of the community.[188] But the following year Houghton with two other Carthusians, Robert Lawrence, prior of Beauvale, and Augustine Webster, prior of Axholme, denied, in Cromwell's presence, that the king, a mere layman, could be the head of the Church of England.

Antiquities of the English Franciscans or Friers Minors, commonly called Grey Friers, with an Appendix concerning the English Nuns of St. Clare, London, 1726, in quarto, with two engravings; Father Cuthbert, O.S.F.C., *The Friars and how they came to England: being a Translation of Thomas of Eccleston's "De adventu FF. minorum in Anglia,"* done into English, with an Essay on the Spirit and Genius of the Franciscan Friars, London, 1903; E. Hutton, *The Franciscans in England,* 1224-1538, London, 1926.

[185] Southampton, Canterbury, Newcastle, Newark, Greenwich, Richmond (Surrey); the seventh is not exactly known. The commission which ordered Bedyll, with Thomas Cromwell and John Tregunwell, chief judge of the Admiralty, to undertake the general visitation of the monasteries and churches, is dated December 1534. Cf. Gee and Hardy, No. LX.

[186] *L. and P.,* VII, No. 49. Amongst these were Peto and Elstow who had publicly resisted the new laws. They returned to their house at Greenwich, under Mary Tudor (cf. Harpsfield, in Bémont, 61 *sq.,* 79 *sq.*). To state "that no prince can have the title and authority of supreme head of the Church" was punished by death "in order to please his Majesty." This happened to more than one religious who was barbarously executed (cf. Ellis, *op. cit.,* 1st Series, II, 85, *sq.*).

[187] This was but justice, Harpsfield remarks (Bémont, 65).

[188] They had been visited by the Bishop of London, Stokesley, and John Edward Lee, Archbishop of York, who persuaded them to take the oath with the restrictive clause.

Imprisoned in the Tower once more (April 13th, 1535) they continued to reject the royal supremacy.[189] John Haile, Vicar of Isleworth,[190] was treated in a similar manner; so, too, was Richard Reynolds, of Sion Abbey, who, when he was asked to name those who thought as he did, replied with sublime simplicity: "All honest people in the realm."[191] All five of them suffered death on May 4th, 1535, with the tortures reserved for those guilty of high treason: *premièrement qui est d'être penduz, sans estrangler, et puis tout vifs fenduz*.[192] Tied to hurdles, they were dragged to the gibbet at Tyburn.[193] There they watched with admirable courage while their brethren were tortured one after the other, and without any change in their features or the tone of their voices they exhorted the people to obey the king in all that was not contrary to the honour of God or of the Church. In a half-strangled state they were placed on the block by the executioner, who proceeded to tear out their heart and bowels. Their bodies were then dismembered, and their head and limbs thrown into a cauldron of boiling tar prior to being exposed on London Bridge and at the gates of the city. The Duke of Norfolk, the Earl of Wiltshire, Anne Boleyn's father, and many

[189] *L. and P.*, VIII, No. 565.

[190] With Haile was arrested Robert Feron, Vicar of Teddington, who obtained pardon by revealing private conversations between the Sion monks and the Vicar of Isleworth.

[191] Reynolds' examination, in *L. and P.*, VIII, No. 566.

[192] Poem by Lancelot de Carles on the death of Anne Boleyn, in G. Ascoli, *op. cit.*, p. 256. Cranmer wanted to save Webster and Reynolds, and told Cromwell that their conversion would influence the public more than the sight of the execution (Cox, *Remains of Cranmer*, No. 303).

[193] On this spot there is now a convent of perpetual adoration in memory of the five hundred priests, religious, and layfolk who suffered martyrdom there, under Henry VIII and Elizabeth, for their fidelity to the Holy See or to the Catholic Faith (cf. P. S. Chandlery, S.J., *The Tower to Tyburn, a London Pilgrimage*, 1920, with forty illustrations; Dom Bede Camm, *Tyburn and the English Martyrs*, 1930).

Henry VIII's legislation on the crime of treason (1531–34), leaving Parliament part of the responsibility for the bloody application of the laws, has been studied by Miss I. D. Thornley in an article in *Transactions of the Royal Hist. Society*, 3rd Series, XI, 1917. J. R. Tanner also devotes a chapter to the *law of treason*, criminal legislation in political matters, which assumed such deadly importance under Henry VIII and Elizabeth in his *Tudor Constitutional Documents A.D. 1485–1603: with an historical commentary*, Cambridge, 1922. The first "statute of treason" belongs to the year 1530. D. Oswald Dykes mentions it in his *Source Book of Constitutional History from 1660*. London, 1930.

other lords and courtiers assisted at this barbarous spectacle by way of passing the time.[194] Three weeks later three other London Carthusians were taken to the Tower, tried and condemned to death (June 19th). Several other monks died in prison through privation and bad treatment.[195]

[194] *L. and P.*, VIII, 661, 666, 726; Hall's *Chronicle*, June 19th, 1535. According to Cromwell's expression (Merriman, *op. cit.*, I, 409, letter dated July 15th, 1535) the execution of the Carthusians and the other martyrs was designed "for the putting the Kynges subiects and other in more terroure ande Feare." These violent measures aroused the indignation of the French, and Continental preachers denounced the king's cruelty (cf. Friedmann, *Anne Boleyn*, II, 65, 69, 73).
More than one writer has remarked upon the "monstrous nature" of this Act on treason, which allowed Henry VIII to silence his subjects and to stifle their conscience (cf. Dixon, I, 234 *sq.*). It became still more detestable as the years passed. "*Il [Henry] ne cessera de mectre la main à sang, tant qu'il sentira en son esperit quelque doubte des siens. . . . De là vient aussi que tous les jours se publient nouveaux edictz si sanguinaires qu'avec mille gardes à peine se peult l'on garder; et avec une seulle légière occasion on se pert*" (Marillac to Montmorency, August 6th, 1540; Kaulek, 211 *sq.*, cf. 209 *sq*). Before Henry VIII's time simple words alone had not sufficed to prove one guilty of high treason; the most that might be said is that certain incriminating words had been considered as a corroboration of the other charges. The statute of 1532 on the crime of high treason had been interpreted in this way in the fifteenth century (cf. Samuel Rezneck, "Constructive treason by words in the fifteenth century," in the *American Hist. Review*, October, 1927).
[195] For the religious martyrs, the following may be consulted: M. Chauncy (one of the London Carthusians) *Historia aliquot Martyrum*, Mainz, 1550, V. M. Doreau's ed., Monstrol, 1888; English trans., 1890; Th. Bourchier, *Historia ecclesiastica de martyrio fratrum ordinis Minorum . . . qui passi sunt ab anno 1536 usque ad annum 1582*, Paris, 1582 and 1586; H. Clifford, *Life of Jane Dormer, Duchess of Feria*, Stevenson's ed., London, 1887; Hendriks, *The London Charterhouse, its monks and martyrs*, London, 1889; V. M. Doreau, *Henri VIII et les martyrs de la Chartreuse de Londres*, Paris, 1890; Card. Gasquet, *Henry VIII and the English Monasteries*, I, chap. VI; J. Gairdner, *Lollardy*, I, 421–37. An account of their martyrdom is to be found in Harpsfield (Bémont, *op. cit.*, 73 *sq.*) and Spillman (*op. cit.*, pp.59–71, 137–47). Froude (*op. cit.*, chap. IX) speaks at length of the Carthusians, following Chauncy, but with his own peculiar trend of mind. J. Gairdner devotes part of chap. III, Bk. I, of his *Lollardy* to them: "Further trials of the Faithful." W. F. Taylor published, in 1912, *The Charterhouse of London, Monastery, Palace and Thomas Sutton's Foundation*, with numerous plates; and, in 1921, G. S. Davies' *Charterhouse in London, Monastery, etc.*, appeared. Donald Benedict Christie has just written, after Maurice Chauncy whose over-rhetorical style he rather imitates, the sufferings and death of the "Proto-martyr of the English Reformation," as Dom Bede Camm calls him: *While the World Revolves: Being the Life and Martyrdom of Blessed John Houghton, Carthusian Monk and Martyr*. With Preface by Dom Bede Camm, London, 1933.
There were only nine Charterhouses in England: Witham, Somerset, the oldest (1178); Hinton, Somerset (1227); Beauvale, Notts. (1345); London (1371); Hull (1378); Coventry (1381); Axholme, Lincolnshire

These are practically the only men martyred for the royal supremacy.[196] By the end of 1534 the bishops, canons, vicars, members of religious orders, professors in colleges, and the staffs of the hospitals and other pious foundations had all recognized the king as the sole spiritual head.

The work was completed when Cromwell was named vicar-general of the king in the following year, i.e. his vicegerent in spiritual matters (January, 1535). All the bishops, including even the Archbishop of Canterbury, had to take their orders from him, especially in all that concerned the royal supremacy. In this way Henry removed from his own shoulders the hateful part of the measures adopted, and at the same time assured their execution.[197]

The bishops were obliged formally to renounce their obedience to the Pope. Not a single one refused (February, 1535). They retracted the oath given to the Holy See at the time of their consecration, an oath which, as we have seen, Henry pretended was incompatible with the one given to the king. They declared "the papacy of Rome not to be ordained of God . . . but to be set up only by man. . . . Furthermore, that the said Bishop of Rome now being, or

(1397); Mountgrace, Yorks. (1397); and Sheen, near London (1414), the most famous after that of London. There was also a Charterhouse in Scotland at Perth (1429), and another in Ireland, at Kinalkin (1280–1321). Cf. E. Margaret Thompson's *The Carthusian Order in England*, London, 1930, in which an account of the suppression of the Order in England and of its martyrs will be found.

[196] The decree of beatification of December 9th, 1886, in addition to Fisher, More, and the Countess of Salisbury (Reginald Pole's mother), names eighteen Carthusians; Reynolds, of the order of St Bridget; the Franciscan, J. Forest; J. Stone, Augustinian; five secular priests; and one layman, G. Gardiner. Another decree of the same date declared venerable twenty other martyrs of the royal supremacy: five Franciscans; eight religious, three of whom were abbots; three secular priests; two Knights of St John; one Knight of Malta; and one layman. [Of these twenty, nine, including the three abbots, four religious, one Knight of St John and the layman, were beatified by a decree of May 13th, 1895; and two more, a secular priest and a Knight of St John, were beatified in 1929—*Translator.*]

[197] The commission naming Cromwell vicar-general has been published by Collier, IX, 119. In the House of Lords Cromwell took his seat at the right hand of the throne, like the bishops, and above the Archbishop of Canterbury (31 Henry VIII, cap. 10). In the House of Commons and in Convocation, where the king did not sit, Cromwell represented him and acted as a lever for him against the higher clergy (Pollard, *The Evolution of Parliament*, 199 *sq.*, 268 *sq.*).

any that shall succeed him hereafter in the said see, is not to be called pope nor supreme bishop, or universal bishop, nor most holy lord, but only ought to be called Bishop of Rome, and fellow brother, as the old manner of the most antient bishops hath been." They bound themselves not to take an oath to any foreign power whatsoever.[198]

"The bishops who did not burn all their bulls obtained from the Holy See," preached George Browne, general of the Mendicant Orders, "and get new ones from the king, deserve very severe punishment; without that they cannot discharge any episcopal duty."[199] Of the thirteen titular bishops acting as auxiliaries, all accepted the supremacy.[200]

New orders were issued in June.[201] The bishops and their clergy, both secular and regular, on every Sunday and festival, were to teach the faithful the royal title of "head of the Church," and at least once a year were to preach against the usurped power of the Bishop of Rome, whose name was deleted in the missals and prayer-books used in the Church. The history of the trial from the time of the legatine court up to the meeting at Marseilles was to be recounted in the

---

[198] This act of the bishops was called *Sponsio* or *Renunciatio Papae*. Wilkins, *Concilia*, III, 780; Rymer, *Foedera*, XIV, 549. See the bishops' letters to Henry VIII in Strype, *Eccles. Mem.*, II, 204 *sq.*; Burnet, VI, 111; H. Ellis, *Original Letters*, 3rd Series, II, 336; *L. and P.*, I, 430.

Rowland Lee, consecrated on April 19th, 1534, was the first bishop to be installed without a Bull. Nine months before the Act of Supremacy was passed he admitted it in these terms: "I acknowledge and recognize your majesty immediately under Almighty God to be the chief and supreme head of the Church of England, and claim to have the bishopric of Chester wholly and only of your gift."

[199] Chapuys' letter January 28th, 1535. *L. and P.*, Henry VIII, 1535, No. 121.

[200] Four of them survived until Mary's reign, and they died in communion with Rome: Thomas Chetham, Bishop of Sidon; Thomas Hallam, Bishop of Philadelphia (both Austin Canons); William Fawell, Bishop of Hippo; and Robert King, Bishop of Rheon (1535), of Osney (1542), and of Oxford (1545). Matthew Mackarell, Bishop of Chalcedon and auxiliary Bishop of Lincoln, died on the scaffold in 1535, one of the victims of the Pilgrimage of Grace. Cf. W. Mazière Brady, *The Episcopal Succession in England, Scotland and Ireland, A.D. 1400 to 1758*, Rome, 1877, Vol. II; W. Gumbley, O.P., F.R.Hist. S., in *The Clergy Review*, August, 1932, p.121.

[201] The first orders, given in general letters, are dated June 1st (Wilkins, *Concilia*, III, 772). They were followed by a second decree of June 3rd (*Remains of Cranmer*, pp. 460, 525; Collier, IV, 282-86. Cf. Strype, *Memorials of Cranmer*, ed. 1848, I, 343, App. 13). Strype gives the date of these documents as 1534. This error was followed by all the writers until Froude. Cranmer was responsible for the wording of these orders.

pulpit, as an injustice committed by the Pope, and in terms
entirely favourable to the king, and was to end thus: "Good
people, I exhort you to stick to the truth and our prince,
according to our bounden duties, and despise these naughty
doings of this Bishop of Rome, and charitably pray that he
and all other abusers of Christ's word and works may have
grace to amend." Public prayers were prescribed for the
king, sole supreme head of the Church, for the Queen Anne
and their daughter Elizabeth.[202]

Meanwhile the justices of peace (June 9th) and the royal
judges (June 25th) were charged, under pain of severe
punishment, to see that the orders against the authority of the
Bishop of Rome, which had been totally extirpated, abolished
and suppressed, were carried out. The bishops also had to
send to the chancellor the sermons they preached on the
subjects imposed on them.[203] After the execution of Fisher
and More, Henry himself addressed a long proclamation to
the people to show them that it was treason to uphold the
authority of the Roman pontiff.[204]

At the end of 1535 the royal supremacy was recognized by

[202] It was moreover forbidden for a year to preach either for or against
the veneration of the saints, the marriage of priests, pilgrimages, miracles,
and justification by faith, on account of the contentions these subjects had
occasioned in the country. H. Jenkyns, *Cranmer's Remains*, I, 247 *sq.*;
Burnet, VI, 86; Collier, IV, 282 *sq.* Cranmer, in his letter to the king
of August 26th, 1535 [1536 according to the Oxford ed.] (Strype *Memorials
of Cranmer*, App. XIII, ed. 1848, p. 343) summarized the discourse he had
uttered in his cathedral against the titles of Christ's Vicar, "Sanctissimus
Papa," "Sancta sedes Romana," and against the "sacros canones" and
"divinas leges" of the Roman Church.

They resorted to various expedients in order to make the Pope's name
opprobrious. The king called him "*communément non seulement evesque de
Rome, qui est encores le titre dont il use en toutes ses lectres, mais par aultres non
moings contumélieux, comme abomination, filz de perdition, ydole et Entechrist, ainsi
que communément ès festes et passetemps qui se font tous les jours l'on a coustume de
faire.*" In order to stir up the people against the popish clergy (Maitland,
Essays on the Reformation, London, 1899, 182 *sq.*) use was made of the theatre
and of songs, of the pulpit and of private conversations, in fact of every
medium which could influence public opinion at that period (Blunt, I,
271 *sq.*).

Although many service-books of this period were destroyed in Mary
Tudor's time, some of these books with the names of the Pope and Thomas
à Becket effaced are still extant. Cf. Wordsworth and Littlehales, *The
Old Service-books of the English Church*, 1904, p. 67.

[203] Wilkins, *Concilia*, III, 752, where this document is called a proclamation; Collier, IV, 280.

[204] Proclamation, of June 25th, 1535 (Burnet VI, 106–110).

the great majority of the nation; the schism was consummated. The defection was general, absolute and complete, and can be explained only by the latent causes of which we have spoken.[205] An entire body of clergy and a whole nation do not become schismatical all of a sudden through the will of one man, even if he be the most absolute potentate on earth, unless there be already in existence a mass of reasons making that religious revolution possible.

The king's will met with no opposition at all, or very little. Henry's quick penetrating eyes, to use Thomas More's words, opened wider and wider on an ever-growing horizon. Nothing makes a ruler more arbitrary than to be persuaded he has no real opposition to fear. To know that much can be done becomes an irresistible reason for wishing to do much. Henry became a dictator. Cromwell, his chief adviser at this epoch, considered the despotism of the Grand Turk as the ideal for a king, and extolled the *quod principi placuit* of the Roman law.[206] England bowed her head before the royal absolutism, which was the consequence and not the cause of the English schism.[207]

[205] See chap. I.

[206] Cf. *L. and P.*, VII, 1554, 1611. Cromwell expressed this idea in a conversation with Gardiner, maintaining that the king's will should be law, whereas the bishop advised Henry contrariwise that the law should be his will (Gardiner's letter to Somerset, after Henry VIII's death. Foxe, VI, 45; cf. J. A. Muller, *op. cit.*, p. 50). More had also told Cromwell that in order to be a good and faithful counsellor, he should incline the king not to what he could, but to what he ought to do (Roper, *Life of Sir Thomas More*).

At the end of the seventeenth century historians compared the King of England's authority over the Church to that of the Grand Turk, which had been Thomas Cromwell's ideal (cf. Collier, IV, 249). When he was a prisoner in the Tower, Cromwell swore that he had wished to make Henry so powerful that the whole world would kneel before him (Burnet, VI, 237).

[207] The *Institution of a Christian Man* (1537) and the *Necessary Erudition* (1543) taught passive obedience. Already in 1535 Cromwell and Henry were boasting before foreigners that they could bend whomever they pleased to their wills. "*Me déclarant d'abondant [ledit Cromwell] l'obeissance et l'union estre telle en ce royaume que, par un petit escrit de luy seulement, il peut mander estre obéi . . .*" (Palamedes Gontier to Admiral Chabot, February 5th, 1535, Le Laboureur, *op. cit.*, I, 409, 411). In 1538 Castillon wrote (Kaulek, *op. cit.*, 54) that "*le roy est résolu pour toutes choses de vivre désormais à son plaisir, et mettre tel ordre en son royaume que les roys d'après luy seront plus riches et plus obéys que ceulx de devant.*" Accordingly Giovanni Micheli observed, in 1557 (Albèri, 1st Series, II, 318, 319), that Parliament had lost its pristine authority: "the kings have become so formidable and powerful that they do as they please."

CHAPTER IV

SUPPRESSION OF THE MONASTERIES

Causes of the suppression of the English monasteries—Visitation of the monasteries (1535-1536)—Dissolution of the lesser monasteries; the Pilgrimage of Grace (1536-1537).—Surrender of the greater monasteries —Results of the abolition of the religious houses.

THE royal supremacy consummated the schism and at the same time was responsible for placing the monasteries in the king's hands. The royal injunctions[1] to those who were to visit the monasteries said "that the abbot, prior, or president and brethren may be declared, by the king's supreme power and authority ecclesiastical, to be absolved and loosed from all manner obedience, oath and profession by them heretofore perchance promised or made to the said Bishop of Rome, or to any other in his stead, or occupying his authority, or to any other foreign power, or person:" and that if any statutes "seem to bind them to obedience, or subjection, or any other recognizance of authority to the said Bishop of Rome, or to any other foreign power, potentate, person or place by any ways: such statutes, by the king's grace's visitors, be utterly annihilate, broken, and declared void and of none effect." The exempt monasteries, depending solely upon Rome, came inevitably under the royal jurisdiction when this was substituted for that of the Holy See.[2] As regards the others, in order to make them directly subject to the king it was necessary only to suspend the power which the bishops had over them, since that power came from the "supreme head of the Church," who could withdraw it when he wished. This was done in 1535.[3] One of the results of the royal supremacy was then to place the monastic wealth within the king's reach.[4]

---

[1] Burnet, IV, 217 sq.

[2] It was in the name of "our most dread sovereign, in earth immediately under Christ supreme head of the Church of England," that the royal commissioners laid hands on the monasteries (Burnet, IV, 263).

[3] See below, p. 157.

[4] The law on Peter's Pence (1534) indeed gave the Crown exclusive

Moreover, monastic life has, in itself, a universal character which ill becomes the particularism of national churches. So despite the eagerness with which the majority of the religious orders renounced papal authority, it was difficult to find room for them in the nationalized English Church.

They were looked upon as smouldering fires which might well be expected to conceal the last traces of an attachment to Roman Catholicism. Lord Herbert said[5] that the members of the religious orders were "looked upon as a reserve army of the Pope's, always ready to appear in his quarrels." Cromwell named them "the Pope's spies."[6]   One of Henry VIII's counsellors observed "how deep these monasteries are in his [the Pope's] interest, and how factiously they contest your [Henry's] supremacy."[7]   "In the rules they followed," wrote Ranke,[8] "in the orders to which they belonged the inter-communion of Latin Christianity had its most living expression, but it was exactly this that the King and Parliament wished to sever . . . in the new order of things there was absolutely no place for the monastic system. It was necessarily sacrificed to the unity of the country." The disappearance of the monasteries was therefore bound to follow the abolition of papal authority, the nationalization of the Church, and the establishment of the royal supremacy, and Henry receives his meed of praise from Anglicans because he "not only shook off the yoke of Rome, but broke the power of that *papal militia*, as the religious orders have been called."[9]

In England a whole series of precedents had unfortunately paved the way for the confiscation of the monastic possessions. "Great buildings commonly crack before they fall," says Fuller,[10] "so was it here in abbeys." As early as the thirteenth century, the cells of the great French monasteries, and absolute control over these monasteries (25 Henry VIII, cap. 19). The 20th article of this law authorized Henry to create commissioners to inspect "the monasteries, priories and exempt religious houses."

The first instructions for the visitation of the monasteries had in view chiefly the exempt houses (Burnet IV, 207).

[5] *Op. cit.*, p. 395; cf. Collier, IV, 288.
[6] Gasquet, *Henry VIII and the English Monasteries*, I, 249.
[7] Collier, IV, 290.
[8] *Englische Geschichte vornehmlich im siebzehnten Jahrhundert*, Leipzic, 1870 (Vol. XL of *Sämmtliche Werke*), p. 154.
[9] Rev. H. Jenkyns, *The Remains of Cranmer*, I, p. XLIII.
[10] *Church History of Britain*, ed. Brewer, Oxford, 1845, III, 345.

known as "alien priories," which had been founded by the
Normans after the Conquest, had been freely used to serve
the royal purposes. These alien priories, numbering between
one hundred and one hundred and fifty,[11] used to send quite
considerable sums of money every year to the mother-house
on the Continent.[12] In time of war this money was confiscated
by the English monarchs.[13] Thus Edward I had seized it
when he undertook to recover the province of Guienne
(1294). Edward II (1307-27),[14] who also tried to obtain
the Templars' possessions,[15] followed his example, and so did
his son Edward III (1327-77), who kept the alien priories in
his hands for twenty-three years.[16] On several occasions
Parliament forbade them to send their money to their houses
on the Continent.[17] Richard II (1377-99) imitated Edward
III and kept them in his own possession.[18] Henry IV (1399-

[11] According to Dugdale's *Monasticon Anglicanum*, 100; according to
Weever (p. 338), 110; according to the "Alien priories" of 1779, 146. For
these priories, see Gasquet, *op. cit.*, I, 40 *sq.*; also a lecture to the Lingard
Society, in the *Dublin Review*, 1928; and R. Graham, "Four Alien Priories
in Monmouthshire" (*Journal of Brit. Archæol. Assoc.*, 1929, 102-121).

[12] The houses of the Cluniac order sent £2,000 sterling every year to
France. Some houses paid an annual tribute called *apportus;* the others
kept only the rent and the tithes for themselves, and gave their money to
the community on the Continent.

[13] According to Dixon (I, 321) King John first confiscated the goods of
eighty-one alien priories and made use of them for his own purposes.

[14] Rymer, *Foedera*, IV, 246. In this Act Edward III restored to their
owners the convents which his father had seized (cf. Dodd, ed. 1737, I, 256).

[15] After the abolition of the Order by Clement V (1312) Edward
instituted proceedings against them (Wilkins, *Concilia*, I, 329) and twenty-
two houses were dissolved. The Pope's Bull ordered their property to be
transferred to the Knights Hospitallers; the king deferred the execution
of it for a year, and when at last he gave way (1313), declared that it was a
concession which in no wise impaired his own rights or those of his subjects.
Eleven years afterwards Parliament decreed in favour of the Hospitallers
(*Statutes of the realm*, 17 Edward II, p. 194); but part of the lands had already
passed out of the king's hands into the laity's (Rymer, *Foedera*, IV, 323;
Dodd, I, 257).

[16] On his accession he re-established a large number of alien priories
(Rymer, *Foedera*, IV, 246) but confiscated them in 1337 when war broke
out. When peace was concluded with France, he restored them to their
owners (1361), only to take them away again eight years later when war
broke out afresh.

[17] Under Edward III and his predecessors; thus in the thirty-second
and thirty-fifth years of Edward I's reign, and in the twenty-fifth and
twenty-eighth years of Edward II's.

[18] About this time the alien abbeys, which were scarcely receiving anything from their cells or dependencies, were trying to rid themselves of these

1413) re-established a certain number of them, but reserved for himself as a subsidy in case of war the amounts they paid to the houses on the Continent in time of peace. In his *Historia Anglicana*, Walsingham records that Henry IV took some of their revenues for the support of his own household in 1408, and that Parliament in 1410, influenced by the doctrines of Wiclif, demanded the abolition of all monastic property, claiming that alone it would suffice for the upkeep of more earls, knights, squires, and houses of alms than the entire kingdom possessed. Finally, Henry V (1413–22) definitely suppressed the alien priories when he revived his claims to the French crown, because he said they were channels through which money was being drained out of England (1414).[19] Although his action was inspired more by policy and by considerations of safety than by thoughts of gain, Fuller remarks that "courtiers, by his bounty tasting on the sweets of abbey-lands, made their breakfasts thereon in the time of Henry V, which increased their appetites to dine on the same in the days of king Henry VIII."[20]

At a later date the Pope allowed certain religious houses in England to be suppressed so that their income might be used for the building of colleges and hospitals. In this way Bishop Waynflete of Winchester founded Magdalen College at Oxford in 1459, and Fisher, St John's at Cambridge.[21] The Archbishop of Canterbury, Chichele (1414–43), and the Bishops of Ely and Lincoln, Alcock (1486-1500) and Smith

latter on the most advantageous conditions. A certain number of convents were naturalized.

[19] *Parliament Rolls*, IV, 22. The monasteries endeavoured, however, to regain their cells, but in vain. Cf. Gasquet, *op. cit.*, I, 55 *sq.*; Fuller III, 349–54.

[20] Fuller, ed. 1837, II, p. 200.

[21] Waynflete made use of the goods of the Augustinian Priory of Selborne for his foundation, in virtue of a Bull of Innocent VIII (July 8th, 1486). He also obtained Sele Priory in Sussex. For Waynflete, cf. R. Chandler, *W. Waynflete*, 1811, with five engravings; Bloxham and Heylin, *Memorials of Bishop Waynflete*, 1851. Fisher founded St John's with the properties of Bromehall in the diocese of Salisbury, and of Lillechurch in that of Rochester. Cf. Fiddes, *Wolsey, Collectanea*, p. 293. Henry VIII and Wolsey authorized Fisher to proceed against the nuns on account of their faults, bad conduct, and dishonourable existence. In December, 1521 he thanked the Bishop of Salisbury for having driven out the prioress and the nuns, because of faults committed by them against their vows (Fiddes, *Collect.*, p. 99). Those same reasons were used by the king fourteen years later for the suppression of the lesser monasteries.

(1495-1514), adopted the same expedient. Henry VII used the monastic properties of Mottisfont and Luffield to build the chantry and hospital at Windsor.[22]

Wolsey's example was more decisive.[23] In 1518, and again in 1525[24] when he was the all-powerful Minister, he obtained faculties from the Pope for the inspection and visitation of all the monasteries. For the first time the people of England beheld the temporal and spiritual authority concentrated in one man, and so when some years later the twofold authority was wielded by Henry, the mass of the people, ignorant of and caring little for distinctions, scarcely noticed the change.

Wolsey, who already found it difficult to obtain the money he needed for the sumptuous palaces he was building, wished to found a magnificent college at Oxford to perpetuate his name,[25] and another in Ipswich, where he was born.[26] The funds for these were to come from the monasteries. Between 1524 and 1528 twenty-nine religious houses were dissolved in various southern counties,[27] despite the murmuring of the inhabitants.[28] As was his way, the cardinal at times employed force to obtain the Bulls of dissolution.[29] He even suppressed three houses by his own authority without waiting for authorization from the Pope.[30] He is said to have contemplated confiscation on a larger scale. In 1528 and 1529, he sought

[22] The Bulls of suppression granted by Alexander VI are dated 1494 (Rymer, *Foedera*, XII, 562).

[23] Cf. Gasquet, *op. cit.*, I, chap. III.

[24] *L. and P.*, II, No. 4399. Rymer, *Foedera*, XIV, 18.

[25] Cardinal's College, now Christ Church. For the foundation of this college the cardinal obtained the dissolution of St Frideswede's monastery— the church of which is now Oxford Cathedral—and of Christ Church Chapel (*L. and P.*, IV, No. 15; Dodd, ed. 1737, pp. 300 *sq.*, where the royal authorization follows).

[26] The Bulls granting the suppression of the religious houses for this foundation are dated May 15th, 1528 (cf. *L. and P.*, IV, 5714).

[27] The list will be found in Gairdner, *History*, 419.

[28] Warham transmitted to the cardinal, on July 2nd and 3rd, 1525, the complaints of the people who preferred to keep their convent, rather than have "forty children of that country educated and after sent to Oxford," as Wolsey promised them (*L. and P.*, IV, Nos. 1470, 1471).

[29] Cardinal Pucci proved to be unmanageable and set Clement VII against fresh suppressions (cf. Rymer, *Foedera*, XIV, 23). When, in 1525, the Pope granted Wolsey the visitation faculties he so ardently desired, he begged Clerk, the cardinal's agent, "for God's sake to use mercy with these friars" (*L. and P.*, IV, No. 610).

[30] *L. and P.*, IV, No. 4920.

permission for the king to suppress all monasteries with less than twelve monks or nuns. They were to be annexed to larger monasteries, or their property used for the building of new cathedrals with an annual revenue of 10,000 ducats. Clement VII gave his assent,[31] but the Bull granting Wolsey the necessary powers (August 31st, 1529) arrived the day following Wolsey's downfall.[32] Among the forty-four articles of impeachment which, according to Lord Herbert, were exhibited in the House of Lords against the cardinal, were the following accusations. He was accused of having visited the monasteries in order to take away the twenty-fifth part of their livelihood (art. 25); of having levied mighty sums of money so that they were no longer able to give hospitality (art. 3)[33]; of having used crafty persuasions to induce the religious to give him money (art. 24)[34]; and of having got them to make false declarations, after their houses had been dissolved, stating that they had willingly given up their house (art. 19).[35] It sounds almost like an indictment against the visitors of 1535-36.

"Here," says Lord Herbert, "certainly began the taste that our king took of governing in chief the clergy, of which, therefore, as well as the dissolution of monasteries, it seems the first arguments and impressions were derived from the cardinal."[36] Wolsey's example certainly had its consequences

[31] The first Bull of November 14th, 1528 (Rymer, *Foedera*, XIV, p. 272) allowed the greater monasteries to annex the religious houses containing less than twelve subjects, and where the rule was little kept; the second Bull of the same date (*ibid.*) referred to the erection of cathedrals, and only authorized Wolsey to make inquiries to see how many monasteries would have to be sacrificed if it were necessary to increase the number of the cathedrals, and if the monks would remain in the cathedrals as canons.

[32] The Bull of June 4th, 1529 (Rymer, *Foedera*, XIV, p. 291) allowed the cathedrals to be built but threw the whole responsibility on the cardinal's conscience. The Bull of the following August 31st granted the annexation of the lesser monasteries by the greater, or their union, as Wolsey pleased, but suppressed the clause *de consensu quorum interest*.

[33] "For if they [the religious] were good," Henry had written to Wolsey, "why should you take their money? And if they were ill, it were a sinful act. Howbeit, your legateship herein might peradventure *apud homines* be a cloak, but not *apud Deum*" (Lord Herbert, *Henry VIII*, p. 164).

[34] Henry had already suspected Wolsey of exempting the monasteries from their payments to the king, in return for large contributions to his colleges (cf. Pollard, *Henry VIII*, 243).

[35] Already the idea of *surrendering* appears (Fiddes, *Wolsey, Collectanea*, 172 and 299).

[36] Lord Herbert, *Henry VIII*, p. 209 (cf. Fuller, III, 355-58).

In the Act of Parliament of 1536 dissolving the lesser monasteries we find, as we shall see later, Wolsey's plan for suppressing all religious houses with less than twelve inmates. Parliament invoked the same reasons as Wolsey, viz., immorality and lack of discipline. "For the cardinal," wrote Strype, " . . . had lately obtained of the Pope a Bull for the dissolving of divers monasteries wherein much vice and wickedness was harboured, *as he informed the Pope, to incline him thereby the easier to grant his request.*"[37] Wolsey had no more thought for the dispersed religious than Henry afterwards showed. Hall relates how the cardinal "suddenly entered by his commissioners into the said houses and put out the religious and took all their goods, moveables, and scarcely gave to the poor wretches anything except it were to the heads of the house."[38]

Finally, the agents employed by Wolsey for the inspection and dissolution of the monasteries were scarcely better than the inquisitors of 1535. The cruel and unjust way in which they treated the monks provoked a general outcry[39]; and even the king blamed the cardinal for it.[40] Fiddes in his *Life of Wolsey* says: "But in the methods of enriching him under the first article (privileges of his visitatorial power) no one contributed so much as his chaplain, John Allen, LL.D., who, accompanied with a great train, and riding in a kind of perpetual progress from one religious house to another, is said to have drawn very large sums for his master's service from them."[41] "This priest," Hall continues, "rode in his gown of velvet, with a great train, and was received into every religion with procession as though the legate had been there. And (he) took such great sums for his visitation that the

[37] Strype, *Eccles. Memorials*, p. 168 (cf. *L. and P.*, IV, No. 4120). In order to dissolve and unite the convent of Pre to the great abbey of St Albans, he told the Pope that the religious discipline was much relaxed therein (cf. Rymer, *Foedera*, XIV, p. 240). For the relaxation of discipline in general and, in certain cases, of morals, in the nunneries, see Miss Power, *Medieval English Nunneries*, chaps. VII-XII.

[38] Hall, *Union of the Families of Lancaster and York*, ed. 1548, p. 137.

[39] Wolsey tried to justify himself (*State Papers*, I, p. 154).

[40] Lord Herbert, *Henry VIII*, p. 164; Fiddes, *Wolsey*, p. 379. Henry addressed these reproaches to Wolsey apropos of the nomination of the Abbess of Wilton (*L. and P.*, IV, 4477, 4488, 4507, 4509; Brewer, *Henry VIII*, II, 283).

[41] Fiddes, *Wolsey*, p. 351.

religious were sore grieved and murmured much against it, and especially for they were charged with great sums of money to the king. And now this sudden visitation or predation clean shaved them."[42]   Allen was afterwards made Archbishop of Dublin, "where his imperiousness and rapacity brought him to a violent end."[43]   In the complaints addressed to the king against the cardinal's agents the name most frequently mentioned was that of Cromwell.[44]   This sinister genius was initiated in his future task of destruction in Wolsey's service.   He who was to be nicknamed *malleus monachorum* acquired then sufficient experience of the elementary principles of monastic confiscation to become a master in the art.   It was his apprenticeship.   His master's fall interrupted the work but he resumed it, on a larger scale, when the king became the "supreme head of the Church of England" and chose Cromwell for his counsellor.

The monastic property, henceforward at the king's mercy, was a prize as rich as it was easy to obtain.   It was less of a gamble than "les mynes d'or qu'il faisoyt chercher,"[45] the gold-mines that he was sending men to find in order to augment his impoverished treasury.   At this period there were nearly eight hundred religious houses in England, and the real property they possessed was considerable, albeit heavily burdened.[46]   "Of the whole area of England, the part owned

[42] Hall, *op. cit.*, ed. 1548, p. 143.

[43] Brewer, *Henry VIII*, II, 278. Speaking of Wolsey's agents, Fuller says (*Church History*, III, ed. 1845, p. 357): "Five they were in number, two whereof challenging the field of each other, one was slain and the other hanged for it. A third throwing himself headlong into a well, perished wilfully. A fourth, formerly wealthy, grew so poor that he begged his bread. The fifth, Dr. Allen, one of especial note, afterwards archbishop of Dublin, was slain in Ireland."

[44] Brewer, *Henry VIII*, II, 394.

[45] J. du Bellay to Montmorency, January 25th, 1529. Le Grand, III, 285; Bourrilly, I, 540. Henry VIII had entrusted this task to Joachim Hochstetter of Augsburg (cf. *L. and P.*, IV, p. 11, No. 5110).

[46] Many lands had been denuded of their tenants by the great plagues in the fourteenth century, which carried off two-thirds of the population, and by the civil wars of the fifteenth century (*L. and P.*, I, 50. E. F. Gay, *The Inquisitions of Depopulation, 1517*, in *Transactions*, New Series, XIV, 231; this answered Leadam's "The Domesday of Inclosure, 1517–18," *Royal Hist. Society*, 1897). The king often gave pensions from the monastery revenues, particularly to the foundation scholars at the universities (*L. and P.*, I, Nos. 49, 60, 106, 615, 920). The founders of the monasteries or their descendants sometimes imposed the obligation of giving help to their

by the monasteries was very large."[47] According to the inventory drawn up in Henry VIII's time, known as the *Valor ecclesiasticus*,[48] the gross revenue from all church property was £320,280 10s. Of this the revenue from the religious houses would be between £150,000 and £200,000,[49] without taking into account all the precious things the piety of the faithful had accumulated through the centuries, such as vestments, gold and silver plate, and precious reliquaries. So that, all told, the monastic property must have been worth some £50,000,000 of our money.[50]

More than once before Church property had been attacked and threatened. Wiclif and the Lollards had demanded its

poor relations, and needy dependents. Gasquet (*op. cit.*, I, 34) gives a curious example. For the monastic debts see Savine, *op. cit.*, pp. 210 *sq.*

[47] Gasquet, *op. cit.*, I, 250.

[48] The inquisitors had no object in exaggerating the revenues, and the commissions exercised a mutual control over each other. We may therefore use this work as a basis: *Valor ecclesiasticus tempore Henrici VIII auctoritate regia institutus*, six vols., 1810-34, which Savine (*English Monasteries on the Eve of the Dissolution*, chaps. I and II) has collated with other documents of the period.

[49] According to Tanner (*Notitia monastica . . . before A.D. 1540*, Oxford, 1695) the monastic revenues amounted to £142,914 12s.; according to Speed (at the end of Henry VIII's chronicle), whom Fuller follows (ed. 1845, III, 329 *sq.*), they were £171,312 4s.; according to Blunt, who places the monasteries and hospitals seized by the king at 1,130 (I, 369) they were £200,000; according to Fisher (*op. cit.*, V, p. 500), £135,000; Savine, the latest historian to study the question, and with the greatest care, keeps the figure at £200,000. Dugdale, in his *Monasticon Anglicanum*, gives the lowest estimate for the monastic revenues. For the revenues of the twenty-seven mitred abbots, according to Speed, see Collier, IX, 159. Cf. Dixon, *op. cit.*, I, 322, for the exaggerated ideas of the monastic fortunes which prevailed at the time of the dissolution.

[50] See Pollard, *Henry VII*, III, No. 52, for a description of the monastic fortunes in the previous reign. An inventory of all the gold and silver objects drawn up by a prior, in Strype (*Memorials of Cranmer*, App. 16), will give an idea of their number and value.

J. Gairdner has given (419 *sq.*) a very interesting list of the chief monasteries: Every town of some importance possessed one or more religious houses, either of the Austin Canons, the Dominicans, the Franciscans, the Carmelites, the Gilbertines or the Benedictines; all these orders or at least several of them sometimes existed together in the same town (pp. 428-431): outside the large towns there were nearly four hundred religious houses for men, and more than a hundred for women, as well as commanderies and preceptories of the Knights of Malta (pp. 420-428). The Anglican Bishop Tanner had previously written the *Notitia monastica or an account of all the abbies, priories and houses of friars . . . before A.D. 1540* (Oxford, 1695).

[For the Carmelite houses, see *The White Friars* by Rev. P. R. McCaffrey, Ord. Carm., Dublin, 1926.—*Translator*.]

suppression. In 1410 Lord Cobham had brought a Bill before Parliament to dispossess a certain number of monasteries for the benefit of the king and his earls. In the reign of Henry V the Lollard party in Parliament again petitioned the king to confiscate monastic and church property.[51] In the early sixteenth century appeared the unfair exaggerations of Simon Fish in his "Supplication of Beggars." He asserted that the Church, which was penniless four centuries before, then possessed one half of the entire wealth of the realm and one-third of all its real property. These wild statements and his diatribes against the mass of mendicants, vagabonds and thieves, who, under cover of their frock, caused a whole crowd of needy, blind, lame and sick folk to starve by begging alms for the repose of the departed souls, were scarcely mitigated by Thomas More's reply, the "Supplication of Poor Souls."[52] Nothing influences public opinion so much as writings which corroborate its own tendencies. The mind of the masses retained the impressions of the Church's fabulous wealth and of the alluring vision of a re-distribution of property. "The Complaynt of Roderick Mors" suggested that the monastic revenues should be used to educate the people[53]; but such was not the idea of the ruling power.

If, in Wolsey's day, Henry had cherished the idea of dissolving the monasteries to augment the crown possessions, Rome would have proved an obstacle to his plans. Now, however, since he had broken away from the Pope there was nothing to hinder his schemes. His conscience could not keep him from an object which would be both to his financial and poli-

---

[51] Cf. above, chap I, pp. 11 sq., and chap. IV, p. 143; Gasquet, op. cit., I, 52, 55. Ecclesiastical property was attacked more especially in Wiclif's Supplementum Triologi sive de dotatione Ecclesiae.

[52] Simon Fish's pamphlet, circa 1524 (cf. Foxe, IV, 763) was entitled: "The Supplication of Beggars, thrown and scattered at the Procession in Westminster, on Candlemas day, before King Henry the Eighth for him to read and peruse. Made and compiled by Master Fish." It is to be found in Foxe (IV, 659–64) and Dodd (ed. 1737, I, 304–309). Sir Thomas More's answer, "The Supplication of Souls," which has been re-edited with the rest of his works, answers Fish's arguments in a humorous and satirical vein, by showing that the monastic property could not be alienated without sacrilege. The "Supplication of Beggars" was condemned in London together with Luther's works and Tyndale's New Testament (cf. Foxe, IV, 667).

[53] The Complaynt of Roderick Mors, E. Eng. Text Soc. ed., pp. 47–52.

tical advantage, for it would fill his coffers and also strengthen his new position as head of the English Church. He had formerly displayed an inclination to secularize Church property. In 1529, he had allowed certain Lutheran writings to circulate at court urging the civil power to despoil the Church; and when Campeggio on that occasion had proved to him that according to the councils and theologians, the Church had a right to possess property, he had replied that all those decrees were the work of churchmen, thereby insinuating that the clergy judged their own case.[54] He approved of the spoliations carried out by the Protestant princes in Germany. He caused search to be made at Oxford for the condemned articles of Wiclif, which attacked the wealth of the Church. In 1533, Chapuys wrote that the king was determined to unite to the Crown all the property which the churchmen held from that same Crown and which his predecessors had not been able to alienate; and that he was obliged to act thus by reason of the oath he had taken on the day of his coronation.[55] He and Cromwell congratulated themselves upon the increase in the royal revenue the breach with Rome brought them,[56] and they looked forward to a vast secularization in the autumn of 1534 which would make bishops merely salaried officials of the Crown, and give to the Crown the episcopal possessions as well as a large share in the revenues of any notable benefice.[57] The religious houses were wealthy and the royal treasury almost empty[58]: what a temptation! This is the period when Cromwell "boasts that he will make his master more wealthy than all the other princes of Christendom."[59] Probably the dissolution of the monasteries was included in this plan, although actually the king was obliged to

[54] Campeggio's Letter of April 3rd, 1529, in Ehses, 76, 77.

[55] L. and P., VI, 235.

[56] Palamades Gontier to Admiral Chabot, February 5th, 1535 (Le Laboureur, op. cit., I, 409, 411). In 1541 Marillac wrote that "the king has taken and applied to himself all the revenues of the abbeys and part of some bishoprics" (Kaulek, 351).

[57] Cf. Fisher, op. cit., pp. 345–46.

[58] The royal farmers could not pay their rents, and the salary of the officials was frequently not paid (cf. Friedmann, II. 137). Catherine's household lived upon loans (L. and P., IX, No. 451).

[59] Cf. L. and P., VII, 1554, 1611. From his prison Cromwell wrote to the king: "If it were in my power to make you so rich as ye might enrich all men, God help me, as I would do it" (Burnet, op. cit., VI, p. 237).

distribute the greater part of the spoils among the noblemen and gentry.

Landlords among the nobility hankered after the monastic properties adjoining their own. Wealthy merchants longed to have estates in the country that they might become gentlemen. None of these men any longer understood the ideals, the religious enthusiasm, or the Christian sentiments which caused the medieval barons to build or endow abbeys. For over a century (1399–1509) not more than eight religious houses had been founded.[60] It seemed to the *nouveaux riches* that no useful purpose was served by these houses, and longing eyes were cast upon the monastic lands. Did anything exist for these men which could not be valued in pounds, shillings, and pence? Men understand least that which most they lack. The envy of the laymen who had been turned out of the monastic domains is expressed in more than one ballad of that period, in which the abbots are ridiculed and depicted as lords, increasing instead of alleviating the poor man's distress.[61] The idea of suppressing the monasteries harmonized therefore with the principles of the governing classes. On several occasions Chapuys averred that the project was about to be submitted to Parliament. But the hour had not yet come; the workman receives his wages only when the work is done. The task of establishing the royal supremacy had been achieved. But it was necessary to secure as firm supporters of the new regime the classes whose parliamentary representatives had helped to found it. Only in this way could any reactionary movements, after the king's death, be foiled. When the iron hand of Henry VIII was no longer there to uphold the structure so laboriously erected, the men who had grown rich on the monastic spoils would be its strongest supporters. "The king," wrote Chapuys in September, 1534, "will distribute among the gentlemen of the kingdom the greater part of the

[60] Donations were made preferably to hospitals and colleges. In 1506 the Bishop of Exeter, Hugh Oldham (1504–19), dissuaded his friend Fox from making legacies to the monks, "who have already more than they can hold."

[61] Serious statistics would probably show that the lands of the peasants produced more or were less burdened than monastic properties (cf. Cunningham, *Growth of English Industry and Commerce*, 1905, I, 530; Fisher, *op. cit.*, 370).

ecclesiastical revenues to gain their good will."[62] The dissolution of the monasteries was in fact, and was probably intended to be, a gigantic bribe designed to bind the most influential classes of English society indissolubly to the religious revolution. Ranke says[63] that the monastic wealth "was sacrificed to the greed of great men." The country squires scented the spoliation of the monasteries from afar; long before the Bill was submitted to Parliament Cromwell was overwhelmed with requests from men desiring to aggrandize their estates by the acquisition of mortmain property. By the time the king died two-thirds of the monastic spoils had been distributed between courtiers, peers, noblemen, merchants and corporations; very few of the common folk had derived the slightest benefit therefrom.[64]

That is one of the chief causes of the dissolution of the monasteries. The pretext for the dissolution was of quite a different order. For three and a half centuries it was believed in this country that the monasteries were suppressed on account of the immorality and crimes of the inmates. Such was the teaching contained in textbooks[65] and general histories,[66] and Burnet, in his *History of the Reformation*, was commonly supposed to have uttered the last word on the subject. This

[62] *L. and P.*, VII, 1141.

[63] Ranke, *Englische Geschichte*, I, 154.

[64] The rest was let out on lease by the Crown. See App. II, Vol. IV, *Political History of England*: "The disposal of monastic lands," by Fisher, based on Alexander Savine's researches (cf. also *ibid.*, p. 381). The numerous gentlemen administrators or the farmers of monastic lands quickly acquired them (cf. Savine, *op. cit.*, 257 *sq.*).

The richest purchaser of the reign was R. Gresham, who bought the estates of three monasteries in Yorkshire (October, 1540).

[65] Cf. Seebohm, *Epochs of History, Era of Prot. Revolution*, 1877, p. 168.

[66] Cf. Froude (*History of England*, IV, 520; *The reign of Henry VIII*, ed. Everyman, II, 123–39). Citing Latimer's words (*Latimer's Sermons*, Parker Society ed., 1845, by G. E. Corrie, I, 123), he says that on the table in the House of Commons was placed the famous "Black Book," which decided the destiny of the monasteries and sent a shudder of horror through the House when it was read (cf. Strype, *Memorials of Cranmer*, ed. 1848, I, 87). Froude, however, adds: "I cannot discuss the insoluble question whether the stories which it contained were true."

Green, in his *Short History of the English People* (ed. 1893, London, II, p. 671), follows the Anglican tradition and says that in the "Black Book": "It was acknowledged that about a third of the religious houses, including the bulk of the larger abbeys, were fairly and decently conducted. The rest were charged with drunkenness, with simony, and with the foulest and most revolting crimes."

belief was based upon the famous "Black Book," which probably never existed, and upon the *Comperta*, or reports of the inquisitors, which all now admit were full of intentional exaggerations.[67] The work of rehabilitation is comparatively recent. It was begun by J. H. Blunt (1869), and continued by Canon Dixon in his *History of the Church of England*, by the editors of *Letters and Papers*, Brewer and Gairdner, and by Dom (afterwards Cardinal) Gasquet in his *Henry VIII and the English Monasteries*. No modern historian repeats the old accusations. It is generally agreed that "when Henry VIII took upon himself to shut up all monasteries throughout the land, to appropriate their possessions, and to turn their inmates adrift, he accomplished his work in a tyrannical, unjust, cruel and covetous manner."[68] "The defaming of the monasteries," remarks J. Gairdner,[68a] "was simply a step towards the confiscation of their endowments; and apart from the gratification of avarice, their suppression was a necessary step in the policy which the king and Cromwell had been carefully engineering." While some of the king's counsellors noted how deeply the religious orders were attached to Rome, that their wealth was one quarter of that of the whole kingdom, that they needed visiting and reforming, and were pleased to see both the religious themselves and their houses decreased in numbers, yet, with the exception of Cromwell, not one of them advised a suppression which no necessity could justify, a suppression by which "scandal would be given to the world" and which would "be construed an encroachment upon public right, and defeating a title which hath both human and divine laws for its establishment."[69]

Yet it cannot be denied that the English monasteries, like many others elsewhere,[70] stood in need of a certain reform. They were no longer the schools of learning they had been,

---

[67] See below, pp. 161 *sq.* Cf. Sander, *op. cit.*, Lewis' trans., 129–30.

[68] Blunt, I, 278. The Protestant Bishop of Hereford, H. Henson, declared (*Church of England*, London, 1917) that the abuses did not cause the fall of the monasteries.

[68a] *Lollardy*, II, 88.

[69] Two speeches by royal councillors, in Collier, IV, 288–91. Cf. speech in the Upper House, Dodd, I, 302 *sq.*

[70] The Council of Trent took their reform in hand (Session XXV, chap. I, 22).

with a reputation commanding respect.[71]   Although the "visitations of religious houses," carried out to correct abuses, notice only the violations of rules and do not mention the many fruits of their strict observance, still the publication of those "visitations," together with Miss Eileen Power's study of them,[72] proves that in the second half of the fifteenth century the number, nature and gravity of the faults committed by the monks and nuns only succeeded in discrediting them in the eyes of their contemporaries, and deterred the latter from founding other religious houses.   When Bishop West of Ely visited the monastery in that city, in 1516, he alluded to deplorable disorders therein.[73]   Ghinucci, the Italian Bishop of Worcester, wrote from Rome, in 1518, saying that he had often been struck by the necessity for reform in the English monasteries.[74]   In 1521, when Henry VIII was still full of zeal for the Church, he thanked the Bishop of Salisbury for putting out and excluding the nuns from their

[71] This reputation had passed to the universities, to which moreover they now sent some of their students.   They no longer wrote chronicles; and with the exception of three Carthusians, Reynolds, Middlemore, and Exmew (cf. *L. and P.*, X, 975; H. Clifford, *Life of Jane Dormer*, ed. Stevenson, p. 17), no English religious are mentioned as contributing to the progress of letters by their culture.   Besides their work in the fields, they did embroidery and engravings and painted or copied manuscripts.

[72] Miss Power (*op. cit.*, pp. 693-97) gives the list of published and unpublished episcopal registers of the visitations.   G. Lohr, O.P. (*Die Kapite der Provinz Saxonia im Zeitalter der Kirchenspaltung, 1513-40*, Leipzic, 1930), observes that the deviations from the regular life, noticeable among the German Dominicans as elsewhere, concerned concrete and individual cases which most frequently proved to be exceptions, and also that the documents designed to reform these abnormal situations in no wise reflect the exact position of the religious orders involved.   We might say the same of the registers of visitations in England.   This is also the opinion of Mr. Cheney, the learned critic who has classified and elucidated a number of documents dealing with the episcopal visitations for the whole medieval period.   He regrets that historians have made use of the records of episcopal visitations solely for the purpose of noting the vices of the monks or the maladministration of the monasteries, whilst neglecting the other sources of information which would have corrected a judgment by far too simplistic (C. R. Cheney, *Episcopal Visitations of Monasteries in the thirteenth century*, Manchester University Press, 1931).   The bibliography of *Episcopal Registers of England and Wales* (S.P.C.K., 1918) has been published by R. C. Fowler in the series "Helps for Students of History," and Clifford J. Offer has drawn from them general conclusions, some of which (first section of the book) concern monastic life: *The Bishops' Register*, S.P.C.K., 1929 (cf. *Ana. Boll.*, 1931, p. 192).

[73] *L. and P.*, II, 1733.

[74] *L. and P.*, II, 4399.

convent at Bromehall "for such enormities as was by them used contrary to their religion."[75] Shortly before the suppression of the monasteries (September 10th, 1535), the Archbishop of York condemned a nun, found guilty of grave immorality, to be placed in confinement and given only abstinence fare. The Franciscan Peto, who had to flee from the king's wrath and who afterwards became a cardinal, admits that there were grave abuses in the monasteries.[76] And the almost universal defection of the religious at the time of the schism proves better than anything else that they had lost their first fervour. <u>These motives might have been a reason for reforming the monasteries, but they were no excuse for dissolving them.</u> If certain people still insist on the faults of a few religious persons here and there, none can maintain that when Cromwell and the king took their property away they were seeking to make the monks better. They were not scandalized by their lives until they were tempted by their wealth.[77]

[75] This was a convent dissolved at Fisher's request, so that the revenue could be applied to St. John's College, Cambridge (*L. and P.*, III, 1863. Cf. also III, 77, 533, 567, 569, 600, 693, 1600; IV, 4900).

[76] Gasquet, *op. cit.*, I, 334. *Dict. of Nat. Biography*, XLV, 89. Cf. Chapuys' letter of 1532 on the Cistercian monasteries (*L. and P.*, III, 361); Sir Thomas More's satires; Bishop R. Fox's letters; chap. XI in the work written by Miss Power, who belongs somewhat to G. G. Coulton's school, of whom we are about to speak (next note).

[77] G. G. Coulton, to whom are due many studies on the Middle Ages (*A Medieval Garner*, London, 1910; *Social Life in Britain from the Conquest to the Reformation*, Cambridge, 1923–27, 2 vols; *The Medieval Village*, Cambridge, 1925; *Art and the Reformation*, Oxford, 1928), and who for quite a long time has undertaken the publication of the episcopal registers dealing with the visitation of the monasteries, has declared a kind of campaign against the work of rehabilitation of which we have just spoken (p. 153). He attacked Blunt, Dixon, and especially Cardinal Gasquet, whom he accused of having given some inaccurate references, and of not knowing sufficiently the registers relating to the episcopal visitations, and whose conclusions, according to him, James Gairdner, at the end of his life, found less convincing than at first (cf. *The Athenæum*, June 22nd and 29th, 1899, and the *Nineteenth Century and After*, July, 1909). In an article in the *Scottish Review* (July, 1928) he resumed the question, and like Creighton before him (cf. *Eng. Hist. Review*, 1888, p. 378), he pretended that the monastic dissolution could not be understood completely till the mass of documents on the episcopal visitations had been exploited and scholars had agreed together upon their strict interpretation. He not only forgets that the visitations, being designed solely to correct faults, are not concerned with what is good and virtuous, but he delights—as Professor Tout, who is himself well versed in the Middle Ages, pointed out when he rebuked him—in piling up hundreds of pages full of wearisome details on the

The work of suppression began with the visitation of the monasteries. This inspection was carried out, not disinterestedly like the visitation by the bishops who sought to correct those of the religious who needed it, but with the formal intention of finding motives for their expulsion.[78]

In January, 1535, Henry VIII named twelve commissioners for the valuation of monastic property, and delegated to Cromwell, his vicar-general, power to visit, personally or by his agents, the monasteries, churches, and clergy[79]; and a royal act, consisting of twenty-six articles, appointed a commission of enquiry for all the religious houses.[80] But the bishops did not seem at all disposed to concede to others their jurisdiction over these houses.[81] It was not until the month of July (1535) that Cromwell authorized Richard Layton, a

monks' vices, his only fear being that he might miss some or else not put them sufficiently in relief in his prefaces and notes. Both Anglicans and Catholics blame these voluminous writings for their violent anti-Catholic prejudices, as well as for the *odium theologicum* with which he pursues Cardinal Gasquet and which tends to weaken the rectitude of his judgments (cf. n. 69, chap. 1). Despite the cardinal's death, in April 1929, the third edition of *Ten Medieval Studies* (1930) renews the attack upon him with greater force and with increasing bitterness. In *Romanism and Truth* (2 vols., Faith Press, 1930 and 1931) G. G. Coulton reproves G. K. Chesterton and Hilaire Belloc; the second volume is entitled *The Struggle against Commonsense*. His arguments are adopted, in no less acrimonious fashion, by the Rev. R. Mercer Wilson (*Before the Reformation.* Lectures recently delivered before the Alumni Association of Wycliffe College, Toronto, 1930). This author attacks Cardinal Gasquet, G. K. Chesterton and Hilaire Belloc. Ch. Reginald Haines' book, *Dover Priory* (1930), is written in much the same vein. The *Times Literary Supplement* (August 21st, 1930) said that it gave a false idea of monastic life in general. The preface was written by G. G. Coulton, whose prejudices are apparent in what he has written, as also in *Five Centuries of Religion* (Cambridge, 1928) and in *Life in the Middle Ages* (4 vols., Cambridge University Press, 1929-30). Another work by G. G. Coulton appeared in 1933: *Scottish Abbeys and Social Life*.

[78] Cf. Gasquet, *op. cit.*, I, 329; see chap. x in Froude, "The Visitation of the Monasteries"; Strype, *Memorials of Cranmer*, I, 73 *sq.*, ed. 1848.

[79] Cf. Collier, IV, 295; Merriman, I, 166. See the appointment of the commissioners for the computation of ecclesiastical and monastic goods, in Collier, IX, 119.

[80] This Act was abundantly corrected and annotated by Cromwell. *L. and P.*, VIII, 75, 76. See the king's two instructions on the visitation of the monasteries, in Burnet, IV, 207, 222.

[81] The King's Council, according to Lord Herbert (cf. *L. and P.*, II, 224), was forced to accept the scheme of dissolution. As the Council's Journal for the period is missing there is no means of verifying this assertion. See, however, p. 153 and n. 69.

clerk of the King's Council,[82] to visit the monasteries in Gloucestershire,[83] and gave a similar mission for Worcestershire to Dr. Leigh,[84] who was accompanied by John Ap Rice.[85] To their number were soon added Dr. London and Bedyll, who had already been employed in receiving the oath given to the "supreme head." In September, the inquisitors suggested to Cromwell that he should suspend the episcopal jurisdiction over the monasteries to prevent the bishops from visiting them at all. They argued that the bishops held their jurisdiction solely from the king, who could take it from them at his pleasure and delegate it to others.[86] The argument met with approval, and thenceforward the royal commissioners visited the religious houses alone.[87] But the haste with which they carried out their enquiries became them better as agents of Cromwell than as conscientious investigators of the truth.

In less than three months (August-October, 1535) Leigh had visited Wiltshire, Hampshire, Berkshire, Surrey, Bedfordshire, Cambridgeshire, Essex, Norfolk and Suffolk. In the same period, Layton called at Cirencester, Bath, Bristol, Bruton, Glastonbury and Oxford. He then proceeded into Surrey and Sussex, where he met with "devilish monks," and on into Kent, where he was able to announce the fall of three religious houses, before the end of October. At this time the universities of Oxford and Cambridge were looked upon almost as monastic institutions. Layton, therefore, visited Oxford and Leigh the sister university. They abolished the study of scholastic philosophy and of canon law, and imposed

[82] He had examined Fisher and More in the Tower.

[83] *L. and P.*, VIII, 822, 1127.

[84] He had examined one of Fisher's servants in the Tower (cf. Sander, *op. cit.*, Lewis' trans., pp. 129–30).

[85] *L. and P.*, IX, 139. In June, Layton had asked Cromwell, but without success, to send him with Leigh to the North, where he had numerous friends, which fact, he said, would facilitate their inquiries (Wright, *Letters relating to the Suppression of Monasteries*, p. 156).

[86] See, in Collier (IV, 294–96) their letter to Cromwell, asking that episcopal jurisdiction should be suspended, and pretending that thus the king's jurisdiction would be made stronger. Generally the order suspending their jurisdiction is transmitted to the bishops by the Primate. Cf. Cromwell's letter to his colleagues, September 18th, 1535 (*ibid.*, IX, 123) and their answer of the following September 24th (Strype, *Eccles. Memorials*, I, Part 2, p. 216).

[87] Cf. Fisher, *op. cit.*, p. 374.

public lectures in Greek and Hebrew.[88]   In the religious
houses all who were twenty-four years old and had taken their
vows before they were twenty were ordered by the commissioners to leave the cloister.[89]   The rest were subjected to
such troublesome rules and so confined to their houses that it
was hoped by these methods to drive them to depart of their
own accord.   They were obliged to answer a questionnaire
consisting of not less than seventy-five questions for monks, and
eighty-six for nuns.[90]   "Although I reckon it well done that
all were out," wrote Ap Rice to Cromwell, "yet I think it were
best that at their own instant suit they might be dismissed to
avoid calumniation and envy.   And so compelling them to
observe these injunctions ye shall have them all to do
shortly."[91]   ". . . They are going to make a reformation of
them so severe and strange that in the end they will go," wrote
Chapuys, "which is the object the king is aiming at, in order
to have better occasion to seize the property without causing
the people to murmur."[92]   Disobedience and lack of discipline

[88] This was confirmed, in 1536, by Parliament, which insisted that the
pure and sincere teaching of the Word of God and of the Scriptures should
proceed.   Duns Scotus represented scholastic philosophy.   "We have sett
Dunce [Duns Scotus] in Bocardo, and have utterly banisshede hym Oxforde
for ever, with all his blinde glosses, and is nowe made a comon servant
to evere man, faste nailede up upon postes in all comon howses of ease-
ment: *id quod oculis meis vidi*.   And the seconde tyme we came to New
Colege, aftter we hade declarede your injunctions, we fownde all the gret
quadrant court full of the leiffes of Dunce, the wynde blowyng them into
evere corner" (Wright, *op. cit.* 61). Cf. B. Landry, *Duns Scot*, Paris, 1922;
E. Longré, *La philosophie de Duns Scot*, Paris, 1924; C. R. S. Harris, *Duns
Scotus*, Oxford, 1927, 2 vols; K. J. Heilig, *Zum Tode des Joannes Duns Scotus*
(*Histor. Jahrbuch*, 1929, fas. 4); A. Calebaut, *Les séjours du b. Duns Scot à
Paris* (*France franciscaine*, Vol. 12, 1929, pp. 353–73); *Revue des Questions
historiques*, April, 1931, pp. 400–11,where a bibliography of the most recent
works will be found.
[89] Cf. Chapuys' letter, *L. and P.*, IX, No. 434. Some, according to Dixon
(I, 372), were content to regain their liberty.   The decree concerning the
age was ambiguous (cf. Ap Rice's letter, *L. and P.*, IX, No. 622).   The
superior, Stów says in his *Chronicle*, had to give "a priest's gown and forty
shillings of money" to the one who was leaving (cf. Sander, *op. cit.*, Lewis'
trans., pp. 129–130).
[90] *Articuli regiae Inquisitionis in monasticam vitam agentes exponendi* (Burnet.
(IV, 207–17) and Collier (IV, 296–300) have given a summary of them
Part of these articles brought the old rules back into force; thus fasting and
abstinence were to be strictly observed; this was because they had fallen
more or less into desuetude.
[91] *L. and P.*, IX, No. 708,
[92] *L. and P.*, IX, No. 434. The 26 articles of the visitors were so vexatious,
says Fuller (III, 381), that monks and nuns "cast off the cowls and veils
and quitted their convents."

were fostered by granting to any monk who wished to complain against his superior or one of the brethren, the right of appeal to the king's vicar-general.[93] Those who did not wish to obey the discipline of the house, by getting up for Matins or carrying out the rule of fasting and abstinence, obtained a dispensation from Cromwell or the inquisitors.[94] Superiors consequently experienced great difficulty in ruling their houses. All nuns below the age of twenty-five were driven out,[95] and certain authors assert that the visitors tried to seduce them.[96] At times the visitors allowed only the oldest nuns to remain in the convent.[97]

As an immediate effect of these visitations the numbers of the religious were considerably reduced, religious houses were impoverished by the despatch of all their valuable objects to London,[98] their right to sell or lease property was trammelled, and their resources exhausted through the extortions of Cromwell or his agents.[99] "There is a report," wrote Chapuys, "that the king intends the religious of all orders to be free to leave their habits and marry. And that if they will stay in their houses they must live in poverty. He intends to take the rest of the revenue."[100] Religious life was disorganized. "We may form some estimate of the discord and demoralization created within the walls of the monasteries by the proceedings of Cromwell's visitors,"[101] says Gairdner. At times teachers

[93] Wilkins, *Concilia*, III, 786–91. Some examples of these denunciations will be found in Wright, *op. cit.*, p. 133, and in *L. and P.*, IX, 321, 322. Cf. Fuller, III, 381 *sq.*

[94] *L. and P.*, X, 321–22. A dispensation was obtained on payment of a certain sum (*ibid.*, Introd., p. 20).

[95] *L. and P.*, IX, No. 873. Ortiz related the rumour circulating in Rome.

[96] Sander, Lewis' trans., p. 130. Fuller, III, 382 *sq.* Cf. Blunt, I, 316; Miss Jacka (*MS. cit.*, ch. iv) disputes this assertion.

[97] Thus it happened at Little Marlow (Wright, *op. cit.*, p. 55). Stow says "the nuns" were "to have such apparel as secular women wear and to go where they will."

[98] Sander, Lewis' trans., p. 130; Harpsfield, in Ch. Bémont, *op. cit.* pp. 84 and 128. Cf. Wright, *op. cit.*, p. 59; Gasquet, *op. cit.*, I, 272 *sq.*

[99] "I submytt myselfe fulle and holle to your mastershipp, as all my refuge, helpe, and socor is yn yow," the Abbot of Rewley wrote to Cromwell, "glad of my voluntarye mynde to be bounde in obligacion of one hunderd powndes to be payed to your mastershipp, so that our house may be sayvd" (Merriman, Nos. 163, 180). According to some writers, many monasteries appear to have disappeared in this way (cf. Blunt, I, 301).

[100] *L. and P.*, IX, 357.

[101] *L. and P.*, IX, Introd., p. xxiii.

or divinity lecturers were appointed to the monasteries who were sent ostensibly "to read the pure and sincere Word of God," but whose real object was to destroy the "popish services" of the monks,[102] in other words to seduce them from the old rules and traditions. The Abbot of Woburn spoke thus to his brethren: "Brethren, this is a perilous time. Such a scourge was never heard since Christ's passion."[103]

Leigh and Layton, after visiting separately the south of England, went together to carry out their mission in Yorkshire and the other northern dioceses. They went quickly to work because Parliament was due to assemble and to decide on the dissolution of the monasteries. Cromwell had himself personally visited some of the religious houses when journeying with the king. "Cromwell goes round about visiting the abbeys," wrote Chapuys, "making inventories of their goods and revenues, instructing them fully in the tenets of this new sect, turning out of the abbeys monks and nuns who made their profession before they were twenty-five, and leaving the rest free to go out or remain."[104] While Cromwell was striving to suppress the lesser monasteries, he accepted from the greater ones—when he did not demand it —a pension for himself and his son.[105]

The inquisitors, on their rounds, sent the results of their

[102] *L. and P.*, IX, No. 747.

[103] Gasquet, *op. cit.*, I, 283.

Yet more than one of the articles imposed by the royal Injunctions (see Burnet, IV, 217-22) had a useful purpose; and although there can be no doubt about Cromwell's intention at that time, yet it cannot be said that Cranmer, and possibly the king, did not intend to bring about a real and rigorous reform. At every meal a chapter was to be read either from the Old or the New Testament, and every day a lecture on Sacred Scripture given, at which all were to assist, as well as an explanation of the rule by the abbot or prior; the abbot and his guests were to eat at the same table, and to refrain always from partaking of rare or dainty dishes; alms were to be given with discrimination so as not to foster idleness on the part of the monastery's habitual clients. Bishop Latimer's Injunctions to his religious houses (*Sermons and Remains of Hugh Latimer*, Cambridge, 1845, II, 204 *sq.*) in particular prescribed the "lecture of scripture every day in English."

[104] *L. and P.*, IX, No. 434. The king and Cromwell travelled in the west and the south from the end of July to the beginning of October, 1535, their object being not only to hunt and to win the affection of the neighbouring population in Wales (*L. and P.*, IX, 58) but also to ascertain the state of the religious houses in that part of England.

[105] The abbot and monastery of Bury St Edmunds to Cromwell, November 26th, 1536 (Collier, IX, 157).

visits, in writing, to the minister.[106]   In addition, they despatched reports, known as *Comperta*, on the morality of the religious houses.[107]   The *Comperta* was the title given to the reports made by the bishops when they visited the monasteries. But whereas the latter aimed at the material and spiritual improvement of the houses visited, the *Comperta* compiled by the royal commissioners had no other end than to encompass their destruction.   The former contained counsels, the latter solely imputations of immorality.

So violent are those imputations that, if they were true, the English monasteries deserved a name other than that of religious houses.   No doubt there were scandals here and there, but there are grave reasons for believing that the visitors purposely exaggerated.[108]   First of all, the accusations were drawn up in such a way that it is impossible to tell whether the fault was committed before or after the person had adopted the religious life; where the women were concerned it frequently happened that they took the veil to efface some previous fault.[109]   In the majority of cases only the names of the guilty persons are given, and the innocent ones are not mentioned, so that it becomes impossible to establish a just and true proportion.   Prompted by the end they had in view, the inquisitors probably made use of every possible means to induce the religious to accuse one another.   Too often they were satisfied with vague rumours and improbable tales.[110] How did they know about those "private and personal vices" with which most of the accused religious persons were charged? Where were their proofs?   "I rather suspect that vices are

[106] The Camden Society published extracts from this correspondence, "The Suppression of the Monasteries," edited by Wright and taken from the Cotton MSS. in the British Museum (Cleop. IV, E). Many letters still remain in the Record Office.

[107] The *Comperta* of fourteen monasteries in the south were published by the Protestant Bishop Bale: "Pageant of Popes," part of which was republished in Speed's History (3rd ed.).   The *Comperta* of the diocese of York, Coventry, Lichfield and Norwich are preserved in the Record Office.   No. 364, Vol. X, *L. and P.*, gives a summary of the letters and reports addressed to Cromwell by his agents.

[108] Under the name of each monastery is given a list of the members living therein, which is divided into two columns, one of which bears the heading "Private and personal vice," and the other "Incontinence." This is followed by the names of those desiring to leave the religious life.

[109] *L. and P.*, X, Introd., p. lxiii.

[110] See examples given by Gasquet, *op. cit.*, I, 343.

feigned or exaggerated," said Edmund Burke,[111] "when profit is looked for in their punishment. An enemy is a bad witness: a robber is a worse." Many of the monasteries, which Layton or Leigh had noted as being very bad, were visited some time afterwards by another commission composed of gentlemen of the neighbourhood, and these men frequently gave quite a different opinion[112]; and more than one religious house condemned by the two inquisitors was still in existence after the law of 1535, which should have caused them to disappear.[113] After the monasteries had been suppressed, eleven priors or abbots were made bishops by Henry.[114] All the religious houses were not visited: "To judge by the proportion in Yorkshire," says Gairdner,[115] "the visitors only examined about four out of ten houses." And even the houses which were visited were seen so rapidly—ninety, for instance, in a fortnight in the diocese of York—that there was no time for a very serious enquiry.[116]

The uniformity of the accusations, on the one hand, renders this kind of hasty catalogue suspect. Whilst, on the other, the numerous crimes with which certain members of the community were charged would have required several weeks' investigation, whereas the inquisitors were running from one house to another. "The investigations," Gairdner observes, "could hardly have been very judicially conducted." Against thirty of the monasteries nothing could be found except their revenues.[117] Of the one hundred and fifty-five monasteries given in the *Compendium Compertorum* forty-three were simply accused of possessing relics. In certain houses the religious life was so much above suspicion and so edifying that the very inquisitors, though little addicted to scruples or sentiment,

[111] *Reflections on the Revolution in France*, 7th ed., 1790, p. 207.
[112] *L. and P.*, X, Introd., p. xlv. The visitors were bound to give the number of monks and the kind of life they led (cf. Wright, *op. cit.*, p. 136).
[113] Cf. Fisher, *op. cit.*, p. 380.
[114] Salcot was made Bishop of Bangor, Kitchin of Llandaff, More of Colchester, Holgate of Llandaff, Hilsey of Rochester, Rugg of Norwich, Holbeach of Rochester, Chambers of Peterborough, Barlow of St David's, Bush of Bristol, Parfew of St Asaph.
[115] *L. and P.*, X, Introd., p. xlv.
[116] The visitors' letters prove that they hastened from one monastery to another. See above, p. 157; Wright, *op. cit.*, p. 72.
[117] Dixon (I, 352 n.) gives a list of them according to a document in the Record Office and in the Cotton Library.

could not help imploring Cromwell's pity for them. "The house of Catesby," the commissioners say, "we found in very perfect order, the prioress a pure, wise, discreet and very religious woman with nine nuns under her obedience, as religious and devout, and with as good obedience as we have in time past seen or belike shall see. The said house standeth in such a quarter much to the relief of the king's people, and his grace's poor subjects there likewise much relieved, as by the reports of divers worshipful (men) near thereunto adjoining, as of all other that is to us openly declared. Wherefore if it should please the king's highness to have any remorse that any such religious house shall stand, we think his grace cannot appoint any house more meet to show his most gracious charity and pity to than to the said house of Catesby."[118] If Cromwell's visitors said nothing of the services rendered by the monasteries which they were appointed to suppress, the Pilgrimage of Grace[119] declared that "the abbeys in the north parts gave great alms to poor men and laudably served God . . . also all gentlemen (were) succoured in their needs . . . and in nunneries their daughters brought up in virtue. . . . And such abbeys as were near the danger of sea banks were great maintainers of sea walls and dykes, maintainers and builders of bridges (and) highways . . . and many of the said abbeys were in mountains and desert places . . ." and "never was in these parts denied either horsemeat or man's meat."[120] Finally the doubtful character of the visitors—their task could have been entrusted to honest men—throws an unfavourable light upon their reports. Layton, the priest—formerly in Wolsey's service with Cromwell—Dr. London, Thomas Leigh and John Ap Rice were all vicious, rapacious,

[118] This letter (Ellis, *Original Letters*, II, p. 72) [cf. Gasquet, *op. cit.*, II 210.—*Translator*] was addressed to Cromwell by E. Knyghtley, Lane, Gyffard and Burgoyn. But this convent of Catesby, despite the permission accorded to fifty-two others to continue after the law against the lesser monasteries (cf. below, p. 168), was suppressed as early as 1536; there could be no better proof that the object the government had in view was less monastic reform than monastic spoliation. Fuller (III, 386 *sq.*), whom Speed follows (*History of Great Britain*) in his serious accusations against certain religious, confesses that more than one monastery gave an example of a life so edifying and useful that the visitors themselves interceded in their favour.

[119] Cf. below, p. 168 *sq.*

[120] *L. and P.*, XII, I, 405, 901. Cf. Savine, *op. cit.*, 224–45, 262 *sq.*

vulgar liars, of doubtful morality. Leigh, who went about with a retinue of twelve servants in livery,[121] was, according to his colleague Ap Rice,[122] "too insolent and pompatique," "a young man of intolerable elation," who was overbearing and insolent towards the abbots and superiors, extorting from them as much money as he could. He became master of Sherburn hospital and in that post robbed the poor of what belonged to them. Layton, who, after holding the living of Harrow-on-the-Hill, became Dean of York, was not less susceptible to bribes, and appropriated the gold and silver crosses of the monasteries. He crudely related to Cromwell, "to make you laugh," all the scandalous stories he thought he had unearthed. It was he who suggested the visitation of the monasteries to Cromwell, and earnestly entreated the latter, for interested motives of his own, to allow Leigh and himself to undertake the work. London, the Dean of Wallingford, who visited many nunneries, was shortly afterwards made to perform public penance for repeated acts of immorality. It was proposed to appoint Ap Rice to some office in the cathedral church of Salisbury, but the dean and chapter vigorously protested.

These inquisitors, always seeking preferment, watching for any blameworthy action, and ready to accept as evident proof every slanderous rumour, were not men whose word could be relied upon. Yet such were the majority of the men, according to their own contemporaries and the statements of English historians, whom the king employed to pave the way for the suppression of the monasteries. "Most of the persons whom he used as his agents in the business were unprincipled men for whom not a word of good can be justly said; and most of those who encouraged and assisted the king in the dissolution did so for selfish objects, and for selfish objects alone . . . the general impression of contemporaries was that they were men

[121] Cf. Burnet, III, 241. In addition to these four principal inquisitors, the following also visited the monasteries: The suffragan Bishop of Dover, Richard Ingworth, William Petre, Thomas Bedyll, George Gyffard, Henry Polsted, John Anthony, Knyghtley, Lane, Robert Burgoyn, John Williams, Richard Pollard, Philip Paris, John Smith, William Hendle, Richard Bellasys, Richard Watkyns and William Parr. The documents prove that it was easy to bribe the inquisitors of 1536. Cf. G. Baskerville, "The dispossessed religious after the suppression of the monasteries," in *Essays in History, presented to Richard Lane Poole*, Oxford, 1927, p. 458.

[122] H. Ellis, *Original Letters*, 3rd Series, II, p. 356.

of no principle, sent out with certain nominal objects in view, but really pledged to foregone conclusions and to the accomplishment of as much confiscation as they could manage."[123] "Men of as prying eyes as afterwards they proved of gripple hands," Fuller describes them,[124] they "were men who well understood the message they were sent on, and would not come back without a satisfactory answer to him who sent them, knowing themselves to be no losers thereby."

For all these reasons there is no modern historian who does not suspect the *Comperta* of falsehood or exaggeration.[125] Yet the English monasteries were tried and condemned on their evidence. As for the "Black Book" which is supposed to have been placed before Parliament in 1536, in all probability it never existed. It is not until Elizabeth's time that the name "Black Book" is mentioned; it first occurs in a document drawn up for the queen's information called the "mode of dissolving the abbeys." "This was showed in parliament," its author asserts, "and the villanies made known and abhorred."[126]

When the inquisitors had finished their task and delivered their reports to Cromwell, a Bill was submitted to Parliament, in its seventh and final session, aiming at the dissolution of the lesser monasteries. The temper of this Parliament, styled the "Long" or "Reformation" Parliament, is already known to

[123] Blunt, I, 279, 296-97, 355-60. Cf. Collier (IV, 292 *sq.*), who summarizes Layton's letter to Cromwell insisting that he be charged with the visitation together with Leigh. The Benedictine Abbess of Godstow's letter, and London's (Wright, pp. 227, 229; Burnet, VI, 192; Ellis, *Original Letters*, 3rd Series, III, p. 233) will give an idea of London's behaviour towards the nuns: Cromwell was obliged to decide against his agent and to forbid him to proceed any further (cf. Dodd, 219 *sq.*).

[124] *Church History*, ed. 1845, III, 369, 380.

[125] It was believed, according to a legend spread abroad in Elizabeth's time, that the *Comperta* were founded on the confessions of religious tormented by their conscience. But the two alleged confessions which survive are documents drawn up at the period of the *surrenders*, not by monks tormented by remorse, but by the royal commissioners, and signed by some of the religious in return for a pension (cf. Gasquet, *op. cit.*, I, 348 *sq.*; Dixon, I, 18-21, 354).

[126] Wright, pp. 112, 114; Gasquet, I, 303. Burnet (II, 547) supposes that the "Black Book" was burnt in Mary Tudor's time; there is nothing to confirm such systematic destruction; the preamble of the law of 1536 does not mention the "Black Book," whereas it cites the *Comperta* (cf. Dixon, I, 342; J. Gairdner, *History*, 166 *sq.*).

us.[127] This same Parliament had assisted Henry, from 1531–1534, in making the schismatic laws. It is not necessary therefore to allege royal pressure in order to explain the passing of this Bill. Of the debate which took place on this occasion we know practically nothing. Sir Henry Spelman, who wrote his *History of Sacrilege* a century later, gives the traditional account thus: Henry "commanded the commons to attend him in the forenoon in his gallery, where he let them wait till late in the afternoon, and then coming out of his chamber, walking a turn or two among them, and looking angrily on them. . . . 'I hear' (saith he) 'that my bill will not pass, but I will have it pass, or I will have some of your heads.' " This account, for which there is no documentary confirmation,[128] appears to be somewhat inconsistent with Henry VIII's character and manner, for he affected an extreme deference towards the Commons, and overwhelmed them with flattery.[129] Besides, if the dissolution of the monasteries was due to the greed of the nobility and gentry,[130] the threat of capital punishment seems to be quite superfluous. But this Act exactly fulfilled the ardent desires of those who passed it. The monastic property was given to the king, the preamble stated, "that his highness may lawfully give, grant, and dispose them, or any of them, at his will and pleasure to the honour of God and the wealth of this realm."[131]   Parliament might have feared that the Crown would become too wealthy, and for that reason have opposed the law; but it was formally promised a share in the spoils, and so the Act passed. Even the great and wealthy abbots, who were a powerful party in the House of Lords (of the fifty-two ecclesiastical peers thirty were abbots), do not appear to have offered any serious resistance. Possibly, as Hall and

[127] See Chap. I.

[128] Sir Henry Spelman's (1564?–1641) *History*, written in 1633, was not published till after his death, in 1698. The passage quoted is on page 183 of that edition, p. 206 of the 1853 ed., and p. 99 of the 1888 ed.

Chapuys, who never misses an occasion of noting anything unfavourable to the king, makes no remark of this kind. And so Gairdner (*Eng. Church in the XVIth cent.*, p. 166) says, "by what pressure the consent of the two Houses was obtained to this measure it might be rash to affirm."

[129] We have a positive instance of pressure; but it concerns the next Parliament, and the author of it was Cromwell, who had made the elections (cf. Gasquet, I, 299).

[130] Cf. above, pp. 151 *sq.*

[131] *Statutes of the Realm*, 27 Henry VIII, cap. 28.

Fuller observe, they hoped to save their abbeys by sacrificing the lesser monasteries. Yet more than one abbot was absent when this business, which affected them so closely, was brought before Parliament. Could they be expected to oppose the dissolution of the monasteries after having consented to renounce the authority of the Pope? Still Dodd does give a speech made by a vigorous opponent of the Bill in the House of Lords.[132]

The enacting clauses of this Bill provided for the suppression of monasteries with a yearly income of less than £200. It was also ordered that the new possessors should provide hospitality and education for the poor, and that occupations and pensions should be given to the monks and nuns not transferred to other monasteries.[133] The preamble of the Act[134] begins by giving what is probably a summary of the grievances brought forward by the government during the debate, and then notes how every attempt at reform for the past two hundred years had been defeated, and contrasts "the vicious, carnal and abominable living" in the smaller religious houses as proved "as well by the compts of the late visitations as by sundry credible informations," with the religious life in the "great, solemn monasteries wherein (thanks be to God) religion is right well kept and observed," as though twelve—the number of inmates which determined, according to the law, whether a house was to be condemned or spared—was also the line of demarcation between virtue and vice.[135] "It

[132] Cf. French ed. of this book, chap. 1, n. 138; Dixon, II, 132. See in Dodd (ed. 1737, I, 302 *sq.*) the speech made in the Upper House against the monastic spoliation. "Catholick honour, the Catholick faith should be so deeply wounded. For God's, and your own goodness' sake, leave not to posterity so great a blemish. . . . If liberty take place of faith, farewell religion. The Turk may then direct us how to guide in rapine, blood and murder."

[133] Among the religious the priests were to receive a post among the secular clergy; the superior alone had a right to a pension. None of the religious was admitted to work in the parishes without a legal dispensation and permission from the Ordinary (Cranmer's Prescriptions for the visitation of the diocese of Hereford, 1538, Burnet, IV, 392).

[134] *Statutes of the realm*, 29 Henry VIII, cap. 28. It is given in full by Fuller (*op. cit.*, ed. 1845, III, pp. 371 *sq.*), Dodd (ed. 1737, I, 303), and Froude, in chap. x of the "Visitation of the Monasteries."

[135] "The smallest convents were the greatest sinners," observes Fuller (ed. 1845, III, 373). "But God first punished great Sodom and spared little Zoar, though probably also in fault. Here Zoar was first punished." See *ibid.*, pp. 373–77, Fuller's various criticisms on the suppression of the

shall be much more to the pleasure of Almighty God that these possessions . . . wasted for increase and maintenance of sin, should be used and converted to better uses, and the unthrifty religious persons so spending the same to be compelled to reform their lives."

Three hundred and twenty-seven religious houses—of which two hundred and twenty-four belonged to men, and one hundred and three to women—having a revenue of less than £200, were affected by the law.[136] The king, however, allowed fifty-two of them to stand in return for the payment of an annual sum,[137] and in 1537 he re-established two that had previously been dissolved.[138] These exceptions appear to indicate that at that time the king had not thought of making the dissolution a general one. The two counties most affected by the law were York and Lincoln. In the former fifty-three religious houses disappeared, and thirty-seven in the latter.[139]

At the same time Parliament created a new administrative department with the significant title "Court of Augmentation," a court, in other words, for augmenting the revenues of the crown. It began to function on April 24th, 1536, and did not cease until 1541, when all the religious houses in

lesser monasteries.—This number, twelve, was evidently suggested by Clement VII's Bull, which authorized Wolsey, in 1528, to suppress the religious houses in which there were less than twelve religious; they were to be transferred to other abbeys (see above, pp. 144–5).

[136] This is the number given in J. Gairdner's list (*History*, pp. 419–24). According to *L. and P.* (X, No. 1238) the number was 362 (360 according to Sander, Lewis' trans., p. 131, n. 1) and 376 according to various authors (Dixon, I, 365; Fisher, 380). See Burnet, IV, pp. 232 *sq.*

[137] Gasquet (II, App. I) and Gairdner (*History*, 420 *sq.*) give, according to Stevens' list (cf. Burnet, IV, 231, n. 9), the fifty-two monasteries which were able to survive the first law; but this number, which is increased by some to one hundred and twenty-three, is reduced by Burnet (IV, 227) whom Dixon (I, 365) follows, to thirty-one; Burnet's list, in which the royal authorizations of 1538–39 are lacking, was completed by Pocock in 1845 from the *Patent Act Rolls*, and comprises fifty-three religious houses (*ibid.*, IV, 230–32; cf. Dugdale, *Monasticon*, II, 454; VI, 378). Others raise the number to one hundred and twenty-three. The revenue varied from £20 to £100.

[138] These last two were the nunnery of Stixwold (Lincolnshire) and the monastery of Bisham (Berks), opened in July and December, 1537, to be closed again by "surrender" the following year (cf. J. Gairdner, *History*, pp. 196 *sq.*, and 420).

[139] Fisher (*op. cit.*) gives a map of the chief religious houses of the north, both of men (Premonstratensians, Cistercians, Canons Regular or Gilbertines) and of women (Gilbertines, Benedictines).

England had been destroyed; even then Mary Tudor's accession was necessary to suppress it (1553). Its officials were numerous and well paid; they cost the crown £7,250 every year. But the wealth they controlled was of little use for the public weal.[140] "He (Henry) ought therefore to have surpassed every prince in Christendom in his wealth of silver and gold"; says Sander,[141] "but it was not so, for by the just judgment of God it was far otherwise with him, for within a few years after the plunder of the monasteries he was a far poorer man than either he himself or his ancestors had ever been before. Yea, he alone laid heavier taxes upon the people than all the kings together had done during the five hundred years that were past."

Instructions were issued immediately (April 24th, 1536) to the various counties. Local commissions were set up, consisting of six visitors, to re-examine the state of the religious houses, draw up an inventory of the property, ascertain which houses were under the annual value of £200, and to ask the monks whether they wished to return to the world or enter another house.[142]

The work of destruction had begun; and it was speedily accomplished. Gold flowed into the Court of Augmentation. The annual receipts were £32,000, and over £100,000 were received as proceeds from the sale of bells, plate and jewels, furniture and material of the religious houses.[143] Two thousand religious were despoiled of their property, and ten thousand servants and tenants lost their means of livelihood.[144]

[140] Cf. Fisher, op. cit., 380-81. For the Court of Augmentation, see Fuller, ed. 1845, III, 464 sq.

[141] Op. cit., Lewis' trans., pp. 155-56.

[142] The commission was made up of three gentlemen of the neighbourhood nominated by the king, and of three royal officials (an auditor, the particular receiver of the county and a secretary). While it was making a sort of counter-enquiry on the conduct and lives of the religious (cf. p. 162) its mission was to draw up an inventory of the properties and rents, and to discover who wished to abandon and who to continue the religious life. The commissioners' reports were used to establish the *Valor ecclesiasticus*, published between 1810 and 1834, which has been studied by Savine. The instructions for this visitation of the monasteries, aiming at their dissolution, will be found in Burnet, IV, 304-308.

[143] These figures are given by Stow (*Chronicle*, 1615, p. 172) and by Lord Herbert (ed. 1863, 441).

[144] Again, these are the figures given by Stow (cf. Gasquet, II, 28; Fisher, op. cit., p. 380).

"It is a lamentable thing," wrote Chapuys at this period, "to see a legion of monks and nuns, who have been chased from their monasteries, wandering miserably hither and thither seeking means to live."[145] The most humble and touching petitions of the poor nuns, brutally snatched from their pious retreats, were unable to move the hearts of Cromwell and the king. The nuns of Legbourne wrote to their patron in these terms[146]: "Where" men recognize "as we do[e] here that all Abbyes and Pryores undir the value of CC[li] be at our most noble Prince's pleasure to subpresse and put downe. Yet if it may pleas your goodness, we trust in God ye shall here no compleynts agaynst us, nother in our lyving nor hospitaltie kepyng. In consideration whereof if it may please your goodness, in our great necessitie, to be a meane and sewter for your owne Powre Pryory, that it may be preserved and stand, you shalbe a more higher Founder to us than he that first foundid oure House. We have noon othir comfort nor refuge but oonly unto your goodnes, and we hooly submyt ourselfs to the pleasure of God, to the pleasure of our Prince, and to the pleasure of you our Founder; and how soever it shall please God that we shalbe orderid, we shall continue your faithfull and dayly bedewomen." There were some pensions promised, but only for the superiors. The ordinary religious were dismissed with a small gratuity. In certain areas the people were roused by these long processions of monks and nuns, from whom they had formerly received alms, work, and pensions, and who now went from door to door begging for food and lodgings. The old monastic chapels

[145] *L. and P.*, XI, 42. "For it would have made a heart of flint to have melted and wept," says a document written in 1591 by one whose father and uncle had witnessed the scenes described (Ellis, *Original Letters*, 3rd Series, III, 33 *sq.*), "to have seen the breaking up of the House and their sorrowful departure; and the sudden spoil that fell the same day of their departure from the House. And every person had everything good cheap except the poor monks, friars, and nuns, that had no money to bestow of anything." All bowed their heads before the storm, with the exception of the Austin Canons of Hexham (Northumberland) who, armed and accompanied by numerous tenants and servants, put the royal commissioners to flight (*L. and P.*, XI, 504). Henry VIII ordered them to "be tied up without further delay or ceremony" (Lemon, *State Papers during the reign of Henry VIII*, I, 537).

[146] The prioress and the Cistercian nuns of Legbourne (Lincoln) to their patron, 1537 (Ellis, *op. cit.*, 1st Series, II, 74).

had been profaned, plundered and dismantled, and now served as pigeon-lofts.[147] The counties of York and Lincoln, in which the greatest number of religious houses had been dissolved, rose in revolt.

The north of England, which was the most religious part of the country and the most faithful to the ancient faith,[148] was also, from the material point of view, the district most affected by the suppression of the religious houses. It was a land of pastures and agriculture, not given to trade like the south, and consequently bound to suffer inevitably from the agrarian disturbance caused by the distribution of the monastic property and its allocation to other purposes. The religious houses in the mountainous districts near the Scottish borders had been particularly useful for the common good.[149] In Lincolnshire, where the rising began, the dissolution of the lesser monasteries had been advantageous to the Treasury[150]; and it was rumoured that after Michaelmas (1536) the larger monasteries were also to be suppressed. Amongst the rebels there were no doubt many tenants who had been evicted from their farms, and workmen deprived of their livelihood.[151] If some of the noblemen, like Darcy and Hussey, thought to turn the discontent of the people to their own advantage,[152] there were many other country gentlemen who were forced by threats to follow or lead this movement, which had really

[147] Cf. Collier, IV, 322. For the pensions, see below, p. 194 and n. 242.

[148] The denunciations of superiors by their subordinates were rare in the north, but not in the south (cf. *L. and P.*, IX, 314, 321, 322). See Froude, chap. XIII: "The Pilgrimage of Grace"; Fisher, chap. XV, under the same heading; the more recent work by the sisters, M. H. Dodds and R. Dodds, *The Pilgrimage of Grace 1536-1537 and the Exeter Conspiracy, 1538*, 2 vols., Cambridge, 1915; J. S. Fletcher's work, *The Cistercians in Yorkshire*, London, 1918, and the article by W. Self Weekes, "Abbot Paslew and the Pilgrimage of Grace," in *Transactions of the Lancashire and Cheshire Antiquarian Society*, Vol. XLVII, 1930-31. Harspfield (Ch. Bémont, 87 *sq.*) also speaks of the Pilgrimage of Grace.

[149] Cf. J. Wilson, *Vict. Co. Hist. of Cumberland*, II, pp. 44-45.

[150] The royal inspector Freeman had collected £8,756 11s. 9¾d.

[151] Cf. Gay, in *Transactions of the R. Hist. Soc.*, New Series, Vol. XVIII, pp. 208 *sq.*

[152] Cf. Friedmann, *op. cit.*, II, pp. 31 *sq.* Up to 1533 Lord Hussey had been chamberlain to Princess Mary. One of the insurgents' demands was that Mary should be acknowledged as legitimate.

originated among the people,[153] and in which both religious motives and social demands played their part.

The new taxes had displeased the people, and they demanded the abolition of first-fruits and the new "Statute of Uses and Wills."[154]   False rumours were circulating in the northern counties, even as far north as the Scottish borders. It was said that every head of cattle would be marked and a tax paid on it to the king; that white bread, geese, capons, and pigs would be taxed; that heavy taxes would be levied on baptisms, weddings and funerals; and that all the chalices, crosses and other jewels of the church would be taken away, and only a tin chalice left in their stead.   Already they had witnessed the demolition of the religious houses and chapels. They had seen the breaking up of the church bells and the melting of the lead roofs and gutters, and had also seen heavy loads of jewels and valuable articles passing through their towns.   When they heard that the bishop's chancellor and a royal commissioner were coming to take the chalices from their churches and to suppress every parish within a radius of six or seven miles, the people of Louth, already inflamed by the suppression of the neighbouring religious houses at Louth Park and Legbourne, rose in revolt and seized hold of Cromwell's commissioner (October 1st, 1536).   Two days later, they joined the people of Caistor in order to seize the royal commissioners, who were due to collect the taxes recently voted by Parliament, but at the first alarm, the latter set spurs to their horses and escaped.   Religious and social reasons together had started in Lincolnshire the first wave of a movement which was to spread throughout the north of England.

The rebels gathered in force at Horncastle, forty thousand

---

[153] Threats were made that their cattle would be taken, their houses burnt, and attempts would be made against their lives. Despite themselves, the leaders could only attempt to keep this movement within bounds, and its success was certainly spoilt by their own moderation (cf. Fisher, *op. cit.*, p. 400).

[154] This law, which gave to the king the right of relief and first seizin, had been passed in Parliament's last session at the same time as the suppression of the lesser monasteries.   It was unpopular because it allowed no interruption in the payment of feudal dues (cf. Lord Herbert, ed. 1683, p. 626). The king, it was said, imposed such burdens that the widow and children of a deceased man had nothing left but to beg their bread (cf. *L. and P.*, XI, 705, 780; XII, 70; XIII, 307).

in number, of whom sixteen thousand were equipped. They were accompanied by seven or eight hundred priests or monks. On October 6th, they entered Lincoln displaying their banner with the Chalice and Host above it, the Five Wounds, and a plough and a horn, all symbolical of their religious and social aspirations. In addition to the abolition of certain taxes,[155] they demanded the restoration of the religious houses, because they had particularly suffered through their suppression, exemption for the Church from payment of first-fruits and tithes, and the banishment from the kingdom of the chancellor of the Court of Augmentation, the Master of the Rolls, Cromwell, and the bishops who had leanings towards the New Learning.[156] At the same time they asserted their loyalty to the king whom they acknowledged as supreme head of the Church.[157] Their movement, which was neither against the king nor ownership, nor any other established institution, was rather conservative than rebellious in character.[158] That was one of the reasons for its failure. The hesitation and delay caused by their loyalty,[159] or the difference of opinion between the gentry and the ordinary folk,[160] the approach of Suffolk's army[161] and the

[155] In their first petition, which was altered and moderated by the gentry, they demanded that taxes should be paid only in time of war.

[156] The insurgents in Yorkshire also demanded that Cromwell and the heretical bishops should be punished (cf. pp. 175 sq.).

[157] Cf. Pollard, Henry VIII, 353; Fisher, op. cit., 399, 401.

[158] Very few acts of violence, the usual consequence of insurrections, accompanied it. The Bishop of Lincoln's chancellor was slain; Dr. Leigh's cook, who had taken a notable part in the suppression of the monasteries, was hanged; and a man named Wolsey, denounced as a spy, almost met a similar fate.

[159] On October 8th they decided to await the king's reply before marching forward lest they should commit an act of treason.

[160] The gentry, drawn into the movement often despite themselves, did all they could to check and moderate it and to take from it whatever might draw down upon them the royal vengeance. They altered and moderated the first demands; they restrained the impetuous movement of the inhabitants of Beverley and Halifax who were going to march the rebel districts against Suffolk; they prevailed upon them to await the royal answer (see previous note) and so lost for them the advantage of rapidity, which ensures success in war (cf. Fisher, p. 401 sq.).

[161] When Suffolk arrived at Huntingdon on October 9th with the nine hundred men he had gathered together in the south, without munitions or artillery, and the Earl of Shrewsbury was unable to quit Nottingham because he had not wherewith to pay his men, the insurgents could easily have driven the royal army back. But three days later Suffolk and the

raising of a second army at Ampthill, both of which threatened "to invade their countries, to burn, spoil, and destroy their goods, wives and children,"[162] the king's assertion that he had never entertained the intentions ascribed to him and the appeal he made to their loyalty by showing that their demands were presumptuous and their conduct unworthy of loyal subjects, these were all reasons that led the gentry and the common folk to return peacefully to their homes. The rising lasted only a fortnight (October 1st-13th, 1536). Instead of burning, spoiling and destroying men, women and children, in accordance with Henry's brutal command,[163] Suffolk adopted a shrewder policy. He flattered the gentry by appealing to them to pacify the district and thus win the king's pardon. To the people he promised equal clemency if they surrendered their leaders. After a detailed enquiry into the causes of the rising, forty-six of the rebels were executed at Louth, Horncastle, and Lincoln, in March, 1537.

Henry had contemptuously scoffed at their demands in his vigorous answer to "the rude commons of one shire, and that one of the most brute and beastly of the whole realm." Was it for people "of least experience, to find fault with your prince for the electing of his counsellors and prelates"? How great was "their madness in trying to make us break the laws agreed to by the nobles, knights and gentlemen of this realm, whom the same chiefly toucheth"! Did they think the government would be so weak and pusillanimous as to remit to one or more counties the taxes agreed upon by Parliament? "As to the suppression of religious houses and monasteries," he added, "this is granted us by act of parliament, and not set forth by any councillors upon their mere will and fantasy, as ye falsely would persuade our realm to believe. And ye allege that the service of God is much thereby diminished; the truth thereof is contrary, for where the most abominable living was used many or most had not more than four or five religious in them, and divers but one, who spent the goods of their house in nourishing vices. . . . And yet were suffered a

Earl of Southampton, with three thousand men, well mounted, armed and paid, and with sufficient artillery, were stationed at Stamford on the Welland, thirty-six miles from Lincoln.

[162] These are Henry VIII's own words to his commissioners at Lincoln.

[163] *L. and P.*, XI, 780.

great many of them, more than we by the act needed, to stand; wherein if they amend not their living we fear we have more to answer for than for the suppression of all the rest."[164]

Lincolnshire was no sooner appeased than Yorkshire, Cumberland and Westmorland arose in turn (between October 9th and 14th, 1536), and for similar reasons. The insurgents adopted the Lincolnshire demands as well as their banner.[165] As at Lincoln, they appealed to all the classes[166] and to the most varied interests.[167] Their demands were both of a religious and of a social nature. Some wanted guarantees against exorbitant taxation, a remedy for the agrarian evils,[168] the suppression of the clauses restricting testamentary freedom,[169] and the restoration of local liberties.[170] Others were more especially anxious about the maintenance of the ancient faith. The government's behaviour in the matter of the royal divorce made them uneasy. They protested in consequence against the laws tending to exclude Catholics from the throne,[171] or which had caused Fisher and More to be beheaded.[172] They demanded the destruction of all heretical books,[173] the banishment of all suspect bishops, the restoration

---

[164] Lemon, *State Papers*, I, 463. *L. and P.*, XI, 780. Cf. Gasquet, *op. cit.* II, 68.

[165] Copies of the Lincolnshire petition had reached them (cf. Fisher, *op. cit.*, p. 485).

[166] As in Lincolnshire, the gentry were enlisted partly by force (see above, pp. 171 *sq.*). The towns taxed themselves, and the gentry had to bear the costs of the venture.

[167] Cf. *L. and P.*, XII, 188, 786, 900; Smith, *Social England*, III, 21 *sq.*

[168] The right of inclosure was universally disliked: in Westmorland the Cumberland county hedges were thrown down; the tithe-barn at Cockermouth was plundered (see Tawney, Part III, *The Agrarian Problem in the Sixteenth Century*, London, 1912).

In Cumberland and Westmorland, where the miners belonged to the poor class (*L. and P.*, XII, 408, 641), the suppression of the heavy payments due for every renewal of a lease, called "gressums," was demanded (cf. *ibid.*, XII, 478, 687 [I, 2]).

[169] Just as in Lincolnshire, they protested against the "Statute of Uses."

[170] The petition of Pomfret (December 2nd, 1536) demanded that the old customs in Durham, Beverley and Ripon should be restored.

[171] In the same Pomfret petition demands were made that Mary Tudor's legitimacy should be acknowledged, and that the law allowing the king to bequeath the crown in his will as he pleased should be repealed (*L. and P.*, XI, 1246).

[172] The same petition also demanded the abolition of the Act of High Treason of 1534, and the punishment of the solicitor-general Rich, who had directed the trial against More and Fisher.

[173] In reply to the king's letter stating that the insurgents' complaints

of Rome's supremacy, and the punishment of the solicitor-general Rich, the chancellor Audeley—who had destroyed all the good laws of the realm and upheld the heretics—as well as of the inquisitors Layton and Leigh. Cromwell, who was hated by all the aristocracy and by all men of conservative tendencies,[174] was held up to public reprobation as the promoter of the new ideas and the man who instigated the suppression of the religious houses. Robert Aske, the leader of the rising, declared that the suppression of the abbeys and the fear of heresy alone would have sufficed to cause the rising, because the mass of the people had fastened on to these two reasons, whereas the other reasons affected only this or that class of people. Hence they called their movement "The Pilgrimage of Grace." With the cross from the parish church or from a neighbouring abbey at their head, and bearing the badge of the Five Wounds and the Chalice and Host on their breasts, they described themselves as pilgrims marching in defence of the old religion and "for the preservation of Christ's Church." What the crown had to fear was that ideas shared by all the different interests might unite the various classes together against the government, which possessed no permanent army.[175]

The Pilgrims of Grace chose for their leader an unknown Yorkshire solicitor, Robert Aske, who in a few short months was destined to become the best known man in England.[176] Lord Darcy, lord-lieutenant of the county, had withdrawn

on matters of religion were not sufficiently precise, the Pomfret petition cited the books of Huss, Luther, Melanchthon, Tyndale, Barnes and St. Germain (L. and P., XI, 1246). See in Dodd, I, 304, the oath taken by the pilgrims "to the restitution of God's church, and to the suppression of erroneous opinions."

[174] This hatred was increased in the county by the fact that Cromwell had imposed a heavy fine on the Yorkshire jury for not obeying his orders in a murder case.

[175] It was considered at that time as the most dangerous insurrection that had ever taken place (L. and P., XI, 585).

[176] After having hunted in the forests of Yorkshire, at William Ellerkar's, he was returning to London with three of his nephews when some of the rebels interrupted his journey and chose him as captain; having repaired to Lincoln there to await and learn the royal answer to Lincolnshire, and being suspected of betraying the "Pilgrimage of Grace" cause, he tried to flee to the north and hid himself in a humble cottage; there he was taken by the insurgents and placed by them at their head (cf. Eng. Hist. Review, V, 330-45, and 550-73).

with Archbishop Edward Lee to Pomfret (or Pontefract) Castle, which was insufficiently provisioned and garrisoned by only one hundred and forty men.[177] With real oratorical talent, Aske explained the causes of the rising and threatened an immediate assault unless Darcy swore to follow the Pilgrimage of Grace. The castle was surrendered after holding out for only two days. Because he had prevailed upon an archbishop and a peer to join the pilgrims, Aske was nicknamed the "great captain." Hull followed Pomfret's lead, and every day fresh adherents were joining the pilgrim ranks. On October 24th, from thirty-four to thirty-five thousand men, "well tried on horseback," were encamped to the north of Doncaster. Lords Neville, Latimer, and Lumley, with the knights and gentlemen from Cleveland and part of Richmond, commanded by Sir Thomas Percy, were in the van; Lord Darcy, Robert Aske, Sir Robert Constable and the knights and noblemen from the North, East and West Ridings, and from Holderness and Ainsty, in the centre; and Lord Scrope, with the men recruited from Ripon, Wensleydale, Swadale, Netherdale, Kirkbyshire and Mashamshire, formed the rearguard. The army thus consisted of all the fighting elements of Northern England. To have attempted a frontal attack on such a force as this might have led to disaster.

The pilgrims—who had protested against the "worthless blood" at the king's side—were indeed opposed by an army under the orders of the Duke of Norfolk, and commanded by some of the greatest English lords, the Marquis of Exeter, and the Earls of Shrewsbury, Huntingdon and Rutland; but it consisted of only eight thousand men, who were without shelter from the fine rain which was continually falling and nearly all in sympathy with the Pilgrimage cause.[178] Norfolk therefore took the advice of his officers and con-

---

[177] Lord Darcy, aged 70, had previously fought against the Moors in Spain. The royal divorce and the religious changes that it foretold displeased him so much that he spoke to the ambassador Chapuys about landing imperial troops (cf. Friedmann, *op. cit.*, II, pp. 31 *sq.*); if the suppression of a few monasteries by Wolsey appeared as detestable to him as the worst of Luther's acts or articles, what must have been his hatred of the law of 1536 and of its author, Cromwell? Fuller (ed. 1845, III, 407-11) proves that, despite the king's assertion, Darcy's titles and fortunes went much further back and that their origin was in no wise due to Henry,

[178] Norfolk himself admitted it.

cluded a truce with Robert Aske, who was equally anxious to avoid a clash with the royal army (October 27th, 1536). A deputation, accompanied by Norfolk and Shrewsbury, journeyed to Windsor to set forth the county's demands.[179] Henry received them very graciously.

Adopting the tactics which had succeeded against the Lincolnshire insurgents—but with less violence, for he was dealing with a stronger party—Henry refuted each of their demands with all the cleverness of a controversialist. His answer, written in his own hand, is a model of political cunning. Their complaints concerning matters of faith were too general for him to answer; but he swore to live and die in the faith of Christ. Was it meet for ignorant people to teach him what he had to believe? The bishops were "just and true executors" of God's law, and those who calumniated them did so from a distance and had never heard them. What did the insurgents mean by Church liberties? Were those liberties in conformity with, or in opposition to, the laws of the realm? "As for our own self," said Henry, "to our own Church we have done not so much prejudice as many of our predecessors have done upon less ground." So far as the common weal was concerned, had any king secured for his subjects prosperity, justice, and peace better or for a longer period than he, or more effectually protected them against foreign enemies? If there were men of lowly birth in his Council, the number of such men was greater when he came to the throne. The king concluded by offering them a general pardon provided they surrendered their ten principal leaders to him.

Henry had probably hoped in this way to cause divisions among the commoners, the nobility and the gentry, as he had done in Lincolnshire. But nothing of the kind happened.[180] His answer was submitted to two hundred delegates who were not at all pleased with it. Some of them were for using force,[181] but prudent counsels prevailed, and a fresh petition was drawn up at Pomfret, on December 2nd, by theologians, noblemen

[179] The members were Ralph Ellerkar and Robert Bowes.

[180] He was greatly vexed; he wrote to Norfolk to use every means to discredit "that villain Aske" before John Latimer and the other nobles.

[181] Sir Robert Constable wanted to take up a strong stand north of the Trent, and he promised the adherence of the counties of Lancashire, Derbyshire and Cheshire.

and gentry, and afterwards read to the commoners.[182] They asked that a Parliament should be called as soon as possible, at York or Nottingham,[183] to undo the disastrous legislation of the past seven years—passed by a Parliament whose authority they disputed[184]—and to give practical shape to all their religious and social aspirations. Nearly forty thousand armed men supported these demands. Norfolk, who was unable to resist them either by force or by cunning, gave way and promised them a free Parliament, and a general amnesty under the king's seal (December 3rd, 1536).[185]

But with the leaders and the majority of the insurgents their attachment to the crown overshadowed every other consideration. Archbishop Lee had already preached in favour of the king.[186] Darcy would have fallen at the king's feet to surrender his sword, if he had met him on the battle-field.[187] At Doncaster, Aske and his friends had knelt to Norfolk before presenting their demands, and these had no sooner been granted than they tore off their badges, exclaiming: "We will wear no badge nor figure but the badge of our sovereign lord." Loyalty had stifled the rising in Lincolnshire in a very few days; it was likewise destined to cause the miscarriage of the more powerful rising in Yorkshire. As shrewd as he was unscrupulous, Henry saw therein a way out of keeping the promise made in his name. First Aske, and then Darcy and Constable, were summoned to court. No man could be more charming than the king when he wished, neither could any man hide resentment better, when there was an interest at stake.

[182] *L. and P.*, XI, 1246. See above, p. 175 and nn. 171, 172. Six lords were present at this gathering at Pomfret: Darcy, Neville, Scrope, Conyers, Latimer, and Lumley, and eighteen knights, including Robert, John, and William Constable, Ralph Ellerkar, and William and Nicholas Fairfax.

[183] This Parliament had, above all, to proclaim an amnesty for all that had taken place during the rebellion and to ratify the agreements between the lords and tenants with regard to the "gressums" on the leases.

[184] See the memorandum submitted to the meeting at Pomfret (*L. and P.*, XI, 1244).

[185] His interview with Robert Aske took place in the Carmelites' house at Doncaster.

[186] He had declared that the unity of the faith was safeguarded by the Confession recently proclaimed (the First Confession or the Articles of 1536).

[187] These are his own words to Bishop Latimer during his imprisonment in the Tower of London (Latimer, *Sermons and Remains*, ed. Corrie, 1845, I, 163).

He quickly won Aske over. Convinced that a Parliament, freely elected, would soon assemble at York, and that the Church would be free to define her doctrine, Aske returned in haste to make the royal promises known to all. The moderate party was satisfied, but the more obstinate among them felt they were being deluded by vain promises and protested that they had been betrayed. The pilgrims were thus divided. Whilst some vainly attempted to capture Hull and Scarborough,[188] the remainder, with Aske, Darcy, Constable, and Ellerkar, used all their power and influence to disperse the insurgents. Norfolk's army did the rest.

When calm was re-established Henry took advantage of the last rising to withdraw his pardon and his promises. It mattered little that they had saved the north from a terrible upheaval by their loyalty; Aske, Lord Darcy, and Sir Robert Constable were put to death as traitors. Darcy was beheaded in the Tower of London. Constable was hanged at Hull, and Aske at York, after being drawn through the streets on hurdles.[189] In the month of February, the king checked a final attempt to revolt, in Cumberland and Westmorland, by striking terror into their hearts: seventy-four insurgents were hanged at Carlisle, and a good many others at Durham and York.[190] It was then the middle of winter, wrote Harpsfield, and yet one might have believed it was autumn, the trees were so laden with these strange fruits which, hanging high up in the branches, threatened to fall upon the heads of

[188] John Hallom, with twenty confederates, entered Hull on a market day, carrying no arms in order to remove all suspicion and thinking he would be able to rouse the people. But the mayor had been warned, and had them arrested (January 16th, 1537). Sir Francis Bigod, after besieging Scarborough, raised the siege on the approach of Sir Ralph Evers, was beaten by Sir Ralph Ellerkar under the walls of Beverley, and fell into Norfolk's hands on February 10th.

[189] At the same time Sir Thomas Percy and Sir Francis Bigod, who had besieged Scarborough (cf. previous note), were executed. For the other victims see Harpsfield's account (Ch. Bémont, *op. cit.*, pp. 88-89, 134-35).

[190] "You shall in any wise," wrote Henry, "cause such dreadful execution to be done upon a good number of the inhabitants of every town, village and hamlet that have offended in this rebellion as well by the hanging of them up in trees as by the quartering of them and the setting of their heads and quarters in every town great and small, as they may be a fearful spectacle to all other hereafter that would practise any like matter." The women who tried at night to take down from the gallows the corpse of a brother or a husband were brought before the justice.

those who passed by.[191] That was the end of the rising. Its
political consequence was a complete change of government
in the north, where the Northern Council was created.[192]
From the religious point of view, however, it had produced
no fruit.

The Pilgrimage of Grace not only failed to stop the dissolution of the monasteries, but it even hastened that dissolution.
Norfolk received orders to expel from the religious houses all
the religious who had returned to them under cover of the
rising.[193] Sir William Fairfax had informed Cromwell that,
together with the clergy, they had been one of the causes
of the rising. Several abbots, who had been implicated in the
disturbance, were attainted,[194] and by a strained and unjust
interpretation of the law of treason, their houses were closed.
In this way were dissolved the abbeys of Jervaulx, Whalley,
Barlings, Bridlington and Kirkstead. The magnificent abbey
of Furness, in Lancashire, and that of Holm Cultram, which
overlooked the waters of the Solway Firth towards Scotland,
surrendered to the king, and were suppressed by him.[195]

[191] Ch. Bémont, *op. cit.*, pp. 89, 135.

[192] The proximity of the ill-guarded borders of Scotland and the
turbulent character of the inhabitants had already in the previous year
inspired Cromwell with the idea of creating a Northern Council (see his
letter to the Duke of Cumberland, June 18th, 1535, in Merriman, *op. cit.*,
I, 407. Cf. *L. and P.*, VIII, 515; XI, 1363). See R. R. Reid, *The King's
Council in the North*, London, 1921, in which there is a complete description
of the council's organization, its competence and procedure (chap. III),
and the sources and bibliography, in Appendix I.

[193] Cf. Gasquet, *op. cit.*, II, 159 *sq.* Aske had given orders for the
monasteries to be restored to the religious, forbidding at the same time all
plundering, and fixing the price of provisions (Fisher, *op. cit.*, p. 408).

[194] The abbot of Jervaulx, Adam Sedbar; a Dominican, Pickering;
the quondam abbot of Fountains, William Thirsk; and the prior of
Gisborough, James Cockerel, had all been tried and executed at the same
time as Robert Aske, Sir Robert Constable and Lord Darcy.

The inscription of the abbot of Jervaulx may be seen in the Tower of
London, where he engraved his name and the year, 1537, in which he
was executed. Blunt (I, 328, n. 8) has reproduced it.

[195] Cf. Gasquet, *op. cit.*, II, 180-88. The Abbot of Holm Cultram,
Thomas Carter, accused of being involved in the Lincolnshire rising, died
before the end of the enquiry; his successor, Gawin Borodale, one of
Cromwell's tools, surrendered the monastery, although the inmates had
asked to be allowed to keep their house as a refuge in case of a Scottish
attack (Ellis, II, 90). The abbot of Furness was obliged, under threat of
death, to give up his monastery (Wright, 153). An excellent edition of the
Furness cartulary, drawn up in 1412 (*The Coucher Book of Furness Abbey*),
was brought out by Atkinson (I, 1886-88) and J. Brownbill (Vol. II and

Henry determined to make a radical clearance of the last traces of monastic life in England. This does not appear to have been his idea at first, since he had allowed fifty-two of the religious houses affected by the law to stand, and had re-established others.

Most of the great religious houses were still standing. The law of 1536 had sanctioned their existence. To suppress them a very special method was used, which conveyed no idea of force, and at the same time did not necessitate intervention by Parliament. Superiors were made voluntarily to surrender their houses, either through threats or promises. This procedure had been suggested by two previous cases. The first dated back to November, 1535, when the Premonstratensians of Langdon, Kent, had been driven by necessity to surrender their houses, revenues, lands and rights of every kind to the king by placing them in the hands of Thomas Bedyll, even before the act had been passed by Parliament. They gave him full freedom and authority to dispose of them as he pleased, and ratified in advance any disposal, conversion, or transfer that he cared to make, and also declared that any objections that might afterwards be made against the surrender were null and void. The second case was that of the Benedictine abbot of Chertsey, Surrey, who surrendered his house to the king, in 1537, in exchange for a large pension, so that its revenues might be applied to the re-established priory of Bisham. The royal commissioners went from one abbey to another with ready-made documents for the abbots and priors, by which they surrendered their houses to the king. The improbable confessions contained in these documents make it perfectly obvious that the so-called voluntary surrenders were wrested from the superiors.[196] A large pension

last, 1918). The ruins of Furness Abbey, the church nave of which is 275 by 70 feet, recently came into Catholic hands again.

[196] Examples of these can be seen in Rymer, VI, Parts III and IV, pp. 15 *sq.*; in *L. and P.*, XIII, XIV, XV; and in Gee and Hardy, No. LXVI (the surrender of Westminster, January 16th, 1540). The surrender of Langdon, which was the first, is not only in Rymer, but also in Burnet (V, 223). Fuller (ed. 1845, III, 396, 398), followed by Blunt (I, 334 *sq.*), gives two which are sufficiently characteristic: priors and monks hand their belongings over to the king, in the first case, because their habit, religious life, and ceremonies are papist and displeasing to God; in the

was the reward for signing these documents, and any hesitation was overcome by threats.[197] The "surrender" itself secured the good graces of Cromwell and the king's favour[198]: it might possibly lead to a bishopric.[199]

other, because repenting of their voluptuous life and of the faults which burden their conscience, they humbly cast themselves at the feet of His Majesty.

A document in Burnet (IV, 263) and in Dugdale's *Monasticon* shows the manner in which the commissioners proceeded to dissolve a monastery after its surrender. This document concerns the important Benedictine monastery of Tewkesbury (Gloucestershire), whose mitred abbot sat in Parliament and which had an annual income of £1,595.

[197] Thus the prior of the Charterhouse of Hinton (Somersetshire) wrote that he and his brethren had refused "freely and voluntarily to give and surrender their house at the motion of the king's commissioners," because of the services it rendered to the honour of God and the deeds of charity done in it to their Christian neighbours; but since, as his brother had told him, the king and Cromwell were highly displeased, he would endeavour not to displease them so that they might have mercy upon them who were henceforth without means of existence (Edward Horde to his brother, 1537, Blunt, I, 339).

There exist even protests against "surrenders" which never really took place. Such is the protest of the abbot of Vale Royal, which is said to have surrendered on September 7th, whereas he wrote to Cromwell on the 9th of the same month as follows: "The truth is, I nor my said brethren have never consented to surrender our monastery, nor yet do, nor never will do by our good wills, unless it shall please the king's grace to give us commandment so to do, which I cannot perceive in the commission of master Holcroft." Wright, I, 338.

[198] This is what Thomas Bedyll, the inquisitor of the London Charterhouse, which was famous for its resistance to the royal supremacy, wrote to Cromwell, in 1537: "My lord (as ye may), I desire you, in the way of charity and none otherwise, to be good lord to the prior of the said Charterhouse, who . . . now, at last, at my exhortation and instigation, constantly moved, and finally persuaded his brethren to surrender their house, lands, and goods into the king's hands, and to trust to his mercy and grace. I beseech you, my lord, that the said prior may be so treated, by your help, that he be not sorry and repent that he hath feared and followed your sore words and my gentle exhortation made unto him to surrender his said house. . . ." (H. Ellis, *Original Letters*, 1st Series, II, 76 *sq*.)

William Trafford, whom Cromwell had named prior in place of the martyred Houghton, indeed induced twenty of his companions to acknowledge the royal supremacy on May 18th, 1537, and on June 10th he surrendered his monastery to the king. But two of his religious, John Rochester and James Walworth, who were implicated in the Pilgrimage of Grace, had been hanged at York in the previous spring, and ten others who refused to recognize the king as supreme head of the Church died in Newgate prison from starvation and want.

[199] Thus More, prior of Walden, became Bishop of Colchester; Holgate, prior of Sempringham, Bishop of Llandaff; Hilsey, prior of the Dominicans at Bristol, Bishop of Rochester; Holbeach, prior of Worcester, Bishop of Rochester (1544–47), and of Lincoln (1547–51); Barlow, prior of Bisham, Bishop of St Asaph (1536) and of St David's (1536–48). Cf.

The majority of the large monasteries disappeared in 1538. Debts or heavy expenses, [200] the vexatious proceedings to which they were subjected, and the terror which the law of attainder inspired caused the religious houses to fall, one after the other, into the king's hands. [201] The story of the dissolution at this period is practically one long list of houses "surrendered." In this way were dissolved the two hundred houses of the mendicant orders, which had not been affected by the law of 1536 because they had no fixed revenues. The Augustinian friar, George Browne—who had journeyed through England with the Dominican Hilsey receiving the royal supremacy oath from the religious—had been appointed general over all the mendicant orders, [202] but it fell to Richard Ingworth, the suffragan Bishop of Dover and former prior of Langley, to disperse the friars in every direction. [203] London and Leigh, famous for their violence and malpractices in the 1535 visitations, finished the work by overcoming all those who until then had resisted every attempt to drive them from their religious retreats. [204]

To make all these actions lawful, a Bill was brought before Parliament in April, 1539 (and passed in May), which secured to the king the property of all the religious houses which had been, or should afterwards be, surrendered into his hands. [205] The preamble of this act stated that this property had been

A. Koszul, "Was Bishop William Barlow Friar Jerome Barlow?" in the *Review of English Studies*, IV, 1928.

[200] Many of these debts were the result of the royal taxes and levies, and of the heavy works necessary to keep the religious houses in good repair. See the Abbot of Faversham's letter to Cromwell, in Wright, *op. cit.*, p. 104; and Blunt, *op. cit.*, p. 311. Cf. Savine, *op. cit.*, pp. 210 *sq.*

[201] In 1538 the prior of Lenton (Nottinghamshire) was accused of high treason and his house dissolved. The same thing happened to the Cistercian abbey of Woburn (Bedfordshire), whose abbot was arrested as a result of malevolent denunciations made by his own monks (June 20th, 1538) (cf. Gasquet, II, 189; Blunt, I, pp. 332 *sq.*). Those who alienated some of their goods in order to prevent confiscation were also punished.

[202] See chap. III. He visited their houses in 1534 (*L. and P.*, VIII, 587 [18]).

[203] Wright, *op. cit.*, pp. 195, 197.

[204] Cf. *L. and P.*, XIII, 758, 767, 911. The abbess of Godstow's complaints against London were so well founded that Cromwell had to admit them (Wright, 230).

[205] At the same time it also recognized that the religious, who by the fact of the dissolution had been released from their vows, had a right to possess property.

taken away from the "slothful and ungodly" religious to
"be turned to better use . . . whereby God's words might
the better be set forth, children brought up in learning . . .
readers of Greek, Hebrew, and Latin to have good stipends,
daily alms to be ministered . . . exhibitions for ministers of
the Church . . . that more bishoprics . . . should be established." [206] These fine promises were sufficient solace for Parliament, and served to procure its sanction for the great
monastic spoliation.

The few surviving monasteries followed the example of the
others. The three Benedictine abbots of Reading, Glastonbury and Colchester resisted. They were attainted, and after a
semblance of a trial, condemned for high treason. [207] Their
heads were exposed over the gateways of their own abbeys,
and their quartered bodies in the surrounding neighbourhood,
as an example to all who might be tempted to restrain the
king's ravenous appetite for wealth. On March 23rd, 1540
the one remaining abbey in the country—that of Waltham
in Essex—was surrendered to the king. Between the years
1537 and 1540 one hundred and fifty-eight large monasteries
for men, not counting their cells or the religious houses in the
towns, [208] had been dissolved, and thirty nunneries; twelve
had been dissolved by attainder. In 1540 forty-three commanderies, belonging to the Knights of Malta, were confiscated. [209] The French ambassador had predicted that not a

[206] *Statutes of the realm*, 31 Henry VIII, cap. 13. *Journals of the Lords*,
p. 108. Fuller, ed. 1845, III, 371; Gee and Hardy, No. LXIV.
[207] Cf. Gasquet, II, 348 *sq.*, 368; *L. and P.*, XIV (II) 206, 399; Wright,
255, 261; Burnet, VI, 234; Ellis, 1st Series, Vol. II, 98; Blunt, I, 345 *sq*;
see Cromwell's "remembrances" in Gasquet, II, 348, and *The last Abbot of
Glastonbury and his Companions*, by the same author, London, 1895; Hurry,
Reading Abbey. See Harpsfield (Bémont, *op. cit.*, 90 *sq.*) for the deplorable
end of Whiting the abbot of Glastonbury. The four quarters of his body
were exposed in four different towns (Ellis, *loc. cit.*).
To attempt to save anything from the spoliation (and this was the case
with abbot Whiting) was a crime in Cromwell's eyes. Moreover, even
before the trial, Cromwell had already, of his own authority, condemned
the abbots to death (cf. Wright, 256, 258, 260; *L. and P.*, XIV, Part II,
399).
[208] Some, like Durham and Norwich, had seven or eight cells. Gairdner
(*History*, 428 *sq.*) gives a separate list of the religious houses in the towns,
where there were often several religious orders. In Burnet (IV, 232–59) the
surrenders, with dates, of one hundred and fifty religious houses, according
to the Court of Augmentation, will be found.
[209] J. Gairdner, *History*, 424–28; Merriman, *op. cit.*, p. 289. The Knights

single abbey would be left standing: "*et si faict bien croire le roy vostre frère qu'il est lieutenant de Dieu en son royaume*"; in April, 1540, he was able to write to Francis I that in the whole of England there was not a single monk who had not exchanged his habit for the dress of a secular priest.[210]

The work was completed. The absolute devastation of the religious houses had been accomplished in five years; it had spread even to Ireland.[211] This spoliation, which, according to Hallam,[212] is incomparable, had caused a torrent of wealth to flow into the rapacious coffers of the Court of Augmentation.[213] "The king," says Burnet,[214] "had then in his hand the greatest opportunity of making royal and noble foundations that ever king of England had." But Henry scarcely took advantage of the opportunity.

In the first place, there was a tremendous amount of wastage. Not only were the treasury agents grossly overpaid, but in addition, the religious houses were frequently plundered. Every one wanted a share in the spoils. When the monks had departed the whole neighbourhood bore down upon the booty. The following account is given of the de-

of Malta, or of St John of Jerusalem, did not give up their houses like the other religious. Parliamentary decrees of April 22nd, 26th and 29th, 1540, suppressed them and allotted considerable pensions to the priors (*Journal of the Lords*, 132 *sq.*).

[210] Kaulek, *op. cit.*, 11, 175.

[211] See F. T. Butler, *Confiscation in Irish History*, London, 1917, which deals with the confiscations in the times of Henry VIII and Charles I; and H. Holloway, *The Reformation in Ireland: a Study of Ecclesiastical Legislation*, London, 1919; the latter writer looks upon the suppression of the Irish monasteries as a fresh cause for enmity against England. P. Rogers, *Henry VIII's Policy in Regard to the Irish Monasteries*, Belfast University thesis (1928–29).

In order to confiscate, with less resistance, the monastic properties which were to enrich the Crown, Cromwell made his friend, George Browne, an Augustinian monk, Archbishop of Dublin, who did his best to reform and to shear his flock. Cf. M. V. Ronan, *The Reformation in Dublin (1536–58) from Original Sources*, London, 1926.

[212] *Constitutional History*, I, 76.

[213] Two laws of 1545 gave to the Crown, first, the hospitals which had belonged to the monasteries; and secondly, the tithes and dues which the tenants formerly paid to each religious house.

"Such was the wretched and unworthy end," Pollini concludes (*Historia ecclesiastica della revoluzione d'Inghilterra*, Rome, 1594, p. 162), "of the monasteries in that unhappy realm of England, where for more than a thousand years the monks, who had brought the Christian faith to it, had grown and spread, thanks to the munificence and liberality of its kings."

[214] *Op. cit.*, I, 430.

struction of Roche Abbey[215]: "It would have pitied any heart to see what tearing up of the lead there was, what plucking up of boards and throwing down of spires. And when the lead was torn off . . . and the tombs in the church all broken . . . all things of price [were] either spoiled, carried away or defaced to the uttermost. . . . All the seats in the choir [were plucked up] and burned. . . . Even such persons were content to spoil them that seemed not two days before to allow their religion and do great worship and reverence at their matins, masses and other services." London wrote[216] that the people, both in the towns and in the country, were all anxious to lay hands on the lead, iron, doors and windows, and that night and day they were continually visiting the dissolved houses, as long as there remained anything to take. The buildings, which had been abandoned in many places, were used as a quarry by the people of the district for the construction of their own houses.[217] At the time of the French Revolution similar scenes of plundering and devastation were witnessed; the same causes produce the same effects.[218]

The king's commissioners seized what they could for the benefit of the royal exchequer,[219] but everything was sold at very low prices. Whilst all the very valuable things were sent to London (nine tons of gold and silver),[220] the sacred vessels, silver plate, vestments, copes and altar linen were given away for nothing, to be used for profane purposes. Bit by bit, the monasteries were parcelled out by auction and passed into rapacious hands. Choir-stalls, bells, wainscoting, stained-glass windows, carvings, ornamental objects, bronze, iron, lead, paving, glass, woodwork, tiles or slates, were all sold to the highest bidders.[221] John Freeman was accom-

[215] The father and uncle of the author, who wrote in 1591, had been witnesses of what he relates (H. Ellis, 3rd Series, III, 33 *sq*; cf. Blunt, I, 344).

[216] H. Ellis, *Original Letters*, 3rd Series, III, 188.

[217] *Blunt*, I, 342, n. 4.

[218] Peter and Poulet, *Histoire religieuse du Département du Nord pendant la Révolution (1789–1802)*, Lille, 1930, I, 100 *sq*.

[219] Cf. Gasquet, II, chap. x *passim*.

[220] Blunt, I, 341.

[221] See Freeman's letter to Cromwell, in H. Ellis, *Original Letters*, 3rd Series, III, 268. Wright (266–78) gives the details of an auction which

panied by a metal refiner and plumber from London. Dr.
London boasted to Cromwell that he had disfigured the
monastic chapels, leaving only the roof and walls for the
king's use, and had sold everything that could be turned into
money.[222] Manuscripts and rare books were all lost in the
storm. Enlightened Anglicans were quick to deplore the
disappearance of these innumerable intellectual treasures,
"the miserable martyrdom of innocent books," the ignorance
and avarice which caused their destruction and which gave
to "learning . . . an incurable wound." "I pray to God
that never good library may lie at the mercy of their [the
back-friends of learning] disposal; lest, having the same
advantage, they play the same prank, to the prejudice of
learning and religion."[223] "Covetousness was at that time,"
says Bishop Bale, "so busy about private commodity that
public wealth, in that [age] most necessary and of respect,
was not any where regarded. A number of them, which
purchased those superstitious mansions, reserved of those
library-books, some to serve their jakes, some to scour their
candlesticks, and some to rub their boots; some they sold to
the grocers and soap-sellers, and some they sent over sea to
the bookbinders, not in small number, but at times whole
ships full . . . I know a merchant-man who shall at this
time be nameless, that bought the contents of two noble
libraries for forty shillings' price: a shame it is to be spoken!
This stuff hath he occupied instead of gray paper, by the
space of more than ten years; and yet he hath store enough
for as many years to come." Merchants, especially the Dutch,
followed Cromwell's agents about, like birds of prey in the
wake of a routed army. All this bartering brought in
£1,423,500 to the Treasury.[224]

tell us quite enough about the royal commissioners' manner of proceeding.
(See also pp. 163 *sq* in the same work.)

[222] Freeman's letter (previous note). London's letter, in H. Ellis,
Original Letters, 3rd Series, III, 131.

[223] Fuller, ed. 1837, II, 246 *sq*; ed. 1845, III, 433–38. The quotation
from Bale which follows is taken from his *Declaration upon Leland's Journey*,
1549 (Bale's *Selected Works*, ed. H. Christmas, Parker Soc., Cambridge,
1849), and quoted by Fuller (ed. 1837, II, 246; ed. 1845, III, 434 *sq*.)
and Blunt (I, 388).

[224] Of this £85,000 came from the sale of silver by weight. To
obtain an approximate equivalent in modern money (pre-war value) the
sixteenth century figures must be multiplied at least twelve times.

In spite of this, Henry VIII left the Treasury heavily in debt. His policy had already made great inroads upon its coffers, and to remedy this Henry had laid hands upon the monasteries. Although the Crown revenues were doubled by this expedient, yet the war against France, Scotland and Ireland, from 1543 to 1546 again emptied the coffers and reduced the king to desperate straits.[225] It was necessary to have recourse to extreme remedies. Large sums were borrowed from foreign countries, all silver plate was stamped, and the coinage debased.[226] Having grown accustomed to spoliation, in 1545 the king laid hands on all the chantries, free chapels and colleges, which had been founded so that Masses might be said for the dead; and what death prevented him from appropriating his son gathered in for the Crown; even the universities feared for their existence.[227] The financial distress became worse under Edward VI and did not improve until the days of Mary Tudor, who strove wisely and energetically to remedy the unhealthy state of affairs created by her father and brother.[228] The spoliation of the monasteries had then, as Sander says, made King Henry a pauper.[229]

Moreover, of the annual revenue of £200,000 he secured

[225] Wriothesley wrote to Sir William Paget, in 1545, "the King's Majesty hath this year and the last year spent £1,300,000 or thereabouts, and his subsidy and benevolence ministering scant £30,000 thereof, as I muse sometime where the rest being so great a sum hath been gotten" (cf. Fisher, *op. cit.*, p. 469).

[226] Money was borrowed from the Fuggers, the big bankers of Augsburg (*L. and P.*, XXI, Part I, 211).

A pound of gold containing 23 carat gold and 1 carat alloy was minted and valued at £28 16s. The debasing of the silver money continued from 1543 to 1545, when silver consisted of 4 ounces of pure silver and 8 ounces alloy (cf. Ruding, *Annals of the Coinage of Great Britain*, 1840, I, 309 *sq.*).

[227] *Statutes of the realm*, 37 Henry VIII, cap. 4; 1 Edward VI, cap. 14. Cf. Fuller, III, 466–80.

In Edward VI's time the monastic goods were used as a means of exchange, the king granted lands, rents and ecclesiastical benefices to individuals, and charitable privileges, etc., to the towns (cf. *Calendar of the patent rolls, Edward VI*, V, London, 1926).

[228] Fr. C. Dietz, *English government finance, 1485–1558*, publication of Illinois University, 1921.

[229] Cf. above, p. 169. "After having estimated in his mind what the great spoliation had produced," wrote Harpsfield (Bémont, *op. cit.*, 84), "the King one day said, 'The treasure of my realm is more than double what it was.' But there is an English proverb which says that a piece of silver found on the ground has been minted from chalices; in other words, ill-gotten goods never go far. And indeed, the Treasury, swollen by such an affluence of wealth, was suddenly exhausted. It was a case of the Danaides' sieves."

only a yearly income of £37,000 for himself. The remainder was used to reward the supporters of the new regime. "The prodigality of Henry VIII was so extravagant that, accumulate what he would of lands and treasure, he was always in need of money."[230] Buildings and churches were given at a low price to the gentry and to all who desired to possess lands of their own. Lords and courtiers received the greater part of the loot and increased their fortunes with the monastic spoils. The king gave them away as presents, as stakes in a game of dice, in exchange for uncultivated and denuded lands, or for practically nothing at all. "It is certain," adds Fuller, who compares the royal munificence to the shower of gold in the legend of Danaë, "that in this age small merits of courtiers met with a prodigious recompense for their service: not only all the cooks, but the meanest turnbroach in the king's kitchen did lick his fingers; yea, the king's servants, to the third and fourth degree, tasted of his liberality."[231] Two things prompted this liberality: he had to reward the majority in Parliament for their vote, by allowing them, like Ruth, "to glean amongst the sheaves"; and he had to gain the good will of the most influential men, by linking up their interests with the dissolution of the monasteries, so that they would become the most ardent champions of that dissolution. There was a scramble for the abbey lands. Audeley, the chancellor, obtained eight religious houses, Cromwell six (amongst them the great Benedictine abbey of Ramsey, afterwards inherited by Oliver Cromwell), Lord Clinton twelve, Norfolk and Somerset thirteen each, and Suffolk, the king's brother-in-law, thirty.[232] "Nothing more is said about the abbeys,"

[230] Blunt, I, 372.

[231] Cf. Fuller, III, 438-42, 464; and above, p. 152 *sq.* Fuller (III, 440) quotes the case of a certain Mrs. Cornwallis, who received from the king a religious house of some value "for presenting him with a dish of puddings which pleased his palate." Amongst those who were enriched we can cite: Sir R. Rich, Sir E. North, Sir T. Pope, Sir J. Williams, Richard and Robert Southwell (these six all belonged to the Court of Augmentation), Sir P. Hobby, Richard Cromwell (Thomas Cromwell's nephew), Sir Richard Long (gentlemen of the Chamber), Sir Ralph Sadler (Henry VIII's secretary), Sir Anthony Browne (Court Steward), and Sir Thomas Cheyney (Treasurer of the Royal Household and Governor of the Cinque Ports) (cf. Fisher, *op. cit.,* 500, based on Savine's work, which may be consulted, *op. cit.,* 258 *sq.*).

[232] Other peers who received monasteries with a revenue of more than

wrote the Venetian ambassador Barbaro,[233] "they are all suppressed and their revenues annexed to the Crown, some being given and usurped by the nobility, who convert them into palaces, furnishing them with the church ornaments." A century later, Sir Henry Spelman and his son observed that the families which had gorged themselves with the monastic spoils had died out or had been decimated; that in the course of twenty years the sword of justice had claimed more victims from their number than in the previous five centuries, from the Conquest to the Dissolution; and that few sons indeed of those who became wealthy in this way had inherited their fathers' goods and titles (not even sixty out of two hundred and seventy, according to Reyner). "Doubtless the Commons have drunk deep in this cup of deadly wine, but they being more numerous and less eminent, are not so obvious to observation."[234]

In this way Henry won over the most influential classes in the country. The nobility, to whom the monastic foundations were due, may have lost the revenues from that source for which their ancestors had made provision, but the gentry, who had looked askance at the suppression of the monasteries, found that it paid and were delighted with the new state of

£200 were: Rutland, Wriothesley, Sussex, Howard, Hertford, George and Francis Shrewsbury, St John, Russell, J. Dudley or Lord Lisle, and Wharton (cf. Fisher, p. 500; Blunt, I, 377 *sq.*).

The High Admiral Thomas Seymour, who became Katherine Parr's fourth husband after Henry VIII's death, was also one of those enriched by monastic spoils (cf. Maclean, *Life of Seymour*, London, 1869; *Annals of Winchcombe and Sudeley*, published by Dent; Pollard, *England under Protector Somerset*, London, 1900, 177 *sq.*).

The revenues of the Abbey of St. Michael's Mount, suppressed at the same time as the Sion Monastery, were given to one of Henry VIII's faithful followers, Humphrey Arundell. Cf. Rev. T. Taylor, *Saint Michael's Mount*, Cambridge, 1932.

[233] An account dated 1551, in Albèri, 1st Series, II, 246. Fuller (ed. 1845, III, 504–13) mentions those who owned the chief abbeys at the time he wrote (1649), together with those who received them from Henry VIII.

[234] Sir Henry Spelman, *De non temerandis Ecclesiis* (*Churches not to be violated*) (1841) and the preface to this book, by his son Clement, p. 72. In his *History and Fate of Sacrilege* (ed. 1888, pp. 109–27) he cites the barons who voted for the suppression of the abbeys and the way in which they died. The Introduction "by two priests of the Church of England" (p. lix *sq.*) shows that 470 peers responsible for the spoliation of the monasteries died childless, and also notes other consequences of the monastic dissolution (cf. Reyner, *Apostolatus Benedictorum in Anglia*, 227 *sq.*; Blunt, I, 379 *sq.*).

things. "This was done," says Fuller, [235] "by the politic counsel of the wise Lord Cromwell, not hoping that these small morsels to so many mouths should satisfy their hunger, but only intending to give them a taste of the sweetness of abbey lands." The king made this work a permanent one by bringing the people into it, and at the same time guarded himself against an attack by any of the Catholic princes on the Continent, [236] which he foresaw might result from his policy.

Another consequence, unforeseen by him, was the founding of a landed aristocracy, which was afterwards to rob the crown of the power the Tudors had wrested from the ancient nobility. And, by not keeping the monastic wealth in the royal Treasury, Henry unwittingly saved England from the absolutism of the Stuarts who, had they been rich, would have done without Parliament. The constitutional monarchy would have foundered. [237]

---

[235] *Church History*, III, 374. Cf. Dugdale, *History of Warwickshire*, p. 802. Fuller (*ibid.*, 411-15) enumerates the obligations imposed upon the monasteries by the founders, which secured abundant revenues for their heirs: pensions or annuities, men and their equipment in time of war, part of the dowry for an eldest daughter, complete armour for the eldest son when knighted by the king, "corrodies" (*a conradendo*) or asylum till the end of their days in the religious houses for old servants whose age prevented them from being any longer useful to their lord, but the tree being henceforth cut down at the root, none of these fruits could be gathered.

[236] For the economic condition of England at this period R. H. Tawney may be consulted, *The Agrarian Problem in the Sixteenth Century*, London, 1912; also W. J. Ashley, *The Economic Organisation of England*, London, 1914, part of which concerns the Tudors; E. Lipson, *An Introduction to the Economic History of England, Vol. I; The Middle Ages*, London, 1915, in which the author links the sixteenth century with the Middle Ages; G. O'Brien, *An Essay on the Economic Effects of the Reformation*, 1923; Oscar Albert Marti, *Economic Causes of the Reformation in England*, Macmillan, 1930, an uncritical work, throwing no fresh light on the subject; R. Baxter, *The Poor Husbandman's Advocate to Rich Rocking Landlord*, ed. F. J. Powick, Manchester, 1926; G. H. Tupling, *The Economic History of Rossendale*, Manchester and London, 1927; Sir Francis L. C. Floud, *The Ministry of Agriculture and Fisheries*, London and New York, 1927.

[237] S. B. Liljegren, in an interesting study (*The Fall of the Monasteries and the Social Changes in England leading up to the Great Revolution*, Lund, 1924), has shown that the political victory of the bourgeoisie, under the Stuarts, was brought about by the confiscation and sale of the monastic properties, of 1536-40, so that Henry VIII and Cromwell, who ruled by absolutism, prepared the defeat of Charles I and Strafford.

For the effects of the suppression of the monasteries, see also Hallam, *Constitutional History of England*, I, chap. II.

Such were the political results of the dissolution of the monasteries. What were the social consequences?

The law passed in May, 1539, to appropriate the monastic property for the common good (the preamble of which, according to Burnet, was written by the King himself) was meant to justify the spoliation, and named the works of general and social interest for which that property would be used.   Old servants were to receive pensions, children education, and large sums were to be distributed as alms, the highways repaired, no new taxes imposed, and bishoprics and university professorships established, and many other things besides. [238]   All these fine promises remained mere projects. Save for a few professorships, [239] nothing was created except bishoprics, and even then only six in lieu of the eighteen Henry had planned. [240]   Certain sums were, however, set aside for the army and navy, and the fortification of the coasts.

The wealthy classes had battened on the spoils, but the others suffered through the suppression of the religious houses. "The poverty of the poor and the wealth of the rich drew away class from class, and introduced that disintegration of society which caused so much trouble in the seventeenth

[238] *Statutes of the realm*, 31 Henry VIII, cap. 13. Cf. above, pp. 184-5. It was thought that part of the revenues might be used to found a school for Ministers of State.   This scheme, which did not materialize, was drawn up by Nicholas Bacon.

[239] Professorships of Greek, Hebrew, Theology, Law and Medicine were founded at Oxford and Cambridge (cf. Pollard, *Henry VIII*, 401). J. R. Tanner (*The Historical Register of the University of Cambridge: being a Supplement to the Calendar, with a Record of University offices, Honours and Distinctions to the year 1920*, Cambridge, 1921) gives a list of the university professorships with their holders from the beginning.

[240] This was a resumption of Wolsey's project.   He had meant to found and endow thirteen new bishoprics with the property of certain small suppressed monasteries (cf. Pollard, *Wolsey*).

The six bishoprics were: Westminster, which lasted only six years; Bristol; Gloucester; Oxford; Peterborough; and Chester.   Their endowment amounted to more than £100,000.   Parliament had authorized the king to erect twenty episcopal sees (cf. Fuller, III, 422 *sq.*; Dixon, II, 218; Blunt, 371 *sq.*).   See the deed for the foundation of the See of Westminster, December 7th, 1540, in Burnet, IV, 500-507. A few days later (December 19th) Thomas Thirlby was named its first and only bishop.   In 1550 he was transferred to Norwich and his first see suppressed.   See *Scheme of Bishopricks with Illustrations of his Assumption of Church property, its Amount and Appropriation*, 1838, limited to 250 copies.

century."[241]   In the first place, the nine or ten thousand monks and nuns who had been driven out received very little, with the exception of the superiors, and many led a deplorable life of vagrancy and poverty.[242]   Of the three million inhabitants, from forty to eighty thousand depended upon the monasteries, because they were sick, or poor, or else employed as servants, and all at once they found themselves deprived of their daily bread.[243]   For numerous branches of industry the abbey was a centre for work, as well as a market for many products. The hospitality of the abbots—"admirable good landlords" Fuller calls them—was proverbially liberal.[244] Their place was taken by tyrannical and exacting landlords, who enclosed their pastures, considerably increased the rents of the farms, and prevented the mass of the commoners from having any cattle or food.[245]   The people sank deeper into

[241] Blunt, I, 389. See the sermon in which Latimer (Sermons, ed. 1824, I, 93) bewailed the poverty of the lower classes.

[242] Cf. Collier, IV, 321 sq. Gasquet, op. cit., II, 449 sq.; Blunt, I, 381. The religious who had entered the religious houses long before (diu antea) the dissolution received an annual pension of from £1 to £8 (Blunt, I, 367). In a large and rich monastery, such as that of Tewkesbury, this pension, save for three of the monks, amounted to £6 13s. 4d., £10, £13, or £16 for the priors, whilst for the abbot it amounted to £266 13s. 4d. (Burnet, 264 sq.). See, in Fuller (III, 449, 459) and Collier (IX, 159) specimens of letters-patent for the pensions of priors and prioresses, given under the great seal and enregistered by the Court of Augmentation (cf. ibid., 447-63).

Geoffrey Baskerville (article quoted, Essays in History, presented to Reginald Lane Poole, Oxford, 1927, 436-66) has tried to find out what became of certain religious disbanded by Henry VIII. He thinks that their pension, paid either by the new owners or by the Crown, was sufficient at that period. Both the new owners and the Crown tried to procure benefices for their creditors so as to be absolved from their obligations. His study shows that the lot of the friars must have been much harder, so, too, must that of the nuns. Bound by the law of the Six Articles to keep their vows of chastity, some of them took advantage of Edward VI's law on celibacy to get married, though public opinion was against it. [For what happened to the religious of the vast diocese of Winchester who were secularized, see Herbert Chitty, Diocesis Wintoniensis Registra Steph. Gardiner et Johannes Poynet, Oxford, 1930.]

[243] Blunt (I, 364) reckons the monastic population at 100,000; Savine (222 sq.) reduces it to 37,000.

[244] Fuller, III, 337-40.

[245] Cf. Blunt, I, 381; Fisher, 500-501. Cf. Tawney; and Eileen Power, Tudor Economic Documents, 1924. Certain obligations of hospitality and husbandry were indeed laid upon the new owners, under penalty of a fine of £6 13s. 4d. a month, but they were so little observed that James I had to suppress them (21 James I, cap. 28).

the slough of poverty whilst the nobility, gentry, and merchants grew rich. Nothing has caused more harm, wrote the
ambassador Barbaro in 1551,[246] than the destruction of the
monasteries which procured work for many people in the
land, kept the poor alive, sheltered travellers, and supplied
the king with subsidies in time of war. "The wholesale destruction of the monasteries . . . filled England with discontent, and helped to sow the seeds of dissent," and increased
the ranks of beggars, who, in Elizabeth's time, had reached a
considerable number.[247] As early as 1540 Parliament had to
assist fifty-seven towns which had fallen on evil days as a
result of the destruction of the abbeys.[248] Whole districts
were impoverished or depopulated. After the monasteries
had fallen, the price not only of eggs and fish but of every
commodity was increased fourfold.[249] The first collection
for the needy was taken in 1538. A short time previously
Henry had enacted two terrible laws, which condemned all
beggars to be punished by mutilation. For a third offence a
beggar received capital punishment "as a felon, and as an
enemy of the commonwealth."[250] Only "aged and impotent
persons" were exempt from these laws, and even they had to
possess a licence.

These consequences of the monastic dispersion have been
recognised by contemporary writers, as well as by all the
Protestant historians of the previous centuries. "The Spital
House" (1535-36), a poem by Robert Copland, recently
published, is an instructive commentary on the social life in
England at the time of the suppression of the monasteries,
and also shows how many "innocent victims" the suppression
made.[251] Nevertheless, now that greater study has been

---

[246] Albèri, *op. cit.*, 1st Series, II, 246.

[247] Rev. Herbert Pole, *The Church of England: Its Catholicity and Continuity*,
1899, pp. 76 *sq.*

[248] *Statutes of the realm*, 32 Henry VIII, cap. 17, 18, 19.

[249] Harpsfield, in Bémont, *op. cit.*, 92. For the high cost of living see
Leadam, *Select Cases in the Star Chamber*, Selden Soc. ed., II (1911), pp. xl *sq.*,
xlvii *sq.*, 224 *sq.*

[250] *Statutes of the realm*, 22 Henry VIII, cap. 12; 27, cap. 25. See also
the volume by A. V. Judges (mentioned below) for the pitiless laws of
Elizabeth which affected alike those who were guilty and those who had
fallen from favour.

[251] It was published by A. V. Judges in *The Elizabethan Underworld*,
London, 1930. To the extraordinary evils from which we are suffering

given to the economic history of England, men are inclined to attribute the distress of the people in the sixteenth century less to that suppression—there are even some who will no longer mention it—than to other causes which, by transforming the conditions of the property-owning and of life itself, would have produced the same effects.[252] Care must be taken therefore not to exaggerate the effect of the laws of 1536 and 1539 upon the lives of the people. It cannot, however, be denied that those laws did at least hasten an economic transformation, which resulted in the distress of the poorer classes. Pauperism, which is one of England's evils at the present day, dates from this period.[253]

The country parsonages, many of which had been maintained by the monks—Tewkesbury abbey alone was responsible for forty-seven in the various counties[254]—were left empty, and the schools, which the religious had also subsidized, were closed. Even at Oxford and Cambridge the numbers fell away, for the religious houses no longer supported scholars at the universities. Bishop Latimer, of Worcester, who on account of his leanings towards the new Learning cannot be suspected of sympathy for the religious, deplored the results of their dispersion: "They maintained scholars and gave them livings; and now that the knowledge of God's Word is brought to light, and many earnestly study and labour to set it forth, now almost no man helpeth to maintain them. It is a pitiful thing to see schools so neglected; every true Christian ought to lament the same . . . to consider

to-day, wrote Harpsfield a few years later (Ch. Bémont, pp. 91 and 137), we cannot attribute any cause other than the destruction of the monasteries.

[252] Oscar A. Marti's work (*Economic Causes of the Reformation in England*, London, 1930) has abundant notes of very unequal value, but tells us nothing more than was already known. References are, however, given in it to good as well as to mediocre works. See G. O'Brien's *An Essay on the Economic Effects of the Reformation*, London, 1923.

[253] For the "Poor Laws," the application of which was left to the parishes till the end of the eighteenth century, see "The Laws concerning the Poor or a Compleat Treatise of the Common and Statute Law relating to the Relief Settlement, etc., of the Poor," 4th ed., very much enlarged, 1720; R. Burn, *The History of the Poor Law*, with observations, 1764; Sir Arthur Newsholme, *The Ministry of Health*, London and New York, 1925; Dorothy Marshall, *The English Poor in the XVIIIth Century*, London, 1926; S. and B. Webb, *English Local Government: English old Poor Law*, Part I, London, 1927.

[254] Burnet, V, 269-72.

what hath been plucked from abbeys, colleges and chantries, it is marvel no more to be bestowed upon this holy office of salvation . . . schools are not maintained; scholars have not exhibitions."[255] The treasures of the monastic libraries had been scattered or destroyed. In 1549, John Bale stigmatized this vandalism:[256] "Yea, what may bring our realm to more shame and rebuke, than to have it noised abroad, that we are despisers of learning? I judge this to be true, and utter it with heaviness, that neither the Britons under the Romans and Saxons, nor yet the English people under the Danes and Normans, had ever such damage of their learned monuments, as we have seen in our time. Our posterity may well curse this wicked fact of our age, this unreasonable spoil of England's most noble antiquities."[257] The few treasures that have survived this universal destruction serve only to revive the regrets and to justify the vehemence of Bale.[258] The abbey church of Waltham, founded before the Conquest by Harold, who was buried therein (1066), enriched by Henry I (1135), Henry II (1189), and numerous queens, was one of the oldest and most beautiful specimens of architecture in England. Although it became a parochial church, and was consequently saved from destruction, yet in the middle of the seventeenth century it was woefully neglected and stood in urgent need of repair, as Fuller, the historian, who was attached to it, sorrowfully records. Several years passed, however, during which its state became worse, before a

---

[255] *Sermons and Remains of Hugh Latimer sometime Bishop of Worcester, Martyr, 1555*, Parker Soc. ed., Cambridge, 1845, I, 291, 349, 478. Cf. *ibid.*, 179, 307, 358, 418, 504.

[256] Fuller, ed. 1845, III, 435. Blunt, I, 388.

[257] Robert Wakefield, Professor of Hebrew at Oxford, saved some Hebrew and Greek MSS. from Ramsey Abbey (Dodd, ed. 1737, I, 225).

[258] The most considerable remnants are in the Durham Chapter Library. R. A. Rye, University of London Librarian, in chap. I of *The Students' Guide to the Libraries of London, with an Account of the most Important Archives and other Aids to Study*, recalls the dispersion and dilapidation of the books caused by the suppression of the monastic orders; even those of the old St Bartholomew's hospice were not spared. Ignorance, carelessness, bigotry and greed contributed to the destruction of the old libraries. Some idea of the destruction of the intellectual treasures, patiently accumulated in the monasteries, will be obtained by reading the list of works belonging to the Charterhouses at Witham, Hinton, London, Coventry, Mountgrace, and Sheen (chap. IX, Miss Margaret Thompson's *The Carthusian Order in England*, London, 1930).

tardy attempt to restore it was made.[259] In scattering the
monastic wealth Henry was well aware that the loss was
irretrievable, since he ordered John Leland, the poet, to save
from oblivion, at his expense, what he himself was dooming to
destruction. Leland's "itineraries" have preserved for us the
aspect and memories of a monastic England that has for ever
disappeared.[260]

In addition to the material and intellectual consequences of
the spoliation of the monasteries, there is one other which is
less frequently mentioned. A nation already too much inclined
to bury itself in questions of a material nature, an excessively
practical race, was deprived of one of the sources of its ideals,
viz. the monastic life, for although Mary Tudor tried to
restore the monastic system, her sister Elizabeth's first care
was to abolish it.[261] The Church of England feels the want
of it so much that for the last three quarters of a century she
has been trying to fill that void in her life; from 1847-99,
thirty monastic and conventual establishments were founded
under her control.[262] There are fifty-four Anglo-Catholic
convents with a total of two thousand nuns, of whom some
practise the contemplative life, and eight monastic establishments, containing eight hundred men. Some of them follow
the rule of St Benedict, since 1898, or that of St Francis. In
1891, a missionary society was organized, and now has
several communities in India of exclusively Indian sisters, as
well as several important centres of apostolate in Africa,
Korea, and Bengal.

"On the whole question," concludes a Protestant historian,
"it may be said that we must ever look back with shame on
that dissolution, as on a series of transactions in which the
sorrow, the waste, the impiety that were wrought, were
enough to make angels weep. . . . A blot and a scandal were

[259] Fuller (III, 519-56) has devoted a long appendix to the history
of Waltham Abbey.

[260] *The Itinerary of John Leland* remained long in manuscript form.
The best edition we have is due to Lucy Toulmin Smith (London, 1907-10,
5 vols.) who added some extracts from *Leland's Collectanea* as an appendix.

[261] Cf. Fuller, III, 480-91.

[262] R. W. Sockman, *The Revival of the Conventual Life in the Church of
England in the Nineteenth Century*, London, 1917. The author gives the
history of these thirty establishments.

indelibly impressed upon our history; and every bare site, every ruined gable, is still a witness to what was nothing less than a great national tragedy."[263]

[263] Blunt, I, 389 *sq.* Hardwick (*A History of the Christian Church*, London, 1886, 377 *sq.*) likewise censures in strong language the enormities and the covetousness of an English monarch which drove him to despoil the Church by confiscating the monastic properties.

The Public Monuments' Commission has had the ruins of Rievaulx and Kirkham Abbeys recently restored. In 1930 the ruins of St. Radegunde's Abbey at Bradsole, near Dover (founded in 1191, dissolved in 1538), were discovered. S. E. Winbolt published a plan of them in *The Times*, October 11th, 1930. There has been a resident warden since 1930 in the Cistercian Abbey of Whalley (Lancs.), which was suppressed in 1537, but "has risen again to new life and service" (cf. J. E. W. Wallis, *A History of the Church in Blackburnshire*, S.P.C.K., 1932).

CHAPTER V

THE CHAMPIONS OF CATHOLIC UNITY

Bishop Fisher—Chancellor Sir Thomas More—Cardinal Reginald Pole

WE have seen how the English schism sprang up, developed, and spread throughout the country, meeting with scarcely any opposition. The entire nation obeyed the wishes of its sovereign, one day acknowledging as lawful what had been unlawful the day before, and admitting his spiritual supremacy as well as his absolutism. Clergy and nobility alike proved to be servile. There was no opposition, because opposition implies the existence of a party, and at this period parties were unknown in England. Opponents, however, there were; very few indeed in number, but in character very great. These opponents were not political leaders—they were too faithful to the king and had too much respect for what was lawful for that,—they were conscientious men who remembered that there are times when there is no obligation to obey earthly kings. "I cannot find in my heart," said More, "the strength to speak other than my conscience dictates."

Fisher and More, *par nobile fratrum*, stand for the passive resistance of an oppressed conscience. Reginald Pole shows a more active form of resistance. The three of them were the most famous champions of Catholic unity against Henry VIII, and other English martyrs sealed it with their blood.

Fisher was born at Beverley, in Yorkshire, in 1459, according to some; in 1469, according to others,[1] of a family of rich

---

[1] Van Ortroy (*Ana. Boll.*, XII, 202, n. 1) gives 1469 as the date, according to Bridgett's *Life of Blessed John Fisher* (London, ed. 1890, p. 6; cf. *ibid.*, pp. 463 *sq.*) and Searle (*History of Queen's College*, p. 133), which would make Fisher seven years old at his father's death, nineteen when he took his bachelor's degree, and sixty-five at his death. But in those days a bachelor's degree was not gained at such an early age. Moreover, his portrait by Holbein bears the words: A^o *aetatis* 74, and as it is not likely that it wa : painted in the Tower, Fisher was at least seventy-five when he died. The first English biography of Fisher (published by Van Ortroy) gives 1459 as the year of his birth.

merchants, judging by the numerous legacies his father left to various religious houses and other pious foundations.[2] He began his university studies at Michael House, Cambridge. In 1487, Fisher became a Bachelor of Arts, and took his degree of Master in 1491. He was afterwards made a fellow of Michael House, and was chosen senior proctor of the university in 1494, and in 1497 became Master of Michael House. In that same year, 1497, the king's mother, the Lady Margaret, attracted by his qualities and his virtues, made him her chaplain and confessor.[3] Henry VII, who held him in great esteem, made him Bishop of Rochester (October 14th, 1504) for his "grete and singular virtue,"[4] and a member of the King's Council. When Henry VII died Fisher preached his funeral sermon in St. Paul's, London (1509).[5]

Fisher was a great scholar and a patron of learning. His name is linked with the revival of letters in England, and with the Humanist movement. As vice-chancellor of Cambridge in 1501, reader in divinity in 1503,[6] chancellor in 1504, and president of Queen's College (1505-1508), he infused new life into the university, which had been on the wane and lacked resources. On the advice of Fisher, the king's mother endowed the Lady Margaret Preachership, so that the laity might receive free instruction in their religion; the teaching of the Gospel being then at a low ebb. He also inspired her with the

---

[2] Lewis-Turner, Life of Dr. John Fisher, ed. Mayor, 1876, pp. 206-88.

[3] The date of this nomination (given by Bridgett, op. cit., p. 19, as 1502) has not been established: it was before 1503, when he became professor of theology and could not therefore be away from Cambridge: as early as 1495 Margaret had invited Fisher to her table as proctor of the university (cf. Cooper, Memoir of the Lady Margaret, p. 5).

[4] This is the date of the pontifical Bull. He was consecrated on November 24th in the same year (Lewis-Turner, II, 254-56).

Fisher was one of the few English bishops who took care of the diocese entrusted to him (Van Ortroy, Ana. Boll., X, 216; Bridgett, op. cit., 53, 61, 64). "He could never be persuaded," says Sander (op. cit., Lewis' trans., p. 121), "to desert the poor church to which God had first called him, though he had been offered more than once a better endowed see."

[5] Funeral Sermons, ed. Hymens, p. 163. The English Works of John Fisher, ed. Mayor, 1876, 206-88.

[6] According to Reginald Pole, Henry VIII thought him the most learned theologian in Europe (Gasquet, op. cit., I, 115). Ellies du Pin (Histoire de l'Église et des auteurs ecclésiastiques du XVIe siècle, Paris, 1701-13, IV, 491-500) says he was one of the best controversialists of his day. The queen-mother Margaret nominated him for the Preachership which she had just founded.

idea of building two splendid colleges at Cambridge, Christ's and St John's. [7] When Lady Margaret died (1509), [8] he overcame all obstacles, carried out her wishes, and completed the work that had been begun. For St John's College he obtained the property of two nunneries and a hospital that were suppressed, and endowed four fellowships and two scholarships, [9] as well as providing for lectures in Greek and Hebrew. He revised the statutes several times, and was still interested in them even while imprisoned in the Tower. [10]

His love for letters was known to all. According to his biographers, his library, which Henry VIII afterwards destroyed, was the finest in Europe; and therein he spent long hours in study. "I know," Erasmus wrote to him in 1524, "how much time you spend in the library, which is to you a very paradise." [11] Fisher gave a sympathetic welcome to the Humanist movement, and to the new spirit of biblical criticism which accompanied the Renaissance. Through him Erasmus became a professor at Cambridge, and it was due to Fisher that the study of Greek did not meet with the same opposition at Cambridge as at Oxford. Despite his advanced age he

[7] The charter of the foundation of Christ's College is dated May 1st, 1505. This college, magnificently endowed by Lady Margaret, was an enlargement of a smaller one (God's House) which had only a proctor and four fellows. Christ's College was able to receive a master, twelve fellows and forty-seven scholars. Fisher was named visitor for life (cf. Cooper, *op. cit.*, pp. 100-22; *Ana. Boll.*, X, Nos. 8, 36-39, 44).

[8] He preached the funeral sermon, three months after that of Henry VII (J. E. B. Mayor, *The English Works of John Fisher*, London, 1876). This funeral sermon on the queen-mother, which testified to her lively faith in the Eucharist and the other sacraments, republished by the Dean of St John's College, Dr. Hymens, was the beginning of Father Bridgett's conversion to Catholicism; he was then a student of the same college.

[9] The two houses dissolved were those of Bromehall (diocese of Salisbury) and of Lillechurch (diocese of Rochester). The hospital dissolved was St John's, Cambridge, from which the college took its name. This college afterwards received various donations, even from Fisher himself (*Ana. Boll.*, X, No. 37).

For St John's College, see Thomas Baker, *History of the College of St John*, ed. J. E. Mayor, 1859; and Mullinger, *The University of Cambridge*, 1879-84, 2 vols.

[10] See J. E. B. Mayor (*Early Statutes of the College of St John the Evangelist*, 1859); *Ana. Boll.*, X, 243, nn. 2 and 3; and Thomas Baker, 100 *sq.*

[11] *Opera Omnia*, Leyden, 1703-1706, III, col. 814. Cf. *ibid.*, col. 1813. See Cooper, *op. cit.*, pp. 186, 196. This library which Fisher had bequeathed to St John's College, Cambridge, was plundered and scattered, his biographers say, whilst he was imprisoned in the Tower.

determined to acquire a knowledge of Greek, and he took advantage of one of Erasmus' visits, in 1516, for this purpose. A year later he was able to read St Paul's Epistles in the Greek text, and even to pick out the mistakes made by Erasmus' printer. Erasmus congratulated him on his constant application, and the venerable pupil was able to give a philological criticism on the Greek text of the Bible.[12]   The bishop's palace, according to his first biographer, "for continency, seemed a very monastery, and for learning a university."

When the New Learning sought to make common cause with the Humanists, Fisher at once severed all connection with it, and constantly proved himself to be very hostile to the religious revolution.   On May 12th, 1521, Wolsey, in the presence of the nuncio, the imperial ambassador, the Archbishop of Canterbury, and the Bishop of London, consigned Luther's books to the flames in St Paul's Churchyard, and Fisher delivered an impassioned speech, denouncing the errors contained in them.[13]   Henry VIII's *Assertio septem sacramentorum* (1521) is quite wrongly supposed to be from Fisher's pen, but he did write several books against Luther: *Lutheranae Assertionis Confutatio* (1523), *Defence of the Sacred Priesthood against Luther* (1524), and finally *A Defence of the Assertions of the King of England against Luther's Babylonian Captivity* (1525).[14]   He also refuted Œcolampadius and Vilenus.[15]   His orthodoxy and his attachment to the papacy remained then unshaken.

Fisher was never a courtier.   Far from flattering those in power, his sympathies were rather with the opposition.   There

[12] Erasmus, *op. cit.*, III, col. 1630, 1813. Cf. Bridgett, p. 95, n.; Kerker, *John Fisher, der Bischof von Rochester und Martyrer für den Kath. Glauben.*

[13] Lewis-Turner, I, 181-83; *Ana. Boll.*, X, 265, 266; Bridgett, *op. cit.*, 50 *sq.* After Henry had attacked the supremacy of the Pope, he caused Cromwell to find and destroy all copies of this sermon (*L. and P.*, VIII, 55; IX, 963).

[14] Fisher's Latin works, edited by Fleischmann, were published, in one volume, at Würzburg, in 1597: *J. Fisherii Roffensis in Anglia episcopi Opera quae hactenus inveniri poterunt omnia.* His English works were published by J. E. B. Mayor, in 1876, Early English Text Society ed., *The English Works of J. Fisher, Bishop of Rochester, now first collected.* Vol. IX of Grauert's *Corpus catholicorum* is a re-edition (1925) by H. Klein of Fisher's *Sacri sacerdotii defensio contra Lutherum*, 1525.

[15] *Ana. Boll.*, X, 268. His *Opera omnia* contain: VI, "De Eucharistia contra J. Œcolampadium libri V."

was always a secret antagonism between himself and Wolsey, due, according to Burnet, to the austere life of the former and the too easy life of the latter. Speaking to the national synod in 1519, Fisher condemned the ambitions, "the indecent and superfluous raiment, delicate fare, and other worldly vanity," and the courtiers' life of the higher clergy. The cardinal thought these remarks were aimed at himself, and so did the rest of Fisher's hearers.[16] In Convocation, in 1523, Fisher opposed Wolsey, who was asking for a subsidy for the war in Flanders.[17]

At the time of the divorce, Fisher proved to be resolute and inflexible. As Catherine's confessor he was her principal confidant, and even the only counsellor upon whose sincerity and honesty she could entirely rely. Wolsey vainly sought to detach him from the queen, and to persuade him that the king was acting only from scruples of conscience.[18] When Catherine had been declared contumacious by Wolsey and Campeggio, the aged bishop was the only one who dared raise his voice in her defence. On June 18th, 1529, he attended the legatine court, and in the presence of Henry VIII declared that "in order not to procure the damnation of his soul, and in order not to be unfaithful to the king," he was obliged, "to affirm, and with forcible reasons to demonstrate to them that this marriage of the king and queen can be dissolved by no power, human or Divine." He added that "the Baptist in olden times regarded it as impossible for him to die more gloriously than in the cause of marriage; and that as it was not so holy at that time as it has now become by the shedding of Christ's Blood, he (the bishop) could encourage himself more ardently, more effectually, and with greater confidence to dare any great or extreme peril whatever."[19] The king,

[16] Burnet, I, 52. Cf. *Ana. Boll.*, X, p. 255, Nos. 2, 257, 258. Van Ortroy does not think that he had Wolsey in view because Polydore Vergil, who had little love for Wolsey, does not mention it.

[17] Hall, *Chronicle*, p. 72.

[18] Cf. *Ana. Boll.*, X, 333. Cf. Collier, IX, 74.

[19] Brewer, *Reign of Henry VIII*, II, 346; *L. and P.*, IV, 2539, 5732 and Introduction, p. ccclxxix; Ehses, Nos. 53, 54. Standish, the Bishop of St Asaph, also spoke and expressed nearly the same opinion, but in briefer terms (Ehses, Nos. 53, 57; *L. and P.*, IV, 5728, 5741).

Fisher's speech made a great impression, and J. du Bellay said it was full of wisdom (*L. and P.*, IV, 5741).

Fisher also wrote a treatise on Catherine's marriage called *Matrimonii*

stung by the comparison between himself and Herod Antipas which the bishop's words suggested, made a violent and bitter reply in the form of a speech to the legates, in which he attacked both Fisher's character and the reasons adduced by the bishop.[20] Fisher's signature alone was missing in the petition sent by the English bishops and noblemen to Clement VII, asking him to grant the divorce.[21]

The energetic prelate's character is wholly revealed in the question of the divorce. He was not one of those unscrupulous churchmen who thought it would have been better for the Holy See to revoke its decision and to sacrifice one woman rather than to lose England. He was not one of those men who travelled across the Continent, going from Wolsey to the Pope, or from the Pope to the King of France, secretly negotiating a suspect cause. He was the first to break the submissive silence observed by public men. He dared to oppose the royal desires. It was a dangerous course to pursue, but how noble and how courageous!

The energy, fearlessness, and nobility of Fisher's soul were reflected in his ascetic figure, and in his large fiery eyes. His biographer gives us his portrait, and Holbein has left us excellent sketches of him.[22] In height he was a little above the average, slender and thin, strong in constitution, well proportioned, with a broad forehead, large mouth, deep grey eyes, hair that was black until he was sent to the Tower, and an emaciated body with little flesh left upon it as a result of his fasting and prolonged mortifications. Fisher bore an expres-

---

cujusdam . . . brevis apologia, which remained in manuscript form in England because Henry VIII had forbidden it to be printed under pain of death. But numerous manuscript copies were circulated throughout the country (Bémont, *op. cit.*, 67); it was printed at Alcala de Henares in 1530, and Harpsfield used it for the first book of his *Treatise on the pretended divorce between Henry VIII and Catherine of Aragon* (cf. Bibliography, chap. II).

[20] The copy of this reply, annotated by Fisher himself, is in the Record Office (cf. Brewer, *op. cit.*, II, pp. 346 *sq.*; *L. and P.*, IV, 5729, and Introd. pp. ccclxxix, cccclxxxii, cccclxxxiv–x). "The whole style of the reply," Brewer remarks (p. 348), "rather resembles the invective of an irritated and angry controversialist than the calm rebuke and dignified bearing of Majesty."

[21] Cf. above, p. 79. *Ana. Boll.*, X, 183; XII, 110.

[22] *Ana. Boll.*, Nos. 195, 196. The best portrait of him, by Holbein, belonged to Queen Victoria and must have remained in the royal family. There are others at St John's College, Queen's, Christ's, Trinity, and the Ven. English College, Rome.

sion of austere gravity which overawed even his superiors.[23]
Gentle and unassuming, he could yet become bitter and
vehement when the interests of God or the Church were at
stake. "I reckon in this realm no man, in wisdom, learning
and long approved virtue together, mete to be matched and
compared with him," said More.[24] Death had no terror for a
soul of this calibre, for every day death had been the subject
of his meditation.[25]

Since the day when Fisher had spoken so strongly in
Catherine's defence, Henry had secretly and persistently
owed him a grudge, and the prelate came to be classed more
and more as an opponent. After Wolsey's fall in 1529, Parliament proposed certain Church reforms. Fisher vigorously
opposed their schemes which he declared were "to the destruction of the Church." He likewise upbraided the Commons for
their lack of faith, and the members protested and complained
to the king.[26] It also appears that he was equally zealous in
opposing the first attempt to seize monastic property, after
which the Crown hankered.[27]   In October, 1530, he was

[23] "And the most of his sustenance was thin pottage, sodden with flesh,
eating of the flesh itself very sparingly. The ordinary fasts appointed by
the Church he kept very roundly (every Friday was then a fast-day in
England, besides very many vigils), and to them joined many other
particular fasts of his own devotion. . . . He wore most commonly a shirt
of hair, and many times he would whip himself in most secret wise."
The inventory of his palace furniture gives a striking picture of his episcopal
poverty, which yet allowed him to be charitable and hospitable towards
the poor (Bridgett, op. cit., pp. 62 sq., 67, according to his first biographers).
[24] English Works, ed. 1557, p. 1437.
[25] "And lest that the memory of death might hap to slip from his mind,"
his biographers say, "he always accustomed to set upon one end of the
altar a dead man's skull, which was also set before him at his table as he
dined or supped." See Rastall's story (Ana. Boll., XII, 267).
[26] Cf. Ana. Boll., X, 337-40. We do not possess the text of this speech, but
the fundamental idea of this protest has been preserved in Hall's Chronicle
(p. 766); the language is more spirited than that given in Fisher's Life
(Ana. Boll., X, 337-40). The king warned Fisher to be moderate (ibid., X,
341); the bishop apologized, but as a man of character who would retract
nothing from what he deemed a principle. Cf. H. A. L. Fisher, op. cit.,
p. 298; Bridgett, op. cit., p. 183; Froude, op. cit., chap. III.
[27] During the same session the bishop most energetically opposed the
king's proposition to alienate monastic goods for a sum of 2,000 florins
(Gasquet, op. cit., I, p. 247).   Van Ortroy, who says that Gasquet does not
mention this motion in Parliament (Ana. Boll., X, 243), missed this passage
in Gasquet in which Fisher's words are recorded. What is true is that there
is no contemporary document in existence which mentions the fact; the
accounts of the Long Parliament have been lost.

arrested, together with the Bishops of Bath and Ely, for having violated the new law relating to church benefices, and for having appealed to the Holy See.[28] That same year it was rumoured that Anne Boleyn had tried to have him put to death. A dish of gruel, of which he did not partake, had poisoned seventeen of his servants, and one of them had died as well as a poor woman to whom the rest of the gruel was given. To give the lie to this rumour, the king had a law passed condemning those guilty of poisoning to be boiled to death in a cauldron of tar; and that same year this barbarous punishment was inflicted.[29]

When the king asked Convocation, in 1531, to recognize him as "supreme head of the Church of England," Fisher foresaw in this a danger for the ecclesiastical hierarchy, and openly declared before them all that in accepting that title the clergy would cut themselves off from the Church. Henry then tried to persuade them that if they granted his request he would not intermeddle in any spiritual jurisdiction, nor assume unto himself any more authority than his predecessors had done. But the Bishop of Rochester remained resolute. What would happen, he asked, "if he should shortly after change his mind, and exercise in deed the supremacy over the Church of this realm?" He rebuked the prelates for their pusillanimity, and, seeing that he could not prevail upon them, is said to have suggested the restrictive clause *quantum per legem Dei licet*, which he also wished to add to his signature.[30] Chapuys wrote to Charles V about this declaration, on

[28] *Ven. Cal.*, IV, Nos. 629, 634.

[29] Sander, French ed., p. 57, apparently not translated by Lewis. Gairdner, *History*, 110 *sq.*

[30] *Ana. Boll.*, X, 176, 177, 351-65 and II, 251, 272 *sq.*; Bridgett, *op. cit.*, pp. 201 *sq.*; cf. Hall, *Chronicle*, pp. 766, 774; and chap. iii of this book, pp. 95 *sq.*

Fisher's attitude at the Convocation of 1531 is known to us through his first biographers, Chapuys and Rastall (*Ana. Boll.*, XII, 251), who, however, are not always favourable to the bishop.

Richard Hilliard (secretary to Tunstall, who was rather ill-disposed towards Fisher) was absent from the Convocation, and he alone presents the bishop in a light which does not seem to agree with either his character or his former conduct. According to him, Fisher feared lest the king should revenge himself on the clergy, and so suggested the clause *quantum per legem Dei licet* in order to gain those who hesitated (*Ana. Boll.*, XII, 272 *sq.*). The original edition of Sander (Cologne, 1585) says nothing about this (cf. Bridgett, *The Tablet*, November 16th and 23rd, 1889). But the subse-

February 21st, 1531: "The Bishop of Rochester is very ill with disappointment at it. He opposes it as much as he can; but being threatened that he and his adherents should be thrown in the river, he was forced to consent to the king's will."[31] Again, a few days later (March 1st), he wrote: "The said Bishop of Rochester is very ill, and has been so ever since the acknowledgment made by the clergy."[32]

When Convocation gave two decisions in favour of the divorce, on March 26th, 1533, Fisher again protested, and he alone was courageous and fearless enough to do so, and he continued to protest until the end. On April 5th he was arrested and handed over, as a prisoner, to the care of the Bishop of Winchester, until June 13th.[33] He was back again in his diocese immediately after Cranmer had pronounced sentence and Anne Boleyn had been crowned (June 1st), and there gave proof of constant fidelity to Catherine's cause. This "paragon of Christian prelates, both for learning and holiness," as Chapuys styled him, alone amongst the English clergy thwarted the royal plans by his opposition and con-

quent editions borrow this passage from Hilliard, which is therefore due, not to Sander, but to his editor, Rishton, who must have known Hilliard in Rome.

In 1888, with this passage from Sander as basis, Mr. W. E. Gladstone raised a lively controversy. Van Ortroy gives the details of it (*Ana. Boll.*, X, 57 *sq.*; XII, 278 *sq.*). Reduced to a theological question, the controversy ended with the conclusion that no ecclesiastical gathering could pronounce that papal jurisdiction was abrogated in any country.

[31] Chapuys to the emperor, February 21st, 1531. *Sp. Cal.*, IV, Part II, No. 641.

[32] Chapuys to the emperor, March 1st, 1531. *Sp. Cal.*, IV, Part II, No. 646.

[33] Chapuys to Charles V, April 10th, 1533. Friedman, I, 197. Cf. J. Gairdner, *History*, p. 141. In 1533 Henry VIII could call himself master of nearly the whole of the episcopate: after Wolsey's fall he had appointed archbishops for York and Canterbury, and bishops for Winchester, London, and Durham; death, and an Act of Parliament against two titular foreigners, Campeggio and Ghinucci (*L. and P.*, VII, 48, 54, 634), had made Bangor, Ely, Coventry, Lichfield, Salisbury and Worcester vacant. Catherine of Aragon's confessor, the Spaniard G. Azequa, Bishop of Llandaff, did not know a word of English; most of the others had taken part in the divorce, such as Longland of Lincoln, the king's confessor, and Clerk, Bishop of Bath and Wells. There was scarcely anybody but Fisher therefore to resist the king on behalf of the Church's liberties.

Winchester House, where Fisher was kept at first, was the London residence of the Bishop of Winchester, Stephen Gardiner, who, three days later, sent him to another of his residences, forbidding him to go more than a mile from it.

stancy, and so the king's followers were only waiting for an opportunity to compromise him; and they had not long to wait.

For some time (1528) there had been much talk of a certain Elizabeth Barton, "the Holy Maid of Kent," who prophesied that dreadful things would happen to the king if he repudiated Catherine. She was a servant-maid to Thomas Cobb, of Aldington, Archbishop Warham's estate-agent. On the recommendation of the archbishop, Elizabeth Barton became a nun at Canterbury (1525). At the age of eighteen she had contracted a nervous disease and used to fall into a state of ecstasy and trance. When she entered the convent she was thought to be cured. She began prophesying, and as she went back occasionally to Aldington many people made pilgrimages thither. A careful study of the documents shows that she was a poor hysterical creature, whose mind was so weakened by her fits that on recovering from them she believed in her own visions and revelations. Hysteria and its effects were little known at that time, and so whilst some believed in her, others taxed her with trickery and hypocrisy.[34] As he stated when he was accused, Fisher believed "this woman to be honest, religious, and of good credence," especially upon the testimony of "My Lord of Canterbury, a man reputed of high wisdom and learning." He had conceived so high an opinion of this woman's holiness that he several times sent his chaplain

---

[34] *L. and P.*, V, 1419, 1445; J. Gairdner, *History*, p. 143; Strype, *Memorials of Cranmer*, Append. VII; A. D. Cheney, "The Holy Maid of Kent," in *Transactions of the R. Hist. Soc.*, new series, XVIII, 107-29; Froude, *op. cit.*, chap. iv (a graphic account, studded with hostile comments); Bridgett, *op. cit.*, chap. xi.

Elizabeth Barton entered the Benedictine house at Canterbury at the age of nineteen. [Fr. Bridgett says she was sixteen, p. 236.—*Translator*.] The rule of enclosure not being strictly kept, as was not seldom the case before the Council of Trent restored the old discipline, she was allowed to leave her monastery fairly frequently. We hear of her near Aldington, and visiting the nuns of Sion, the Charterhouse monks at Sheen, the Archbishop of Canterbury, More, Fisher, and even the king. During her lifetime she was, and still continues to be, an object of discussion (cf. Bridgett, *op. cit.*, 234, 486; Froude, *loc. cit.*). Fisher's first biographers prudently reserve judgment as to the reality of her visions: "Quod ad me attinet in neutram partem propendebo, quia multa utrinque tam pro ea quam contra eam a viris probis narrata audivi" (*Ana. Boll.*, *loc. cit.*). If her visions were the outcome of illness, as Gairdner remarks (*loc. cit.*), then the question of deceit is excluded. Cf. Le Grand, I, 279 *sq.*

to her to see if her revelations were supernatural.[35] The king paid very little heed to Elizabeth Barton's oracles as long as he was not concerned in them,[36] but his opinion of her changed when she proclaimed that he would be dethroned a month after the divorce, and driven from the country by his own subjects, and that his place in hell was already determined.[37] The people were already much inflamed against Anne Boleyn. There were many who believed in the Holy Maid of Kent, even amongst the highest classes. Her adherents ranged from most venerable and learned prelates to the lowliest farm-hand. A book relating her visions was circulated among the people. On the subject of the divorce she had held conversations with Wolsey, and had written to the Pope, and the people were whispering one to another her prophecies against the king.[38] To destroy the bad impressions all these facts might create, they tried to brand her as a hypocrite and a liar. To terrify all those who had had close or distant relations with her, mention was made of a plot against the State. In September, 1533, Elizabeth Barton was imprisoned in London, together with her confessor, a penitentiary of Canterbury, and the parson of Aldington, Richard Masters.[39] Confessions were extracted from them by torture,[40] and on the strength of these other persons were arrested, and a list of

[35] Letter from Fisher to the Upper House in H. Ellis, 3rd Series, II, 289. *L. and P.*, VII, 240, and Bridgett, *op. cit.*, p. 248. Cromwell's reply (February, 1531) to Fisher's lost letter on the Holy Maid of Kent, in Merriman, *op. cit.*, I, 373-79; Wright, *op. cit.*, 27; Burnet, IV, 195.

[36] Thomas More to Cromwell (Burnet, V, 431 *sq.*).

[37] *Statutes of the realm*, 25 Henry VIII, cap. 12. Chapuys' letters to Charles V on November 12th and 20th, 1533, in *L. and P.*, VI, 1419, 1445. Cf. *ibid.*, Nos. 1466, 1468, 1470; Strype, *Memorials of Cranmer*, p. 336; *Ana. Boll.*, XII, 101, n. 1; Froude, *op. cit.*, chap. vi.

[38] Cranmer to Archdeacon Hawkyns, December 20th, 1533. Cranmer's *Works*, II, letter lxxxiii; Strype, *Memorials of Cranmer*, Append. VII; *L. and P.*, VI, 1519.

[39] In July Archbishop Cranmer subjected her to a first examination in which she maintained the reality of her visions and revelations, and he pretended to believe in them (*L. and P.*, VI, 869, 967; cf. Friedmann, I, pp. 244-45).
Her confessor, Dr. Bocking, was a Benedictine monk of Christ Church, Canterbury. The penitentiary's name was Hadley, but he was not among those condemned for treason. Richard Masters was not so fortunate, but he was pardoned.

[40] This is admitted by one of Henry VIII's partisans, Richard Morison (cf. *Apomaxis calumniarum convitiorumque*, London, 1537, p. 75).

accused people was secretly drawn up. On November 23rd, the nun and six of her companions were made to do public penance on a scaffold erected at St Paul's Cross. Dr. Capon, a friend of Anne Boleyn and the new Bishop of Bangor, read the written confession which Elizabeth had given him, and in the presence of an immense crowd poured scorn upon the hypocrisy of the nun and the disloyalty of those who had listened to but had not denounced her. [41]

Henry wished to exploit the nun's confession in order to spread terror amongst all who had believed in her either from overweening confidence, or curiosity, or political motives. Was it not the best way to break down the opposition, [42] and to make Parliament declare without resistance that his first marriage was invalid? [43] As the judges could not easily be brought to declare all those who had believed in Elizabeth's revelations guilty of heresy, or those who had imprudently quoted them guilty of treason, a Bill of Attainder was passed in the House of Lords, on March 12th, 1534, None of the accused persons had been allowed a hearing; the peers blindly relied upon the enquiry made by the Privy Council. [44]

It was easy to be embroiled in a charge of treason in those days. "Every accusation in this country is called treason," wrote the French ambassador. [45] In addition to those who were attainted, many others might have been condemned. But Henry was concerned less with the number of victims

[41] L. and P., VI, 1460; cf. ibid., VII, 72.
The confession had been drawn up long before (Gasquet, op. cit., I, 134). In it Elizabeth Barton admitted that she had been "the original of all this mischief, and by my falsehood have deceived all these persons here and many more" (L. and P., VI, 72 [11]). In the previous month she had been questioned in the Star Chamber and forced to confess that she had never had a vision in her life, but that they were all feigned in order to take advantage of those who listened to her and to gain a reputation (L. and P., VII, 54 [31], 532). On the day of her execution she repeated more briefly the confession which had been read for her on November 23rd, 1533 (Hall, Chronicle, 814).

[42] And in fact Cromwell was soon receiving letters or testimonies of humble submission (cf. Friedmann, op. cit., I, p. 246 and n. 5, pp. 273–74).

[43] The Act of Succession was indeed passed just when Elizabeth Barton and her partisans were attainted, in March, 1534.

[44] See the opinions of the judges in the consultation to which Henry VIII summoned them, in L. and P., VI, No. 1445, Chapuys' letters of November 20th and 24th, ibid., No. 1460; the indictment in Statutes of the realm, 25 Henry VIII, cap. 12. Cf. J. Gairdner, History, p. 144.

[45] Marillac to Montmorency, March 21st, 1540 (Kaulek, 185).

than with discrediting certain embarrassing people.   The Bill of Attainder bore the names of Fisher, More, the Marquis of Exeter, the Countesses of Derby and Salisbury, and Lord and Lady Hussey.[46] Elizabeth Barton and six of her followers were condemned to death,[47] six others were indicted for misprision of treason, and thus stood to lose their property and their lives. Misprision of treason was the crime of concealing anything that might be dangerous from a political point of view. Of these six accused persons Fisher's name was first on the list.[48]

The bishop had no difficulty in showing the absurdity of such an accusation. Why should one be bound to reveal what, according to the nun's own indictment, was already public knowledge? "But this was the very cause why I came not to your grace," Fisher observed in his letter to the king, "for, in good faith, I dreaded lest I should thereby have provoked your grace to farther displeasure against me."[49] Cromwell did all he could to persuade the bishop to follow the Marquis of Exeter's example and write a humble letter to the king, asking for pardon and submitting himself to the royal mercy, for he knew that thus Fisher's opposition would be overcome and his mouth silenced both in Parliament and in Convocation. "I dare undertake," Cromwell wrote, "that his highness shall

[46] The Marquis of Exeter, Edward IV's grandson, was, together with Norfolk, the most powerful lord in the kingdom. Attempts were indeed made to compromise Catherine and her daughter (*L. and P.*, VI, 1372, 1419) but the queen protested, and Cromwell was obliged later to acknowledge Mary's innocence.

[47] The parson of Aldington was pardoned.   The others, Bocking, Elizabeth's confessor; Dering, another Benedictine of Canterbury; the two Franciscans, Rich and Risby, who were offered their lives, according to Father Bourchier (*Hist. Ecc. de Martyrio FF. Ord. Min.*, 1583), on condition that they accepted Henry as supreme head of the English Church; and the parson of Aldermary, were executed, together with Elizabeth Barton, at Tyburn, on April 20th, 1534 (cf. *Ana. Boll.*, XII, 106, 107, 108; *L. and P.*, VI, 1445; Froude, chap. vi).

[48] Cf. *Ana. Boll.*, XII, p. 105.

[49] In this same letter (*L. and P.*, VII, 2397; Lewis-Turner, *op. cit.*, II, 336 *sq.*) as well as in his letter to the Lords already referred to, the bishop declared that he would have disclosed to Henry what he knew if Elizabeth Barton had not assured him that she herself had told the king. J. Bruce (*Archaeologia*, XXV, pp. 65–70) shows that the accusation was not based on any serious grounds. Fisher again told Cromwell (letter of January 31st, 1534, reproduced by both Bruce and Bridgett, *op. cit.*, p. 250) that through motives of delicacy he had refrained from mentioning the question of the divorce, upon which the king and he could not agree.

benignly accept you into his gracious favour, all matter of displeasure before this time forgotten and forgiven." But if the bishop sought to justify his conduct as though it were not blameworthy, Cromwell could make him no promises. "If the matter come to trial," he added, "your own confession in these letters, besides the witnesses which are against you, will be sufficient to condemn you."[50] Fisher nobly refused; he was not a man to abase himself. He fell ill, and was unable to make the journey to London. To defend himself he sent a letter addressed to the House of Lords.[51] "I sought not for this woman's coming unto me," he told them, "nor thought in her any manner of deceit. . . . And as I will answer before the throne of Christ, I knew not of any malice or evil that was intended by her, or by any other earthly creature unto the king's highness." Why repeat to the king what she declared she had already told him? He pointed out that laws or interpretations of laws which infringed upon the constitutional freedom were as dangerous for themselves—Cromwell was one day to experience this—as for him. "And therefore eftsoons I beseech all your benign charities to tender this my most humble suit as you would be tendered if you were in the same danger yourselves." Tried in his absence, he was condemned to be imprisoned and to have all his property confiscated.[52] The king, however, commuted the penalty into a fine of £300.[53]

[50] Cromwell to Fisher, February, 1534, in Burnet, IV, 195 *sq.*; Wright, *op. cit.*, 27; and Merriman, I, 373 *sq.* Three times in this same letter Cromwell insisted on the necessity of relying upon the king's pardon, and laboured to refute the bishop's vindication point by point, and to prove that he had given credence to Elizabeth's revelations because they agreed with his own manner of thinking (cf. Collier, IV, 274). On November 12th, 1533 Chapuys wrote (*L. and P.*, VI, 1419) that he was seriously afraid for the "good bishop of Rochester."

[51] This letter is in Collier, IX, 244–48; Ellis, 3rd Series, II, 289; and *L. and P.*, VIII, 240.

[52] Although he asked that before any sentence were passed against him his cause should be well and duly heard, the House of Lords decided that the bishop's letter was equivalent to his having been heard (*Journals of the House of Lords*). Lord Campbell (*Life of Audeley*) observes that Henry VIII's law on treason, which suppressed all proofs and judicial forms, was a very convenient instrument of tyranny.

[53] *L. and P.*, II, 70; *Ana. Boll.*, XII, p. 108. Cf. Lewis-Turner, chap. xxxII. Edward Thwaites who, together with Elizabeth Barton, had undergone the public penance and humiliation at St Paul's Cross, regained his liberty by paying 10,000 marks (*L. and P.*, VII, 386). Such instances of penalties being commuted are not rare (see *ibid.*, VI, 1519, 1666).

He had scarcely escaped this peril before he fell into another and a greater one. In attacking Fisher they had hoped to bring to the ground the steadfast defender of Catherine of Aragon; the Act of Succession of March 30th, 1534, enabled them to strike at him with more sureness. This law, in spite of the Pope's authority, declared Henry's marriage with Catherine of Aragon to be unlawful, and also forbade "faith, truth and obedience" to be given to any foreign authority, i.e. to the Pope.[54] All whose loyalty was suspect had to take an oath immediately to maintain, defend and keep this act. Like More, Fisher accepted that portion of the oath which settled the succession on the heirs of the king and Anne Boleyn, for a contest over the succession to the throne might prove a danger for the State. This much then he conceded—although inwardly he deplored it—since it was already a *fait accompli*.[55] But he rejected the clause concerning Catherine's marriage and the Pope.[56] On April 4th news reached London that Clement VII had confirmed the validity of Henry VIII's first marriage.[57] The following day Fisher, weakened by illness, had to go to London, whither the Archbishop of Canterbury summoned him.[58] On the 13th he appeared before the commission at Lambeth appointed to receive the oath.[59] When he refused to take it in its entirety, he was given

[54] *Statutes*, 25 Henry VIII, cap. 22. Cf. *L. and P.*, VII, 51; Froude, chap. VII.

[55] Alluding to the Wars of the Roses, the king said that the uncertainty of succession would cause the realm the worst calamities, the shedding of human blood, the loss of a mass of subjects, and the destruction of the nobility. Fisher answered in writing that he had always been ready to acknowledge upon oath the succession to the throne as it had been decreed by Parliament (Strype, *Memorials of Cranmer*, ed. 1848, Append. IX, X).

[56] Strype, *ibid.*, Append. X and XI; *L. and P.*, VII, 499.

[57] This decision on the validity of Henry's marriage with Catherine was given on March 23rd, 1534. Henry VIII was greatly exasperated thereby and gave orders to speak against the Pope; the preachers, Chapuys wrote (*L. and P.*, VII, 469), have acquitted themselves desperately, saying the most outrageous and abominable things in the world. Woe to those who crossed the king at that time, says Froude (*loc. cit.*).

[58] His early biographers give affecting accounts of his farewell to, and separation from, his episcopal city, and all thought the separation was a final one: "nothing was there to be heard but lamentation and mourning on all sides." They also describe his frugal meal in the open air (*Ana. Boll.*, XII, 128-31). According to R. Pole (*Pro Ecclesiae unitatis defensione*, Bk. III, f. cxvi) Fisher, worn out with fatigue, fainted on the journey.

[59] The formula of this oath, due to the chancellor Audeley, Archbishop Cranmer, and the Dukes of Suffolk and Norfolk, and subsequent to the

into Cranmer's charge. The archbishop was inclined to be gentle, and when after a few days' reflexion Fisher still accepted only part of the oath, Cranmer advised the others to be satisfied with that. "If all the realm with one accord would apprehend the said succession, in my judgment it is a thing to be amplected and embraced" unto which thing "might not a little avail the consent and oaths of these two persons, the Bishop of Rochester and Master More, with their adherents, or rather, confederates."[60] But Henry VIII opined that to pass over the other clauses in silence was tantamount to disapproving his second marriage and admitting the authority of Rome. On the night of April 17th Fisher slept in the Tower.[61] From that time onward his lot was coupled with that of More.

His ill-health and his advanced years did not save him from the rigorous treatment meted out to political prisoners. He wrote to Cromwell[62]: "I have neither shirt nor sute, nor yett other cloths, that ar necessary for me to wear, but that bee ragged and rent to shamefully . . . and noo in myn age my stomake may nott awaye but with a few kynd of meates, which if I want I decaye forthwith, and fall into coafes [coughs] and diseases of my bodye, and kan not keep myself in health . . . I byseche you to have sum pittee uppon me, and latt me have such thyngs ass ar necessary for me in myn age, and specially for my health." Roland Lee, Bishop of Coventry and Lichfield (1534-43), saw him in prison and said that he looked like a skeleton, "the body cannot bear clothes on his back" so thin had he become; "the man is nigh going and doubtless

---

Act of Succession, had not been approved by Parliament (it was added to another law passed in the following December; *Lords' Journal*, I, p. 82): for this reason both Fisher and Sir Thomas More held that they were not legally bound to take the oath as it was.

[60] Cranmer to Thomas Cromwell, April 17th, 1534. Strype, *Memorials of Cranmer*, Append. XI. Cf. *Ana. Boll.*, XIII, 132, 136.

[61] Cromwell to Cranmer, April 1534. Merriman, I, No. 71. *L. and P.*, VII, No. 500.
The bishop's prison house in the Tower of London, very little changed is still shown.

[62] Letter dated December 22nd, 1534, in Dodd (ed. 1737, I, 311) and Bridgett (*op. cit.*, 290 *sq.*). State prisoners were obliged to pay high prices for the necessaries of life. Deprived of his belongings by confiscation, the bishop had nothing left; his brother, Robert Fisher, did what he could to help him.

cannot continue unless the king and his council be merciful unto him."[63] Fisher fell ill and had to be seen by doctors.[64] His privations and his bodily sufferings—and these were not alleviated by the rites of religion, which were denied all prisoners[65]—did not prevent him from spending his leisure hours in writing two spiritual treatises on Christian perfection.[66]

When the Act of Supremacy was passed (November 1534), which made the king the spiritual head of the Church in England, Fisher's indictment for a political offence entered upon a new phase. During the same session Parliament condemned him, together with Thomas More, to perpetual imprisonment for not having accepted in its entirety the oath of succession. In order, however, to avoid a more serious punishment for them, the word "maliciously" was introduced into the Bill on the supremacy, so that opinions uttered with no idea of rebellion could not be considered treason; it was sufficiently detestable that for the first time mere words should constitute a treasonable crime. It was made then high treason[67] "for any person after the first day of February next coming [1535] *maliciously* to wish, will, or desire by words or writing . . . to deprive them [the king, the queen, or their heirs apparent] or any of them of their dignity, title or name of their royal estate." A futile precaution indeed, for in the tyrannical hands of Henry VIII the weapon was not less deadly. By their arbitrary interpretations Henry's ministers converted this law—which even Froude called an "extreme measure"—into the two-edged sword of which More spoke, "if a man answer one way it will confound his soul, and if the other way it will confound his body."

Fisher was urged to recognize the royal supremacy. Several of his episcopal brethren, Stokesley, Gardiner, and Tunstall,

---

[63] Strype, *Memorials of Cranmer*, Append. X.

[64] *Anna. Boll.*, XII, 166, n. 1.

[65] For the denial of all religious consolations to the prisoners, whatever their rank in society, see Bridgett, *ibid.*, 296 *sq.*

[66] The first, *A Spiritual Consolation*, dedicated to his sister, a nun, is the fifth English work published in 1876 by Turner. The second treatise, *The Ways of Perfect Religion*, is the sixth publication of this series.

[67] *Statutes of the realm*, 26 Henry VIII, cap. 13. Somerset had this law abolished immediately after the king's death (1 Edward VI, cap. 12).

came on behalf of the king and begged him to do so.[68] Shameless representations were made to him that More had decided to take the oath,[69] but he maintained a close silence. He was then deprived of all the privileges belonging to his episcopal dignity, and the see of Rochester was declared vacant (January 2nd, 1534). It was hoped that he would at least utter some compromising words. Those who attended his wants watched him closely and afterwards gave testimony at the trial. At all costs a verbal refusal had to be extracted from him which could be reckoned as treason. That the law considered mere wishes as treason was not sufficient[70]; an expressed opinion, albeit forced, would incur the penalty of high treason. On May 7th, 1535 Cromwell and some of the members of the Privy Council overstepped their rights and the duties of their office, and subjected the aged bishop to a real mental torture in order to manufacture a non-existent indictment against him. Was it on this occasion that Fisher declared "the king was not supreme head in earth of the Church of England"?[71] Or was it, as his biographer and Lord Campbell assert,[72] before one witness alone, the solicitor-general, Rich, "one of the most sordid as well as unprincipled men who have ever held the office of lord chancellor in England,"[73] who assured him that the king wished to know his opinion to set his conscience at rest, and that any words he uttered would never be repeated, and who afterwards made the bishop's confidences known at the trial? These interviews could not be avowed openly, nor could they prove Fisher's guilt. Mr.

[68] *Ana. Boll.*, XII, 155 *sq.*

[69] The same trick was played upon Sir Thomas More, who was assured that Fisher had at last acknowledged the king's supremacy (*ibid.*, XII, 152 *sq.*).

[70] Bruce (*Archaeologia*, XXV, 82) criticizes the "atrocious character" of this law, which "evidences a state of society but little removed from actual barbarism."

[71] The official bill of indictment says it was on May 7th "and in the presence of several of His Majesty's subjects." The indictment against Sir Thomas More sets forth that on May 12th he learnt that John Fisher "being examined, had denied to accept the king as before mentioned." Fisher denied that he had said those words (*L. and P.*, VIII, 856; cf. *ibid.*, VIII, 886). On May 5th it was intended to deal with Fisher and More in the same way as the Carthusians, if they did not take the oath of the Royal Supremacy (*L. and P.*, VIII, 666).

[72] *Ana. Boll.*, XII, 172 *sq.*

[73] Lord Campbell's words in *English State Trials*.

Gairdner asks[74]: "How could Fisher . . . have been justly said to 'publish and pronounce' an opinion for which he had been expressly asked in prison by members of the king's Privy Council?" Lord Macaulay calls the State trials of those days "murder preceded by mummery."

Henry appears to have hesitated before condemning Fisher and More. But in the consistory held on May 20th, 1535 Paul III created Fisher a cardinal, with the title of St Vitalis. Later, the Pope asserted that he was ignorant of the extreme tension existing in the relations between the bishop and the king, and that he had not wished to give any offence at all to the latter.[75] When the news of the Bishop of Rochester's elevation reached England, Henry grew extremely angry and ordered all messengers from the Pope to be stopped at Calais, and "bishops, curates, and others . . . to preach certain articles against the Church, and schoolmasters to instruct their scholars to revile apostolic authority," and threatened to send the bishop's "head afterwards to Rome for the cardinal's hat." Fisher's fate, as well as More's, was settled: either their conscience yielded, or else it meant death.[76]

On June 14th, Fisher was again questioned by two recorders of the council, Thomas Bedyll and Layton—afterwards

[74] *L. and P.*, VIII, Introd., p. xxxiii.

[75] Gregory Casale to Cromwell, May 29th, 1535. Denonville, Bishop of Macon and ambassador to Paul III, May 29th, 1535. *L. and P.*, VII, 425; Friedmann, II, 72; Bridgett, *op. cit.*, 354–60. Cf. Friedmann; Chacon-Oldoin, *Vitae et res gestae Pontificum Romanorum et S. R. E. cardinalium*, Rome, 1677, III, col. 573, 575.

[76] Chapuys to Charles V, June 16th, 1535. *L. and P.*, VIII, 76, 742, 876; and chaps. XXXIV, XXXV and XXXVI in Lewis.

The first Life of Fisher relates that, when Cromwell asked what he would do if the Pope sent him a cardinal's hat, Fisher replied: "Sir, I know myself far unworthy of any such dignity, that I think nothing less than such matters; but if he so send it me, assure yourself I will work with it by all the means I can to benefit the Church of Christ; and in that respect I will receive it upon my knees." When informed of this answer, the king said with great indignation: "Yea, is he yet so lusty? Well, let the pope send him a hat when he will . . . he shall wear it on his shoulders, for head he shall have none to set it on" (*Ana. Boll.*, XII, 163 *sq.*; Baily, *op. cit.*, 171). According to Lewis (II, 412) Fisher's answer proves that he had never desired to be a cardinal. Sander also says the same (*op. cit.*, French ed., 1587, f. 73. [Apparently not in Lewis' trans.—*Translator*.]). To find out if Fisher "*a fait poursuyte du chappeaul*," Chapuys wrote on June 16th, 1535 (*L. and P.*, VIII, 76; Friedmann, *op. cit.*, I, 87, n. 1), "*sont constituez plusieurs prisonniers tant de ses parents que de ceux qui le gardoient en prison.*" Naturally nothing could be learnt from them.

famous for their share in the suppression of the monasteries—
but with no better result.[77] On the 17th, albeit weakened by
his illness and long captivity, Fisher appeared at Westminster
before a jury of twelve freeholders, chosen, by Cromwell's
orders, from the quarter around the Tower. Accused of high
treason for having said: "The king our sovereign lord is not
supreme head in earth of the Church of England," he pleaded
"Not Guilty." "Though I had spoken the words, indeed, the
same being not spoken maliciously, but in the way of advice
and counsel. . . . And that favour the very words of the
statute do give me, being made only against such as shall
maliciously gainsay the king's supremacy."[78] The odious
speech of the lord chancellor, Audeley, gave the jury clearly
to understand what was expected from them, and they condemned Fisher to a traitor's death. The king commuted the
sentence and ordered him to be beheaded. After he had
denied that malice against the State could be imputed to him,
Fisher admitted his faith in the presence of the judges, and
told them that if he had not taken the oath in support of the
new statutes, he had refused "with truth and holy intention,
as they were opposed to Scriptures and our faith."[79] "I
think, indeed," said he, "and always have thought, and do
now lastly affirm, that his grace cannot justly claim any such
supremacy over the Church of God as he now taketh upon
him, neither hath been seen or heard of, that any temporal
prince before his days hath presumed to that dignity."[80]
When he left Westminster an immense crowd of men and
women followed him weeping and begging him to bless them

[77] The lieutenant of the Tower and several other witnesses assisted at
this examination, which we still possess with the answers signed by Fisher
(cf. Bridgett, *op. cit.*, 365).

[78] Account of the trial in *Ana. Boll.*, XII, 173 *sq.* Cf. *L. and P.*, VIII,
1075; Bruce's article in *Archæologia Britannica*, XXV.

[79] Chapuys to Ortiz, imperial Ambassador in Rome (*L. and P.*, VIII,
1075).

[80] According to the biography frequently mentioned (*Ana. Boll.*, XII,
184) which records these words, they were pronounced after the verdict.
And thus Fisher did what More was afterwards to do. According to
Chapuys (letter referred to in the previous note), and the anonymous Life
of Fisher, the fragments of which are preserved in the British Museum,
and Cardinal Pole (Quirini, *R. Poli Epistolae*, Brescia, 1744-51, IV, 79,
and Bridgett, 386) they were uttered before the verdict. "For him," says
Pole, speaking of Fisher, "the time to speak out was immediately when he
was questioned, for this befitted his character of bishop."

as he made his way back to the Tower. He himself "seemed rather to have come from a great feast or a banquet than from his arraignment."[81]

He spent his last four days in prayer and quietness. One day a false rumour was circulated that he was to be executed that very day, and his servant hearing it prepared no dinner for him. Fisher advised the man not to listen to such reports: "Make it ready as thou art wont to do, and if thou see me dead when thou comest, then eat it thyself; but I promise thee if I be alive, I mind by God's grace to eat never a bit the less." On June 22nd, at 5 a.m. the lieutenant of the Tower, Sir William Kingston, came to inform him that it was the king's pleasure he should die that day. He begged the lieutenant to allow him to sleep an hour or two because he had had little sleep during the night. When he awoke he told his man to take away his hair shirt, and to give him a clean white shirt and his best apparel. "Dost thou not mark that this is our wedding-day," he asked, "and that it behoveth us, therefore, to use more cleanliness for solemnity of the marriage?" He asked also for his fur tippet to put round his neck, and when Kingston expressed his surprise that the bishop should trouble about his health an hour before death, he remarked that health was a gift of God, which we are not allowed to jeopardize: "I will prolong the same as long as I can by such reasonable ways and means as Almighty God hath provided for me." At nine o'clock, whilst waiting to proceed to Tower Hill, he opened his New Testament and besought God to aid him to find a comforting thought. His eyes fell upon these words of St John[82]: *Haec est autem vita aeterna: ut cognoscant te solum Deum verum et quem misisti Jesum Christum. Ego te clarificavi super terram; opus consummavi, quod dedisti mihi ut faciam; et nunc clarifica me, tu Pater, apud temetipsum claritate quam habui, priusquam mundus esset, apud te.*[83]

[81] Chapuys' letter to Ortiz previously referred to (*Ana. Boll.*, X, 185).

[82] Chap. xvii, vv. 3, 4, 5.

[83] All this and most of what follows is known to us through the early biographers, who took the accounts of eye-witnesses. *Ana. Boll.* XII, 186 *sq.* The accounts of Maurice Chauncy and Baily agree in their testimony to the calm, dignity, and Christian resignation of the holy bishop in the days and moments before his martyrdom. Chapter xxxvii of Lewis' *Life of Fisher* is devoted to his death and taken mostly from the MS. 1266 in Cambridge University, which contains an account of the martyrdom of

He mounted the steps to the scaffold without any help, and with a surprising liveliness for one so old and weak. At that moment the sun shone on his face and he murmured the words of the Psalmist: *Accedite ad eum, et illuminamini et facies vestrae non confundentur.* It was eleven o'clock. His last hour had arrived. They offered him life and liberty if he would acknowledge the royal supremacy.[84] But turning to the crowd: "Christian people," said he in a voice that was wonderfully strong for "so weak and sickly an old body," "I am come hither to die for the faith of Christ's holy Catholic Church, and I thank God . . . I have not feared death; wherefore I do desire you all to help and assist me with your prayers, that at the very point and instant of death's stroke, I may in that very moment stand steadfast without fainting in any one point of the Catholic faith, free from any fear. And I beseech Almighty God of His infinite goodness to save the king and this realm . . . and send the king good counsel."[85] He then recited the *Te Deum* and the psalm *In Te Domine speravi*, the words of which were most apposite for him, e.g., *In eo dum convenirent simul adversum me, accipere animam meam consiliati sunt.* At the sight of his "long, lean, and slender body . . . a very image of death . . . monstrous was it thought that the king could be so cruel as to put such a man to death." The executioner bandaged his eyes. After addressing a few short and fervent invocations to God, the bishop knelt, and quietly and courageously laid his head on the block. One blow of the axe severed it from the body. By the

---

Fisher and More. A long Latin letter of 1535—attributed for a long time to Erasmus (Bridgett, 365) but which was not from his pen (cf. Van Ortroy, *Vie de Jean Fisher*, Brussels, 1893, p. 35)—retraces the last days of "John Fisher, Bishop of Rochester, a man who proved himself a true bishop by the sanctity and austerity of his life . . . and his assiduity in teaching both by word and writings, and by his wonderful liberality to the poor and kindness to students."

[84] "*Il fut sollicité à merveille, depuis qu'il fut sur l'échaffault, de consentir à ce que vouloit le roy, luy offrant sa grâce. Mais yl n'y eust ordre, et mourut très vertueusement.*" Chapuys to Charles V, June 30th, 1535.

[85] Dodd, ed. 1737, I, 311. The papal nuncio in France (1535–37), Rodolfo Pio di Carpi, wrote that Fisher died "to preserve the honour of God and the Holy See."

A. Vittorelli (quoted by Chacon-Oldoin, *op. cit.*, III, col. 575) said of the Bishop of Rochester: "*Christi pugil invictissimus, qui . . . Christi Domini fidem, sanctae sedis Apostolicae dignitatem . . . moriens suo sanguine consignavit.*"

king's order, the bishop's head was exposed at the end of a pole for fourteen days on London Bridge.[86]

By the king's orders also, the body, which had been left on the scaffold until eight o'clock at night, was carried "upon a halbert" to Barking cemetery by two of the watchers, who "without any reverence tumbled the body of this holy prelate and blessed martyr all naked and flat upon his belly, without either sheet or other accustomed thing belonging to a Christian man's burial" into its grave. Some time afterwards it was removed to the church of St Peter ad Vincula in the Tower, where Thomas Cromwell and Anne Boleyn were also laid to rest in due course.[87]

The inventory written during the bishop's imprisonment[88] mentions "A St John's head standing at the end of the altar," which Fisher kept in his chapel in memory of the beheading of St John the Baptist. He himself had declared, before Henry VIII, that he was ready, like John the Baptist, to uphold the

---

[86] The early biography (*Ana. Boll.*, XII, 201), from which the whole of this account is taken, adds that "his cheeks being beautified with a comely red, the face looked as if it had beholden the people passing by and would have spoken to them, which many took for a miracle (cf. Friedensburg, *Nuntiaturberichte*, I, 518) . . . at the end of fourteen days the executioner was commanded to throw down the head in the night-time into the river of the Thames." Richard Morison, who wrote his *Apomaxis calumniarum* in 1537, in defence of Henry VIII, denies this last fact, which is recorded both by John Cochlœus (1536) and by Justice Rastall; but there are a number of other erroneous assertions which, together with his partiality towards the king, render Morison suspect, and it is admitted that the Bishop of Rochester's head was thrown into the river (cf. Chacon-Oldoin, *op. cit.*, III, col. 574; Friedensburg, I, 518).

Cosimo Gherio, Bishop of Fano (1528–37), writing to Archbishop Beccadelli, on June 18th, 1537 (Morandi, *Monumenti di varia Letteratura*, Bologna, 1797–1804, I, Part 1, 319 *sq.*), tells how an English priest then in his service, who had been in Fisher's service and had been ordained by him, had fallen into schism and a thousand excesses, but that the Bishop of Rochester had appeared to him on several occasions after his death and upbraided him for his errors and the life he was leading. Wherefore he had left England and come to Rome to do penance.

[87] According to some the body was removed a fortnight later; according to others, only after seven years; "the soil itself . . . for seven years brought forth no grass." Anonymous Life of Fisher in Latin (Arundel MS., 152, f. 233 *sq.*). Chacon-Oldoin, *op. cit.*, IV, col. 574. Cf. *Ana. Boll.*, X, 202, 203, and n. 1.

St Peter ad Vincula is to-day used as a church for the troops in the Tower.

[88] This inventory of the bishop's palace at Rochester, of April 27th, 1534, has been printed by Lewis-Turner, *op. cit.*, II, 221–22, and reproduced by Bridgett, *op. cit.*, 62, 63, 64

indissolubility of marriage with the sacrifice of his life. And it is said that Anne Boleyn ordered the martyr's bleeding head to be brought before her, and addressed it thus: "Is this the head that so often exclaimed against me? I trust it shall never do me more harm"; and striking the head with the back of her hand, received a wound from a prominent tooth which left a scar for the rest of her life. Whether this be true or not,[89] this report shows that the people saw in Anne Boleyn another Herodias, and in Fisher another defender of the marriage laws. His early biographers compared his death to that of the Baptist, and stigmatized Henry whose cruelty was greater than that of Herod.[90]

Thomas More was born on February 7th, 1478, in the heat of the civil Wars of the Roses.[91] His father had followed the law and became a judge in the King's Bench, London, and was anxious that his son should follow in his footsteps. A crayon sketch of the father made by Holbein, when the former was in his seventy-sixth year, still exists. At the age of thirteen Thomas More was admitted into the household of Cardinal Morton, Chancellor and Archbishop of Canterbury. The Cardinal delighted in his "wit and towardness" and was wont to say frequently to the nobles dining at his table: "This child here waiting at the table, whoever shall live to see it, will

[89] J. H. Blunt (p. 422) gives this as a true story. Chacon-Oldoin had previously related it, taking it from the early biography of Fisher (*Ana. Boll.*, XII, 198 *sq.*). Lewis, in his Life of Fisher, disputes the probability of it. Bridgett (*op. cit.*, pp. 398, 499) does not attempt to prove its authenticity, and Van Ortroy attributes it (*Ana. Boll.*, X, p. 129) to popular malice.

[90] *Ana. Boll.*, XII, 226–33.

"Et a nonnullis comparatur Joanni Baptistae; ambobus enim fuit commune nomen, ambobus eadem sors et casus, qui capite truncati pro veritate et justitia similiter occubuerunt; utrobique ab adulteris justus occiditur utrobique odium peperit veritas, nec potuit aequo animo tolerari quod homo Dei sanctus monebat" (Chacon-Oldoin, III, col. 577); cf. Letter from Paul III to Ferdinand of Hungary, "King of the Romans," April 22nd, 1535 (*ibid.*, col. 575; Bucholtz, *Gesch. der Regierung Ferdinands des Ersten*, Vienna, 1831–38, IX, 15).

[91] This date, February, 1478, has been fixed by A. Wright, *Notes and Queries*, 4th Series, II, 365. Thomas was the only surviving son of Sir John More. His master at St Anthony's School—the best in London according to Stow—was the Humanist Nicholas Holt who had been Colet's and Latimer's professor, and who was the author of a Latin Grammar with he alluring title *Lac puerorum*.

prove a marvellous man."[92]   After a year the cardinal sent More to Oxford University.   There he studied under the famous Greek scholars, Thomas Linacre and William Grocyn, who had recently returned from Italy where Politian had taught them Greek.[93]   More loved Greek, and writing to Van Dorpius said that if he were to recount all that a man lacked who knew not Greek, he would never end.[94]   He spoke Latin with the same facility as his own language, and we know from Erasmus that he strove long to render the writing of it easy and harmonious.   He also learnt French, mathematics, geometry, and history, and could play both on the viol and the flute.[95]   At the age of eighteen he was recalled from Oxford by his father, who had no love for Greek (according to Erasmus) and feared lest his son's love of literature should weaken his faith and lead him to neglect his legal studies. In February, 1496, More was placed in Lincoln's Inn.   Five years later, having been called to the bar, he was appointed reader at Furnivall's Inn.[96]   At the same time he delivered

[92] W. Roper, Life of Sir Thomas More, Lumby ed. of Utopia, Cambridge, 1908, VI. For John Morton, Cardinal (1499) and Archbishop of Canterbury (1486–1500) see A. F. Pollard's article in the 11th edition of the Encl. Brit., XVIII, 881, and the portrait of him given by More in terms of admiration in "The first Booke" of Utopia.   He had a great influence upon More.   Cf. Hutton, Life of Thomas More, London, 1895, p. 9; A. Wood, ed. 1691, I, 547 sq.;   Registrum annalium collegii Mertonensis, 1483–1521, 1923.

[93] Cf. Gasquet, The Old English Bible, Essay XIII.   For W. Grocyn (†1519) see A. Wood, I, 13 sq.; and for Linacre, ibid., 17 sq.; W. Osler, Thomas Linacre (1460?–1524), physician and classical scholar, Cambridge, 1908, with eleven engravings.

[94] Dorpius, a Flemish scholar and linguist, fearing the movement which was drawing men's minds towards Paganism, had at first denounced Greek studies.   The long Latin letter which More wrote to him is a kind of treatise in defence of Erasmus' critical studies on the New Testament and the Fathers.   Dorpius admitted More's arguments and publicly retracted what he had written against Erasmus.   The Thomae Mori dissertatio epistolica de aliquot sui temporis theologastrorum ineptiis. . . . Ad Martinum Derpium is at the end of the London edition of Erasmus' letters, in More's Opera omnia. Cf. Pace, De fructu qui ex doctrina percipitur, Basle, 1517, p. 82;   Bridgett, Bl. Thomas More, 3rd ed., 89–94.

[95] Stapleton, Hallett's trans., 1928, p. 15.   In a letter to Ulrich von Hutten on July 23rd, 1519 (Erasmi Epistolae, Leyden, 1706, I, 472), Erasmus wrote of him: "Ad Musicam vocalem a natura non videtur esse compositus, etiamsi delectatur omni Musices genere."

[96] Erasmus, writing of the Bar in England, said: "Quae professio, ut est a veris litteris alienissima, ita apud Britannos cum primis habentur magni, clarique qui in hoc genere sibi pararunt auctoritatem, nec temere apud illos alia via ad rem ac gloriam parandum magis idonea."   The nobility, he adds, are very addicted to it (Erasmi Epistolae, ed. Leyden, 1706, p. 472).

another course of lectures, with great success, on St Augustine's *De Civitate Dei*,[97] in the Church of St Lawrence. In 1504 he entered Parliament.[98]

His great talents assured his success as a barrister, the career he had adopted out of deference to his father's wishes.[99] "Nature never made any one so ready of wit, so keen sighted, so shrewd," says Erasmus. "His intellect is equalled by his power of speech; and his suavity is so great, his humour so keen yet so innocuous, that he has every quality of a perfect advocate." His humour was universally known. His delight in refined merriment and his pleasure in witty repartees were inexhaustible, and these together with a charming tenderness, a highly cultivated mind, and his sense of honour have made Thomas More one of the most attractive figures in the history of England.[100]

He had had thoughts at first of becoming a Franciscan, and then a priest. For four years he lived near the London Charterhouse and shared the religious life of the community.[101] At this time he began to wear a hair shirt, a practice he continued for the rest of his life. (This shirt is

[97] "More's lectures were so well attended and highly esteemed that even Grocyn, whose supremacy had hitherto been undisputed, found his audience leaving him for More" (Stapleton, Hallett's trans., p. 9; cf. Erasmus' letter mentioned above).

[98] He caused a bill to be rejected which granted £113,000 for the marriage of Margaret, Henry VIII's sister, to the King of Scotland; the marriage took place in 1502. Henry VII bore him malice for this, and his father, Sir John More, was imprisoned in the Tower on some pretext or other and made to pay a fine of £100. He himself, having made several vain attempts to be reconciled with the king, had thought of going overseas, but then the king died (Roper, Lumby ed., *Utopia*, pp. vii–viii).

[99] See what Stapleton says about this, chap. VI, Hallett's trans., pp. 16–17.

[100] As an instance of his humour it is said that when one of his friends was criticizing all women Sir Thomas replied: "You exaggerate, there is only one bad woman, and that is the one every man complains he has married." Erasmus called him Democritus ["the laughing philosopher"]. Stapleton (*op. cit.*, Hallett's trans., pp. 132 *sq.*), like Cresacre More, devoted a chapter (the 13th) to "The Keen Humour" of Thomas More. "Nullus comes festivior" was Erasmus' description of him (letter to von Hutten July 23rd, 1519). Cf. T. E. Bridgett, *Wisdom and Wit of Sir Thomas More*, London, 1893.

[101] Erasmus' letter of July 23rd, 1519, already mentioned, and Roper, in his *Life of Sir Thomas More* (ed. Lumby, *Utopia*, p. vi).

preserved in St Augustine's Priory, Newton Abbot.)[102] His friend and confessor, John Colet, the Humanist, persuaded him to remain in the world.[103] Erasmus tells us that though in the world he yet remained deeply religious and was wont each day to recite the canonical hours; that when speaking to his friends about the life to come his lively faith and sturdy hope were always in evidence, and then, Erasmus adds, there are people who think real Christians are to be found only in monasteries. The Duke of Norfolk once met him in Chelsea Church in a surplice singing in the choir. "God's body, God's body!" said the Duke on leaving the church, "my Lord Chancellor a parish clarke, a parish clarke, you dishonour the king and his office." "Ney," quoth Sir Thomas More, smiling upon the Duke, "your Grace may not think that the Kinge your Master and myne, will with me for serving God his Master be offended, or thereby count his office dishonoured."[104] When his son-in-law, Roper, displayed leanings towards Lutheranism, More's prayers brought him back into the right path.[105] Stapleton gives many instances of his piety, his deep faith, and his charity towards those upon whom nature or fortune had frowned,[106] and one of the last things he wrote during his imprisonment concerned love for one's enemies.

More's ascetic qualities are revealed in both his marriages. Mr. Colt, who hoped he might have the brilliant young barrister for a son-in-law, used frequently to invite him to his house. He had three eligible daughters. More preferred the youngest, the most beautiful and most gifted of the three, but he married the eldest, saying that if he had married the

[102] Only his eldest daughter, Margaret, knew that he wore a hair shirt and gave himself the discipline (Roper, xxviii *sq.*).

[103] See chap. III in Bridgett (*op. cit.*, pp. 19 *sq.*) where he refutes certain assertions by Seebohm in his *Oxford Reformers*. Stapleton (Hallett's trans., pp. 11 *sq.*) quotes a long letter by More which shows his great friendship for John Colet.

[104] Roper, ed. Lumby, p. xxx. Cf. Stapleton, Hallett's trans., p. 68.

[105] This is stated by Stapleton, Harpsfield and Cresacre More (Stapleton, *op. cit.*, Hallett's trans., 70). Roper himself relates (Lumby ed. *Utopia*, xviii-xix) how his wife, given up by the doctors, "miraculously" recovered her health thanks to her father's fervent prayers. Roper had married Margaret More on July 2nd, 1521 (*Times Literary Suppl.*, April 3rd, 1930, p. 298).

[106] Chap. VI, Thomas More's *Holiness of Life*, Hallett's trans., 65, 72.

youngest, her eldest sister, Jane, would have been grieved and shamed. A feeling akin to pity therefore decided his choice.[107] Jane was the *uxorcula Mori*, whose frail, delicate, and gracious picture is recalled by Erasmus. She died five years after the marriage, leaving three daughters and one son. More took for his second wife, in 1510, a widow, Alice Middleton, seven years his senior, neither young nor handsome, as he would laughingly say to Erasmus, "but an active and vigilant house-wife." With her, Erasmus informs us, "he lives as pleasantly and sweetly as if she had all the charms of youth. You will scarcely find a husband who, by authority or severity, has gained such ready compliance as More by playful flattery." Any disturbances or strife were immediately appeased in that household.[108]

More moved from Bucklersbury to Crosby Place, and again in 1523 to Chelsea. There, between the hills on the banks of the Thames, he built for himself a house, *domicilium musarum et omnium virtutum et charitatum*, which became known far and wide. It stood in an orchard and a large garden, in which More loved to have all kinds of animals. "One of his great delights," wrote Erasmus, "is to consider the forms, the habits, and the instincts of different kinds of animals. There is hardly a species of bird that he does not keep in his house, and rare animals such as monkeys, foxes, ferrets, weasels and the like."

He built a chapel, a library, and a gallery near the big building which housed his large family. The celebrated sketch by Holbein, in the museum at Basle, depicts ten members of that family.[109] Neither William Roper, the husband

[107] Roper, Lumby ed., p. vi. In the first line of the epitaph he composed for his first wife More called her *uxorcula*:

> *Chara Thomae jacet hic Joanna uxorcula Mori,*
> *Qui tumulum Aliciae hunc destino, quique mihi.*

[108] Letter already quoted, July 23rd, 1519. In another letter to Budée, at the end of 1521, Erasmus also says: "His wife [Alice Middleton], who excels in good sense and experience rather than in learning, governs the little company with wonderful tact, assigning to each a task and requiring its performance, allowing no one to be idle or to be occupied in trifles." See Stapleton, chap. IX, and Bridgett, chap. VIII.

[109] In this sketch we see Elizabeth, the younger sister, who married William Daunce (or Daunsey) September 29th, 1525; Cecily, the third daughter, who, on the same day, married Giles Heron, who was foreman of the jury which tried Anne Boleyn and who was martyred at Tyburn on August 4th, 1540; and John, Sir Thomas' only son, to whom Erasmus dedicated his edition of *Aristotle*. John married Anne Cresacre, was im-

of Margaret, More's eldest and favourite daughter, nor the
eleven grandchildren who lived under that patriarchal roof,
appear in that sketch, nor, needless to say, the many friends
for whom there was always a welcome in More's home, a
home, in the words of Erasmus, *ad amicitiam natus, factusque
videtur.* All who lived under the family roof at Chelsea were
united by their common liking for literature and piety.
"More had all his daughters educated from their infancy; first
paying great attention to their morals, and then to their learning. . . . Titus Livius is ever in their hands. They have
advanced so far that they can read such authors and understand them without a translation, unless there occurs some
such word as would perhaps perplex myself." For this
Erasmus is once again our authority. A short time previously
each of them had written a Latin letter to him, unprompted
and uncorrected by their father. The letters contained
nothing silly or girlish and the style was such that Erasmus
was charmed: "Believe me, dear Budée, I was never more
surprised."[110] At table a passage from the *Lives of the Saints*

prisoned in the Tower for not taking the oath, like his father, and then
released. We also see an orphan girl and relative of the family, Margaret
Gigey, or Gigs, who was adopted by Sir Thomas, and from whom Stapleton
obtained several traits of More's piety and virtues; her future husband, John
Clements, who had been a tutor in More's family, became professor of
Greek at Oxford, and suffered exile for the faith under Edward VI and
Elizabeth; and More's secretary, John Harris. According to the fashion
of the time, More had also his "fool," Henry Patenson, whose features have
been portrayed by Holbein. When he became chancellor More handed
his jester over to his father, and on the latter's death gave him to the
Lord Mayor (cf. Bridgett, 124 *sq.*; Stapleton, Hallett's trans., 97, 158).
All the members of the More family, save John (still in his teens and comparatively little gifted), belonged to the Reformation Parliament, which was
opened by More, as Chancellor, in 1529 (A. F. Pollard, "Sir Thomas
More's Family," *Times Literary Suppl.*, March 27th, 1930).

[110] Letter to Budée at the end of 1521, already referred to. Erasmus
said that More's house was "a school for the knowledge and practice of
the Christian faith" (cf. Stapleton, Hallett's trans., p. 98). More personally
superintended the education and instruction of his children, and with
such care that twice he thought of leaving the court and government in
order to attend to it more fully. He wanted them to write in Latin, and so
he wisely praised and advised them in order to make them reach the degree
of perfection which he desired of them. Much in advance of those who
held that "erudition in women was a new thing," he gave his daughters a
strong literary culture, at the same time warning them against false knowledge and stupid vanity, which is "ridiculous and miserable" (see his
letters to his children and to William Gunnell, who was tutor in his family
after John Clements, in Stapleton, chap. x, Hallett's trans., pp. 101 *sq.*,

or a commentary was read by one of his daughters, in monastic fashion. Morning and night prayers were said for the family, with certain psalms and collects. On Sundays they all went to Mass and Vespers. More himself spent "the greater part of every Friday . . . meditating on the Passion . . . with prayers and sacred penitential exercises." Every year on Good Friday the family and household staff were assembled for the reading of the Passion, and More would afterwards comment on certain passages with a few words of meditation. When he found any of the children crying or sad he would gently take their hands and remind them that the creature cannot fare better than the Creator: "We may not looke at our pleasure to go to heaven in fether beddes, it is not the way."[111]

More was fond of art, and his house became a kind of museum. "If he meets with anything foreign," wrote Erasmus, "or in any way remarkable, he eagerly buys it, so that his house is full of such things, and at every turn they attract the eye of visitors." Artists found favour with him. One day he received a letter from Erasmus in which the latter informed More that the bearer of the letter was the man who had painted his portrait. Erasmus protested that he had no desire to weary More by singing the artist's praises, though he was a famous artist. The arts were in a bad way at Basle, and so the painter was going to England to try and earn a little money. This letter was dated, Basle, 1526. This artist, who was unable to pay his way at Basle, was none other than the inimitable Holbein. More received him, fed and housed him and brought him to the notice of Henry VIII. Holbein became the fashionable artist, the artist of the English Court, and thenceforward gold flowed into his coffers.

More was a Humanist. "If More had the means he would be a great Mæcenas of learning."[112] As a young man he used to compose Latin epigrams and write small comedies.[113] When

105 sq.). Margaret, who wrote with rare elegance in Greek and Latin, was a model of learning and modesty (cf. ibid., chap. XI, Hallett's trans., 112 sq.; cf. L. and P., III, No. 1527).

111 Roper, ed. quoted, pp. xvii sq.; Stapleton, op. cit., chap. IX, Hallett's trans., 94 sq.; Cresacre More's Biography of More.

112 Erasmus, in his letter to Budée in 1521.

113 Erasmus, in the letter of July 23rd, 1519, to von Hutten, already referred to. With his friend, William Lilly, he translated into Latin verse

he was occupied with affairs of State he still found time to
write, and he whiled away the hours of his imprisonment by
writing spiritual treatises. His *English Works* fill a quarto
volume of one thousand five hundred pages, and his Latin
works are equally lengthy. They are a noble achievement for
a man who was a writer only in his leisure moments. More,
it has been said, opened "all the paths through the wilds of
our old English speech." His talents as a humorist, a controversialist, and a narrator were displayed in his writings on
various topics, but the same sparkling humour, warmth, and
vitality ran through them all. Although the English language
was in course of formation at that period, yet More's style was
simple and unrestrained, and can still be easily understood
by all.[114]

His best known work, which has long been a classic, was

the anthology: *Progymnastica Thomae Mori et Gulielmi Lilii Sodalium*. After
having studied Greek and Latin in Rhodes and Rome, Lilly taught in
London with such success that John Colet placed him at the head of the
school he had just founded (1512); he taught there for about ten years
(cf. A. Wood, I, 14 *sq.*).

[114] "He is the first Englishman who knew how to write prose," says
Ranke (*Englische Geschichte*, Leipzic, 1870, I, 148). At the age of thirty-
eight (1510) he translated from Latin into English the Life of John Picus,
Earl of Mirandula, who died in 1494, and whose Christian mysticism,
allied to his love of antiquity, had fascinated More (cf. M. Kullnick, *Thomas
Morus' Picus Earl of Mirandula*, in the *Archiv für die Studien der neueren Sprachen*,
1908 and 1909). In 1513, while he was under-sheriff, he composed his
History of Richard III both in English and Latin. This was not finished,
however, and was printed only after his death. His witty and caustic mind
was very suitable indeed for controversy, hence his letter to Dorpius in
defence of Erasmus; he also attacked the heretics of that period. Several
times did his piety prompt his talents in writing either on the psalms or
on the Passion of Our Lord to comfort souls in their trials or to prepare
them for sacramental and spiritual communion. See Stapleton's fourth
chapter: "Thomas More's Wide Literary Labours," with notes and
remarks by Audin (French ed., 1849, pp. 79-113; Hallett's trans., p. 30);
Ellies Du Pin, *op. cit.*, IV, 501 *sq.*; Bridgett, chap. VII, "Literary"; and
Brémond, chap. VI. A bibliography of More's works will be found in
Gillow's *A Literary and Biographical History or Biographical Dictionary of the
English Catholics* (V, 99 *sq.*). The complete edition of Thomas More's *Works*
was published at Basle, 1563, and following years, but the Frankfort and
Leipzic edition, 1689, is better. See also J. Gairdner, *Lollardy*, Bk. II,
chap. v, "Sir Thomas More's Writings."

An edition of *The English Works of Sir Thomas More* in seven volumes is
now in course of publication. They are reproduced in facsimile from
William Rastell's edition of 1557, and edited, with a modern version of the
same, by W. E. Campbell; with introductions, notes, essays, etc., by
Professors A. W. Reed and R. W. Chambers and Mr. Doyle-Davidson,
2 vols., 1931.

the one for which he coined a word that has since passed into everyday speech, "Utopia." This "undiscoverable island" is a pure fiction, in which the author's most intimate convictions are to be found nestling with idle fancies, witticisms, and paradoxes. It is impossible to say how seriously he means the theories of this book to be taken. It is a work of imagination combining an adaptation of Plato's *Republic* with reminiscences of St Augustine's *De Civitate Dei*.[115] In this book the author remains as much an enigma to us as he was to his wife, who never knew, so Stapleton says, "whether he was speaking in jest or in earnest." *Utopia* is a blend of wisdom and irony, of shrewd philosophy and banter, and of various teachings and hypotheses, bordering now on the ridiculous, now on the sublime, and passing so naturally from one to the other that the reader is often puzzled to know where he stands. Were we to judge the author's principles by these figments of his imagination, and to draw from them conclusions diametrically opposed to his beliefs, we should be erring only less naïvely, albeit more seriously, than those good English priests who, perceiving a close affinity between the religion of the Utopians and the true teaching, were anxious to go and convert them.[116] The work appeared in Latin at Louvain in 1516,

[115] Cf. Lina Berger, "Thomas Morus und Plato," in *Zeitschrift für gesamte Staatswissenschaft*, 1879, XXXV, pp. 187 *sq.*, 405 *sq.*; Kleinvächter, *Die Staatsromane*, 1891. The social theories of *Utopia* were studied by the socialist Kautsky (*Thomas More und seine Utopie mit einer historischen Einleitung*, 1888, 2nd ed., 1907), and in a Treatise at Erlangen University (1904) by H. Cruse, *Die Utopie des Thomas More und die soziale Frage*. If this work was "the gospel of the followers of Fourier and Saint-Simon and of the communists of every age," if "it extolled Communism and the six hours' day as early as 1516" (editor of *Utopia*, 1927, in the *Scripta Manent* series) its author did not foresee it. M. Freund ("Zur Deutung der Utopia des Thomas Morus" in *Historische Zeitschrift*, 1930, No. 2) sees in *Utopia* the development of England's state policy. W. E. Campbell (*More's Utopia and his Social Teaching*, London, 1930) says that *Utopia* "is probably the most misrepresented book in the world." The life and faith of Thomas More help us to ascertain the real social views of the chancellor. See also *More's Utopia*, by Professors Chambers and Reed, 1931.

[116] Burnet, in his *History of the Reformation*, and Seebohm, in his *Oxford Reformers*, have put forward opinions which are easily refuted. Cf. Audin, in his edition of Stapleton, pp. 90 *sq.*; J. Spillmann, p. 40; Bridgett, pp. 103-107; R. Hercourt, *L'Utopie de Thomas Morus* (Thesis, Poitiers, 1911); R. W. Chambers, "The saga and the myth of Sir Thomas More," extract from the *Proceedings of the British Academy*, 1927. See *Thomas Morus et l'île d'Utopie* (Paris, 1912) by F. Flach, and E. Dermenghem, *Thomas Morus et les Utopistes de la Renaissance*, Paris, 1927 (a popular edition). C. Fink

through the kind offices of some devoted friends of More, who were themselves men of letters.[117] It passed through innumerable editions, and was translated into French, Italian, German, Spanish and English. Praise was showered upon it from every side.[118]

His best friends were the celebrated Humanists, who gathered round him and formed a kind of Greek academy. They were John Colet, the Dean of St Paul's, and his confessor; Grocyn, the Greek scholar and vicar of St Lawrence's church in London; Linacre, his former tutor; the Greek scholar William Lilly, the youngest of them all; and Erasmus, his *erasmiotatos* (untranslatable),[119] whom he called "my darling." He also maintained a friendly correspondence with those who dwelt abroad, such as Budée, Beatus Rhenanus, and John Cochlæus.[120]

Erasmus first met the young student when he visited England in 1497, at the house of William Blount, Lord Mountjoy, who had been his pupil in Paris.[121] The great Humanist

("Die Utopie Thomas Morus und die Klosterrepublik auf dem Berge Athos," in *Hist. Jahrbuch*, 1930, 2nd fasc.) proves against H. Brockhaus that *Utopia* owes nothing to the monastic republic of Athos.

[117] In particular, Peter Giles (Egidius) and Jerome Busleyden, Canon of Brussels, Malines and Cambrai, ambassador in London under Henry VIII and founder of the trilingual college at Louvain.

[118] More wrote his work in Latin because he intended it only for discerning minds. The English translation appeared only in 1551, from the pen of Ralph Robynson, with Roper's biography of More at the beginning. In 1879 Lumby added an introduction, notes and a glossary, and from that date down to 1908 there were thirteen editions. Lupton also brought out an edition of Ralph Robynson, with introduction and notes (Oxford, 1895), which are the result of real scholarly labour. For the various English editions of *Utopia*, G. Wolf may be consulted, *Quellenkunde der deutschen Reformationsgeschichte*, Gotha, 1915–16, I, 350, n. 2.

[119] Superlative of ἐράσμιος (beloved), and a pun on the name of Erasmus. Erasmus called More the "dearest of mortals." The edition of *Erasmi Epistolae*, London, 1642, gives More's correspondence with Erasmus, in 70 pages: "Auctarium Epistolarum ex Thoma Moro."

[120] Cf. Stapleton, Hallett's trans., pp. 51 *sq.*; Bridgett, *op. cit.*, 185 *sq.*; Rebitté, *Guillaume Budé, réstaurateur des études grecques en France*, 1846; L. Delaruelle, *Guillaume Budé: les origines, les débuts, les idées maîtresses* (fasc. 162, "École des Hautes Études" Library), Paris, 1907 (goes only as far as 1519); J. Plattard, *Guillaume Budé et les origines de l'humanisme français*, Paris, 1923 (very short). Budée wished to publish More's letters with his own; the latter, however, hesitated, wanting to revise them, and in the end they were not printed. But L. Delaruelle has published the *Répertoire analytique et chronologique de la correspondance de Guillaume Budé*, Paris, 1907, which is very useful.

[121] For Erasmus' relations with Lord Mountjoy, see *Erasmi Epistolae*,

was charmed with More's gracious bearing, wit, and extensive knowledge, and that day saw the beginning of the strong and tender friendship between them which was broken only by death. Erasmus left England after two or three years at Oxford. He returned in 1505, and for a year lived with More's family as one of the household. The two friends undertook various literary labours, and translated several of Lucian's dialogues into Latin. In 1508 Erasmus was again beneath the hospitable roof at Chelsea. There he wrote his *Praise of Folly*, or the *Encomium Moriae*, and the little joke on More's name indicates that it was written in More's house and, as it were, with his collaboration. The work was attacked, and More defended it. At that time Reformation was not a synonym for revolt, and the monk of Wittenberg was still unknown.[122]

When Luther rebelled, the two friends remained in the ranks of orthodoxy.[123] Under the assumed name of William Ross, More wrote a reply to Luther's scurrilous attack upon Henry VIII's *Assertio septem Sacramentorum*, and defended the

ed. Leyden, 1742, I, 56, 102, 122, 135, 142, 145, 184, 220, 305, 402, 574, 684, 732. During one of his visits Erasmus saw for the first time in a country house near to Mountjoy's, the future Henry VIII, then nine years old, with his two sisters, Margaret and Mary.

[122] After More had amused himself writing a Declamation in imitation of Lucian on Tyrannicide, he wanted Erasmus to do the same. In 1506 More dedicated four Latin translations of Lucian's dialogues to Thomas Ruthal, secretary to Henry VII and a member of the Privy Council, afterwards Bishop of Durham (1509–29). For this translation and the *Encomium Moriae*, see Bridgett, pp. 80–87; A. Renaudet, *Préréforme et Humanisme à Paris (1494–1517)*, Paris, 1916, pp. 488, 491 sq. In his Letter to Dorpius, More defends the *Encomium Moriae*, which the Sorbonne afterwards censured in 1543 (cf. H. Reusch, *Die Indices librorum prohibitorum des sechzehnten Jahrhunderts*, Tubingen, 1886, p. 85). Holbein illustrated a copy of this work with humorous pen sketches.

[123] For Erasmus' attitude towards the New Learning, see Emerton (*Desiderius Erasmus of Rotterdam*, 1899), who is inclined to exaggerate in the Protestant sense. Cardinal Gasquet's chapter on Erasmus, in *The Eve of the Reformation*, restores the balance. In the face of Luther and of Rome, Erasmus clearly and boldly defined his attitude in his letter to George, Duke of Saxony, on September 3rd, 1522, which is published in *Opus epistolarum Desiderii Erasmi*, by P. S. Allen. Cf. Paul Kalkoff, *Die Stellung der deutschen Humanisten zur Reformation*, Vol. XLVI of *Zeitschrift für Kirchengeschichte*. Some good bibliographical information will be found in G. Wolf, *Quellenkunde der deutschen Reformationsgeschichte*, I, pp. 363 sq. The following have appeared since: Renaudet's *Préréforme*, already mentioned; J. B. Pineau's *Erasme. La Pensée religieuse* (Paris, 1924); Alb. Hyma, *The Youth of Erasmus* (University of Michigan publication, 1930); and various other works (cf. n. 64, chap. 1).

papacy, praying "that God may raise up such Popes as befit
the Christian cause and the dignity of the Apostolic office."[124]
Some years later he refuted Simon Fish, Tyndale and his
followers, Frith and George Jay (or Joye), and continued
these controversial writings till the end of his life.[125] He
deserved the title he gave himself in his own epitaph: *hæretici
molestus;* he himself thought that death was preferable to the
power of sowing seditious heresies.[126]

More was about forty years old when he came to court and
entered public life. This is the description Erasmus gives of
him at that age, in his letter (447) to Ulrich von Hutten[127]:
"To begin, then, with what is least known to you, in stature

[124] More had no share in Henry's book, as he himself said at the time of
his trial (Roper, ed. quoted, p. xxxvii); he had arranged the index for it
after it was written (cf. Bruce in *Archaeologia Britannica*, XXIII, 67). During
his lifetime none knew that the *Reply to Luther* was by More; More himself
referred several times to William Ross's book without any suspecting that
he was the author (cf. Bridgett, p. 222, n.2).

[125] See Hutton, "The Religious Writings of Sir Thomas More," in the
Eng. Hist. Review, 1889; and the French edition of this book, p. 512. See
J. Gairdner, *Lollardy*, Bk. II, chap. v, "Sir Thomas More's Writings." A
critical edition of the *Dialogue touching . . . Luther and Tyndale* was brought
out by W. E. Campbell, London, 1927.

[126] "I detest the whole tribe of them [heretics]," More wrote to Erasmus,
"so much that there is no one to whom I wish to be more hostile than to
them, unless they renounce their errors." Stapleton, Hallett's trans., 29.
For More's zeal for the faith, see Bridgett, pp. 273 *sq.* As chancellor More
incurred the reproaches of the innovators. More's adversaries also blamed
him for the way in which he treated heretics. That is not what he preached,
they said. *Utopia* indeed praised toleration. But this was merely an idea
belonging to the kingdom of Utopia; More did not believe it could be
applied (his theological treatises show this) to a country which was held
together by a common faith and in which heresy, recalling the Lollardist
revolt, appeared to threaten both the political and social order and religion.
Moreover, during his period of office as chancellor, only four heretics were
executed; and these were men previously convicted of heresy, and against
such the law was formal (see Stapleton, Hallett's trans., p. 29, n. 2).   In
his *Apology* More asserts that he always tried to reclaim those who had
erred by speaking a good word to them, and that he never delivered any to
the secular arm before trying the effects of extreme kindness upon them.
See Bridgett, chap. XIV: "Treatment of heretics"; and the works by
Professor R. W. Chambers, already mentioned. Yet Luther, in his *Table
Talks*, reproaches More for having shed the innocent blood of a great
number of confessors of the Gospel, and he was possibly the only one of the
Reformers who did not show his disapproval of More's execution.

[127] Leyden edition, 1706, I, 472. Stapleton, chap. xx (Hallett's trans.,
p. 216), gives a portrait of More in a few lines, from details handed down
by eye-witnesses, but less lifelike than that of Erasmus. Pollini (*Historia
ecclesiastica de la Revoluzion d'Inghilterra*, Rome, 1594, p. 119) reproduced it.

he is not tall, though not remarkably short. His limbs are
formed with such perfect symmetry as to leave nothing to be
desired. His complexion is white, his face fair rather than
pale, and though by no means ruddy, a faint flush of pink
appears beneath the whiteness of his skin. His hair is dark
brown, or brownish black. The eyes are grayish blue, with
some spots, a kind which betokens singular talent, and among
the English is considered attractive, whereas Germans generally prefer black. It is said that none are so free from vice.
His countenance is in harmony with his character, being
always expressive of an amiable joyousness, and even an
incipient laughter, and, to speak candidly, it is better framed
for gladness than for gravity and dignity, though without any
approach to folly or buffoonery. The right shoulder is a little
higher than the left, especially when he walks. This is not a
defect of birth, but the result of habit, such as we often contract. In the rest of his person there is nothing to offend. His
hands are the least refined part of his body. . . . I never saw
anyone so indifferent about food. Until he was a young man he
delighted in drinking water, but that was natural to him.
Yet not to seem singular or morose, he would hide his temperance from his guests by drinking out of a pewter vessel
beer almost as light as water, or often pure water. . . . He
likes to eat corned beef and coarse bread much leavened,
rather than what most people count delicacies. . . . His
voice is neither loud nor very weak, but penetrating; not
resounding or soft, but that of a clear speaker. . . . He speaks
with great clearness and perfect articulation, without rapidity
or hesitation. He likes a simple dress, using neither silk nor
purple nor gold chain, except when it may not be omitted.
It is wonderful how negligent he is as regards all the cere-
monious forms in which most men make politeness to consist.
He does not require them from others, nor is he anxious to
use them himself, at interviews or banquets, though he is not
unacquainted with them when necessary. . . . In society
he is so polite, so sweet-mannered, that no one is of so melan-
choly a disposition as not to be cheered by him, and there is
no misfortune that he does not alleviate." In another letter
Erasmus describes him as the ideal sociable man, *omnibus
omnium horarum homo.*

More quickly became one of the most prominent citizens. Though he neither desired nor sought to be a statesman, he soon became one. In 1515 he was sent to Flanders to settle some commercial disputes. In 1517 he was commissioned by the Privy Council to discover the causes of a disturbance in the city.[128] In 1518 he became a member of the Privy Council, and in the following year he was so absorbed in court matters that he resigned his office of under-sheriff.[129] Honours and offices then followed rapidly. In 1518 he was made Master of the Requests, Vice-Treasurer in 1521, and was elected Speaker in the House of Commons in 1523, and two years later became Chancellor of the Duchy of Lancaster.[130]

Henry had long been attracted by More and desired to make a conquest of him. Soon he was treating More with exceptional familiarity. More's son-in-law, Roper, has left an unforgettable account of the long intimacy between Henry VIII and More[131]: "The king," he says, "upon holidayes, when he had done his owne devotions, used to send for him into his traverse, and there sometyme in matters of Astronimie, Geometrie, Divinitie, and such other Faculties, and sometyme in his worldly affayeres, to sitt and conferr with him; and otherwhiles would he in the night have him up into the leades, there to consider with him the diversities, courses, motions and operations of the Starrs and Planetts. And because he was of a pleasant disposition yt pleased the Kinge and Queene after the Counsell had suppt, at the tyme

[128] Hall's *Chronicle* and More's *Apology*, chap. XLVII. Four months later (August, 1517) he was included in an embassy sent to Calais to settle certain disputes with the French envoys (Brewer, *Reign of Henry VIII*, I, 188).

[129] He had held this office since 1509. At that time the under-sheriff was one of the body of magistrates. He was elected, sat once a week, and judged most of the civil causes.

[130] Roper (ed. quoted, pp. ix, x, xiv) gives More's speech at the opening of Parliament (cf. Bridgett, pp. 153-79).

[131] Ed. quoted pp. IX, XIV *sq*. Erasmus, in the letter to Ulrich von Hutten, also speaks of his intimacy with the king, who greatly appreciated him for serious matters and delighted in his witty conversation. The king greatly fascinated the most eminent men around him. "The king," said More, "is so courteous and kindly to all that everyone who is in any way hopeful finds a ground for imagining that he is in the king's good graces" (cf. Stapleton, Hallett's trans., p. 77). When he entered the king's service Henry told him "first to look unto God and after God unto him." More recalled these words, the most virtuous lesson ever given by a prince to his servant, when Henry tried to urge him to declare in favour of the divorce (cf. Roper, ed. quoted, p. xxix.

of there supper for there pleasure commonly to call for him, and to be merry with them. . . . And for the pleasure he tooke in his Companie, would his Grace sodenly sometimes come home to his house at Chelsie to be merry with him, withere on a tyme unlooked for he came to dinner, and after dinner in a faire garden of his walked with him by the space of an howre holdinge his arme about his neck."

But the royal favours did not upset the balanced mind of Thomas More. His son-in-law remarked "how happy he was whom the king had so familiarly entertained, as I had never seene him to do to any before, except Cardinall Wolsey, whom I saw his Grace once walk with arme in arme." "Soone Roper," quoth he, "I may tell thee, I have no cause to be prowde thereof. For yf my head would winne him a Castle in Fraunce (for then there was wars betweene us) yt should not fayle to go."[132]

After playing a subordinate part in several diplomatic missions, More was named chancellor (October 26th, 1529) on the fall of Wolsey.[133] It was the first time in the history of England that the seal had been given to a layman. More declared that his thoughts were always for his duty, and the service of God and the king. The Duke of Norfolk publicly stated, in the king's name, "how much all Englande was beholden to Sir Thomas Moore for his good service." To which the chancellor modestly replied that "he had done no more than was his duty."[134]

---

[132] Roper, ed. quoted, pp. xiv–xv.

[133] In the same year he had signed the Treaty of Cambrai as plenipotentiary. He had previously formed part of embassies to Calais (1517), to Bruges (1521), and to France (1527). He also assisted at the meeting of the Field of the Cloth of Gold (1520), where Erasmus introduced him to Francis I's secretary, the famous Greek scholar, Budée. See Bridgett, chap x.

More's power as chancellor cannot be compared to that of Wolsey. Norfolk, the president of the Council, had assumed a preponderant influence therein.

[134] Roper, pp. xxiv sq. Cf. Bridgett, chap. xii. Stapleton, Hallett's trans., pp. 20 sq. "I do indeed congratulate England, for a better or holier judge could not have been appointed," Erasmus wrote on the nomination of the new chancellor (Erasmi Epistolae, letter 1034). And indeed the functions of chancellor were never better carried out. When More resigned nothing was in arrears. The poor man who sought him was given a ready entry and obtained prompt judgment. More made a decree in one case against his son-in-law, Giles Heron, who was presuming on Sir Thomas's favour. He always tried to reconcile opposing parties, to make them come to

These honours, however, were the rumblings before the storm. Henry had already on several occasions asked him his views on the divorce, and More, after consideration, had replied that he could not favour the king's ideas. This first difference of opinion was fraught with fatal consequences. More's refusal to yield to the royal whims in the question of the divorce was, according to Stapleton, "the origin of the king's anger and vengeful proceedings against Sir Thomas More."[135]

When Henry VIII obtained the title of "supreme head of the Church of England" from Convocation (February 1531), More desired to resign his office; he retained it, however, a little while longer. "The chancellor is so mortified at it," wrote Chapuys, "that he is anxious above all things to resign his office."

A year later, he strenuously opposed the Bill on the Submission of the Clergy before the whole King's Council, and together with Gardiner, caused it to be rejected in the House of Lords. "The king is very angry," wrote Chapuys to Charles V, "especially with the chancellor and the Bishop of Winchester, and is determined to carry the matter." Three days later (May 16th, 1532) More resigned. "Seeing the Kinge fully determined to proceed forth in the Marriage of Queen Ann . . . doubting least farther attempts should after follow,

some arrangement, just as when he was a barrister. Stapleton gives more than one testimony to his irreproachable integrity (cf. *Notes and Queries,* 1st Series, VII, 85; X, 173, 393; Roper, ed. quoted, pp. xxiv sq., pp. xxxiv sq.; Stapleton, Hallett's trans., 26 sq.).

When he resigned his office the king expressed his gratitude to him for his good and loyal services. He assured him that he would always have his protection, and asked him to call upon the king on every occasion when his interests or his honour were threatened (Roper, p. xxx; Stapleton, chap. vi, Hallett's trans., 28).

[135] Stapleton, Hallett's trans., p. 145. J. Gairdner agrees with Stapleton (Bridgett, ed. 1904, p. xxvii). More had always been against the divorce (cf. *L. and P.,* VII, 289; More, *English Works,* p. 1247). When he saw the king fatally bent upon the downward course he was greatly perturbed for the religious future of England, as his conversations with Roper, his son-in-law, show. At the king's request he examined the case and informed him that he could not in conscience favour his views, and in vain did theologians and bishops, like Stokesley, try to make him alter his ideas. Although the king avoided using unpleasant words, More did not shut his eyes to the danger which would result from a difference of opinion in such a serious matter (Roper, ed. quoted, pp. xvi sq., xxiii, xxix; Stapleton, chap. xiv, Hallett's trans., 145 sq.).

which, contrarie to his conscience, by reason of his office he was likely to be put unto, he made sutte to the Duke of Norfolk to be a meane to the Kinge, that he might, with his Grace's favour, be discharged of that chargeable Roome of Chancellorship, wherein for certaine infirmities of his bodie, he pretended himselfe unable any longer to serve."[136] He had been chancellor for two and a half years. "Everyone is concerned," again wrote Chapuys, "for there never was a better man in the office."[137]

Returning to Chelsea, More announced his resignation to his family with apparent indifference, and proceeded at once to moderate their way of living.[138] He was determined to live a retired life away from the court, where he was hated by Anne Boleyn. He gave his reasons for this in the epitaph which he composed for himself: "He, therefore, irked and weary of worldly business, giving up his promotions . . . that he might have some years of his life free, in which he . . . might continually remember the immortality of the life to come."

---

[136] Roper, p. xxix sq.

[137] L. and P., V, 112, 1013, 1046; Brewer, I, 149: Friedmann, op. cit., I, p. 186 and nn. 1, 2. He had read the king's message at the opening of Parliament on March 30th.

[138] Almost immediately on his return to Chelsea Stapleton relates (chap. XIII, Hallett's trans., 139) that he went at once to the church. Vespers were being sung. . . . At the end of the office he made for the pew reserved for the chancellor's family and occupied by his wife and daughters, "and said to his wife, as usually one of his servants would say, 'If you please, Madam, my Lord Chancellor is gone.' Seeing him making the announcement in person, she thought he was joking. 'No doubt it pleases you, Mr. More,' she said, 'to joke in this fashion.' He replied: 'I speak seriously and it is as I say: my Lord Chancellor is gone and is no longer here.' " (Roper, p. xxxii).

More had given up his lucrative position as a famous barrister (£400) for the king's service and had spent a good deal of his own resources on diplomatic missions, says Roper (pp. xxxi sq.), and so had only about £100 annual income. He called together the many members of his family, made known to them the change in his fortune, and proposed to go on living together, even if it meant restricting themselves more and more, changing their residence, or even begging with a bag on their back and singing the Salve Regina from door to door to obtain alms. But his sons-in-law left the paternal roof, even Roper, though he remained in Chelsea. More sold his gold and silver plate for £400 (Stapleton, chap. xv, Hallett's trans., 158). A short while before he had refused a sum of £5,000 which the clergy had subscribed as a testimonial in gratitude for his labours against heretics. He energetically repelled the earnest solicitations of the Bishops of Durham, Bath and Exeter, threatening to throw the money into the Thames, so that it had to be given back to the subscribers (Roper, pp xxvii sq.).

Roper tells us[139] he used then to "talke with his Wife and Children of the joyes of Heaven and the paines of Hell, of the lives of holy Martiers, and of theire greevous Martirdome, of theire marveilous patience, and of theire passiones and deaths, that they suffered rather than they would offend God, and what an happie and a blessed thinge it was for the love of God to suffer losse of goods, imprisonment, loss of lands, and life also. . . . He shewed them afore what trouble might fall unto him."

The calm did not last for long, though he avoided all opposition, straining his conscience as far as he could.[140]   In February, 1534, he was accused of writing a pamphlet which had been published by his nephew Rastall.[141]   Had he not avoided appearing at the queen's coronation?[142]   Shortly afterwards he was compromised in the Holy Maid of Kent affair, because he had visited her in the house of the Sion Fathers.   He proved to Cromwell that he had exhorted the nun to concern herself solely with spiritual things and to leave political matters alone.[143]   His name appeared, never-

[139] Roper, p. xxxii. Cf. his letter to the king, March 5th, 1534, Ellis, I, 48; Stapleton, chap. xv, Hallett's trans., 159.

[140] "Our Lord advised His disciples," he had written (passage from his *English Works*, quoted by Bridgett, p. 316), "that if they were pursued in one city, they should not come forth and foolhardily put themselves in peril of denying Christ by impatience of some intolerable torments, but rather flee thence into some other place, where they might serve Him in quiet, till He should suffer them to fall in such point that there were no way to escape. And then He would have them abide by their tackling like mighty champions, wherein they shall not in such case fail of His help." This was the teaching of St Athanasius in his *Apologia de fuga sua*.

[141] William Rastall was the son of John Rastall and Elizabeth More. He afterwards became a lawyer and a judge. At this time he was engaged in running his father's business as publisher. On this occasion (February 1st, 1534) More wrote to Cromwell (*English Works*, p. 1422) "that on my faith I never made any such book nor never thought to do." This book refuted a proclamation by the King's Council (Christmas, 1533) in favour of the divorce.

[142] Tunstall, Clerk and Gardiner, Bishops of Durham, Bath and Winchester, Roper relates (p. xxxiii), invited him to join them in the coronation procession, and sent him at the same time £20 to defray the cost of clothes. He thanked them and accepted the gift, but remained quietly at home. When he met the bishops he said jokingly to them: "You required two things of me, the one whereof sith I was so well contented to graunt you, th' other therefore I thought I might to be boulder to deny you."

[143] In a long letter to Cromwell (*L. and P.*, VII, 287; Burnet, V, 431-40, published it, according to a manuscript which no longer exists; cf. Fisher,

theless, for misprision of treason in the Bill of Attainder presented to Parliament, and was deleted only on the third reading in the House of Lords (March, 1534). Henry had thought that he could force More to approve his second marriage, either through fear or menaces, "wherein," Roper remarks,[144] "His Grace was much deceived." His resentment accordingly became much stronger, and it was only fear of certain defeat in Parliament that made him withdraw his former chancellor's name from the Bill.[145] *Quod differtur non aufertur*, was More's comment to his daughter. And when Norfolk reminded him of the words of Scripture: *Indignatio principis mors est*. "Is that all, my lord?" asked More, "then, in good faith, between Your Grace and me is but this, that I shall die to-day and you to-morrow."[146] The fatal hour was indeed approaching.

On Low Sunday (April 12th, 1534), as he was coming away from Vespers, he was warned to appear at Lambeth on the morrow in order to take the oath to the Bill of Succession which implied the denial of papal authority. As was his wont in all serious matters, he went to Confession, heard Mass, and received Holy Communion, and then, without bidding his wife or children farewell, went by boat with Roper and four servants to Lambeth. He sat silently for a while as the boat glided along, and then suddenly turned to his son-in-law

---

op. cit., pp. 334 *sq.*) he minutely and candidly sets forth his part in the affair of "The Holy Maid of Kent"; his good faith, loyalty, and caution are evident.

More also wrote to Henry VIII on March 5th, 1534 (Ellis, 1st Series, II, 48-52) to assure him of his loyalty, and that he would prefer to "lose goods, lands, libertie, and my life withall" rather than the king's good opinion. He also reminded him of his promise to protect his former chancellor against any attack upon his honour (cf. above, n. 134). Yet a fortnight later (February 21st, 1534) the Bill of Attainder was introduced in the House of Lords.

[144] Roper ed. quoted, p. xxxvi (cf. p. xxxiii).

[145] See Appendix D (c), pp. 482 *sq.*

[146] Roper, ed. quoted, pp. xxxix *sq.* The Duke of Norfolk's son, the Earl of Surrey, was beheaded on January 19th, 1547. Norfolk was himself condemned to death (January 27th, 1547), but Henry VIII died a few hours before the time fixed for the execution (January 28th). In his unfinished work on *Ecclesiastes*, published in 1557 but written in 1522, More compared the unsettled length of life to two execution stakes, situated the one a mile and the other a hundred miles away. The condemned man who had a hundred miles to walk had not very much greater reason for rejoicing than he who had the shorter distance to cover.

and whispered in his ear: "Son Roper, I thank our Lord the field is won."[147]

Soon he was in the presence of the commissioners: Audeley, the Lord Chancellor; Benson, the Abbot of Westminster; Thomas Cromwell; and Cranmer, the Archbishop of Canterbury. Before these men, noblemen and priests had blithely denied the Bishop of Rome's authority. More himself describes the scene in a letter to his daughter[148]: "I saw Master Dr. Latimer[149] come into the garden, and there walked he with divers other doctors and chaplains of my lord of Canterbury. And very merry I saw him, for he laughed and took one or twain about the neck so handsomely, that if they had been women I would have weened he had been waxen wanton . . . I heard also that Master Vicar of Croydon and all the remnant of the priests of London that were sent for, were sworn; and that they had such favour at the Council's hand, that they were not lingered or made to dance any long attendance to their travail and cost, as suitors were sometimes wont to be, but were sped apace to their great comfort; so far forth that Master Vicar of Croydon, either for gladness or for dryness, or else that it might be seen, *Quod ille notus erat pontifici*, went to my lord's buttery bar and called for drink, and drank *valde familiariter*."

More, like Fisher, was willing to recognize the new order of succession, but not the whole of the statute as it stood, on account of the attack upon papal authority contained in the preamble. "Then said my lord of Westminster to me," wrote More, "that . . . I had cause to fear that mine own mind was erroneous, when I see the great Council of the realm determine of my mind the contrary, and that therefore I ought to change my conscience. To that I answered . . . I am not bounden to change my conscience and conform it to the Council of one realm against the general council of Christendom." When More refused to take the oath Thomas Cromwell "said and sware a great oath."[150]

---

[147] Roper, ed. quoted, p. xl. These words recall the *Allons, gardes, c'est fait* in *Polyeucte* (Act. IV., Sc. IV.).

[148] *English Works*, p. 1428. In part in Stapleton, chap. xv.

[149] Shortly afterwards Bishop of Worcester.

[150] *L. and P.*, VII, 575. Letter referred to from More to his daughter, in which he relates in detail the various attempts made, whilst he was at

Sir Thomas was then given into the custody of the Abbot of Westminster. On April 17th Cranmer advised Cromwell to tender a modified form of the oath to the king, which could be signed by More without any scruples. "And, per-adventure, it should be a good quietation to many others within this realm, if such men should say that the succession comprised within the said Act is good and according to God's laws. For then, I think, there is not one within this realm that would once reclaim against it."[151] But Henry refused, influenced possibly by Anne Boleyn and Cromwell.[152] More was committed to the Tower that same day, April 17th. At the Tower gate the porter, according to custom, demanded his upper garment. "Mr. Porter," quoth he, "here it is," and he offered his cap, saying: "I am very sorry it is no better for thee." When the lieutenant of the Tower apologized because he could not "make him good cheer," More replied: "I do not mislike my cheer; but whensoever I do so, then thrust me out of your doors."[153]

No means were spared to make the ex-chancellor side with the king, and to overcome his constancy. Temptation came to him in many guises. First, it was the good Lady More, mature in age and somewhat worldly in her outlook, who could not understand why her husband did not follow the lead of many honest folks of their acquaintance. "What a good year! Mr. More," was her greeting, "I marvel that you, that hitherto have been taken for a wise man, will now so play the fool, to lie here in this close, filthy prison, and be content thus to be shut up among mice and rats, when you

Lambeth, to influence him by different arguments and the example of others to utter compromising words. Stapleton observes (Hallett's trans., 158): "Nothing could show more clearly the honour and respect that More enjoyed in the eyes of the king, the Parliament and the people, and at the same time his firmness and constancy in the cause of God and the truth."

[151] Strype, *Memorials of Cranmer*, Append. I. Cf. above, p. 214.

[152] Queen Anne, says Roper (p. xlii), so exasperated the king against him by her tiresome clamourings that, contrary to his first resolve, he demanded the oath of supremacy.

[153] Roper, pp. xlii and xliii. Cf. Harpsfield, ed. Bémont, p. 68.
The prisoner was allowed to have one of his old servants to attend him, John Wood, who could neither read nor write, and who was made to swear that he would denounce his master if he heard him utter anything against the king, the council, or the State (*ibid.*, p. xli).

might be abroad at your liberty, and with the favour and goodwill both of the king and his Council, if you would but do as all the bishops and best learned of this realm have done. And seeing you have at Chelsea a right fair house, your library, your gallery, garden, orchard, and all other necessaries so handsome about you, where you might in the company of me, your wife, your children, and household, be merry, I muse what (a God's name!) you mean here still thus fondly to tarry." To this outburst More quietly replied: "Is not this house as nigh heaven as mine own?"[154]

Next it was Margaret's turn, the "dear Meg" whom More loved so tenderly, whose mind he had moulded on his own, and who shared his most secret thoughts. The authorities had great hopes that the intervention of his favourite daughter would overcome the prisoner's resistance; but they were mistaken. More laughingly addressed her as "Mistress Eve!" and parried her arguments with his characteristic humour. Then adopting a serious and earnest tone, "Daughter Margaret," he said, "we two have talked of this thing more than twice or thrice, and I have told you that if it were possible for me to do the thing that might content the king's Grace, and God not offended, no man had taken this oath more gladly than I would do."[155] On another occasion he wrote to her in the following affectionate terms: "Our Lord bless you. If I had not been, my dearly beloved daughter, at a firm and fast point, I trust in God's great mercy this good great while before, your lamentable letter had not a little abashed me, surely far above all other things, of which I hear divers times not a few terrible towards me. But surely they all touched me never so near, nor were so grievous unto me, as to see you, my well beloved child, in such vehement piteous manner, labour to persuade unto me that thing wherein I have, of pure necessity for respect unto mine own soul, so often given you so precise answer before. Wherein as touching the points of your letter, I can make none answer. For I doubt not but you well remember that the matters which

[154] Roper, p. xlv (cf. Stapleton, chap. xvi, Hallett's trans., 176), and Sander (Lewis' trans., p. 123).

[155] Margaret Roper to Lady Alington, More's stepdaughter (1534), in More's *English Works*, p. 1433.

move my conscience . . . I have sundry times showed you that I will disclose them to no man."[156]

Nothing, indeed, could shake More's constancy, neither the affection of his own family, nor the snares of his adversaries. No argument, were it never so subtle, could convince him.[157] Feeling that he himself was weak, he had placed all his confidence in God.[158] "For this I am very sure that if ever I should swear it [the oath], I should swear deadly sore against mine own conscience. For I am very sure in my mind, that I shall never be able to change myne own conscience to the contrary."[159] And in a short meditation of two pages, *Quod mors pro fide non sit fugienda*, he penned the following lines: "If you save your life to-day by offending God, you will hate it to-morrow, and lament that you did not undergo yesterday. . . . What folly by trying to avoid temporal death to incur death eternal, while you do not really avoid temporal death but merely postpone it!"

On November 3rd, 1534, Parliament declared that the oath offered to More and Fisher was the only one in conformity with the Act of Succession. More was accused at the same time of misprision of treason, and the king took from him the lands he had given to him in 1522 and 1525, in order to bestow them upon one of his favourites, Henry Norris, and upon the queen's brother.[160] Soon Lady More was compelled to sell even her apparel so that she might pay for her husband's board. The letters she wrote to the king (at the end of 1534) and to Cromwell (May, 1535) to implore their pity were not answered. Henry confiscated their hospitable home at

---

[156] *English Works*, p. 1431; Bridgett, p. 374; Stapleton, chap. xvi, Hallett's trans., 162.

More's letters during his stay in the Tower and Margaret Roper's were printed, in 1557, by his nephew Rastall, in his *English Works*, but without dates. Two only are dated: Lady Alington's to Margaret Roper (August 10th, 1534), and Sir Thomas More's to a priest named Leader (January 16th, 1535). When pens, ink, books and paper were taken from him he still found means to write short messages full of affection, piety and resignation, on scraps of paper with charcoal or coal (Bridgett, 378 *sq.*).

[157] See Appendix D (*c*), p. 482 *sq.*

[158] More to Margaret Roper, *English Works*, p. 1446.

[159] More to a priest named Leader, January 16th, 1535 (*English Works*, p. 1450).

[160] Cf. Roper, p. xliii.

Chelsea, and in 1538 gave it to the French ambassador, Castillon, as a residence.[161]

In November, 1534, Parliament conferred the title of "supreme head of the Church" upon the king, and made it high treason for any one *maliciously* to deny it.[162] It was becoming increasingly difficult for More to evade his enemies.

Cromwell went to the Tower, on April 30th, 1535, to question More upon this Act of Parliament. The prisoner refused to answer. He was asked his opinion on the divorce or on the Pope's authority, but all to no purpose. "I am the king's true, faithful subject and daily bedesman," he replied, "and pray for His Highness, and all his, and all the realm. I do nobody no harm, I say none harm, I think none harm, but wish everybody good. And if this be not enough to keep a man alive, in good faith I long not to live."[163] Similar scenes occurred on May 7th and June 3rd. Cromwell swore that the king would make him speak, and that he should either acknowledge and confess it lawful that His Highness should be supreme head of the Church of England, or else utter plainly his malignity. "Whereto I answered that I had no malignity, and, therefore, I could utter none."[164] Meanwhile his correspondence with Fisher had been discovered, and in consequence he was more closely watched and confined.[165] Books, paper, and ink were all taken from him. In order therefore to meditate more freely upon the joys of heaven Sir Thomas closed the shutter of his narrow window, and to the lieutenant who expressed surprise at this action he merrily replied that as all the wares were gone the shop windows might as well be shut.[166]

---

[161] Kaulek, *op. cit.*, 70 *sq.*

[162] See above, p. 216 *sq.*

[163] More to Margaret Roper (Bridgett, 402-403); he relates his interview with Cromwell, and concludes thus: "That that shall follow lieth in the hand of God, whom I beseech to put in the King's Grace's mind that thing that may be to His high pleasure, and in mine to mind only the weal of my soul. . . ."

[164] More to Margaret Roper (Bridgett, pp. 405 *sq.*).

[165] The letters that passed between them were carried by George Golde. Fisher, More, and their servants, Wilson and Wood, were severely examined in an attempt to find proofs of treason or conspiracy. But nothing came of it (June, 1535) (*L. and P.*, VIII, 856, 858).

[166] Roper, p. xlvi. Sander, Lewis trans., p. 123. Stapleton, Hallett's trans., 140.

Rich, the solicitor-general, held a conversation with More on June 12th. Roper thus describes it: " 'Mr. Moore,' sayd Mr. Riche, 'it is well knowne that you are a man both wise and well learned, as well in the Lawes of the Realme as otherwise, I pray you therefore, Sir, lett me be soe bould as of good will to put unto you this case. Admitt there were, Sir, an Acte of Parliament, that all the Realme should take me for the King, would not you take me for the King?'—'Yes, Sir,' quoth Sir Thomas Moore, 'that would I.' 'I put the case further,' quoth Mr. Rich, 'that there weare an Acte of Parliament that all the Realme should take me for the Pope; would then not you, Mr. Moore, take me for the Pope?' 'To your first case,' quoth Sir Thomas Moore, 'the Parliament may well meddle with the stat of temporall Princes; but to make aunsweare to your second case, I will put you this case: suppose the Parliament would make a law that God should not be God, would you then, Mr. Rich, saye God weare not God?'—'Noe, Sir,' quoth he, 'that would I not, sithe noe Parlement may make any such Law.'—'Noe more,' sayd Sir Thomas More (as Mr. Rich reported of him), 'could the Parliament make the Kinge suppreame head of the Church.' "

It was upon this conversation, witnessed by none and held by More to be perjury, this report of one man, "a great dicer and of noe commendable fame," that the judgment, which Lord Campbell called a "judicial murder," was largely based. In vain did More prove to his judges that he had uttered nothing *maliciously, traiterouslie and diabolicallye*, as he had been accused of doing.[167]

The special commission, consisting of nineteen members, contained several of More's former friends or colleagues: Audeley, the chancellor; the Duke of Norfolk; the Duke of Suffolk; Anne Boleyn's father and brother; the Earl of Huntingdon; Lord Montague; and Thomas Cromwell, secretary.

The indictment was extremely long[168] and bore charges under three headings:

[167] Roper, pp. xlvi–xlix. He appears to have extracted it all from the indictment against More (*Baga de Secretis*). Cf. Stapleton, Hallett's trans., 175–76.

[168] The original Latin document is in the *Baga de Secretis* at the Record Office. Bridgett (417 *sq.*) gives a summary of it; the complete text is given

(1) That, being examined on the king's supremacy, on May 7th, he replied: "I will not meddle with such matters."

(2) That he had written to Fisher, on May 12th, advising him to remain silent.

(3) That he had used the expression: "The Act of Parliament is like a two-edged sword, for if a man answer one way it will confound his soul, and if the other way it will confound his body."

To the first charge, More answered that there was no law condemning silence, and observed that though our speech and actions may be man's concern, our secret thoughts belong to God alone.

To the second, he admitted writing to Fisher, but the letters were about private affairs.

To the third he replied that the meaning of his words had been altered, and he assured them that he had never done or said anything maliciously against the statute of supremacy.[169] He was condemned to death (July 1st, 1535).

Until then More had considered it his duty, so as not to tempt God, to defend himself by making use of the subtilty of speech which had stood him in good stead as a barrister.[170] Now that this had failed, he was free to speak his mind, and his voice rang out in Westminster Hall carrying echoes to the confines of the Christian world: "This indictement is grounded upon an Act of Parliament, directly oppugnaunt to the lawes of God and his holye Church, the supreame governement of

in Append. III of *The Life and Death of Sr. Thomas Moore,* written by N. Harpsfield and edited by E. V. Hitchcock and R. W. Chambers, 1932.

[169] See *Récit du procez de Thomas More . . . envoyé de Londres la mesme année par un témoin de ses dernières paroles et de sa mort,* in Le Laboureur's *Mémoires de Castelnau,* Brussels, 1731, I, 416. This account was translated into English by J. Gairdner from a MS. in the *Bibl. Nat.,* Paris (*L. and P.,* VIII, p. 394). Cf. Stapleton, Hallett's trans., 192 *sq.*

A German account is also extant, which was printed in the sixteenth century, but the place of publication is not given: *Beschreibung des Urtheils Herrn Th. Morus.*

[170] Cardinal Pole also answered the Bishop of Badajoz, who did not approve More's long and studied silence. "I cannot think that More was wanting in his duty to the Church because he did not immediately answer that their decree was against the Divine law; for about this he was not asked, nor was he called to account for violating Divine, but human, law. When he understood that the protection of human law was taken from him, and that he was condemned contrary to the right of human law, then, in the proper time, as it seems to me, he used ecclesiastical arms" (Quirini, *R. Poli Epistolae,* Brescia, 1744-51, IV, 79).

which, or of any part thereof, maye no temporall Prince presume by any lawe to take uponn him as rightfully belonginge to the See of Rome . . .; it is contrary to *Magna Charta*, and contrary to that sacred oath which the King's Heighness himselfe, and every other Christian Prince allwayes at their Coronations received; noe more might this Realme ot England refuse obedience to the See of Rome, than mighs the Childe refuse obedience to his naturall father.   Thif Realme, beinge but one member and small parte of the Church might not make a particular lawe dischargable with the generall law of Christ's holye Catholique Church, no more then the Cittie of London, being but one poore member in respect of the whole Realme might make a law against an Act of Parliament. . . . And therefore am I not bound, my Lords, to conforme my conscience to the Councell of one realme against the generall councell of Christendoome." To the chancellor who asked him if he wished to be considered wiser and of better conscience than all the bishops and nobles, he replied: "My lord, for one bishop of your opinion I have a hundred saints of mine; and for one parliament of yours, and God knows of what kind, I have all the General Councils for 1,000 years; and for one kingdom I have France and all the kingdoms of Christendom."[171]

Before he left he reminded them of St Paul witnessing and consenting to the martyrdom of St Stephen, and added that those two saints were united in heaven, "so I shall therefore right hertily praye that, though your Lordships have now in earth beene judges to my condemnation, we may yete hereafter in heaven merily all meete togither to our everlastinge salvation."

His daughter Meg was waiting for him when he left Westminster after his trial, and breaking through the ranks of the guards, ran to him, "embraced him, and took him about the neck and kissed him." He blessed her and tried to comfort her with words of resignation, beseeching her to have patience, not to worry, and to look upon it as God's will.   Thereupon

[171] Roper (pp. l-lii) says that the words he records were related to him by Sir Anthonie Sumtleger, Knight; Sir Richard Heywood and John Webb, gentlemen; as well as by other trustworthy men, who all heard them. Stapleton, Hallett's trans., 196-7. *Récit du procès de Thomas Morus* in Le Laboureur, *op. cit.*, I, p. 417; and Sander, Lewis' trans., p. 125.

she left him.   Then not being satisfied, she turned back again, and caring nothing for the press of people, kissed him lovingly several times. The onlookers could not help weeping at the sight. On the eve of his death More reminded her of this incident: "I never liked your manner towards me better than when you kissed me last; for I love when daughterly love and dear charity hath no leisure to look to worldly courtesy."[172]

In this same letter, written with a charred stick (July 5th, 1535), he blessed them all, wife, sons-in-law, children and grandchildren, and recommended himself to their prayers, and added: "to-morrow . . . is St Thomas's even, and the utas [octave day] of St Peter; and, therefore, to-morrow long I to go to God. It were a day very meet and convenient for me."[173] Early in the morning of July 6th, his friend, Sir Thomas Pope, came to the Tower, by order of the king, to inform him that the execution would take place before nine o'clock. More expressed his gratitude to the king for placing him where he could prepare for his last end. "And so, God help me, am I bounden to His Highness most of all that it pleaseth him so shortly to rid me from the miseries of this wretched world." More had indeed prepared himself for his last end by constant meditation, and his treatise on the Passion reveals some of his thoughts.[174] All his life he had

---

[172] Roper, pp. lii and liii. Cf. *Récit du procès de Thomas Morus, loc. cit.;* Stapleton, Hallett's trans., 199-200. Sanders, Lewis' trans., pp. 125-26.

To Sir William Kingston, constable of the Tower, who bade him farewell with tears running down his cheeks, he said, "Good Mr. Kingston, trouble not your selfe, but be of good cheere. For I will pray for you and for my good Ladie your wif, that we may meete in heaven togeather, where we shall be merrie for ever and ever." Meeting Roper shortly afterwards Kingston said: "In faith, Mr. Roper, I was ashamed of my selfe that at my departure from your father, I found my harte soe feeble and his soe strong, that he was fayne to comfort me which should rather have comforted him" (Roper, p. lii).

[173] The Feast of the Translation of St Thomas à Becket was celebrated in England on July 7th (and is still, in certain dioceses).

With his letter More sent his hair shirt, which is still preserved. Cf. p. 225-6.

[174] In his treatise on the Passion, he wrote learned and pious reflections on each word, quoting a number of passages from the Latin and Greek Fathers. "When he had written the story of the Passion as far as those words of the Gospel, 'They laid hands on Jesus,' hands were laid on him, and he was not allowed to add another word." His own passion was soon to follow. Cf. Sander, Lewis' trans., p. 124. *The Dialogue of Comfort against*

longed for the joys of heaven, and Erasmus tells us he loved to speak of them frequently and at length with his friends. When the Carthusians passed beneath his window singing the *Te Deum* on the way to their execution, he could not help envying them before his daughter: "Loe, dost thou not see, Megg, that these blessed fathers be now as cheerefull goeinge to there deathes, as brydegromes to their marriages? . . . Thie sillie father, God thinking him not worthie soe soone to come to that eternall felicitie leaveth him here yet, still in the world further to be plunged and turmoyled with miserie."[175]

He, too, as though he had been invited to a banquet, wished to put on his best dress, which his friend Bonvisi[176] had given him. The lieutenant of the Tower advised him not to don it, because it would become the perquisite of the headsman. "Were it cloth of gold," he replied, "I should think it well bestowed on him." He yielded, however, and consented to wear rough frieze, that he might be more like our Lord, but insisted on giving a gold angel to the headsman, "as St. Cyprian did who gave his executioner thirty pieces of

Tribulation develops the idea that he is not more a prisoner now than he was before or than other men are, since all are prisoners of the Divine Jailer who punishes them in various ways for their faults. This treatise, which is in the 1557 edition of the *English Works*, was separately printed at Antwerp in 1573, and in modern spelling by Dolman in 1847.

These two treatises, together with the letters written in charcoal, were published in London in Mary Tudor's reign (1557) by Thomas More's granddaughter, Mary Roper, who had married James Basset, the stepson of Lord Lisle [†1542]. James Basset was twelve years in the service of Gardiner, Bishop of Winchester (cf. Bémont, *op. cit.*, p. 114, No. 1; J. A. Muller, *op. cit.*, pp. 69, 352). More's last letters have been republished by W. E. Campbell, with an introduction by Cardinal Gasquet, 1924: *The Last Letters of Blessed Thomas More*. Six unpublished letters of Thomas More are given in H. de Vocht's *Literae virorum eruditorum ad Franciscum Cranevel-dium*, 1522–28, Louvain, 1928, Vol. I.

[175] Roper, p. xliv. When he heard of Fisher's martyrdom he "began to pray, saying: 'I confess to Thee, O Lord, that I am not worthy of so great a crown, for I am not just and holy as is thy servant the bishop of Rochester, whom Thou hast chosen for Thyself out of the whole kingdom, a man after Thine own heart; nevertheless, O Lord, if it be Thy will, give me a share in Thy chalice.'" (Sander, Lewis' trans., pp. 122–23).

[176] Antonio Bonvisi, a rich Italian scholar who had settled as a merchant in London, had been a friend of More for forty years. He sent many things to him during his captivity, as well as to Fisher. One of the last letters written in the Tower was to him (*English Works*, p. 1455, and Stapleton, Hallett's trans., 188, 209).

gold." One woman offered him a glass of wine out of com-
passion, whilst he was on his way to the block, but he refused
it saying: "Christ in his passion was given not wine, but
vinegar, to drink." Margaret Clements afterwards recalled
his pale and emaciated face and long beard, as he advanced
with his eyes raised to heaven, and carrying a red cross in his
hand.[177]

He arrived at the place of execution calm, unexcited, his
feelings completely under control, and his last words revealed
the strength and serenity of his soul. The scaffold appeared to
him to be rather unsteady, "I praye you, Mr. Lieuetenannt,"
said he jokingly, "see mee safe upp, and for my cominge
downe lett me shift for myself." Sir Thomas Pope had
warned him: "The king's pleasure is . . . that at your
execution you shall not use many words." More therefore
merely desired the people to bear witness with him that he
was suffering death *in* and *for* the faith of the Catholic Church,
as a faithful servant of God and the king. He then knelt down
and fervently said the *Miserere*. He rose again cheerfully, and
when the executioner begged his pardon, More kissed him
and said: "Pluck upp thie spirittes, man, and be not affrayed
to doe thine office, my necke is very short. Take heede therefore thou scute not awrie for savinge thine honestie." With
joy in his soul, he gladly received the fatal blow, and his soul
sped aloft to heaven.[178] "Thus died the most honourable
and the most innocent man known in those days," wrote
Harpsfield, "the man I should like most to resemble."[179]

---

[177] Roper, pp. liv *sq*. Stapleton, Hallett's trans., pp. 208, 209. See also
the *Expositio fidelis de morte D. Thomae Mori et quorumdam insignium virorum in
Anglia*, place of publication not given 1535, Antwerp 1536, in Beyschlag,
Sylloge variorum opusculorum, Halle, 1829, I, 236 *sq*. The letter of dedication,
signed P. M., is dated Paris, July 23rd. The author notes the great number
of leaflets, of private letters, and of tracts distributed everywhere, which
tell of the chancellor's condemnation and death, and on which his work is
based. Stapleton (chap. xvi) says that everybody in England saw Erasmus
in this author (which was a mistake). The initials P. M. at the end of the
letter might stand for Paul Manutius (Paolo Manuzio), and Paris might
be a disguise for Venice or Rome, where Manutius was living in 1535.

[178] Roper, p. lv; Stapleton, Hallett's trans., 211; account of More's
trial in Le Laboureur, I, 418; Foxe V, 100; *Glaubwuerdiger Bericht von dem
Todt T. Mori*, Strasbourg, 1535. According to Cresacre More (*Life and
Death of More*, p. 281) and Foxe (ed. Pratt, V, 100; Froude, chap. xv;
Bridgett, p. 435, n. 2), when the axe was raised, More bade the executioner
stay till he had removed his beard, saying that it had committed no treason.

[179] Harpsfield (Bémont, p. 73).

After his head had been exhibited on London Bridge, Meg acquired possession of it, and kept it until her death.[180] His body was laid with Fisher's in the chapel of St Peter ad Vincula by Margaret, her adopted sister Margaret Clements, and Dorothy Harris.[181]

Stapleton[182] relates that the king was playing at dice when the execution took place. He got up suddenly from his seat, glared at Anne Boleyn and said: "You are the cause of that man's death," and then retired to another room to weep. Baldinucci, in his *Artists' Lives*,[183] adds that Anne Boleyn also rose and as she passed before Holbein's portrait of More (now in the Louvre) thought she detected in his eyes a look of reproach. Seized with terror, she took the portrait down and threw it out of the window, exclaiming: "He looks as though he were still living."

The execution of Fisher and More, who were universally known and respected, raised a storm of reprobation, not in England where the people were forced to hide their feelings,

[180] Stapleton (chap. xx) says that she was summoned before the council for having procured her father's head. She replied that she had taken it merely that she might bury it. Her noble attitude and the influence of powerful friends soon brought about her release. Henry had More's head parboiled so that it should not retain the appearances of life as Fisher's had done (Vergerio to Ricalcati, September 24th, 1535, Friedensburg, I, 518).

[181] Roper, p. liv. Dorothy Harris, wrote Stapleton (Hallett's trans., pp. xv, 214), "is still living in Douai," she possesses "the shirt in which he died, stained with his blood, and gave me a large portion of it." "Again and again she has told me these details" of an incident connected with the burial "which may well be regarded as miraculous" (pp. 213-14). "Margaret Roper from earliest morning had been going from church to church and distributing such generous alms to the poor that her purse was now empty. . . . She hastened to the Tower to bury her father's body. . . . In her hurry she forgot to replenish her purse, and found that she had no winding-sheet for the body." At Margaret's suggestion and hoping for credit, Dorothy entered a neighbouring shop, bought the necessary linen, and then put her hand into her purse as if to look for money. "Although the maid was quite certain that she had absolutely no money, yet in her purse she found exactly the price of the linen, not one farthing more or less. . . ." Sander (Lewis' trans., p. 127) also relates this incident. So, too, does Pollini, *op. cit.*, p. 114.

[182] Stapleton, Hallett's trans., 212. Pollini, *op. cit.*, p. 112. Blunt, I, 424.

[183] Filippo Baldinucci resumed Vasari's work, to complete and correct it, in his *Artists' Lives*, in six vols., three of which were published after his death (1696); the second edition appeared in 1731.

but abroad, in France, Spain, Italy and even amongst the Protestants in Germany.[184]

"This is the reward then, O unjust and bloody King," one of them (J. Rivius, †1553) exclaimed, "that you reserved for his fidelity and devotion." "It is abundantly clear," wrote Erasmus, "that More and Fisher were guilty of no ill-will towards the king, but, if they erred, it was by following their conscience in all sincerity. It was their firm persuasion and deep conviction that the opinion they defended was holy. . . . But More's death is deplored even by those whose views he combated with the greatest possible vigour. . . . I myself have seen many shed tears who had never seen More nor had any intercourse with him."[185]　Francis I made use of very strong language in the presence of the ambassador John Wallop.[186]　When Charles V heard of More's death he told the English ambassador he "would rather have lost the best

[184] Stapleton (Hallett's trans., 218 *sq.*) devotes his twenty-first and last chapter to "The Verdict of Famous Scholars upon More's Death." Audin completed this in the French edition, pp. 437 *sq.* For the feelings of Protestants abroad, see Friedmann, *Anne Boleyn*, II, 83 *sq.*

[185] Stapleton, Hallett's trans., 219 *sq.* (cf. n. 177). In the following year (September, 1536) appeared the *D. Erasmi Rotherdarmii in sanctissimorum martyrum Rofensis episcopi ac Thomae Mori . . . Carmen.* John Cochlaeus, the celebrated German Humanist and controversialist (1479–1552), also wrote against Henry VIII, reproaching him with his victims (*Defensio Joannis episcopi Roffensis et Thomae Mori*); Pole congratulated him upon his book: "in quo contra Pharaonis Angliae impiam crudelitatem pietatis jacula fortiter torsisti" (Quirini, III, 1).

[186] Cf. *Ana. Boll.*, XII, 206; Friedmann, II, 80. "The King of France on numerous occasions severely blamed these acts of tyranny." Cardinal Ehrard van der Mark, Bishop of Liége (†1538), told Vergerio (Friedensburg, *Nuntiaturberichte*, I, 518) that Cromwell wrote a long letter to Wallop on August 25th, 1535, justifying Henry and begging Francis I not to listen to vain rumours and idle tales, but to the truth which His Majesty and his council asserted.

Numerous pamphlets telling of Sir Thomas More's execution were circulated in France, and an anonymous poet composed an "Elegy on the late master Thomas More, in his lifetime Chancellor of England," which G. Ascoli has published, pp. 227–31; cf. *ibid.*, p. 62. François de Belleforest, in Vol. II of his *XVIII Histoires tragiques extraites des oeuvres italiennes de Bandel* [Bandello] (Paris, 1566–83), calls Henry VIII *"un monstre de nature,"* whose *"cruauté le rendait si redouté des siens et haï de ses voisins que je crois jamais la vie de Néron n'avoir été plus détestée que celle de cestuici."* He goes on to praise the martyrs of the Faith, Fisher *"la sainteté duquel laisse si bon témoignage à l'Eglise qu'avec la doctrine il peut être égalé à ces premiers martyrs qui ont répandu leur sang pour la confession de la verité . . ., ce grand et excellent en tout savoir Thomas Morus, son chancelier, décapité parce qu'il contredisait aux cruautés et ribauderies de son prince"* (cf. Ascoli, *op. cit.*, pp. 73 *sq.*).

Cittie of our Dominiones, then have lost such a worthie Councellor."[187] "From that day forward the king's name was held in shame and ignominy by all the Christian princes and nations." "O City of London," cried Reginald Pole, "ye have put to death him who was the noblest of all the English."[188]

Henry was affected by this universal outburst and felt he ought to justify himself. Several accounts were published in order to whitewash the king.[189] Gardiner, the lawyer-bishop, had to prove to Francis I that the execution of his episcopal brother was necessary.[190] England's representatives abroad, as well as the various tribunals in England, received orders to denounce Fisher and More as rebels and traitors, who were a danger to their country and condemned by her laws "well

[187] Roper, pp. lv sq. Stapleton, Hallett's trans., 226. Ana. Boll., XII, 205 sq. In 1535 the ambassador in Germany was not Thomas Elyot (†1546), as these authors allege, but Richard Pate (†1565). Elyot had returned to England in March, 1532, two months prior to More's resignation from the chancellorship (cf. Pollard, Times Lit. Suppl., July 17th, 1930). The Dict. of Nat. Biogr. mentions, however, second a diplomatic mission undertaken by Elyot in 1535. It is quite possible that Elyot related the words spoken by Charles V to Pate, and that Roper (from whom Stapleton had it) believed they were addressed to Elyot, "which matter was bye Sir Thomas Elliot to my selfe reported."

[188] Reginald Pole, in the fourth chapter of Book III of his de Unitate Ecclesiae, a chapter which he devotes entirely to More (cf. Stapleton, Hallett's trans., p. 219). The previous sentence is from Fisher's early biographers in Ana. Boll., XII, 206.

[189] At this time Sir Richard Morison wrote his Apomaxis calumniarum, of which we have already spoken.

Certain works were addressed to Catholics. One of these asserted that, contrary to the Holy See's statement, Francis I had taken no steps on behalf of the Bishop of Rochester. The King of France was thus placed in a false position. If he denied this assertion he would lose all credit with the English court; if he kept silent he would appear to approve Fisher's execution. The writings destined for Protestants represented Fisher and More as despisers of the Gospel: More "a cruel and ferocious character," had "invented cruel tortures to punish those whom he saw leaning towards the Gospel truth." The contemporaries gave no credence to all these accusations, and the king did not even recover the costs of his slanders. P. Friedmann, op. cit., II, pp. 83–88. Cf. Froude, chap. IX. The Lutheran Seckendorf (Commentarius historicus et apologeticus de Lutheranismo, Frankfort and Leipzic, 1688) ranks Henry VIII "inter malos principes."

[190] The rough draft published in L. and P. (VIII, No. 1118), where it is said to be by Wriothesley, was identified by R. H. Brodie as being by Gardiner, and again later by M. P. Janelle, who republished it, in Latin and in English, with notes and comments, in Three Political Tracts by Bishop Stephen Gardiner, Cambridge, 1930. Cf. Collier, IV, 275; J. A. Muller, Stephen Gardiner, London, 1926, pp. 60 and 350, n. 26.

worthy, if they had had a thousand lives, to have suffered ten times a more terrible death."[191] They were more formidable in death to the king than they had been in life, and no better panegyric than that could be pronounced over these noble victims.

When Cardinal Tournon related the details of Fisher's death in consistory, all his hearers were moved to tears.[192] With Fisher's death and that of the chancellor all hopes of reconciliation with the Holy See vanished. Paul III and the cardinals thought of depriving Henry, *christiani nominis opprobrium*, of his kingdom, and sought the aid of Charles V for this.[193] Reginald Pole was shortly afterwards dispatched to the various European Courts to urge them to decide upon concerted action against England for the overthrow of the king.

Reginald Pole, who was born in March, 1500, was the third son of Sir Richard Pole,[194] and could claim to be of

[191] Order to the royal representatives (Strype, *Eccles. Mem.* I, Append.). Cromwell to John Wallop, August 23rd, 1535 (Burnet, VI, 116). Cromwell to Foxe, Bishop of Hereford, envoy to the Lutheran princes of Germany, in Froude, ed. Everyman, II, p. 98, n. 3. Cromwell to G. Casale at Rome, in *L. and P.*, VII, p. 633.

[192] G. Casale to Cromwell, *L. and P.*, VII, p. 260.

[193] Ricalcati to Vergerio, Rome, July 31st and August 3rd, 1535. Friedensburg, *Nuntiaturberichte*, I, 436, 467.

See Paul III's Bull (August, 1535), the publication of which was delayed at the request of Francis I, in Sander, French ed., 1587, 79; Pollini, p. 120; Burnet, IV, p. 319 (final Bull of 1538); Dodd, ed. 1737, I, 295, 296. *L. and P.*, IX, No. 207; cf. X, Nos. 82, 107. Altered in December 1535, the Bull was submitted to the consistory; although Francis I no longer raised objections and had, in March, 1536, recalled Cardinal du Bellay, who had unceasingly placed obstacles in the way, the Bull was not published until 1538, because the Pope continued to hope for signs of improvement on the king's part, especially after Anne Boleyn's disgrace (Cf. *L. and P.*, VII, 628; Collier, IV, 286 *sq.*; Friedmann, *op. cit.*, II, pp. 80 *sq.*; Fisher, 536). Whatever he may have said, the papal excommunication troubled Henry, for in the definition of the Church annotated in his handwriting, he altered the phrase "Ecclesia accipitur pro congregatione omnium hominum qui baptizati sunt in Christo . . . nec sunt excommunicati," to "nec sunt *juste* excommunicati aut *obstinati*" (Burnet, IV, 408).

[194] T. Philipps (I, 3) is wrong in saying he was the fourth son. The eldest was Lord Montague. The second son died young; the youngest was called Geoffrey. The only daughter, Ursula, married her cousin, the son of the Duke of Buckingham, whose hopes of the crown and Henry VIII's suspicious policy cost him his life [1521] (Cf. *L. and P.*, III, p. lxvi, and Nos. 1, 1284, 1356).

royal blood through his mother, Margaret, Countess of Salisbury.[195] Henry VIII took an interest in his education at an early age. The king paid for his first lessons with the Carthusians at Sheen, sent him to Magdalen College, Oxford,[196] and then bestowed a large pension upon him as well as numerous ecclesiastical benefices[197] to enable him to frequent the famous Italian universities.[198]

Pole stayed in Padua from April, 1521,[199] until the autumn of 1526, and there improved his intellectual qualities by mixing with the most famous men of the time. Leonico Tomeo completed his philosophical studies, and Romolo Amaseo his Greek and Latin. The Humanists, Marcantonio Flaminio and Lazzaro Buonamici, were favourite friends of his and often dined at his table, as also did some of the talented young men, such as Longolius (de Longueil), who afterwards died in his house and whose "Life," written by Pole, is one of the most appreciated of the latter's works from a literary point of view. He made the acquaintance of Stanislaus Hosius, afterwards Bishop of Ermland. The famous poet Bembo, "whose beautiful Latin was the joy of Italy," sought his company, and Matteo Ghiberti, the friend of the Renaissance scholars, was anxious to be counted among his friends.[200] Erasmus, in

[195] The countess (1473-1541) was the daughter of George Plantagenet, Duke of Clarence (†1478) and brother to Edward IV. Henry VII married her to her cousin, Sir Richard Pole, whose mother was step-sister to the queen-mother, Margaret Beaufort. Her brother, the Earl of Warwick, had been beheaded in 1499 by Henry VII (R. Pole's genealogy in Philipps).

Richard Pole (†1505) was Prince Arthur's chamberlain, and the countess became one of Catherine of Aragon's ladies-in-waiting, and afterwards governess to Princess Mary until 1534.

[196] L. and P., I, 4190. At Oxford Pole was under the Humanists Linacre (†1524) and William Latimer (†1545). According to Wood (Athenae Oxon. I, 92) he became a Master of Arts in June, 1515. On leaving the university he defended a thesis on Moral Theology and Logic which lasted thirty days, Sundays and festivals excepted (Beccadelli, op. cit., I, Part 2, p. 281).

[197] Pole seems to have been destined for the Church at an early age (L. and P., XI, No. 92). So, although young and a layman, he was presented to the collegiate church at Wimborne as dean (February 12th, 1518, L. and P., II, No. 3943) and to two prebends at Salisbury (March 19th, 1518 and April 10th, 1519).

[198] At his own desire Henry VIII sent him to Italy on February 21st, 1521, and guaranteed him £100 a year (L. and P., III, 1544; cf. Beccadelli, I, Part 2, p. 282).

[199] His letter to Henry VIII announcing his arrival at Padua is dated April 27th, 1521 (L. and P., III, 4190).

[200] For these Humanists, see the French ed. of this book, pp. 540 sq.,

a letter to him, addressed him as, "My dear Pole, you whom I esteem above all others."[201] Bembo saw in him the most virtuous, the most learned, and the most serious of young men,[202] and he was "sought after more than the other nobles who are drawn to this city by its literary fame."[203]

Beccadelli, who lived with him for a long while,[204] says that when he returned to England his refined manners and the extensive learning he had acquired in Italy pleased the Court and all with whom he came in contact.   He was of average height, thin, with rather a long face, like the average Englishman,[205] of reddish complexion, with a fair beard and eyes glowing with vitality and kindness.   Healthy but not strong in body, he was frequently indisposed and suffered from rheumatism in his arms, and fasting was a trial to him. He slept but little, and often rose before dawn to meditate and study.   His morals were always above suspicion.   Of a generous nature, he spent what he had, was liberal with donations and anxious that his staff should be well treated.   Debts he avoided, and regulated his manner of living by his income, which was never very large after his breach with Henry VIII.   He was an unassuming man, who never gave way to anger but always mastered his feelings.   Some people thought he was much too humble, but he based his life upon that of Christ and never harboured ill-feelings for any injuries he received. His conversation was both pleasing and lively, and as he had

where a bibliography will be found.   For Longolius, Th. Simar's work must be included, *Christophe de Longueil, humaniste (1488–1522)*, Louvain, 1911.

[201] A letter dated 1525.   Erasmus had begun correspondence with Pole through the medium of Richard Pace's secretary, Thomas Lupset, "more eloquent, learned, and pious than any other Englishman" (cf. Beccadelli, I, Part 2, p. 282;   Dom Biron, p. 24, in which an interesting chapter (pp. 14 *sq.*) will be found on Pole's sojourn in Italy).   Cardinal Gasquet's work, *Cardinal Pole and His Early Friends*, 1927, based upon N. Leonico Tomeo's correspondence, is of particular interest for Pole's sojourn at Padua.

[202] Bembo's expressions.

[203] *L. and P.*, IV, No. 1529.

[204] The description that follows is from Beccadelli, ed. Morandi, I, Part 2, pp. 284, 322–33.

[205] The text says "la facia haveva alquanto larghetta"; but Pole's portraits, even those showing the full face, reveal a countenance that is neither large nor full, but elongated and emaciated, with prominent cheek-bones.   Possibly it is to this last peculiarity that Beccadelli alludes when he says "alquanto larghetta."

been much in society and had read a great deal he could always captivate his hearers. Beccadelli asserts that he knew none more prompt at repartee or able to use more gracious comparisons or figures of speech. As a friend he was sincere and genuine. Flattery and falsehood were abhorrent to him, and his opinions were always so delicately expressed that he never gave offence to those who disagreed with him. His cardinal's vote was always so freely and so unassumingly given in consistory that none could be displeased. He was so gentle and kind that when attempts were made upon his life he interceded for the culprits.[206] When Paul IV suspected him of heresy he defended himself rather sharply, but after reflecting for a few days threw what he had written into the fire. His large-hearted charity caused him to love one and all without distinction. When the meanest of his servants was ill, Pole would himself visit and care for the invalid. That same charity made him look with a blind eye upon the faults of others, and men sometimes took advantage of this leniency. He was anxious to be of service to all, and would gently seek to correct those who erred, without hurting their feelings. So courageous was he that, according to Beccadelli, none of his contemporaries could be compared with him, neither was this the courage of the Stoic or the warrior, but real Christian courage. With the eyes of faith—and his was a very lively faith indeed—he looked upon everything that God sent or permitted and found it good. Calumny, exile, persecution, or the death of his relations and friends, all these he bore without complaining and even with a certain joy. His prudence and serious ways commanded the respect of the cardinals, and even of the Pope, and were equalled only by his moderation and forbearance. He showed greater leanings to study and to meditation than to action, and was fond of being alone. As a young man he loved Aristotle and Plato, but in his later years their place was taken by the Sacred Scriptures, which he was constantly reading, and his perfect knowledge of them is shown in his writings. In the solitude of his room

[206] At Viterbo Beccadelli tells us (p. 325) he caused three Italians to be released who had plotted against him. And at Capranica he intervened on behalf of two Englishmen sent from England to assassinate him: "This is a personal affront: I wish their lives to be spared." Thanks to him they were condemned to the galleys only for a very short period.

he devoted much time to prayer and meditation. Every Sunday he received Holy Communion, and after his ordination (1555) he continued this practice by saying Mass every Sunday also. Charles V averred that he knew no better priest than the English cardinal in the whole of Christendom. Beccadelli observed that in his day many retained memories of Pole as of an angel, and that recollection has persisted through the centuries: *Non anglus sed angelus vocetur*.[207]

As a young man he avoided the Court—Beccadelli[208] is our authority for this—and loved to frequent the religious houses. He began his studies in the Charterhouse at Sheen, and thither he returned after his delightful stay in Italy to spend a couple of years (1527-29) in the pleasant house that John Colet (1519) had built for himself as a refuge from the world in his old age and as a rendezvous for a few choice friends.[209] He was still Henry's protégé, and after securing Colet's charming little place for him the king made him Dean of Exeter, on August 12th, 1527. Clouds were gathering, however, on the horizon.

The sorry business of the divorce began in June, 1527, bringing in its wake the intrigues and disturbances which were soon to spread from the court through the whole country. There can be no question that the support and assistance in this matter of such a man as Pole, the scion of one of the most noble families in England, esteemed by all, and destined by his rank and learning to the highest ecclesiastical offices, would have been invaluable. Cromwell, prompted possibly by the king, tried to win him to their side. During the course of a long conversation, preserved in the *Apologia ad Carolum V*,[210] Cromwell suggested that Pole should forget the

[207] C. M. Antony's biography of Pole (London, 1909) is entitled: *The Angelical Cardinal*. In his speech for the abjuration of schism, Gardiner called Pole "the angel of England." Sadolet in a letter to Priuli, July 4th, 1559 (Quirini, I, p. 343) called him "an angelic mind." And Cardinal Seripando, writing to St Thomas of Villanova (Beccadelli, II, Part 2, p. 333, n. 64), said "every time he hears Reginald speak of the things of God he thinks he hears not a man but an angel from Heaven bringing the eternal Gospel to men." Wood (*op. cit.*, ed. 1691, I, 92) wrote that Reginald Pole's "piety, learning and integrity of life did make him more illustrious than the splendour of his royal blood."

[208] *Op. cit.*, II, Part l, p. 330.

[209] Letter 435 from Erasmus to J. Jonas of Erfurt.

[210] *Apologia R. Poli ad Carolum V Caesarem supra quattuor libris a se scriptis*

principles he had learnt, which might be good enough for universities, and showed him that the way to royal favour and to honours lay in following the principles of Machiavelli, a copy of whose *Prince*[211] he offered to lend him.   But Pole foresaw that at any moment he might find his honesty and his conscience conflicting with his gratitude and friendship for the king, and so after staying two years in England he asked to be allowed to go to Paris to continue his studies.[212]

He had evaded the divorce crisis, but was unable entirely to escape it.   Henry sought his assistance to obtain from the Sorbonne a decision against Catherine of Aragon.   Pole tried to avoid this mission and apologized for not being properly qualified to serve the king in such an important affair.[213] Henry then sent Edward Foxe, afterwards Bishop of Hereford, to join him, and Pole passed all the responsibility on to Foxe.[214] Under the influence of Francis I, the university decided in Henry's favour.   Pole returned to the Charterhouse at Sheen in the month of July (1530).

Henry still meant to win Pole to his side.   When Wolsey died, the king offered Pole Winchester or the Archbishopric

---

de Unitate Ecclesiae, Louvain, 1569, republished by Quirini, *op. cit.*, I, 166. "R. Pole and Cromwell" (*Amer. Hist. Review*, July, 1904).

[211] *Il Principe*, written in 1514, was not published till 1532, but Cromwell had managed to obtain a copy.   He did not send a copy to Pole as he had promised, but the latter obtained one in order to judge the principles, the latent poison of which Cromwell had made known to him.   Cf. Meinecke, *Der Fürst und Kleinere Schriften von Machiavelli*, Berlin, 1923; F. Ercole, *Il Principe di Machiavelli*, in *Revue des Sciences politiques*, 1925-6, and also Ercole's *La Politica di Machiavelli*, Rome, 1926; Ettore Janni, *Machiavelli*, Eng. trans., by Marion Enthoven, London, 1930; F. Chabod, *Del "Principe" di Niccolo Machiavelli*, Milan, 1926, and *Sulla composizione de "Il Principe"* in *Archiv. Romanicum*, 1927; French ed. of *Il Principe*, with preface by Mussolini, Paris, 1929; and F. Battaglia, *Studi sul Machiavelli* in *Nuovi Studi di Economia e Politica*, 1928-9; and L. Russo, *Prolegomeni a Machiavelli*, Florence, 1931.

[212] The king not only gave permission but granted him £1,000 a year (*L. and P.*, IV, No. 6003, V, No. 315).

[213] Beccadelli, p. 284.

[214] In his *De Unitate Ecclesiae* (Bk. III, chap. III) and in his *Epistola ad Eduardum VI*, he very clearly says that if the king had not freed him from his mission he would have preferred to die rather than accept the responsibility of a cause which he considered illegal.   When he speaks of the measures taken by Foxe and their success, merely to inform Henry, he uses terms which do not imply that he approves the divorce (cf. Brewer, *Land. P.*, Nos. 6252, 6394, 6483, 6505).   For certain Anglican criticisms of Pole's conduct in these circumstances (especially Hook's in his *Lives of the Archbishops of Canterbury*) see Dom Biron's reply, *op. cit.*, 42 *sq.*

of York. Norfolk conveyed this offer to him and hinted that
the king would not tolerate any one in that high office who
was against the divorce. Pole preferred not to accept either
See, and the duke then showed him how dangerous such a
refusal would be for his own family, and gave him a month
for reflection. Meanwhile Pole's relations began to pester
him over his refusal, Lord Montague in particular. Harassed
and worried, Reginald thought he had discovered a solution
to the difficulty which would satisfy both his own conscience
and the king, and he agreed therefore to see the latter at
York Palace. When, however, he tried to say what he had
made up his mind to tell the king, he could not open his lips
and his paralysed tongue could only murmur words of
caution to the king against an error which was perilous for
his soul. Henry's face grew stern, and his hand sought his
dagger. Pole departed in tears.[215] He had definitely fallen
from the king's good graces.

In a secret letter to Henry he still maintained his opinion,
but it was so sincerely worded and manifested such an ardent
desire to safeguard the king's honour that the latter could not
take offence at it.[216] Towards the spring of 1532, he even
obtained permission to leave England, upon the plea of
studying, and was allowed to retain the revenue of his deanery
at Exeter and received a yearly pension of four hundred
ducats.[217] Powerless on a fatal slope, the country was fast

[215] Beccadelli, pp. 285 sq.; Quirini, I, 251 sq.; L. and P., XII, Part 1,
No. 444; Dodd, I, 473; Dom Biron, 47 sq.

[216] Henry himself informed Lord Montague of this (Quirini, I, 182,
327 sq.). Pole's arguments touched him so much that he ordered Cranmer
to examine them. They were written "with that eloquence," said the
archbishop, "that if it were set forth and known to the common people,
it were not possible to persuade them to the contrary." Pole tried to move
the king by political considerations; then he refuted one after the other
the reasons in favour of the divorce, and ended by proposing every means
of saving the king's honour which his affection could suggest (Cranmer to
Anne Boleyn's father, June 13th, 1531. Strype, Memorials of Cranmer,
chap. II and Append. I). Pole's arguments are known only through this
letter of Cranmer, in which the latter resumes and endeavours to refute
them, for the writing itself has never been found. The king probably
destroyed it (cf. ibid., p. 11, n. h; Beccadelli, I, Part 2, p. 286).

[217] L. and P., V, No. 737. The king's kindness was tinged with a certain
prudence, for Chapuys tells us that Pole had stated that if he were present
in Parliament (February, 1532), he would openly give his opinion on the
divorce should the question be raised (cf. Fisher, p. 421; Dom Biron, p. 56).

moving towards schism.[218] Pole did not come back again until Mary Tudor's reign.

He spent several months in the papal town of Avignon, where he studied theology under famous professors. At Carpentras he made the acquaintance of the learned Bishop Sadolet, who remained one of his best friends.[219] As, however, the climate and the winds in the south of France did not suit his health, and as, moreover, he still longed for the province of Venice, his second motherland, it was not long before he went to Padua, the city that always lived in his memory.[220] There he discovered his old friends, Bembo, Flaminio, and Buonamici. New friends he also made, among them Cosimo Gherio, the young Bishop of Fano; Gregorio Cortese, the Benedictine Abbot of San Giorgio Maggiore in Venice; Gasparo Contarini, afterwards cardinal (May 31st, 1535); Ludovico Beccadelli, who was Pole's secretary before he became Archbishop of Ragusa and who afterwards wrote the Life of Pole; and the most faithful of all, Alvise Priuli, the young patrician of Venice, whom no offers of dignities,

---

[218] On February 11th, 1531 Convocation gave the king the title of *Supremum caput Ecclesiae post Deum*. On May 15th, 1532, it passed the *Submission of the Clergy*, which subjected the Church to the State (see above, pp. 95-105). Despite Burnet's assertion Reginald Pole, as Dean of Exeter, did not assist at the deliberations of the clergy, as is proved by the list of those who were present (*L. and P.*, IV, No. 2699).

[219] Sadolet (1477-1547), who was made a cardinal two years later, at once appreciated Pole's eminent qualities: "nihil mihi accedere possit optatius quam me abs te tali viro diligi" (letter to R. Pole, November 23rd, 1534). Although he was much older than Pole, and also his superior, yet he submitted to him his manuscript, *De liberis recte instituendis*, which appeared in 1533, and welcomed his friendly comments. He followed his advice and devoted himself thenceforward to sacred in preference to profane studies. In 1536 he met him again on the commission called together by Paul III to reform the Church. Cf. *J. Sadoleti Epistolae*, ed. V. A. Costanzi, Rome, 1759-67, Part 2, pp. 184, 221, 236; Part 3, pp. 159, 164, 174, 181, 348; Append., p. 261. Tiraboschi, *Storia della letteratura italiana*, Naples, 1777-86, VII, Part I, pp. 16 *sq.*, 187, 244 *sq.*; Part 3, p. 356. Friedensburg, *Nuntiaturberichte*, II, pp. 40, 49, 56, 88, 151, 230 *sq.*, 320. G. von Schulten-Rechberg, *Der Kardinal Jacopo Sadoleto*, Zurich, 1909. S. Ritter, *Un Umanista teologo, Jacopo Sadoleto (1477-1547)*, Rome, 1912. Al Ferrajoli, *Jacopo Sadoleto in Il ruolo della Corte di Leone X* (*Archiv. della R. Società romana di storia patria*, Vol. 38 (1915), pp. 215-81, 425-52). Fern. Benoît, *Le cardinal Jacques Sadolet, évêque de Carpentras* (*Annuaire de la Société des Amis du Palais des Papes*, 1925, pp. 35-47, with an unpublished portrait).

[220] Beccadelli, 287; Quirini, II, 2 *sq.*; Dom Biron, 108 *sq.* He remained less than a year in the neighbourhood of Avignon.

not even the cardinalate, could separate from Pole until the latter's death.[221]

Here in the peace and quietness of this friendly circle echoes of the turmoil in England reached him. Henry had not lost sight of this subject whose influence he feared for the time to come.[222] He sent a special messenger to Pole ordering him to give his opinion, and without fail, upon the new title of Head of the Church of England, and he demanded his complete and precise opinion, without mental reservations or a shadow of dissimulation. Reginald's former chaplain, Thomas Starkey, was commissioned to obtain this formal statement, and his letters to Pole became increasingly insistent.[223] The reply was promised on April 12th, 1535, but appeared only in the following year (May, 1536).[224] It was the famous *De Unitate Ecclesiae*, which clearly solved the question: "No temporal prince can be the supreme head of the Church in his own country (Bk. I); according to Sacred Writ, tradition, and history, the Pope is the successor of Peter and the Vicar of Christ (Bk. II)[225]; would that Henry, whom

---

[221] For these men, see the French ed., p. 549 *sq*. P. Paschini has devoted much time to research on Priuli and has published a collection of documents of importance for his relations with Reginald Pole, *Un amico del Cardinale Polo: Alvise Priuli*, Rome, 1921.

[222] Chapuys wrote to the emperor on September 27th, 1533 (Friedmann, I, 234) that Catherine of Aragon had designs upon Pole, that she wanted to marry him to Princess Mary because he was related to the King. The malcontents founded their hopes on him. The imperial ambassador recommended him to Charles V's notice.

[223] Beccadelli, I, Part 2, p. 288. Cf. *L. and P.*, VIII, Nos. 218, 535, 574; cf. Zimmermann, *Kardinal Pole*, 75 *sq*.; Fisher, *op. cit.*, 422; Dom Biron, 76 *sq*.

[224] The martyrdom of Fisher and More caused Pole to write it (cf. Beccadelli, 289; Fisher, p. 422). Pole's work was not then divided into books and chapters as it was when it was printed. (*Ad Henricum Octavum Britanniae regem, pro ecclesiasticae Unitatis defensione libri quattuor*.)

It was delivered to the king in May 1536. This is also usually given as the date when it was completed (cf. *Dictionary of National Biography*). But Pole submitted it to the Pope before April of that year (Quirini, I, 442); and Beccadelli (*op. cit.*, p. 289) says it was written in "four months." Pole wrote it near Verona, in the pleasant country house at Treville, which belonged to his friend Priuli.

[225] These two first books are a refutation of the *Oratio de dignitate et potestate regis* by Sampson, Dean of the Chapel Royal and afterwards Bishop of Chichester (1536-43), which the king had sent to him, and of Gardiner's *De vera obedientia*, as Pole informed Contarini when he wrote to him on February 8th, 1536 (Quirini, I, 460). During the conclave in 1550 he wrote his *De Summo Pontifice*, a dialogue between the Cardinal of Urbino and

an unfortunate passion had led astray and who had caused
the deaths of the most saintly and the purest of men, might
listen to him and repent !" (Bks. III and IV).[226] The facts
were accurate and the arguments powerful, but his strong
vehement style was reminiscent of the Philippics. The work
was too rhetorical and hardly calculated to change a man of
Henry VIII's temperament. In it the king was compared to
Cerberus, the Grand Turk, Domitian, Nero, and Satan himself, and it was hinted that his subjects were on the verge of
rebellion. After hesitating for a while, Pole ordered an English
gentleman in his service, Michael Throckmorton, to deliver
the work into the king's own hands so that others should not
know what he had written.[227] Henry concealed his feelings
and insisted that Pole should return at once to England,
while Starkey and Bishop Tunstall, to whom the refutation
of Pole had been entrusted, reproached him with having
forsaken his country, his relations, and such an excellent

himself, Louvain, 1569 (J. Th. Rocaberti, O.P., *Bibliotheca maxima Pontificia*,
Rome, 1697–99, XVIII, p. 144; Quirini, I, 66–71), in which he places
the power of the Popes far above that of kings. See especially chaps. VII
and L.

[226] In these books Henry is more directly taken to task, both as regards
the divorce and the victims of the royal supremacy. A whole chapter is
devoted to Thomas More.

[227] Beccadelli, *op. cit.*, ed. Morandi, p. 290. He had thought of throwing
it into the fire. Priuli and Contarini, to whom he submitted the manuscript,
criticized the tone of certain passages. The silence of the Pope, to whom
he had also sent it, made him anxious. But when Anne Boleyn was beheaded (May 19th, 1536) he decided to take action (Quirini, I, 422;
Beccadelli, p. 290, n. 17). The document was not published till 1538
(Rome) when all bonds with Henry had been broken. It was reprinted at
Strasbourg in 1555 by Vergerio and again at Ingolstadt in 1597, after
Pole's death.

Throckmorton left Venice with a letter from Reginald Pole to Henry VIII
dated May 27th, 1536 (J. P. C., *Nine historical letters of the reign of Henry VIII*,
p. 1; these nine letters of R. Pole were handed over to the State Paper
Office in 1859); see Pole's instructions to his messenger (in Burnet, VI, 172),
in which he assured him that he was giving his opinion with truth as his
only consideration, in order to obey the king's will and in the hope that the
king would allow himself to be persuaded. Yet he had no illusions about it,
for a few days later, June 8th (Quirini, I, 455), he told Contarini that he
had lost all hope of seeing England again, and that he would go back
there only after the king had been converted. On the same day he wrote
to the Bishop of Durham, Tunstall (*L. and P.*, XI, 210), saying "that if God
would give his Grace to taste but one tear of pure penance he would say
all the pleasure and comfort that ever he had from childhood, or the whole
world could give, were not to be compared to the sweetness thereof."

prince.[228]   But Pole saw danger ahead, and acting on his friends' advice stayed in Italy.[229]

His position thenceforward was a very delicate one.   The ties binding him to England and to the king were fast losing their hold upon him.   He saw, as Beccadelli remarks, the snares England held out to him to bring him down and to make him an open rebel against the king.   He thought of his own family, who shortly afterwards—and probably at Henry's instigation—sent him bitter reproaches well calculated to trouble his tender heart.[230]   Accordingly when Paul III summoned him to Rome, albeit as a layman, to take part in the commission which was to discuss Church reforms (July, 1536), he hesitated, delayed his departure, and consulted his friends.   He informed both the king and Cromwell, and they replied in a warning tone in which threats were but thinly veiled.   He yielded at last to the insistence of his friends who showed him where his duty lay, viz. in obedience to the Pope.[231]   To reward him for the active part he had played in that commission, Paul III wished to make him a cardinal, but Pole begged him to postpone the nomination on account of the evident peril for his family, and the inconvenience his relations with England would suffer.   The Pope yielded to his objections, but

[228] Pole to Contarini, June 8th, 1536.   Henry VIII to Pole, June 15th, 1536.   Quirini, I, 75, 455, 755.   Strype, *Eccles. Mem.*, Append. LXXI. Burnet, VI, 177.   The refutation of Tunstall, who had been More's and Pole's friend, is in Foxe, V, 90-99.

[229] "Per Deum immortalem," Contarini wrote to him in Paul III's name (Beccadelli, p. 290, n. 17), "te obtestor ne te objicias manifestissimo imo compertissimo periculo."   Chapuys wrote to the emperor on July 23rd saying that if Pole were so imprudent Henry would make him a cardinal in the same way as he had the Bishop of Rochester.

[230] *L. and P.*, XI, Nos. 93, 157; XIII, Part 2, No. 328.   Cf. Pole's letter to Contarini, October 10th, 1536; Beccadelli, p. 291, n. 18; Dom Biron, 78 *sq*.   His mother and his brother, Lord Montague, rebuked him for accepting the Pope's invitation to go to Rome, and begged him not to comply with the request.

[231] Cf. Quirini, I, 483; II, 32.   Dom Biron, pp. 96 *sq*.   The Pope had summoned him (July 19th, 1536) *in virtute sanctae obedientiae*.   It was in Verona, in October, when he was about to set out for Rome with Ghiberti, Caraffa and Cortese, that he received the letters from Cromwell, Tunstall, his mother, and Lord Montague, which caused him extreme anxiety (cf. Beccadelli, p. 291, n. 18; Quirini, *loc. cit.*).   The commission to which Pole had been summoned was designed to prepare the council to be held at Mantua; the *Consilium de emendenda Ecclesia* was drawn up by it (cf. G. Constant's *La Légation de Morone près l'empereur et le concile de Trent*, Paris, 1922, p. xxii, n. 3).

on the morning of the consistory (December 26th, 1536) decided to carry out his first intention, and sent a prelate to find Pole and accompany him to the barber's to have the tonsure cut. "I was present," says Beccadelli, "and the good lord was amazed, but obeyed *tanquam agnus coram tondente*."[232] In spite of the annoyance it caused the king and Cromwell, he was made cardinal. He did not, however, break off relations with them on that account; he vindicated his actions and met their violent reproaches.[233] When, two months later (February 15th, 1537), he was nominated legate for England, he openly declared his affection for and attachment to the king, and constantly hoped for the latter's return to the Roman obedience.[234]

The Pilgrimage of Grace was at its height. With the north in revolt, possibly the presence of a legate and the assistance of the foreign powers might have seriously jeopardized Henry VIII's safety. "Things are going very badly for the king in England," wrote Paul III's secretary on March 11th, 1537, "the legate we are sending might be very useful there."[235] But when Pole left Rome (March 31st), all chance

[232] Beccadelli, pp. 292 *sq.* Pole was a layman, as has been said. The same thing had happened in Contarini's case (1535). Bembo was ordained priest after he had been made a cardinal (1538). At that time there was nothing extraordinary in such cases. Cf. Chacon-Oldoin, *op. cit.*, III, col. 656. Together with Pole, the learned Sadolet and two men afterwards Popes, Giovanni Ciocchi dal Monte (Julius III) and Giovanni Pietro Caraffa (Paul IV), were made cardinals.

[233] The Bishops of Durham and London, Tunstall and Stokesley, and the King's Council violently upbraided him for becoming the tool of the one who wanted to stir up the country. He answered in a pamphlet known as *Apologia ad Angliae Parliamentum* [this should be *ad Consilium*] (Quirini, I, 179–87; *L. and P.*, XII, Part 1, No. 144), the moderate tone of which differs from that of *De Unitate*. He had acted only as every Catholic is bound to act, in obedience to the Vicar of Jesus Christ. Was it not possible to be both a friend of the king and of the Pope, who had nothing but the feelings of a father for Henry and for the English nation? (cf. Quirini, I, xcvii *sq.*).

[234] R. Pole to Cromwell, Rome, February 16th, 1537; Cambrai, May 2nd, 1537; Liége, May 29th, 1537; and no address or date [1537]; J. P. C., *Nine Historical Letters of the reign of Henry VIII*, pp. 3, 6, 12; and Burnet, VI, p. 185. R. Pole to the Privy Council, February 16th, 1537 (*L. and P.*, XII, Part 1, No. 444).

Pole again explained to Edward VI the treatise he had had to write against the latter's father, Henry VIII: *R. Poli cardinalis britannici epistola ad Eduardum VI Angliae regem de opere adversus Henricum patrem scripto*, in Schelhorn, *Amoenitates historiae ecclesiasticae et literariae*, Frankfort and Leipzic, 1737, pp. 191–277; and Quirini, IV, 306–53.

[235] Ambrogio Ricalcati to Morone, Friedensburg, II, 126. Cf. J. Gaird-

of success had disappeared. The rebels had been dispersed, and the war between the emperor and the King of France (1536-38) gave Henry the upper hand. Henry warned each of the rivals that if either received Pole, all relations with himself would be broken off. Fearing to have England against them, they both accordingly refused to see the legate. Francis I openly explained his difficulty, but Charles V was all excuses and evasions.[236] Knowing how afraid Francis was lest England should form an alliance with the emperor, Henry VIII went so far as to demand that the legate should be arrested as a traitor when he passed through France.[237] To the Regent of Flanders he made an offer to pay for ten thousand infantry-men for ten months, if Pole were delivered into his hands. Orders to assassinate the legate reached Calais, and a huge price was placed on his head. "The King is much mistaken," Pole quietly observed when he heard the news, "if he thinks to harm me by procuring rest for me; it is as though he were helping a man to go to bed who was very anxious to sleep."[238] He took refuge first at Cambrai, but the bishop, Robert de Croy (†1556), had no desire to keep him there when he had heard how the emperor viewed the matter; then, after waiting nearly two months for permission from the Council of Flanders, he went on to Liége, where the Bishop, Ehrard van der Marck (†1538), showed him every consideration.[239]

ner, *History*, 204, 206; and *Lollardy*, II, 41 *sq.*, 107 *sq.*; Fisher, *op. cit.*, p. 423. The Pope realized that "if the legate were not supported by those who could and ought to support him, his activity would serve no purpose" (Friedensburg, II, 116). Consequently he directed him to Charles V and the King of France.

Ghiberti and Priuli accompanied Pole on his legation (cf. Beccadelli, p. 293).

[236] He congratulated the Council of Flanders on the discreet manner in which they nullified the measures taken by the legate and rendered his mission futile in order not to arouse the king's suspicions. See the French ed. of this book, p. 558.

[237] Pallavicini, *Istoria del concilio di Trento*, Rome, 1656-57, Bk. 4, chap. IV, No. 7. *L. and P.*, XII, Part I, No. 939. Francis I was too chivalrous to consent to such behests. He even sent an escort to accompany the legate to Cambrai.

[238] Beccadelli, p. 295; Dodd, I, 474; *L. and P.*, VII, 697, 701.

[239] Quirini, II, 48, 104; Beccadelli, 195, n. 24, 196, n. 25. For Ehrard, see L. Halkin's *Le cardinal de la Marck, prince-évêque de Liége (1505-38)*, Liége, 1930; and E. Fairon's *Supplément au Recueil des ordonnances de la Principauté de Liége promulgées par Ehrard de la Marck* (Bulletin de la Commission royale des anciennes lois et ordonnances de Belgique, 1930, XIII, p. 263 *sq.*).

He had hoped to be able to cross over to England, but events there were more and more prejudicial to his office. Paul III recalled him in July (1537). He set out for Rome on August 22nd, via Germany, Trent, Ferrara, Ravenna, and Loreto, to give the Pope an account of the mission in which he had failed through no fault of his own (October, 1537).[240]

Henry could not lay hands on him, so he wreaked his vengeance upon Pole's family. The cardinal's younger brother, Sir Geoffrey, was sent to the Tower in August, 1538. The confinement and the rigorous examinations to which he was submitted soon preyed upon his neurotic mind,[241] and under threat of torture he was induced to confess. His confessions led to the arrest of Lords Montague, Courtenay, and Neville, all heads of powerful families connected with the House of York (November 3rd, 1538).[242] Courtenay, Marquis of Exeter, a grandson of Edward IV (whose grandnephews the Poles also were), had already been accused, in 1531, of aspiring to the throne.[243] George Neville, third Baron of Abergavenny, was the son-in-law of the Poles' uncle, the Duke of Buckingham, who had been beheaded, in 1521, on account of his claim to the throne. Neville himself had already been suspected of treason. Certain phrases of private conversations—more or less faithfully reported—against those in the king's circle or against the new

---

[240] Quirini, II, 59, 273. Letter from Pole to Contarini, July 21st, 1537, *ibid.* II, 73; Merriman, *op. cit.*, II, Nos. 217, 218; Rinaldi, *ad. ann. 1537*, §44; Friedensburg, *Nuntiaturberichte*, II, 191; Dom Biron, chap. VII; G. M. Mouti, *La legazione del Polo e del Ghiberti in Francia e in Flandra nel 1537* (*Archivio storico Italiano*, 1929, pp. 293–309), from Ghiberti's letters, nearly all unpublished, in the Vatican archives.

[241] He attempted to commit suicide several times in prison (*L. and P.* XIII, Part 2, Nos. 703, 875; XIV, Part 1, No. 19). His wife declared, in her petition of January 4th, 1539 (Foley, *Records of the English Province of the Society of Jesus*, III, 790 *sq.*) that he was incurable.

[242] Cf. Ellis, *Original Letters*, 1st Series, I, p. 96.

[243] Cf. Thomas Willoughby to Cromwell, March 16th, 1539. Ellis, I, 105; *L. and P.*, V, No. 416; XIII, Part 2, No. 961; *Archaeologia*, II, 20 *sq.*; Fisher, *op. cit.*, 428; Pollard, *Henry VIII*, 374.
Amongst his ancestors was Hugh de Courtenay, who married Edward I's granddaughter (1325). His mother Catherine, a daughter of Edward IV (1461–83), was sister to Elizabeth, Henry VII's wife, who had thus united in herself the blood and rights of the Houses of York and Lancaster. For the Courtenay family, of Norman origin, which followed William the Conqueror, see Le Laboureur, *Mémoires de Castelnau*, I, 419 *sq.*

religious policy, sufficed to bring a charge against the speakers and to condemn them. "The laws," said the French ambassador, "were so sanguinary that a few words, often perhaps spoken inadvertently or in good faith, could be construed into the crime of high treason."[244] Lord Montague, however, knew that the king's resentment against Reginald endangered his own position and had consequently left no stone unturned to avert suspicion and to win the favour of Cromwell. In the end the only charge they could bring against him was that he had delighted in the works of Thomas More and had not sufficiently disapproved the actions of his brother, the cardinal.[245] Montague, Courtenay, and Neville were all beheaded five weeks after their arrest (December 9th, 1538). Six months later a Bill of Attainder was passed legalizing this execution, which had been as summary as the sentence itself. Their children were thrown into prison. The Marchioness o Exeter, Courtenay's wife, languished and died in the Tower.[246] Cromwell strove to conceal the hateful part played by the king in these proceedings by presenting contradictory excuses to the ambassadors and to the people.[247] The man who was the most involved in the whole business, Geoffrey Pole, whose confessions had caused his kinsmen's deaths, received a royal pardon. His nervous disorders were increased by the

[244] Marillac to Montmorency, June 23rd, 1540; Kaulek, *op. cit.*, pp 193 *sq.* Burnet (III, 210) admits that the king's wrath against Pole drove him to great excesses and to commit many acts of injustice and cruelty (cf. Fisher, *op. cit.*, 428 *sq.*).

[245] Cf. Fisher, *op. cit.*, pp. 429 *sq.*

[246] Cf. Kaulek, *op. cit.*, p. 176. Montague's son died in the Tower. Courtenay's son, Edward, was liberated by Mary Tudor fourteen years later when she reached the capital.

In 1540 Lord Lisle (Arthur Plantagenet, Edward IV's natural son), deputy of Calais from 1533 to 1542 [†1542], was also accused of having "received secret intelligence from Cardinal Pole, who was a near relation of his." He was thrown into the Tower with "master Ly [Lee]" who had "been acquainted with the said cardinal Pole . . . in Italy . . . where he had lived for ten or twelve years" (Kaulek, 184 *sq.*).

[247] He told the French ambassador that Courtenay, who aspired to the Crown, had wanted to marry his son to Princess Mary, whose resistance to her father's wishes was to be attributed to him. To the imperial ambassador he asserted, on the contrary, that Courtenay and Montague had plotted the death of the king and of his three children, Edward, Mary and Elizabeth. A proclamation of December 16th, 1538, gave the people quite different reasons for the three beheadings of the 9th (cf. J. Gairdner, *Lollardy*, II, 156 *sq.*; Fisher, pp. 430 *sq.*; Dom Biron, p. 140).

ignominy of such a pardon, and he continued to live in a state bordering on insanity.[248]

Pole's mother, the Countess of Salisbury, who had already suffered a great deal through her children, was not destined to escape the king's resentment. In striking the mother Henry hoped to wound her son Reginald. It mattered little that he had frequently referred to her as the saintliest woman in his realm, or entrusted her with the education of his daughter, Mary. Two inquisitors were sent to her (November 13th, 1538), Bishop Goodrich of Ely and Admiral Fitzwilliam. They could discover nothing against her. They admired her sang-froid, and reported that they ought rather to call her a man of resolution than a woman. Not a single compromising word could they extract from her regarding her son the cardinal; she would only admit that her maternal heart could not help rejoicing when he escaped the assassin's dagger. Her house at Warblington was searched from cellar to ceiling. A few undated papal Bulls were found there. Her neighbours and servants were closely questioned, and it was alleged that she had forbidden her tenants to read the New Testament in English. She was taken from her residence and given into the custody of Fitzwilliam, who was converted from an admiral into a gaoler and a spy. A few months later she was sent to the Tower, and she never left it again. On May 10th, 1539, Cromwell presented a Bill of Attainder against her and her kinsmen who had already been beheaded. Two days later he lodged a charge against her, holding in his hand a white silk tunic, found amongst the countess's clothes, on which had been embroidered, together with the arms of England encircled by a wreath of pansies and marigolds, the five wounds of the Saviour, the Pilgrimage of Grace badge.[249]

[248] He withdrew to his property at Lordington (Sussex), where he was to be seen wandering about like one hallucinated. Leaving his wife and children, he fled to Flanders, and then to Rome, where he confessed all his remorse to his brother. The latter got the Pope to absolve him and then confided him to the Bishop of Liége, to whom Pole paid 40 crowns monthly. On Edward VI's death he came back to England (1553) and died at Lordington, in 1558, a short while before Reginald. Two of his five sons were arrested by Elizabeth for their claims to the Crown and they died in the Tower. Another son, Geoffrey, saved the lives of several priests (cf. Dom Biron, pp. 140 sq.).

[249] The pansies represented Reginald Pole, and the marigolds the

This was enough for Parliament and sentence of death was passed (June, 1539). For close upon two years the countess languished and pined in the Tower in utter destitution, for everything belonging to her had been confiscated.[250] Henry VIII made a revolt in Yorkshire, in April 1541, an excuse for notifying her that her execution would take place at dawn on the following May 28th. She protested that she was innocent, and walked quite steadily to the block laid ready on the ground. No scaffold had been erected, and the headsman was away from London. The imperial ambassador reported that a wild youth atrociously hacked her neck and shoulders, and that as she rose to her feet, frantic with pain and her hair all dishevelled, he pursued her and struck at her with his axe until her head fell. This barbarous spectacle, the beheading of one of the most noble women in the country, whose seventy years had not saved her, disgusted the foreign ambassadors.[251] The remains of the countess were not allowed to rest at Christchurch, in the splendid tomb carved by Pietro Torregiano, Michelangelo's rival. The sculptures were even smashed by Cromwell's order. "I was with Cardinal Pole," wrote Beccadelli,[252] "when he heard of his mother's death. To me he said: 'Hitherto I thought God had given me the grace to be the son of one of the best and most honourable ladies in England, and I gloried in that fact and thanked God for it. Now, however, He has honoured me still more and increased my debt of gratitude to Him, for He has made me the son of a martyr. For her constancy in the Catholic faith the King has caused her to be publicly beheaded, in spite of her seventy years. Blessed and thanked be God for ever!' " The Church has since confirmed the admirable words of that son, whose

Princess Mary, both of whom, according to the desire of the countess, were to restore the old religion. This was the interpretation Cromwell put upon the embroideries (*L. and P.*, XIV, Part 1, No. 980 [cf. Dom Bede Camm, *Lives of the English Martyrs*, Vol. I, pp. 527 *sq.*, and 529, n.—*Translator.*]; cf. Kaulek, 99, 100).

[250] Kaulek, *op. cit.*, p. 102.

[251] Cf. *L. and P.*, XVI, No. 897; *Sp. Cal.*, VI, Part 2, No. 331; Kaulek, p. 309. "However, Sire," the French ambassador wrote to Francis I, "neither sex, nor age, nor blood, nor long imprisonment, nor any other considerations prevented them from shortening the few days she had to live. . . ."

[252] *Op. cit.*, pp. 328 *sq.*

courage and Christian resignation Beccadelli could not sufficiently praise.

In 1538 Paul III had at last been able to bring together the two irreconcilable adversaries whose antagonism was endangering Christendom. Taking advantage of their mutual exhaustion, he had made them conclude a truce for ten years (June 18th, 1538), at the meeting at Nice, which he himself attended "without consideration for his advanced age, his supreme dignity, the difficulties and discomforts of a long journey, or hardships of every kind." He was accompanied by Cardinals Contarini, Sadolet and Pole. Charles V and Francis I gave him hopes that they would break with Henry VIII once the sentence of excommunication had been pronounced. The Pope returned to Rome full of joy.[253] After the profanation by Henry VIII of the relics of St Thomas of Canterbury—the defender of the Church's liberties —the Pope published in December the Bull which had been prepared three years previously. He also sent Pole as legate to the Spanish and French Courts to urge the two princes to sever their business relations with, and to establish a continental league against England.[254] At the same time a papal envoy was sent to Scotland, France's ally and England's rival, to deliver the biretta to the new Cardinal Beaton, who had great influence with James V.[255] Towards the end

[253] For the meetings at Nice and Aiguesmortes, the truce concluded at that time, and Francis I's difficult position, see the French edition of this book, pp. 564-71, where information is given from documents seldom consulted. At the meeting at Aiguesmortes Rabelais was in close attendance upon Francis I.

[254] Paul III made the king's sacrilegious behaviour known in the consistory of October 25th, and delegated four cardinals, Ghinucci, Campeggio, Contarini, and Caraffa, to carry out the sentence of excommunication (cf. Sander, Lewis' trans., pp. 142 sq.; Pallavicini, Bk. IV, chap. VII; Pollard, Henry VIII, pp. 372, 377; Fisher, pp. 426 sq.). The Bull was published in Rome on December 17th, 1538 (L. and P., Part 2, No. 1087; Introd., p. xli; Pallavicini, loc. cit.) but, contrary to plan, not in Flanders, Spain, or France. Pole pointed out to Granvelle how harmful to the Holy See the non-execution of the censures would be, and the Royal Council replied that they would beg the Pope to delay publication, and in effect it was not published outside Rome (R. Pole to Cardinal Farnese, Carpentras, 1538, Beccadelli, 340 sq.). Instructio pro Rmo Pole ad Ces. Mtem proficiente, preserved in the Vatican Archives, and published by the Rev. Paul Van Dyke under the title, "The Mission of Cardinal Pole to enforce the Bull of Deposition against Henry VIII (1539)" in the Eng. Hist. Review, XXXVII (1922), 422 sq. (cf. J. Gairdner, Lollardy, II, 181 sq.).

[255] James V, whose marriage with Francis I's daughter, Magdalen

of 1538, it was open to question whether Henry VIII's religious policy would not be suddenly checked by the combined action of the emperor and the Kings of France and Scotland.

Shortly afterwards by the Treaty of Toledo (January 12th, 1539) Charles V and Francis I promised that neither would make any agreement or alliance with England without the consent of the other. The emperor stopped the negotiations for the marriage between his niece Christina, the Duchess of Milan, and the schismatic king, by alleging the necessity for a dispensation. Christina, bearing Anne Boleyn in mind, is said to have replied to Henry: "Sire, if I had two heads, I would willingly place one at your Majesty's disposal."[256] Francis I showed no enthusiasm for a union between Henry VIII and a French princess.[257]   Various rumours of an

(†July 7th, 1537), had lasted but six months, took for his second wife the Duke of Guise's daughter, Mary of Lorraine, the Duke of Longueville's widow. Through her a French and Catholic influence dominated Scottish politics. Scotland began war with England just when the peace between France and the empire was broken (1542). Cf. E. Bapst, *Les mariages de Jacques V*, Paris, 1889; G. Ascoli, *op. cit.*, pp. 74-79. Marot and Ronsard, who followed James V to Scotland as pages, sang the praises of his marriage with *"Madame Magdeleine la première fille de France,"* a marriage which Henry VIII had tried to prevent (cf. *Mémoires de du Bellay*, pp. 243, 247), and which caused him great annoyance (*Nuntiaturberichte*, II, 94). On January 30th, 1543, Cardinal Beaton, Archbishop of St. Andrew's, was appointed legate *a latere* with very extensive faculties. See his Bull of nomination in Burnet, V, 409. For the cardinal himself, cf. J. Herkless, *Cardinal Beaton, Priest and Politician*, Edinburgh, 1891.

For the line of conduct which Paul III took towards the King of England, see chap. III (pp. 33-53): "De Pauli aequitate et prudentia in Anglicani schismatis per Henricum VIII invecti negotio," in Quirini's work entitled: *Imago Pauli III Farnesii ad primos tantum quinque annos ejus Pontificatus spectantibus*, Brescia, 1545.

[256] Christina was noted for her beauty. She was the daughter of Isabella, one of Charles V's sisters, who was married to Christian II, the deposed King (1523) of Denmark (†1559). She was the widow of Francis Sforza, and was but sixteen years old (cf. Kaulek, 24, 35, 74, 77, 79; Turba, *Venetianische Depeschen vom Kaiserhofe*, Vienna, 1889-95, I, 217, 232). A few months previously Henry had sent Holbein, who for several years had been "servant to the King's Majesty" with a salary of £40, to Brussels to paint Christina's portrait, which is now in the National Gallery.

[257] The King of England put forward this scheme when Francis I was on his way to the meeting at Nice (Kaulek, pp. 47 *sq.*; cf. Turba, I, 217). He asked for the hand of the Duchess of Longueville, Mary of Lorraine, who was promised to James V, in order to loosen the bonds between France and Scotland, which were continually growing tighter. When all hope in that quarter was taken from him, Henry spoke of marrying Louisa of Lorraine (1520-42), the Duchess of Longueville's sister, or Mary of

approaching invasion came to the troubled ears of the King of England from several European courts.[258] The meeting at Nice had already thrown him into a state of "great suspicion and doubt," to use the King of France's own expression. He had tried in every possible way to hinder that meeting and to make it unsuccessful. He besought Francis not to attend it, or at least to make him, Henry, a third contracting party in the agreement. He argued that no good purpose could be served by bringing the Pope into this business; the Duchy of Milan was the core of the negotiations, and his daughter, Mary, would obtain that by her marriage with the Infante of Portugal; the emperor had only ensnared the King of France by promising it to him. Resuming the see-saw tactics which had already served him in good stead, he pretended to be on the best of terms with Charles V, to whom he was making advances, whilst at the same time he declared that he had never been more friendly towards France, and flattered the French ambassador and promised England's assistance in the event of a breach and war with Charles, but his offer appeared to Castillon and Francis I vague and insufficient. Even after Nice and Aiguesmortes he did not relinquish his idea of "breaking the friendship between the king and the emperor, which was not at all pleasing to him." But Francis I and the Constable of France, Montmorency, saw through his game and refused to lay themselves open to any breach. All Henry's proposals and plans for a meeting between the two Kings of France and England were turned aside, for any such meeting would have thrown suspicion upon the interview with Charles V which Francis had had shortly before. Even at the English Court the imperial and French ambassadors were required to maintain "all the usual courteous relations . . . necessary to show the friendship between their two masters," because the two sovereigns were on the best possible terms.

Bourbon, Anthony of Navarre's sister (Kaulek, pp. 48 *sq.*, 51, 53, 64, 68, 71, 75, 76, 80, 81, 82, 83). Their portraits were willingly sent to him (*ibid.*, 69, 75), but when he asked to see them either in England or at Calais, Francis I categorically refused (*ibid.*, 68, 73, 76, 77, 80 *sq.*, 83): '*ce ne sont point hacquenées à vendre*," wrote the Constable of France (July 29th, 1538; *ibid.*, p. 76; cf. pp. 80–82).

[258] Cf. Kaulek, pp. 89 *sq.*; Fisher, p. 431. Henry was kept informed in an extraordinary manner, said the French ambassador, Marillac (Kaulek, p. 128).

"You will make the king's letters known to the emperor's ambassador, who is there," were the orders given to Castillon by the Constable of France, "and you will continue to entertain him as you have hitherto done, in accordance with the good and great friendship existing between their two majesties." The rivalry and division between Charles and Francis had favoured Henry VIII and his designs, but their rapprochement altogether upset the English plans. There was great anxiety in the King's Council, and even amongst the people. "Many people are astonished and know not how they stand," the French ambassador wrote to his king; "I have seen the king in a state of great uncertainty, and the nation as well, both on account of the truces and of the meeting between yourself and the emperor.—Their bearing indicates that we shall easily get the better of them. . . . No kingdom was ever a better bargain. I marvel that the Pope does not get to work on his own account." Castillon suggested that advantage should be taken of the opportunity in order to "redeem in an amiable manner the pension" which the King of France had for many years been paying to the King of England: "He must certainly pay us for friendship instead of our paying him for it, and he must think more now of preserving his kingdom than of receiving pensions from others." Henry's nervousness was shown in his demand to the bishops that they should declare the Bull of excommunication null and void, in the displeasure he manifested over the meetings at Nice and Aiguesmortes, and in his suddenly recalling from Paris his representatives, who had been unable to prevent the odious agreement between the two rivals. Henry was mortally afraid lest England should be isolated. "I can assure you, Sire," Castillon wrote to Francis I, "that he will spare no effort not to be left alone." The sudden departure, in February, 1539, of the French and imperial ambassadors, who did not wait for their successors, capped all the English suspicions and fears: "It was thought that war was about to commence." One would have thought "the enemy was at their gate," Castillon's successor wrote immediately he arrived in London; "the cause of this agitation and the opinion this king has conceived" arise from the fact that "he thinks the king [of France], the emperor and the Pope are joining forces against him to drive him out of his kingdom, and principally, as this king himself has told me he has heard from people who are in a better position to know than others, because the king [of France] is only arranging with the emperor to make war upon him [Henry]." The preparations of the imperial fleet and the rumours to which they gave rise "have very much disturbed this prince's brain, and moreover he is afraid he will be invaded from Scotland." Warlike preparations were made at every point where danger threatened. The fortresses on the coast and on the borders of Scotland were placed in a state of defence. Works of fortification, for which material from the dissolved monasteries was at times used, were feverishly expedited at Calais, Berwick, Carlisle, Calshot, Camber, and Hurst. The king visited the ports. The fleet, consisting of one hundred and fifty sails, fully manned and armed, awaited the order to weigh anchor. "The king's ships and a few other vessels . . . have left" the Thames "for Portsmouth. Five or six guard-ships do nothing but sail round this country," so that they might send up fire signals to "those who watch at night" should any landing be attempted. Henry asked Parliament for subsidies. "The cost of these preparations and fortifications in this country may now amount to at least two hundred thousand crowns," Marillac wrote on April 15th, and he added that on his way from Dover, wherever "I passed, I saw that they were displaying all the king's subjects who were capable of bearing arms . . . enrolling all who were over seventeen or eighteen, and not excepting any aged man. . . . On the way I met a band of men going to take up garrison duty on the Downs . . . and they said they numbered from five to six thousand men." Again on May 20th he wrote: "Displays have been held all over the country, and recently here in the city of London, where I counted . . . about fifteen thousand Englishmen . . . and about ten thousand of them were armed from head to foot." Henry himself had said, "I have good men and good trenches."[259]

When the uneasiness in England was at its height, Reginald Pole, accompanied by his faithful friends Priuli and Beccadelli and travelling incognito, set out for Spain (January, 1539), although he knew that assassins awaited him along the

[259] For details concerning all these incidents, see French ed., pp. 574–84.

route.[260]   After a long, perilous, and hard journey "in the severity of winter," he took a coach when three hundred miles from the court in order to reach Toledo more quickly. He arrived on February 14th.   Henry had written asking Charles V to expel him from the country as a traitor and not to listen to him; the English representative in Spain, Thomas Wyatt, even demanded that Pole be surrendered to him.   The emperor replied that he would grant even his own enemy an audience, if he came on behalf of the Holy See.   But that was all.   From his lips came an icy refusal.   The Pope had been imprudent in publishing censures which he could not enforce; he, Charles, already had his hands full with the Lutherans and Turks, and was not at all anxious to incur the enmity of England, unless he could be sure that Francis I would help him.   Pole soon understood that though the two adversaries had been reconciled for a while, the rivalry between them was merely dormant, and that it might blaze up again at the first opportunity and so destroy the harmony which Paul III had with great difficulty established at Nice.   "The emperor is afraid he may arouse the jealousy of the other princes, who might suspect him of trying to usurp the English crown."   The drain of the recent wars upon his resources made Charles anxious not to hurt the King of France's feelings, but he himself was quite as sensitive as his rival.   When Pole spoke of enlisting the assistance of France if Charles refused to help, the lords in council, with Granvelle as president, gave him clearly to understand that a combined attack by the Kings of France and Scotland would be most displeasing to them. They even took umbrage at the thought of his going as legate to the French Court, and dissuaded him on the plea that "I might do more harm to Christendom than good to England,

[260] The king's agent at Venice, Harvel, had entrusted three well-known Italian condottieri with the task of ridding Henry of the cardinal. They were Lodovico dell'Armi of Bologna, Count Bernardo di San Bonifacio of Verona, and Filippo Pini of Lucca (*Sp. Cal.*, VIII, No. 33; cf. Turba, I, 444). As long as Henry VIII was alive Pole had to fear the assassin's dagger and was obliged to have around him men upon whom he could rely. The Pope desired that Pole should travel incognito, "so that the chismatic king, the cardinal's implacable enemy, could not make an attempt on his life." He reached Bologna on January 6th and Barcelona on the 19th. A. Giganti, *Vita di Monsig. L. Beccadelli*, in Morandi, *op. cit.*, I, Part 1, pp. 16 *sq.*; Beccadelli, pp. 297 *sq.*; Quirini, II, p. 85; Tiraboschi, VII, Part 3, p. 249; Turba, I, 284.

if perchance the means I employed did not meet with the complete approval of their Imperial and Most Christian Majesties." The cardinal therefore considered it wise not to see Francis I. "As for my journey to France," he replied to the imperial council, "I have no desire to create discord between their two majesties; I am certainly not one of those *fuorusciti* of Florence or Milan, who would upset any country and the whole world in order to return home; I will go back to my country only if God's cause leads me there . . . and that cause I intend to serve only by such means as will promote God's honour and harmony between their two majesties; such also is the will of His Holiness, who is especially anxious for this union and sent me to the emperor and the King of France hoping that this action undertaken by common consent would but bring their majesties closer together."[261]

The political situation then had changed since Pole left Rome; for, in delegating him, the Pope "was persuaded that the emperor would allow the censures to be published and also break off all relations with the excommunicated King of England." Reginald concluded that it was "necessary to await fresh instructions from His Holiness." Instead of repairing to the French Court through Guienne, he returned the way he had come. From Gerona he dispatched Perpaglia, the Abbot of San Solvatore, to Francis I to acquaint him with the object of his mission. In order to banish all suspicion from the emperor's mind, a copy of the letter to the French king was sent to Toledo.[262] Meanwhile, in the peaceful surroundings of the Franciscan Observants' monastery at Carpentras, with his friend Sadolet near at hand, he awaited Perpaglia's return and orders from Rome. Francis I's reply was couched in the same terms as Charles V's. He was

[261] R. Pole to ardinal Farnese, Carpentras, March 1539. Beccadelli, pp. 300 *sq.*, 338 *sq.*; *L. and P.*, XIV, Part I, Introd., pp. XI *sq.*; Quirini, II, pp. cclxxi and cclxxxvii; Turba, I, 287 *sq.*

[262] Cf. Beccadelli, p. 300, and also Pole's letter to Cardinal Farnese.
For Perpaglia, the Abbot of S. Solvatore, near Turin, who was long in the cardinal's service, see Maitland's article in the *Eng. Hist. Review*, XV, 795 *sq.*; G. Constant, *La nonciature de Perpaglia auprès d'Élisabeth* (1560) in *Mélanges Bémont*, Paris, 1913, 509 *sq.*; *Concilium Tridentinum*, Vol. X, by G. Buschbell, Freiburg, 1916, pp. 288, n. 3, 548, n. 4, 613, n. 3, 623, n. 5, 631, 633, nn. 1 and 5, 918.

anxious for peace and desired "the kind and great friendship" of the emperor, and would therefore avoid anything at which the latter might take umbrage. An isolated attack upon England would offend the emperor; he promised his assistance on condition that Charles V also helped.

Meantime, in order to ward off the danger of a combined action, Henry VIII had been busy making advances to the two rivals, to which they might be inclined to listen sooner or later. He offered an alliance to each of them in order to make them mutually distrustful. While they were anxious to avoid anything that might jeopardize the recent pact made at Nice, "they were not less preoccupied, through fear of each other, in preserving the King of England's friendship."[263] Even while Francis I was writing to his ambassador that he would leave nothing undone to keep Henry VIII well disposed towards himself, the latter was priding himself upon the good relations existing between Charles and England, and openly demonstrating them. "These lords fawn upon the emperor's ambassador in a marvellous manner. . . . A service was held here, with obsequies, honours, very great ceremonies and solemnity, for the late empress, and the most eminent men in the country attended it . . . with quite fifteen to twenty bishops; and it is said that mourning will be worn for quite a fortnight."[264]

Possibly Henry VIII's friendship meant more to the emperor than to Francis I, for when the latter suggested making a truce with the Turks and "undertaking the English business," Charles thought he saw a trap therein and complained "that they were trying in this way to make him the King of England's enemy." As soon as the sentence of excommunication was promulgated, Francis I began to worry about putting it into effect: on January 6th, 1539, before Pole had even left Bologna, one of Montmorency's secretaries was already in Toledo trying to arrange for the application of the Bull. "The nuncio and the French ambassador attend the council every day," the representative of Venice observed with a certain anxiety, "and very secretly negotiate all that

---

[263] Turba, I, 304. *L. and P.*, VIII, No. 130; XIV, Part 1, No. 104. Kaulek, 179. Beccadelli, 300.

[264] Kaulek, p. 97, No. 112, pp. 103 *sq*. Cf. Turba, I, 311, 317, 321, 323.

concerns the English business; from various sources I learn that preparations for the war in the Levant have considerably diminished, and that His Majesty is now thinking of war against England." Up to the time of Pole's arrival he continued to note "the great diligence" in the negotiations between the nuncio G. Poggio and the ambassador Castelnau on the one side, and His Majesty and the imperial counsellors on the other, and definitely affirmed that "these very active dealings were intended to make the emperor declare war upon the King of England; it is openly spoken of, and much more so than the offensive against the infidels." When Pole undertook his mission and began to negotiate with the emperor, the King of France gave nothing but very evident signs of goodwill. Venice, on the contrary, feared that the excommunication would "upset the venture against the Turk." The Venetian ambassador at the Spanish Court curried favour with his English colleague "gentilissimo signore," who quietly told him that in order to help the Signory against Soliman Henry was prepared to pay for ten thousand lansquenets. As for the emperor, from the very beginning (January 16th) he declared his mind to Mocenigo: "Ambassador, my sole idea is to war against the Turks alone; the King of France would like me to attack England; why, I know not, but as for myself, I do not wish it." His answer to Pole at the first interview left no hope: "He who wages war knows that it is more easy to start a war than to bring it to a good ending." Short of money and worried over the Turks, against whom Venice was constantly asking his help, Charles considered "the expedition against England costly, full of danger, and likely to turn out badly." And when the Pope continued to insist after Pole's departure, Charles again replied "that he wished to concern himself solely with the Turks, to defend his States, and had no desire to start a venture which might cause him great difficulties with Francis I even if it were only in sharing their common gains." Finally, when Paul III's nephew, Cardinal Farnese, begged him at least to send two representatives to England, accompanied by two more from the King of France, to bring Henry back to the unity of the Church, Charles met him with a masked refusal: if Francis was willing, then he was. By February 6th, the English ambassador considered the game won.[265] The failure of Pole's mission is therefore less imputable to the King of France than to the emperor, who in virtue of his title and office should have defended the Church, but yet never gave the Pope any solid hopes of assistance against the schismatic king.

Henry VIII was not slow to realize how matters stood. Threatened with commercial isolation, as a bait to the merchants of Flanders he held out visions of great profits by promising to abolish all tariffs for seven years; that sufficed to allay the empire's hostility.[266] In April he was again worried "by a rumour that a truce had been arranged" with the Turks, for "here the most indigestible thing in the world is the news of good friendship between the king and the emperor and that things are quiet in the Levant"; but by the month of May both he and the lords of the council were "beyond fear": "their brains seem to have been wholly cleared of the anxiety thay had conceived." Warlike preparations were not continued; only in a few places were the fortifications carried on in order to finish what had been begun. In June he was playing the braggart and scoffing at what a little while before had caused him such anxiety. In his presence on the Thames, two royal galleys manned by his men "one bearing the royal arms, and the other those of the Pope and several cardinals' hats," staged a battle in which "the king's men were victorious, and the Pope and cardinals were all thrown into the water with their arms to show the people by this spectacle that this king's forces are able to

[265] Kaulek, 109 *sq.*; Turba, I, 267, 278, 280, 281, 284 *sq.*, 387 *sq.*, 294, 297-99, 301, 310, 326, 336. Fisher, *op. cit.*, p. 432.

[266] The French ambassador had writen on April 26th, 1538 (Kaulek, p. 41) that the best means of bringing Henry to his senses would be to place an interdict upon all who had business dealings with the English, "even from the Flanders region." That was what the Pope had desired and hoped for in sending Pole to Spain and Flanders (Beccadelli, p. 300; Pole's letter to Farnese, *ibid.*, p. 366 and *L. and P.*, XIV, Part I, p. xi; Turba, I, p. 287). The nuncio Vergerio's secretary, Ottonello Vida, had written in 1535 (Friedensburg, I, 519 *sq.*) that to forbid the Flemish to have business dealings with England "would do incredible harm to the country," for although Flanders would lose by it still they had other markets, whereas "the English isolated in Christendom are, as it were, separated from the world." The censures would therefore either make them revolt or else make the king repent.

confound and abolish entirely the power and name of the Holy Father and of those with him." Finally, in July, the fleet was dismantled and "the ten thousand men ready to go aboard dismissed." On June 9th the French ambassador observed that the king, who hitherto "had been alone and pensive, now strives to take as much recreation as he possibly can, going every evening to play upon the Thames, with harps, singers, and all other kinds of music and amusements." The uneasiness caused by "the fervent friendship" between the king and the emperor was a thing of the past.[267]

Pole was greatly distressed by the failure of his mission, which he had hoped would remedy "the sorry condition of religion and liberty in England." He did not conceal from his friend Contarini the bitterness and great disappointment he felt. No longer able to rely upon the princes "whose real thoughts are never known" and in whom he had placed all his hopes, he applied the first verse of Psalm xi to them: *Defecit sanctus, quoniam diminutae sunt veritates a filiis hominum.* The sad news which reached him from England concerning the deaths of his relations and the sorry state of affairs there made him desire to prolong indefinitely his retreat which was spent in meditation and work.[268] His *Apologia ad Carolum V Caesarem super quattuor libris a se scriptis de Unitate Ecclesiae* dates from that period.[269] He would have preferred to remain in the shade, convinced as he was that he "could no longer be of service." Paul III was of another opinion. After leaving him at Carpentras for six months to find solace in the company of his friend Sadolet, he recalled him to Rome (October, 1539), and then sent him as legate to Viterbo. In later years (1542 and 1545) he made him the third legate at the Council of Trent.[270] Pole, indeed, according to Pallavicini, was "very

[267] Kaulek, *op. cit.*, pp. 92, 96, 98, 103, 105, 108–111, 116, 122.

[268] Quirini, *op. cit.*, II, 154, 186 *sq.*

[269] Published in Louvain in 1569, it was republished by Quirini in his first volume, pp. 66–172. It is, so to speak, a preface to the *De Unitate Ecclesiae* (cf. *ibid.*, p. lxxxvii) and a criticism of the king's acts (cf. Zimmermann, *op. cit.*, p. 173). Another preface of the *De Unitate* is addressed to the King of Scotland (*Proœmium alterum ejusdem Libri a R. Polo transmissi ad Regem Scotiae*, Quirini, I, 172–78).

[270] See *Concilium Tridentinum*, ed. Görres-Gesellschaft, Freiburg, 1901 *sq.*, Vols. I, II, IV, V, X; *Documenta ad legationem Poli Spectantia*, Rome, 1896; Pallavicini, Sarpi, and the biographies of Pole already mentioned.

Pole went to Trent in 1542 with the two other legates, Cardinals Parisio

conversant with theology, and deserved to be revered for the holiness of his life, his noble birth, and the glory of exile and persecutions suffered in defence of the see of Rome."[271]

All attempts to overthrow the King of England's spiritual supremacy had been useless. The Pope's efforts abroad to band the Catholic princes together had broken down before the rivalry of the opposing powers; whilst at home the resistance of the most noble characters was stifled in blood and brought to nothing by the servile submission of the great majority of the nation. Nevertheless, the names of Reginald Pole, of Fisher and More more particularly, have their place in history. The calm and serene vigour of the chancellor and the bishop has won the admiration of all men, whatever their religion. They are heroes of the human conscience, and particularly of the Catholic conscience. And Leo XIII, by a decree dated December 9th, 1889, set them up for the imitation and veneration of the faithful. J. Gairdner, the historian, asks: "Were not these great Christian heroes altogether in the right? To give them half-hearted sympathy is ignoble. To suppose that they did not judge truly the merits of the cause for which they died is to suppose something very strange in the history of martyrdom. Yet to admit that they were right altogether seems at first sight to destroy the position of English Protestantism entirely and we are led to the conclusion that generation after generation among ourselves have been brought up in a mutilated, unhealthy Christianity during the last three hundred years."[272]

and Morone, but the council could not be held owing to the troubles in Germany. He was again nominated as legate in 1545, together with dal Monte, afterwards Julius III, and Marcello Cervini, afterwards Marcellus II.

[271] Pallavicini, Bk. V, chap. 1, No. 7. Burnet, for his part, admits that he was famous for his knowledge, modesty, kindness and humility, and that he was as virtuous as any man of his century.

[272] *Lollardy and the Reformation in England*, I, 505.

CHAPTER VI

THE ADVANCED PARTY IN THE SCHISM

Thomas Cromwell, Earl of Essex, the king's vicar-general—Thomas
Cranmer, Archbishop of Canterbury—Their friends—Their share in the
Reformation.

In the English schism there were two distinct parties in
frequent conflict, which though not open was nevertheless
real.[1] The ultimate triumph of one or the other depended
entirely upon Henry. On the one hand, there was the
advanced party which favoured Protestant teaching and
Protestant policy, and, on the other the moderate or conservative party, which desired to retain the dogma, discipline, and
rites of Catholicism and was merely schismatic in character.
A study of these two parties will enable us to understand the
teaching of the Church of England under Henry VIII, and
what the Reformation really meant for that Church at that
period.

The two leaders of the advanced party were Thomas
Cromwell and the Archbishop of Canterbury, Thomas
Cranmer.

I

Thomas Cromwell was born about 1485 on the outskirts of
London, at Putney. He was the son of Walter Cromwell, a
brewer, blacksmith, and fuller,[2] who appears to have been of a

---

[1] The French ambassador mentions their *envye et division irréconciliable*
(Kaulek, p. 188).

[2] Being a blacksmith, he was often known by the name of Smith. The
Court Roll has "Walter Cromwell, alias Walter Smith." Chapuys wrote
to Granvelle on November 21st, 1535 (Merriman, I, 17; *L. and P.*, V,
No. 228) that "*Me Cremuel est filz dung poure marechal*"; and Bandello
(*Novella* XXXIV della 2ª parte delle Novelle, X, p. 251) said he was
"*figliuolo d'un povero cimatore di panni*" (cf. Foxe, V, 362). A number of
entries in the Court Rolls mention fines Walter incurred for slight assaults.

quarrelsome nature. Chapuys asserts that Thomas's uncle was Archbishop Warham's cook. He had several brothers and sisters, and one of his nephews, Richard Williams, who prior to 1536 changed his name to that of Cromwell, was the great grandfather of Oliver Cromwell the Protector.

Little is known about his early years, save that he had been wild and dissipated, as he afterwards admitted to Cranmer, and spent some time in Italy, where he joined the French army and took part in the battle of Garigliano (December 28th–29th, 1503).[3] He afterwards became book-keeper to a rich merchant in Venice, whom Cardinal Pole knew, and then worked as a merchant in Antwerp, and a lawyer in London. About 1512 he married Elizabeth Wykys, the daughter of a fuller, who died of the sweating fever about 1528.[4] By her he had two daughters, who did not live long, and one son, Gregory, a dull and idle lad, who was nevertheless created a peer of the realm in 1539, and made an advantageous marriage with Jane Seymour's sister.[5] It was on him that Cromwell based all his hopes for the future of the family.

After his marriage, in addition to his legal calling, Cromwell adopted his father-in-law's trade. This strange combination of occupations, together with the various other callings which he had successively followed, was in keeping with his versatile character and was also the means of bringing him into contact with people of widely varying conditions. The "struggle for life" gave him at once a thorough knowledge of men and things and an extraordinary knack of adapting everything to suit his own plans. In this way he was formed for his future career as a minister. He had brought back from his sojourn in foreign parts a knowledge of French and Italian, and had also established relations with the continental merchants which enabled him to grow wealthy.

In 1520 he was in Wolsey's service, and in all matters entrusted to him by the cardinal he showed himself an accom-

That did not prevent him, however, from being a magistrate and a juryman.

For Richard Williams and his enrichment from the monastic spoils, see Vol. II of *The Victoria County History of Huntingdon*, London, 1932.

[3] Foxe, V, 362 *sq.*; Chapuys' letter of November 21st, 1535; Bandello, *Novella XXXIV*; Reginald Pole in his *Apologia ad Carolum V.*

[4] *"fille dung tondeur de draps."* *Apologia ad Carolum V;* Chapuys' letter mentioned above; Merriman, I, 56; *L. and P.*, IV, 772.

[5] She was Sir Anthony Ughtred's widow (*L. and P.*, XIII, Part 2, 423).

plished and experienced lawyer. None was more clever or speedy in collecting debts, establishing title-deeds, or examining and surveying property.[6] He gave up trade altogether, but retained his legal profession and became the cardinal-minister's confidential agent, purveyor of his bounties, and the channel through which all the cardinal's favours flowed. Letters addressed to him from 1524 onwards show that it was necessary to have Cromwell's support in order to gain his master's.[7] Petitioners besieged him; and by a shrewd distribution of gifts and pensions he gained great influence over the predominant party at Court.

It was not long before he took his seat in the House of Commons (1523). There he distinguished himself by a speech he made when the king, who was Charles V's ally, demanded a large subsidy of £800,000 for the purpose of invading France. That speech revealed his political genius. Under a veneer of clever and discreet flattery he displayed discerning and just views upon the interests of the State, a knowledge of detail and economic principles seldom found at that period, and prudence in practical counsels.[8] Such a speech was bound to attract attention, and the man who uttered it could not for long escape the king's keen eye.

[6] Cf. *L. and P.*, III, 1026, 1940, 1963, 2241, 3657. We know nothing of him from 1512 to 1520. Neither do we know how he entered into relations with the cardinal. However, it was probably through his cousin, Robert Cromwell, collector of taxes for Wolsey, that he was presented to him. According to Singer (Cavendish, *Life of Wolsey*, I, 193, n.), the cardinal met Cromwell in France; and according to Ellis, Lord Henry Percy, an intimate friend of the cardinal, brought him to the cardinal's notice. J. Gairdner, in his article in the *Dictionary of National Biography*, mistakes him for his cousin Robert when he says he was collector of taxes for Wolsey in 1514.

[7] Cf. *L. and P.*, IV, 294, 388, 979, 1385, 1620, 1768, 2347–48, 2379, 2387.

[8] Merriman, I, 30 *sq.*; *L. and P.*, III. For this request for a subsidy and the cold manner in which it was received by the House of Commons, of which More was Speaker, see *L. and P.*, III, Introd., pp. 243, 253, 278; Fisher, pp. 242 *sq.* In reality England, allied to Charles V and the Duke of Bourbon, paid all the costs of the war by loans to the emperor and the duke, and by putting the northern frontiers in a state of defence. These expenses had emptied the Treasury, and no attack on France would have been possible without an extraordinary subsidy. Hence Wolsey, who had not summoned a Parliament since 1515, was obliged to summon one in 1523. In order to obtain the subsidy he had relied upon the king's popularity and the national hatred of France (cf. Creighton, *Twelve English Statesmen Series*, London, 1888, pp. 128 *sq.*).

For more than four years (January 1525–October 1529) Cromwell was employed by Wolsey in suppressing the twenty-nine religious houses which served to build the cardinal's two colleges at Oxford and Ipswich. No one was better fitted for this task than the man afterwards known as the *monachorum malleus*. "He was certainly born," says Pole,[9] "with an aptitude for ruin and destruction." He had no scruples, and pity was unknown to him. Moreover, he possessed a thorough knowledge of the laws concerning property. It was his business, as liquidator, to survey and measure the confiscated lands, to draw up an inventory of them, value, and then sell or let them. He had also to sell all the movables, such as altars, bells, tapestries and furniture. Cromwell was employed in this occupation or in supervising the work at Oxford and Ipswich[10] until the time of Wolsey's disgrace. The suppression of the religious houses was most unpopular, and the people's feelings were further aggravated by the manner in which that suppression was carried out. Cromwell made use of his powers in order to increase his fortune. So intense was the feeling of hatred against him that, in 1527, men spoke of assassinating him, and in London, according to Pole, the rumour spread that he had been thrown into prison for extortion.[11] Yet where Wolsey was concerned, far from being under a cloud, Cromwell's position was only enhanced, and abbots and lords used to come to him before applying to the cardinal.[12] The fall of Wolsey would have been fatal for anybody else,[13] but for Cromwell it served as a stepping-

[9] *Apologia ad Carolum V*, Quirini, I, 127.

[10] *L. and P.*, IV, 3198, 3461, 3475, 3535, 3676, 4117, 4135, 4275, 4441, 4570, 4573, 4697, 4778, 5186, 5330, 5399, 5411.

[11] Merriman, I, 18, 19. Very moderate at first, his fortune increased considerably, as is shown by the inventory of his belongings in 1527 (*L. and P.*, IV, 3197) and his will in 1529 (Merriman, I, 56; Froude, *Henry VIII*, Append. to chap. IV). Cromwell was not the only one to grow rich on the spoils of the suppressed religious houses. The commissioners who helped him in his task, especially Dr. Allen, followed his example (cf. *L. and P.*, IV, 3360).

[12] Cf. *L. and P.*, IV, 3072, 3119, 4201, 5169, 5365, 5456. In April, 1527, Henry Lacy wrote in his favour, and in May of the same year revenues were assigned to him.

[13] As Wolsey's agent he was detested. Cf. Letter from his friend, Stephen Vaughan, October 3rd, 1529, in *L. and P.*, IV, 6036; and Thomas Bush's letter giving an account of the evil rumours which were being spread about him (*ibid.*, IV, 6110).

stone. While appearing busy with his master's interests, he was in reality looking after his own.

Throughout the cardinal's disgrace Cromwell's thoughts were all for himself, as the following account from Cavendish[14] clearly shows. "It chanced me," he says, "upon All-hallowne day to come into the *Great Chamber* at Esher, in the morning, to give mine attendance, where I found Mr. Cromwell leaning in the great windowe with a Primer in his hand, saying our Lady mattens; which had bine a strange sight in hime afore . . . . He prayed no more earnestly, than he distilled teares as fast from his eyes. . . . To whom I saide: 'Why, Mr. Cromwell, what meaneth this dole? Is my lord in any danger that ye doe lament for him?' . . . 'Nay,' quoth he, 'it is for my unhappy adventure. For I am like to lose all that I have laboured for, all the daies of my life, for doing of my master true and diligent service. . . . Every thing is as it is taken; and this I knowe well, that I am disdained withal for my master's sake. . . . But this much I will say to you, that I will this afternoone, when my lord hath dined, ride to London and to the courte, where I will *either make or marre*, or ever I come againe.' "

He was made. Had he betrayed his master, he would have alienated everybody; he appeared to serve him, but in such a way that everything turned to his own advantage.[15] First he killed two birds with one stone by obtaining a seat in Parliament through the good offices of Norfolk, Wolsey's worst enemy and thenceforward the most influential man in the King's Council. Then, having learnt that in his innermost heart Henry VIII did not wish to proceed to extreme measures, he caused the Bill of Attainder against Wolsey to be rejected in the House of Commons, and presented to the king the cardinal's written confession, in which the latter admitted his alleged offences against the statute of *praemunire*. In this way Crom-

---

[14] *Life of Wolsey*, ed. Singer, 1827, I, 192; ed. 1852, I, 169 *sq.* Shakespeare (*Henry VIII*, III, 2) and Froude follow Cavendish. Cf. Maitland, *Essays on Subjects connected with the Reformation in England*, 1849, 176–82, 236.

[15] Yet, according to Fisher's biography (*Ana. Boll.*, X, 355 and n. 1), he did betray him. Cardinal Gasquet also insinuates as much in his *Henry VIII and the English Monasteries*, I, 385 *sq.* "But," Van Ortroy observes, "no one suspects Cromwell of treachery so black as that described by Fisher's biographer."

well acquired the reputation of having saved his master in the hour of danger. That was the first advantage he gained.[16]

He secured his second advantage by winning the Boleyn party to his side, though apparently preserving his fidelity to Wolsey at the same time. Acting on Cromwell's advice, the Cardinal bestowed pensions upon his worst enemies from what remained of his wealth. A few hundred pounds were not sufficient to mitigate their hatred, but sufficed to make them favourably disposed towards the agent who had procured the money.[17]

On the death of Wolsey, Cromwell obtained an interview with the king and succeeded by some masterly stroke in winning the royal favour. The imperial ambassador says that he fascinated Henry by "promising to make him the richest king in the world." According to Reginald Pole, he suggested that in order to put an end to the divorce business Henry should declare himself head of the Church of England: the kingdom of England was actually a two-headed monster; but if the king took the Pope's usurped authority in hand, the present difficulties would disappear, and churchmen would

---

[16] Cavendish, *op. cit.*, ed. 1852, 179 *sq.* *L. and P.*, 6098, 6203, 6249. Cf. Dixon, I, 48 *sq.*; W. Stubbs, *Seventeen Lectures on the study of medieval and modern History*, Oxford, 1887, p. 315. He represented the Borough of Taunton in the Commons.

[17] Cf. *L. and P.*, IV, Introd., pp. 549 *sq.* See Wolsey's letters to Cromwell, in December 1529 and January, 1530, in *L. and P.*, I, No. 351; IV, No. 6181. The draft of the donations to Anne Boleyn's brother is in *L. and P.*, IV, 6115.

After his fall Wolsey seemed to be dependent upon his former servant. If he dared to insinuate that Cromwell was not looking after his interests Cromwell replied by veiled threats (cf. Merriman, I, 326–28). If he got someone else to undertake anything concerning his position without informing Cromwell, he very humbly explained his reasons for doing so to Cromwell (*L. and P.*, IV, 6203). Towards his former master Cromwell adopted the tone of a selfish and arrogant counsellor (Merriman, I, 326–35). The confiscation of the possessions of St Albans and of Winchester, or of the colleges at Oxford and Ipswich, gave Cromwell yet another opportunity for advancement, as Cavendish observes. The annuities and allowances granted by the king from those possessions had no value, according to the law, after Wolsey's death. To obtain confirmation of their grants, all those interested had recourse to Cromwell, to whom had been given the administration of all property confiscated from the cardinal. Whilst he created for himself a clientele of applicants, he did not cease to grow in favour with the king by his clever dealings, for these negotiations gave him continual access to the king's person (Cavendish, ed. 1852, p. 198. Cf. Gasquet, I, 392–93).

become the servile ministers of his will.[18]   Cromwell may
even have suggested both these ideas.   Whatever happened,
the interview ended with Cromwell's nomination to the Privy
Council.

Certain historians affirm that after Cromwell had become
one of the king's counsellors, he inspired the whole of the
schismatic policy dating from 1530 to 1533, which loosened
and broke by degrees the bonds uniting the Church in England
to Rome.   Against this opinion objections might be raised on
the score that the ambassadors attached to the English Court
do not mention Cromwell in this rôle, and that the common
impression amongst the people throughout the country was
that responsibility rested entirely with the king.   We might
meet these objections by saying that, in order to prevent any
revolt against these revolutionary and unpopular measures,
it was necessary for the king to appear alone, so that his
authority might carry weight.   Important innovations require
high sanctions.   No good purpose could be served by associat-
ing the obscure name of an upstart lawyer, who was little
esteemed by the people and little worthy of esteem, with a
policy which undermined all the old and respected principles
and which dared to brave and contend with the highest power
in Christendom.   In an action such as that the best place for a
minister like Cromwell was in the background and the shade.[19]

This much is certain, that in 1533 Chapuys noted that
Cromwell had great power with the king.   Later he again
wrote that since he had been appointed to the Privy Council
(1530), "he has been constantly rising in power, so much so
that he has now more influence with his master than the
cardinal ever had; for in the latter's time there were Compton,
the Duke of Suffolk, and others, to whose advice the king
occasionally listened, whereas now-a-days everything is done
at his bidding.   The chancellor (Audeley) is but a tool in his
hands."[20]   The French ambassadors also reported that
Cromwell "had principally managed the country's affairs
since the cardinal's death," and that "he alone could do more

[18] *Apologia ad Carolum V*, chap. xxix.   Cf. Lingard, Vol. VI, p. 283;
Merriman, I, 92; Fisher, p. 295.
[19] Cf. Merriman, chap. vi; Fisher, p. 296.
[20] *Sp. Cal.* V, 228; *L. and P.*, VI, No. 351.

than any other with his master the king; and that never was
the late Cardinal of York in better favour or standing." In
after years Francis I was delighted when "such a wicked and
wretched tool" of a fatal policy fell, and he expected that his
downfall would bring "to the common good of the Church,
the princes, noblemen, and in general the whole people of
England, rest, peace, and calm."[21]   The emperor and
Granvelle showed similar signs of satisfaction; and Paul III
began to hope again.[22]   In the eyes of his contemporaries
then Cromwell was the chief agent and instigator of the royal
despotism.

Cromwell owed his power to the fact that his theories
agreed with the king's and tended to make Henry all-powerful.
He was convinced that it was necessary for the king to be all-
powerful in order to assure England's safety, and his term of
office was the golden age of Tudor absolutism; had he not,
moreover, as his ideal the despotism of the Grand Turk?
From Wolsey he had learnt what the king's disposition was;
and he always flattered it, according to Machiavelli's principle, as he himself boasted in the presence of Reginald Pole.[23]
He considered Plato's *Republic* as nothing compared to
Machiavelli's *Prince*. His judgment of life was harsh and had
nothing idealistic about it; neither sentiment nor morality
affected him.   Covetous, cunning, active, and determined,
he had a precision for details that amounted to a passion.
Without an atom of pity, cruel even, he went straight to the
mark, steeling the will of his sovereign, and supporting him
in his steady progress towards the ideal of a one-man government. He was accustomed to say that for a man of experience
a few words were as good as big books or even whole volumes
of philosophy.   Convinced that wealth meant power, he
determined to load the Treasury with Church property, and
since the monarch's sway was limited by the spiritual authority
of Rome, to abolish the latter in favour of the king. Certain
minds might rebel against the royal despotism, but sanguinary
laws, such as only tyranny can invent, would crush them. If

[21] Kaulek, 189, 191. Le Laboureur, I, 409.
[22] L. Cardauns, *Nuntiaturberichte*, V, 307, 320, 336.
[23] *Apologia ad Carolum V*, Quirini, I, 132 *sq.* Cf. Pollard, *Henry VIII*, 323.

he was less diplomatic than Wolsey and less able to see the difficulties of foreign policy, yet in matters of domestic policy he was a past master. This position he owed to his extreme cleverness in creating new sources of revenue, to a thorough knowledge of the nobility, the business world, and the clergy, which he had acquired through his quite peculiar gift of surveying and inventorying, and through his previous occupations as money-lender, lawyer, merchant and business man; that knowledge was further increased when he became vicar-general to the supreme head of the Church. For ten years he held undisputed sway, and tried to direct Parliament's activities. He had behind him an army of partisan lackeys, as arrogant and unpopular as himself, but docile, swift, and inexorable in carrying out his orders. They applied his principles and methods to landed property, taking it from the monasteries and bestowing it upon a new aristocracy. Cromwell dominated the council by his iron will and his ability for work, and the members saw that all their functions were passing into his hands. The chancellor, Audeley, admitted that Cromwell had singularly reduced his office. Norfolk detested him, but bowed before him, and in Cromwell's presence the Lord Admiral was wont "to go with the wind." Cromwell's fall surprised all who had provoked it: "It is certainly all the more wonderful," wrote the French ambassador, "because it happened contrary to everybody's opinion and expectancy."[24]

As Parliament alone counterbalanced the royal authority Cromwell sought to reduce its office and to render it more docile, or, to use his own word, more "tractable." He intervened directly in the elections of 1536 and more especially in those of 1539.[25] In the latter year he caused Parliament to

---

[24] Kaulek, p. 190.

[25] Cf. above, chap. 1. In a letter to the inhabitants of Canterbury on May 18th, 1536 (Merriman, II, 13; cf. I, 126 sq.) he asked for the annulment of an election in favour of two candidates, who were both unanimously elected (L. and P., X, 929). One of the petitions in the Pilgrimage of Grace was that every one of the king's pensioners should be ineligible (L. and P., XI, 1143, 1182 [15], 1244, 1246). During the elections of 1539 both threats and jugs of wine were used (cf. E. and A. Porritt, The Unreformed House of Commons, 1903), but this did not prevent the House of Commons from passing the Act of the Six Articles, contrary to Cromwell's opinions, nor from passing a Bill of Attainder against him and condemning him to death (cf. Pollard, Cranmer, 127 sq.).

pass a measure that he had long contemplated and which in
many matters left Parliament only a recording right. By a
parliamentary vote force of law was given to all royal
proclamations, save for those concerning life, property,
liberty or established laws; even these exceptions did not
apply to anybody prosecuted for heresy.[26] This Act of Parliament, to which Hume applied the epithet "detestable,"
because it would have meant the total destruction of the
English constitution, was so unpopular that the king made
little use of it, and it was abolished immediately after his
death. But the despot Cromwell's great constitutional idea
was to rule through the King's Council rather than through
Parliament.[27]

In order to be an absolute ruler a king must possess wealth.
So Cromwell, who had promised to make Henry the richest
king England, or even Christendom, had ever seen, began by
transferring to the Crown all that had hitherto been paid to the
Roman Curia. Chapuys asserted that he was responsible for
the two laws on the Annates and Peter's Pence: "These are

[26] *Statutes of the realm*, III, 726. Burnet, I, 422. Parliament declared that
with the advice of his council the king could issue proclamations having
the same force of law as the parliamentary decrees; that he could enforce
them by corporal or financial sanctions, but that they could neither
contradict nor abolish existing laws, nor deprive any subject of his goods,
liberty, or rights. All who left the country in violation of those proclamations would be treated as State criminals. If Henry VIII's successor was a
minor, his council could issue proclamations in the king's name, which
would have the same force of law. This act was passed only after discussions
which lasted a fortnight and after the first Bill had been rejected (*L. and P.*,
XIV, Part 1, No. 1158. Cf. *Lords' Journals*, 1539). One reason which
made Parliament accept the Act was the fact that it would assure that
union and agreement of opinions which had been the object of the Act of
the Six Articles passed at the same period, and that by it Henry would
become the mainstay of orthodoxy so that England would be united in
strict conformity of opinion against all outside enemies. There was but one
kind of offence against the proclamations which could be punished by
death, viz. the offences of those who violated any proclamation of His
Majesty, his heirs or successors, concerning any kind of heresy against
Christian doctrine. For the exact meaning of this statute, its scope and the
use made of it during Henry VIII's reign, and for its suppression by
Somerset in the first year of Edward VI's reign, see chap. 1, n. 118. For the
origin of this Bill, see French ed. of this book, pp. 599 *sq.*

[27] In 1534 he put forward his idea of including in the King's ordinary
Council all the most important gentlemen in each county (*L. and P.*, VII,
420). See the draft of his Bill for a new court "of conservators of the
commonwealth," and for a more rigid execution of the laws (*ibid.*, VII,
1611).

devices of Cromwell."[28]   He then concerned himself with
the minting of money,[29] and the passing of the much-disputed
and unpopular "Statute of Uses" (1536), which restored the
ancient feudal rights to the Crown.[30] We have already seen
the part he played in the suppression of the monasteries in
order to fill the royal Treasury; the Pilgrimage of Grace in
1536 denounced him as the author of that suppression and
demanded his death.[31]

Whether that complement and refinement of despotism, the
king's supremacy in the Church, was inspired by Cromwell or
not, he at least was responsible for its triumph. He applied its
laws with implacable severity and barbarous brutality. The
London Carthusians, the Holy Maid of Kent, Fisher, More,
and the other victims of the royal supremacy were all prosecuted, examined, tried and condemned at his direction. His
"Remembrances," the indictments, and the examinations are
clear proofs of this. The verdict was dictated beforehand, and
the sentence was a mere formality. The following entries
occur in Cromwell's "Remembrances": "*Item*. The Abbot
Redyng [Reading] to be sent down to be *tried and executed* at
Redyng with his complices. . . . *Item*. The Abbot of Glaston
[Glastonbury] to be *tried* at Glaston, and *also executed* there."
Another more astounding entry reads: "*Item*. To see that the
evidence be *well sorted* and the indictments *well drawn* against
the said abbots and their accomplices." The claims of justice
did not worry Cromwell: "*Item*. What the king his pleasure
shall be touching the learned man in the Tower." That
learned man was Thomas More.[32]

[28] *L. and P.*, VII, 1554; *Sp. Cal.*, V, 228; Merriman, I, 17. Cromwell
had made a note of these laws (*Statutes of the realm*, 23 Henry VIII, cap. 20;
25 Henry VIII, cap. 20; 26 Henry VIII, cap. 3. Cf. *L. and P.*, V, 879,
VI, 793. See above chap. III) in his "Remembrances" either to get them
passed or else to draw up the Bills for them (cf. *L. and P.*, VI, 299; IX, 725.
Merriman, I, 134 and n. 1).

[29] *L. and P.*, VII, 1304; IX, 144, 183; X, 1170; XII, Part 2, 1151.
Cf. G. Schanz, *Englische Handelspolitik gegen Ende des Mittelalters*, Leipzic,
1881, I, 518, 535-37.

[30] Cromwell's "Remembrances" mention it for the year previous to
the decisive vote [1535] (*L. and P.*, VIII, 892; IX, 725). This was one of
the grievances of the Pilgrimage of Grace against Cromwell.

[31] Cf. Merriman, I, p. 182.

[32] *L. and P.*, XIV, 399. His favourite author, Machiavelli, had said
(*On Titus Livy*, chap. XLI): "All means are good provided the motherland

Cromwell established a secret police system to carry out his orders, and made denunciation almost a part of State machinery. Not only was every subject bound to inform against anybody who violated the minister's orders and who might be reckoned as siding with the Bishop of Rome,[33] but the whole country was also enmeshed in the toils of a treacherous and complicated spy system. "In every county and village," writes Dean Hook,[34] "almost in every homestead he had a secret force of informers and spies." His agents were ubiquitous and reported on sermons that were preached, conversations between gentlemen at table, complaints and murmurings against his tyranny, jokes about him, and any words uttered in admiration of his victims. Suspects were ordered immediately to take the oath of royal supremacy, and whilst they were summoned to appear before the council in London their houses were ransacked and plundered. A man living in Worcester was prosecuted for having, in a private conversation, spoken ill of the desecration of a shrine. The Abbot of Colchester was hanged at the gateway of his own abbey for not having concealed his sympathy with More and Fisher.[35] Although Parliament was not altogether excluded from public affairs,[36] yet Cromwell's government, particularly from 1534 to 1540, marks a unique period in English history, a period of fierce despotism, gloomy and sad compared with the brilliant beginnings of the reign, becoming more and more enshrouded in an atmosphere of suspicion, violence and plunder. Terror sat at every hearth and daunted the whole nation. "Cromwell," said Mendez Silva, "freely carried out his atrocities, giving people to understand that they were beneficial to the

be defended; when it is a question of deciding its destiny, no consideration of justice or injustice, of humanity or cruelty, of shame or of glory, must tand in the way."

[33] The Injunctions of 1538, Article 11. Cf. Froude, *op. cit.*, chap. IX. For Cromwell, papist and traitor were synonymous terms (*L. and P.*, XIII, Part 1, No. 120).

[34] *Lives of the Archbishops of Canterbury*, VI, 98. Cf. Froude, *Henry VIII*, chap. v. The members of the council blamed him for sending people to death for "a few words, often perhaps spoken inadvertently or in good faith."

[35] Cf. Gasquet, *Henry VIII and the English Monasteries*, II, 377–78.

[36] The 1529 Parliament lasted until 1536. Two others were summoned in 1539 and 1540.

prince, in order to make the crown more secure and to subject his subjects."[37]

As the king's vicar-general in spiritual matters (1535) he possessed unequalled power. He shared in the royal supremacy, which he in turn could delegate. He had power to "exercise all spiritual jurisdiction belonging to the king for the due administration of justice in all cases touching ecclesiastical jurisdiction, and godly reformation, and redress of errors, heresies, and abuses in the said church." As vicegerent in ecclesiastical causes, his authority was not confined solely to the time of ecclesiastical visitations.[38] These unprecedented powers gave him a position immediately after that of the king, whose temporal and spiritual powers were, by delegation, concentrated in Cromwell's hands. His position is certainly unique in English history. In Convocation he sat above the archbishops and bishops, and his was the first signature on all documents. In Parliament he took precedence of the nobility of every rank, and the Act of Parliament of 1539 concerning precedence gave him a place immediately after the princes of the royal blood.[39] He could enquire into the morals and opinions of the clergy, reform church laws, designate the bishops who were to be elected and then invest them. The edicts issued by his authority on ecclesiastical

---

[37] Cf. Merriman, I, 123, note in Spanish. Machiavelli's *Prince*, his favourite book, was precisely the vindication of inquisitorial and corrupt tyranny. Cf. J. R. Charbonnel, *La pensée italienne au XVIe siècle et le courant libertin*, Paris, 1919, p. 393.

[38] In order to have an eye upon and to correct the abuses in the Church the king, as "Kinges Grace Vicarius Christi," made Cromwell his vicar-general in 1535, and thereby delegated to him all the jurisdiction and authority inherent in the supreme head of the Church of England. Cromwell in turn delegated other commissioners. Both he and they had full power to make visitations in order to enquire into the life and conduct of every ecclesiastic, no matter what his rank or dignity, "quocunque nomine et dignitate, etiamsi archiepiscopali vel episcopali præfulgeant." Whilst they were on visitation, every cause pertaining to the ecclesiastical forum, resignations, vacancies of and pensions from benefices, elections and investitures, depended upon them (Wilkins, *Concilia*, III, 784). See Cromwell's nomination as vicar-general in Wilkins, *loc. cit.*; Burnet, V, 456, cf. II, 547 *sq.*; and Collier, IX, 119.

[39] Wilkins, *Concilia*, III, 803; Ellis, *Original Letters*, 3rd Series, III, 196–202; *Statutes of the realm*, 29 Henry VIII, cap. 10. Cf. Burnet, I, 422. He wrote to the Bishop of Llandaff January 7th, 1538 (Burnet, IV, 394) saying "it hath pleased his majesty to appoint and constitute me in the room and place of his supreme and principal minister, in all matters that may touch any thing his clergy, or their doings."

matters were called Injunctions. Even the Primate of England had to take orders from him. Never was a layman of such lowly origin possessed of such exorbitant powers.

As a Minister of State he was likewise all-powerful. His office of Secretary of State alone was greater than the three similar offices which do the same work at the present day. All correspondence was handed to Cromwell, who selected and prepared what he thought the king should see. Everything was scrutinized by him, whether it came from foreign countries or from within the realm, and he effaced whatever he wished and had copies prepared for submission to the king. As secretary he was every day in touch with Henry, whom he could approach at any hour. His influence increased to such a degree that soon all officials were set aside. During his ten years as minister he never left the king for very long, and at the same time succeeded in removing his two chief rivals, the leaders of the moderate party, Norfolk and Gardiner. In 1535, the duke had to retire to his estate at Kenninghall,[40] and Gardiner was sent to France as an ambassador.[41]

Cromwell's rise, wrote Lord Campbell, "more resembled that of a slave at once constituted grand vizier in an Eastern despotism than of a minister of state promoted in a constitutional government where law, usage, and public opinion check the capricious humours of the sovereign." Privy Councillor in 1531, he became Master of the King's Jewels in the following year, a member of the Exchequer and Master of the King's Wards in 1533, Chancellor of the Exchequer, Secretary of State and Master of the Rolls in 1534, Vicar-General in 1535, Lord Privy Seal, the King's Vicegerent in ecclesiastical causes, and Baron Cromwell of Okeham in 1536, a Knight of the Garter in August 1537, and a peer of the realm with the title of Earl of Essex in 1540.[42] During his seven last years as a

[40] Cf. *L. and P.*, VI, 1510. At the time of the rising in Yorkshire the Duke of Norfolk raised men at his own expense (*L. and P.*, XI, 793, 800, 864) in order to regain the royal favour and to be able to return to London. But he was ordered to send his son to court and to stay at home himself (*ibid.*, XI, 601-602). Cromwell feared his return (*ibid.*, XI, 909).

[41] For this Gardiner bore him a grudge, and this played no small part in the downfall of the all-powerful minister.

[42] Cf. Lord Herbert of Cherbury, *op. cit.*, p. 202; Burnet, I, 292 *sq.*; Dixon, I, 244-47; G. W. Child, *Church and State under the Tudors, London*, 1890, pp. 78 *sq.*

minister he received no less than nineteen lucrative offices, which considerably swelled his private fortune.

His financial status had also been increased by the spoils of the monasteries. Abbots and priors showered donations, pensions, and gifts upon the vicar-general, in the hope that they would be spared.[43] Numerous valuable articles, such as crosses and reliquaries, were forwarded to him by his agents, and were found in his house after his death. He converted to his own use seven religious houses and their cells in various counties.[44] His son, who took up residence in one of them, wrote saying that Mrs. Cromwell, his wife, had settled down very comfortably. All who needed a recommendation from Cromwell knew how to obtain it. Presents rained upon him from all sides: Irish hawks from Bath, geldings from Tewkesbury, fish from Croyland [Crowland], apples from Kingslangley, partridges and pheasants from Harrow, and even cheeses.[45]

Cromwell lived in great style, distributing princely gifts, spending money on his pleasures regardless of the cost, and building sumptuous houses for himself which he furnished in a luxurious manner.[46] He loved to make a display of rich and exquisite works of art: rare specimens of jewellery and goldsmiths' articles, valuable manuscripts, and celebrated works

[43] To prevent the suppression of his house, the Cistercian abbot of Pipwell (Northumberland) offered £200 (Wright, p. 179), the abbot of Rewley, Oxford, £100 (*ibid.*, p. 73), the prior of Durham an annuity of £10 (Ellis, *Original Letters*, 3rd Series, III, 44); the prioress of Catesby (Northumberland), "a hundred marks to buy a gelding" (*ibid.*, p. 50); the abbot of Leicester followed their example (*ibid.*, II, p. 313). Cromwell, in return for remunerations, spared the priories of St Faith (September 23rd, 1536; *L. and P.*, XI, 484, and Merriman, II, No. 163) and of Coxford (1536; *L. and P.*, XI, 485, and Merriman, II, No. 180).
The account book of Cromwell's steward, Thomas Avery, shows that he received large sums of money by way of presents (Gasquet, *op. cit.*, I, 413).

[44] Cromwell took possession of the rich priory of Lewes, in Sussex, with its cell at Melton Mowbray, in Leicestershire; and of the priories of Mickelham, in Sussex; Lound, in Leicestershire; Modenham, in Kent; St Osithe's, in Essex; Alcester, in Warwick; and of Yarmouth, in Norfolk. (Cf. Merriman, 168; Blunt, I, 377).

[45] Gasquet, *op. cit.*, I, 418; Blunt, I, 377 n. 4. Cromwell's "Remembrances" (Gasquet, *op. cit.*, I, 419-20) show that sums of money passed between himself and his agents, which has a suspicious look.

[46] *L. and P.*, XI, Nos. 478, 862; XIV, Part i, No. 5. "His household cost him, for some time at least, more than £100 a month," a heavy sum for that period.

by the Italian Humanists.[47] The appointed court artist,
Holbein, painted his portrait in 1534.[48] The former cloth-
carder had a princely demeanour; his house was besieged by
people seeking his favour. In 1536 Chapuys reported to
Charles V that it was rumoured that he was about to wed the
king's daughter, the Princess Mary.[49]

In addition to Holbein, the imperial ambassador has also
left us a living portrait of Cromwell: short, corpulent, with
broad clean-shaven features and close-cropped hair, and a
small cruel mouth with an excessively protruding upper lip,
and grey eyes that aroused attention by their extreme mobility.
His odd and clumsy manners seemed to indicate a certain
dullness of mind, but his face lit up in conversation and
assumed an expression of intelligence and subtle shrewdness
which contrasted with his ordinary appearance. His speech
was easy, witty, even amiable, and was often accompanied
by a knowing, sidelong glance. His quick-changing features
were an index of the ease with which he could adapt himself
to his surroundings, altering the tone of his voice, his attitude
and his behaviour according to circumstances and the company he was in. None knew better than he how to flatter, if
anything were to be gained thereby. None could be more
harsh or cruel when there was occasion to bully and command
without running any risks. Utilitarianism was his essential
characteristic, and he openly admitted it to Reginald Pole.[50]
He had adopted and made his own the thoughts of Machiavelli: "Bad faith is necessary for all who would rise from medio-
crity to power. You must act as a maniac, and praise, speak,
see, and act contrary to your own opinions in order to please
the prince. Thus is peace assured, and you share all his good
fortune without any risk. When a man's actions appear against

[47] Various inventories taken of his goods denote this and prove that he
had a considerable fortune (cf. L. and P., IV, 6346, 6613, 6744).

[48] This portrait, the face of which has been repainted, is at Tittenhanger
Park (Hertfordshire) in the Countess of Caledon's collection. It has been
reproduced by P. Ganz, Gemälde des Meisters Hans Holbein d. J., p. 106,
and by Pollard, Thomas Cranmer, p. 138.

[49] L. and P., VIII, 108; XI, 41; and XV, 801. But it does not seem that
Cromwell seriously entertained the idea of marrying the princess (cf.
Merriman, I, 294, n. 3).

[50] Apologia ad Carolum V, chap. xxix. Stow gives examples of this in his
Chronicle.

him, if he is fortunate, the result justifies him."[51] These were the maxims of the man who controlled the destinies of England for ten years, and who was, in the words of Foxe, "a mighty pillar set up in the Church of Christ."[52]

In matters of religion Cromwell was, with Cranmer, the leader of the advanced party. Whatever his own personal feelings may have been—politics were chiefly his religion— he was looked upon, at home and abroad, as a protagonist of the New Learning. He was denounced to the king as such by the northern rebels. Melanchthon and the German princes eulogised him, whilst Francis I and Charles V loathed him.[53] As a matter of fact, the conflict between himself and his adversaries was in reality the conflict between the reforming and the orthodox or moderate parties; and his fall coincided with the triumph of the reaction.

As vicegerent of the supreme head of the Church of England, Cromwell intervened in matters of dogma and ecclesiastical discipline and played an important part in the Reformation; his rôle would have been still more important had he not been overthrown by the king at the zenith of his greatness.

The First Confession of Faith (1536) was a kind of compromise between the old and the new faith, and if it was not really Protestant in tone it was because the vicar-general and Cranmer dared not go against the theology of the supreme head himself.[54] When it was discussed in Convocation, Cromwell brought in a Scot, Alexander Alane (Alesius), to influence the members. He was to preach on the sacraments and faith from the Lutheran standpoint; but after his first speech the bishops excluded him as a foreigner and an intruder.[55] The Six Articles of 1539, which showed a retro-

[51] *On Titus Livy*, chap. XIII, iii, ix.

[52] *Op. cit.*, V, 144.

[53] *L. and P.*, XV, 785. The disappearance "*d'ung si meschant et malheureux instrument*" could result only in "*le bien de l'Eglise.*" Francis I to Marillac, June 15th, 1540. Kaulek, 191. Cf. below, n. 104.

[54] See chap. VIII.

[55] Alexander Alane, known as Alesius, once a canon of St Andrews and lecturer in Cambridge University, had come from Flanders the previous year at Cromwell's behest. The first day he spoke on the sacraments in order to refute what he called "an old rusty sophistry and unwritten

grade tendency, were presented to Parliament not by Cromwell, but by his greatest adversary, the Duke of Norfolk.[56]

At Oxford, and especially at Cambridge, where he became chancellor upon the death of Fisher, Cromwell abolished canon law and the scholastic philosophy with "its frivolous questions and obscure glosses," and developed biblical studies. Frequent public lectures in Greek and Hebrew were inaugurated, and thenceforward theology was to be taught with the Scripture alone as a basis, and in accordance with the meaning of the text and not as Duns Scotus had taught it. Professors, rules, and professorships were all changed, and Cromwell's faithful lackeys, Leigh and Ap Rice, who were noted for their abrupt and haughty manners, saw that his orders were executed (September, 1535).[57]

Cromwell reformed the veneration of the saints and their images, without altogether abolishing it. The Injunctions issued in 1536 ordered the clergy to cease paying honour to images or relics from motives of superstition or gain, to dissuade the people from pilgrimages and to persuade them to give their money to the poor instead of to all these superstitions and hypocrisies, and to cease observing the superstitious feast days, i.e. the saints' days.[58] The orders laid down for the visitation of the monasteries (1536) likewise forbade the religious to display relics for the purpose of soliciting

verities." The next day he had promised to prove that the Christian faith rested only on the Bible (cf. J. Gairdner, *History*, p. 125). A little later Alane wrote a pamphlet against Bishop Bonner: *Of the Authoritie of the Word of God, against the bishop of London*, Leipzic, 1542.

[56] The secret history of the Six Articles shows that Cromwell's influence at that period was badly shaken. He concealed his own preferences in face of the king's orthodoxy (cf. Stubbs, *Medieval and Modern History*, 3rd ed., 1900, pp. 329 *sq.*).

[57] Cf. *L. and P.*, IX, 615; Strype, *Eccles. Mem.*, I, Part 1, p. 322, Part 2, pp. 218 *sq.*; Wilson, *Magdalen College*, p. 80; Davis, *Balliol College*, pp. 82-86; *Fasti Oxonienses*, I, 86; Merriman, I, 406, No. 104, II, Nos. 325, 326. Fisher, then in the Tower, refused to sign the regulations for Cambridge, which Cromwell had altered and which had been partly drawn up by Leigh and Ap Rice. Parliament, which had just been dissolved (April 14th, 1536), approved them and thus reformed the universities.

[58] Burnet, IV, p. 309; Gerdes, *op. cit.*, IV, 474; *L. and P.*, IX, 377; Merriman, II, No. 159; Gee and Hardy, No. LXII. These are the first "Injunctions" of the Tudors. Latimer, in Convocation, had preached in favour of the restriction of the number of holy days (cf. J. Gairdner, *History*, p. 177).

alms.[59]   The Injunctions of 1538 obliged every vicar to preach, at least once a quarter, against the practice of offering money or candles to relics or images.   The use of lighted candles was expressly forbidden everywhere save before the Blessed Sacrament.   The *ora pro nobis* after the numerous names of saints in the litanies was suppressed so that more attention might be paid to the subsequent prayers.[60]   "Surely the want of the knowledge hath been the occasion of many great abuses and superstitions among Christian people," said *The Institution of a Christian Man* (1537).

From 1538 onwards the crusade against relics and images went hand in hand with the dissolution of the monasteries. Certain false relics and superstitious devotions were the pretext for an almost universal destruction.   The famous "Rood of Boxley" (Kent), with a jointed figure of Christ whose eyes and lips were made to move by an ingenious piece of mechanism, was publicly displayed at Maidstone and then taken to London and ridiculed before a mob at St Paul's. They subsequently tore it to pieces whilst Bishop Hilsey of Rochester thundered against the veneration of relics and images from the pulpit.[61]   The "Holy Blood of Hayles" was also destroyed.   This was commonly held to be the Blood of Christ, though as the abbot himself proved to Cromwell it was not used for fraudulent purposes.   Hilsey declared at St Paul's Cross that it was "honey clarified and coloured with saffron."[62]   A wooden statue, the "Darvel Gadarn" (or Gathern), which was considered by the Welsh people to have the power of withdrawing souls from hell, was dragged to

[59] Burnet, IV, 221; Wilkins, III, 815 (where the date is given, 1536); Gee and Hardy, No. LXIII.

[60] Burnet, IV, 343; Wilkins, *Concilia*, III, 815.   If they had formerly preached in favour of relics, images and pilgrimages the parochial clergy were to retract their utterances and to declare that the Scriptures do not mention them and that they themselves had erred or acted for gain. Whoever infringed these injunctions was an abettor of the Bishop of Rome and would be prosecuted as such (Articles 10 and 11).

[61] *L. and P.*, XIII, Part 1, Nos. 231, 348, 694, 864, Part 2, No. 111; Burnet, VI, 194; Bridgett, *Blunders and Forgeries*, and an article in the *Dublin Review*, 1887.   J. Gairdner, *History*, 199; and the same author's *Lollardy*, II, 122-33.

[62] Cf. R. Holinshed, *Chronicles of England, Ireland and Scotland*, 2nd ed., 1587, p. 946; *L. and P.*, XIII, Part 1, Nos. 347, 540, 564, Part 2, Nos. 186, 409, 488, 709, 710, 856; Gasquet, *Henry VIII and the English Monasteries*, II, Append. II, p. 536; J. Gairdner, *Lollardy*, II, 142-45; Dixon, II, 48 *sq.*

London and thrown on the fire in which John Forest, one of the martyrs of the royal supremacy, was burning, and at the same time the Bishop of Worcester railed against the Pope and superstition.[63] The reformers exulted. "The Azotic Dagon," wrote one of them,[64] "falls down everywhere in this country. That Babylonian Bel has already been broken to pieces."

From devotions that were superstitious they passed to others that were not. Certain celebrated sanctuaries, such as Our Lady's at Ipswich, St Anne's at Buxton, and Our Lady of Walsingham were all desecrated. The reliquaries of St Richard at Chichester, St Swithun at Winchester, and St Cuthbert at Durham were emptied of their relics and sent to the Tower of London (1538).[65] St Thomas à Becket's shrine at Canterbury was the richest and the most famous of all. It was of pure gold and covered with precious stones. Its chief adornment was an extremely beautiful ruby, the "Regal

[63] Ellis, *Original Letters*, 1st series, II, p. 82; cf. Hall, *Chronicle*, May 30th, 1538; J. Gairdner, *History*, p. 200; by the same author, *Lollardy*, II, 146–49; Fisher, 426.

St Darvel (Gadarn means "the powerful" in Welsh) came from Llantwit Major, on the coast of Glamorganshire, and fought as a warrior at the Battle of Camlan in 537. He was the patron saint of Landerfeld (diocese of St Asaph) where certain remains of the old statue, a horse and a staff, are still preserved. He was honoured at Plovézet (Finistère) under the name of Dervel (cf. Baring-Gould and Fisher, *Lives of British Saints*, II, 333 *sq.*).

[64] John Hoker of Maidstone to Bullinger. G. C. Gorham, *Reformation Gleanings*, London, 1857, p. 17; Burnet, VI, 194 *sq.*; *Original Letters*, ed. Parker Society, II, 609; Pollard, *Cranmer*, p. 117; J. Gairdner, *Lollardy*, II, 149 *sq.*

[65] Cf. Wright, *Three Chapters of Letters*, p. 218; Williams, *Monastic Treasures*, pp. 40, 43. See John London's letter to Cromwell on the destruction of the shrine at Walsingham, in Ellis, *Original Letters*, 1st series, II, 79. In 1931 the Anglo-Catholics placed a Latin inscription on the building at Walsingham, which they wish to make again a pilgrimage centre; translated, it reads as follows:

"This shrine, founded in the year 1061 at the will of the Blessed Virgin Mother of God in honour of the Mystery of the Sacred Incarnation, St Edward, King and Confessor and Lord of this Manor having reigned nineteen years, and afterwards utterly overturned by the king who raged with the most foul love of gain (on whose soul may God have mercy), now for the first time in the year 1931 was restored." Cf. *The Universe*, July 31st, 1931.

Henley, at Durham, wished to cast St Cuthbert's relics to the winds, but when the body was found to be whole and incorrupt, the prior and the monks buried it in the earth on the very spot where the reliquary had formerly stood (*Rites of Durham*, pp. 3 *sq.*, 79, 86. Cf. Ch. Eyre, *The History of Saint Cuthbert*, 3rd ed., 1887, with six maps and plans).

of France," given by Louis VII in 1179.[66] The shrine was smashed to pieces, and the gold and precious stones sent to the Treasury. St Thomas himself was declared a traitor because, during his lifetime, he had dared to resist the king and defend the Church's liberties. His festival and office, and all prayers in his honour were suppressed. His body was taken out and burnt, and the ashes scattered to the winds (autumn, 1538).[67] There are no grounds, however, for the alleged judicial farce, in which the king is supposed to have summoned St Thomas to appear, and to have caused a proxy to appear for him after thirty days had elapsed.[68]

[66] He came to visit the shrine with Henry II. Henry VIII wore the *royal de France* [an immense ruby] on his finger. Later it was set in a necklace and Mary Tudor used it for pious purposes (*Erasmus' Pilgrimages*, ed. Nichols, Introd., p. 86). Erasmus (ed. quoted), Polydore Vergil (Bk. XIII, ed. Ghent, 1556, pp. 557 *sq.*), and an Italian account of the previous reign (Pollard, *Henry VII*, III, No. 52) give a description of St Thomas à Becket's shrine. See Dr. Tancred Borenius' "St Thomas Becket in Art," London, 1932.

[67] Proclamation and a letter from the king, November 16th and December, 1538, Burnet, VI, 220, 223; Morris, *The Relics of Saint Thomas*; Dixon, II, 63 *sq.* Article 15 of the 1538 Injunctions abolished and forbade the feast and the cult of St Thomas à Becket. The royal decree declaring him a traitor is dated November 10th of that same year (Wilkins, *Concilia*, III, 848; cf. Wriothesley, *Chronicle*, ed. Camden Society, 1875, p. 87). On December 17th it was decided to publish the Bull of Excommunication (J. Gairdner, *Lollardy*, II, 151–57).

Because Thomas à Becket represented the cause of the Church's liberties —a cause supported for generations by the feelings of the crowds which flocked to his tomb (cf. Jusserand, *La vie nomade et les routes d'Angleterre*, p. 213)—Cromwell and the king laid the blame upon him as though he were a living person.

In his panegyric of St Thomas (December 29th, 1668) Bossuet recalled the theological principles governing the relations between the Church and State, and once again attacked the schism from Rome (cf. Dom Cabrol, "Bossuet, ses relations avec l'Angleterre," *Revue d'Hist. eccles.*, July, 1931, pp. 538 *sq.*).

[68] Cf. Wilkins, *Concilia*, III, 835. If it had been true, it lent itself too readily to the oratorical developments which Reginald Pole liked for the *Apologia ad Carolum V* not to mention it when alluding to the saint. J. H. Pollen, S.J. (*King Henry VIII and Saint Thomas Becket*, London, 1921, which appeared first as articles in *The Month*, February and April, 1921) is inclined to think that the suit against Thomas à Becket is a pure invention on the part of Crisostomo Henriquez, but he does not explain how the very precise details of the proceedings were imagined. A. J. Mason, *What became of the Bones of St Thomas? a Contribution to his 15th jubilee*, 1920; V. H. Hutton, *Thomas Becket, Archbishop of Canterbury*, Cambridge, 1926 (decides, as does Pollen, against the authenticity of the relics found in 1888 by A. J. Mason). See also Sidney Dark's recent work, *Saint Thomas of Canterbury*, London, 1927; H. Prentout, *Thomas Becket et ses historiens*

Cromwell showed great zeal in publishing and spreading the English version of the Bible. During the Convocation of 1534 he and Cranmer insisted on asking the king to allow an English translation.[69] In the following year he adopted the translation of one of his friends, Miles Coverdale, which was a combination of the Vulgate and Luther's version.[70] But as it was not adopted by Convocation in 1536, Cromwell replaced it, in 1537, by John Rogers' version (Matthews' Bible), which combined the texts of Coverdale and Tyndale. Tyndale had been burnt as a heretic in the previous year, at

(Société bibliographique et critique de Normandie, Caen, 1929, pp. 370–93); E. Walberg, in the Introduction to *La vie de Saint Thomas le martyr* by Guernes de Pont-Sainte-Maxence, cleric, poet and juggler (Upsala, 1922), examines the historical sources of this medieval poem consisting of 6,180 Alexandrines. C. J. Webb has recently (1931) published a Life of *John of Salisbury* (†1180), Becket's friend who was present at his martyrdom and was also his first biographer.

For present-day shrines, see B. C. Boulter's *Pilgrim Shrines of England described and illustrated*, 1928.

[69] *L. and P.*, VII, 1555.

[70] The "Holy Bible truly translated by Myles Coverdale" was printed in London in 1535. In 1847 Bayster, the publisher, brought out a facsimile edition with Coverdale's portrait.

The passages in favour of Catherine of Aragon's case had been given quite a contrary meaning in the translation (*L. and P.*, X, 352, 698; XIV, Part 1, No. 186 [V]). This was the edition which Cromwell reckoned on making every parochial church buy before August 1st, 1537, as prescribed by the final clause (Art. 7) of the "Injunctions" of 1536 (Burnet, IV, 311 and VI, 216).

In Wolsey's time Coverdale had been secretary to Dr. Barnes who was burnt as a heretic on July 30th, 1540. Like Barnes, he was originally an Augustinian friar of Cambridge. He spent several years abroad translating the Bible "out of Dutch [i.e. German] and Latin into English," as he says in the Preface. Of the original Hebrew and Greek Coverdale took no account. His task was finished by October, 1535. He was one of Cromwell's most zealous spies (see above, p. 293) in the war against the veneration of images.

The only editions of Coverdale's Bible appear to be those of 1550 and 1553, in Edward VI's time, when he was very much in favour and became Bishop of Exeter (1551–53). (Cf. John Lewis, *A complete History of the several Translations of the Holy Bible and New Testament into English*; Burrow, *A Summary of Christian Faith and Practice*, 1882, Introd., p. xxvii; F. Fry, *The Bible by Coverdale, MDXXXV: Remarks on the Titles, the Year of Publication, the Preliminary, the Watermarks, etc.*, London, 1867, with 15 facsimile plates.) But J. Gairdner (*op. cit.*, p. 192) mentions an edition in 1537, in which "the name of Queen Anne had to be awkwardly altered into Queen Jane in the dedication."

A parchment copy of Coverdale's Bible is preserved in St John's College, Cambridge.

Vilvorde near Brussels.[71] There were not, however, sufficient copies of this edition to supply the whole nation, and moreover certain forewords and notes gave too much offence, so a London printer named Grafton obtained permission to publish a bigger Bible in Paris, where better paper and type were obtainable than in England (1537).[72] The work was thought to be nearly completed and Cromwell had already prescribed

[71] In 1526 Tyndale translated the New Testament from the Greek, and between 1530 and 1534 the Pentateuch and other books of the Old Testament from the Hebrew. He evidently designed his translation to depreciate all ideas of an organized or hierarchical Church (the familiar terms "priests," "church," "do penance," were replaced by "seniors" or "elders," "congregation," and "repent"), and his translation was twice burnt in London, at the instance of Tunstall and More (cf. Foxe, IV, pp. 666 sq.). Nevertheless it went through seven editions in Antwerp between 1536 and 1538 (cf. J. C. de Hoop Scheffer, in the Studiën en Bijdragen op't gebeid der historische theologie, Amsterdam, for the year 1872, pp. 415 sq.; Rev. R. Demaus, Life of Tyndale, ed. Lovett).
In 1536 John Rogers, for several years in charge of a "Reformation" school in Germany and afterwards a prebendary of St Paul's, who was the first to be burnt as a heretic in Mary Tudor's reign (February 4th, 1555), was ordered by Cromwell to resume the translation which had been entrusted to Coverdale. "The first books of the Old Testament, and the whole of the New, were a reprint of Tyndale's; the rest was Coverdale's text with some alterations" (J. Gairdner, History, p. 192). But by this time Tyndale had been burnt for heresy, in Flanders (October 6th, 1536). Rogers therefore prudently suppressed both Tyndale's name and his own and used a nom-de-plume: Thomas Matthews. There were 1,500 copies of this edition, which was printed at Hamburg by Grafton and White-church, two London printers, and it cost £500. [J. Gairdner, History, p. 192, says of it, "The printing . . . seems to have been begun abroad, but after Isaiah had been completed, to have been continued in London."— Translator.] Grafton, who hoped to make a good thing out of it, asked Cromwell (1537, Strype, Memorials of Cranmer, Append. No. XX) to make it obligatory for every parish to buy one and for every abbey to buy six, and also to give him the sole authorization to sell the Bible in English for three years. For there was another translation, brought out by the Dutch, printed on bad paper and full of inaccuracies and linguistic errors, which threatened it as a rival.—George Offor brought out an edition of Tyndale's version, in 1836, "with proceedings and correspondence of Henry VIII, More and Cromwell"; and F. Fry published Tyndale's New Testament in 1862 (rare). J. I. Mombert did the same for some of Tyndale's books of the Old Testament, in New York, in 1884 (500 numbered copies): "Five Books of Moses called the Pentateuch, a verbatim reprint of the edition of 1530, compared with Tyndale's Genesis of 1534, etc., with collations and prolegomena."—For English translations of the Bible before Tyndale, see the French ed. of this book, pp. 612 sq., where a bibliography will be found for the several translations of the Bible into English.
[72] L. and P., XII, Part 2, p. 593, and Append. 35. The licence granted by Francis I will be found in Strype, Mem. of Cranmer, Append. No. XXX; cf. ibid., chap. XXI.

its purchase[73] when the French printer, Regnault, was summoned before the Inquisitor-General and his edition (2,500 copies) burnt in the *Place Maubert*.[74] The Englishmen fled. Cromwell, who had paid six hundred marks from his own pocket, protested, and Bonner, the new Bishop of Hereford, eventually secured the plates and brought over some French printers who finished the printing in London, in April 1539.[75] This Bible in-folio, known as the Great Bible,[76] was the only authorised edition. In 1538 every parish church was ordered to buy one and place it in a position where all the faithful could easily read it. The bishops were to see that there was one in every house.[77] Thanks to Cromwell and Cranmer,[78] Tyndale's translation, which had previously been condemned and burnt in England, thus became the official version.

[73] The "Injunctions" of 1538. Merriman, II, 273.

[74] Only a few copies escaped which had been sold to a haberdasher as packing-paper (Strype, *Mem. of Cranmer*, chap. xxi).

[75] *L. and P.*, XIII, Part 2, No. 1163; XIV, Part 1, No. 37; Kaulek, 97, 108; Eadie, *The English Bible*, 1876, I, 360; Dixon, II, p. 77; Strype, *Mem. of Cranmer*, chaps. xvii, xxi; H. J. Todd, *Life of Archbishop Cranmer*, I, chap. xi; Gairdner, *Lollardy*, Bk. IV, chap. i.

[76] This expression was probably used to distinguish Grafton's Bible from the smaller ones of his rivals, against which he had asked to be protected. It has also been called "Cranmer's Bible" on account of the Preface written by Archbishop Cranmer for the 1540 edition (cf. Strype, *Mem. of Cranmer*, chap. xxi).

[77] Burnet, IV, 341, 343; *L. and P.*, XIII, Part 1, No. 1304, Part 2, No. 281; Merriman, II, 146 and Nos. 266, 273. Cf. Dixon, II, 77 *sq.* In 1536 Cromwell had ordered the priest in every parish to obtain a Bible in Latin and in English and to place it at the disposal of the faithful (Burnet, 309). His decrees for the monasteries prescribed that the Bible should be read during meals and that one hour should be given to the study of the Scriptures every day (*ibid.*, IV, 218). The Bishop of Worcester, Latimer, perceiving in 1537 that these orders were being neglected, renewed them for the religious houses under his jurisdiction, in his own name and under the penalties prescribed by the law (*ibid.*, V, 442; Latimer, *Sermons and Remains*, II, 240). The price of the "Great Bible" was fixed at ten shillings for an unbound and twelve shillings for a bound copy (Strype, *Mem. of Cranmer*, chap. xxi). By royal decree Cromwell was ordered to see that, for five years, no Bible which he had not approved was printed (Burnet, IV, 314; cf. I, 432; Rymer, XIV, 649).

See in Burnet (VI, 199 216) the orders of the Archbishop of York and of the Bishops of Coventry, Lichfield and Salisbury in conformity with Cromwell's "Injunctions" as regards the Bible, superstitious practices, and the prayers and ceremonies used in divine worship.

[78] For details of all this, see J. Gairdner, *Lollardy*, II, 221–304, and Bk. IV, chap. i, "The Story of the English Bible."

All these reforms, Lutheran in character, together with the dissolution of the monasteries and the breach with Rome, had made the German Protestants well disposed towards England. They hoped that there would soon be a doctrinal understanding, hence the conferences at Wittenberg (1536) and London (1538).[79] Cromwell had strong leanings towards them. To promote an alliance with them against Charles V was his policy, whereas that of Henry VIII and Wolsey had consisted in taking advantage of the rivalry between Francis I and the emperor in order to make alliances now with the one and now with the other, and thus maintain a balance which protected England from a combined attack by the two adversaries.[80] But Francis and Charles seemed to have become reconciled and united. The truce of Nice and the meeting at Aiguesmortes (1538) had already alarmed the whole of England. The chivalrous King of France had recently allowed the emperor to pass through his realm in order to go to the aid of Flanders. The two monarchs had met at Loches and given each other mutual signs of friendship, and Francis accompanied the emperor on his journey to the north. On New Year's Day (1540) they entered Paris together and eight days were spent in jousts, festivals, and balls. England watched these manifestations of mutual friendship with an anxious eye.[81] It was the hour when Cromwell's policy was about to triumph.

As soon as Cromwell had noticed the rapprochement between France and the empire, he had begun negotiations for a marriage between the king and the Elector of Saxony's sister-in-law, Anne of Cleves, which would lay the foundations for a future alliance with the Protestant princes of Germany. The king had fallen in with the plan in order to increase Charles' anxiety and to deter him from making an

---

[79] See chap. VIII.

[80] A whole lot of correspondence with the "German lords who adhered to Luther's doctrines" was found in Cromwell's house, and when he fell he was blamed for being "very fond of the German Lutherans' party" (Kaulek, p. 190). On July 28th, 1533, one of Cromwell's friends and clients, Stephen Vaughan, left London to negotiate an alliance with the Elector of Saxony, the Landgrave of Hesse, the Duke of Brunswick-Luneburg and the other princes in the Smalcaldic League (cf. Friedmann, *Anne Boleyn*, I, 226).

[81] See French ed., pp. 615–17.

alliance with Francis against England.[82]   Fear of such an alliance hastened a marriage which was primarily a political affair.   The day the emperor entered Paris, Henry took the road to Rochester to meet his fiancée.[83]   Anne was thirty-three years old, and was wont to spend her time at needlework. She knew no foreign or ancient language, and could neither sing nor play a musical instrument.[84]   Her portrait by Holbein in the Louvre, though flattering, certainly does not depict the extraordinarily beautiful woman that Cromwell pretended he was giving the king as wife.[85]   "Everyone praises the lady's beauty," he had written on the previous March 18th,[86] "both of face and body.   One said she excelled the Duchess

[82] Cf. Merriman, II, 235, 242; Pollard, pp. 381 *sq.*   By raising Anne, sister to the Duke of Cleves and to the Duchess of Saxony, to the royal dignity, Cromwell reckoned on gaining a powerful support and assistance which would overcome his adversaries (cf. Burnet, I, 433).

[83] This idea of marriage with Anne of Cleves waxes and wanes according to the foreign policy of the moment.   It follows the varying probabilities of the threatened anti-English alliance between Francis and Charles.   In March, 1539, at the time of Cardinal Pole's legation, it was looked upon as certain to take place.   Two months later it was said to be doubtful, and at the end of June improbable.   But, in the autumn Cromwell's plans were defeated by the news of the Franco-Imperial diplomacy, and on October 4th "the marriage treaty was concluded and settled" (Kaulek, 133-35). A few days later the king clearly stated the purpose of this marriage to the French ambassador: he desired a "league with the German princes and lords . . . by which he could prevent the attempt which was being designed against him" (*ibid.*, 137).   When Henry's marriage with Anne was dissolved, he said that he had been forced into it through fear of a Franco-Imperial alliance under the Pope's direction (Burnet, IV, 430).   See French ed., p. 617.   At that same period Henry was seeking a partner for his daughter, Princess Mary, in Germany (cf. Kaulek pp. 148 *sq.*. 152, 154 *sq.*, 158, 168, 170, 176, 244, 319).

[84] *L. and P.*, XIV, Part 2, No. 33; Ellis, *Original Letters*, 1st Series, II, 121 *sq.*

[85] Henry VIII had commissioned Holbein to paint Anne of Cleves' portrait, which is now in the Louvre (Holbein room, No. XXXIII). "I learnt, in truth, how a painter, excellent in his art, whom the king had sent to Germany to bring back a living likeness of the Duke of Cleves' sister, arrived back in court during the last few days" (Marillac to Francis I, September, 1539, Kaulek, p. 125).   The ambassador Wotton thought the portrait a fine likeness (*L. and P.*, XIV, Part 2, No. 33).   Anne's marriage seems to have caused Holbein's disgrace, as it did Cromwell's, for the king terminated his engagement as "servant to the king's Majesty" which he had held since 1536 with a salary of £40 (cf. *Histoire de l'Art*, by A. Michel, V, p. 348).   In The Victoria and Albert Museum there is a medallion of Anne painted by Holbein, which was reproduced by P. Ganz in his *Gemälde des Meisters Hans Holbein d.j.*, p. 148.

[86] *L. and P.*, XIV, Part 1, No. 552.

[of Milan] as the golden sun did the silver moon." Disappointment was immediately felt. "She was not so young as had been believed," wrote the French ambassador, "neither was her beauty as great as all had affirmed," and he commented upon the lack of elegance among the members of her suite.[87] Heavy, common, and unversed in the art of pleasing, she made a most disagreeable impression upon the king, who did "not say twenty words to her" at their first meeting. Cromwell asked the king how he liked the Lady Anne and Henry replied "hevelye And not plesantlye nothing so well as she was spoken of."[88] The council was hurriedly summoned to find a way out, but none was found. "Is there no remedy," asked the king, "and must I accept this yoke in spite of myself?" On January 6th, 1540, Henry reluctantly proceeded with the marriage ceremony. "She pleased me not before," said Henry to Cromwell on the morrow, "but she displeases me even more now." Henry did not forgive the man who was responsible for this unpleasant adventure. The means chosen by Cromwell to raise and maintain himself in power proved to be the cause of his downfall.[89]

In the next few months the political horizon grew clearer, and it became more apparent every day that no useful purpose could be served by this union for which the king had an increasing dislike. Charles had smothered the revolt in Flanders, and was preparing to oppose the princes of the Smalcaldic League and therefore no longer thought of rewarding Francis for his magnanimity. He had decided not to give up the Duchy of Milan after which the King of France still hankered. Henry was quick to notice the division between the

[87] Kaulek, 151.

[88] Anne's betrothal to the young Duke of Lorraine, Francis I, was indeed alleged, but Cleves' agents asserted that it had been broken off and that there had been no contract (cf. Kaulek, 66, 201).

[89] Merriman, II, 268 sq. The king had told Cromwell that had he not feared he would throw her brother into the arms of the emperor and the King of France, who were then but one, he would never have consented to marry her (Froude, op. cit., chap. XVII, ed. Everyman, III, p. 65).

"Ce dernier mariaige, par ou s'en est ensuivye la ruyne du feu Cramvel" (Kaulek, 242) was undoubtedly the beginning of the all-powerful minister's downfall (cf. Sander, French trans., 1587, f. 109).

For Anne of Cleves' marriage, see Burnet, I, 410, 433 sq., 440 sq.; Froude, chap. XVII, "Anne of Cleves and the Fall of Cromwell"; Pollard, Henry VIII, 384 sq.; Fisher, pp. 440 sq.

two friends, and thinking that an alliance with the emperor would be more sure than one with the German princes he resolved to throw over Anne of Cleves, whom he had never loved, and also to sacrifice his minister's Protestant policy.[90] At home that policy had done nothing but produce a dangerous disagreement of opinions, which had to be remedied by the Six Articles of 1539, and now it was on the point of failing abroad.[91] Henry therefore decided to jettison both the policy and the minister responsible for it.

At the same time Cromwell's adversaries, the moderate party with Gardiner, who had come back from his French embassy, as its leader, were doing their utmost to overthrow him and destroy his power. In April, 1540, the French ambassador wrote that Cromwell was beginning to totter.[92]

However, before this all-powerful minister fell, his authority waxed and waned in a very strong and remarkable manner, very much as was the case with Robespierre in France. By the part he played in the elections of 1539 the vicegerent had secured a following for himself. Both the court and the government were filled with men who owed their position to him. In the Church he appointed the bishops-elect to the vacant sees, and there were at least half a dozen bishops, with Cranmer at their head, who were in favour of his religious policy. In the council both Audeley, the chancellor, and Wriothesley shared his views; and a group of reformers, few

[90] In April Marillac noted "the joy and satisfaction" of the court at the rumour which "is being spread that matters between the king [Francis I] and the emperor have cooled down, so that they are hoping rather that there will be war between the said lords than that the fervent friendship which recently existed between them will continue" (Kaulek, 179).

Before April, 1540, Henry was convinced that to abandon the Lutheran league would not mean that France and the emperor would unite against him, for the latter was wholly absorbed in pacifying Germany and the Low Countries. While he assured Francis I of his friendship, he let it be known to Charles that he was much more in favour of an alliance with him than with the Protestant princes. Accordingly, in May he very coldly received the request from Cleves' ambassadors that he should give his support in favour of the duchy of Gelderland (L. and P., XV, 735).

[91] See the reasons given by Henry VIII himself to the French ambassador when Cromwell was arrested (Kaulek, 189; cf. ibid., p. 194). Cromwell's policy had for sole basis the necessity of counterbalancing the union between Francis I and the emperor. When that necessity disappeared the policy itself also went by the board.

[92] Ribier, Lettres et mémoires d'Estat, 1537-59, Paris, 1666, I, 513. L. and P., XV, 486. Kaulek, 179. Merriman, 290. Cf. below, chap. VII.

in number but very zealous and noisy, did their best, in ballads and sermons, to prove that the people were desirous of even a more radical reform.[93] The Privy Council, Marillac wrote at this period, was divided into two parties, each of which was striving to destroy the other, and one of them was bound to fall.[94] The king allowed them to fight their battles until he thought the moment had arrived for him to intervene. Then neither Cromwell's cleverness nor his financial expedients sufficed to give him preference in the king's eyes over unity in the council and the preservation of orthodox teaching.

In February, 1540, Barnes, the most zealous of the Lutheran preachers, and Gardiner met at St. Paul's in a theological debate. Barnes had to recant what he had said and was sent to the Tower. Two months later Gardiner became a member of the Privy Council, from which he had been excluded, and Tunstall was mentioned as a successor to Cromwell in the rôle of vicegerent.[95] Parliament assembled a few days later and Cromwell recovered himself, for he was a past master in the art of managing the House. Within a very short space of time, the property of the Knights of St John was confiscated and new taxes were imposed and, as a result the Treasury benefited to the extent of three million pounds. Two of his intimate friends, Wriothesley and Sadler, became Secretaries of State, and he himself was created a peer of the realm with the title of Earl of Essex. In May, Bishop Sampson of Chichester, Gardiner's best friend, was en route for the Tower with two other opponents, and Cranmer replaced him in the pulpit at St Paul's. There was mention also of restoring to Barnes his liberty and to Latimer his former see. Marillac thought the scales were turning in favour of Cromwell, who had never had more "credit and authority" with the king.[96]

But on June 10th, the Captain of the Guard arrested Cromwell in the midst of the council. He protested vehemently and, "very annoyed, threw his hat on the floor"; then seeing there was no hope of escape, he demanded that the matter should be quickly ended. The Duke of Norfolk tore the order of St

---

[93] Cf. Dixon, II, 246 *sq.*; Merriman, 288 *sq.*; Pollard, *Henry VIII*, 393 *sq.*; Fisher, 441 *sq.*
[94] Kaulek, 188.
[95] Kaulek, 169, 171, 175 *sq. L. and P.*, XIV, Part 2, p. 141; XV, No. 486.
[96] Kaulek, 179, 189.

George from his neck, and the Earl of Southampton, "as great an enemy in adversity as he was a friend in prosperity," took the Garter from him. Some of the council cried out that he was a traitor, and others demanded that he should be judged "by the sanguinary laws he had made himself." From Westminster he went to the Tower, and before night fell an inventory was made of his belongings and furniture, amongst which were found "crosses, chalices, mitres, vases, and other things from the spoils of the Church," a sure sign, according to the French ambassador, that no pardon would be granted him. The king stripped him of all his titles, and gave orders that he was to be known quite simply as "Thomas Cromwell, cloth-carder."[97]

Amongst many other things he was accused of having opposed the king's views in matters of religion, of having said that he would impose his own upon him and "would make him come down to the new doctrines, even if he had to take arms against himself," of having favoured heresy and its supporters, of disbelieving "in the most holy and blessed Sacrament of the altar and other articles of the Christian religion," in fine, of having violated the Six Articles of 1539.[98]

As he was likewise accused of revealing secrets which the king had confided in him concerning Anne of Cleves, Henry took advantage of this to extract from him proofs of the royal "lack of consent" to a marriage which was repugnant to the king, and then to have it annulled by ecclesiastical authority and by Parliament; these two authorities alleged lack of freedom and non-consummation (July 9th and 12th, 1540).[99] On the eve of this decision by Parliament, Henry's union

[97] Marillac to Francis I and to the Constable of France, June 11th and 23rd, 1540. Kaulek, 189, 191, 193 *sq*. Cf. Pollard, *Cranmer*, X, 138; Fisher, 443 *sq*. The Earl of Southampton, who took the Order of the Garter from Cromwell, was Admiral Fitzwilliam; he took Cromwell's place as Lord Privy Seal.

[98] Marillac's letters of June 11th and 23rd, 1540, mentioned above. In one of his letters to the Protestant princes, he assured them that the king would shortly embrace their belief or else he (Cromwell) would make him do so by force of arms, so wrote Cervini on June 24th, 1540 (L. Cardauns, *Nuntiaturberichte*, V, 304). Cf. Burnet, I, 444; IV, 415 *sq*.

[99] Gardiner, who was very conversant with Canon Law, took upon himself to discover, by questioning Cromwell, causes of nullity (defective consent and previous contract), and these were pronounced on July 9th (1540) by the united Convocations of Canterbury and York (Wilkins,

with the Duke of Norfolk's niece, Catherine Howard, the king's fifth wife, was already being mentioned. Anne willingly consented to everything, received a pension, honours, and certain manors, and settled down in England to end her days in peace (1558). Of all the women who were sacrificed to the whims of Henry VIII, she had least cause for complaint.[100]

Cromwell proved to be as cowardly and spiritless in adversity as he had been proud and arrogant in the days of success. He whined for mercy.[101] The very form of trial which he himself, as minister, had instituted against Reginald Pole's mother was used in his own case, and Parliament condemned him without a hearing (June 17th to 29th, 1540).

Nec lex est justior ulla
Quam necis artifices arte perire sua.

He was declared to be a heretic and a traitor, and as such either the stake or the gibbet awaited him. But the king commuted the punishment, and on the morning of July 29th, five days after the dissolution of Parliament, his head fell under the headsman's axe.[102] On the scaffold he protested that he was dying in the ancient faith and that he had not

---

Concilia, III, 851-55; Burnet, IV, 430-40; Collier, IX, 174 *sq*.). Two days later Parliament passed a Bill "for the dissolution of the pretended marriage with Lady Anne of Cleves" (Kaulek, 200-202, 210, 213 *sq*., 217 *sq*., 224; Merriman, II, 268 *sq*.; Burnet, I, 446 *sq*. and IV, 424). For the way the king proceeded to obtain Anne's consent, see Ellis, 2nd series, II, 158; Lemon, *State Papers*, I, 635, 637 *sq*., 643.

[100] Henry gave her an income of £400, the castles at Richmond and Bletchingley, and the first rank after the queen and his daughter Mary, that is above all the ladies in the kingdom. A few months later Marillac wrote "that she shows signs of being not less joyful than usual, and seeks to take all the recreation she can in divers garments and pastimes" (Kaulek, 217, cf. 214). She frequented the court and amused herself there, and several times the rumour was circulated that Henry would take her back again (*ibid.*, pp. 228, 231, 258 *sq*., 270, 285, 288, 353, 367, 368, 372, 374 *sq*., 381-83).

[101] The letter in which he cried "mercy, mercy" to the king is dated June 30th, 1540. Burnet, IV, 424, and Ellis, 2nd series, II, p. 160, who gives the more accurate version. See another letter written from the Tower, *ibid.*, VI, 237; Ellis, 2nd series, II, 160; Merriman, II, 264.

[102] The text of the condemnation is in Burnet, IV, 415-24. They wanted to treat him as though he were not a nobleman, and to hang and quarter him as a traitor. But *"il luy a esté faicte grâce sur la façon de mourir"* (Kaulek, 194, 198, 207. Cf. Cardauns, *Nuntiaturberichte*, V, 352).

favoured heresy at all,[103] although everybody looked upon him then—and time has not altered the verdict—as "the chief author of all the innovations in religion."[104]

Envied by the nobility on account of his rapid rise, hated by all who were attached to the ancient belief and by all whom the destruction of the monasteries or his sanguinary laws had affected, Cromwell witnessed in a single day the collapse of all his former greatness and power. His adversaries vied with one another in repeating the words of the psalm: *Vidi impium superexaltatum et elevatum sicut cedros Libani. Et transivi, et ecce non erat* (Ps. xxxvi). Not one of his partisans had dared to say a word in his defence, save Cranmer, his most faithful follower, who wrote a timid letter to the king (June 14th).[105]

Cranmer, like Cromwell, had been a leader of the advanced party. Was he not destined to share the lot of his friend and ally?

II

In the small hamlet of Aslacton, between Grantham and Nottingham, was born on July 2nd, 1489, Thomas Cranmer, "the first Protestant archbishop of this kingdom," as Strype describes him, "and the greatest instrument, under God, of the happy Reformation of this Church of England: in whose piety, learning, wisdom, conduct and blood, the foundation of it was laid. . . . It is true what the Romanists say in

[103] Burnet, I, 453. Hall, *Chronicle*, 839; Beccadelli, I, 344; Dodd, I, 312.

Friedmann says (*op. cit.*, II, p. 286) that those condemned to death were allowed to speak only "if they promised not to say anything against the king or in opposition to the sentence they had received." So Reginald Pole was dubious about Cromwell's repentance (Quirini, III, 62).

[104] Kaulek, 189. Cf. Strype, *Mem. of Cranmer*, chaps. xx, xxii.

Although Cromwell's religion was chiefly dictated by his politics (Merriman, 286; Kaulek, 190; Pollard, *Cranmer*, 136) yet he favoured the Reformation and it made great strides in the country, thanks to him (Merriman, 306). Henry looked upon him as a heretic (Merriman, 293 *sq.*; Kaulek, 194), and the decree of Parliament condemned him for heresy and for supporting the heretics (Burnet, I, 444 and IV, 415).

[105] He recalled all his past services without exonerating him from the charges hanging over him. "I loved him as my friend, for so I took him to be; I chiefly loved him for the love which I thought I saw him bear ever towards your Grace, singularly above all other. But now, if he be a traitor, I am sorry that ever I loved him or trusted him, and I am very glad that his treason is discovered in time" (H. Jenkyns, *Cranmer's Remains*, I, 298 *sq.*). Five days later he voted for the Bill against Cromwell. Numerous

obloquy of this archbishop, and we Protestants say it to his eternal fame, that he was the first of all the Archbishops of Canterbury that made a defection from the Papal chair; thereby vindicating this crown from a base dependence upon a foreign jurisdiction. . . . Cranmer is the father of the Reformation here in England."[106] Todd adds[107]: "Imperishable is the memory of Cranmer . . . who was the chief promoter and the ablest advocate of the Reformation."

Thomas Cranmer, whose arms show a Chevron and three Cranes,[107a] belonged to a needy family of the gentry. He had four brothers and two sisters, and as he was a younger brother, he was destined, together with his youngest brother Edmund, for the Church. Edmund followed his brother Thomas to Cambridge University, became imbued with the New Learning, took a wife, and afterwards became Archdeacon of Canterbury. He fled to the Continent in Mary Tudor's reign, and died abroad in 1571.

Thomas Cranmer received his early education from "a marvellous severe and cruel schoolmaster." About the year 1504 he entered Jesus College, Cambridge. There he met Thomas Elyot, the friend of Ascham and More and the translator of Isocrates and Plutarch; Thomas Goodrich, afterwards Bishop of Ely and chancellor; and John Bale, the ardent heretical bishop. Cranmer was in his twenty-first year when Erasmus was appointed to the Lady Margaret readership, but no relations were established between them. He was fonder of a young girl, a relation of the landlady of the Dolphin Inn, than of studying Greek, and he made her his wife; but she died a year later.[108]

Cranmer then began to study the Bible, and at the age of thirty-four became a lecturer in divinity. He took Orders in or before 1520,[108a] and four years later Wolsey invited him to

letters are given by Jenkyns (*op. cit.*, I) from Cranmer to Cromwell, with whom he maintained a continuous correspondence (cf. Burnet, I, 442, 443, n.67).

[106] Strype, *Mem. of Cranmer*, chap. 1, letter of dedication to the Archbishop of Canterbury, John Tillotson (†1694); and Preface to the 1st ed.

[107] *Op. cit.*, Preface.

[107a] An heraldic pun on the name: The Marsh of Cranes. Cf. Pollard, *Cranmer*, p. 3; H. Belloc, *Cranmer*, p. 4.

[108] Strype, I, 3 *sq.*

[108a] Pollard, *Cranmer*, p. 20.

become a fellow of the college which the cardinal had founded at Oxford, but he refused. He himself afterwards declared that the new doctrines had already affected him at this period.[109] Outwardly, however, he gave no signs of this, and when, between 1525 and 1528, certain young students, known as the "Germans," who used secretly to meet at the White Horse Inn, were driven out of Cambridge, no suspicion of heterodoxy fell upon Cranmer. At Cambridge, in fact, in this small circle of minds trained in the germanic teachings, the first sparks of the Reformation were struck.[110]

In 1529, the plague known as the sweating sickness broke out. Cranmer took refuge at Waltham, in the house of a relation named Cressy, whose two sons had been entrusted to him for their education. There he unexpectedly met with good fortune. Just at that time the sudden closing of the legatine court had robbed the king of all hope that the question of the divorce could be solved so as to meet with Rome's approval. The king happened to be hunting at Waltham. His secretary, Gardiner, and the Lord High Almoner, Edward Foxe, were lodging at Cressy's house. Both of these men knew Cranmer, for Foxe was the Rector of King's College, Cambridge, and Gardiner had been a professor at Trinity Hall. The royal divorce was discussed by the three friends at table, and Cranmer was asked to state his views. He replied that he had not studied the case at all, but, being a theologian and not a canonist, he could not understand all these delays and the perplexity of the canonists, who would probably contribute but little towards a solution. He maintained that the question should be taken out of their hands and submitted to the great theologians at the universities. Their opinion could soon be obtained without any difficulty, and it would ease the king's conscience. Gardiner and Foxe repeated Cranmer's words to the king a few days later. Henry summoned him to London, lodged him with Anne Boleyn's father, whose chaplain he was, and made him write a book on the divorce. Meanwhile the royal agents

[109] *Cranmer's Works*, II, 327.

[110] Tyndale, Coverdale, Latimer, Barnes, Bilney, Crome and Lambert, all leaders of the Lutheran movement in England, belonged to this circle.

scoured Europe to obtain favourable decisions from the universities.[111]

Cranmer is undoubtedly the "extraordinarily virtuous and wise man," whose counsels Henry said that he was following at that time. When the treatise was finished, manuscript copies of it were given to the heads of Cambridge University, and Cranmer went in person to defend his arguments, and his success was such that in one day he gained the support of five professors and a few others for the royal cause.[112]

From that moment Cranmer's fortune was made; it was only a matter of time.[113] In December, 1530, he went with the Earl of Wiltshire, Anne Boleyn's father, Bishop Stokesley of London, and Edward Lee, the Archbishop of York, on their embassy to the Pope and the emperor.[114] When this mission was ended, he rejoined his friend, the learned Croke, at Venice, so that he might help him to obtain an opinion in favour of the divorce from the Italian doctors. Thence he returned to England via Rome, where he tried to obtain a Brief from the Pope for Henry.[115] As a reward for his services, he was made Archdeacon of Taunton, the town which was then represented in Parliament by his friend, Thomas Cromwell, who was soon to become his ally.

In 1532 he was appointed ambassador to the imperial court in place of Sir Thomas Elyot, and was secretly commissioned to secure an alliance with the Protestant princes of the Smalcaldic League against Charles V, and at the same time to contrive to obtain from the Lutheran doctors an opinion in favour of the divorce.[116] Cranmer met Charles V

[111] See chap. II. Cf. Strype, I, 6 *sq.*; Pollard, Cranmer, 38 *sq.*; Fisher 287 *sq.*

[112] Strype, I, 10. It does not seem to have been printed then. Strype and Pocock (Burnet, IV, 146 *sq.*; VII, 239) believe that the treatise on the divorce in the Cotton MSS. (Vespasien B.V.) in the British Museum signed *Thomas Cantuariensis*, is the original.

[113] At the first audience the king, Strype says (I, p. 7), "having heard him discourse upon the marriage, and well observing the gravity and modesty, as well as learning of the man, resolved to cherish and make much of him."

[114] *L. and P.*, V, 317.

[115] *L. and P.*, IV, 6531; Pocock, *Records of the Reformation*, No. CXXX.

[116] His instructions were dated January 24th, 1532. For his secret negotiations with the Duke of Saxony and the Protestant princes, see Strype, chap. III. Chapuys, who feared that he had been commissioned, in visiting the universities of Germany, to win them over to his own opinion,

at Ratisbon, and followed him to the Diet of Nuremberg. There he became acquainted with the famous Lutheran, Osiander, who dedicated his Concordance of the four Gospels to Cranmer a few years later (1537). Cranmer won his adhesion to the king's cause, although he was boldly proclaiming all the while at the court that he was opposed to the divorce.[117] Osiander's teaching doubtlessly influenced Cranmer's theological ideas; and his niece Margaret had a similar influence upon Cranmer's life, for although he was a priest, Cranmer married her.[118] In September, 1532, he followed Charles to Linz, Vienna, and Villach, and thence to Italy. The emperor, with an army of three hundred thousand men, was preparing to drive out the invading Turks. But in the middle of November, Cranmer received orders, at Mantua, to return to London without delay.[119]

Henry, knowing that he could rely upon his support in the question of the divorce, had chosen him to succeed Warham in the primatial see of Canterbury. In this affair which no longer brooked delay, Henry needed a man of lively and cunning intelligence but no strength of character. "Of

advised the emperor "to keep an eye" on him. Friedmann, *op. cit.*, I, 175, n. 3. Sir Thomas Elyot was no longer *persona grata* with the king and his favourite (*ibid.*).

[117] Osiander declared Henry VIII's marriage with Catherine of Aragon unlawful in a book that was censured. Cranmer also won Cornelius Agrippa over to the king's opinion (Strype, *op. cit.*, chap. III).

Granvelle was surprised that in Rome they considered Cranmer as being in favour of the divorce "*actendu que, durant le temps qu'il estoit résident en ceste court, il blasmoit mirablement que le roy dangleterre, son maistre et ses autres ministres faisoient en laffaire du divorce encontre les dictes Royne et Princesse*" (Friedmann, I, 179, n. 1).

[118] Strype, chap. III. Cf. Friedmann, *op. cit.*, I, p. 177. Th. Kolde, in his article in the *Realencyclopädie* (3rd ed., IV, p. 321), states that his researches in the marriage registers of Nuremberg were all in vain.

[119] Strype, Append. II. Cf. *ibid.*, chap. III. The emperor begged the King of England to give him some assistance against the enemy of Christendom. Cranmer transmitted the request and the details; and William Paget, afterwards Secretary of State, went to see Charles V about it. In a letter dated October 20th, 1532 (Pocock, *Records*, No. CCXCIII) he drew a lurid picture of the havoc wrought by the troops and related the dangers he himself was running.

Cranmer took leave of the emperor on November 18th and landed in England the following January. His successor was the Archdeacon of Ely, Nicholas Hawkyns, whom Cranmer kept constantly informed on the divorce (Strype, Append. Nos. III, VII). On his way from Spain a few weeks later, Charles V went to see Clement VII at Bologna.

ready wit, a good controversialist, and withal elegant, graceful, and insinuating," Cranmer, who was already over forty, was considered to be the man for the situation. He was "timorous by nature, but capable of outbreaks of audacity as timid persons often are: a gentle and lovable man, but lacking in that robust self-confidence needed by one who would take a resolutely independent line; . . . such a character, brought under the direct influence of a powerful will and a magnetic personality, is readily led to see everything as it is desired that he should see it, and at the worst to differ from the master-mind only with submission."[120] In spite of Chapuy's efforts—he had warned the emperor and sent a messenger to Rome—and to the great disgust of those who were defending Catherine, the papal Bulls confirming Cranmer's election were issued in consistory on February 21st, 1533.[121] Charles V had offered no opposition, for Cranmer had lulled his suspicions and won his favour. The new archbishop was consecrated by Longland on March 30th.[122] Twelve days later he took the question of the divorce in hand; and on May 23rd, he declared Catherine's marriage with Henry invalid, and Anne Boleyn's valid. In his *De Unitate Ecclesiae*, Reginald Pole consequently blamed him vehemently for the schism and all its lamentable effects: "Are you not guilty of all these evils?"

Cranmer slavishly ministered to the king's desires, and the royal will became his supreme law,[123] and thenceforward his mission in life was the making and unmaking of the royal marriages.

Indeed Henry had not yet reached the end of his matrimonial difficulties. After moving heaven and earth, besides breaking with Rome, in order to marry Anne Boleyn, he soon

[120] Friedmann, *Anne Boleyn*, I, p. 176. Cf. A. D. Innes, *England under the Tudors* (1905), p. 121.

[121] Friedmann, *op. cit.*, I, p. 179; cf. *ibid.*, 182. Warham had died in August. Normally Henry waited a year or more before appointing anybody to a vacant see. He had managed to overcome the nuncio's distrust and also to flatter the hopes of the Pope (cf. Friedmann, *op. cit.*, I, p. 180; Pollard, *Henry VIII*, 297).

[122] Friedmann, *op. cit.*, I, pp. 179, 182 *sq.* At the consecration the Bishop of Lincoln was assisted by the Bishops of Exeter and of St Asaph, John Woysey (1519–51 and 1553–54) and Standish (1518–35).

[123] "Others condemned Cranmer," says Burnet (I, 331), "as a man that obsequiously followed all the king's appetites . . . whose conscience was governed by the king's pleasure as his supreme law."

grew tired of her. At an early stage he had complained of her arrogance and had hurled harsh and bitter words at her. His whim had been gratified, and Anne's miscarriages only made him more and more bad tempered. He was still without a male heir. Under the king's suspicious eye and the hostile eyes of her adversaries, Anne was soon frightened that her place would be taken by another and she herself lost.[124] She had rejoiced at the death of her rival, Catherine (January 8th, 1536); and speaking of Princess Mary, had observed that if she herself soon had a son, as she hoped, she knew what would happen to the princess. But the son she brought into the world on January 29th, 1536, was still-born.[125] From that moment she was lost. On that very day, although he was unaware of the misfortune which had occurred, Chapuys wrote that it was rumoured in court circles that there would soon be another divorce. As on the first occasion, Henry was again alleging scruples, saying that he had been carried away by passion and that his marriage must of necessity be null because God did not give him a male heir. He had already some time before fallen in love with Jane Seymour, a lady-in-waiting to Anne, as Anne herself had formerly been to Catherine; and the lords, who hated the Boleyn party, favoured these intrigues.[126] Anne was suddenly arrested and sent to the Tower on May 2nd, 1536. She was accused of incestuous relations with her brother, Lord Rochford, and of adultery with Sir Francis Weston, Henry Norris, William Brereton, and Mark Smeton. Her accomplices were all condemned to death for high treason on May 12th. Three days later, a jury of twenty-six peers, presided over by her uncle, the Duke of Norfolk, pronounced a verdict of "guilty" against Anne Boleyn, and on May 19th a queen's head fell on the scaffold for the first time in England.[127]

[124] Cf. Le Laboureur, I, 412; *L. and P.*, V, No. 216, VII, 1279; Friedmann, *op. cit.*, II, pp. 35 *sq.*

[125] Friedmann, *op. cit.*, II, pp. 195 *sq.* Sander, Lewis' trans., pp. 131–32. For Catherine of Aragon's death, see P. Friedmann, *Anne Boleyn*, II, chap. xiv; Sander, Lewis' trans., p. 131; Dodd, I, 311.

[126] *L. and P.*, X, 199. Cf. Friedmann, *op. cit.*, II, pp. 200 *sq.* For the intrigue with Jane Seymour, see *ibid.*, II, 138, 200–202, 239, 252 *sq.*, 282. Her portrait by Holbein is now in Vienna; there is a pencil sketch of her in the museum at Basle, which bears no indication but can be easily recognized.

[127] Cf. Sander, Lewis' trans., pp. 133–34; Friedmann, *op. cit.*, II.

The unfortunate woman had been little more than a plaything in the hands of avaricious relations and unscrupulous politicians, who had looked upon her marriage as well as the new ideas simply as means of securing power. It appears to be evident that she was unjustly condemned. Only one of her accomplices, the musician Smeton, could be induced by torture to make any admission; the others denied the charge even in the face of death. The king had vainly compromised his reputation and his popularity for the sake of Anne, and now he felt only a growing aversion for her. A divorce would seem to prove that the Pope had been right after all, and would have confirmed his sentence. Cromwell's authority was in danger, and in order to establish it more firmly he coldly resolved to sacrifice the woman who had largely made his fortune, and he devised the plan destined to satisfy at once the nation, the emperor, and the king. Both before and after receiving Communion Anne declared on the salvation of her soul that she had never been unfaithful to the king. If the letter "From my doleful prison in the Tower, May 6th [1536]," which has been attributed to her was not written by her, at least it shows the feelings which she did not cease to manifest until the end of her life: "Do not imagine that your poor wife will ever confess a fault which she never even imagined."[128] On the scaffold, where the executioner's sword fascinated her, she did not recant. She was sorry she was ever born and regretted having caused the deaths of innocent persons. "She began to raise her eyes to Heaven and cry mercy to God and to the king for the offence she had done, desiring the people always to pray to God for the king, for he was a good, gentle, gracious, and amiable prince."

pp. 137 *sq.*, and chaps. XVII and XVIII; Froude, chap. XI; Pollard, *Henry VIII*, 342 *sq.*; Fisher, 348 *sq.* See also Major Hume, *The Wives of Henry VIII*, London, 1905; W. Jerrold, *Henry VIII and His Wives*, London, 1933.

The documents relating to Anne Boleyn's attainder, taken from the *Baga de Secretis*, were printed as an appendix to Wriothesley's *Chronicle*, Camden Soc. ed., I. On May 12th Ferdinand's Court heard, not without joy, of Anne Boleyn's arrest, and on June 11th of her execution (Friedensburg, I, 571, 573; Bucholtz, *Geschichte der Regierung Ferdinands I*, Vienna, 1831–38, V, 99).

[128] Burnet, IV, p. 291; Dodd, I, 312. Cf. *L. and P.*, X, 808, n. 2. "That this letter was not really either written or composed by Anne Boleyn the handwriting and the style alike indicate beyond any reasonable doubt"; also Friedmann, I, p. xx, where he refers "to the letter (printed by Burnet)

The "good, gentle, gracious and amiable prince" had spent the previous days in noisy nocturnal carousals upon the Thames, to the disgust of even the queen's enemies. On the morning of the execution he dressed in white, and the following day he became betrothed to Jane Seymour, whom he married ten days later.[129] This was a disappointment for Paul III, who had hoped that on the fall of Anne Boleyn Henry would come back to the unity of the Church by wedding Magdalen, the daughter of Francis I.[130]

Forty-eight hours before the death of Anne Boleyn, Cranmer, who had at first interceded for her,[131] declared, with the support of an ecclesiastical court, that the marraige which three years previously he had solemnly pronounced as valid was now null and void. His judicial reasons—which had been carefully kept secret—for the annulment were Anne's previous engagement to Percy, Earl of Nothumberland, an engagement which the latter denied upon oath, or the impediment of affinity resulting from the king's relations with Anne Boleyn's sister. Clement VII had already dispensed from this impediment (1528), but as in the meantime the Church of England had repudiated papal authority, the canonical impediment still stood.[132] Cranmer's decision was approved

which Anne Boleyn was formerly supposed to have written from her prison in the Tower, but which is now generally admitted to be a forgery." See French ed., pp. 630-35. The best edition of Francis Hargrave's *State Trials* is the fourth, with two new alphabetical tables and new Preface: *Complete Collection of State Trials and Proceedings for High Treason, and other Crimes and Misdemeanours, from 1388 to 1776,* 11 vols., 1776-81.

[129] Friedmann II, 282, 283 and n. 1, 302, n. 3; Ellis, 1st series, II, 66. For the people's judgment of the king on this occasion, see Burnet, I, 206.

[130] Cf. Collier, IV, 333; Burnet, I, 337 *sq.*; Friedmann II, 302-307.

[131] "I am in such a perplexity that my mind is clean amazed; for I never had better opinion in woman than I had in her; which maketh me to think that she should not be culpable." Cranmer's *Works,* Parker Soc. II, 324; Jenkyn's *Cranmer's Remains,* I, 163; Strype, *op. cit.,* Append. XVIII; Burnet, I, 320. Cf. Friedmann II, 272. Cranmer saw Anne Boleyn on May 16th in order to get from her some proof for her divorce. He must have made her think her life would be spared because that same day she spoke of retiring to Antwerp (Kingston to Cromwell, May 16th, 1536; Ellis, 1st series, II, 63; cf. Friedmann, *op. cit.,* II, pp. 288 *sq.*).

[132] Chapuys gives this last reason (*L. and P.,* XI, 41) and it is also the one that Lingard puts forward (*History of England,* IV, Append. Note K). Friedmann (*op. cit.,* II, Append. E; cf. pp. 288 *sq.*) maintains this reason against Froude (*op. cit.,* chaps. II, XI and Append.); and nowadays it is admitted to be the most probable one. Cf. Pollard, *Cranmer,* 99 *sq., Henry VIII,* 344 *sq.;* Fisher, 388. Cf. Strype, chap. XII, I, p. 101 and n. Z.

by Convocation, and Parliament passed a law confirming it on July 1st, 1536. Elizabeth, like Mary, was illegitimate.[133]

On the very day Anne Boleyn was beheaded, Cranmer granted the king a dispensation from consanguinity so that he might marry Jane Seymour, who was a descendant of Edward III.[134] To the king's great joy, a son was born on October 12th, 1537, the future Edward VI, and Cranmer stood as godfather to the child. Nine days later the queen died. According to Lord Herbert, she was the most reserved, the most unassuming, and the most beautiful of all the wives of Henry.[135] Had she lived, she might possibly have saved Henry from the tragi-comedy of Anne of Cleves and the tragedy of Catherine Howard.

As he was married for political motives to a German princess who displeased him (January 6th, 1540), Henry took advantage of Cromwell's fall to have that union declared null. And Cranmer, who had blessed the union and urged it upon the king in order to advance the Reformation in England, was the first to vote for its annulment (July 9th, 1540).[136]

---

[133] Wilkins, *Concilia*, III, 804. *Statutes of the realm*, 28 Henry VIII, cap. 7.

People have wondered why Henry VIII was not satisfied with Anne Boleyn's execution and why he made Cranmer and Parliament give a decision which, together with that of 1533, made his two daughters illegitimate. It is believed that this was done to satisfy public opinion which, even among the Lutherans, held Anne Boleyn's marriage to be illegal, or so as to avoid the hateful necessity of signing his own wife's death warrant, or else to assure the succession of his illegitimate son, the Duke of Richmond (†July 22nd, 1536), to the detriment of Mary and Elizabeth (cf. Pollard, *Cranmer*, 99; Fisher, 388; Friedmann, *op. cit.*, II, p. 287).

[134] *L. and P.*, X, 915, 926, 933, 1000. She was the daughter of Sir John Seymour of Wolf Hall, Wiltshire, and a descendant of Edward III on her mother's side; and Cranmer dispensed from the third and fourth degrees of consanguinity. Her brother, Edward Seymour, had been growing more and more in favour with the king for several years, and became Protector in Edward VI's reign. For Jane Seymour, see Agnes Strickland, *Lives of the Queens of England*, 1-31. Calvin wrote to Jane Seymour (see *J. Calvini opera*, ed. Baum, Cunitz, Reuss, letter No. 1207).

[135] The following witticism was engraved upon her tomb at Windsor, by way of epitaph:

> *Phoenix Jana jacet nato Phoenice; dolendum est,*
> *Soecula Phoenices nulla tulisse duos.*

For Edward's birth and the queen's death, see P. Heylvn, *Ecclesia restaurata*, ed. 1849, I, 12 *sq*. The precise date of her death is controverted (cf. Davey, *Lady Jane Grey*, London, 1909, p. 14, n.).

[136] This time Henry pleaded lack of intention: he had not really

Nineteen days after the annulment of his marriage by Convocation, Henry VIII embarked on another matrimonial adventure. At Oatlands without any solemnity, he married the Duke of Norfolk's niece, "a lady of great beauty," Catherine Howard,[137] who was his junior by thirty-one years. This time all was happiness. The king expressed his joy and full satisfaction to everybody.[138] On All Saints' Day, 1540, he ordered his chaplain, the Bishop of Lincoln, to sing the *Te Deum* in thanksgiving for the very pleasant life the queen had given him and would certainly continue to give him for many more years to come. Twenty-four hours later, Cranmer informed the king of Catherine Howard's infidelity: she had misconducted herself before her marriage. The Archbishop received orders to obtain a confession from the queen. It was complete, and a commission of inquiry was held—which historians must not trust—which tried to prove that the queen had been unfaithful after her marriage.[139] For several days

wished to marry Anne of Cleves, but exterior circumstances, the fear of a combined attack by Charles V and Francis I, had driven him to do so. He even pretended that the marriage had not been consummated (*State Papers*, I, 635). After Catherine Howard's execution, the Duke of Cleves tried to get Henry to marry his sister again (Jenkyns, *op. cit.*, I, 311 *sq.*). Gardiner was the one who sought reasons for an annulment and laid them before Convocation (Wilkins, *Concilia*, III, p. 851), but Cranmer, as Primate, was the first to give a decision (cf. Strype, *Eccles. Memorials*, I, Part 2, pp. 452 *sq.*).

Anne of Cleves was buried at Westminster (1558). For details concerning her, see Bautewerk, *Anna von Cleves* (1515–57), in the *Zeitschrift des Bergischen Geschichtsvereins*, IV, 337–413; Agnes Strickland, III, 31–98. The letter she wrote to the king about her divorce may be seen in Miss Everett Wood's *Letters of royal and illustrious Ladies of Great Britain*, 1846, III, 160 (cf. Anne of Cleves' *Oraison et remonstrance*, published in France in 1545 and 1552).

[137] Marillac, who announced the marriage on July 21st (Kaulek, 202; cf. 213), gives a portrait of Catherine in his letters of September 3rd and November 22nd (*ibid.*, 218). Henry had been thinking of this marriage for some time (L. Cardauns, *Nuntiaturberichte*, 344, 352). There is a portrait of Catherine Howard, by Holbein, in Windsor Castle and another in the possession of the Duke of Buccleuch. Cf. P. Ganz, *Gemälde des Meisters Hans Holbein d j.*, 148, 149. Gardiner had been "*ung des princippaulx aucteurs de ce dernier mariaige où s'en est ensuivye la ruyne du feu Cramvel*" (Marillac to Francis I, November 16th, 1540, Kaulek, 242). Catherine and the king frequently met under his roof (*Original Letters*, Parker Soc., I, 202; cf. *L. and P.*, XV, 613).

[138] "*De laquelle ce roy est tant amoureux qu'il ne sçait par quelque bon traitement qu'il soit luy faire assez grande démonstration de l'affection qui luy porte, qui excède, par ce qu'on veoit, toutes les caresses qu'il a faict aux aultres*" (Marillac to Montmorency, September 3rd, 1540, Kaulek, 218).

[139] Nicolas, *Proceedings of the Privy Council*, VII, p. 352; Kaulek, pp. 338,

Henry refused to admit the truth. He then gave way to such tempers that it was feared "his mind was impaired": now "he would demand a sword, saying that he would kill her whom he had loved so much," now "he would suddenly ask for horses, without saying whither he intended to go," now he would call the queen a "nasty, vile" woman, and then bursting into sobs "regret his misfortune in meeting such ill-conditioned women and would throw all the blame for his latest mishap on the members of his Council."[140] The entire Norfolk family was in danger. The duke himself escaped by denouncing his niece's repeated breaches of faith, by taking a most active part in the trial, and by approving the proceedings against his own mother, for "such is the custom in this country, that it is right for those who are related by blood to maintain that attitude and to go against their nature, in order that they may thus show they have no part in their relations' crimes." But his mother, the dowager Duchess of Norfolk; his brother, William Howard; his sister, the Countess of Bridgewater; and his sister-in-law were all condemned to perpetual imprisonment and to have their property confiscated because they had been silent on the queen's conduct. Parliament once again made use of the very elastic law on treason, and construing a moral lapse into a crime of high treason brought in a Bill of Attainder against Catherine Howard (January 16th, 1542) who was the second of Henry's wives to be beheaded. "Transported by night to an old convent of nuns which used to be called Syon," she remained there until two days before her death. When she was taken to the Tower, a fit of despair caused a certain hesitation about the day of her execution: "she cries, shrieks, and frets in a wretched mannner without interruption." They allowed her leisure "and convenience to make up her mind and to think about her conscience" and then, on February 13th, "at nine o'clock in the morning,"

352-57, 363-67; L. and P., XVII, Nos. 19, 28, 197. See article in Dict. of Nat. Biog., where it is stated "the evidence of adultery was vainly sought."

[140] Marillac to Francis I, December 7th, 1541. Kaulek, 370. Norfolk himself told Marillac (ibid., 356) of "the great disappointment, regret and sorrow of his master, who loved her with such affection that he cannot speak of her without weeping bitterly." In order to show his great grief at "l'ennuy qu'en prent le roy d'Angleterre, mon bon frère," Francis I sent a gentleman with his condolences to Henry (ibid., 369 sq., 378).

this nineteen-year-old queen was dragged to the scaffold. She was "so weak she could scarcely speak." She turned, however, towards the people "admitting in a few words that she had deserved not one death, but a hundred . . . because she had so unfortunately offended the king her lord, who had treated her so graciously." Then in the presence of the Dukes of Norfolk and Surrey, her uncle and her first cousin respectively, "her head was struck off with an axe, according to the custom of the country." Lady Rochford, whose husband had been beheaded because of Anne Boleyn, herself suffered a similar fate on account of Catherine Howard. Thus ended "this piteous tragedy."[141]

After prudently waiting for a year and a half, Henry at length came safely into harbour by taking unto himself a sixth wife, Katherine Parr. She had been twice widowed, and although twenty years younger than Henry, was quite matronly and stout and "far from being as beautiful as Anne of Cleves," according to the imperial ambassador. Although her second husband, Lord Latimer, had been one of the leaders of the Pilgrimage of Grace, yet she was suspected, and not without reason, of being in sympathy with the new ideas.[142] Reserved, always ready to forestall her royal husband's fits of temper or to alleviate his premature infirmities, gentle and disciplined in mind, very fond of religion and of books, she had withal an influence over the king which she discreetly used to help those who favoured the New Learning. The education of Edward and Elizabeth bore her stamp; and Cranmer found an ally in Katherine Parr. Yet it was not he who married her, but, by one of fate's pranks, that office was performed by the most determined adversary of the innovators, Stephen Gardiner.

[141] Marillac to Francis I, February 11th and 13th, 1542; Kaulek, 366, 371, 383, 388 *sq.*; see French ed., 640 *sq.* Agnes Strickland, III, 98-175 and Madox Hueffer's notable psychological novel, *The Fifth Queen*, London, 1906, may be read for details of Catherine Howard.

[142] According to Foxe (553-61) Katherine Parr was nearly sent to the Tower in 1545 (cf. J. Gairdner, *History*, 227; Fisher, 477). This rumour was spread in Rome in July 1546 (Friedensburg, *Nuntiaturberichte*, IX, 107, n. 1). J. Foxe (V, 561) accuses Gardiner and the other Henricians of this "pestiferous purpose against the queen." See Agnes Strickland, III, 175-301; J. Gairdner, *Lollardy*, II, 357-467, chap. III, Bk. IV: "Katherine Parr and the new learning."

Cranmer was one of the warmest partisans of the royal supremacy. He himself related how, when he was a professor at Cambridge, he secretly prayed for the abolition of the papal power within the realm.[143] Four days before his consecration Cranmer with his own hand wrote a protest, in which he declared that the oath of obedience to the Pope which he had to take was a mere formality and that it would still leave him free to do as he pleased so far as reforming the religion and government of the Church of England was concerned: he declared that he wished to hold his archbishopric from none but the king.[144] When he had pronounced sentence against Catherine of Aragon, he appealed from the Pope to a Council, for "I stand in dread lest our holy father the Pope do intend to make some manner of prejudicial process against me and my church."[145] Shortly afterwards he drew up the form of oath for the renunciation of papal authority which every bishop had to take,[146] and composed the litanies in English, with the clause: "From the tyranny of the Bishop of Rome and all his detestable enormities, Lord deliver us."[147] He went

[143] *Cranmer's Works*, Parker Soc. ed., II, p. 327.

[144] Original in Latin. Wilkins, *Concilia*, III, 757. Strype, Appends. V, VI, VII; cf. chap. IV. Collier, IX, 101. Dodd, I, 312. At the time of his trial he corroborated *viva voce* these documents preserved in his archiepiscopal registers. Foxe, VIII, 55. Cf. Cranmer's letter to Mary Tudor, September, 1555, in Jenkyns, I, 369 and Strype, *Mem. of Cranmer*, Append. LXXXVIII.

[145] See Strype (*Mem. of Cranmer*, chap. v) who gives Cranmer's letter (November 27th, 1533; also in *Cranmer's Works*, II, 268) to Bonner, whom Henry VIII had instructed, at the time of the meeting between Clement VII and Francis I at Marseilles, to appeal to the council that was to be summoned. Cranmer knew what his intervention in a case pending at Rome would lead to. A Bull in September, 1533, deprived him of his see and excommunicated him (*L. and P.*, VII, 1104).

[146] As regards the actual taking of the oath, Cranmer advocated moderation, being opposed to the violent methods of Cromwell and of the king. He intervened in favour of Fisher and More, and wanted the others to be satisfied with their readiness to take the oath; he would have liked to save them (Strype, chap. VI) as well as the Carthusians Webster and Reynolds (Cox, *Remains of Cranmer*, Letter No. 303).

[147] These litanies are largely an adaptation of the Latin litanies of the saints. They are in the Primer of 1545, the English prayer book drawn up by Cranmer himself to take the place of the old *Hours* in individual use. These English *Hours* existed long before the Reformation. (Dixon, II, p. 360, quotes eight different books existing before 1460.) See H. Littlehales, *The prymer in English about A.D. 1400*, with introduction and notes, 2 vols., 1891–92. Three of these books appeared in Henry VIII's time: The "Goodly Prymer," 1535; the "Manual of Prayers," 1539; and the "King

through his diocese preaching the schism and denouncing to the king all who contradicted it.[148] In order to refute the Pope, he made use of his knowledge of Canon Law and asserted in Parliament, in 1533, that "both by the word of God, and consent of the primitive Church, this usurped power of the pope is a mere tyranny, and directly against the law of God; and that the power of emperors and kings is the highest power here upon earth, unto which bishops, priests, popes and cardinals ought to submit themselves." The issue of this declaration was the abolition of that foreign papal power, and the expulsion of it out of this realm by the full consent of Parliament.[149]

The suppression of papal jurisdiction meant the increase of Cranmer's own jurisdiction for a while. The Archbishop of Canterbury's court became the supreme court for ecclesiastical causes in England.[150] Appeals from all the other dioceses were addressed to Canterbury. The bishops of the conservative or moderate party were keen on opposing all authority of the suspect primate which exceeded their own. They blamed him for "calling of poor men from the furthest parts of the realm to London for an half-penny candle, or for a little opprobrious word, as was declared and proved plainly in this Parliament." They added that his Court of Audience, which was a delegation of papal power, no longer had any foundation and was contrary to the vicegerent's rights. They argued that if the

---

Henry's Prymer," 1545 (cf. *Three Primers put forth in the reign of Henry VIII*, Oxford, 1848).—The deprecation "From the Tyranny of the Bishop of Rome . . ." was suppressed in the 1559 edition; the invocations to the Blessed Virgin, the Angels and the Patriarchs had been suppressed in the first Book of Common Prayer (1549). The remainder has not been changed. And Cranmer's English Litanies still retain the charm of their beautiful English and quaint wording of the sixteenth century for those who frequent Anglican churches (cf. Strype, chap. xxiv; Dixon, II, 351; Gairdner "Henry VIII's Litanies," in Vol. XXIII (1908) of the *English Hist. Review*, p. 530, and *History*, 230 and n. 1; Pollard, *Cranmer*, 172 *sq*.; Belloc, *Cranmer*). In the nineteenth century the Rev. T. Mayo published the English Litanies and their different chants: *Book of the Litany, with various musical notations*, Frome-Selwood, 1874.

[148] Strype, *op. cit.*, chap. viii; H. Jenkyns, *Cranmer's Remains*, I, 167 *sq*., 183.

[149] Strype, *op. cit.*, chap. v. For his study of Canon Law so that he might make use of it against the Holy See, see French ed., pp. 643 *sq*.

[150] The Archbishop had two courts: the Court of Arches and the Court of Audience.

king wished to maintain it, he ought to transfer it to somebody else so as to show that the authority of that court came from himself and not from Rome.[151]   Although Henry upheld Cranmer and the latter's claims against his adversaries, yet in the end the primate's judicial powers were passed to the royal chancery.[152]   Neither was he more successful in retaining the title of *legatus natus* for any length of time.   This did not, however, prevent him from imitating the Pope, in 1544, by sending the pallium to the Archbishop of York.[153]

Cranmer shared with Cromwell the position of leader of the advanced or reforming party, but less openly and more slyly than his friend.   "The archbishop was gradually leaning towards Lutheran doctrine, and Cromwell believed in a Lutheran policy if not in the Lutheran creed."[154]

During the years 1533 and 1534 he made a general visitation of the dioceses belonging to his metropolitan see, in order to make sure that papal authority had been abolished and that the new doctrines were being developed.   Two bishops of the moderate party, Gardiner and Stokesley, tried to oppose him in their own dioceses.   They contended that the titles *totius Angliae primas* and *Apostolicae sedi legatus*, in virtue of which Cranmer brought them under his jurisdiction, were "against the crown of our sovereign, his regality, statutes, or customs of his realm."[155]   Henry decided against them.

By a pastoral letter of 1534, the archbishop ordered all priests to maintain the most absolute silence with regard to Masses for the dead, the veneration of the saints and of their images, and ecclesiastical celibacy.   He hoped that there would be soon nothing left of those practices and observances, and he urged Henry to suppress them.   Finding the faithful

---

[151] *A reply to the archbishop against his Court of Audience*, Strype, *op. cit.*, Append. XVII.   Cf. *ibid.*, chap. x.   This attack, which came from the Lower House of Convocation, was inspired by Gardiner.

[152] Cf. Pollard, *Cranmer*, p. 96; MacColl, *The Reformation Settlement*, 10th ed., p. 567.   Ecclesiastical dispensations, which hitherto had come from Rome, were still being granted by the Archbishops of Canterbury under the Tudors and the Stuarts, but in the king's name (cf. E. F. Churchill's article in the *Eng. Hist. Review* for July 1919).

[153] Cf. Mason, *Cranmer*, London, 1896, 53; Pollard, *Cranmer*, 74.   This title of *legatus natus* existed from the twelfth century (cf. Dixon, I, 239 *sq.*).

[154] *An English Garner—Tudor Tracts 1532–1588*.   With an introduction by A. F. Pollard (1903), p. xv.

[155] Strype, *op. cit.*, chap. VIII and Append. XV; *L. and P.*, V, 850.

and the clergy in his diocese "very obstinately given to observe
and keep with solemnity the holidays lately abrogated," he
reprimanded the former and threatened the latter with "pain
of deprivation of their benefices."[155a] In February, 1536, he
preached at St Paul's against the Pope, purgatory, and
indulgences. In that same year the Pilgrimage of Grace
denounced him to the king as a heretic, and demanded that he
should be either surrendered or else banished from the
realm.[156] Both in Parliament and in Convocation he offered
the strongest opposition to the passing of the Six Articles (1539)
which betokened a Catholic reaction. They were passed in
spite of Cranmer and his followers. "The side of the favourers
of the gospel at this time was the weaker," Strype sorrowfully
observes, "the king was inclining more to the other party."[157]
Shortly before Cromwell fell, Cranmer was "appointed
preacher and reader" at St Paul's, and there he "put forward
the contrary" of what Bishop Gardiner, the leader of the
orthodox party, had "preached there in Lent last."[158] After
Cromwell had disappeared, he tried to restrict the veneration
of the saints, and of their relics, and their festivals, pretending
thus to avoid "childish superstitions."[159] If he alone had
been responsible, no doubt all the shrines in the kingdom
would have suffered the fate of St Thomas à Becket's in his
cathedral church at Canterbury. In the very month in which
Henry VIII died, he tried to make him abolish certain customs or ceremonies connected with the departed and with
the veneration of the cross. If the rites of the Anglican Church

---

[155a] H. Jenkyns, *Cranmer's Remains*, I, 201.

[156] *L. and P.*, XI, 786, 1182. The decree of 1535 on images and purgatory
is attributed to him (cf. Dixon, I, 257). Neither Cranmer nor his reforming
tendencies were ever popular, even in London (cf. Pollard, *Cranmer*, 136;
Jenkyns, *Cranmer's Remains*, I, 206–222).

[157] See chap. VIII; Strype, *op. cit.*, chap. XIX; Pollard, *Cranmer*, 128 *sq.*;
Fisher, 435.

[158] Marillac to Montmorency, June 1st, 1540, Kaulek, 188.

[159] In July, 1541, he drew up a regulation suppressing certain feasts of
saints, and in the following October he was authorized to take away relics
and reliquaries "superstitiously venerated," and to forbid the lighting of
candles anywhere "but only to the blessed sacrament of the altar" (cf.
Strype, *op. cit.*, chap. XXIII; *L. and P.*, 1540–41, Nos. 78, 1022, 1027, 1062).
He had long and frequent discussions with the king, who was greatly in
favour of the veneration of statues and of the Cross, according to Strype
(*ibid.*, chap. XXX), and he endeavoured to modify his ideas.

were not notably changed at that period, it was not because Cranmer had not formed plans for changing them.[160]

He and Cromwell prevailed upon Convocation and then upon the king to publish an English version of the Bible and to have it circulated throughout the country. His injunctions for the diocese of Hereford in 1538, whilst that see was vacant, commanded all churchmen to study a chapter a day and to exhort their parishioners to read it but to refrain from futile discussions.[161] The editions of 1540 and 1541 bore his name: "Cranmer's Bible." He wrote the preface for them,[162] and in it recognized that, although the custom of reading the Scriptures had been lost, yet it had existed for centuries in England, as many translations in the vernacular testified. Thomas More had asserted that long before Wiclif's time many virtuous and learned men had translated the whole of the Bible into English and that a number of honest folk read it devoutly, seriously, and with respect.[163] In 1542, Convocation declared that the new translation could be no longer tolerated without scandal, so it had to be corrected, and the task of revising the text was entrusted to a committee over which Gardiner and Tunstall presided. But three weeks later Cranmer produced a message from the king ordering the universities to undertake the revision. Convocation made a vain protest and nothing

[160] Strype, *Mem. of Cranmer*, chap. xxx; Jenkyns, I, 318–22; J. Gairdner, *History*, p. 238, and French ed. of this book, p. 645.

[161] Cf. Burnet, IV, 392.

[162] H. J. Todd gives this preface in an Appendix to Vol. I of his *Life of Archbishop Cranmer*, 1831. The title of the 1539 Bible was: "The Bible in Englyshe, that is to say, the content of all the holy scrypture both of ye olde and newe testament, truly translated after the veryte of the Hebrue and Greke textes, by ye dylygent studye of dyverse excellent learned men expert in the forsayde tonges.—Prynted by Richard Grafton and Edward Whitechurch. Cum privilegio ad imprimendum solum. 1539."

[163] The deformed translation of the Bible by Wiclif and his followers was forbidden by the provincial Council of Oxford, in 1408, as well as any new unauthorized translation (Wilkins, III, 317). Later all the Protestant Bibles "which certain sons of iniquity, ministers of the Lutheran faction," were endeavouring to spread (Archbishop of York's Mandate, November 3rd, 1526, *The Register of Charles Bothe bishop of Hereford*, ed. by A. T. Bannister, 1921, p. 187) were seized in order to be destroyed. But this did not affect either the versions prior to Wiclif's or those which might be approved. And Blunt (*op. cit.*, I, chap. x) has fully proved how greatly mistaken are those who believe that the clergy and the laity had no knowledge of the Scriptures before the Reformation. See French ed. of this book, pp. 611 *sq.*

was asked of the universities, so that Cranmer's text remained as it was.[164]

Through Cromwell the archbishop was able to bestow mitres upon many of his friends who were, as he knew, partisans of the New Learning: Latimer of Worcester, Shaxton of Salisbury, Foxe of Hereford, Hilsey of Rochester, Barlow of St Davids, and Goodrich of Ely. In the debates which preceded the various Confessions of Faith, Cranmer and his followers always voted in a Lutheran sense[165]; and it was not their fault that England did not become Protestant at an earlier date.

Cranmer no longer believed in transubstantiation, yet he admitted the Real Presence with Luther, i.e. the concomitance of the Body of Christ and the bread. "There are strong reasons," says Jenkyns, "for believing that for some portion at least of Henry VIII's reign, his tenets on the Eucharist were Lutheran."[166] In the last year of the reign he drew up "a form for the alteration of the Mass into a Communion service."[167] He was anxious to abolish ecclesiastical celibacy, and "his greatest distress," says Sander,[167a] "was that he could not show abroad as his wife the woman who was living with him. The king would not allow him to do so. He must therefore keep her secretly in his house. When he went abroad he was compelled to carry her from place to place hidden from

[164] Cf. Blunt, I, 518 sq.; Pollard, Cranmer, pp. 166 sq. Before the royal message was received the translation of the New Testament had been divided amongst fifteen bishops, whose names are given by Fuller from the Convocation registers now destroyed (Fuller, ed. 1845, III, 198); and the examination of the Old and New Testaments was entrusted to two committees of bishops and theologians, some of whom afterwards revised the 1549 Prayer Book.

[165] Cf. Dixon, I, 412. Cranmer helped Latimer when poverty befell him (ibid., II, 139 sq.). The Parker Society published, between 1844 and 1845, Latimer's Sermons and Remains.

[166] Jenkyns, I, p. lxxiv sq. See Cranmer's letter, in 1537, to Joachim von Watt (†1551), a disciple of Zwingli, on the Eucharistic controversy amongst the Swiss, in Jenkyns, I, 193 sq., and Strype, op. cit., Append. XXV, and also chap. xvii in the same work.

In 1538 he was ordered by Henry to refute John Lambert's arguments against the Real Presence. Referring to this occasion at his trial under Mary Tudor, he said, "I maintained then the papists' doctrine" (Strype, op. cit., I, 144, n.).

[167] Strype, op. cit., chap. xxx. Cf. G. Constant's article: "Transformation du culte anglican sous Édouard VI," Revue d'histoire ecclésiastique, XII, 46 sq.

[167a] Lewis' trans., p. 181.

sight in a chest." Harpsfield also tells the same story. Cranmer protected those who preached against the letter and the spirit of the Six Articles in Kent, personally opposed the voting of this law both in Parliament and in Convocation, and at the king's request set forth in writing the reasons for his opposition. He just escaped paying dearly for what he wrote. His secretary, Morice, was carrying the manuscript when it fell into the Thames. It was recovered by one of the archbishop's adversaries, and would have been handed over to one of the Henricians on the council as a proof that Cranmer was a heretic, if Cromwell, warned by Morice, had not had it restored to its owner.[168]

In the last years of the reign he prepared his Book of Homilies, the first Book of Common Prayer, and his revision of the canonical laws. All these works were definitely Lutheran in tone. They were afterwards published in Edward VI's reign, and brought the Reformation spirit into England. The Book of Homilies was written about 1539, submitted to Convocation in 1543, but not approved by that assembly, and finally appeared in July 1547. It contained twelve homilies, three of which are printed in *Cranmer's Works* and deal with salvation, faith, and good works. Gardiner attacked them as innovations, but Bucer eulogized them later.[169] The two projects for religious services were to serve as a foundation for the first Book of Common Prayer (1549). The influence of the German liturgy is easily recognizable therein, especially that of Bugenhagen's *Ordinatio ecclesiastica* (1535), which was followed in Denmark, Norway, Schleswig-Holstein, and Pomerania. The copy which the archbishop probably consulted was a gift to Henry VIII from Bugenhagen and is now in the British Museum.[170]

[168] Foxe (*Acts and Monuments*, V, 388-91), whose account of "How the Lord Cromwell helped Archbishop Cranmer's secretary" has come down to us (quoted by Burnet, I, 424, reprinted by Ed. Arber in *An English Garner*, 1896, VIII, 25-31, and by Pollard in his *Tudor Tracts*, 1903, 29-35; see also Merriman, I, 255), tells how during a bear-baiting the bear broke loose from the dogs, dashed into the river and upset Morice's wherry when he was on his way to the court to deliver the famous manuscript into the king's hands. The royal request would not have saved Cranmer any more than Henry's authorization had protected Wolsey from *Praemunire*. Cranmer had argued for three days in Parliament against the Six Articles.

[169] Cf. Dixon, II, 426; Pollard, *Cranmer*, 166, 194 *sq.*

[170] J. Wickham Legg, who wrote *The second recension of the Quignon*

The *Reformatio legum ecclesiasticarum*, which was revised by
Peter Martyr in the following reign, was meant to give the
country church laws from which all traces of Roman authority
had been banished.[171]

When Cromwell fell, Cranmer himself was in great danger,
and abroad it was rumoured that he had been executed.[171a]
His friends, Bishops Shaxton and Latimer, were arrested and
condemned as heretics, and he himself was furiously attacked
by the moderate party.[172]　Henry, however, protected him.
He was thrice accused of heresy.　The first charge was brought
against him by the canons of his own cathedral, the justices

breviary, 2 vols., in 1905 and 1912, has made a special study of *Cranmer's
liturgical Products* (London, 1915) from the MS. in the British Museum, the
preface of which was previously published by Gasquet and Bishop
(*Edward VI and the Book of Common Prayer*, London, 1890, pp. 356-71)
after comparing it with those of Cardinal Quiñones. Wickham Legg
compared Cranmer's first project with various Lutheran services (pp. xxviii
sq.) given by W. Löhe (*Agende für christliche Gemeinden des lutherischen
Bekenntnisses*), and came to the conclusion that Bugenhagen's conformed
most to Cranmer's ideas (p. xxxiv). He then gives the text of the manuscript, with an appendix and notes. Wickham Legg's two works constitute
Volumes XXXV and L of the Henry Bradshaw Society's publications.
This society has been editing rare liturgical texts since 1890.

[171] This *Reformatio*, for which Cranmer took numerous extracts from
the *Corpus juris canonici* (Strype, *Mem. of Cranmer*, ed. 1848-54, III, pp. 741-
872; cf. chap. xxx), was not published till 1571, by Archbishop Parker.
It was reprinted in 1640 and Cardwell brought out an edition of it in 1850
which agreed with that of April, 1571 and was compared with the MS.
which Cranmer had written *circa* 1551 [Harleian MS. 426, British Museum]:
The Reformation of the Ecclesiastical Laws. The 1640 edition contains additions
by William Haddon and a preface by John Foxe: *Reformatio Legum ecclesiasticarum, ex authoritate primum Henrici 8 inchoata, deinde per regem Eduardum 6
provecta, adauctaque in hunc modum, atque nunc ad pleniorem ipsarum reformationem
in lucem oedita. Londini, impensis L. Sadler.* It was in 1534, 1536 and 1544 that
Parliament had charged the king to form a commission of ecclesiastics
and laymen in equal numbers, for the revision of the canonical laws, but
it was never formed in Henry VIII's time (cf. J. Gairdner, *History*, pp. 229
sq., 239; Pollard, *Cranmer*, pp. 165 *sq.*, 214).

[171a] Jenkyns, I, 300 and n. *n*.

[172] Cf. Dixon, II, 344 *sq.* Latimer had been deprived of his see in 1539
for not having subscribed "to what the others had decreed in conformity
with the ecclesiastical constitutions," i.e. to the Six Articles. Eleven days
before Cromwell fell Marillac wrote that Latimer "*doibt au premier jour estre de
nouveau faict evesque*" (Kaulek, p. 188). But when Cromwell had been
arrested Latimer remained six years in compulsory retirement and was condemned to prison in 1546. He was released in Edward VI's reign, on
January 1st, 1548, and his voice, which had been silent so long, was again
heard at St Paul's Cross. As for the Bishop of Salisbury, N. Shaxton, he
was condemned as a Zwinglian in June, 1546, but recanted and vainly
tried to persuade Anne Askew to follow his example.

of the peace, and the orthodox clergy of his diocese.[173]   "O my chaplain," said the king jokingly to him, "now I know who is the greatest heretic in Kent"; and he placed the document in the hands of the archbishop, who himself nominated the examiners and the judges. Those who had accused him made honourable amends and begged his pardon.[174]   Dr. London, warden of New College, Oxford; and a canon of Windsor, who had instigated the "plot," died miserable deaths in prison; and Gardiner's nephew was executed for copying out the articles against Cranmer, on the plea that he had denied the royal supremacy. On the second occasion, Sir John Gostwick, the parliamentary representative for Bedfordshire, but probably speaking for the adversaries of the archbishop since he himself had not heard one of his sermons, complained in Parliament, in 1545, of the doctrine preached by Cranmer. Henry flew into a rage and was then supposed to have delivered the famous sermon preserved by Hall and Lord Herbert[175]: "*Charity is gentle, charity is not envious, charity is not proud* (1 Cor. xiii, 4). . . . Behold, then, what love and charity is amongst you, when one calleth another heretic and anabaptist, and he called him again papist, hypocrite and Pharisee? Be these tokens of Charity amongst you? Are these signs of fraternal love amongst you?" Gostwick recanted; and Cranmer obtained the king's pardon for him, but not without difficulty.[176]   The third accusation against Cranmer has been dramatized by Shakespeare in Henry VIII (Act V, Sc. 1 and 2): Cranmer was summoned to appear before the council and kept waiting half an hour amongst the lackeys in the lobby

[173] Known as the "Prebendaries' Plot" and detailed at length by Strype (*Mem. of Cranmer*, chaps. XXVI and XXVII).

[174] Strype (*op. cit.*, Append. XXXIII) gives the recantations and letters of submission of Dr. Willoughby, a Kentish incumbent and king's chaplain; of William Gardiner and John Milles, Canons of Canterbury; and of the preacher, Edmund Shether, who had been one of the most zealous adversaries of the archbishop. William Gardiner must not be confused with Germain Gardiner, the Bishop of Winchester's nephew and secretary.

[175] Pollard reproduced part of it in his *Henry VIII*, pp. 419 *sq.* The whole of it is in Dodd, *op. cit.*, ed. 1737, I, pp. 315 *sq.*, and a summary in Collier, V, 149 *sq.* J. Gairdner (*History*, 232) believes the discourse was delivered on this occasion.

[176] See Strype (*op. cit.*, chap. XXVIII) who follows Foxe in taking Morice's account.

outside the council chamber. The council had decided to
send him to the Tower for heresy, when the archbishop
exhibited the ring given to him by the king that very night
as a sign that Henry had taken the matter into his own
hands.[177]   The king reprimanded the councillors and
threatened them: "I would you would well understand that I
account my Lord of Canterbury as faithful a man towards me
as ever was prelate in this realm." The Duke of Norfolk's only
excuse was that he was pretending to send Cranmer to the
Tower in order to assure him the glory of a triumphal
acquittal. Each man then shook hands with the archbishop.
As a sign of reconciliation the king invited them all to his
table. From that day forward Cranmer lived in peace, and as
long as Henry lived no man dared trouble him again.[178]

Cranmer had long secured the king's friendship. "You
were born in a happy hour," said Cromwell to him, "you do
and say what you will, the king will always take it well at
your hand. . . . His Majesty will never give credit against
you, whatsoever is laid to your charge; but let me or any other
of the Council be complained of, His Grace will most seriously
chide and fall out with us. And therefore you are most happy
if you can keep you in this estate." There were two main
reasons for this friendship. First, the archbishop was humble
and devoid of ambition; he had not wished to be made a
bishop.[179]   The autocratic Henry, who had broken both
Wolsey and Cromwell, had no cause to fear that Cranmer's
will would be in opposition to his own, nor that he would be
dominated by it. Cranmer was his docile servant; he had been
so frequently useful to the king in his matrimonial adventures

[177] There are other instances of a ring given by Henry VIII in similar
cases, as Nichols shows in his edition of *Narratives of the Reformation* (Camden
Society, 1860, pp. 56, 256). According to another version, the king suddenly
entered the Council Chamber.

[178] See Pollard, *Cranmer*, 154 *sq.*, according to Morice's account in
Narratives of the Reformation. From Morice's account came that of Foxe,
who inspired Shakespeare and was useful to Strype for his twenty-eighth
chapter. According to Strype, this happened in 1544. In any case it cannot
be later than 1545, for Dr. Butts, the king's physician, who saw Cranmer
waiting at the door of the Council Chamber among the valets and told
Henry (*ibid.*, p. 274), died in 1545.

[179] Burnet (I, 214) says that six months elapsed before Cranmer consented
to accept the See of Canterbury. He came back from Germany as slowly
as he could, hoping the king would change his mind.

that he had to be a little beholden to him. Secondly, Cranmer was the most zealous partisan of the royal supremacy; moreover, he was the living example of it. Of advanced opinions himself and a Protestant at the bottom of his soul, yet in all things he yielded to the will of the king, whom he looked upon as the sole spiritual head in the realm. He signed the confessions of faith which he had opposed in Convocation. He saw that they were observed, and he tried and condemned heretics who were much the same way of thinking as himself. In fine, he set aside his own beliefs in order to obey the supreme head of the Church of England. He even dared to write: "All Christian princes have committed unto them immediately of God the whole cure of all their subjects, as well concerning the administration of God's word for the cure of souls, as concerning the ministration of things political and civil governance. . . . Mine opinion and sentence, I do not temerariously define, and do remit the judgement thereof wholly unto your majesty."[180]

Henry was consequently devoted to him. On his deathbed it was the archbishop he sent for to come and bid him a last adieu and to help him; with his failing hand he pressed that of the man who had been his servant and his ally in the harsh conquest of power.[181]

Speaking of Cranmer, J. Le Grand remarks: "If Protestants are to be believed, he was the equal of the early Fathers of the Church, and if we listen to Catholics, no man ever had less religion than he." Then he adds: "It was thought that Cranmer would follow closely in the steps of Cromwell; he himself feared this and withdrew from the court for a while. But this insincere prelate knew so well how to adapt himself to the king's mind that he always stood his ground. . . .

[180] Questions and answers on the Sacraments, the nomination and power of bishops and priests (Append. XXVI in Strype's *Mem. of Cranmer*). The sentence, "Mine opinion . . ." has his signature before and after it, and is written in his own hand. In sending his reflections on various passages in the King's Book of 1537 he humbly apologises to Cromwell: "I trust the king's highness will pardon my presumption, that I have been so scrupulous and, as it were a picker of quarrels to his Grace's book, making a great matter of every light fault, or rather where no fault is at all. . . . And I refer all mine annotations again to his Grace's most exact judgment" (Strype, *ibid.*, chap. XIII; Jenkyns, *op. cit.*, I, 227 *sq.*).

[181] Strype, chap. xxx

Although a Lutheran, he signed the different professions which were made during Henry's reign, put both Catholics and heretics to death, and in all his judgments recognized no law other than the whims of this prince."[182]

Cranmer did not possess the soul of a leader, and his friends were more apt to create difficulties for him than to assist him. Latimer was as simple as he was feeble, Shaxton was proud and disputatious, and Barlow imprudent, and most of the preachers protected by the archbishop were either over-zealous or else immoderate in their use of suspect terms. All these compromised the Reformation more than they favoured it. When Cromwell disappeared, the advanced party was without a head and seemed destined to perish.[183] But with the accession of Edward VI, Cranmer returned to power and dominated the moderate party, which had hitherto had the upper hand and, together with Henry, had prevented the Church of England from becoming what it afterwards became.

[182] Le Grand, I, pp. 245, 286 sq. "Everyone expected to see him go next. And it is very probable that had not the incontinence of Catherine Howard broken out not long after, he had been sacrificed the next session of Parliament" (Burnet, I, 454 sq.).

[183] Cf. Burnet, I, 409. For William Barlow, see A. Wood, ed. 1691, I, 122 sq.; J. R. Lunn, Bishop Barlowe's Dialogue on the Lutheran Factions, published 1531, with an Introduction on Anglican Orders, 1897. After Cromwell's fall Cervini, observing the orthodoxy of the Six Articles, hoped that England would return to the unity of the Church, but the royal supremacy over the Church remained the obstacle (cf. L. Cardauns, Nuntiaturberichte, V, 305).

CHAPTER VII

THE MODERATE PARTY IN THE SCHISM

The Henricians: Gardiner, Bishop of Winchester; Stokesley, Bishop of London; Bonner, Bishop of Hereford; Tunstall, Bishop of Durham—How they influenced the movement

THE part played by the moderate party in the English schism was more important than people suspect or generally assert. The majority forget to study this party, to bring out its salient features, or to reveal the motives behind it, and thus leave in the background one of the most characteristic traits of the Reformation under Henry VIII, a trait without which we should but ill understand what the Reformation really was. If the maintenance of Catholic dogma and discipline during this period appear to us somewhat of a puzzle, to be explained only by exterior circumstances which had little or nothing to do with it, it is because one of the factors of the religious revolution has been overlooked, viz., the moderate party or the Henricians.

The term Henrician was first applied to Cranmer by Sander.[1] To-day it is used to denote the prelates holding contrary ideas to Cranmer. In doctrine they were Catholics, yet by word of mouth and in writing they defended the schismatic acts of Henry VIII.

Chief among them were Bishop Gardiner of Winchester; Bishop Stokesley of London; Bishop Bonner of Hereford, who became Bishop of London on the death of Stokesley; and Bishop Tunstall of Durham.

They were worthy men, and their talents, learning, and qualities of all kinds attracted the attention of Wolsey, who was a good judge of men, and also qualified them for episcopal honours.

[1] "Hitherto, indeed, Cranmer himself had been a Henrician, that is, a follower of Henry VIII, from whose instructions he never dared to depart even a hair's breadth in anything" (Sander, Lewis' trans., p. 180).

Stephen Gardiner, who studied civil and canon law at Trinity Hall, Cambridge, was an eminent jurist and was looked upon as the best canonist in England. University professor in 1524, he was appointed master of Trinity Hall the following year, a post he retained until his death.[2] The Duke of Norfolk, to whom he was always greatly attached, entrusted him with the education of one of his sons, in 1524, and introduced him to Wolsey, who shortly afterwards chose him for his private secretary. In this capacity Gardiner, archdeacon of Taunton, took part in the trial of the heretics in 1526,[3] and accompanied the Cardinal to France, from July to September, 1527. Wolsey had a high opinion of him. He presented him to Clement VII as *mei dimidium*, and looked upon him as the only man capable of carrying out certain delicate missions.[4] In July, 1528, he appointed him to the commission formed to draw up the statutes for the colleges of Ipswich and Oxford. In a letter dated September 3rd, 1527, Erasmus congratulated Gardiner upon the great credit he enjoyed with their common patron.[5] Gardiner's intellectual qualities were so eminent that even his worst slanderers recognized them. Foxe, author of *The Book of Martyrs*, described him as being full of vice and "the enemy of God's word," but paid great tribute to his natural mental gifts, his great wisdom, and his excellent memory, the latter being necessary for all knowledge since *tantum scimus quantum memi-*

[2] Save for the break from 1549 to 1553 during his imprisonment in Edward VI's reign. As a doctor he was incorporated in Oxford University in 1531. For Gardiner's birth, and the legend about him, see French ed. of this book, pp. 652 *sq.*

[3] He took advantage of his influence over Wolsey to save from the stake Barnes and Joye, whom he had known at Cambridge. From the former he obtained, with a certain amount of difficulty, a recantation, whilst he helped the latter to take refuge on the Continent (Muller, *op. cit.*, chap. III).

[4] *L. and P.*, IV, 3912. While he was in France (1527) Wolsey wrote to the king saying that Gardiner was the only one he could send to London to receive Henry's secret instructions. In the matter of the divorce he constantly had recourse to his services.

[5] In 1511 Gardiner made the acquaintance of Erasmus, who was then staying in Paris with an Englishman named Eden in order to have his *Encomium Moriae* printed. Gardiner, then fourteen years old, had been entrusted to Eden by his father to learn French. Every day the child, whom "a mass of Greek and Latin books" acquired by the Humanist intrigued, used to prepare a lettuce salad for him, with "butter and sour wine, delicious to my taste," as Erasmus wrote sixteen years afterwards (J. A. Muller, *op. cit.*, chap. I: "A Salad for Erasmus," and p. 339, nn. 10 and 11).

nimus.[6] Stephen Gardiner, says Lodge, "was the most refined politician of his time; one of the many eminent persons selected from the multitude by Wolsey's unerring judgment."

Stokesley studied at Oxford and occupied various important posts at Magdalen College,[7] of which he became a fellow, and was then successively lecturer in divinity (1498) and in philosophy (1505), dean of divinity (1503), vice-president (1505), as well as principal and bursar of Magdalen Hall (1498 and 1502).[8] According to Erasmus, he knew three languages and his company was much sought by learned men.[9] He was ordained priest in 1505, and in the following year received two benefices from the university.[10] When Henry came to the throne (1509), Stokesley was appointed chaplain and almoner to the king, and a member of his council. In this capacity he accompanied Henry to the Field of the Cloth of Gold (1520), and to the interview with Charles V a few months later. Stokesley was dean of the chapel royal in 1524, and Erasmus asserts that he was one of the most influential men at court.[11]

Bonner studied at Pembroke College, Oxford, where he took his degrees in civil and canon law. He received Orders about the year 1519.[12] Ten years later he was chosen by Wolsey as chaplain, and entrusted with messages for the king.

---

[6] Foxe, VII, 585. Sir John Harington, *Nugae antiquae*, I, ed. 1792, p. 49, and ed. 1804, p. 64. See Ellies Du Pin, *Histoire de l'Église et des auteurs ecclésiastiques du XVIe siècle*, V (Paris, 1703), pp. 83 *sq.*

[7] *Illustrations of British History, Biography and Manners*, London, 1838, I, 125, n.

[8] Bloxam and Macray, *Register of Magdalen College*, I, 37–60; II, 20–24. For his birth, see French ed. of this book, pp. 654 *sq.*

[9] *L. and P.*, II, 4340.

[10] The livings of Willoughby (Warwickshire) and of Slimbridge, in Gloucestershire. On March 23rd, 1524, he received the living of Ivychurch (Kent).

[11] *L. and P.*, III, 394.

[12] Said to be the illegitimate son of George Savage, Rector of Daven-ham (Cheshire), and of Elizabeth Frodsham, who afterwards married Edmund Bonner, a long-sawyer of Hanleyd, in Worcestershire. Strype asserts that Bonner was a legitimate son, according to the papers of Nicholas Lachmore, Baron of the Exchequer. For Bonner, see A. Wood, ed. 1691, I, 123 *sq.* Bachelor of Canon Law and of Civil Law on June 12th and 13th, 1519, he took his Doctorate of Civil Law on July 2nd, 1525. Bonner studied Italian: in April, 1530, he reminded Cromwell of his promise to lend him Petrarch and to make him fluent in Italian (Ellis, 3rd series, II, 177; *L. and P.*, IV, 6346).

When everybody else abandoned the cardinal on his fall, Bonner remained in his service and often acted as a go-between for Wolsey and Cromwell. He accompanied the cardinal, when the latter retired to his see at York, and was at his side when he was arrested; and another two years elapsed before the king employed him in his service on various diplomatic missions.

Cuthbert Tunstall belonged to a noble Lancashire family. He began his studies at Oxford (1491) and Cambridge and finished them at the celebrated university of Padua, where he took his doctor's degree.[13] He was a learned theologian and orator, and conversant with Greek, Hebrew, jurisprudence, and mathematics. He wrote a book on mathematics which brought him fame even on the Continent (*De arte supputandi*, 1522).[14] Wood spoke of him as "a singular ornament to his country," Erasmus, who housed him in Brussels, whilst he was on a mission to the Low Countries, placed him among the leaders of the Renaissance in England, ranking him with More, Linacre, and Colet. With these three Tunstall was on friendly terms. He also had relations with Warham and certain learned men on the Continent, such as Budée and Beatus Rhenanus.[15] In a letter to Erasmus, Thomas More asserted that none was more conversant with good literature than Tunstall, or more austere in life or morals, or more pleasing in speech. "A man doutlesse out of comparison,"

[13] The illegitimate son of Thomas Tunstall, of Thurland Castle (Lancashire). His grandfather, Sir Richard Tunstall, had lost Thurland Castle through attainder, because of his attachment to the House of Lancaster (*Cal. Patent Rolls*, Edward IV, Part 1, 333, 422 *sq.*). He was born at Hackforth, Yorkshire, in 1474. His legitimate brother, Brian Tunstall, inherited Thurland Castle and was killed at the Battle of Flodden Field (September 9th, 1513); he made Cuthbert the executor of his will and the guardian of his son Marmaduke (*L. and P.*, I, No. 5288).

[14] His treatise was inspired by the Franciscan, Luca Paciulo (†1514), whose scientific *Summa* was the standard work at that time. Godwin (*op. cit.*, Part 2, p. 138), who says he was "ob animi virtutes quamplurimas merito celeberrimus," praises his learning: "Ad literarum cognitionem quod attinet, Graecae linguae fuit peritissimus; Hebraïcae non ignarus; Mathematicae ad miraculum usque scientissimus, ac Arithmeticae praesertim, de qua conscriptus ab eo libellus multum celebratur; eloquentia tam potens ut clarissimis sui temporis oratoribus potuerit annumerari; juris prudentissimus, ideoque legum doctor creatus; theologiae denique cognitione tantus, quantum eum ostendunt edita ab illo opuscu'a."

[15] *Erasmi Epistolae*, ed. 1642, Part 1, col. 27, 120, 148, 172, 173, 400 582, 783, 1158, 1509.

is the description given of him in *Utopia*. When he returned from Italy, he received various benefices and became chancellor to the Archbishop of Canterbury (August 25th, 1511), who introduced him to court.[16] Thenceforward he climbed rapidly. When he was Archdeacon of Chester, in 1515, he was sent to Brussels as ambassador to the Prince of Castile, afterwards Charles V. He was already considered a shrewd politician.[17] Although he had been appointed Master of the Rolls (May 12th, 1516), he was obliged to leave England again on various diplomatic missions. In 1517, he was at Maximilian's Court. The following year he spoke in London on the betrothal of the Dauphin of France to the Princess Mary.[18] In 1519, he accompanied Charles V to Cologne, and then to the Diet of Worms (1520–21). As a reward for his services, he was made Dean of Salisbury (May, 1521), Bishop of London (1522), and Lord Privy Seal (May 25th, 1523); in this last capacity he delivered the speech at the opening of Parliament in 1523. After the defeat at Pavia, Tunstall rejoined the emperor in Toledo (May 24th, 1525): his mission was to propose the dismemberment of France and the exclu-

[16] Although he was not a sub-deacon until 1509, yet on December 25th, 1506 he was presented to the living of Barmston, in Yorkshire. In 1507 he gave up Barmston, and in 1508 received the living of Stanhope, Co. Durham. In 1509 he changed the benefice of Aldridge, Staffordshire, for that of Steeple-Langford in Wiltshire (*L. and P.*, I, 1007). On December 6th, 1511 he was appointed to Harrow-on-the-Hill. In 1514 (April 15th) he received one of Wolsey's prebends in Lincoln Cathedral.

[17] *L. and P.*, II, 422. Tunstall was to negotiate for the continuation of the treaties passed between Henry VIII and the late King of Castile, Philip the Handsome, and then to dissuade Charles from entering into relations with France. His colleague was Thomas More, who says that the mission was not much to Tunstall's liking (More to Erasmus, Ep. II, 16), and who also recalls it at the beginning of his *Utopia*. The embassy was prolonged well into 1516 (Brewer, *Henry VIII*, 65 *sq.*; *L. and P.*, II, *passim*).

When Henry and Wolsey wished to take part in Italy's affairs at their own expense, Tunstall wondered why the king should undertake to uphold the cause of others (*L. and P.*, II, 2270). In 1517 Henry, incensed at Maximilian's treachery, wrote him some unpleasant letters in which he displayed his anger. Tunstall, certain that they would produce a bad effect, retained them, and the king did not blame him for doing so (Pollard, *Henry VIII*, 133).

[18] *C. Tunstalli in laudem matrimonii Oratio habita in sponsalibus Mariae et Francisci*, London, 1518; 2nd ed., Basle, 1519. On the occasion of the Treaty between France and England (October 8th, 1518). The betrothal was celebrated by proxy, on October 5th, between Mary, who was two years old, and the Dauphin Francis, born on February 28th of the previous year.

sion of Francis I and his son from the throne.[19] Two years later, he accompanied Wolsey to France, and was one of the English plenipotentiaries at the treaty of Cambrai (1529). His qualities were so outstanding that even his religious adversaries were overawed by them. Bishop Godwin, who could not speak harshly enough of Bonner, describes Tunstall in terms of eulogy; and his epitaph, composed in the days of Elizabeth (who had deprived him of both his liberty and his see), crowned his white hairs with a golden halo.[20]

Such men as Tunstall, Bonner, Stokesley, and Gardiner were the strength of the party.

The Henricians had three characteristics: (1) They favoured Henry VIII's divorce; (2) they contributed to the establishment of the royal supremacy in the country; (3) but they energetically maintained Catholic dogma against the advanced party. Thus they were at once abettors of the schism and guardians of orthodoxy.

First of all, they had an active, effective, and preponderant part in the divorce.

Gardiner displayed extreme cleverness in his errand to Clement VII, in 1528. It was through him that Wolsey, together with Campeggio, was empowered to try the divorce case. He was also instrumental in obtaining the famous secret Decretal deciding the case in Henry's favour in advance, and which Clement afterwards regretted having granted.[21]

---

[19] *L. and P.*, IV, 1212, 1249, 1255, 1264, 1296; British Museum, Stowe MS., 147, fol. 67, 86. If Wolsey's scheme was serious, Charles had not the least desire to see it realized. He did not intend to allow England to profit by his victory, in making Henry King of France or lord of certain French provinces. The emperor no longer even wanted to marry Mary, as laid down in the Treaty of Windsor. Tunstall was accompanied by Sir Richard Wingfield; he came back in January, 1526.

[20] Godwin, *op. cit.*, Part 2, pp. 138-40.

> ANGLIA CUTHBERTUM TUNSTALLUM MÆSTA REQUIRIT
> CUJUS SUMMA DOMI LAUS ERAT ATQUE FORIS.
> RHETOR, ARITHMETICUS, JURIS CONSULTUS ET ÆQUI.
> LEGATUSQUE FUIT, DENIQUE PRÆSUL ERAT.
> ANNORUM SATUR ET MAGNORUM PLENUS HONORUM
> VERTETUR IN CINERES AUREUS ISTE SENEX.

[21] *L. and P.*, IV, 4345; Pocock, *Records*, I, 167; Ehses, *Röm. Dokumente*, No. 22, 23; *Eng. Hist. Review*, XII, 9; see chap. II. At Orvieto, whither Clement had fled, the ruined palace, in which he had three small chambers, "all naked and unhanged," with the ceiling fallen, the long private

Although his colleague, Edward Foxe, took precedence over him as royal secretary and the first named in the king's letters, yet Wolsey had given Gardiner priority in "speech and utterance," i.e. in the execution of instructions; the cardinal knew his powers of debate and his rare qualities as a diplomatist. The king openly expressed his entire satisfaction with Gardiner for the manner in which he had succeeded in such a difficult mission, and made him Archdeacon of Worcester, and then of Norfolk.[22] Campeggio's errand bristled with difficulties; and Gardiner was sent back to Clement VII at the beginning of 1529, to try and overcome them. He was recalled in May, after vainly attempting to remedy the situation, and after warning Wolsey that the case was about to be cited before the Roman court. His presence in London was more useful.[23] When he returned, Henry appointed him principal clerk of the court for the divorce proceedings, and shortly afterwards made him his chief secretary (July 28th, 1529).[24] From that time onwards he is frequently mentioned in public correspondence under the name of Mr. Stephens. Gardiner was so successful in his new appointment that when he was away Henry said he had had lost his right hand.[25]

conversations to which the Pope had to submit in his bed-chamber, the furniture of which, "bed and all," was not worth "twenty nobles," the scarcity of food, the absolute lack of comfort, and the fear of the imperial troops, all made a strong impression upon Gardiner and Foxe, and tended to diminish their respect for the supreme authority and to make them even bolder.

[22] Pocock, *Records*, I, 147; Strype, *Eccles. Memorials*, I, 2, p. 119.
At the end of 1528 he was called Archdeacon of Worcester (*L. and P.*, IV, 4736, 4737). According to Le Neve (*Fasti Ecclesiae Anglicanae*, ed. Hardy, Oxford, 1854, II, p. 484), he was made Archdeacon of Norfolk on March 1st, 1529, but on the Convocation list in the November of that year Wolsey's son, Thomas Wynter, was still given as occupying that post (cf. Muller, *op. cit.*, pp. 42, 346, n. 4).

[23] Gardiner to Henry VIII, May 4th, 1529, Burnet, VI, 23. Henry VIII to Clement VII, May 20th, 1529, Theiner, *Vetera Monumenta Hibernorum*, p. 563, No. 1000. The messenger bearing the letter to Gardiner and Brian recalling them left London on May 13th (Ehses, No. 42). See French ed., pp. 659 *sq*. We know from Gardiner's will that the man who carried his letters while he was in Rome was called Robert Massie.

[24] Gardiner informed Peter Vannes on July 28th, 1529 (Pocock, *Records*, I, 265), that he was taking office at the court that very day, "fortunae nostrae progressum tu ut spero brevi videbis." He had reached London on June 22nd.

[25] Merriman, I, 344. Cf. Muller, *op. cit.*, chap. VII: "The right hand of the king."

His influence rapidly increased. In August, 1530, the ambassador from Milan compared it to that of Norfolk and Thomas Boleyn.[26] After Wolsey had fallen into disgrace, he applied to Gardiner on several occasions to obtain for him the favour of the king, and in spite of what has been said, Gardiner certainly did his best to help his former master, who was crippled with debts and also in the clutches of the Norfolk-Boleyn faction as well as of the envious aristocracy. He saved one of the cardinal's colleges, Christ Church, Oxford, but vainly pleaded for the other at Ipswich.[27] In March, 1531, he was Archdeacon of Leicester, and in that same year (October 23rd) he obtained the bishopric of Winchester, and was consecrated on November 27th.[28] A few months later, he was sent on an embassy to Francis I (December 29th, 1531–March 7th, 1532). He had to forestall the consequences of the divorce and, by entering into a close alliance with France, to protect England from being attacked by the emperor.[29] The

[26] *Calendar of State Papers and manuscripts existing in the Archives and Collections of Milan*, London, 1913, p. 52. At the Boulogne meeting, together with Norfolk and Suffolk, he held diplomatic conversations with the French representatives (*L. and P.*, V, 1256, 1523).

[27] The last letter in which Gardiner's efforts for Ipswich are mentioned bears the date, October 17th, 1530 (Sir Thomas Arundel to Wolsey, *L. and P.*, IV, 6688). The cardinal died on the 29th of the following month. Muller (chap. VII, "The fall of the cardinal"), in a true critical spirit, gives a sound appreciation of Gardiner's conduct in those delicate circumstances, and defends him against the malignant insinuations of certain historians (*ibid.*, pp. 36 and 345). Gardiner's own talents and his zeal in the matter of the divorce were sufficient to cause his advancement; there was no need for him to turn against Wolsey, whose downfall would have happened inevitably through the hatred his enemies bore him.

[28] Henry VIII to Clement VII, September 12th, 1531 (Theiner, 598); Clement VII to Henry VIII, October 23rd, 1531 (Ehses, No. 108; Pocock, *Records*, II, 137); Clement VII to Gardiner, October 23rd, 1531 (Ehses, No. 109, cf. p. 207). Although he received £1,300 less than his predecessor, Richard Fox, Gardiner had to pay the king £366 13s. 4d. in dues (*L. and P.*, V, 507).

[29] Francis I to de la Pommeraye, January 13th, 1532, *Bibl. Nat.*, Fr. MS. 4126, fol. 5. The treaty, negotiated by Gardiner, was concluded at Greenwich in April, 1532. France was represented by Gilles de la Pommeraye, and England by the Earl of Wiltshire and Dr. Foxe (Camusat, *Meslanges historiques*, II, 84–88). Francis I bound himself to supply 500 lances and a fleet of 1,500 men if the emperor attacked Henry. If France were attacked Henry was to send the same number of naval ratings and 5,000 archers. On September 1st Henry and the French ambassador took the oath of mutual alliance on the altar, after the Mass celebrated at Windsor by Gardiner, who had previously read the warrant conferring the title of Marquis of Pembroke upon Anne Boleyn (cf. Muller, 41 *sq.*, 48).

king congratulated him on the success of his errand. He had once more placed his knowledge as a jurist at the disposal of his sovereign against Catherine in order to prevent the consequences of the king's citation before the Roman court. With a retinue of twenty-four men, Gardiner accompanied Henry VIII and Anne Boleyn to the interview at Boulogne (October 1532), where Henry made up his mind to proceed with the divorce in view of Francis I's friendship.[30] In Convocation (April, 1533) he stated his opinion, as a canonist, that the marriage between Catherine and Arthur had been consummated. In the following May he was a member of the court, with Cranmer as president, which pronounced Catherine of Aragon's marriage invalid; and he was the new queen's train-bearer at her coronation.[31] He was then one of the chief promoters of the divorce, and Anne Boleyn had reason to thank him for the "willing and faithful mind" he had shown towards her throughout the whole business.[32]

Stokesley likewise sided with the king on the divorce question. In collaboration with Edward Foxe, Bishop of Hereford, and Nicolas de Burgo, he wrote a Latin book in favour of the divorce. Cranmer translated it into English, with certain additions and corrections, and it was printed in London, in 1531, and entitled *The determinations of the most excellent Universities*. In 1529, Stokesley went with George Boleyn to France to induce Francis I to oppose the holding of a Council on account of the emperor's influence over the Pope, and to ask him to recommend the divorce question to the French universities.[33] In the following year he accompanied Anne Boleyn's

[30] A month previously the Pope had said that Gardiner had changed his opinions about the divorce and had been obliged to leave the court (*L. and P.*, V, 561; cf. *ibid.*, 696). The same rumour was spread abroad several times in 1532, after Gardiner's attitude in Convocation at the time of "The Supplication against the Ordinaries" (cf. *L. and P.*, V, 738, 834, 1058, 1291).

[31] Hall's *Chronicle*, II, 238. According to Cranmer (letter to Archdeacon Hawkyns, in Strype, *Mem. of Cranmer*, Append. III), on entering Westminster the queen was supported on one side by Stokesley, Bishop of London, and on the other by Gardiner.

[32] Anne Boleyn to Gardiner, April 4th, 1529 (Burnet, V, 444; *L. and P.*, IV, 5422). When he was successful at Orvieto, she had declared that he deserved a "large recompense" (cf. Friedmann, *op. cit.*, I, 70 *sq.*).

[33] *L. and P.*, IV, Nos. 5983, 6026. He was also to prevent any league between France and Scotland (cf. Friedmann, *op. cit.*, I, 105).

father on the latter's embassy to Clement VII and the emperor, at Bologna, and undertook to inform the Pope of the reasons for the divorce.[34] He then travelled about Italy obtaining the opinions of the universities and doctors. More than a hundred references in Vol. IV (Part III) of *Letters and Papers* bear witness to his activities in Bologna, Padua, Venice, and other cities. He himself said that he aroused the King's cause which had been allowed to sleep in the hands of the ambassadors in a seemingly hopeless state.[35] On his return to England he made use of the declarations he had obtained from the universities in favour of the divorce in order to give fresh impetus to the matter in the Upper House (March 31st, 1531). He espoused the cause with such warmth that he brought forth protests from Standish and Clerk, Bishops of St Asaph and of Bath, who said that Parliament had no right to discuss the question.[36]

Stokesley had already been given a bishopric as a reward for his zeal. He had been appointed to the see of London (July, 1530) on the transfer of Tunstall to Durham, and was consecrated Bishop of London on November 27th, 1530. He continued to be a fervent advocate of the divorce. When Convocation met in March, 1533, it was Stokesley who proposed that they should discuss the validity of Catherine's marriage. Some of the members objected that it was not permitted to discuss a cause pending in the Roman court. Thereupon Stokesley produced a four-year-old Brief, which had been annulled by the Pope, authorizing certain classes of

[34] That the Pope refused to listen to them, as Henry complained (Theiner, *Vetera Mon. Hibernorum*, p. 591, No. 1016; Pocock, II, 630), is rather doubtful, if we are to believe Charles V's letter to Chapuys on March 25th (Friedmann, *op. cit.*, I, 106–107), and Cardinal Grammont's to Francis I on March 27th, from Bologna (Le Grand, III, 399 *sq.*). Stokesley, on the contrary, seems to have been well received, and Campeggio allowed him the two hundred gold florins which were due to himself as cardinal protector for the recent nomination of the bishop in London (Ehses, 277, 278). Stokesley was considered to be an influential person and one who ought to be treated carefully: "judico sarà bene, venendo a Roma, accarezzarlo." Campeggio to Salviati, Innsbruck, May 4th, 1530, Ehses, 145.

[35] *L. and P.*, VII, 15.

[36] *L. and P.*, V, 171. The Duke of Norfolk had to intervene and explain that the king had submitted the opinions of the universities to the Lords, not for them to discuss the case, but so that they should know the motives which inspired him.

people to give their opinions, and boldly commented upon it: *Summus pontifex voluit unumquemque declarare mentem suam et opiniones suas in dicta causa libere et impune.*[37] A month later he was one of the assessors who sat on Cranmer's court at Dunstable, and delivered judgment against Catherine. On September 10th, he baptized Anne Boleyn's daughter, Elizabeth.

Bonner in his various missions helped to further the cause of the divorce. He was in Rome in 1532, and protested against Henry VIII being summoned before the Curia. In the following year he was commissioned by Henry to inform Clement VII that the king intended to appeal to a council.[38] His brutal and violent character fitted him for an office of this nature. He took advantage of the meeting between Francis I and the Pope at Marseilles (November, 1533) to force himself, unannounced, upon the Pope, and to inform him, pointblank, of Henry VIII's appeal (November 7th). The Pope became exceedingly angry. It is said that he threatened to have Bonner thrown into a cauldron of molten lead; however, he did nothing more than rapidly fold and unfold his handkerchief, as was his wont in moments of frenzy.[39] On his return to England Bonner was given the living of East Dereham in Norfolk,[40] and in 1535, he was made Archdeacon of Leicester.

Tunstall was one of the few bishops who were considered favourable to Catherine, so the queen chose him as her counsellor.[41] Yet he persuaded her not to appeal to Rome, and in no way opposed the king's plans. Tunstall was transferred from London to Durham, a see held by Wolsey *in commendam* since 1523.[42]

Just as the Henricians had upheld Henry VIII on the divorce, so, by their whole-hearted submission, were they responsible for the triumph of the spiritual supremacy.

[37] Friedmann, *Anne Boleyn*, I, 196.

[38] Bonner received these instructions at Lyons, together with the order to join Gardiner at Marseilles (Strype, *Mem. of Cranmer*, I, Append. No. IV; Pocock, *Records*, Append. No. XXXV; *L. and P.*, VI, p. 525).

[39] Bonner to Henry VIII, November 13th, 1533. Burnet, VI, 56-68. Cf. *L. and P.*, VI, 721, 998; chap. III, p. 106.

[40] *L. and P.*, VII, No. 545.

[41] Cf. *L. and P.*, V, 696. Ehses, No. 31.

[42] The transference took place in the Consistory of February 16th, 1530. *Acta Consistorialia*, Arch. Vat., Sec. XII, Vol. CXXII, fol. 171.

Gardiner's *De vera obedientia* was the party's manifesto. This treatise was an attempt to make the title and office of "supreme head of the Church" legitimate, and to find a basis for them in theology. No work had more to do with establishing and vindicating the king's new authority; it was regarded as the last word on the subject. Cromwell placed it in the hands of the foreign ambassadors in England, and had numerous copies distributed on the Continent.[43] Another Henrician, Sampson, dean of the chapel royal, also wrote in defence of the spiritual supremacy. His work, *Oratio de dignitate et potestate regis* (1535),[44] won for him the see of Chichester and was sent abroad to the European courts; but it was both dull and weak. The first part, which is extremely long, appears to be a piece of patchwork made up of old sermons having nothing to do with the subject. Sampson holds forth interminably upon the love of God and the love of one's neighbour, the foundation of the new law, in order at length to reach the question: How am I to love God? By keeping the commandments, is the Gospel answer. Then follows an enumeration of the commandments of God. At length, touching upon the commandment of obedience, the author comes to the point he has long been trying to make: "Obey those that are in authority. Honour the king. Whatever the king says and commands, that believe and do."[45] Reginald Pole ridiculed the author, in his *De Unitate Ecclesiae* (Bk. I): "Sampson," he says, "has a very long spear; the beginning of his book is of immense length; 'the supreme head' is the iron point of that long spear. Armed with this unbearable weapon, he is no longer a Sampson, but a Goliath advancing to challenge the sons of Israel, the children of the Church. Sampson is a priest who betrays his master: he is a Judas; but he sold him for a very small price, for he wanted Norwich, and he received only Chichester. Sampson is not a Hercules, but he may play at being a Cacus: he drags the sheep of Christ into the King's den by their tails. But the sheep may bleat and awaken

[43] *L. and P.*, IX, 848, 964, 965; X, 7; XII, Part 2, 620; Merriman, I, No. 126, II, No. 217. Cromwell even tried to convert Reginald Pole to the Royal Supremacy with this treatise (Merriman, *loc. cit.*).

[44] *L. and P.*, IX, 848.

[45] Strype, *Eccles. Mem.*, Append. XLII. Gerdes, *op. cit.*, IV (148)–(163). Cf. Schelhorn, *Amœnitates historiae ecclesiasticae*, 1737–38, I, 27.

Hercules." Gardiner's work was incontestably far superior to Sampson's.

Before definitely adhering to the royal supremacy, Gardiner had wavered somewhat, and his attitude aroused the king's suspicions. He had appeared in this light on account of his attempts to defend the privileges of his Order, to which he had always been very attached. When the famous *Supplication against the Ordinaries* (an attack upon the legislative power of the Church by the Commons) appeared, in 1532, Gardiner, as a canonist, had been called upon to answer it. And he maintained that the clergy's right to legislate for the good of souls was "grounded upon the Scripture of God and the determination of Holy Church" and was, moreover, "a duty certainly prescribed by God." He held that bishops "may not submit their charges to his Highness's assent."[46] Gardiner was made to feel that he had displeased the king. By way of reply he sent a slightly ironical letter to the king, in which he said that in giving his opinion he had followed only the most important authorities, the Council of Constance and the king himself in his book against Luther; if meanwhile the king had discovered reasons against it, he, being more learned in law than in theology, would consider them, but that until better authorities were forthcoming to prove the contrary, he would rely upon those he had, which were so good and so strong.[47] The king (or Cromwell) then discovered that, on account of the oath they gave to the Pope, the bishops were not his subjects, and aired this grievance in the House of Commons. Gardiner went a step further. Together with Sir Thomas More, he caused the Submission of the Clergy Bill, which had been passed by Convocation, to be rejected in the House of Lords. A few days later, he withdrew in disgrace to Esher,[48]

---

[46] Gee and Hardy, *op. cit.*, No. XLVII: "Answer of the Ordinaries," which is very long, and will be found abridged in Wilkins (*op. cit.*, III, 748 *sq.*) and F. Atterbury (*The Rights, Powers and Privileges of an English Convocation*, London, 1701, p. 86). Cf. chap. III, pp. 100-1. On April 15th Gardiner submitted the first part of his reply to the Upper House of Convocation, which adopted it immediately. The Lower House passed it four days later (cf. J. A. Muller, *op. cit.*, p. 348).

[47] Convocation thought that Gardiner's reply was so good that it made in its own. Hence it appears in Wilkins, *op. cit.*, III, 752.

[48] *L. and P.*, V, 1013. Cf. above, chap. III; J. A. Muller, chap. VIII. Gardiner is mentioned as being present at Greenwich (this may be an

in his own diocese. Three months afterwards, Warham died.
With Reginald Pole in voluntary exile, it seemed that the
primatial see of Canterbury must fall to Gardiner, then the
most prominent prelate in England, and not, as it did, to
Cranmer, who was still unknown. It is quite possible that
there is some truth in the statement that Gardiner's subsequent feelings towards the archbishop and the latter's reforming ideas were accentuated by this unpleasant memory.

In the following year, however, on account of his ability
as a diplomatist and canonist, Gardiner was sent on a mission
to France, at the time of the meeting between Francis I and
the Pope at Marseilles. After a month of fruitless negotiations
for the divorce, Gardiner made Bonner read to Clement VII
the king's appeal to the council, which he himself had probably written (November 7th, 1533). He opposed Francis I,
and the latter, displeased with the appeal and the annoyance
it had caused his august guest, begged Henry to recall Gardiner on account of his behaviour.[49] On his return to England,
Gardiner found another enemy in Cromwell, whose power
was growing every day, but who was secretly jealous of the
bishop; he was therefore obliged to resign his office as chief
secretary to the king and withdraw once more to his diocese.[50]
He was suspected of being secretly attached to the papal
primacy, and on several occasions they tried to find fault with
his ideas concerning the king's supremacy or succession, but
all to no purpose.[51] He took the oath with regard to the royal
succession, and made "the abbots, priors, vicars, and curates

error, cf. Muller, 348, n. 5), when Henry transferred the great seal to
Audeley, after Thomas More had resigned (May 20th).

[49] Friedmann, *Anne Boleyn*, I, pp. 252 *sq*. Cf. above, chap. III; J. A.
Muller, pp. 51 *sq*.

[50] Yet, in April, 1534, he was one of the judges appointed to settle the
dispute between the clergy and laity of London over the tithe-gatherers.
Cf. *L. and P.*, VII, 425; *Victoria Hist. of the Counties of England*, I, London,
1907, pp. 247 *sq*.

[51] John Mores, receiver of the monastery of Sion (Middlesex), on the
borders of the Winchester diocese, was questioned by Cromwell and the
king to ascertain what Gardiner had said to him about the Pope's primacy.
Mores replied that Gardiner had shown him "that the primacy of the
Bishop of Rome began by the policy of man, and since then clerks have
applied scripture to make it appear that the primacy had the beginning of
God: which he thought could not be truly maintained." Cf. Ellis, *Orig.
Let.*, 2nd series, II, 85; J. A. Muller, *op. cit.*, p. 57 *sq*.

of all the churches and chapels in the county" also take it. It was rumoured that his arrest was imminent.[52]

Gardiner then took the decisive step. On February 10th, 1535, he signed a formal renouncement of the Bishop of Rome, and wrote some verses exalting the royal supremacy[53] for his students at Winchester College. In the same year he published. *The Oration on True Obedience*, and he himself faithfully practised that "true obedience" during Henry VIII's reign. This work was brought out by the king's printer in 1535, and contained one of Holbein's engravings.[54] In it the author

---

[52] Cf. *L. and P.*, VII, 441, 483, 522. Palmer says (P. Janelle in the *Bulletin of the Institute of Historical Research*, June, 1928) that the king sent Latimer to him to convince him of the royal supremacy, and that Gardiner, who admitted that his competence in knowledge of the law was greater than in theology, yielded, and was obliged by the King's Council to preach on the royal supremacy at St Paul's Cross by way of recantation.

[53] Wilkins, *Concilia*, III, 780. His letter to the king, *State Papers*, I, 438.

[54] Strype (*Eccles. Mem.*, I, Part 1, 264), Anthony Wood (*Athenae Oxonienses*, ed. 1691, I, 124, ed. Bliss, I, 370), and Lord Herbert give the date as 1534. There is probably some confusion with Bishop Foxe's *De vera differentia*, which did appear in 1534.

The title was short: *Stephani Wintoniensis episcopi De Vera obedientia Oratio*, London, 1535, in 4to. The 1536 edition, of which the title, on the contrary, was very long, bears the inscription *Hamburg, ex officina Francisci Rhodi*. It was probably printed in London itself by some anonymous heretic (Maitland, *Essays on the Reformation*, London, 1849, pp. 277 *sq.*). In the seventeenth century editions appeared in 1612 and 1690. The work may be consulted in Gratianus, *Fascic. rerum expetendarum*, Hamburg, 1690, ed. Brown, II, 800 *sq.*, or in Goldast, *Monarchia S. Romani Imperii*, Hanover, 1612 and 1611, I, 716; Frankfort, 1621 and 1668. The first English translation of *De vera obedientia* appeared in 1553 (*Chronicle of Queen Jane*, ed. Nichols, p. 33); Maitland (*Essays*, p. 280) says it is very crude, so imperfect is the translation. There were two editions of it, one at Roane (Rouen) and the other at Rome "before the Castle of Saint Angel." The latter name is fictitious, but it is not certain, as has been asserted (cf. Ame, *Typographical Antiquities*, ed. Dibdin, III, p. 290, IV, p. 29), that it stands for London. The translator, who conceals himself under the pseudonym of Michael Wood, was Bishop Bale, according to Maitland (*op. cit.*, pp. 281 *sq.*; cf. Gairdner, *History*, 326 *sq.*), but at that time Bale was under supervision in Flanders. Cf. P. Janelle, pp. ix, xxxi, xl. The reprint of this translation by William Stevens, in his *Life of Bradford*, 1832, is scandalously inaccurate. The editor has displayed the most absolute ignorance and the greatest incompetence, as anyone may see in the examples quoted by Maitland (*Essays*, p. 283, n. 1). A good but very scarce re-edition of the English version is that by B. A. Heywood (the last ed. 1870, London), with the title: *The royal Supremacy in matters ecclesiastical in Pre-Reformation times. Bishop Gardiner's Oration on True Obedience, with Bonner's Preface.* Cf. J. A. Muller, *op. cit.*, Append. II. In 1929 the Cambridge University Press published the Latin text, with Bale's first version, with a large number of corrections and annotations by P. Janelle (*Obedience in*

vindicated both the king's divorce and his title of "supreme head of the Church of England," in order to show that the controversy between the king and the Bishop of Rome was quite different from what the ordinary people thought.[55] He allowed as did Melanchthon,[55a] that the Pope might have some kind of primacy among bishops, but he rejected a primacy that would make him the universal head of the Church. Three conclusions could be drawn from his arguments: (1) All traditions of men must be considered inferior to the divine precepts, and the papal authority claimed by the Pope was merely one of those traditions. (2) The Roman Pontiff has no power or jurisdiction over the other churches, and therefore the oath of obedience given to him was worthless. (3) Every prince possessed supremacy over the Church in his realm, and was bound to make religion his first care.

The crafty prelate is easily recognized in the arguments he uses. "How absurd," he exclaims, "to say that a certain man, qua John, is a subject of the prince who is head of the country, but that the same man, qua Christian, is no longer a subject of the king! He belongs to the country because he lives in England, and since he is a Christian, he belongs to the Church of England. But what is the Church of England, save an assembly of men and women, of churchmen and laymen, united in the profession of the Christian religion? To say the prince is head of the realm but not of the Church would be to make him head of infidels. How numerous, in fact, are the old English laws relating to the Church and religion which were promulgated and applied by royal authority! Will it be said that the kings made those laws only as defenders of the

Church and State). The De vera obedientia has at times been confused (cf. Maitland, op. cit., 272 and 276) with Foxe's De vera differentia (1534), of which the full title is: Opus eximium De vera differentia regiae potestatis et ecclesiasticae, et quae sit ipsa veritas ac virtus utriusque, also printed by Berthelet, and translated between 1540 and 1550 (1548, according to the old Bodleian catalogue) under the title: The true dyfferens between the regal power and the ecclesiastical power translated out of latyn by Henry Lord Stafforde.

[55] In qua (oratione) ostenditur causam controversiae quae inter ipsam serenissimam Regiam Majestatem et Episcopum Romanum exstitit, longe aliter ac diversius se habere, quam hactenus a vulgo putatum sit. (Title page of the Hamburg edition.)

[55a] Cf. H. Volz, Luthers Schmalkaldische Artikel und Melanchthons "Tractatus de potestate papae." Gotha, 1931. Melanchthon recognized the Pope's primacy de jure humano.

Church, and not as heads of that Church? But where then are the heads who possessed the highest authority at that time? Not the bishops of England, since the king is acknowledged to be above them all. Had the bishop of Rome that pre-eminence? In that case, how strange that our ancestors should have made so many laws against him . . . to prevent him from seeing too far outside the watch-tower in which they believed God had placed him! Legislation against a superior is not lawful . . . I do not mean to reject absolutely the term Primacy, because it is supported by great examples; but in order to explain I turn to the Gospel, where I find it has two meanings. Granted that Christ conferred the Primacy upon Peter, what is the consequence? Has he domination and pre-eminence on that account? When he received the order to confirm his brethren, did he also receive the order to be their lord? That Peter has a primacy of zeal, that he is the advance soldier of Christ, the first in the office of preaching and teaching, the first to defend the Church against heresy and to shed his blood in time of persecution, like the former bishops of Rome, who, almost alone, resisted the fury of the tyrants clad in purple: in all those things, certainly, the premier place belongs to the first man, and the Primacy to the successors of the prince of Apostles. But, if the bishops of Rome try to undermine the rights of others, if they endeavour to maintain their Primacy by force and dissimulation, then they will be brought down to the level justified and fixed by truth. I could augur even worse, but I refrain." [56]

Although, according to Reginald Pole, the *De vera obedientia* contains nothing that an intelligent man could not refute and

[56] Translated from the French. The original text is in Latin, but Bale's translation of it is defective. Goldast, I, pp. 722, 723, 728, etc.; P. Janelle, 68–172 *passim*. Gardiner concludes his treatise in these terms (Goldast, p. 733; P. Janelle, 171): "Tantum abest, ut aliorum convitia pertimescam, dum huic uni (veritati) mea probem officia, et secundum eam Principi supremo ecclesiae anglicanae in terris capiti obediendo, alias simul obedientiae verae partes obire contendam, quae sunt homines proprie christiani, ut emensis in obedientia et veritate hujus vitae spatiis, potiri valeam aeterna vita; cujus author est et dator Jesus Christus, qui ut omnes ad patrem traheret, patri per omnia factus obediens mortem pro nobis obiit salutiferam, nec facto minus quam verbo eam docuit obedientiam, quae veritatis plena cum sit, ad ipsam omnes quotquot in fide adhaeserint tandem evehet veritatem, qui est Deus benedictus in saecula. Amen" (cf. J. A. Muller, *op. cit.*, chap. xi).

is in more than one argument definitely paradoxical and un-convincing,[57] yet it was a plausible and formidable work when it appeared; Pole considered it cleverly and skilfully written. Continental Protestants welcomed it with enthusiasm; in addition to their theory of Peter's Primacy, they found the principle applied in Germany, *cujus regio hujus religio*, con-firmed in it. In 1536, the princes of northern Germany had it printed at Hamburg with a preface by Bonner, who happened to be there on a mission. In the same year the Swiss reformers, Capito, Hedio, and Bucer, brought out an edition at Stras-bourg; and in the foreword warmly recommended the work as the finest account of the true theory of the privileges and duties of a bishop in the early days.[58] Of all Gardiner's works this was the most read and the most frequently published.

Until then Catholics had reckoned Gardiner amongst the prelates most in favour of the papal cause. Thenceforward they stigmatized him and attributed his work to cowardice and the fear of death. On his return from his embassy to Charles V (1541), he stayed in Louvain for a few days, and the university cordially offered him hospitality. He distributed copies of his book, and thus caused great scandal among the doctors, against whom he maintained and defended his opinion; "minding to say Mass in St. Peter's Church, they did deny unto him as to an excommunicate person the ornaments and vestments meet for the same; wherewith being highly offended he suddenly hastened his journey from thence."[59]

By preaching many sermons Gardiner upheld the royal supremacy and urged the destruction of Rome's authority. He helped Henry VIII in his schemes. The king was anxious to keep in force certain papal Bulls, and the bishop

---

[57] Quirini, I, 460. Collier (*op. cit.*, IV, 388–91), who gives a short analysis of it, notes the paradoxical nature of, and the lack of force in, more than one argument, and marks Gardiner down as "a better statesman than controversial divine." The best refutation of Gardiner is possibly the Rev. Herbert Scott's, in his *Eastern Churches and the Papacy*, London, 1928.

[58] It is to be found in Goldast, *op. cit.*, I, 716, but not in Janelle.

[59] Evidence given by witnesses at Gardiner's trial under Edward VI. Foxe, VI, 105, 140, 168, 185, 198, 202, 223. F. Driander to Edmund Crispin, September 22nd, 1541; *ibid.* VI, 139. Cf. Maitland, *Essays, etc.*, chap. xix; J. A. Muller, 65; article by P. Janelle in *Revue des sciences religieuses*, Strasbourg, July, 1927, p. 458.

suggested he might promulgate them afresh, substituting his own name for the Pope's; and he drew up a rough draft for the purpose (1536).[60]

The other Henricians likewise championed the royal supremacy, either by word of mouth or else in writing.

Stokesley, as Bishop of London, zealously saw that all the projects for abolishing papal authority were carried out. With the Archbishop of York, he persuaded the London Carthusians not to resist any longer and to take the oath, with the restrictive clause *quantum per legem Dei licet*. He assisted at the dissolution of the monasteries of Reading and Godstow, and of other houses in Lincolnshire.[61] In 1537, he and Tunstall wrote to Reginald Pole, severely admonishing him for his book *De Unitate Ecclesiae* and for his elevation to the cardinalate.[62]

Bonner, in turn, preached the new doctrine of the royal supremacy, and wrote for the second edition of *De vera obedientia* (1536)[63] a preface far more violent than the book itself. In this he eulogized Henry's marriage with "the most excellent and most noble lady Anne Boleyn," and attacked "the false and pretended supremacy of the bishop of Rome . . . this Olympian Jupiter who had assumed a power which exceeded the imagination of man." Bonner, in his embassies, sought to preserve the king's supremacy from all foreign attacks. He was in Hamburg in 1536 preparing an agreement between the Protestants of Denmark and those of northern

[60] Evidence given by William Medow, Gardiner's chaplain, on the article relating to the royal supremacy (Foxe, VI, 202; *L. and P.*, X, 1089). Foxe (VI, 594 *sq.*) notes, as much with malice as with care, all Gardiner's attacks on papal authority.

[61] British Museum, Cotton MS. Cleopatra, E, IV, fol. 223, 225, 234-37. Arundel MS. 249, fol. 82, 84.

[62] Printed in Bernard Garter's "New Year's Gift," 1571, and Foxe, V, 90-99. Cf. Pole's letter to Contarini, August 4th, 1536 (Quirini, I, 470), in which Pole states that Tunstall had not read his book.

[63] His oath against papal authority is in Wilkins, III, 781. Maitland has raised doubts about attributing the above-mentioned preface to Bonner (301 *sq.*). Yet it appeared in London, in 1536, with the name "Edmund Bonner, Archdeacon of Leicester." Bonner did not protest, and when, in 1556 (March 28th), he examined William Tyms, Rector of Hockley, who was accused of heresy, Tyms challenged him to deny that he was the author of that preface. "The book is extant, and you cannot deny it." Bonner admitted it (Foxe, VIII, 110; cf. Godwin, *op. cit.*, p. 250). See also what J. A. Muller says, 310 *sq.*

Germany.[64] Two years later, he went with the Dean of Exeter, Dr. Haynes, to persuade Charles V not to accept the council which the Pope had just summoned at Vicenza; but the emperor would not allow him into his presence. In the same year (1538) he took Gardiner's place in Paris, and his mission was to prevent a union between Francis and Charles, which would have been disastrous for the King of England.[65] But his arrogant tone, and his stern and abrupt manners drew down upon him more than one unpleasant answer from Francis I. He forgot, Montmorency remarks,[66] that every good ambassador "ought to try to make himself agreeable to the prince with whom he is dealing and to conduct his negotiations in all modesty." "But for the consideration due to his master," said the King of France, "Bonner would already have received more than a hundred strokes of the halberd."[67]

[64] He wrote his preface to *De vera obedientia* during this embassy. "Edmund Bonner, archdeacon of Leicester, the King of England his most excellent majesties ambassadour in Denmarke. To the sincere, gentle herted and godly Reader" (cf. Freidmann, *Anne Boleyn*, II, pp. 187–8, 190–1, *sq.*).

[65] Cf. Burnet, I, 398. Thomas Wyatt, recently recalled from Spain, was instructed to help him (*L. and P.*, XIV, Part 2, p. 524). But the jealousy between Bonner and Wyatt was more apt to hinder than to promote the success of the mission (G. F. Nott, *Memoirs of the life of Sir Thomas Wyatt*, 1811, II, 44, 52).

After the meeting at Nice, which they had not been able to prevent, Gardiner, Thirlby and Brian were recalled and their places taken by Bonner, who was then under Cromwell's protection. Bonner's description to Cromwell of his meeting with Gardiner near Lyons should be read (Foxe, V, 154 *sq.*; cf. Dixon, II, 8; Muller, 74 *sq.*). The latter could hardly disguise his vexation and refused to give up his mules and harness in spite of the king's request, pretending that he needed the former and that the latter bore the episcopal arms. The two of them became so heated that the flesh of Gardiner's cheek "began to swell and tremble, and he looked upon me as he would have run me through. And I came and stood even by him and said: 'Trow you, my Lord, that I fear your great looks?'" "Bonner and Winchester were the greatest enemies that might be" (Foxe, V, 413). When a little later, Bonner was promoted to the see of Hereford, Gardiner "cast down his head making a plaicemouth with his lip." See S. R. Maitland, *op. cit.*, chaps. XVII and XVIII: "Gardiner and Bonner."

[66] Kaulek, p. 159.

[67] Henry had demanded that a certain Brancetor should be arrested. He was an English subject, a follower of Charles V, and had been attainted in 1539. Francis I agreed to the request of Bonner and Wyatt. But Brancetor protested to the emperor, whom alone he pretended to look upon as his master. Charles objected to his arrest, and the King of France seleased him. Bonner was so upset because he had not succeeded that he remonstrated with Francis I in a rude and churlish manner. The king, he raid, acted in this business entirely against God, reason, and duty, and

He had to be replaced by Sir John Wallop. At the beginning of his embassy in France, Bonner had been appointed to the see of Hereford (November, 1538); on his return, he was transferred to the see of London, of which the bishop, Stokesley, had just died.[68]

Among the services rendered by all the Henricians to the cause of the royal supremacy Tunstall's were certainly not the least. After the deaths of Warham and Fisher, he was indisputably the most respected and esteemed of the English prelates. Venerable on account of his age—he was over sixty—known and valued by the Humanists, he was considered to be the most learned man in the country, so Pole wrote to Ghiberti in 1536.[69] Thomas More had a high opinion of his virtue and knowledge, and was on intimate terms with him. The bishop's "invincible moderation" gave, moreover, considerable importance to his attitude on the religious question.

Tunstall began by protesting against the title of "supreme head of the Church"; this happened in the Convocation at York in 1531. He declared that those words should be clearly understood to mean that the king was, after Christ, the supreme head of his realm and of the English clergy in temporal and earthly matters.[70] Henry, who showed a keen appreciation for Tunstall's judgment, was so affected by this protest that he wrote to Tunstall, answering his arguments and reassuring him. He also averred that the restriction *in temporalibus* demanded by the bishop was superfluous since he had no intention of encroaching upon the spiritual jurisdiction.[71]

that it was iniquitous and unjust, and against the treaties in existence between his master and the King of France. This bluntness and lack of manner drew down upon him the hatred of the whole court, and he was unable to stay there any longer. Francis I himself asked that he should be recalled. And Henry was grieved because Bonner had shown such little skill in his duties of negotiation. Although Cromwell spoke for him and tried to excuse him, Bonner was recalled in the beginning of February, 1540 (Kaulek, pp. 153, 156–62, 164, 171; cf. Merriman, I, 282; *L. and P.*, XV, 86).

[68] His transference was confirmed on November 11th, 1539, and he was consecrated in St Paul's, on April 4th, 1540 (Burnet, I, 409).

[69] *Ven. Cal.*, 1534–54, No. 116.

[70] This protest is given in full in Latin in Wilkins, *Concilia*, III, 745. Cf. Chapuys to Charles V, May 22nd, 1531 (Stow MS. 141, fol. 36).

[71] "In using words," said the king, "we ought to regard and consider the expression of the truth in convenient speech and sentences, without overmuch scruple of superperverse interpretations as the malice of men

After Parliament had recognized the king's new title, Tunstall, at heart a constitutionalist, yielded; he signed a solemn renunciation of the Bishop of Rome and preached against papal authority in his own diocese.[72] Thenceforward his zeal was so little suspect that he was chosen to speak in the presence of the Carthusians who had been condemned to death, on Quinquagesima Sunday, 1536.[73] Three years afterwards, on Palm Sunday, he preached a famous sermon on the royal supremacy in Henry's presence, which was printed by Berthelet, the court printer.[74] He upbraided Reginald Pole for his *De Unitate Ecclesiae*, and said that it manifested an ignorance of the first councils; he advised him to burn it, and alleged that the king had in no wise broken the Church's unity.[75] "I never was more deceived," wrote Pole to Con-

may excogitate." And to show that titles are not to be taken literally he gave these instances: "when we write to the pope 'sanctissimo' we mean not holier than St Peter, though it sound so; and he that in our letters should object that, should be thought ridiculous. . . . Hath not the pope been called 'Caput ecclesiae' and who hath put any addition to it? Have not men said that the pope may dispence 'cum jure divino'? and yet in a part 'juris divini viz. moralis et naturalis' the same man would say he might not dispence. . . . And why . . . doth the pope suffer any other besides himself to be called archbishop, seeing that he himself challengeth to be 'Princeps apostolorum et episcoporum' in Peter's stead, which the name of an archbishop utterly denieth? . . ." (Wilkins, II, 762).

[72] He protested that he looked "for no mutation, nor new world," i.e. the restoration of papal jurisdiction (Strype, *Eccl. Memorials*, I, 204 *sq.*; Ellis, *Original Letters*, 3rd series, II, 336). Even under Edward VI he accepted some of the religious reforms, which he had previously voted against, after Parliament had sanctioned them. Gardiner blamed him for being too submissive. Although, for instance, he had been opposed to the Act of Uniformity in the Upper House (*Lords' Journal*, January 15th and February 19th, 1549), yet once it had become law he applied it in his diocese.

[73] Wriothesley, *Chronicle*, I, 34.

[74] Berthelet, 1539. London, in 8vo; republished in 1633, in London, in 4to. Strype (*Eccl. Mem.*, I, p. 336 in the old edition) gives a more or less accurate extract. There is a 1539 copy in the library at Lambeth Palace.

[75] Strype, *Eccl. Mem.*, I, Part 2, p. 306. J. Foxe, V, 90-99. Cf. Quirini, I, 470; Schelhorn, *Amoenitates historiae ecclesiasticae et literariae*, I, 76; Bridgett, *Life of Bl. Th. More*, p. 347. Tunstall's treatise, sent to Pole in the form of a letter, was published by Reginald Wolf, a year after the author's death, in 1560, and reprinted in the Appendix to Knight's *Erasmus*. In another letter of the same period to Reginald Pole (Bridgett, *Life of Bl. Th. More*, p. 347), Tunstall declared that the king was desirous "to reduce his Church of England out of all captivity of foreign powers. . . . Would to God you had been exercised in reading the ancient councils, that you might have known from the beginning, from age to age, the continuance and progress of the Catholic Church, by which you would have perceived

tarini, "for I always thought Tunstall was full of zeal for the religion. Whereas he contests my belief or rather the Church's belief in the Pope's authority, which he desires to see wholly destroyed." Thus Tunstall, like the rest of the Henricians, accepted the theory of and practised passive obedience to the civil powers.[75a]

The submission of such learned, moderate, and venerable prelates did more to establish the royal supremacy than the execution of Fisher and More. In the Upper House the spiritual lords, bishops and abbots, were in the majority. The fate of the country's schismatic laws was entirely in their hands. Faced with examples such as these, the confusion of the public conscience can be easily understood. How many people must have repeated to themselves the words of Lady More to her husband: Why not do "as all the bishops and best learned of this realm have done?"[76]

The bishops spread abroad the false doctrine of the royal supremacy, and caused the clergy under them to do the same. The Bishop of Chichester wrote to Cromwell, on June 28th, 1535, saying he had "preached the Word of God openly in his cathedral of Chichester, and published the King's most dreadful commandment as to the union of the supreme head of the Church of England to the Imperial Crown, and the abolition of the bishop of Rome's authority." He had "also sent forth his suffragan to preach and publish the same. By this day every abbot, prior, dean, parson, etc., in his diocese has

---

that the Church of Rome had never of old such a monarchy as of late it hath usurped." Tunstall was here expressing the opinion of modern Anglicans. Pole answered Tunstall's treatise (Quirini, I, p. 483; cf. p. 477).

[75a] An Englishman at Louvain University wrote to Pole in 1537 in these terms: "Leus (Lee) et Tonstallus, gravissimi alioqui et doctissimi antistites serviliter homini adulantes . . . sanctissimorum Patrum decreta totius Ecclesiae consensu approbata ac confirmata impugnant, et tot jam soeculis receptam Romani Pontificis authoritatem elevant imo abrogant" (Letter affixed to that of R. Pole to Contarini, July 21st, 1537, Quirini, *op. cit.*, II, 73, 77).

[76] W. Roper, Lumby's ed. of *Utopia*, Cambridge, 1908, p. xlv. "The disputes," Cardinal Pole says, "that the conduct of Henry has aroused in England have brought everything into doubt; men do not know what to believe, which side to take. How can we know, they ask, when clever men, learned men, and, as far as we can see, good men, take opposite sides?"

received similar orders."[77]   In those days when the printed word could not be widely and rapidly circulated, the pulpit was the most powerful means of influencing the crowd. What the press, tracts, posters, and meetings do to-day was done then through the pulpit. So Henry VIII and Cromwell made use of it to form the opinions of the people, who through the non-residence of the clergy and the too frequent lack of sermons had been allowed to wallow in ignorance of religious matters. Thus with the blind leading the blind, the mass of the simple people were drawn into the common abyss of schism.[78]   By their authority and example the Henricians were largely responsible for this plunge into the abyss.

Though they were the servants and the defenders of the royal supremacy, the Henricians remained attached, nevertheless, to the privileges of their Order, and secretly hoped one day to see them revived. Even during Henry's lifetime, and despite the fact that he objected to it as being contrary to his supremacy, Gardiner maintained that the bishops held their powers from God alone.[79] The king was no sooner dead than the bishop wrote to the Protector Somerset (1547) asking whether the king's powers, as spiritual head of the Church, were not limited by the same constitutional laws as his temporal powers.[80]   Gardiner, Bonner, Tunstall, and Thirlby contended that the King's Council could make no innovations in religious matters during the prince's minority,[81] for the king *in person* was the supreme head of the Church. Until the prince came of age, that spiritual authority was in abeyance, and could not therefore be exercised by either the council or the protector in the king's name. In this way the Henricians hoped to able sooner or later to check and limit the royal supremacy and to keep it, as it were, within constitutional

[77] Robert Sherborn adds that he had two thousand copies of the declaration of the royal supremacy distributed (*L. and P.*, VIII, Nos. 941, 963).

[78] Under cover of charity and religion, wrote Chapuys on February 4th, 1534, the new doctrines are taught to the simple people; it is much to be feared that everything here will go to wrack and ruin.

[79] Strype, *Eccl. Mem.*, I, Part 1, 332; Part 2, 220. Cf. R. C. Usher: *The supposed origin of the Doctrine of the divine right of Bishops*, in *Mélanges Bémont*, Paris, 1913, p. 541.

[80] Foxe, VI, 42.

[81] Pollard, *England under Protector Somerset*, 1900, 112 *sq.*; cf. 96   Thomas Thirlby was then Bishop of Westminster.

bounds, which would permit the bishops to regain some of the freedom they had lost.   They disliked the theories which tended to subject the Church to the State.

They were not at all partisans of absolute monarchy.   Once when Cromwell was lauding the *quod principi placuit* of the Roman law and advising Henry to make his will and desires the law, Gardiner, who happened to be present, told the king "to make the laws his will was more sure and quiet," as well as less dangerous and more in keeping with his people's nature. Henry preferred the latter counsel.[82]

The Henricians had approved the breach with Rome, the king's authority in spiritual matters, the dissolution of the monasteries,[83] and the destruction of images which pandered to superstition. Further than that they would not go. They maintained the dogma, and so Strype and Foxe speak of them as "the popish bishops."   They were all determined adversaries of Lutheranism. In 1520, Tunstall was at Worms as ambassador to the emperor, and he informed Erasmus of the progress that heresy was making in Germany and invited him to write against Luther. He did not wish a single copy of the *Babylonian Captivity* to cross the Channel.[84] Six years later, he prohibited and hounded down in his diocese Tyndale's New Testament, Simon Fish's *Supplication of Beggars*, and all Protestant books.[85] He induced Thomas More to use his talents as a writer to defend the faith "against the impious spoilers of the Church" and to refute the writings of the Lutherans.[86] He always upheld the Real Presence against the innovators, and vigorously maintained it in his *De Veritate corporis et sanguinis D.N.J.Ch. in Eucharistia*. According to Chapuys, Stokesley was sorry that he had favoured Anne Boleyn's marriage, because she and her relations were inclined to Lutheranism[87]; and

[82] *L. and P.*, VII, 1554. Foxe, VI, 46.

[83] Gardiner inveighed against the religious orders, in 1538 (Burnet, I, 400).

[84] *Erasmi Epistolae*, I, col. 759. Gairdner, *History*, p. 78.

[85] This prohibition is printed in *Four Supplications of the Commons*, Early English Text Society, 1871, pp. x–xi.

[86] For this reason he gave him permission to read all those writings. Burnet, IV, 13; Wilkins, *Concilia*, III, 711. Cf. Bridgett, *Th. More*, 281–82; Gairdner, *History*, 124.

[87] "The said bishop was the chief cause and instrument of the first

he had Tynedale's brother arrested for selling Protestant Bibles in London.[88] Gardiner attacked Bucer, the theologian-diplomatist *par excellence*, in several treatises and turned his specious arguments against him.[89] On various occasions he strenuously defended the Catholic doctrine of the Eucharist against Peter Martyr and the other innovators. He asserted that the devil persuaded men that Christ meant to say something different from the meaning expressed by his words when he said: "This is my body"; and that those whom the devil had seduced asked, like the Jews at Capharnaum: "How can this man give us his flesh to eat?" To establish a contradiction between Christ's presence in heaven and His presence in the consecrated Host was a fallacy of the devil. The addition of the adverb "but" to the words "Do this in remembrance of me" in order to show that the sacrament was merely a memory or a reminder and nothing more was also a diabolical fallacy; and it was equally diabolical to add to the words of one of the fathers, who spoke of the Eucharist as a sign and a figure, the commentary *"but* a sign, *but* a figure."[90]

divorce, for which he is heartily sorry and would like to go on with this one, because the said concubine and all her family are so abominably Lutheran" (Chapuys to Charles V, April 29th, 1536, *Staats-archiv* in Vienna, P.C. 230, fol. 78).

[88] Merriman, *op. cit.*, p. 100. Cf. *L. and P.*, V, 65.

[89] Bucer's theological abilities were such that he was used to bring about a rapprochement between the Lutherans and the Zwinglians, that they might have a doctrinal understanding between themselves. Cf. G. Constant's article, "La Transformation du culte anglican sous Edouard VI" in the *Revue d'histoire ecclésiastique*, XII (1911), pp. 252 *sq.* See the French ed. of this book (p. 674) for Gardiner's treatises against Bucer, and also P. Janelle (*Obedience in Church and State*, pp. lxv *sq.*, 174-212): Gardiner's answer to Bucer. *Contemptum humanae legis justa authoritate latae gravius et severius vindicandum quam divinae legis qualemcumque transgressionem*, see p. 389, n. 172.

[90] This appears in *A Detection of the Devil's Sophistrie, where with he robbeth the unlearned people of the true byleef in the most blessed Sacrament of the aulter*, London, 1546, which treatise was answered by John Hooper, afterwards Bishop of Gloucester (1550-54) and of Worcester (1552-54), under Edward VI (*An answer unto my lord of Wynchester booke intytlyd a detection of the devyls Sophistrie*, Zurich, 1547, reprinted in the Parker Society edition, 1843-52, of Hooper's *Works*), and also by Anthony Gilby, a violent controversialist of the Reformers' school, who attacked the Anglican Church under Elizabeth for being too conservative from his point of view. (*An answer to the devilish detection of Stephane Gardiner . . . compiled by A. G.*, London, 1547.) See French ed. of this book (pp. 675 *sq.*) for the refutations written by Gardiner against Peter Martyr and Cranmer on the Eucharist. Two manuscript treatises by Gardiner on the Eucharist (1550), one

He had a horror of the new opinions: faith alone did not suffice for justification, charity was also needed; predestination is a mystery which we must not be ashamed to recognize as such, but we can most certainly say "to any man particularly: Thou mayest be damned by thine own sin, and likewise to every particular man: Thou mayest be saved by God's mercy." A great number of errors are due to individual interpretations of the Scriptures: "I protest openly and take God to record that I never yet durst be so bold to gather any sense of Scripture but such as I have read gathered already in good authors, whose spirit I durst better trust than mine own. I knowledge and confess my own poverty therein. . . . Scripture is to me over dark to understand it alone."[91] None fought more than he against any religious understanding with the German Protestants. When Henry VIII consulted him in 1536 on the proposed alliance with them, the bishop replied by making use of arguments *ad hominem* capable of affecting him[92]: in England, the king was an emperor and head of the Church; if he entered the Smalcaldic League he would bind the Church to Germany and would be unable to do anything without the consent of that country. "You are asked," he said, "to accept the Augsburg confession. Would you not thus be binding England to Germany's way of thinking and accepting the word of God on conditions? The Bishop of Rome would not fail to take advantage of that. You are asked to make a contract, but the contracting parties are not on equal terms. On one side there is the King of

against Hooper and the other against Œcolampadius, are in the Record Office and the Brit. Mus. (cf. Muller, 315 *sq.*).

[91] *A declaration of suche true articles as George Joye hath gone about to confute as false*, London, 1546. In this treatise Gardiner still speaks of justification, good works, the Eucharist, purgatory, the invocation of the saints, the impeccability of the Blessed Virgin, and ecclesiastical celibacy. It is preceded by an introduction by Henry Joliffe, and was written at the end of 1552, but published after the author's death under the title: *Responsio venerabilium sacerdotum Henrici Joliffi et Roberti Ionson sub protestatione facta ad illos articulos Joannis Hoperi, episcopi Vigorniae nomen gerentis, in quibus a catholica fide dissentiebat: una cum confutationibus ejusdem Hoperi et replicationibus reverendissimi in Christo patris, bonae memoriae, Stephani Gardineri episcopi Vintoniensis, tunc temporis pro confessione fidei in carcere detenti*, Antwerp, 1564. In spite of Gardiner's very clear attitude, Foxe, who is bitterly hostile to him, tries to point out his contradictions on various points, especially on the Eucharist (*Acts and Monuments*, VII, 597–604).

[92] Gardiner was then away on an embassy to Francis I.

England, who is the head of his own Church. On the other, only dukes and other subordinates dependent upon the emperor, who is the head of the Church of Germany. How can you pretend to contract a religious agreement without his consent?"[93]

Gardiner was always for confining the alliance with the Protestants to purely political matters, and the failure of the negotiations between the Lutherans and the English was attributed to him.[94] His relations with the German Reformers, in 1539, did not affect his doctrinal ideas in any way at all. On the first Sunday in Lent in the following year (February 15th), he preached a very strong sermon against Luther's errors at St Paul's Cross, which considerably annoyed Dr. Barnes. He took his text from the Gospel for the day dealing with Christ's temptation. "Nowadays," he said, "the devil tempteth the world and biddeth them cast themself backward. There is no foreward in the new teaching, but all backward. Now the devil teacheth, come back from fasting, come back from praying, come back from confession, come back from weeping for thy sins. . . . The devil hath excogitate to offer heaven without works. To be in heaven needs no works at all, but only belief, only, only, nothing else."[95]

[93] Gardiner's opinion on the articles presented to His Majesty by the German princes. [This is translated from the French text, which is not a literal translation of the original.—*Translator*.] Strype, *Eccl. Mem.*, II, 3; Collier, IX, 131; Merriman, II, 3; cf. J. A. Muller, 66 *sq*.

[94] We have just seen what he wrote for the first conference, at Wittenberg (1536). He brought about the defeat of the second (London, 1538), according to Burnet and Dixon, by extolling a civil league before touching upon the religious question (Dixon, II, 5). He is even said to have supported Charles V's efforts to reconcile England with the Holy See, in 1541 (Morone's despatch, in Dittrich, *Histor. Jahrbuch*, IV, 627). He received a letter from Paul III which nearly caused him grave difficulties. And because at that time he listened to Granvelle's proposals, they tried to pick quarrels with him in the last years of the reign (cf. J. A. Muller, chap. XIV and p. 141).

[95] Gardiner recalls this sermon in his *Declaration* against George Joye, mentioned above. He mentions also the virulent reply by Barnes, forced by the king to recant and kindly treated by Gardiner, who tried in a friendly manner to withdraw him from error, but in the end he was carried away by his friends and by Cromwell's protection, in whose downfall he was also involved. Barnes was burnt, together with Garrard and Jerome, two days after Cromwell's execution (July 30th, 1540). Cf. Kaulek, 169, 171, 174 *sq*., 188, 207, 208; J. A. Muller, chap. XIII.

All who sided with the New Learning were ferreted out by the Henricians. Gardiner and Stokesley tried Frith, at St Paul's on June 20th, 1533, for erroneous opinions on transubstantiation and purgatory.[96] Together with Tunstall, they instigated the proceedings against John Lambert, who was condemned at Westminster in November, 1538, for denying the Real Presence. Barnes was sent on a mission to Germany; and Gardiner impugned his nomination, before the whole Council, because he was accused of heresy; and some time afterwards (February, 1540), in a theological debate, Gardiner made Barnes admit his errors.[97] The persecution of the Windsor heretics, in 1543, was also attributed to Gardiner.[98] Foxe, author of *The Book of Martyrs*, relates that Stokesley, on his deathbed, congratulated himself upon the execution of more than thirty heretics.[99] Bonner, who had become Bishop of London, opened the sessions at the Guildhall, in 1541, against the Reformers; and the following year he ordered all the vicars in his diocese to discover, and also to denounce, all who possessed suspect books, especially the works of Luther, Calvin, Tyndale, Joye, Roye, Simon Fish, and John Frith.[99a] Shortly afterwards he had a boy of fifteen, Richard Mekins, consigned to the flames for speaking against the Eucharist and for saying that Barnes died a martyr's death.[100] He likewise condemned John Porter for reading aloud at St. Paul's one of the Bibles placed there for the use of the faithful, and for

[96] Gardiner did all he could to save Frith, who had been his pupil at Cambridge (*L. and P.*, VI, 600); Stokesley, on the contrary, was very vehement against him (*ibid.*, VI, 761; Foxe, V, 16). Frith was burnt in July, 1533. Cf. J. A. Muller, 52 *sq.* In 1531, Stokesley had condemned a whole series of books, including Frith's and Tyndale's "The Supplication of Beggars." Cf. J. Gairdner, *Three Fifteenth Century Chronicles*, Camden Soc., 1880, pp. 89 *sq.*

[97] *L. and P.*, XV, 306, 312, 334. Cf. Merriman, I, 287.

[98] Foxe, V, 486.

[99] Foxe, III, 104. Cf. Laurentius Humfredus [Dr. Humphrey], *Vita Juelli*, p. 268; Schelhorn, *Amoenitates eccles.*, I, 86. For Stokesley's action against heretics, cf. *L. and P.*, V, 65.

[99a] Cf. Burnet, IV, 517 *sq.*; H. Reusch, *Die Indices librorum prohibitorum des sechzehnten Jahrhunderts*, Tubingen, 1886, pp. 19 *sq.*

[100] At the stake he admitted his error and acknowledged the kindness and charity shown to him by the bishop to help him to die a good death (Hall, *Chronicle*, 841). Hall pretends that he had been coached to say that, but he could not have derived any benefit from it. The harshness of this deed must be attributed more to the act of the Six Articles (1539) than to Bonner.

commenting upon it in his own words despite the episcopal injunctions. Porter, loaded with chains and attached to the dungeon wall by a collar of iron, died, so Foxe says, after five or six days.

Of the Henricians, Gardiner and Bonner have left the most galling memories for their firm stand against heresy. Protestant historians have continually depicted them in the worst possible light, even down to our own times. The attempt to justify and vindicate their actions by showing that they simply applied the laws which then existed, and that they were at times even merciful is of comparatively recent date.[101]

Foxe says that Gardiner "had a vile nature and pestilent pride, joined with malice and disdain, intolerable, great vices, as pride, envie and cruelty, flattering to his Prince, submisse to his superiours, envious to his equals and haughty to his inferiours," in fine, Gardiner, according to Foxe, was "the enemy of God's word."[102] Foxe and Strype allege that, at the end of his life, Henry VIII hated Gardiner more than any layman, on account of his action against the Windsor

[101] Maitland (*Essays*, chap. xx) takes the older writers to task for their exaggerations. He is followed in this by Gardiner's latest biographer, J. A. Muller, who fully shows the Bishop of Winchester's condescension, and his efforts to retrieve from error those especially whom he had known at Cambridge (cf. *op. cit.*, pp. 52 *sq.*, chaps. III, XIII, XIX). If at times the innovators by their replies and their obstinacy unnerved him so much that he lost his patience, he was rather reproached for being "too gentle and good" (*ibid.*, pp. 146, 270, 273). *The Life and Defense of the conduct and principles of the venerable and calumniated Ed. Bonner by a tractarian British critic* (London, 1842) is merely a sarcastic work, more controversial than biographical, which is attributed to Townsend of Durham, Foxe's editor.

[102] Foxe, VII, 585. These words are recorded by Sir John Harington, ed. 1792 of the *Nugae Antiquae*, I, 49; ed. T. Park, 1804, 64; Foxe, V, 160 *sq.* Sir John Harington is not inclined to say much good of Gardiner, "who persecuted me before I was born." Because of their attachment to Queen Elizabeth, his father had spent a twelvemonth in the Tower, and his mother had been kept from the future queen, "as a hereticke," owing to the Bishop of Winchester's influence, during Mary Tudor's reign (*ibid.*, ed. 1792, I, p. 50). He concludes his remarks on Gardiner by quoting some lines written by his father in memory of his imprisonment, and two pieces of poetry, each containing twenty-six verses. The second piece, which is a reply to the first, curses Gardiner, whom the author, "one Mr. Prideaux," places right in the centre of Hell for his cruelties:

> "O thou devourer of the good
> Thy wrongs in earth do dwell,
> Thy cruel thirst of guiltless blood
> Now must thou quench in hell."

heretics.[103] The story told of Gardiner's attempt to put to death Katherine Parr—a decided partisan of the Reformation —appears also to have been invented by Protestants.[104] "His hatred of the true religion was such," wrote Bishop Godwin, "that he was not satisfied with sending a number of excellent men to the stake, but strained every nerve to suppress the future Queen Elizabeth, saying that it was no use cutting off the leaves and branches, unless the root were also pulled up, which was the heretics' only hope. . . . If he himself had not been prematurely suppressed by Divine Providence, there is no knowing what might have happened."[105] Sir John Harington, who was only a child when Bonner died, says that Bonner was more hated and feared than Gardiner, and that the former was merely Gardiner's agent in the execution of the papist barbarities. "He was so hated,"[106] he says, "that every ill-favoured fat fellow that went in the street, they would say that was Bonner." Anglicans have, in fact, been most embittered against Bonner, who tried and condemned many heretics in the days of Mary Tudor.[107] Thomas Preston, in his tragedy *Cambyses*, compared him to the Persian tyrant:

"He was a kin to bishop Bonner, I think verily
For bothe their delights was to shed blood
But never intended to do any good."
(Last Scene.)

[103] Cf. the evidence given by witnesses when Gardiner was deprived of his see (Foxe, V, 486, 496; VI, 164, 173, 176). Maitland (*op. cit.*, 239 *sq.*) refutes this assertion.

[104] Foxe, V, 533. If it had been true, John Bale, Gardiner's enemy, would not have failed to speak about it in his article on Katherine Parr (Bale, *Scripta*, ed. 1548, fol. 234). When Gardiner was tried, under Edward VI, no allusion was made to this (*Biographia Britannica*, p. 2104, art. "Gardiner"; cf. Maitland, *op. cit.*, 243 *sq.*; Froude, *History of England*, chap. XXVII; and J. A. Muller, pp. 138 *sq.*).

[105] Original text in Latin. Godwin, *De Praesulibus Angliae Commentarius*, London, 1616, 298 *sq.* That Gardiner sought to make attempts on Elizabeth's life while she was at Woodstock is one of Foxe's tales, who moreover bases his story solely upon hearsay and suppositions (cf. Mumby, *The Girlhood of Queen Elizabeth*, London, 1909, pp. 125, 184 *sq.*). But he did think it necessary to keep her from the throne; accordingly a few weeks before he died he proposed to Parliament that she should be excluded from succession (cf. J. A. Muller, 287 *sq.*).

[106] Ed. 1792 of *Nugae Antiquae*, I, pp. 18 *sq.*, 53.

[107] Bale, *Scripta*, p. 40; Ponet, *Treatise of Politicke Power*, 1556, ed. 1642,

Foxe, in turn, compared him to Porsenna and inveighed against "his great rage" and "his raging heat" and depicted him as "one clean void of all humanity." He termed his efforts to persuade heretics "the subtle snares of that bloody wolf," and epitomized his life thus:

"This cannibal, in three years' space, three hundred martyrs slew;
They were his food; he loved so blood, he spared none he knew."[108]

Godwin[109] followed after Foxe and, improving upon his predecessor, styled the bishop *martyromastix truculentus*, and *carnifex sanguinarius*; "more cruel than the cruellest hired assassin, he sent more victims to the stake than all the other bishops of England together." Fuller was unable to find expressions sufficiently strong to brand the man "whom all generations shall call bloody. We may say that a lion, tiger, wolf, bear, yea, a whole forest of wild beasts met in Bonner, killing two hundred in the compass of three years."[110] For three centuries Bonner's cruelties were used as a "bogey" to cow naughty English children, much as ogres are flaunted before children of other lands.[111]

Bonner, according to Foxe, was in truth the enemy of the Holy Ghost, i.e. the Reformation. Those words may be applied to all the Henricians, for they strenuously opposed all changes of doctrine. When the various Confessions of Faith

p. 57; Traheron, *Works*, p. 65; Burnet; Strype; Foxe; Fuller; Heylin, etc.

[108] Foxe, V, 765; VI, 718 *sq.*; VIII, 414, 482. Bonner, he adds (V, 414) "made the reading of the Bible a trap or snare to entangle many good men and to bring them to ruin and destruction."

[109] *Op. cit.*, 250 *sq.*

[110] Fuller, IV, 185: "And as if his cruelty hade made him metropolitan of all England," continues Fuller, "he stood not on distinction of dioceses, but martyred all wheresoever he met them. . . . No sex, quality, age escaped him." Dr. Laurence Humphrey, who lived in Elizabeth's time, wrote that Stokesley, too, "had sacrificed to the god of hell above three hundred" (cf. A. Wood, ed. 1691, I, 576).

[111] Maitland (*Essays*, chap. xv) has undertaken to refute these accusations. Although Bonner condemned many heretics, it does not follow that he delighted in their tortures, as Foxe asserts (cf. Gairdner, *History*, 220). But he was unpopular, and London was the centre of contempt for episcopal authority. When the bishops met at Highgate, Elizabeth refused to offer her hand to him.

were debated during this reign, they were always on the side of orthodoxy. In the discussion upon the Ten Articles, in 1536, Stokesley maintained[112] that the sacraments were seven in number against the attacks of the opposing party.[112] He vigorously refuted Alexander Alane, whom Cromwell had brought to the meeting to uphold the new teaching.[113] "It is false and not to be allowed that all sacraments ought either to have a manifest ground in Scripture, or shew forth some signification of the remission of sins." "Sacraments," said Alane, "are seals ascertaining us of God's will: without the Word there is no certainty of God's good will: therefore without the Word there be no sacraments." "And is there none other word of God," fiercely answered Stokesley, "but that which every sutor and cobbler read in their mother tongue? If ye think that nothing pertaineth to the Christian faith but that only that is written in the Bible, ye err with the Lutherans."[115] "Scripture," Gardiner also said,[116] "is a sweet pure flower whereof spiders gather poison and bees honey. . . . Go thither instructed with wholesome doctrine and there thou shalt see it confirmed. Go thither infect with malicious opinions and there thou shalt writhe out matter wherewith to maintain them." He explained that the partisans of the new doctrines took texts here and there from the Scriptures to support those teachings and interpreted them according to their fancy, paying no attention to the Church's traditions. The Bishop of London and Tunstall endeavoured to give to the Second Confession of 1537 a Catholic tone and appearance. On this occasion, Tunstall upheld the divine

[112] He was followed by Edward Lee, Archbishop of York; Longland, Bishop of Lincoln; J. Clerk, Bishop of Bath; Sampson, Bishop of Chichester; and even it appears, by William Rugg, of Norwich, who shortly afterwards sided with the Reformers.

[113] Cranmer; Latimer, Bishop of Worcester; Shaxton, Bishop of Salisbury; Edward Foxe, Bishop of Hereford; and Thomas Goodrich, Bishop of Ely.

[114] Alane is better known under the name of Alesius or Aless. Gardiner debated with him, as well as with Bucer, at the Diet of Ratisbon (1541); and he concluded that he had never in all his life debated with such a fool (cf. Gardiner, *Exetasis testimoniorum quae M. Bucerus ex S. Patribus non sancte edidit, ut patrocinetur opinioni de coelibatus dono*, Louvain, 1554; J. A. Muller, *op. cit.*, pp. 97 *sq.*).

[115] Cf. Dixon, I, 522 *sq.*

[116] *A declaration of suche true articles as George Joye hath gon about to confute as false*, London, 1546. Cf. J. A. Muller, 129.

institution of auricular confession in a long statement, which the king annotated in his own hand and which may be seen in the British Museum.[117]

When the articles were considered before the final formulary of faith (1543), Bonner, like Tunstall and the other Henricians,[118] gave orthodox replies to the daring questions placed before the Commission by Cranmer. He confessed that he believed the doctrine of the seven sacraments to be based upon Scripture; that consecration was necessary in Holy Orders and that the Apostles had been made bishops by Christ; that sinners were bound to confess their secret sins; and that Extreme Unction was a sacrament mentioned in the Scriptures.[119] The Six Articles (1539), marking the extreme point reached by the Catholic reaction under Henry VIII, were in keeping with the aspirations of the moderate party. Gardiner was said to have compiled them[120]; and Bonner applied them in his diocese with such severity that he became unpopular. Fl. Volusenus [Wilson], the Scotch scholar, dedicated his commentary on the 50th Psalm of David (1532) to Gardiner, and praised his strength and the example of firmness he had given to the other prelates. When Cromwell fell, the Bishop of Winchester was chancellor of Cambridge, and he was so alarmed at the progress the new doctrines were making that he adopted a retrograde policy in the university rules.[121] In 1545, it was rumoured that Cranmer had again secured the ear of the king, and that he was about to give a fresh impetus

[117] Cotton MS., Cleopatra, E, V, fol. 125.

[118] Especially Edward Lee, Archbishop of York; the Bishop of Carlisle, Robert Aldrich; and Thirlby, Bishop-elect of Westminster. For Gardiner's silence, see Dixon, II, 309, n.

[119] Burnet, IV, 457, 460, 478, 494; VI, 245 sq. Lee and Aldrich were of the same opinion as Tunstall.

[120] By W. Turner, e.g. in his Rescuynge of the rhomishe fox, 1545, and by the Vice-Chancellor of Saxony, who was in London when the law was passed (L. and P., XIV, Part 2, 423), Bucer, Melanchthon, and other Continental Protestants (ibid., 186, 379, 444). Cf. J. A. Muller, 81, 353 sq.

[121] He even forbade the new method of pronouncing Greek which Thomas Smith and Cheke had introduced and which had nothing to do with the faith (cf. Strype, Eccl. Mem., I, Part 2, p. 479; J. A. Muller, chap. XVII). He wrote in his De pronuntiatione Graecae linguae in 1542, and it was published in 1555 at Basle with Cheke's reply (J. Cheki . . . de pronuntiatione Graecae potissimum linguae disputationes cum Stephano Wintoniensi episcopo). Smith's treatise was published in Paris in 1568. All three are given in Havercamp's Sylloge altera Scriptorum, 1740. Cf. J. Bywater's The Erasmian Pronunciation of Greek, London, 1908.

to the New Learning. Gardiner, who was then ambassador to Charles V (October, 1545 - March, 1546), immediately warned Henry that any innovation in religion would imperil the negotiations for peace, and drive the emperor to side with France—then at war with England—and thus leave England without an ally. It was through him, according to Strype and Burnet, that the king made no change.[122] Burchardus, writing to Bullinger, said that "unless he [Winchester] . . . be caught, the evangelical truth cannot be restored."[123]

The Henricians showed great caution with regard to the translation of the Bible (1533). Tunstall even refused to have any share in it. He would not undertake the translation of the Acts of the Apostles which Cranmer had entrusted to him. Stokesley argued that the reading of the Scriptures in English would infect the people with heresies. Gardiner translated St Luke and St John, but informed Cromwell that his health and fatigue prevented him from further translations.[124] After Cromwell's death, Convocation, in 1542, condemned the great Bible, edited by Cromwell and Cranmer, as being full of errors. The task of revising it was to be given to the most prominent Hebrew and Greek scholars.[125] Gardiner, who presided over the Commission with Tunstall, objected that many words in the Latin version of the Vulgate had an ecclesiastical meaning which could not easily be given in English. He drew up a list of them and demanded that the Latin word for them be retained or else that they be altered as little as possible in translation, *quam accommodatissime fieri possit*. The English translation was therefore overloaded with so many Latin words, according to both Burnet and Fuller, that the people could hardly understand it any better than the Latin text itself; and the same authors attribute the failure of the Commission to Gardiner.

[122] Strype, *Cranmer*, Bk. I, chap. xxx; Burnet, I, 507, 524; Nichols, *Narratives of the Reformation*, 342; Foxe, V, 561 *sq*. Cf. Pollard, *Cranmer*, 218; Gairdner, *History*, 238 *sq*.

[123] *Original Letters*, Parker Soc. (1847), II, 639, Letter ccxcv.

[124] Nichols, *Narratives of the Reformation*, 277, 278. Gardiner's letter to Cromwell was dated June 10th, 1535.

[125] Wilkins, *Concilia*, III, 860. Fuller (III, 198) gives the list of the bishops commissioned to undertake the revision, from the Convocation documents since lost.

It is possible that they exaggerate.[126] At all events, by objecting thus, Gardiner, in opposition to the Lutherans,
endeavoured to retain the traditional meaning of the most
important words, and to preserve the doctrinal import which
the Church attributed to them. In this way they avoided the
errors of Tyndale and the other Protestants, who translated
πρεσβύτερος (*presbyter*), for instance, as "elder" instead of
"priest," ἐκκλησία (*ecclesia*) as "assembly" instead of "church,"
μετανοεῖν (*facere penitentiam*) as "to repent" instead of "to do
penance," and ἀγάπη (*caritas*) as "love" instead of "charity."
These errors, reproduced in part in the Great Bible, were
important dogmatically; Gardiner therefore wished to
counteract the evil by keeping for the essential words their
Catholic meaning.[127]

The opposition between the new and the old teaching
caused contention among the respective supporters of these
teachings. As long as Henry VIII lived the members of the
reforming and the moderate parties were at variance. The
bishops of one party looked upon their episcopal brethren in
the other as irreconcilable adversaries. Latimer accused
Gardiner of trying to take his see from him; and they all
reached such a pitch of rivalry and hopeless division that the

---

[126] Burnet, I, 455, 498. Fuller, III, 199 *sq.* gives the list of Latin words,
from Wilkins, III, 860. The anxieties of the scholar and the philologist
are also recognizable in Gardiner. When he was questioning Marbeck,
the heretic (1543) about his English concordance of the Gospels, he
exclaimed that to translate an expression into English in such a manner
destroyed the Latin tongue.
At the end of a month the king stopped the work that had been commenced, on the plea of entrusting it to the Universities of Oxford and
Cambridge. All, with the exception of Cranmer, Goodrich and Barlow,
protested that Convocation was more fitted for the task than the universities,
i.e. that truth should prevail over learning (*L. and P.*, 1542, No. 176).

[127] In the "Great Bible" *charitas* is translated "love," 1 Cor. xiii;
communio, "partaking," 1 Cor. x, 16; *sacramentum* frequently "mystery," as
in the passage of the Epistle to the Ephesians, v, 32, which speaks of
marriage (*Hoc est magnum sacramentum:* "this is a great mystery"); *confessio*,
"to knowledge with the mouth," Rom. x, 10; *ecclesia*, always "congregation"; *parabola*, at times "similitude." Precisely all these words are found
in Gardiner's list.
Gardiner's principle was afterwards adopted for a certain number of
words, as Blunt observes (*Plain account*, 56). Thus "Resurrection" was
retained instead of the "Again rising" in the old versions, and "Redeemer"
instead of "Again buyer." But those words already had their English
equivalent, and their doctrinal import was not contested by Protestants
(cf. J. A. Muller, *op. cit.*, pp. 104 *sq.*).

people were puzzled to know what to believe.[128] It was chiefly against Cranmer and Cromwell that the Henricians combined. In 1534, Gardiner and Stokesley objected to the metropolitan, Cranmer, visiting their dioceses, knowing that he favoured the new ideas. Gardiner alleged that the title of primate, in virtue of which Cranmer claimed to make his visitation, was derogatory to the royal supremacy. Stokesley disputed the title of *legatus natus* of the Apostolic See, which, as it had not been abolished, placed the Archbishop above the other prelates.[129] The king, however, upheld Cranmer; and the visitation was carried out in the usual way.

Cromwell detested the Henricians, and sought to keep them from the court, fearing that their influence might counterbalance his own. Their diplomatic abilities provided him with excellent excuses. From 1536 to 1540, Bonner was sent upon various missions which kept him constantly out of England.[130] Tunstall was given certain duties upon the Scotch borders which kept him fully occupied.[131] Gardiner was ambassador in France from 1535 until the end of 1538, and in 1539 he was sent to Germany.[132] He was Cromwell's chief rival, and the latter had a particular aversion for him. Cromwell managed to arouse distrust and suspicion of him in Henry VIII's mind. In 1534 Gardiner had to hand over his post as the king's chief secretary to Cromwell, and leave the court. Some time later Henry expressed his pleasure and

[128] "*L'estat de religion cependant demoure en ceste malheurté, les évesques en envye et division irréconciliable et le peuple en doubte de ce qu'il doibt tenir.*" Marillac to the Constable of France, Montmorency, June 1st, 1540. Kaulek, *op. cit.* p. 188, *L. and P.*, XV, 737. The contest in the King's Council between the moderate party and the Protestants, from 1545 to 1547, may be followed in Vol. VIII, *L. and P.* Cf. *Eng. Hist. Review*, 1906, p. 800.

[129] Strype, *Mem. of Cranmer*, Append. XIV, XV, and chap. VIII. Cf. *L. and P.*, V, 850.

[130] Yet, according to Foxe, Bonner was on friendly terms with Cromwell, whom he considered as being partly the cause of his preferment (Foxe, V, 414; VII, 587). In 1536, Bonner was at Hamburg, and at the King of Denmark's Court; in 1538, he was at the emperor's court, and then in France until the beginning of 1540.

[131] He was made President of the Northern Council after the Pilgrimage of Grace (Merriman, I, 200; cf. II, 99).

[132] Speaking of his mission in France, in 1533, Friedmann says: "As Gardiner, next to Norfolk, was the chief rival of Cromwell, the latter was not sorry to get rid of him for a time. With Cranmer, Audeley, and Wiltshire at his back, Cromwell expected to be more than a match for the duke alone" (*Anne Boleyn*, I, 227). Cf. Merriman, I, 129.

satisfaction with Gardiner for the way he had carried out the negotiations in France; but the all-powerful minister succeeded once more in arousing Henry's suspicions, and the bishop withdrew to Winchester, scarcely able to conceal his annoyance and full of resentment (1538). He proved to be one of the chief agents of Cromwell's downfall.[133]

Stokesley was likewise at enmity with Cromwell, who pestered him with all sorts of vexatious proceedings. In 1535, he was ordered to send to the court a copy of a sermon he had just preached. The bishop replied that he never wrote his speeches, and that even if he did he could not deliver them as they were written, because a thousand things came into his mind whilst he was speaking which had not been foreseen in the preparation.[134] Three years later (May 29th, 1538), the solicitor-general accused him of violating statutes 16 of Richard II and 28 of Henry VIII, by executing a Bull of Martin V. Imprisoned and then released with a caution, he was able to produce the king's pardon when the judges summoned him before them. He died in the following year (September 8th, 1539).[135]

Cromwell feared Tunstall's influence and his moderation. When Parliament was voting on the dissolution of the monasteries (1536), he wrote to tell Tunstall that the king dispensed him from making the journey on account of his age. The bishop was only a few miles outside London when he received this letter. While he was trying to decide what to do, he re-

---

[133] Wriothesley, "a satellite of Cromwell," met him on the way to Winchester between Sittingbourne and Rochester, with a "very gallant train" which seemed rather "strange" to him. When he told him that the king was at Greenwich, Gardiner "said he heard so," but appeared to be very little anxious to go and see him. Wriothesley took Thirlby apart, and tried to extract from him a few words that would compromise Gardiner, but he did not succeed, for Thirlby lauded his friend's prudent wisdom (Wriothesley to Cromwell, September 27th, 1538. *L. and P.*, VIII, 51; cf. Muller, 76 *sq.*).

The enmity between the two antagonists was latent, but constant. "Gardiner, bishop of Winchester," says Foxe, "*who never favoured Cromwell*" (V, 414). "Gardiner . . . envious to his equalls, namely to Cromwell" (Sir John Harington, ed. 1792 of *Nugae antiquae*, p. 49, and ed. 1804, p. 64).

[134] *L. and P.*, VIII, 1054.

[135] *L. and P.*, XIII, Part 1, 1095. He was buried in London, in St Paul's. There is a translation of his Latin epitaph in A. Wood, ed. 1691, I, 576, ed. Bliss, II, 749. His portrait by Holbein is at Windsor; Magdalen College, Oxford, possesses a copy of it.

ceived a peremptory order to go back to his diocese without delay.[136]

The passing of the Six Articles (1539) marked the zenith of the conflict between the Henricians and the Reformers, which continued unabated. At the beginning of the following year, the French ambassador noted "the great contest in which the bishops of this country are engaged, some wishing to maintain their doctrine as true, whilst the rest condemn it as erroneous and false."[137] To triumph over an adversary became a matter of life or death. For the Henricians, it was a question of overthrowing Cromwell, and for Cromwell, a question of suppressing the Henricians. The struggle lasted a year.

Cranmer and Cromwell managed to make the Six Articles a dead letter, and to prevent the Protestant preachers from being troubled. "The papistical faction," wrote the Lutheran Burchardus to Melanchthon from London (October, 1539), "has nowise obtained its hoped-for tyranny, nor, God willing, ever will in England";[138] the law was passed, but not executed. Gardiner and his ally, Bishop Sampson of Chichester, were excluded from the council.[139] Cromwell hoped that the marriage with Anne of Cleves would bind Henry indissolubly to the anti-Catholic cause, and he endeavoured to make sure

[136] Richard Hilliard's (or Hillyard's) account—secretary to Tunstall—preserved in Arundel MS. 152, fol. 312, and printed by Van Ortroy, *Ana. Boll.*, XII, 272, 273. This account is confirmed by two of Chapuy's letters (*L. and P.*, VII, Nos. 221 and 690). Hilliard was in Scotland, in 1543, as an outlaw and afterwards became Rector of the English Hospice in Rome (Bridgett and Knox, *Queen Elizabeth and the Catholic Hierarchy*, 214). There he wrote a religious history of Henry VIII's reign, now lost, but an extract from it is preserved in the Arundel MS., and Rishton, Sander's Roman editor, made good use of it. The *Athenae Cantabrigienses* (I, 534) contains an account of Richard Hilliard.

[137] Marillac to the king, April 24th, 1540 (Kaulek, 178). In his letter dated May 8th (*ibid.*, 181) he also speaks of "*la contention où les évesques en ce parlement, sont entrez sur aucunes propositions qui concernent la religion.*" Burnet (I, 405) notes that the influence of the moderate party was already increasing at court in the previous year.

[138] *L. and P.*, XIV, Part II, No. 423. Burchardus, Vice-Chancellor of Saxony, had been sent to London to try and arrange an agreement between Henry VIII and the Protestant princes in Germany (cf. chap. VIII).

[139] Because of their attacks on the reforming party (*L. and P.*, XIV, Part 2, p. 279). Sampson was accused of keeping too much to the old ceremonies in matters of worship (cf. Strype, *Eccles. Mem.*, I, 499; II, 378, 381, 627).

that in the elections of 1539 there should be a majority against the reactionary party in the council. The Henricians united for a final effort. All the episcopal nominations in 1539 and 1540 were in their favour. Two reactionaries, Bell and Capon, took the places of Latimer and Shaxton at Worcester and Salisbury, for these had been obliged to resign after the Six Articles were passed.[140] Another Henrician, Skip, received the see of Hereford. Bonner, who became Bishop of London on the death of Stokesley in September, 1539, was more forceful and more unmerciful to the heretics than his predecessor. Heath, who became chancellor in Mary Tudor's reign, was appointed to Rochester in the place of Hilsey, the former provincial of the Black Friars who favoured the new ideas. Both of them, in addition to Wriothesley, had become reconciled with Gardiner; and the latter consecrated them on April 4th, 1540.[141] Cromwell himself sought Gardiner's friendship, and dined and spent four hours in conversation with him on March 30th, 1540. A commission was sent to Calais to cleanse the town of all ideas of the New Learning, which Cranmer's commissary had encouraged there. In 1540, Gardiner was re-admitted to the Council; and there was in existence a scheme to make Tunstall the king's vicar-general in lieu of Cromwell.[142]

A few days later Cromwell became "Earl of Essex and great Chamberlain of England, enjoying greater credit and authority with his master than ever; a position he had come near to losing through the Bishop of Winchester." He sent Bishop Sampson of Chichester to the Tower with two other opponents, and declared that five bishops would be going very soon in the same direction. "These bishops are in

[140] Foxe was the first to characterize Latimer's resignation as voluntary and a sacrifice to his principles: "He did of his own free accord resign and renounce his pastorship." But Latimer himself said he was forced to resign (*State Papers*, I, 489; cf. *Latimer's Sermons and Remains*, Parker Society ed., 1845, I, 136). Melanchthon reproached Henry VIII for his treatment of Latimer and Shaxton: *Audio viros excellenti dotrina et pietate praeditos, Latimerum, Saxtonum, Cromerum et alios, teneri in custodia* (*Melanchtoni Opera*, IV, 837).

[141] Nott, *The Works of Henry Howard, Earl of Surrey, and of Sir Thomas Wyatt the Elder*, London, 1815–16, I, 306. For these prelates, see J. Le Neve, *Fasti ecclesiae anglicanae*, ed. Hardy, Oxford, 1854.

[142] Merriman, I, 288 *sq.* *L. and P.*, XV, 249, 486, 804; XIV, Part 2, p. 141.

marvellous trouble." Every day, wrote the ambassador Marillac, fresh arrests are expected, and things have reached such a pitch that one or other of the parties must succumb.[143] It was Cromwell's party that eventually succumbed (June 10th, 1540).[144]

The moderate party's triumph was the triumph of orthodoxy. Whatever his own personal views may have been on religion, Cromwell was looked upon by all as the representative of the reforming party.[145] As such Gardiner attacked him: he accused him of holding principles which contradicted the principles of the Six Articles, of upholding the Reformers, and of always showing favour to those who preached the erroneous opinions and of opposing those who taught the traditional doctrines.[146] "It had been good that he had been dispatched long ago," said Bonner of Cromwell, "who loved him [Bonner] very dearly."[147] The Duke of Norfolk and Gardiner, long since on friendly terms, ruled the council without any rivals. Norfolk, who displayed his hatred of heresy, was the queen's uncle and the king's principal minister. Gardiner, save for a few passing cloudy intervals, remained in the king's favour for the remainder of the reign; "no man could do me hurt during his life," he afterwards wrote to Somerset.[148] All the reformers looked upon him as their most

[143] Marillac to Francis I, April 24th, 1540, to Montmorency, June 1st, 1540. Kaulek, 179, 187. *L. and P.*, XV, 737. Cf. *State Papers*, I, 637; Strype, *Eccl. Mem.*, II, 378 *sq.*

[144] Cf. chap. VI. "*Maintenant,*" wrote Marillac on June 11th (Kaulek, 190), "*s'est vérifié ce que par mes précédentes il vous aura pleu entendre touchant la division qui estoit entre les ministres de ce roy, dont les ungs taschoient destruire les aultres. Le party du sieur Cramvel . . . est quasi du tout abatu pour la prinse dudit sieur Cramvel qui estoit le chef de sa bende, et ne sont restez de son costé que l'archevêque de Canturbery qui n'ose plus ouvrir la bouche et le seigneur admiral qui de long temps s'est très bien aprins de ployer à tous ventz. . . . C'est certes une chose d'aultant plus merveilleuse qu'elle est venue contre l'oppinion et expectation de tout le monde.*"

[145] Merriman, whose thesis is to make politics the centre of everything in Cromwell's life, admits this fact: "He was commonly looked upon as the greatest friend and helper that the Protestants had" (I, 286).

[146] These reasons which Gardiner suggested (Merriman, I, 294) were used by the king to explain Cromwell's fall. Marillac's letter, June 1st, 1540, *L. and P.*, XV, 766 and Kaulek, 189. Letter from the Council to Sir John Wallop, *L. and P.*, VIII, 349, 350. Cf. Merriman, I, 286, 288.

[147] Foxe, V, 413.

[148] Foxe, VI, 36. In 1543 his nephew and secretary, Germain Gardiner, a priest, was accused, with three other clerics, of having denied the royal supremacy. The three others were acquitted, but he was condemned and

formidable adversary. Anglicans speak of this period as the time of Catholic reaction. Barnes, Garrard, and Jerome were burnt. Because Dr. Crome had said that belief in purgatory contradicted the abolition of the chantries, he was forced to recant before the whole of the King's Council. The former Bishop of Worcester, Latimer, was thrown into prison,[149] whilst Shaxton, the previous Bishop of Salisbury, was tried and condemned, and then made his abjuration (1546). Heretics were rigorously persecuted; and the Continental Protestants compared Henry VIII to Nero. Tyndale's and Coverdale's New Testament, as well as all the works of Wiclif, Frith, George Joye, William Roye, Barnes, William Turner, and Richard Tracy were consigned to the flames.[150] In 1542 Convocation declared that the translation in the Great Bible was scandalous and needed revising. It was withdrawn from the churches; and Grafton, the man who printed it, was given six months' imprisonment and fined £300.[151] To be in possession of an anabaptist book meant a fine of £5. Severe penal laws checked the abuses of Holy Writ in sermons, books, ballads, theatrical plays, and songs. In the preface to the Third Confession of Faith, the king condemned "an inclination to sinister understanding of Scripture, presumption, arrogancy, carnal liberty and contention," which needed curbing because the people had become imbued with it and had forgotten the difference between teachers and those who were

---

executed (Strype, *Mem. of Cranmer*, I, 176; Foxe, V, 526, 690; Burnet, I, 567). Gardiner's enemies took advantage of this to attack his loyalty. But it is not true, as Strype asserts (*loc. cit.*), that the bishop fell into disgrace for ever after. Foxe (*loc. cit.*) says just the opposite: "*He still kept in with the king* to the great inquietation of the public state of the realm, and especially of Christ's church" (cf. Maitland, *Essays*, 240–42). In November, 1546, Gardiner had a little dispute with Henry over an exchange of lands (cf. Maitland, 254 *sq.*; *State Papers*, I, 883, 884; vindication of Gardiner in Foxe, VI, 188); and this was probably the reason why he was excluded from the Regency Council in the king's will (December 26th, 1546), which document is considered suspect by more than one historian. A contemporary copy of this will is in the Stow MSS (cf. Foxe, V, 603, 691).

[149] Wriothesley, *Chronicle*, I, 167–68. Cf. R. M. Carlyle, *Hugh Latimer*. For Barnes, Garrard, and Jerome, see Foxe, V, 414–38.

[150] Cf. Strype, *Mem. of Cranmer*, Bk. II, chap. xxiv; Foxe, IV, 666, 753, V, 414 *sq.*, 565 *sq.*, 696, and Append. III. The injunctions against heretical books had appeared in 1539. Wilkins, III, 847; Strype, *Eccl. Mem.*, I, 537.

[151] Strype, *op. cit.*, chap. xxi. Gairdner, *History*, 223 *sq.*; Kaulek, 02.

taught.[152]   In the same year (1543) Parliament forbade women and common folk to read the Bible, even at home.[153] The Henricians had the advantage. "A man may now travel from the east of England to the west, and from the north to the south," wrote one of the Reformers to Bullinger, "without being able to discover a single preacher, who out of a pure heart and faith unfeigned is seeking the glory of our God. He [the king] has taken them all away."[154] These words may be somewhat exaggerated, but at least they express the opinion common amongst the Reformers and the general tendency at the end of this reign.[155]

When Henry's reign ended Protestantism had been unable to make any impression upon the dogma of the English Church; and this was due largely to the Henricians.

We may wonder how it was that bishops, who were so energetic and constant in defence of the Church's teaching, were yet so feeble when faced with the royal supremacy and so ready to repudiate the Pope's authority. We may not be able to justify the Henricians, but we must at least try to explain their behaviour.

First of all, in judging bygone centuries we must be careful not to consider them as identical with our own if we wish to avoid anachronisms, which would be historical errors. In the sixteenth century, the primacy of the Sovereign Pontiff was not seen with the same clearness as Catholics have viewed it since the Vatican Council. This truth had become befogged during the troubled times of the Great Schism, and in the discussions of the Councils of Constance and Basle which followed on that schism and wherein papal authority received more than one setback.[156] The Council of Florence (1439), in its last session, had affirmed the Pope's primacy, but that council had practically no authority for all who looked upon

[152] Lloyd, *Formularies of Faith in the reign of Henry VIII*, 215.

[153] *Statutes of the realm*, 34 and 35 Henry VIII. Cf. Dodd, ed. 1737, I, 269 *sq.*

[154] Letter cv, from Richard Hilles, *Original Letters*, Parker Society ed. 1846, I, 204.

[155] The struggle between the two parties in the autumn of 1546 (cf. Foxe, V) is known to us only by foreign accounts (*Correspondance d'Odet de Selve*, and the *Sp. Cal.*, 1545–47).

[156] Cf. Bridgett, *Bl. Thomas More*, 346 *sq.*

the Council of Basle as a legitimate council.[157] "It must not be forgotten," said Cardinal Manning, "that at this time the minds of men had been so distracted by the great western schism, by the frequent subtraction of obedience, by the doubtful election of the popes, and the simultaneous existence of two or even three claimants to the holy see, that the supreme pontifical authority had become a matter of academical discussion *hinc inde*. Nothing but such preludes could have instigated Gerson to write on the thesis *de Auferabilitate Papae* [whether the Pope could be deposed]."[158] "Owing either to the false principles which had become current since the great schism," says the Rev. T. E. Bridgett,[159] "to the want of deep theological studies at the universities, or to the contempt of ancient ways that then prevailed among the disciples of the Renaissance, the importance of the supremacy of the Holy See for the maintenance of unity was less felt than in former ages in England. Tunstall and others considered it to be of merely ecclesiastical institution, like the patriarchical and metropolitan authority, and, in their exaggerated spirit of nationalism, thought that it might be set aside and replaced by that of Catholic kings." Yet one of the most famous English theologians, Thomas Netter of Walden (†1430), greatly esteemed by Henry VI, who chose him as confessor, had strenuously maintained the papal primacy against Wiclif.[160] When Henry VIII upheld this same doctrine in his

[157] This was the Gallicans' case. During the Council of Trent, in April 1563, Cardinal Lorraine wrote that "the Council of Florence has little authority for those who admit the doctrine of the Council of Basle as legitimate and œcumenical, especially when it is a question of the Roman Pontiff's power" (G. Constant, *La légation du cardinal Morone près l'empereur et le concile de Trente*, Paris, 1922, p. 59). With a number of others, he opposed the renewing of the decree of Florence and the adoption of the title "pastor Ecclesiae universalis."

[158] The *Dublin Review*, January, 1888, p. 245. "For in the next General Council," More wrote shortly before his martyrdom, "it may well happen that this Pope may be deposed and another substituted in his room, with whom the King's Highness may be very well content. For albeit that I have for my own part such opinion of the Pope's primacy as I have showed you, yet never thought I the Pope above the General Council . . ." (More, *English Works*, p. 1426). This letter of More to Cromwell was printed in his *English Works* from the rough draft; the original, slightly corrected, is in the British Museum, MS. Cleopatra E, VI, ff. 150–52; it is reproduced by Bridgett in *Bl. Thomas More*, 343 *sq.*

[159] Bridgett, *Bl. John Fisher*, 325.

[160] In his *Doctrinale antiquitatum fidei* (1415–29) he addresses Wiclif in

book against Luther, Thomas More, who afterwards died in
defence of the doctrine, pointed out to the king that there
was a danger, from a political point of view, in overrating the
Pope's authority in the Church.[161] The king is believed to
have stressed the Pope's primacy less from personal convictions
than from a desire to obtain a title such as the Kings of France
and Spain possessed, and, in fact, he was given that of "Defender of the Faith."[162] "I have never doubted the Pope's
(spiritual) royalty," wrote Erasmus; "but elsewhere I have
wondered whether this royalty was acknowledged in St.
Jerome's time."[163] More's answer when he was sentenced to
death throws a singular light upon the state of mind of his
contemporaries. "I have, by the grace of God, been always a

these terms: "Cur ergo contra Romanum Primatum insurgis? Cur sic
irasceris audiens quod Episcopus Romanae Ecclesiae præeminat capitaliter
super omnes alios episcopos? Sanctissimi Christi pontifices hunc Primatum
in universa Ecclesia confessi sunt. Beatus Augustinus fuit; et huic Primatui
non invidit, sed eum humillime recognovit." Then, quoting St Augustine
and other Fathers, he adds: "Quid ergo inflatur superbus hæreticus contra
præeminentiam primae Sedis? Non est nova ista præeminentia, quae tunc
temporis Augustino et sanctis Patribus fuit sine omni dubitatione cer-
tissima."

[161] "At the first reading whereof I moved the King's Highness either
to leave out that point or else to touch it more slenderly, for doubt of such
things as after might hap to fall in question between His Highness and
some Pope. . . . And in my book against the Masker I wrote not, I wot
well, five lines, and yet of no more but only St Peter himself, from whose
person many take not the primacy, even of those who grant it none of his
successors. . . . But whereas I had written thereof at length in my con-
futation before, and for the proof thereof had compiled together all that I
could find therefor, at such time as I little looked that there should fall
between the King's Highness and the Pope such a breach as is fallen since;
when I after that saw the thing likely to draw towards such displeasure
between them I suppressed it utterly, and never put word thereof in my
book, but put out the remnant without it" (Thomas More's letter to
Cromwell, already mentioned above (n. 158).

[162] Henry replied to More's objection by revealing to him the secret
reason for his behaviour, viz. his ambition for the title. The title of *Defensor
fidei*, given to him by Leo X on October 3rd, 1521, was personal to the
king (Rymer, *Foedera*, ed. 1712, XIII, 756). Clement VII confirmed it in
1523, with, however, no mention of hereditary right, qualifying it only
with the ambiguous word "perpetuum." The title was made hereditary
by Act of Parliament (1543). Cf. *Dan. Guil. Molleri Disput. tio de titulo
Defensoris fidei*, Vol. II, fasc. 1, pp. 25-73 of Beyschlag's *Sylloge variorum
opusculorum*, 1829; Lingard, *History of England*, ed. 1849, p. 466; Brown,
Transactions of the Royal Hist. Society, 1880, pp. 242 *sq*.

[163] "Sed ut alicubi noto quod videtur facere ad hanc opinionem, ita
rursus aliis locis annoto quae faciunt ad diversam opinionem. Et tot aliis
locis voco Petrum principem apostolici ordinis, pontificem Romanum,
vicarium Christi et Ecclesiae principem" (*Erasmi Epistolae*, 667).

Catholic, never out of communion with the Roman Pontiff; but I have heard it said at times that the authority of the Roman Pontiff was certainly lawful and to be respected, but still an authority derived from human law, and not standing upon a divine prescription. (This was partly Gardiner's thesis in *De vera obedientia*.) Then, when I observed that public affairs were so ordered that the sources of the power of the Roman Pontiff would necessarily be examined, I gave myself up to a most diligent examination of that question for the space of seven years, and found that the authority of the Roman Pontiff, which you rashly—I will not use stronger language—have set aside, is not only lawful, to be respected, and necessary, but also grounded on the divine law and prescription. That is *my opinion;* that is the belief in which, by the grace of God, I shall die."[164]

Faced thus with a truth which the errors of the day had overclouded, the fear of death made the majority incline towards the side which was safer for the body, if not for the soul. Those who denied the royal supremacy were adjudged traitors by the law.[165] In Mary Tudor's time, Bonner was reproached by a heretic for serving the Pope whereas he had previously written against him, and he replied in these terms: "My lord of Winchester (Gardiner) being a great learned man, did write a book against the supremacy of the pope's holiness, and I also did write a preface before the same book, tending to the same effect. And thus did we, because of the perilous world that then was: for then was it made treason by the laws of this realm to maintain the pope's authority, and great danger it was to be suspected a favourer of the see of Rome; and therefore fear compelled us to bear with the time, for otherwise there had been no way but one. You know when any uttered his conscience in maintaining the pope's authority, he suffered death for it."[166] The nuncio in France averred

---

[164] The *Dublin Review*, January, 1888, p. 245. Cf. Gasquet, *Henry VIII and the English Monasteries*, II, 334, n.; Bridgett, *Bl. Th. More*, 300 *sq.*, 346 *sq.* According to Bridgett (p. 347), the opinion of Tunstall, with whom he was on terms of intimate familiarity, at first influenced Thomas More. Henry VIII's book against Luther first set him studying the papal primacy. Cf. Brown, in *Transactions of the Royal Hist. Society*, 1880, p. 258.

[165] Cf. *An invective agenste the great and detestable vice treason* . . . London, 1539.

[166] Foxe, VIII, 110.

that it was through fear of death that Gardiner wrote his *De vera obedientia*.[167] "What! my country, were you not a spectator of this," exclaims Reginald Pole,[167a] eulogizing Fisher and More, "when every deceit was practised, every snare was spread—on one side the favour of the prince, power, honour, and whatever is delightful to men, and on the other side prison torment, infamy, and death, or rather deaths?"

Many saved their lives and salved their conscience by a mental reservation. They made a tacit distinction between the Church of England and the Catholic Church, between *in temporalibus* and *in spiritualibus*, in other words, inwardly they acknowledged the king as the supreme head of the Church in temporal, but not in spiritual, matters. On being asked, "What did you for saving your conscience when you were sworn to take the king for Supreme Head?" John Rugg replied: "I added this condition in my mind, to take him for Supreme Head in temporal things, but not in spiritual things."[168] In a long harangue on the execution of the three Benedictine abbots occurs the following: "I cannot think the contrary, but the old bishop of London, Stokesley, when he was alive, used the pretty medicine that his fellow, friar Forest, was wont to use, and to work with an inward man and an outward man; that is to say, to speak one thing with their mouth and then another thing with their heart . . . what time as the spiritualty were sworn to take the king's grace for the supreme head, immediately next under God of this Church of England, Hugh Cook receiving the same oath, added prettily in his own conscience these words following: 'of the temporal church,' saith he, 'but not of the spiritual church.' "[169]

I doubt if a subterfuge such as that satisfied the conscience

---

[167] *L. and P.*, X, 570; cf. *ibid.*, 956. The nuncio in France, Pio di Carpi, had conversed with Gardiner, then ambassador at Francis I's court.

[167a] Original in Latin.

[168] Gasquet, *Henry VIII and the English Monasteries*, II, 371, n. John Rugg had been a prebendary of Chichester, but he gave up this post to retire to Reading. He was condemned to death with the Abbot of Reading for having finally denied Henry VIII's spiritual supremacy, "ob negatam Henrici pontificiam potestatem," to quote the original edition of Sander. Other instances of the state of mind of the contemporaries and the plausible excuses they made for taking the oath may be seen in *L. and P.*, Nos. 277, 387.

[169] Record Office, *State Papers*, Dom. 1530, V, 208, f. 23.

of men so enlightened and learned as were the Henricians, who, moreover, did not confine themselves to an oath but were militant defenders of the royal supremacy. But during the quarrel over investitures and in the discussions on the ecclesiastical communities, had not their predecessors in the episcopacy in England been servile followers of the Crown, at Rockingham in St Anselm's time, and at Northampton in the days of St Thomas of Canterbury? But Englishmen of the Renaissance period had such respect for the law that when it was pointed out to Gardiner that the Pope's primacy had been recognized by a general council, he replied "that an Act of Parliament discharges his conscience and that of all the king's subjects."[170] And in his *De vera obedientia* he asserted that if the king's orders were contrary to the Divine Will, the king himself, and not the subjects who obeyed him, would have to give an account to God. His friend Thirlby relates that, in the Upper House, he "was earnest against alterations as well concerning the bishop of Rome, as other orders in religion, yet, after those matters were established and set forth, by the acts, statutes and laws of this realm accordingly he was bound."[171] Possibly he and the other Henricians thought that, once the breach with Rome was consummated, in upholding Henry they would be maintaining the ancient faith, to which the king seemed to be sincerely attached. They wished to make his supremacy a breakwater against the waves of heresy which had swamped Germany. They defended the royal authority in matters of religion against the Reformers, because Henry VIII was using his authority more to

[170] J. A. Muller, p. 58. And when, in Mary Tudor's reign, England was restored to the Catholic unity with Parliament's consent, his comment on this restoration was that when Parliament had made a decision no individual had any right to question that decision as to whether it was right or wrong. ". . . shuld, whã a pliamête hath cõcluded a thinge, one or any private pson have authoritie to discusse whether yt they had done righte or wronge? no, yt may not be." (J. L. Chester, *John Rogers*, London, 1861, p. 306.) W. Palmer's poem on Gardiner, which is quoted by M. P. Janelle (cf. Bibliography, F, pp. 463 *sq.*). is a confirmation of the Henricians' way of thinking. Gardiner speaks thus:

> We crye a law / a lawe must be obeyde
> and not to brynge that / agayne in questione
> which by parlement / ys determynde,
> for then we say / we shoulde ever have dissencion.

[171] J. Foxe, VI, 190.

preserve religion than to introduce innovations.[172] The upholding of the king's claims appeared to them to be a means of preventing him from relying exclusively upon the advanced party, which would have led him to make changes in doctrine. When the moderate party in any country places itself in opposition, then the government inevitably veers round to the extreme parties. Henry VIII was not a reformer because the moderate party was on his side.

The calculations and the tactics of the Henricians seemed to be justified by events so long as Henry VIII lived; but with Edward VI things were different. In the latter's time the royal supremacy was no longer a prop for Catholic dogmas; on the contrary it was used to destroy and overthrow the old religion. Then, with one accord, the Henricians resisted. They were deprived of their sees and imprisoned.[173] The fundamental innovations accomplished in Edward VI's reign, still under cover of the royal supremacy, opened their eyes at length to the real nature of that supremacy. "The logic of facts was a more eloquent teacher than that of words." In Mary Tudor's reign they returned to the Roman communion and thenceforward remained faithful in their allegiance to the Pope. On his death-bed (1555), Gardiner interrupted the reading of the Passion at Peter's denial, and said with a sigh: "Negavi cum Petro, exivi cum Petro, sed nondum flevi cum Petro"; and these words were felt by all to be expressive of the remorse he felt for having formerly renounced papal authority.[174] Bonner and Tunstall were still living when Elizabeth, who definitely established Protestantism in Eng-

[172] After the Six Articles of 1539, when the last Confession of that reign was being elaborated—and together these marked the extreme point reached by the doctrinal reaction—Gardiner wrote a treatise against Bucer and Calvin, with the object of placing the king's authority above private interpretation of the Scriptures (1541): *Contemptum humanae legis justa authoritate latae gravius et severius vindincandum quam divinae legis qualemcunque transgressionem.* This treatise, the manuscript of which is preserved at Corpus Christi College, Cambridge, was published by M. P. Janelle in 1930 in *Obedience in Church and State.*

[173] *Acts of the Privy Council*, ed. Dasent, II; Le Neve, *Fasti Ecclesiae anglicanae*, II; Pollard, *England under Protector Somerset*, 21, 113, 114, 263.

[174] T. Stapleton's *A Counterblast to M. Horne's vayne Blast against M. Fekenham*, 1567, p. 368. Cf. Foxe, VIII, 635. J. A. Muller (291 *sq.*) is the first historian who does not take the prelate's words in their obvious meaning and sees in them little regret for the breach with Rome.

land, ascended the throne. Together with all the bishops of the previous reign save one, they refused to take the oath they had formerly sworn to Henry VIII. Their eyes were opened. They saw that a schism could not remain a schism but must inevitably go further in the Europe of those days, convulsed by the reforming movement of the sixteenth century.[175] They understood that the orthodox teaching of Henry VIII's reign was something essentially personal to the king and as short-lived as the king himself. They knew whither the Scriptures, adopted as the supreme authority, led; and their own authority, severed from Rome and the remainder of Christendom, was feeble indeed unless supported by the king's, and when opposed by the latter they were entirely disabled. They concluded that, if they were not Roman, they were not Catholic; and so preferred to die in prison. The Henricians had been schismatic, but at heart they remained Catholic, and the majority of them ended their lives in communion with Rome.[176]

[175] At the examination of Roland Taylor, a Suffolk rector, Gardiner confessed that he had accepted the royal supremacy because Henry VIII had taken all responsibility for it upon himself, but that the arbitrary proceedings of Edward VI had convinced him that the constitution of Church and State had been upset.

[176] Sir John Harington called the Henricians "Catholick Protestant or Protesting Catholick" (*Nugae antiquae*, ed. 1792, p. 50, and ed. 1804, p. 64).

CHAPTER VIII

THE CHURCH OF ENGLAND'S DOGMA UNDER HENRY VIII

Errors of certain historians—Orthodoxy and *autos-da-fe*—Attempts to unite the Churches of England and Germany: Conferences at Wittenberg (1536) and London (1538)—The First Confession or the Ten Articles of 1536—The Second Confession, "The Godly and Pious Institution of a Christian Man" (1537); the Thirteen Articles of 1538; the Six Articles (1539)—The Third Confession "The Necessary Erudition of a Christian Man" (1543).

ONE of the prerogatives of the royal supremacy was the defining of the tenets to be believed by the king's subjects. Henry VIII, being "supreme head of the Church of England," fixed that Church's doctrine. He certainly consulted the assembled bishops and asked their advice, but carefully revised and annotated their resolutions; it was his own opinion that finally prevailed, so much so that at the end of his reign the usual term for orthodoxy was "the King's doctrine." When the bishops "contested any propositions concerning religion" and were consequently "in envy and irreconcilable division," the king intervened and gave a decision as the "head of this party."[1] Every injunction or doctrinal proclamation was issued, according to the formula then in vogue, "by the King's authority as supreme head in earth of the Church of England, with the assent and consent of the prelates and clergy of the realm assembled in Convocation." The title given by Convocation to the First Confession in 1536 was "Articles about religion set out by the Convocation and published by the King's authority." Henry altered it to: "Articles devised by the Kinges Highnes Majestie . . . approved by the consent and determination of the hole clergie of this realme." The Second Confession of Faith (1537) stated that the king had not only to defend justice and to procure the

[1] Kaulek, 102, 181, 188.

public good, but also and especially to defend Christ's faith and religion, and carefully to preserve his true teaching. The First Confession of 1536 had previously affirmed that it was the duty of princes, according to Scripture, to see that the true religion and the right doctrines were maintained and taught.

Henry was always very anxious to preserve in his realm unity of belief, for he was convinced, as were all the princes of that period, that it was necessary as a foundation for political unity. Hence the various formularies of this reign, all of which tended, at times by the most rigorous means, to destroy the elements of division which were beginning to unsettle the country. He severely recommended the bishops to see that great caution was observed by themselves and by their clergy in their manner of speaking during the ecclesiastical rites and ceremonies, so that nothing might happen to "engender a diversity of opinion, whereby there ensued contention."[2] "Among other cures appertaining unto this our princely office," said the king in the First Confession, "we have always esteemed and thought . . . that unity and concord in opinion, namely in such things as doth concern our religion, may increase and go forthward, and all occasion of dissent and discord touching the same be repressed and utterly extinguished." The very title of the Ten Articles indicates with sufficient clearness the ruling thought in the king's mind: "Articles devised by the Kinges Highnes Majestie, to stablyshe Christen quietnes and unitie amonge us, and to avoid contentious opinions." "The king," said the message read by Cromwell to Convocation on June 21st, 1536, "studieth day and night to set a quietness in the Church; his special desire is to set a stay for the unlearned people, whose consciences are in doubt what they may believe." The aim of the Second Confession of 1537 was "the perfect establishing of said subjects in good unity and concord." The Six Articles

[2] Henry VIII to some of the bishops, Windsor, November 19th, 1537. *L. and P.*, XI, No. 1110, and Burnet, IV, 396; Collier, IX, 150.

The royal Injunctions of 1536 (Burnet, IV, 309 *sq.*; cf. I, p. 361) show how difficult it was to instruct the people upon the essential dogmas. And, in the letter to the bishops, mentioned above, of November 19th, 1537, Henry discloses the religious discord and disunion brought about "owing to a contemptuous manner of speaking against certain laudable ceremonies and customs of the Church."

menaced anyone preventing "true unity and sincere concord, which consequently redound to the commonwealth of this most noble realm." Finally, in the preface to the Third Confession Henry made a great attack upon all who presumptuously used the Scriptures to excite contention and disputes.[3]

The Church of England's dogma under Henry VIII has given rise to many erroneous judgments.

It is particularly important, in studying this dogma, to remember the doctrinal evolution through which the Reformation passed in England. "In order to avoid serious errors in history," says Michelet, "periods must be specified." Dogma under Henry VIII bears no relation to the dogma in Edward VI's or Elizabeth's time. Various historians do not appear to have made this distinction. It is also possible that, where the controverted points are concerned, they have failed to compare adequately the various doctrines. The Calvinists thought that certain Confessions of Henry's reign reflected their doctrine, while in the same Confessions the Lutherans saw their own particular teachings.[4] Catholic historians, like Butler and Lingard, knowing Catholic dogma better, have been sounder in their judgments.[5] Nearly all English

---

[3] Cf. Wilkins, III, 868; Dixon, I, 417 *sq.*; Pollard, *Henry VIII*, 378 *sq.*; Merriman, I, 253.

"A sermon against Contention and Brawling" complained of the religious discussions which were taking place in taverns and other places, "not so much pertaining to edification as to vain-glory," and which were causing quarrels and strife. After instancing St Paul's dislike of discord and dissension among the Corinthians, when one man said 'I am of Apollo' and another 'I am of Christ,' the preacher asked what St Paul would have said had he heard the discordant words then in every mouth: "He is a Pharisee; he is a Gospeller; he is of the new sort; he is of the old faith; he is a new-broached brother; he is a good Catholic fellow; he is a papist; he is a heretic."

In one of his last speeches in Parliament, as we have already seen (p. 337), Henry made the same reproaches to his subjects, commenting upon St Paul's words: "Charity is patient" (Dodd, *op. cit.*, ed. 1737, I, 316).

[4] See Kolde's article on Cranmer in the *Realencyclopädie*, 3rd ed., IV, 323 *sq.*; Laurence (Archbishop of Cashel), *An attempt to illustrate those Articles of the Church of England which the Calvinists improperly consider as calvinistical;* Todd, *Life of Cranmer*, I, 168 *sq.* An idea of the various interpretations placed upon the change in religion in this reign may be obtained by reading the articles by H. Birrel, J. H. Round, and G. W. E. Russell in the *Nineteenth Century*, 1896.

[5] See particularly chaps. VIII and X in Lingard. The Rev. H. A. Moreton, an Anglican, is of the same opinion. See his *Réforme anglicane au XVI. siècle*, 1930, chap. VII.

historians agree to-day in admitting that the doctrine prior to Edward's accession was orthodox. Yet the Germans, from the time of Ranke,[6] have persisted in maintaining the contrary for the First Confession or the Ten Articles of 1536. F. Makower, for instance, puts forward this opinion in a very important work on the constitution of the Church of England,[7] as also does Mentz in a study of the Wittenberg Articles, about which we shall shortly have something to say.[8] Professor T. F. Tout, of Manchester, in his *History of England*, which he wrote with F. York Powell, follows their opinion and for no valid reason whatsoever perpetuates it.[8a]

The German opinion does not represent the facts at all. All his life Henry upheld the orthodox teaching and persecuted the partisans of the new doctrines. Those who remained faithful to the Pope were looked upon as traitors, but the Reformers were condemned as heretics. A striking illustration of this was given to the people on July 30th, 1540. On that day, at the same time, three priests were hanged for denying the royal supremacy and three heretics were burnt for attacking the Catholic faith. Sander says that a heretic and a Catholic were bound together and dragged on the same hurdle. "Certainly it was a wonderful sight to see those who adhered to two contrary parties put to death on the same day and at the same hour."[9] So men were forbidden, under pain of death, to be Roman but had to remain orthodox.

---

[6] *Englische Geschichte*, I, chap. v (*Sämmtliche Werke*, XIV), 149 *sq.*, 153 *sq.* *Deutsche Geschichte*, IV, 40.

[7] *Verfassung der Kirche von England*, 1894, English transl.: *Constitutional History of the Church of England*, London, 1895, 177.

[8] *Die Wittenberger Artikel von 1536* in the *Quellen und Schriften zur Geschichte des Protestantismus* by J. Kunze and Stange, 1905.

[8a] Bk. VI, chap. II, "The Ten Articles and the Bishops' Book." He sees the new ideas in the Ten Articles because four sacraments are quietly ignored therein, which is not true as we shall see later, and because the old belief is not so much maintained as explained and justified, as though explaining and justifying a belief were not equivalent to maintaining it. The same tendency towards a moderate doctrinal reformation also appears, according to Professor Tout, in the Bishops' Book of 1537. This proves that he has not read these formularies of faith, or else that he does not know Catholic teaching.

[9] Marillac to Francis I, August 6th, 1540. Kaulek, 208. The three priests were Edward Powell, who had written against the royal divorce; Thomas Abell, Catherine of Aragon's chaplain, a prisoner in the Tower for eight years; Richard Fetherstone, also chaplain to Catherine and tutor to

It would be an historical error to think, as some writers have alleged, that the king maintained Catholic teaching solely to avert an attack from the Continent[9a]; for just when the emperor and the King of France appeared to be on the point of joining forces against England, Henry VIII got in touch with the German Reformers and exchanged ambassadors, but while holding out visions of a possible alliance with the Lutherans he was careful always to see that it did not materialize. As soon as danger disappeared, Henry, in his professions of faith, strongly asserted his Catholicism and mercilessly pursued heretics and sent them to the stake.

These rapprochements with the German Lutherans occurred in fact, only at such times as Henry feared a Continental coalition between Charles V and Francis I, and they were meant to divert the emperor's attention. Even his own personal inclinations were sacrificed for this purpose, for, although he loathed the union, he married Anne of Cleves.

He had inherited his policy from Wolsey, and it consisted in holding the balance, as far as possible, between the two powerful rivals, or as he himself put it "in being their mediator for the peace and happiness of Christendom"; a handsome expression which meant that he did not neglect any opportunity of setting Francis and Charles at variance. When either appeared to threaten him, he made overtures to the other. This stratagem was as easy for him as it was profitable, for thus he was able to safeguard England from foreign attacks at very little cost.[10]

Catherine's divorce had, however, complicated matters. Henry could no longer go from one rival to the other in the same free and easy manner, nor even intervene between them. While Catherine lived, reconciliation with the emperor was out of the question. Her death was mentioned openly before it occurred, and even in August, 1534, the imperial

Princess Mary. Cf. Wriothesley's *Chronicle*, Camden Soc. ed., I, 120 *sq.*; Kaulek, 211; Dodd, ed. 1737, I, 208 *sq.*; 222; Friedmann, *op. cit.*, II p. 70; Foxe, IV, 438 *sq.*

The three heretics were Robert Barnes; William Jerome, Rector of Stepney; and Thomas Garrard, or Garret. Cf. Burnet, IV, 497 *sq.*; Foxe, V, 414 *sq.*

[9a] Trésal, *Les origines du schisme anglican*, Paris, 1908, pp. 192 *sq.*

[10] Cf. Merriman, I, 223, 233.

ambassador Chapuys heard it discussed as a fortunate *dénoue-ment* for the English policy.[11]

There remained France. But Francis I's friendship for his "good brother," the King of England, had cooled off in a singular manner. He had been hurt by the insolent behaviour of the English ambassadors at his meeting with Clement VII at Marseilles; and the Pope had given him a glimpse of Calais as a reward for his breach with Henry. The rivalry between France and the empire had, it is true, inspired him to seek an Anglo-French alliance, but Henry did not relish the proposal that the Duke of Orleans or the Dauphin should marry either Princess Mary or Princess Elizabeth; the two extraordinary missions sent from France for this purpose came to nothing.[12] Meanwhile, the horrible deaths of the Carthusians and the execution of Fisher and More had raised a general storm of reprobation and had accentuated the strained relations between the French Court and England; Francis I used very strong language to the English ambassador, Sir John Wallop.[13] The new Pope, Paul III, was trying to band the Catholic princes together in order to carry out the sentence of deposition against Henry. Several Briefs had been published already, in which the Pope had censured Henry for his conduct and his crimes and forbidden all communication with him.[14] Francis I received one of these Briefs and sent an embassy to Henry to inform him of its contents and to let him know that he would hold his hand only on one condition, to wit, if England consented to join in an expedition against Milan, in other words, to provide £33,000 a month. This was

---

[11] Chapuys to Charles V, January 17th, 1534. *L. and P.*, VII, No. 1095. P. Friedmann, *Anne Boleyn*, II, pp. 139, n. 1, 141 *sq.*

[12] Neither Admiral Chabot, nor subsequently his secretary, Palamede Gontier, succeeded in getting Henry to accept Francis I's conditions; Henry thought them too burdensome (1534). Dinteville's attempt, in 1535, met with no greater success. Cf. P. Friedmann, *op. cit.*, II, pp. 39 *sq.*, 43 *sq.*, 51 *sq.*, 67-71, 122 *sq.*, 134 *sq.*; *L. and P.*, VII, Nos. 1483, 1507, 1554; VIII, Nos. 174, 557; Merriman, I, 224 *sq.* Charles V was urging Mary's marriage with the Duke of Angoulême, which indirectly entailed recognition of the princess' legitimacy and of the validity of Catherine's marriage. Henry in consequence, although he did not openly refuse, yet answered in an evasive fashion which left little hope. Cf. *L. and P.*, VII, No. 1060; H. Baumgarten, *Geschichte Karls V*, Stuttgart, 1885-92, III, 146.

[13] Cf. Friedmann, *op. cit.*, II, pp. 80 *sq.*

[14] Cf. Rinaldi, *ad. ann. 1535*, No. XXXIII.

an ultimatum. Henry, with an income of only £140,000, refused, and bitter words were exchanged.[15] Cromwell, always inclined towards an anti-French policy, quarrelled with the French ambassadors. They complained loudly of his insolence. Diplomatic relations were strained and a rupture with France seemed imminent.[16] Urged by Paul III, Francis I approached the emperor, who was more formidable than ever since his successful expedition at Tunis (July 1535), an expedition which had sown such consternation in the hearts of the king and Cromwell that they looked like "dogs that had tumbled out of a window."[17] Henry felt that he was isolated.

He chose this moment to enter into closer relations with the German Protestants. The events just mentioned happened between the months of August and October, 1535. The first English embassy which attempted to come to a doctrinal understanding with the Lutherans was dispatched in the November of that same year.

Cromwell was for ever striving to form an alliance with the Smalcaldic League so as to put an end to Henry VIII's dangerous policy, which might result in the complete isolation of England. In moments of serious danger the king thought that such an alliance might be useful. But, like Gardiner, the leader of the moderate party, he would have preferred that alliance to be purely political, whereas the Lutherans were anxious for a preliminary agreement upon doctrine.[18]

[15] Cf. P. Friedmann, *op. cit.*, II, pp. 115-123; Merriman, I, 226.

[16] Cf. P. Friedmann, *op. cit.*, II, pp. 136 *sq.* When Cromwell fell Francis I asserted that he had been the "cause of all the suspicions and malice that he [Henry] has entertained against his friends" (Kaulek, 191). According to Merriman (I, 258) there was a general aversion to France and a general friendly feeling towards Spain among the lower classes.

[17] Chapuys to Granvelle, September 13th, 1535. P. Friedmann, *op. cit.*, II, p. 113 and n. 3. Cf. Weiss, *Papiers d'État de Granvelle*, II, 361 *sq.*

[18] Cf. Burnet, I, 405 *sq.*; Collier, IX, 131 *sq.*; Merriman, I, 238. Already in the previous year (January, 1534) Heath and the German Mundt, who had been sent to the courts of Bavaria, Saxony, Hesse, Cologne, Treves and Mainz, and Sir William Paget, who had been sent to Poland, to the Dukes of Pomerania and Prussia and to the free towns of Germany, had maintained the king's just rights in the matter of the divorce, begged those who were going to the council to uphold Henry, and assured the Lutherans of Henry's sympathies, as he was an enemy of the Pope and desirous of uniting with them in order to extirpate false doctrines (*L. and P.*,

The first negotiations for this understanding lasted from December, 1535, until April, 1536.

Robert Barnes, a zealous agent between England and France, Edward Foxe, the new Bishop of Hereford (1535-38), who had been sent to Rome on a mission to Clement VII at the time of the divorce, Nicholas Heath, Archdeacon of Canterbury and afterwards Archbishop of York (1555-58), were commissioned to lay the foundations for this accord. They reached Erfurt on November 28th, 1535, and accompanied the Elector John Frederick to the Diet at Schmalkalden.[19] The ideas which they put forth there, from the very outset, upon the council summoned by Paul III at Mantua were too much like the Lutherans' own ideas for the latter not to hope that agreement could be reached. Three years previously Henry had appealed to a council; now, however, when it was being assembled by the Pope and the emperor, he was afraid. So, whilst he clamoured for "a free and godly Council,"—just as the Protestants did during the Council of Trent—to "procure a wholesome remedy for the present evils and to restore the peace of the Catholic Church," he spurned the Mantuan Council a priori. Full of bitterness for Paul III— "I will have nothing to do with that man"—and preoccupied with his own title of supreme head of the Church of England, he rejected all councils "rashly assembled, in an invalid and iniquitous manner"[19a] to confirm "the usurped honour, power,

VII, No. 21; Burnet, VI, 91–103). But these declarations were coldly received, so suspect did the king's sympathy with the Reformation appear to Protestants. Cf. Merriman, I, 220.

[19] Barnes, who suffered the death-penalty of heretics at Smithfield on July 30th, 1540, had scarcely been elected Prior of the Augustinians at Cambridge before he was denounced to Wolsey as being imbued with Lutheranism (1525) and obliged to recant. Although Foxe was partial to the new ideas, Heath, the Bishop of Rochester (1540–43), and of Worcester (1543–51), was rather an Henrician. Imprisoned under Edward VI, he was afterwards raised by Mary to the most important see after that of Canterbury. See what Melanchthon thought of these envoys, in Dixon, I, 311, n.

Luther informed Vergerio of Barnes' visit in the early days of November, 1535 (Friedensburg, I, 542; cf. Köstlin, Martin Luther, sein Leben und seine Schriften, Elberfeld, 1875, II, 373). As the Elector John Frederick was at Vienna when the English delegates arrived at Erfurt, they were received by Councillors Brück and Burchardt, on December 9th. L. and P., IX, No. 1018. For the Elector, see Eells, The attitude of Martin Bucer toward the bigamy of Philip of Hesse, 1925.

[19a] Original in Latin.

jurisdiction, and primacy." If he did not reject what was decided to be in conformity with the Gospel, "he repelled beforehand, condemned, and held as invalid and worthless" anything that might be defined contrary to Scripture, particularly with regard to the papal primacy.[20] In a speech to the assembled States, Foxe represented the king's alliance with the Protestant league as a possibility. He asked that an embassy should be sent to England to come to an understanding on matters of religion, and that a conference should be held beforehand in Germany itself, *ut alias meliore otio et occasione audiant ipsos; nam de his rebus cumulatius, data facultate ipsis, dicturos.*[21] In their answer consisting of thirteen articles (December 25th), the Lutherans expressed the joy they felt at the good will manifested by Henry, and their desire to see him propagate the Gospel in his kingdom, according to

---

[20] On December 15th the English delegates, in accordance with their instructions (*L. and P.*, IX, No. 213; Burnet, VI, 142), had already insisted on the need for a common action at the council, which necessitated a previous agreement on the essential points of doctrine (*Corpus Reformatorum*, II, col. 1008; cf. A. Duchesne, *Histoire d'Angleterre*, ed. 1614, p. 1297). Foxe spoke in such a way as to turn the Protestants from the council, in accordance with the book which the king had published (A. Duchesne, p. 1306). The title of it (a copy [Berthelet's, London, 1538] is preserved in the *Bibl. Nat.*, in Paris) was: *Henrici VIII . . . ad Carolum Cæsarem Augustum, cæterosque orbis christiani monarchos, populumque christianum, epistola, qua rex facile causas ostendit et cur is Vincentiam, ad concilium falso nomine generale appellatum, non sit venturus, et quam periculosum sit aliis qui veram Christi doctrinam profitentur, eo sese conferre. Additus est et libellus ille quem . . . rex sereniss. universique Brytanniae proceres de Mantuanensi concilio aediderunt* (Cf. Collier, IX, 141–50). Morone sent it to Rome on October 30th, 1537, labelling it "poisonous." (Friedensburg, II, 235.) Gardiner did not agree to taking part in a council "convoked by the emperor" (see his reasons in Collier, *op. cit.*, IX, p. 132). In the same way, Bishops Cranmer, Stokesley, Tunstall, Clerk, Goodrich, Capon, Shaxton, Latimer and Hilsey, as well as several other ecclesiastics whom Henry consulted, thought that the power of convoking a council, which formerly belonged to the emperor when Rome ruled the evangelized world, and was subsequently usurped by the Bishop of Rome, belonged thenceforth to all the princes of Christendom who, on the motion of one or more of their number, would agree to call a council together (see their opinion, *ibid.*, IX, 139–41). In the following year Luther, in turn, wrote a pamphlet against the primacy of the Pope in case the council, summoned at Mantua, should assemble: "Articles of Christian Doctrine, destined to be presented in the event of a Council being assembled at Mantua or elsewhere, and which indicate what we can, and what we cannot, accept or grant" (cf. *Les articles de Smalkalde par le Dr Martin Luther*, translated and annotated by Ed. Roerich, Caen and Paris, 1928).

[21] *Corpus Reformatorum*, II, col. 1028.

the Augsburg Confession; they agreed to an immediate conference between the English ambassadors and the German theologians.[22]

This was held at Wittenberg, which the English envoys reached on January 1st, 1536. After the reasons for a divorce from Catherine of Aragon had been exposed at length (Henry was always seeking the approval of the Lutherans, but in vain),[23] they dealt with questions of more general interest from the middle of February until April 8th. Their instructions insisted on the need for a common understanding between them at the council which Paul III was trying to assemble at Mantua.[24] For this, the Lutherans were to abandon certain articles which could not possibly be defended, such as de libero arbitrio and de potestate ecclesiastica, in order more strongly to maintain the others. On March 12th, 1536 Henry VIII wrote to the Smalcaldic Confederates expressing his desire for a doctrinal unity between the Churches of England and Germany, which, he said, could he realized only by toning down certain affirmations in the Augsburg Confession, and in its Apologia.[25] In this request the king's anxiety for the orthodox teaching will be recognized. Luther had been kept informed of all these negotiations, and he concluded that no good would ensue from the royal recommendations, although he admitted the possibility of certain concessions.[26]

[22] Ibid., II, col. 968 sq., 1032. Burnet, VI, 150. Cf. J. F. Roos, a German abridgment of Seckendorf's Commentarius de Lutheranismo, Tübingen, 1788, §189, pp. 442 sq.

[23] In addition to the instructions already mentioned, see Seckendorf, loc. cit., Roos' German abridgment, §197; A. Duchesne, ed. 1614, p. 1300. Despite their great desire to please Henry, the Lutherans replied that marriage with a brother's widow seemed to them to be indeed contrary to divine law and that amongst themselves it was forbidden, but that they dared not give a decision as regards divorce after a marriage contracted in the conditions of His Majesty's, and they asked to be allowed to think it over. Lutheran opinions on the king's marriage in Collier, IX, 145. Cf. J. Gairdner, History, 162 sq.

[24] This was the object of P. Vergerio's journey through Germany in 1534 and 1535 (see P. Friedensburg, Nuntiaturberichte, I; Ehses, Concilium Tridentinum, IV, cxi sq.). The English envoys happened to be at Schmalkalden when the Lutheran states replied, on December 21st, to Vergerio's proposals for the council (Ehses, IV, pp. cxvi sq.).

[25] Corpus Reformatorum, III, col. 48. Burnet, VI, 155 and 158.

[26] Luther to the Elector John Frederick and to Burchardt, April, 1536. Erlanger-Frankfort ed. o Luther's Works, LV, 129, 133.

The German delegates did all they could to gain a country such as England to their cause. For a long time they set aside the articles which they thought would be most repugnant to the king: the Mass, Communion under two kinds, marriage of priests, and monastic vows.[27] Then, while maintaining the essential doctrine of Lutheranism, they endeavoured to mitigate its mould, so that at times they even made it ambiguous. The Wittenberg theologians, who had charge of these negotiations, consulted Luther, Melanchthon, Bugenhagen, Jonas, and Cruziger.[28] But it was Melanchthon who recapitulated the negotiations and drew up the articles known as the Wittenberg Articles. An intrinsic examination of these Articles, and a comparison with the Augsburg Confession and the Apologia of that Confession as well as with the *Loci communes* (all works of Melanchthon), amply demonstrate their origin.[29] Although Luther's spirit is not to be found in them, yet he approved them and they are even entitled: "Articles of Christian doctrine debated by the English ambassadors with Dr. Martin, in the year 1536."[30]

The Wittenberg Articles were discovered by Mentz in 1905 in the archives at Weimar. There are two incomplete copies in Latin, completed by the German translation of the Vice-Chancellor of Saxony, Franz Burchardt. In the seventeenth century Seckendorf alone was acquainted with them. He published the article on the Eucharist, together with the four articles concerning the Mass, communion under both kinds,

[27] Cf. Dixon, I, 311.

[28] *Corpus Reformatorum*, III, col. 795.

[29] Melanchthon also drew up the letter to Henry VIII, dated September 1st, 1536, from the confederates of Schmalkalden, demanding a prompt reply on the agreement reached by his envoys at Wittenberg. Cf. Seckendorf, *loc. cit.*; Strype, *Eccl. Mem.*, Appendices Nos. 94-102. Th. Kolde produced an edition of the Latin and German texts of the Augsburg Confession, with some short explanations and four appendices (*Die Augburgische Confession deutsch und lateinisch Kurz erläutert*, Gotha, 1896). Melanchthon's *L'Apologie de la Confession d'Augsbourg* was translated into French and published by Ed. Roerich, together with the *Articles de Smalkalde*, 1928 (see n. 20). The Augsburg Confession will also be found in Vol. I of *Bekenntnisschriften der evangelisch-lutherischen Kirche*, Hrsg . . . im Gedenkjahr der Augsburgischen Konfession, 1930, Göttingen.—In the previous year Cromwell had insisted on Melanchthon coming to England (Cromwell to John Wallop, August 23rd, 1535. Burnet, VI, 116 *sq.*).

[30] *Artikel der christlichen Lehr, von welchen die Legatten aus Engelland mit dem Herrn Dr. Martino gehandelt anno 1536*. Luther to the Elector John Frederick, March 28th, 1536, Erlanger-Francfort ed. of Luther's *Works*, LV, p. 129.

the marriage of priests, and monastic vows; but these last were erroneously attributed by him to the theologians of John Frederick, who was supposed to have sent them to Henry VIII, in his letter dated April 14th, 1540.[31] English historians do not yet seem to know them.[32]

The English ambassadors accepted the Wittenberg Articles, but on condition that these were approved by the king, an approbation which, according to them, would be obtained without any great difficulty.[33] But nothing of the sort happened: despite his desire for an alliance with the German Protestants, the king refused the Lutheran confession, mitigated and ambiguous as it was. That is the reason why the Wittenberg Articles have been forgotten.

Yet the king manifested his good will towards his German friends by making a few apparent concessions. At that time the clergy were assembled to discuss the First Confession of Faith. Foxe arrived from Germany on July 4th, and on the 11th he read a short treatise in ten articles (the Ten Articles of 1536), in which the evident and certain influence of the Wittenberg Articles is noticeable.[34]

The essential question is to determine accurately what that influence is. Mentz, who published the Wittenberg Articles, noticed that certain passages in the Ten Articles corresponded, almost word for word, with the Wittenberg Articles,

---

[31] *Commentarius historicus et apologeticus de Lutheranismo*, III, 111 *sq.* Cf. Roos' German abridgment of this, Tübingen, 1788, §197, pp. 489 *sq.* Strype (*Eccl. Mem.*, I, 361) and Jenkyns (*Cranmer's Remains*, I, xxi) know only Seckendorf's quotation. The *Corpus Reformatorum* (III, col. 1005) repeats Seckendorf's mistake. A. Duchesne (*op. cit.*, ed. 1614, p. 1299) gives a brief summary of the Wittenberg Conference, probably from Seckendorf.

[32] The articles cited by Dixon (I, 311) are not the Wittenberg articles. He resumes what Collier (IV, 322, 326 *sq.*) says. J. Gairdner (*History*, 162 *sq.*) merely notes the English delegates' presence in Schmalkalden, and their stay in Germany till the spring of 1536, but in *Lollardy* (II, 316) he cites the articles as well as Mentz's study, which he does not appear to have made use of. P. Friedmann (*Anne Boleyn*, II, pp. 104 *sq.*) vaguely alludes to the English delegation to the Elector of Saxony; but Barnes is the only one known to him. Fisher (p. 361) simply says that Foxe, Heath and Barnes "laboured for religious concord at Wittenberg," and he appears to be unaware of Mentz's work, who alone has seriously studied the question.

[33] *Corpus Reformatorum*, cols. 62, 145, 795.

[34] Fuller (Bk. V, sect. 34, ed. Brewer, III, 140) calls them "medley religion."

and he concluded that the Ten Articles were Lutheran.[35] He was too hasty in his conclusion.

The corresponding passages are those on which there is no dispute between Catholics and Protestants. They refer to the common points of belief, such as certain developments of the Apostolic, the Nicean and the Athanasian Creeds, Baptism or the Real Presence in the Eucharist. But just where doctrinal differences begin the concordance of the two texts ceases. That is what we find after carefully collating the two texts.

The first apparent concession, then, was the borrowing of certain non-heretical passages from the Wittenberg text. The second consisted in mentioning only three sacraments in the Ten Articles: Baptism, Penance, and the Eucharist. The other four were not suppressed. The text concerning them was ready and had been signed by Cromwell; but Henry delayed publication in order not to offend the German Reformers, for it would have meant a complete break with them, so different was the doctrine from their own. There was an omission, but no denial. Finally, the third concession consisted in not alluding at all to transubstantiation or consubstantiation in the article on the Eucharist. The difference between these two concerns the manner in which Christ is present, and not the Real Presence itself, which is admitted in both cases.[36]

Thus the king's good will, his desire to please the Lutherans, and his adoption of Melanchthon's formulas on points which were not disputed by Catholics, show the profound divergence between the English and the Germans better than the other points which had to be passed over in silence in order to avoid a breach. To exercise an influence in doctrine is to modify the adverse opinion upon certain disputed questions. But the Wittenberg Articles did not cause the king's orthodoxy or

[35] He adds that the origin of the Ten Articles, which Jenkyns (I, xxii) and Hardwick (*History of the Articles of Religion*) thought so obscure, must be sought and seen in the Wittenberg Articles.

[36] Luther set up against the Catholic teaching of transubstantiation, which Henry VIII still maintained, the doctrine of consubstantiation, or impanation, which he expounded to Melanchthon in these terms, in 1534 (Burnet, VI, 279, 282): "Nostra autem sententia est corpus ita cum pane, seu in pane esse, ut revera cum pane manducetur; et quaecunque motum vel actionem panis habet, eandem et corpus Christi; ut corpus Christi vere dicatur ferri, dari, accipi, manducari, quando panis fertur, datur, accipitur, manducatur; id est *Hoc est corpus meum*."

that of the Henricians to waver on a single one of those questions. Cranmer, Fox, and certain other bishops of the advanced party inclined towards those articles as early as 1536. They did not, however, prevail. Henry had already given the Lutherans to understand that he would allow no foreigner to impose a creed upon his country.[37]

The First Confession of Faith or the Ten Articles is divided into two parts; the first deals with things necessary for salvation, the second with ceremonies.[38]

The first part consists of the rule of faith, justification, and the sacraments.

The rule of faith is the canon of the Scriptures (first difference from Protestants, who do not admit various books in that canon), the Apostles', the Nicean, and the Athanasian Creeds, the authority of the Fathers (another difference from Protestants, who reject tradition), and finally, the four great Councils of Nicea, Constantinople, Ephesus, and Chalcedon, and all the other councils in conformity with these.

The number of the sacraments is not mentioned, and only three are defined, viz. Baptism, Penance, and the Eucharist. The doctrine is entirely orthodox. For the Eucharist, e.g. the Fourth Article, based upon the Wittenberg Articles, states: "under the form and figure of bread and wine, which we there presently do see and perceive by outward senses, is verily, substantially, and really contained and comprehended, the very self-same body and blood of our Saviour Jesus Christ, which was born of the Virgin Mary, and suffered upon the cross for our redemption, and that under the same form and

[37] Dixon, II, 411 sq.; Merriman, I, 130. Cf. Fisher, 361.

[38] The Ten Articles were printed for the first time in 1536, by Berthelet, with this title: "Articles devised by the Kinges Highnes Majestie, to stablyshe Christen quietnes and unitie amonge us, and to avoyde contentious opinions, which Articles be also approved by the consent and determination of the hole Clergie of this Realme. Anno MDXXXVI." Burnet (IV, 272, n. 1), who gives them in his *Collection of Records*, also mentions the other editions which subsequently appeared. They may be seen in Wilkins, *Concilia*, III, 817; Fuller, Bk. V, sect. 3; Collier, IV, 343; Strype, *Eccles. Mem.*, II, 260 (cf. also his *Mem. of Cranmer*, chap. xi; Cardwell, *Formularies of Faith*, II). Makower indicates other sources and references for the formularies of faith of this reign. See the opinion of the northern clergy on the Ten Articles, in Wilkins, III, 812, and Strype, *Eccles. Mem.*, I, Appendix, p. 179.

figure of bread and wine, the very self-same body and blood of Christ is corporally, really, and in the very substance exhibited, distributed and received of all of them which receive the said sacrament; and that therefore the said sacrament is to be used with all due reverence and honour, and that every man ought first to prove and examine himself, and religiously to try and search his own conscience, before he shall receive the same; according to the saying of St. Paul."

With regard to Penance, the Ten Articles broke clean away from the Lutherans by adopting three parts to this sacrament: auricular confession, contrition with a firm purpose of amendment, and satisfaction. Moreover, it was asserted, again in contradistinction to the Protestants, that this sacrament was of divine institution and necessary for salvation.

The definition of justification, borrowed from Melanchthon, did not specify how it was effected and thus remained orthodox: "This word Justification signifieth remission of our sins, and our acceptation or reconciliation unto the grace and favour of God, that is to say, our perfect renovation in Christ." It was not stated that this reconciliation was wrought by faith alone, as the Lutherans believed; and in the same article insistence is laid upon the necessity of good works (Art. X).

The second part of the Ten Articles "concerning the laudable ceremonies used in the Church," dealt with devotion to the saints and their images, sacramentals and purgatory. On all these points, they contradicted the Lutheran teaching.[39]

The veneration of images in the churches, especially those representing our Lord and the Blessed Virgin, is excellent: it is a means of raising our souls to things beyond our senses. The people are to be taught that the honour given to images is given not to the material image itself, but to God and His saints (Arts. VI and VII).[40]

---

[39] Cf. *The ceremonies to be used in the Churche of England*, in J. Collier's *Ecclesiastical History*, IV, 352 *sq.*; Cardwell, pp. xxviii *sq.*, 13 *sq.*; Strype, *Mem. of Cranmer*, ed. 1848, I, 87 *sq.*

[40] To preach against the veneration of the saints and against pilgrimages was an heresy which came under Henry IV's law *de heretico comburendo*. But Article IV of the Injunctions to the clergy of 1536 pretended to prevent the abuses arising from superstition (Burnet, IV, 309 *sq.*; cf. I, 361).

The saints were to be honoured, not with the honour due to God alone, but as the elect of Christ, as our models, predecessors, and as interceding with God for us. To pray to the saints was a laudable practice; but there must be no superstition in such prayers nor must we think that God would listen to any saint better than to His Son. The feast-days of the saints were to be observed as holidays; but as during the ages they had increased considerably, their number was reduced, especially during the harvest season and whilst the courts were in session (Art. VIII).[41]

The traditional ceremonies of the Church, which certain Reformers had attacked—and the clergy had complained to the king in consequence—were retained, as were also the sacramentals. Thus holy water, blessed bread, candles on Candlemas Day, the ashes, the blessed palms, the veneration

Henry referred to it again in the Preface of the 2nd Confession (Wilkins, III, 830).

The veneration of the saints was looked upon as superstition by Luther, and he blamed the corporations who took a saint for their patron and the Christians who invoked the saint whose name they received in Baptism (Weimar ed. of Luther's *Works*, I, 149, 415, 418, 420, etc.). Melanchthon wrote to Henry VIII, in April, 1539 (Burnet, IV, 347) stating what ought to be thought about it; without denying the intercession of the saints, he considered that there was no foundation in Scripture for venerating them, and that such a practice was merely a remnant of paganism (*Confessio Augustana*, Art. XXI; *Apologia Confessionis Augustanae* in *Corpus Reformatorum*, XXVII, 1859, col. 289, 587, 595; *Loci theologici, ibid.* XXI, 1854, col. 979). Bullinger (*De origine erroris, libri duo*, Zurich (1529), revised ed. 1539, fol. 2vo, 74 , 105–16vo) and Calvin (*Institutiones christianae*, Bks. I, XI, §§9–16; Bk. IV, chaps. x, xiii, xix. Treatise on relics in his *Opera*, Vol. XXXIV, 1867, of *Corpus Reformatorum*, col. 402–52) see a pagan and Jewish origin in such veneration. The *Decima Centuriae Magdeburgenses* (ed. 1567, col. 322 *sq.*) mentions the relics of saints and their translation, but without comment; but there is one chapter (*ibid.*, col. 686 *sq.*) *De miraculis superstitiosis et fabulosis pro stabiliendo errore de Sanctorum intercessione.*

[41] See the feast-days that were suppressed, in Wilkins (III, 827). Cf. Burnet, I, 360 *sq.*; IV, 309; Dixon, I, 424. The big feasts were still: Christmas, Easter, Ascension Day, Trinity, Nativity of St John the Baptist, and St Michael. The feasts of local patrons, or those which fell during harvest-time, from June 1st to September 29th, with the exception of St George, the feasts of the Apostles and of the Blessed Virgin, were suppressed. The dedication of the churches was still fixed for the first Sunday in October. It was really another edition, with different expressions, of the 1362 canon (Wilkins, III, 823. Cf. Blunt, I, 489). The clergy were to explain to the people why certain feasts were no longer days on which servile work ceased (royal injunction to the clergy, Burnet, IV, 309). For the veneration of the saints, see C. Hardwick, *History of the Christian Church*, 298 *sq.*; H. R. Percival, *The Invocation of Saints, treated theologically and historically.*

of the Cross on Good Friday, the blessing of the font, and other rites of a similar nature were all preserved and their meaning explained. "These customs, rites and ceremonies be not to be condemned and cast away, but to be used and continued as things good and laudable, to put us in remembrance of those spiritual things that they do signify; not suffering them to be forgotten, or to be put in oblivion, but renewing them in our memories from time to time. None of these ceremonies have power to remit sin, but only to stir and lift up our minds unto God, by whom only our sins be forgiven" (Art. IX).[42]

As regards purgatory, the doctrine is not less explicitly anti-Lutheran and contrary to the future Articles of Elizabeth. The commandment of charity, it is stated, not less than the voice of Scripture, prescribes that we should pray for the dead and have Masses said for the repose of their souls. Henry himself set the example the following year when he had twelve hundred Masses said for Jane Seymour. As to the whereabouts of purgatory and the nature of the suffering there, nothing was defined by Scripture, and those questions were left to the wisdom of the Almighty. Papal indulgences were rejected in consequence of the schism (Art. X).[43]

Such was the First Confession in this reign. Of all the Confessions it was the least explicitly Catholic on account of the desire to promote an understanding with the German Protestants.

The day after the Ten Articles had been accepted by Convocation the king gave orders that no priest was to preach until the said Articles had been published, so as "to repress all occasions of dissent and discord" and to establish a good and Catholic uniformity. The Injunctions issued in the month of August ordered every priest having charge of souls to read the Articles from the pulpit at least once every three months under pain of suspension, and to comment upon them twice a quarter.[44]

[42] For an explanation of their mystical meaning, see Cardwell, 15 sq. Cf. Strype, Mem. of Cranmer, I, 89.

[43] Burnet, IV, 285. Cf. A. J. Mason, Purgatory, The State of the Faithful Dead, Invocation of Saints, Three Lectures.

[44] Cf. Burnet, IV, 308; Dixon, I, 417 sq., 422, 425.

The Ten Articles bear the signature of Cromwell, of fifty-eight members of the Upper House (bishops, abbots and priors) and of fifty-one members of the Lower House of Convocation.

Two months later (October, 1536) came the rising in the north. The "Pilgrims of Grace" demanded the preservation of the ancient faith and the death of certain bishops, who were reputed to be heretics. The need of doctrinal unity became more pressing than ever. To meet this need, the Second Confession of Faith was drawn up in the following year (1537). As the continental danger appeared to have been averted, Catholic doctrine was more explicitly set forth in this than in the previous Confession.

Yet the preliminary discussion upon the dogma had afforded a spectacle and a proof of the wide divergence of opinions which was beginning to creep into the bishops' ranks, and of the antagonism between the old and the new teachings as well as between the moderate and the reforming parties. The gathering of bishops and theologians, which sat from February until July, 1537, was chiefly occupied in examining the four sacraments passed over in the Ten Articles; Confirmation, Holy Orders, Matrimony and Extreme Unction. Three questions were asked with regard to these sacraments: (1) "Is it a sacrament of the New Law?" (2) "What the external signs and inward graces be in every of the said sacraments." (3) "What promises be made to the receivers of them by God, and of what efficacy they be of." In order to avoid a public debate, each man had to answer in writing.[45]

The answers, preserved in a manuscript in the British Museum, show the two opposing tendencies which divided the episcopacy. Whilst the Henricians, such as Stokesley, Tunstall and Longland maintained the Catholic dogma in its entirety,[46] the advanced party, with Cranmer, William Barlow, Hilsey, Rugg, and Goodrich, were inclined towards the Lutheran doctrine. Cranmer, for instance, asserted that

[45] Strype, *Eccles. Mem.*, I, chap. xli; Burnet, IV, 293. Other questions by Cranmer for the reform of certain abuses (Burnet, IV, 293) were added to those on the Sacraments. They dealt with confession, images, tithes, councils, the ecclesiastical forum, monasteries, residence and the nominations to livings and other ecclesiastical offices. All of which seem to be an attempt to introduce a Lutheran reform, on the plea of combating popery.

[46] Tunstall's reply especially was very much against the new ideas. Stokesley, after he had recalled the matter and form of Confirmation, declared that it was a sacrament which conferred the gifts of the Holy Ghost; such "is the continual belief of the university of the same Catholic Church from the time of the apostles hitherto, without contradiction of any man (ignorants and suspects of heresy only except)." Burnet, IV, 297.

Confirmation was not of divine institution, that the chrism used by the Church as an outward sign was nowhere mentioned in the Scriptures, and that the rite had no effect beyond the power of the bishop's prayer.[47] Capon, Bishop of Bangor, said that this sacrament was not instituted by Christ, but by the Fathers of the Church.[48] Barlow, the former prior of the Austin Canons at Bisham and Bishop of St David's, maintained that ordination was not necessary in order to fulfil the Church's ministry, and that any cobbler could be a bishop without receiving any Orders, provided he were designated by the king.[49] "It is a troublesome thing," observed Latimer,[50] "to agree upon a doctrine in things of such controversy, with judgments of such diversity, every man, I trust, meaning well, and yet not all meaning one way." During these theological debates the Plague broke out, and people were dying at the door of Lambeth Palace, wherein the commission was holding its meetings.[51]

Despite the heretical character of the discussions, the Confession which resulted was orthodox, because the supreme head had willed that it should be. Where doctrine was concerned he was always on the side of the Henricians. He himself contributed to the final wording of the formulary of faith: "We were constrained to put our own pen to the book, and to conceive certain articles, which were by all you the bishops and whole clergy of this our realm in Convocation agreed on as Catholic"[52]; many corrections and annotations in the king's own writing may be seen in the British Museum.[53]

However, as Henry VIII had not had sufficient time to revise the bishops' conclusions, he did not consider the work

[47] Strype, *Mem. of Cranmer*, Append. XXVIII; *Eccles. Mem.*, I, 234; Burnet, IV, 296.

[48] Cf. Dixon, I, 527.

[49] Strype, *Eccles. Mem.*, II, 273; Dixon, I, 522.

[50] Letter to Cromwell. Strype, *Mem. of Cranmer*, ed. 1848, I, 107, n. 1.

[51] Cranmer wrote to Cromwell that people were dying "everywhere in London and Westminster, and in Lambeth they die at my gate and even at the next house to me. I would fain see the King's Highness at my departing, but I fear me I shall not, by cause that I shall come from this smoky air" (Strype, *Mem. of Cranmer*, I, 107, n. 1).

[52] Henry VIII's letter to the bishops, Windsor, November 19th, 1537. *L. and P.*, XI, No. 1110; Burnet, IV, 396; and Collier, IX, 150 (where the date is given as November 20th). Cf. Strype, *Mem. of Cranmer*, I, 108.

[53] Cotton MSS., Cleopatra, E, V and VII.

as final, and ordered it to be read every Sunday, but only for three years.[54] This Second Confession, which was not submitted either to Convocation or to Parliament, was signed by the two archbishops, all the bishops, and by twenty-five doctors on behalf of the high ecclesiastical dignitaries of the country. It was attributed to the bishops, and called the "Bishops' Book."[55]

It was printed by Berthelet in 1537 and entitled *The Godly and Pious Institution of a Christian Man*.[56] As its name indicates, it was more a pious than an instructive work, very developed (about two hundred pages in octavo) and intended more especially for the faithful. The Confession of the previous year was reproduced in it, but developed and divided in a different way, and certain things were added. In the main it was merely a reshuffling of and a complement to the Ten Articles of 1536.

The "pious Institution" gave an orthodox statement of the Creed,[57] the seven sacraments,[58] the ten commandments of

[54] Shortly after it was printed the king annotated the *Institution* in a copy (preserved at the Bodleian) which he sent to Cranmer. The latter in turn made certain observations, and the manuscript containing them is at Corpus Christi College, Cambridge (cf. Jenkyns, II, 21, n.). These annotations were published, as well as Cranmer's, in the Parker Society's edition of Cranmer's *Works*, II, 83 *sq.*; and in Jenkyns' edition, II, 21-65. Cf. Burnet, I, 420; IV, 408 *sq.*; *L. and P.*, XIII, Nos. 403, 404; Dixon, II, 310. The contemporaries attributed the maintenance of the old doctrine to the king, as is proved by the passage in the Life of Cranmer by an unknown writer, taken from Foxe's manuscripts, and quoted by Strype (*Mem. of Cranmer*, chap. XIII).

[55] This is the name given to it in the instruction to his clergy of John Voysey, Bishop of Exeter, in 1538, and in Bonner's, in 1542 (Wilkins, III, 844, 864). Lord Herbert points out that there was another "Bishops' Book" in the previous year (1536) written in reply to Reginald Pole's *De Unitate* on the royal supremacy. Cf. Strype, *Mem. of Cranmer*, chap. XIII, I, 107, n. 1, 112, 115 *sq.* The king's mandate for the examination of the Second Confession was addressed to the bishops and theologians, and not to Convocation, which did not assemble that year. Burnet, I, 389, n. 47.

[56] Cf. *L. and P.*, XII [II]; Dixon, I, 518-30. Three copies of the 1537 edition are at Lambeth Palace and one of them (XXVIII, 1, 13, in 8vo) bears Archbishop Bancroft's arms on the cover. The *Institution*, the preface of which is given by Wilkins (III, 830), is in Hardwick (*op. cit.*, 186 *sq.*), and Cardwell (21-212). It was reprinted in 1543.

[57] The explanation of the creed followed by observations (53 pages in 8vo) is surcharged with corrections in the king's own writing. Cf. Burnet, I, 420.

[58] The efficacy of the Sacraments *ex opere operato* was explicitly recognized in the Article *De Ecclesia* of the Thirteen Articles (1538). Cf. Burnet, IV, 408. The doctrine on the Sacraments takes up 47 pages in 8vo.

God, the Our Father,[59] the Hail Mary,[60] justification, and purgatory.[61]   The disagreement of 1533 reappeared in the explanation of the Creed and of Holy Orders, for the Church of Rome was there looked upon as "only a particular member" of the Catholic Church and not the "head"; "the other churches of Christ" are "all free from any subjection unto the said Church of Rome. . . . It was many hundred years after Christ before the bishop of Rome could acquire or set any primacy or governance above any other bishops out of his province in Italy." In his letter of the following November 9th,[62] Henry strongly blamed "the diversity of opinion which was only engendered by a certain contentious manner of speaking against honest, laudable and tolerable ceremonies, usages and customs of the Church," and ordered the bishops to go through their dioceses preaching the preservation of those customs. He forbade them to make use of words, even in private conversation, which might be badly interpreted, and threatened with loss of benefices any cleric who despised or considered those customs as immaterial.

In keeping thus to the seven Sacraments, the Hail Mary, and the ancient rites of the Church, the Church of England

[59] The Pater Noster was developed at length in paraphrases which filled twenty-four pages. After God had been asked to grant temporal goods, mentioned in detail: Bread, drink, clothes, money, fruits, flocks, etc., He was asked to give the food of the soul: Grace, "that it may appear in all the acts and deeds of our life." "Grant that the holy sacrament of the altar, which is the bread of life, and the very flesh and blood of thy Son Jesu Christ, may be purely ministered and distributed to the comfort and benefit of all us thy people . . . and specially against our death, so that we may enjoy the life everlasting. . . . Grant this also, merciful Father that all false doctrine, contrary to thy word, which feedeth not but poisoneth and killed the soul, may be utterly extinct and cast away out of thy Church."

[60] Five pages were devoted to a development of the *Ave Maria*, which "the Church hath used to adjoin to the end of the *Pater Noster*, as an hymn, laud, and praise, partly of our Lord and Saviour Jesu Christ for our redemption, and partly of the blessed Virgin for her humble consent given and expressed to the angel at this salutation." The *Ave Maria* was also mentioned in the Preface (Wilkins, III, 831).

[61] The last Injunctions had the same import. Cf. Dixon, I, 524. The king had a Latin translation of the *Institution of a Christian Man* sent to his ambassador at Charles V's court (*L. and P.*, IX, No. 615) "to the intent it might appear to the emperor how conformable to Christ's doctrine, the institution of His holy Church, the learning is which his Majesty hath ordained to be taught to his Highness' people."

[62] Burnet, IV, 396; *L. and P.*, XI, No. 1110.

further emphasized its difference from the German churches. Henry VIII no longer gave a thought to the few concessions of 1536. Catherine of Aragon was dead. He could therefore resume his former policy of maintaining the balance, since the obstacle which prevented a reconciliation with the emperor had disappeared. So when he heard of Catherine's death he thanked God for delivering him from all fear of war; he was under the impression that he would be able to manage the King of France better in future, by making him fear an alliance between the empire and England. His joy was so lively and so indecent that he was accused of having hastened Catherine's end, of having poisoned her. The day after her death he attired himself in bright yellow and wore a white feather in his hat. A ball was held at Court in the afternoon, and the following days were given up to brilliant tournaments. Henry resumed his rôle of arbitrator between France and Spain; in other words, he seized every opportunity to set them at variance, so that he might rule in peace. At this period Francis I was engaged in his third war with Charles V (1536–38), during which the imperial troops advanced as far as Marseilles.[63]

But, in 1538, fresh clouds were gathering on the political horizon. Paul III had intervened and had made the two adversaries conclude the truce of Nice. Some time afterwards the meeting had occurred at Aiguesmortes, at which the emperor and Francis had exchanged their decorations of the Fleece and of St. Michael, and had given each other mutual tokens of warm friendship. Jane Seymour was dead, and Henry, being a widower, was contemplating marriage with the Duke of Lorraine's daughter, in order to safeguard himself against France, or with the Duchess of Milan, so as to be on good terms with Charles V. This twofold project succeeded only in making Henry look ridiculous. Then Cromwell, continually haunted by fear of an invasion and constantly advocating a league with the German Protestant princes, induced the king to resume the relations of 1536.

[63] Friedmann, *op. cit.*, II, pp. 165 *sq.*; Merriman, I, 233. Cf. *L. and P.*, VII, No. 1095.

Towards the end of her life Catherine had for enforced residences Buckden and Kimbolton, details of which will be found in Vol. II, *Victoria County Hist. of Huntingdon*, 1932.

Was it not the best way to ward off a coalition between Francis and Charles, which boded ill for both English and German freedom? It was to the interest of Henry and the Lutherans alike to band themselves together against the common enemy.[64] The king's manifesto against the Pope's right to summon a council had been hailed with enthusiasm in Germany, and had run through three editions; and whilst Bullinger dedicated his work on the Scriptures "against the superstition of the Roman tyranny" to Henry, the Elector of Saxony and the Landgrave of Hesse were urging him to adopt a common policy.[65] They therefore set themselves to work on the scheme, outlined in 1536, for a conference in London between German and English theologians with a view to a doctrinal understanding.

Henry invited the Protestant princes to send delegates to discuss the contested points with him, so that he might enter the Smalcaldic League.[66] A delegation set out for England in May. It consisted of the Vice-Chancellor of Saxony, Franz Buchardt; George von Boyneburg; and F. Myconius, the pastor of Gotha, one of Luther's fellow citizens and his faithful assistant.[67] Melanchthon gave them a letter of recommenda-

[64] Merriman, I, 233 sq., 238. Henry, abandoning theological discussions, informed the French ambassador Castillon that the German delegates of the 1538 conference "are here to form some defensive alliance for the first to be assailed for not obeying the Pope" (Kaulek, p. 59). Charles V was well aware of the bond which drew Henry and the Lutherans together and which would make them unite against anyone who attacked either side. "The aim of the Lutherans and of the King of England," said he to Cardinal Alexander Farnese, "is not so much to discuss the doctrines of the Church or any article of faith as to usurp ecclesiastical property and to shake off the yoke of the Apostolic See so that they may live as they like. . . . This common aim of theirs will keep them from ever abandoning each other when one or the other side is molested" (Farnese to Paul III, Toledo, June 25th, 1539. Quirini, I, p. cclxxxvii).

[65] Particularly after the Bull of excommunication and R. Pole's mission, Henry was so afraid lest the Lutherans and the Holy See should be reconciled that he did all he could to prevent it (Friedensburg, III, 114). In February, 1538 it was rumoured that Henry had joined the Smalcaldic League and had given a subsidy to it (ibid., pp. 440 sq.). An Anglo-Lutheran league which would uphold France, either openly or in secret, was feared as a catastrophe (ibid., p. 455). Henry showed his great opposition to the council and his complete hatred of Paul III, until the end (ibid., IX, p. 242). Bullinger's work was called: De Scripturae sanctae authoritate, certitudine, firmitate contra superstitionem tyrannidis romanae, Zurich, 1538.

[66] L. and P., I, No. 367.

[67] For Friedrich Myconius (1490–1546), a Reformer of Thuringia, see

tion. They were given a great welcome. Three bishops and four doctors represented the Church of England. The London conference lasted two months. [68]

By order of the Elector of Saxony, the Germans brought the Wittenberg Articles with them, and used them as a basis for their theological discussions. If these Articles are compared with those of 1538, an evident concordance will be noticed, which is also frequently a literal one. [69]

Three points, upon which agreement would have been difficult, were set aside: free will; the veneration of the saints and their images; as well as the "abuses" mentioned in the second part of the Augsburg Confession, a covering word for ecclesiastical ceremonies. [70]

The Thirteen Articles of 1538 were the outcome of this conference. [71] Henry did not accept them and would take no inspiration from them.

On August 5th, when they were about to depart, the German theologians wrote a long letter to the king. In it they denounced the abuses which still needed suppressing in order to exterminate "the scourge of the Roman antichrist," and upon which no agreement had been possible. They were communion under both kinds, private Masses and ecclesiastical celibacy. In order to arouse Henry, they invoked the

Kawerau's article in the 3rd edition of the *Realencyklopädie*. John Eck called him "pessimus apostata ex Minoribus" (Friedensburg, IV, 567, n.). He was the author of the *Historia Reformationis* of 1517–47, which has remained in manuscript in the library at Gotha.

[68] On May 31st Castillon announced the arrival of the German delegates. Kaulek, 59. W. Möller (*Lehrbuch der Kirchengeschichte*, Freiburg, 2nd ed. 1893–1902, III, 188) indicates the sources which relate to this conference in London. See also Dixon, II, 1 *sq.*; *Zeitschrift für Kirchengeschichte*, V, 164 *sq.*; *L. and P.*, XIII.

[69] Especially as regards the Eucharist, Baptism, the use of sacramentals and the *ministerium Ecclesiae*. Jenkyns, who published the Articles of 1538 (*Cranmer's Remains*, IV, Append. XIII), and Hardwick, who reprinted them (261–77), both note how they agree with the Wittenberg article on the Last Supper, which Seckendorf cites, as we have said before.

The Elector John Frederick's Instructions, which are in the Archives at Weimar, are dated May 11th (Mentz, *op. cit.*, 14).

[70] Jenkyns, I, 260; Strype, *Eccles. Mem.*, Append. XC.

[71] According to Mentz, these articles came from the English theologians. Dixon (II, 5, n.) maintains, on the contrary, that they came from the German delegates. Strype (*Eccles Mem.*, I, 551) gratuitously assumes that they were the work of the Commission which drew up *The King's Book* two years afterwards.

practice of the Greek Church and conjured up the papal "bogey." "Your royal Majesty easily perceives that purity of doctrine cannot exist or subsist where abuses are not suppressed, which are diametrically opposed to the word of God and which engender the tyranny or the idolatry of the Roman antichrist. . . . Unless they be suppressed, the deplorable domination of the bishop of Rome cannot be completely exterminated."[72]   But, with Tunstall's help, Henry sent them a long answer, written partly in his own hand, in which he strenuously maintained the three points denounced by the Lutherans: "We who in our own realm have greatly endeavoured to banish the tyranny of the bishop of Rome . . . shall strive, with the help of God, to abolish all abuses emanating from the bishop of Rome or from any other, and we shall not consult those who pretend to hate the bishop of Rome and who utter truths which they do not accept in their hearts."[73]

Those last words emphasize the futility of attempting to agree with the German theologians.   The latter returned from London, their hopes frustrated, with bitterness in their hearts and severely condemning the king.   Like the conference of 1536, its successor in 1538 ended in failure.

The destinies of the English Church were, nevertheless, not unaffected by that conference.   It proved to be the channel through which Luther's doctrine infiltrated.   The Thirteen Articles which emanated from that conference served as a basis for the Forty-two Articles of Edward VI (1553): certain sentences are identical.[74]   Moreover, the German and English theologians had compiled a "Book containing divers Articles," the thirty Articles of which correspond to those of the Augsburg Confession.[75]   They inspired the Forty-two Articles of

[72] Original text in Latin. Burnet, IV, 352-73; cf. I, 407.

[73] Original text in Latin. Burnet, *op. cit.*, IV, pp. 373-92.   Cf. *ibid.*, I, 408; Lingard, V, 106.

[74] Jenkyns (I, xxiii) had already remarked upon this.   Cf. Dixon, II, 6.   The Thirteen Articles may be compared with the Augsburg Confession in Hardwick (260) who indicates the passages which correspond (cf. nn. 20 and 29).   Mentz thinks (p. 15) that the Thirteen Articles do not reflect the complete theological agreement of the conference, according to the Latin and German copy at Weimar, but rather the propositions of the English bishops, with which the German delegates did not altogether agree.

[75] This "Book" will be found in Strype's *Eccles. Mem.* and in *Cranmer's*

Edward VI and the Thirty-nine Articles of Elizabeth (1563). The seeds of the Lutheran influence then were imported at this time, but bore their fruit only in the following reigns.

A few months after the return of the German delegates, Melanchthon wrote to the king to induce him to undertake a more extensive reform, on the lines of the Augsburg Confession and the conferences of 1536 and 1538. He said the Mass should be abolished, together with ecclesiastical celibacy and the veneration of the saints. "It is astonishing that although the author of the abuses has been rejected, the abuses themselves are still retained. . . . Let the divinely instituted rites be retained, as well as certain rules made by man for the preservation of good order; but it is meet that barbarity be driven from the churches, together with the other useless and inept rites. . . . I therefore beseech Your Majesty to have the Roman impiety taken out of the churches. . . . In order that posterity may detest the tyranny of the bishop of Rome, it is most important that the laws which are the nerves of his authority should disappear."[76]

But the King of England no longer had any faith in a doctrinal understanding. He gave up all idea of entering the Smalcaldic League, and turned his thoughts to a purely political alliance with the German princes. His marriage with Anne of Cleves had no other purpose; the same was true of the relations he sought to establish with Philip of Hesse, John Frederick of Saxony, and Philip, heir of Bavaria.[77]

As for reforming the Church of England in accordance with Melanchthon's advice, he took good care not to do anything of the kind. The elements of discord, which threatened more and more to break the unity of faith, perturbed him, and he resolved to establish uniformity by violent and rigorous means.

Remains (IV, 273-92) by Jenkyns, who has added the *Augsburg Confession* of 1531, and has given in italics the words that are to be found in the Forty-two Articles of Edward VI.

[76] Original in Latin. Melanchthon to Henry VIII, April 1st, 1539. Burnet, IV, 347-52.

[77] Cf. Merriman, I, 257, 259, 268 *sq.* Kaulek, 95, 101, 148 *sq.*, 152, 154, 155, 158, 168, 170, 176, 244, 319. See Baumbach's mission, in Merriman (264 *sq.*). Philip of Bavaria, son of the Palatine Robert (†1504) and of Elizabeth of Bavaria, defended Vienna against the Turks, in 1529, and died nine years later (1538). Cf. Turba, *Venetianische Depeschen vom Kaiserhofe*, Vienna. 1889-95, I, 230, 232.

In May, 1539, only a few months after the departure of the German theologians, Parliament passed the famous Act of the Six Articles, nicknamed by Protestants "the Whip with six strings," and styled "rigorous and barbarous" by Lingard and "terrible and bloody" by Strype. [78]

Its object was sufficiently clear from the title: "Act for abolishing diversity of opinions in certain articles concerning Christian religion." [79] The preamble stated that discord and religious errors were a perpetual danger not only for the peace of the realm, but also for the souls seduced by heresy. [80]

To abolish them, Henry had recourse to an authority which neither of the first Confessions possessed. On May 16th, the Duke of Norfolk—and not Cromwell, who should have done it as vicegerent—proposed the following points for discussion in the House of Lords [81]: "Whether in the eucharist Christ's real body was present without any transubstantiation?— Whether that sacrament was to be given to the laity in both kinds?—Whether the vows of chastity made either by men or women ought to be observed by the law of God?—Whether, by the law of God, private Masses ought to be celebrated?— Whether priests, by the law of God, might marry?—Whether auricular confession was necessary by the law of God?"

[78] Lingard, V, 129. Strype, *Mem. of Cranmer*, chap. xix.

[79] Wilkins, III, 848; *Statutes of the realm*, 31 Henry VIII, cap. 14; Collier, V, 37-40; Dodd, ed. 1737, I, 314 *sq*.; Hardwick, 189; Gee and Hardy, No. LXV. For the Six Articles see chap. xvi of Froude's *The Reign of Henry VIII*; Burnet, I, 410 *sq*.; J. Gairdner, *Lollardy* (II, 170-221) Bk. III, chap. iv: "German Protestantism and the Act of the Six Articles."

[80] The king's letter of November 19th, 1537 (Burnet, IV, 396; cf. I, 409) and Cromwell's, of January 7th, 1538, to the Bishop of Llandaff (*ibid*., IV, 394; cf. I, 409), prove that numerous complaints had arisen on nearly every side against those who favoured the new ideas.

[81] Thus was rendered futile the expedient, to which Cromwell had resorted in trying to combine the two opposite tendencies in a committee of bishops instructed to draw up a Bill. Cranmer and Lee, the two arch-bishops, were on this committee, together with Tunstall (Durham), Gardiner (Winchester), Clerk (Bath and Wells), Bird (Bangor), Aldrich (Carlisle), Barlow (St David's), Goodrich (Ely), Hilsey (Rochester), Shaxton (Salisbury), and Latimer (Worcester). After a discussion lasting eleven days Cranmer had to admit that agreement was impossible. Cf. Blunt, I, 473 *sq*.—Marillac wrote to Francis I (Kaulek, 95) that the Duke of Norfolk was present every day in Parliament.

The text of these six questions is taken from Burnet (I, 411). The text given at the beginning of the act (Gee and Hardy, p. 304) is slightly different, and the question concerning the marriage of priests is the third and not the fifth.

The discussion was taken up by the Henricians, Lee, Gardiner, Tunstall, Stokesley, Sampson, Rugg, and Aldrich, and by the bishops of Lutheran tendencies, Cranmer, Latimer, Barlow, Goodrich, Hilsey, and Shaxton; the temporal Lords did not intervene in the debate. "The bishops of this country have been in great altercation, some being entirely for keeping the Mass, the others for making a new one," the French ambassador wrote to Francis I on June 9th.[82] Cranmer maintained the debate for three days.[83] The king, "the supreme head," himself decided whether victory was with the moderate or with the advanced party by going in person to the House. "The king's most royal majesty," says the text of the act, "most graciously vouchsafed, in his own princely person, to descend and come into his said High Court of Parliament and council, and there, like a prince of most high prudence and no less learning, opened and declared many things of high learning and great knowledge touching the said Articles."[84] His feelings were known. Holy water and the blessed bread were given every Sunday in his chapel. He had served Mass on his knees the previous Good Friday; and a citizen of London had just been hanged for breaking the Friday abstinence.[85] He upheld the orthodox teaching and demanded that the doctrinal declaration should be sanctioned by corporal punishments. Neither Cromwell nor the chancellor Audeley dared oppose him. "This king as the head of this party has made such a declaration as was befitting . . . and imposed silence with threats of death for all who would open their mouths to the contrary."[86] The innovators were

[82] Kaulek, 101. Cf. Dodd, I, 121.

[81] See his reasons in Burnet, I, 411-13, and especially in Foxe, V, 264 sq., 365, 379, 388, 398, 410, 439, 462, 501, 506, 508 sq., 561 sq., 605. Foxe (ibid., 265-362) adds a long dissertation, with documents to show that the Six Articles were "pernicious, new fangled, erroneous, and heretic." Cf. Collier, V, 36.

[84] The king annotated several articles in his own hand. Two drafts of the Six Articles, corrected by him, are still extant (Burnet, I, 420). L. and P. (XIV, No. 868) mention only one.

[85] A year later Marillac wrote (Kaulek, 175, 185) that those who "avoient mangé chair au caresme, en adhérent aulx doctrines nouvelles, en mespris du commandement que leur roy, comme chief de l'Église anglicanne leur avoir fait" were arrested and punished, as well as those who had not "faict leurs Pasques."

[86] Marillac to Francis I, June 9th, 1539. Kaulek, 102. Strype, Mem. of Cranmer, p. 163 and Append. XXV.

forced to keep silent. "His Highness confounded them all with God's learning," wrote one of the temporal peers of the Upper House,[87] "I assure you never prince shewed himself so wise a man, so well learned, and so catholic, as the king hath done in this Parliament. With my pen I cannot express his marvellous goodness which is come to such effect, that we shall have an Act of Parliament so spiritual." Even abroad, the king was spoken of as "the king catholic, in all that does not concern his own advantage or His Holiness." Some even, counting upon his orthodoxy, conceived great hopes that he would return to the unity of the Church. At the Diet of Ratisbon (1541), Granvelle proposed to act as a go-between to reconcile Henry with Rome, and the English ambassador received a letter there from the Pope.[88]

The first of the Six Articles clearly enunciated transubstantiation: "In the most blessed Sacrament of the altar, by the strength and efficacy of Christ's mighty word (it being spoken by the priest), is present really, under the form of bread and

[87] Strype, *ibid.*, Append. XXVI. Cf. chap. xix; *L. and P.*, XIV, No. 1040; Froude, chap. xvi; Pollard, *Cranmer*, 128 *sq.*; Fisher, 435.

[88] Farnese to Aleandre, Vienna, March 22nd, 1539. Friedensburg, III, 506. B. Maffeo to Farnese, July 11th, 1546, *ibid.*, IX, 107, n. 1. J. A. Muller, chap. xiv. In that same year, 1546, the papal envoy in France, Gurone Bertano, visited Henry VIII (A. Pieper, *Zur Entstehungsgeschichte der standigen Nuntiaturen*, Freiburg, 1894, p. 130, and Friedensburg, IX, 413, n. 3).

According to Gardiner, who knew well the trend of the king's religious thoughts, Henry several times thought of returning to the unity of the Church. In his famous speech before the whole court, on December 2nd, 1554, he said: "When the tumult was in the North, in the time of King Henry VIII, I am sure the king was determined to have given over the supremacy again to the pope: but the hour was not then come, and therefore it went not forward, lest some would have said that he did it for fear. After this, master Knevet and I were sent ambassadors unto the emperor [1541] to desire him that he would be a mean between the pope's holiness and the king, to bring the king to obedience of the see of Rome: but the time was neither then come; for it might have been said that it had been done for a civil policy." Foxe, VI, 587. Cf. below, n. 137. With dilatory courtesy, Henry replied to Granvelle's proposals that he would instruct the emperor to reconcile England with Rome when the Princes of Germany had recognized the papal primacy. An understanding between Protestants and Catholics was never so nearly reached as at this Diet of Ratisbon, where the legate Contarini accepted a formula of agreement upon justification, which Rome did not afterwards approve. Gardiner received, very secretly, a letter from Paul III. Knyvet, who was with him, got wind of it and, in 1551, the bishop's adversaries, by recalling this incident, tried to have him condemned for high treason. Cf. Foxe, VI, 165-68; J.A. Muller, chap. xiv; M. P. Janelle, *op. cit.*, p. xliii *sq.*

wine, the natural body and blood of our Saviour Jesus Christ, conceived of the Virgin Mary; and after the consecration there remaineth no substance of bread or wine, nor any substance, but the substance of Christ, God and man."[89]

The second Article declared that communion under both kinds was not necessary for salvation. "It is to be believed, and no doubted of, but that in the flesh, under the form of bread, is the very blood; and with the blood, under the form of wine, is the very flesh; as well apart, as though they were both together."

The third Article stated that the priest, after receiving Orders, could not marry.[90]

The fourth prohibited marriage for men and women who had taken the vow of chastity.

The fifth asserted that private Masses were pleasing to God.

The sixth taught that auricular confession in use in the Church came from God.[91]

[89] Marillac (Kaulek, 102) said "*l'on eust à croire, adorer et révérer ledit Sainct-Sacrement avec les cérémonies accoustumées, ainsi que l'Église de si long temps l'a inviolablement observé.*" One of the temporal peers wrote (Strype, *Mem. of Cranmer*, I, Append. XXV): "We shall have an act of parliament so spiritual that I think none shall dare say, in the Blessed Sacrament of the Altar doth remain either bread or wine after the Consecration." Sander says of the king (*op. cit.*, Lewis' trans., pp. 161–62): "His reverence for the Sacrament of the Eucharist was always most profound. Shortly before he died, when about to communicate, as he always did, under one kind, he rose up from his chair and fell on his knees to adore the Body of our Lord. The Zwinglians who were present said that his majesty, by reason of his bodily weakness, might make his communion sitting in his chair. The king's answer was, 'If I could throw myself down, not only on the ground, but under the ground, I should not then think that I gave honour enough to the most Holy Sacrament.'"

[90] Henry always disliked communion under two kinds, as well as the non-observance of ecclesiastical celibacy (cf. Burnet, I, 406). In November 1537, he had already instructed the bishops to make serious enquiries about the clergy in their diocese, and to seize and send to him those who "have presumed to marry themselves contrary to the custom of our Church of England" (Henry VIII's letter to the bishops, November 19th, 1537). *L. and P.*, X, No. 1110.

[91] Article V of Cromwell's Injunctions in 1538 (Burnet, IV, 342) already dealt with the Easter Confession. In the same year a declaration of the two archbishops, eleven bishops, and twenty theologians and canonists (*ibid.*, IV, 336–41) spoke of "ministers, which have special power to loose and absoile from sin all persons which be duly penitent and sorry for the same." In the 1539 Parliament Tunstall wrote a paper to prove, by Scripture and by the Fathers (Bede, Origen and St Cyprian) that auricular confession was of divine law. Henry read it and added his own reflections

These Six Articles are the very opposite of the corresponding Articles in the Augsburg Confession. Nothing could be more anti-Lutheran, as Cervini observed when he sent them to Cardinal Farnese.[92] And Charles Butler, the Catholic historian, remarks that they all agree with the teaching of the Roman Church.[93]

The "whip with six strings" severely lashed the Reformers. Any one denying the first article on transubstantiation would be burnt and his property confiscated; even abjuration could not save him from the stake. For the first offence against the five other articles the penalty was confiscation of property and imprisonment, according to the king's good pleasure; a second offence was punished by the death reserved for traitors, without the assistance of the priest.[94]

No serious opposition was manifested. "We of the temporalty," wrote one of the temporal peers,[95] "have been all of one opinion." In the Lower House of Convocation there were only two dissentient voices. In the Bishops' House, only Cranmer, Shaxton, Latimer, Hilsey, and Barlow again asserted that the marriage of priests was lawful, and Cranmer and Barlow alone were anxious for Communion under both kinds. As for the people, they showed great delight in the Six Articles, being "much more inclined to the old religion," said Marillac, "than to the new opinions which are maintained by only a few bishops." "Finally, all in England have cause to thank God and most heartily to rejoice of the king's most godly proceedings."[96] The reforming movement had then only a very small minority behind it at this period.

The law was enforced immediately, and a court consisting of laymen displayed extraordinary zeal. Anyone who went

in the form of marginal notes; he even wrote a letter to the bishop on the same subject. All this will be found in Burnet, IV, 400–408. Cf. *ibid.*, I, 413.

[92] L. Cardauns, *Nuntiaturberichte*, V, 305.

[93] *An historical and literary account of the Formularies*, 1816, p. 71. "All of which," says A. Duchesne (*op. cit.*, ed. 1614, p. 1303), "being directly ordered against the Lutherans, prevented this Prince from sending his embassies to their gathering at Frankfort."

[94] Wilkins, III, 848; *Journal of Lords*, 113 *sq.*; Burnet, 414 *sq.*

[95] Letter already quoted. Strype, *Mem. of Cranmer*, I, 416.

[96] Kaulek, 103, and letter mentioned in previous note.

but seldom to Mass or who did not bow down at the consecration was denounced. Within a fortnight there were five
hundred arrests in the city of London, and the majority were
convicted of heresy. They shrank from the hateful idea of a
mass execution, and so the prisoners were set at liberty. But
Bishop Shaxton of Salisbury and Bishop Latimer of Worcester
resigned. They were thrown into prison, where one remained
until the king's death and the other not quite so long.[97] Only
the special affection which the king had always shown for
Cranmer saved the latter. Even so, he was obliged to send his
wife to Germany for a time. A year later Cromwell fell under
the ban of the Six Articles. He was accused of having spread,
in writing, a torrent of errors on the Eucharist, and of having
led the people astray from the true faith in this sacrament and
"other articles of Christian religion most graciously declared
by your Majesty, by authority of Parliament."[98]

The Six Articles were the cause of intermittent persecutions
during the last eight years of the reign, and also kept the
Reformers in a constant state of fear. Although the king often
restricted their application,[99] yet they sent more than one
Reformer to death, for example, Barnes, Garrard, and Jerome,
as well as unknown persons "of very lowly condition . . .
for having spoken against the honour and reverence due to the
Holy Sacrament, and for not having consented to revoke their
errors either before or after their condemnation."[100] These

[97] Cf. Burnet, I, 462 sq. Shaxton (†1556) did not relapse into his error.
Taylor, afterwards Bishop of Lincoln (1552–1554), and Dr. Crome were
also obliged to recant. Cf. J. A. Muller, 135–37.

[98] See the text of Cromwell's condemnation, June 29th, 1540, in Burnet,
IV, 415–24. Cf. Merriman, I, 286.

[99] The legend established by Foxe that the persecution of those who
belonged to the reformed religion did not cease from 1539 to 1547 was
refuted by Dixon (II, chaps. x and xi). With the exception of a few in-
stances in 1540, 1543 and 1546 the Six Articles were scarcely applied
(L. and P., XVIII, Part 1, Introd. p. xlix; part 2, Introd. p. xxxiv; Orig.
Letters, Parker Soc. II, 614, 627; Strype, Mem. of Cranmer, 168 sq.; Pollard,
Henry VIII, 401, n. 1, 415 sq.; Cranmer, 143 and n. 1; Makower, 179).
Whilst he was alive, Cromwell did his best to make the law a dead letter.
Cf. Froude, op. cit., chap. xvi.

[100] Kaulek, 181. A Frenchman, an Italian and an Englishman were
burnt on May 3rd, 1540, two Flemish and an Englishman on May 8th,
and a man named Collins on July 7th; R. Mekins, despite his 15 years,
did not escape death; a priest, Saxy, arrested in virtue of the Six Articles,
hanged himself in prison on April 12th (Wriothesley, Chronicle, ed. Hamilton,
I, 115, 118 sq.; Kaulek, loc. cit.; Stow, General Chronicle, ed. 1615, p. 579;

same Articles caused the last fires of this reign to be lit at Smithfield for Anne Askew (July 16, 1546), who belonged to a very well-connected family of Lincolnshire. She refused every attempt to save her by means of a recantation, and torture was powerless to make her speak even to the end.[101] The law remained in force during the lifetime of Henry VIII, and was repealed only after Edward VI had ascended the throne, in 1547.

The German Protestants were extremely offended by the violently reactionary character of the Six Articles. All hope of an understanding disappeared. The law had scarcely been passed when the ambassadors of Hesse and Saxony hastily left London "as displeased and dissatisfied with the King as it is possible to say . . . much to the displeasure of the lords belonging to the king's council."[102] Melanchthon sent a severe remonstrance to the king, which annoyed the latter very much. He reminded him of the scene of the Athenians revoking the unjust decree against Mytilene, and implored him to repeal "a barbarous statute" which the devil in his rage was using against the Church of Christ to massacre and exterminate her members. The zeal of the prelates, he added, was insincere, and their love for truth mere hypocrisy, for their articles were "erroneous, false, and impious."[103] After the execution of Barnes certain Reformers called the

Foxe, V, 530; Agrippa d'Aubigné, *Histoire universelle*, ed. A. de Ruble, I, 108; J. A. Muller, 355).

[101] Cf. J. Bale, *Select Works*, Parker Soc. ed., 1849, where the *Examinations of Anne Askew* will be found, as well as in Foxe, V, 537-50; Blunt, I, 538 *sq.*; J. Gairdner, *History*, 234 *sq.*; and *Lollardy*, II, 426-30, 446-55, 461 *sq.*; Fisher, 476 *sq.*; chap. v in R. Davey's *The Nine Days Queen, Lady Jane Grey, and her Times*, London, 1910.—According to Blunt (I, 479) very few were condemned in virtue of the Six Articles, which inspired rather a salutary fear. Moreover, the law *de heretico comburendo* sufficed to burn heretics such as Anne Askew. Whatever Foxe may say, the Six Articles, repealed under Edward VI, had nothing to do with the executions in Mary Tudor's time.

[102] Marillac to Francis I and the Constable of France, June 9th, 1539. Kaulek, 102, 103.

[103] *Melanchtoni Opera*, IV, 837; *Corpus Reformatorum*, III, 804. There is a translation in Foxe, V, 350-58. Cf. Cardauns, *Nuntiaturberichte*, V, 117; Froude, chap. XVI; Dixon, II, 159 *sq.* Grafton, the publisher, was accused of translating this letter. Nothing could be more disagreeable for Henry than to see Melanchthon's reproofs circulated in print. The British Museum preserves the *Defensio conjugii sacerdotum . . . missa ad regem Angliae*, 1540 (3905 a. 75) and *The Epistle . . . of Melanchton made unto . . . Kinge Henry the VIIIth*, 1547.

King Nero. Henry's marriage to Anne of Cleves (January 6th, 1540), which appeared to set the seal on a reconciliation between the king and the German princes, had quite the opposite effect.[104] The divorce which ensued and Cromwell's fall (June, 1540) consummated the division. Cromwell had been the instigator and an ardent partisan of an understanding with the Lutherans. When he disappeared, all endeavours to promote a doctrinal agreement between the Churches of England and Germany ceased. In order to alienate the king still more, Gardiner represented to him that he ought not to lower his dignity and his learning before the little princes of Germany, nor allow them to impose laws concerning religion on his own land. They would never acknowledge the king's supremacy, he said, because they would not like to have to submit to that of the emperor.[105]

Moreover, the king's fears were allayed. He understood at last that the rivalry between Charles and Francis would last as long as they lived, and that their friendship was essentially of a passing nature. No serious coalition was therefore to be feared between such irreconcilable adversaries. He resumed his former policy. In 1543 he formed an alliance with Charles V, invaded France (1544) and captured Boulogne. Finding himself alone at war with Francis I, after the latter had made a separate peace with the emperor (1544), Henry again entered into negotiations with the Lutheran princes, but without allowing them to exercise any religious influence over the Church of England.[106]

[104] A month before Cromwell fell, the Lutheran Princes, together with John Frederick of Saxony, sent to Henry VIII various "articles resolved in their assemblies and diets, with letters in which they invite him to follow them as regards the said religion." But the king and the Henricians immediately discovered "several erroneous doctrines" in those articles (Marillac to Montmorency, May 21st, 1540. Kaulek, 184).

[105] Cf. Burnet, I, 432 *sq.*

[106] Cf. A. Hasenclever, *Die Politik der Schmalkaldener vor Ausbruch des Schmalkaldischen Krieges*, Berlin, 1901; *Der Schmalkaldener zwischen Frankreich und England, 1545*, in *Zeitschrift für Geschichte des Oberrheins*, Neue Folge, XX; Stein, *Heinrich VIII und der Schmalkaldische Bund;* P. Singer, *Beziehung des Schmalkaldischen Bundes zu England, 1539*, Griefswald Dissertation, 1901; Pollard, *Henry VIII*, 411 *sq.*; *Cranmer*, 18 *sq.*; J. Gairdner, *History*, 230 *sq.*; L. Cardauns, *Von Nizza bis Crepy. Europäische Politik in den Jahren 1534 bis 1544*, Rome, 1923.—The negotiations for peace between England and France took place in 1546 and the treaty was signed on June 7th. Cf. W. Friedensburg, *Nuntiaturberichte*, IX, 40, 57, 123, 171, 271 and 583.

This last period of the reign saw the Third Confession, which was the final formulary: "The Necessary Erudition of a Christian Man" (1543).

The Second Confession, or the "Bishops' Book," of 1537 had been merely provisional, and the king had authorized it for three years only. So, in 1540, he ordered a commission of bishops and theologians to revise it. They were three years at their task.[107]

Cranmer had set seventeen questions, which each man had to answer in writing, as in 1537, so as to avoid disputes in public. These questions sufficiently reveal the primate of England's advanced opinions, not to mention his scepticism. The following are a few of the questions relating to Holy Orders:

"Whether the apostles lacking a higher power, as in not having a Christian king among them, made bishops by that necessity, or by authority given them by God?—Whether a bishop hath authority to make a priest by the Scripture, or no? and whether any other, but only a bishop, may make a priest? Whether in the New Testament be required any consecration of a bishop and priest, or only appointing to the office be sufficient?—Whether (if it befortuned a prince Christian-learned to conquer certain dominions of infidels, having none but temporal-learned men with him), it be defended [forbidden] by God's law, that he and they should preach and teach the word of God there, or no? and also make and constitute priests, or no?—Whether it be forfended by God's law, that (if it so fortuned that all the bishops and priests of a region were dead, and that the word of God should remain there unpreached, the Sacrament of Baptism and other

[107] In the commission were the two archbishops; Bonner, Bishop of London; Tunstall, Bishop of Durham; Gardiner, Bishop of Winchester; Heath, Bishop of Rochester; Skipp, Bishop of Hereford; Barlow, Bishop of St. David's; Drs. Thirlby, Robinson, Cocks, Wilson, Day, Oglethorp and other well-known theologians. A second commission, composed of six bishops of reforming tendencies, was charged to revise the religious ceremonies. Cf. J. Gairdner, *History*, 216.

The text of the deliberations which preceded the formulary of faith is in Burnet, IV, 443–497. Strype, who attributed the articles of the conference with the Germans in London (1538) to the 1541–43 Commission, has caused extreme confusion on the deliberations of this commission. Cf. Dixon, II, 310, n.

unministered), that the king of that region should make bishops and priests to supply the same, or no?"[108]

These questions revolved upon the royal supremacy, and Cranmer answered them in terms which flattered that prerogative of the king, and exaggerated it by attributing to Henry rights which the latter, with the little common sense he had left, had never dreamt of claiming.[109] "There is no more promise of God," said Cranmer, "that grace is given in the committing of the ecclesiastical office, than it is in the committing of the civil office. All officers and ministers, as well of the one sort [ecclesiastic] as of the other [civil] be appointed, assigned and elected, and in every place, by the laws and orders of kings and princes. In the admission of many of these officers, be divers comely ceremonies and solemnities used, which be not of necessity, but only for a good order and seemly fashion. A bishop may make a priest by the Scripture, and so may princes and governors also, and that by the authority of God committed to them, and the people also by their election. To be a bishop or a priest needeth no consecration, by the Scripture; for election or appointing thereunto is sufficient. If it so fortuned that all the bishops and priests of a region were dead, and that the word of God should remain there unpreached, the king of that region should make bishops and priests to supply the same."[110] It is difficult to deny the sacrament of Holy Orders more peremptorily than that. At

---

[108] Strype, *Mem. of Cranmer*, Append. XXVI, XXVII, XXVIII; Burnet, IV, 443–97, where the answers are given after the questions. The author consulted a manuscript in Lambeth Palace library.

[109] *The Institution of a Christian Man*, of 1537, said: "We may not think that it doth appertain unto the office of kings and princes to preach and teach, to administer the sacraments, to absoyle, to excommunicate, ann such other things belonging to the office and administration of bishops and priests; but we must think and believe that God hath constituted and made Christian kings and princes to be as the chief heads and overlookers over the said priests and bishops, to cause them to administer their office and power committed unto them purely and sincerely."

[110] Strype, Append. XXVI. Burnet, IV, 467 *sq.*, 471 *sq.*, 475 *sq.*, 478, 481, 485.

It is well known that since 1908 the question of women ministering in the Church has been frequently discussed amongst Anglicans. The commission appointed by the Archbishop of Canterbury settled the controversy negatively. Its report was published in 1919. All the arguments for and against will be found therein. (See also H. L. Goudge's collective work: *The Place of Women in the Church*, London, 1917; and Mrs. E. Louie Acre's *Some Questions and Answers concerning Women and Priesthood*, London, 1931.)

this time Cranmer was Lutheran in his belief, if not already tending towards Zwinglianism.

He was followed by Barlow and all the reforming clan. The Henricians, as always, remained inviolably faithful to the traditional teaching of the Church.[111] The "supreme head" was on their side. Consequently orthodoxy triumphed as usual. And the people could have had no idea of the strange division amongst the bishops and theologians, who were supposed to have produced the Third Confession. Besides, the advanced party, with Cranmer at their head, had signed the Confession contrary to their own opinions. That was one of the effects of the royal supremacy.

Henry had carefully perused the written considerations, and had annotated them in his own hand in the margin. In "the matter of the said religion," the French ambassador wrote, "the bishops have not yet agreed upon conformity of opinion, so from day to day it seems that they would put things more in doubt, if this king did not keep them close [in hand], wishing to hear and examine reasons and foundation of their opinion, adding to them and determining as seems good to him, as the above-mentioned lords his ministers asserted to me then, saying that soon a book would appear authorized by parliament, in which all that must be held in the said religion will be determined."[112] The final formulary was submitted to the king, who wrote the preface for it. Hence the popular name by which it was known, the "King's Book." Parliament in 1543 decreed that to speak against the doctrine contained in it was a crime, for which an ecclesiastic would be sent to the stake and a layman to perpetual imprisonment.[113]

The official title of the "King's Book," which was approved

---

[111] Cf. Strype, Append. XXVII and XXVIII; Burnet, IV, 443-97.

[112] Marillac to Montmorency, May 21st, 1540. Kaulek, 184. A few days before (*ibid.*, 178) Marillac had told Francis I of "*la grande contention où les evesques de ce pays sont entrez, les ungs voullant mainctenir leur doctrine comme véritable, les autres la réprouver comme erronée et faulse.*"

[113] 34 and 35 Henry VIII, cap. 1 and 23.—The same name, *The King's Book*, had been given, in 1533, to Foxe's book on the royal supremacy (see chap. VII, n. 54). Strype (*Mem. of Cranmer*) speaks of "the necessary erudition" in his twenty-fourth chapter; and Appendix XXXI contains three speeches by Cranmer on faith, justification and forgiveness of injuries, on the occasion of this formulary of faith.

by Convocation on May 12th, 1543, was: *A necessary Doctrine and Erudition for any Christian Man, set forth by the King's Majesty of England* (May 27th, 1543). It was written better than the "Bishop's Book" of 1537, and the style was finer, clearer and more resolute. The Catholic doctrine was still specified in it.[114] It gave a more complete explanation of the Sacraments, particularly of the Eucharist; and it began with a long article on faith, immediately after the preface.[115] In this article, as well as in the last but one "of good works," the conclusions of Dr. Redman were adopted. He was the most judicious and learned of the English theologians. On this occasion he wrote his *De justificatione opus*, which was published at Antwerp, after his death, in 1555. After speaking of faith united with penance and charity, and after asserting the existence of free will, Redman declares the necessity of good works: "That faith alone justifies and suffices for salvation cannot be affirmed without great danger and scandal for souls; for it is manifestly contrary to Scripture, which says: *Justificatur homo ex operibus et non ex fide tantum.* If the ancient authors sometimes use the expression *sola fides justificat*, they oppose it to the Judaical doctrine of justification by works of the Law, but they did not at all intend to exclude the works of faith."[116] Redman

[114] Makower (61, n. 27; cf. Perry, *History of the English Church*, ed, 1887–88, II, 179) says it is a recasting of the *Institution of a Christian Man*, with a more marked tendency for the traditional doctrine. It was published by Berthelet in 1543, and the Latin translation in 1544, with some additions on free-will and good works: *Pia et catholica christiani hominis Institutio.* Copies, with Archbishop Bancroft's arms on them, are to be found in Lambeth Palace. This formulary of faith was reprinted at Oxford, in 1825 and 1856, in C. Lloyd's *Formularies of Faith*, ed. Cardwell, already mentioned, 213–78. Two verses from Psalms xix and xx, applicable to the king, follow the title: "Lord, preserve the king; and hear us when we call upon thee. Lord, in thy strength the king shall rejoice, and be marvellous glad through thy salvation."

[115] *Quidam doctrinae christianae articuli pro Ecclesia anglicana* had been examined by the commission of 1540: I *De Ecclesia.* II *De Justificatione.* III *De Eucharistia.* IV *De Baptismo.* V *De Penitentia.* VI *De Sacramentorum usu.* They are in Strype (*Eccles. Mem.*, I, chap. XLVIII); and Burnet (IV, 408) gives the first one.

[116] He deals with this question from page 20 onwards (*De bonis operibus et perseverantia*). "Manifestum est bona opera ad justitiam et gratiam in quam sumus vocati tuendam et conservandam plurimum facere. . . . Fides, si bona opera continentur adhibeas, conservatur; sin minus, sensim obscuratur et tandem penitus evanescit atque extinguitur. . . . Bona opera justitiam augent et perficiunt. Opera fidei et charitatis faciunt ut melius et certius Dei misericordiam apprehendamus. . . . Dementia est

denounced as an iniquitous mystery the new teaching: "believe, and you are saved," a teaching which aimed at "burying free will." On the contrary, according to the teaching of the apostle, the people must be exhorted to do good works "which are the gifts of God, calling us to his kingdom and his glory, leading us to eternal life."[117]

The "Necessary Doctrine" appeared to Pole himself to be so consistent with the true doctrine that he ordered it to be read in the pulpit in Mary Tudor's time, whilst waiting for a book of homilies to be published. The Reformers attributed it to the leader of the Henricians, Gardiner.[118]

This "Necessary Doctrine" was a re-shuffling of the Second

asserere quod nullis omnino cum Deo operibus agendum sit, sed tantum cum proximo; cum oratio, confessio, gratiarum actio sacrificia laudis et crucis [Masses], sint opera quibus cum Deo agimus. . . . *Opera a justificatione non rejicienda.* Quamvis operum fiduciam, id est propriae dignitatis praesumptionem damnamus, opera tamen ipsa . . . non damnamus. . . . Fiducia omnis in solo datore atque ipsius gratia et non in dono collocanda est, quare et ab operibus et ab ipsa fide, quatenus fides etiam in nobis donum est, in solam Dei bonitatem et gratiam transferenda est. . . . Quamvis autem bona opera tantopere praedicamus gratiae tamen nihil detrahimus . . . imo vero gratiam et Christi beneficium quam maxime illustramus, dum operum bonitatem soli gratiae ascribimus, et Christum qui nobis morte sua spiritum fidei et charitatis promeruit, per bona opera ipsius in nobis virtutem inhabitantem ostendentes, pure adoramus. Nec tamen in nobis ipsis aut nostris operibus gloriandum quicquam esse dicimus sed in sola gratia Domini nostri Jesu Christi: gratia enim Dei sumus id quod sumus" (*Joannis Redmani Angli s. theologiae professoris de justificatione opus*, Antwerp, 1555 (in 4to), pp. 6, 9, 12, 24, 28, 37, 39, 42, 46). In a letter to the council, in 1547 (cf. J. A. Muller, 360) Gardiner said that, in addition to Redman, Drs. Cox and Robinson and Bishops Heath, Thirlby and Day collaborated in this article.

[117] Henry VIII asserted his belief in good works when he left alms in his will for the salvation of his soul (*ibid.*, pp. 42, 44, 47). The work finishes (pp. 48-55) with a hymn "in quo peccator justificationem quaerens rudi imagine describitur."—Luther expounded the doctrine of justification in *De captivate Babylonis* (chapter on "Baptism"), in his sermon *De novo Testamento*, etc. See E. F. Fischer, *Melanchthons Lehre von der Bekehrung*, Tübingen, 1905; A. Ritschl, *Die Christliche Lehre von der Rechtfertigung und Versöhnung*, 1870-71, 3 vols. (the second and third volumes were translated into English, in 1874 and 1900, at Edinburgh: (a) *A critical History of the Christian Doctrine of Justification and Reconciliation;* (b) *The Christian Doctrine of Justification and Reconciliation*).

[118] R. Pole's Injunctions for the diocese of Gloucester (*Lambeth Documents*, London, 1838, pp. 146, 148).

In this Confession the mind, doctrine and influence of Gardiner are certainly to be found. As for indicating the exact part he took in it, this is all the more difficult because he was away on an embassy at the imperial Court part of the time during which it was prepared (cf. J. A. Muller, *op. cit.*, 106, 360).

Confession, which in turn was merely a revision and a complement of the First Confession; so that the three formularies of
faith were really one and the same, but developed, elucidated,
and determined according to the circumstances and needs of
the day. Not one of them was abrogated by those that
followed, and the later Confessions merely supplemented the
earlier ones.

These Confessions of Faith firmly and clearly enunciate
transubstantiation, communion under one kind, veneration
of the saints, the Mass, purgatory, religious vows, ecclesiastical celibacy and other articles which the Lutherans contested.
In 1543, the separation between the latter and the English
Church was complete. The Council of Trent had not yet
spoken, and already the Reformation, despite its efforts to
penetrate into the Church of England, was condemned.

But did not Henry VIII authorize the destruction of
images? All he meant to do was to suppress certain superstitious devotions.[119] The Confessions of Faith prescribed
that the images should be kept in the churches and taught that
it was good to venerate them.[120] He himself began his will
with these words: "In the name of God, and of the glorious
and blessed Virgin our Lady Saint Marie, and all the holy
companie of Heaven."[121]

---

[119] See Articles VI, VII, and VIII of the Ten Articles. Here, again,
as in the case of the monasteries, the desire to fill the royal treasury played
a part: "*Après que ce roy a prins et appliqué à soy tout le revenu des abbayes et
partye de celluy d'aucuns éveschez,*" wrote Marillac on October 23rd, 1541
(Kaulek, 351), "*il s'est estendu sur les chasses d'or et d'argent qui restoient, où les
relicques d'aucuns corps sainctz estoient encloses, et disent ceulx cy qu'ilz mettront
les ossemens des dictz sainctz dans des monumens de pierre, où ilz pensent qu'elles
seront plus décentes que ès lieux où estoient.*"

[120] Images must not be prohibited, said *The Institution of a Christian Man*
(on the 2nd Commandment of God), but they must be placed in our
churches "to yield thanks to our Lord, and to praise him and his saints,
and to remember and lament our sins and offences, and to pray God that
we may have grace to follow their goodness and holy living. . . . The said
images may well be set up in churches, to be as books for unlearned people,
to put them in remembrance of those saints, of whom they may learn
examples of faith, humility, charity, patience, temperance and of all other
their virtues. . . . And whereas we used to cense the said images, and to
kneel before them, we must know that such things be not done to the
image itself, but to God and in his honour."

[121] Fuller, III, 214; Dodd, ed. 1737, I, 317. Redman, in the book
on Justification (p. 25), referred to above, had said: "Somniant quidam
omnes fideles qualicunque fide praediti fuerunt, virtute tamen et justitia

Henry suppressed the monasteries, but from motives of gain and without invoking any doctrinal principle, as was done in Germany. The expelled monks and nuns were still bound by their vows of chastity; if they failed therein, they were liable to imprisonment and to have their property confiscated, and in the case of a relapse the punishment was death. Thus was it decreed by Article III of the Six Articles, which came out precisely in the year in which the suppression of the monasteries was most ruthlessly carried out.

At the same time as the Third Confession of Faith a *Rationale* for the liturgy was drawn up in Convocation. It did no more than justify the rites and ceremonies then in use, and explained them without making any alteration or modification. All the old ceremonies were retained. Marillac was able to write to Francis I: "The ecclesiastical service after all conforms entirely to the Latin Church, except the mentioning of the Pope, which is all changed and transferred to the name and authority of this king."[122] The *Rationale* successively examined the Pontifical, the Breviary and the Missal, and explained clearly and even in a beautiful manner the different parts of Catholic worship.[123] It displeased Cranmer, who prevented it from appearing. In the first year of Edward VI's reign, Convocation re-demanded it but the archbishop did not present it.[124]

If, together with the worship, the Creed was also main-

pares esse, ita ut non vereantur omnes foeminas beatae Virgini aequare. Sed procul absit a christianis mentibus ejusmodi blasphemia." The *Necessary Doctrine* explains "The Salutation of the Angel to the blessed Virgin Mary" as does also the *Institution of a Christian Man* of 1537.

[122] Kaulek, 351. He had already written to the king on April 10th, 1540 (*ibid.*, 175 and cf. 115): "*On reduit icy l'affaire de la religion en tout conforme à la façon de l'Église,*" save obedience to Rome and the preservation of the monasteries. All that was done under Henry VIII, says the Rev. H. Pole (*The Book of Common Prayer*, London, 1902, p. 8), was to take the Pope's name out of the old liturgical books; no change in ceremonies took place until the following reign.

[123] The mystical meaning of the ceremonies of the Mass and cf the priestly vestments is explained. In 1910 C. S. Cobb published it, in Vol. XVIII of the "Publications of the Alcuin Club": *The Rationale of Ceremonial, 1540–43.* Collier (II, 191 in the ed. in folio of 1708, and Vol. V, pp. 104–22 in the Lathbury edition, 1852), and Strype, in his *Eccles. Mem.*, had previously extracted it from the manuscripts for its historical interest.

[124] The *Book of Homilies* was also begun in the 1543 Convocation. There was, moreover, a desire to entrust the revision of ecclesiastical laws to thirty-two men. Cf. Dixon, II, 313 *sq.*; Blunt, I, 492 *sq.*

tained, it was because the Henricians always defended the
traditional teaching against the new ideas. Gardiner, Stokesley, Bonner, Tunstall and their friends were schismatics, but
they remained orthodox.

The Henricians were supported by Henry. The king had
never the least sympathy with Lutheranism. He had attacked
Luther in his *Assertio septem sacramentorum*, and he never forgot
the invectives and insults that the Wittenberg monk hurled at
him.[125] The attempts at a rapprochement with the Protestants of Germany were inspired by Cromwell. They were
dictated by political motives, and finally failed.

Henry VIII had received a serious theological education
in his young days. According to Lord Herbert, his father had
destined him for the Church.[126] All his life through he
remained imbued with that first powerful training. His work
against Luther displays the soundest theology. The numerous
annotations which he made on the writings of the bishops,
who were gathered together for the various Confessions of
Faith, are a proof of the continual interest he took in doctrinal
discussions, and his constant intervention in favour of the
Henricians seems indeed to show his attachment to the orthodox teaching. "The king's majesty," said the message read
by Cromwell to Convocation in June, 1536, "by his excellent
learning, knoweth these controversies well enough; yet he will
suffer no common alteration, but by the consent of you and of
his whole Parliament."[127] The innovators who recanted knew
that they had been overcome by his learning, joined to that of
the other theologians.[128] Reginald Pole never reproached
him with adhering to the Reformation, even in his most
violent attacks[129]; he was even delighted with the First

[125] See W. Walther, *Heinrich VIII von England und Luther*, Leipzic, 1908
(cf. P. Smith, in the *Eng. Hist. Review*, XXV).

[126] See n. 28, chap. II.

[127] Foxe V, 379.

[128] *Recantatio* of Barnes, Jerome and Garrard, who were afterwards burnt
at Smithfield for having relapsed (Burnet, IV, 497, and Foxe, V, Append.
VII).

[129] These articles admit, Pole wrote to his friend Contarini (Quirini, I,
458; cf. 479), and they profess all the dogmas of the Church, save the
unity of the Church and the Vicar of Jesus-Christ, which they do not
mention; they clearly show the royal way of thinking. "Henry . . .", says
Sander (*op. cit.*, Lewis' trans., p. 171), "had left . . . in cities and towns,
in colleges, in villages, a very large number of churches unrifled, which

Confession of Faith, though it was the least explicit of all. The Reformers disowned Henry. One of them said that all the publications issued by the royal authority had been subject to the jealous revision of a prince who was more opposed to the papal power than to the doctrinal corruption of the Roman religion; not a single one of those books could be called Protestant until the accession of Edward VI. "It is needless to observe," remarked Dr. Lloyd,[130] the Anglican Bishop of Oxford, "that these documents cannot pretend to any authority in the present day. Nothing antecedent to the reign of Edward VI has any title to that character." The Lutherans did not look upon Henry as one of their own, as both the letters of Melanchthon and the bitter reflexions of Myconius testify.[131] The letter *Germaniae ad Angliam de restituta Evangelii luce Gratulatio* of 1559 spoke in glowing terms of Elizabeth, her brother Edward, and her mother Anne Boleyn, but was silent concerning Henry VIII.[132]

By a unity of belief Henry meant to maintain a political unity. Was not the upholding of the ancient faith the surest means of assuring that unity? The newborn Reformation was leading already to doctrinal dissensions and to a division into sects. Nothing could inspire the king with more horror and disgust.

The majority of the people were attached to the ancient faith; they needed to be reassured and shown that one could renounce the authority of the Bishop of Rome and yet remain orthodox. Henry displayed a certain affectation in keeping himself orthodox. "The chief topic put forward by this king," the French ambassador wrote in 1539,[133] "was to complain of the Pope, who was trying to recall the emperor and the king,

our forefathers had built; and he had preserved their furniture undamaged, crucifixes, pictures, vessels, vestments. He also held in honour the seven sacraments, and checked and suppressed almost every heresy except that which related to the supremacy of the Roman Pontiff and the religious orders."

[130] Ch. Lloyd, *Formularies of Faith*, 1825 and 1856, p. iv. The first quotation is from Burrow's *A Summary of Christian Faith*, I, p. 1. Henry was certainly not a Protestant, and it cannot be said that he made the Church of England Protestant, says the Rev. H. Pole (*The Church of England*, London, 1899). Cf. Dodd, I, 127 *sq.*

[131] Cf. above, pp. 416 *sq.*, 423.

[132] "Experiamur laudatissimae Reginae, matris tuae, Annae Boleniae, in te virtutes . . ." (p. 16).

[133] Kaulek, 114 *sq.*

his friends, from their alliance and their devotedness to wage
war against him, on the plea that all here were heretics and
infidels, of which [statement] in order to show the contrary he
requested that the opinions which were to be held in religion
should be fixed, so that each one might know what to hold."
The Confessions of Faith taught his subjects that the king's
doctrine remained inflexible and contrary to all reforming
movements.

Finally, Henry seems to have remained always opposed to
new ideas. In solemn session, surrounded by bishops and
peers, he himself, attired all in white, tried John Lambert,
who was accused of denying the Real Presence and of maintaining, with Luther, that it was a sin to pray to the saints; he
condemned him either to recant or to go to the stake.[134]
Every morning he was accustomed "to hear Mass at seven
o'clock."[135] Some of his wives had a leaning towards heresy,
but he himself never wavered. Katherine Parr, who had
undertaken to convert him, was threatened with the stake.
In his will he ordered numerous Masses to be said for himself.
If he did not make himself head of the English Church, wrote
Cervini (afterwards Marcellus II), apropos of the Six Articles,
his opinions would be Catholic.[136] Sander even relates that
in his last illness Henry thought of being reconciled to Rome,
when he saw how the bonds of Church unity had been broken
by his actions.[137]

He probably had visions of a schismatic Church, like the

[134] Cf. Strype, *Mem. of Cranmer*, chap. xvii, Append. No. XXIV; J.
Gairdner, *History*, 204; Fischer, 434.

[135] Marillac to Francis I, December 4th, 1540. Kaulek, 247.

[136] Cervini to Farnese, Brussels, June 24th, 1540. L. Cardauns,
Nuntiaturberichte, V, 305.

[137] Sander, Lewis' trans., 160 *sq.* Rinaldi (*ad ann. 1547*, No. CXX)
quotes Sander, and A. Duchesne (*op. cit.*, ed. 1614, p. 1334) also follows
his account. "The majority feared that a snare had been laid for them,"
Sander adds. But "it is said that Gardiner persuaded him . . . to call his
Parliament together if possible and to communicate to it a matter of that
importance," or at least "to express his resolution in writing. . . ." This
appears to be sufficiently in keeping with Gardiner's character, who had
good reason to fear that the true doctrine would suffer from the results
of the schism when Henry was dead. The king's wishes expressed in writing
would have been a powerful argument against the innovators, who were
going to take advantage of Edward VI's minority to introduce the
Reformation. "But as soon as the bishop [Gardiner] had gone," Sander
continues, "the crowd of flatterers came around him [Henry] and afraid
that the return of the kingdom to the obedience of the Holy See would
force them to part with the ecclesiastical lands, these men persuaded him

Greek or Russian Church. Was it possible in the Europe of that period, agitated by the clash of opinions and unsettled by the great religious revolution of the sixteenth century? Lutheran infiltrations were already apparent in the Church of England. The courts against heresy were never more active than during the last years of this reign. The episcopate itself did not go unscathed: two bishops were obliged to resign; but others, partisans of the Reformation, remained, and with them the primate, Cranmer, who signed and promulgated the Confessions of orthodox faith, although at heart a Lutheran, if not a Zwinglian. Once the king was dead, the Church of England would be unable to retain her creed. Rome then had reason to consider the English schism as not less to be feared than the German heresy.[138] "By leaping out of Peter's ship," said Archbishop Heath in the first of Elizabeth's Parliaments (March, 1559), "we hazard ourselves to be drowned in the waters of schism, sects and divisions." And Sander wrote that, in spite of his severe laws, Henry was not able for long to preserve the Church of England, because "the bulwarks and embankments of the Church being broken, various heresies impetuously entered in."[139] And in 1669, in his funeral sermon for Henrietta of France, Bossuet pointed to England "more agitated in her lands and even in her ports than the ocean which surrounds her, and inundated with the overflow of a thousand fantastic sects."

Henry VIII died on January 28th, 1547. With him the schismatic and orthodox Church of England was destined to disappear.

to allow no such scruples to enter his mind" (cf. Cardauns, *Nuntiaturberichte*, V, 352).

Richard Hall (†1604), who translated Fisher's first biography, adds this detail which confirms Sander's words: "Stephanus Wintoniensis episcopus, qui erat ei [regi] familiarissimus, narrare saepe solebat habuisse quidem illum animum redeundi ad Ecclesiae gremium, sed, dum expectaret quoad ab aliis ad hoc invitaretur, potius quam ut ipse sua sponte id petere videretur, morte preventum fuisse" (*Ana. Boll.*, XII, 243; cf. *ibid.*, X, 194).

[138] Friedensburg, *Nuntiaturberichte*, II, 423. Several times in his letters to R. Pole, Contarini bewailed the obstinacy of the king who, after the Lutheran defection, had separated from the Church one of its chief members, the realm of England: "Ingemisco et doleo quantum scis, immo fortasse quantum nescis" (Quirini, I, 464, and II, 30, July 8th, 1536 and May 12th, 1537).

[139] Sander (*op. cit.*, French trans., 1587, f. 91, 92, apparently not translated by Lewis). Heath's discourse has been printed by Strype, *Annals*, 1558-1603, I, Part 2, pp. 399-407.

APPENDICES

APPENDIX I

BIBLIOGRAPHY

			PAGE
A.	GENERAL BIBLIOGRAPHY	. . . . .	439
B.	BIBLIOGRAPHY, CHAPTER II		441
C.	BIBLIOGRAPHY, CHAPTER IV		447
D.	BIBLIOGRAPHY, CHAPTER V		449
	(a) Cardinal John Fisher		449
	(b) Sir Thomas More		451
	(c) Cardinal Reginald Pole		455
E.	BIBLIOGRAPHY, CHAPTER VI		457
	(a) Thomas Cromwell		457
	(b) Thomas Cranmer		458
F.	BIBLIOGRAPHY, CHAPTER VII		459
G.	BIBLIOGRAPHY, CHAPTER VIII		461

APPENDIX II

COULD CLEMENT VII ANNUL HENRY VIII'S MARRIAGE? . 469

APPENDIX III

THOMAS MORE AND PAPAL AUTHORITY . . . 482

CHRONOLOGICAL TABLE OF EVENTS IN THE RELIGIOUS HISTORY OF HENRY VIII'S REIGN 485

APPENDIX I

BIBLIOGRAPHY

The notes to this Appendix will be found on pages 462–468

A

GENERAL BIBLIOGRAPHY

There are numerous works in English relating to the sixteenth century. The old Church Histories, such as those of Burnet,[1] Fuller,[2] Collier,[3] and Dodd[4], are out of date, but are, nevertheless, valuable for the documents they contain. These writers also refer us to J. Foxe[5] and Strype, and J. S. Brewer considers the latter an "indispensable authority."[6] Between 1819 and 1830 John Lingard, a Catholic priest who studied at Douai until the outbreak of the French Revolution and then became successively vice-president of Ushaw College and Rector of Hornby in Lancashire, wrote his *History of England from the first invasion by the Romans to the year 1688*, in ten vols. (London). Many editions and translations of this work were published and are still read. The best edition of the nineteenth century was the fifth (1849-51); it was re-published in 1883 with an etched portrait at the beginning of each volume. The last edition, due to Hilaire Belloc, was in eleven volumes. For Lingard, see Martin Haile and Edwin Bonney, *The Life and Letters of John Lingard, 1771-1851*, London, 1890 and 1911, with five illustrations. From the High Church point of view, Canon Dixon wrote his six volumes on the *History of the Church of England from the Abolition of the Roman Jurisdiction* (London, 1878-1902), covering the period from 1529 to 1570[7]; and J. Gairdner, the well-known editor of *Letters and Papers*, who had spent forty years of his life in publishing the documents of that period, made use of his knowledge, with great impartiality, for the fourth volume of the *History of the English Church*, edited by W. Stephens and W. Hunt.[8]

The publication of the documents (*Letters and Papers*) just

439

mentioned, which was begun by the brothers Lemon (*State Papers during the reign of Henry VIII*, 11 vols., 1830–52),[9] was not confined eventually to State papers, and became known by the more general title *Letters and Papers* (*Letters and Papers. foreign and domestic of the reign of Henry VIII preserved in the P. Record Office, the British Museum and elsewhere in England*, 1509–47, London, 1862–1910).[10]   The first four volumes were edited by J. S. Brewer and the remaining seventeen by J. Gairdner, assisted towards the end by R. H. Brodie, who began, in 1920, a new edition of the whole collection, considerably augmented, For the reign of Henry VIII alone we are already confronted with about 50,000 documents, analysed in 20,000 crowded pages, and with more than a million facts.   To the foregoing publications must be added the series of *Calendars* containing the correspondence of foreign ambassadors preserved in the archives of Spain and Italy,[11] the collection of treaties, laws, decrees, acts of the Privy Council,[12] and ecclesiastical statutes,[13] the parliamentary minutes,[14] and the contemporary Chronicles of Hall (†1547),[15] Wriothesley,[16] Stow,[17] and Holinshed,[18] not to mention others.[19]   This enormous mass of documents has been further augmented by the publication of private archives,[20] and the zeal of historical societies,[21] such as the Camden, the Parker, and the Royal Historical Societies.   This last society has published amongst other things, and in addition to its periodical *Transactions*, *The Domesday of Inclosures*, 1517–18 (ed. J. S. Leadam, 1897).[22] To this extensive collection of documents has been added a number of either general or particular studies[23]; and these almost continuous contributions did not cease during the Great War.   At the same time as the French edition of this book appeared, a university thesis was published by an Anglican, the Rev. H. A. Moreton: *La Réforme anglicane au XVI⁰ siècle* (Paris, 1930).

Special bibliographies will be found in this appendix for the chapters requiring them.   With regard to a general bibliography, after the indications already given, it seems useless to give one here, particularly as we already possess bibliographies by J. Gairdner in Volume II of the *Cambridge Modern History* (pp. 789 *sq.*) and at the end of the chapters in *The English Church in the Sixteenth Century*, and by Fisher in Volume V of the *Political History of England* (pp. 488 *sq.*).[24] M. Charles Bémont has given the chief sources for this reign in his Introduction to the *Chronique latine sur le premier divorce de Henri VIII*.[25]

Several portraits of Henry VIII are given in the *Croquis de Chantilly*, by Morone-Laton; and in *Portraits of illustrious personages of the court of Henry VIII*, edited by E. Lodge and J. Chamberlaine (London, 1828), will be found portraits by Holbein of sixty-nine court personages of those days.

A hundred years after Henry VIII's death, Lord Herbert of Cherbury wrote his life (*Life and Reign of Henry VIII*, London, 1649), with the help of documents which have since partly disappeared.[26] J. A. Froude, whose talent as an historian is as undeniable as his Protestant bias, gave a highly coloured rather than a truthful description of the reign.[27] Its first years were elucidated by J. S. Brewer's able prefaces,[28] while those written by J. Gairdner, which by order of the government were less developed, merely gave a brief summary of the salient events. Two and a half centuries after Lord Herbert, A. F. Pollard published his *Henry VIII* (London, 1902), with fine illustrations by Goupil.[29] In the preface (p. ix) the author says that, for England, an adequate and impartial history of what is called the Reformation remains to be written.[30] Francis Hackett, the Irish sociologist and novelist, who wrote literary criticism for the Chicago "Evening News," has taken many quotations from *Letters and Papers* for his *Henry the Eighth* (London, 1929; 12 photogravures); but a great deal of the book comes from his own imagination and intuitions, as he himself admits. It is more amusing to read than trustworthy, and trivialities are not always avoided. As for *King Henry the Rake* (London, 1930), by Clement Wood, this is a kind of historical novel, in which the king is depicted as a stupid and ravenous clown, whose love affairs were his sole policy. *The Private Character of Henry the Eighth*, by Frederick Chamberlin (1932), tells us no more about Henry's disease or his character than we knew before.

B

BIBLIOGRAPHY FOR CHAPTER II

One of the registers of Verzosa (Simancas, Estado 2016)—who founded the Spanish archives in Rome in Philip II's time (cf. G. Constant's Report on a scientific mission to the *Archives of Austria and of Spain*, in Vol. XVIII of *Nouvelles Archives des Missions scientifiques et littéraires*, pp. 525 *sq.*)—contains a certain number of documents belonging to the case, which were copied by him in the Vatican Archives. "Continet etiam ea quae acta fuerunt super validitate matrimonii Henrici regis Angliae." In 1870 N. Pocock published some of the documents relating to the divorce: *Records of the Reformation. The divorce 1527-1533, mostly now for the first time printed from MSS. in the British Museum, the Public Record Office, the Venetian archives and other Libraries*, 2 vols., Oxford, 1870. To-day, besides the abundant collection of *State Papers during the reign of Henry VIII* (11 vols., 1830-52) due to the brothers Lemon, the *Letters and Papers*, of which the first four volumes are by Brewer, the next nine by James Gairdner, and the last eight by Gairdner and Brodie, the *Calendars*, (a) *Venetian* (b) *Spanish*, taken from the Simanacas archives and due to Bergenroth [the first two volumes and their supplement, 1868, contain documents relating to Catherine of Aragon before and after her marriage with Henry VIII]; and to Don Pascual de Gayangos [Vols. III and IV, 1525-38, very important, concern the divorce period]; and a few other documents also taken from the Vatican archives; we have the correspondence of Cardinal Lorenzo Campeggio, whom Clement VII ordered to try the case in England together with Wolsey (October 8th, 1528-October 5th, 1529), correspondence that has been hitherto but imperfectly known or edited (H. Lämmer, *Monumenta Vaticana historiam ecclesiasticam saeculi XVI illustrantia*, Freiburg, 1861; A. Theiner, *Vetera monumenta Hibernorum et Scotorum historiam illustrantia, 1216-1547*, Rome 1864), and afterwards published by Mgr. S. Ehses with all possible care and with all the criticism that can be desired. *Römische Dokumente zur Geschichte der Ehescheidung Heinrichs VIII von England, 1517-34*, Paderborn, 1893. *The Life of Blessed John Fisher* (*Analecta Bollandiana*, Vols. X and XII), the vigorous defender of Catherine of Aragon, is an important source (see chap v). "The first embassy in England (1527-29) of Jean du Bellay", Bishop of Bayonne (1526-32) and of Paris (1532-51), afterwards cardinal (1555-†1560), of which Le Grand made great use (*Preuves de l'Histoire du divorce, de la Defense de Sanderus et de la Réfutation de M. Burnet*, i.e. Vol. III of his *Histoire du divorce*, Paris, 1688), was published, in 1905, by V. L. Bourrilly and P. de Vaissière (History of France archives).

Fisher's passionate defence of Catherine's marriage with Henry VIII was published, in 1530, at Alcala de Henares before a definite judgment had been given in the case (John Fisher, *De causa matrimonii regis Angliae liber*). Harpsfield,

Archdeacon of Canterbury (1554), summarized it, without adding to it, in the first book of his *Treatise of the pretended divorce between Henry and Catherine of Aragon* (edition Pocock, Camden Society, 2nd Series, Vol. XXI, 1878); and he wrote an "Historical discourse on the Divorce" (end of Book II and Book III of the same treatise), in which are analysed a large number of official documents which he consulted in Mary Tudor's time. On the same subject he drew up a Latin Chronicle, which is preserved in the *Bibliothèque Nationale;* Joachim Le Grand, of the Congregation of the Oratory, consulted it for his *Histoire du divorce de Henri VIII*, but erroneously attributed it to Thomas Harding; Charles Bémont published it with a French translation, explanatory notes, and a learned introduction, in which he shows who the author was (Fasc. 221, *Bibliothèque de l'École des Hautes Études*, 1917).

In Mary Tudor's time, a few publications in favour of her mother, Catherine of Aragon, had already appeared: Grillanderus, *Repudio della reina d'Inghilterra e difesa*, Bologna, 1553; *Goretii Oratio de matrimonio regis ac reginae Angliae*, London, 1554.

At about the same period as Harpsfield (1576) Nicolas Sander, or Sanders [1530?–1581] (cf. Pollen, *Nicholas Sanders*, in the *Eng. Hist. Review*, Vol. VI, 1891, pp. 36 *sq.*; Guilday, *The English Catholic Refugees on the Continent, 1558–1795*, London, 1914, *passim*), a Catholic theologian who had taken refuge on the Continent and made a report on England under Elizabeth (1562) [printed in the *Rome Calendar*], published at Louvain, in 1571: *de visibili monarchia libri octo*, wrote, in Madrid, his *De origine et progressu schismati anglicani*, "in all sincerity as I have gathered it from public records or from the testimony, oral and written, of men of the greatest consideration, or at least from my own knowledge and observation" [Lewis' trans., p. cxlvii]; this work was published after his death, with a continuation (Book III, 1568–85), by another Catholic priest, his friend E. Rishton, whose pen is very violent (Cologne, 1585 and 1590; Rome, 1586; Ingolstadt, 1588). "I have also left out some of the discussions which seemed tedious, in order to preserve more closely the order of the story, adding much, especially those things that took place after the death of Dr. Sander" (Lewis' trans. p. cxliii). The work was slightly altered and augmented by Father Pedro de Ribadeneira (†1611, aged 80), a friend and collaborator of Sander, who made use of certain anecdotes of the Spanish chroniclers who had lived in England (*Historia ecclesiastica del cisma del regno de Inglaterra*, Madrid and Valentia, 1588). He is the source of Bernardo Davanzati's History of the English Schism (codex 250 of the Corsini Library in Rome has a copy of 1602: *Schisma d'Inghilterra sino alla morte della Regina Maria descritto in lingua Florentina da Bernardo Davanzati*, beginning with Arthur's betrothal), and of the *Historia ecclesiastica della Rivoluzione d'Inghilterra divisa in libri quattro* (Florence, 1591; Rome, 1594) by Girolamo Pollini, a Dominican belonging to the Province of Tuscany, a book which Elizabeth tried to suppress (Elizabeth to the Duke of Florence, April 6th, 1592. Cf. A. O. Meyer, *England und die katholische Kirche unter Elisabeth*, Rome, 1911, pp. 317–18). Sander's work was translated into many languages; the oldest French translation is dated 1587, and is by I.T.A.C. Canon Maucroix of Rheims brought out a second translation, in 1676. David Lewis translated it into English, with notes and an introduction, in 1877. The success of Sander's work brought forth a reply, the *Anti-Sanderus*, an anonymous publication which came out shortly after Ribadeneira's *Histoire*, and in which were published documents relating to the case (Julius II's dispensation, December 25th, 1503, Clement VII's Bull "De secundis nuptiis contrahendis constante nullitate primi matrimonii," and the pronounce-ments of the universities of Orleans, Paris, Bourges, Toulouse, Bologna, and Padua). When, in 1679, there was a rumour on the Continent of a Catholic king ascending the English throne, Charles II's chaplain, Gilbert Burnet, moved by Maucroix's translation which brought fresh fame to Sander, decided to write his *History of the Reformation of the Church of England* in an endeavour to refute Sander "whom he accused," says Bossuet (*Histoire des Variations des Églises protestantes*, Bk. VII), "of having invented atrocious facts in order to render the English Reformation detestable." If at times Sander showed so little moderation that he made the king's passion for Anne Boleyn seem very unlikely, it is admitted nowadays that the replies which he provoked were equally lacking in moderation (cf. Sander, *op. cit.*, Lewis' trans., pp. xxiv, *sq.*; G. Ascoli, *op. cit.*, pp. 154 *sq.*; Ch. Bémont, *op. cit.*, p. 40. It was chiefly the augmented edition which contained the idle tales and the village gossip. Cf. Gasquet: *Henry VIII and the English Monasteries*, ed. 1889, 2 vols., II, p. 351). J. Le Grand, defending Sander, published his *Histoire du divorce de Henri VIII roy d'Angleterre et de Catherine d'Aragon, avec la Défense de Sanderus, la Réfutation des deux premier, livres de l'Histoire de la Réformation de M. Burnet et les Preuves* (Paris, 1688); these "proofs," to-day in the *Bibliothèque Nationale*, were given to him by Thévenot, keeper of the king's library, to whom the book is dedicated. He intended to publish in a final volume, "since this collection is already too large," many other documents, such as Henry VIII's letters to Anne Boleyn, the Bishop of Tarbes' dispatches, and those of MM. de Castillon and de Marillac: but this was not done (cf. Le Grand, *Lettres à M. Burnet touchant l'histoire des variations, l'histoire de la réformation et l'histoire du divorce de Henri VIII et de Catherine d'Aragon*, Paris, 1691). But Dodd took the question up again in 1737, and in an authoritative manner (cf. Bibliography A, n. 4). The Chronicles of Edward Hall, of Stow, and of Wriothesley, studied by Ch. Bémont in his Introduction to Harpsfield's Latin Chronicle, certain works of Strype (*Annals of the Reformation*, 4 vols., 1709-31; *Ecclesiastical Memorials relating chiefly to religion and the reformation of it*, 2 vols., 1711-33; *Memorials of Thomas Cranmer*, 3 vols., 1694), not to mention the general histories already referred to (Bibliography A, nn. 1, 2, 3, 4), provide documents or explanations on the history of the divorce.

After Agnes Strickland's *Lives of the Queens of England*, ed. 1878, II, pp. 458-704, W. H. Dixon published four volumes (3rd ed., London, 1873-74) on the *History of two Queens: Catherine of Aragon; Anne Boleyn*; and Paul Friedmann, with the aid of Chapuy's correspondence preserved in the *Staatsarchiv* of Vienna, wrote, in 1884, *Anne Boleyn, a chapter of English History*, a learned and impartial book. Miss Benger had previously, in 1821, published *Memoirs of the Life of Anne Boleyn, Queen of Henry VIII*, two volumes, with portrait. Du Boys' History (*Catherine d'Aragon et les origines du schisme anglican*, Geneva, 1880, English translation in 2 vols., 1881) is obsolete; J. A. Froude's *The divorce of Catherine of Aragon*, 1st ed., 1891, lacks neither talent nor bias. Dom, later Cardinal, Gasquet edited Mrs. Hope's *The first Divorce of Henry VIII as told in the State papers*. J. Gairdner had written in the *Eng. Hist. Review* (Vols. XI and XII) his *New Lights on the divorce of Henry VIII* and in the *Transactions of the Royal Historical Society* (new series, Vol. XIV, 1899, pp. 75-103), *The Fall of Cardinal Wolsey*. He also speaks of the royal divorce in *Lollardy and the Reformation in England*, I, 376-87. W. Busch, in the *Historisches Taschenbuch* (VIte Folge, VIII, 271-327, IX, 39-114), studied the origin of the divorce (*Der Ursprung der Ehescheidung Königs Heinrichs VIII von England*), Wolsey's fall (*Der Sturz des Cardinals*

Wolsey), whose policies were well known to him (*Drei Jahre englischer Vermittlungspolitik, 1518–1521*, Bonn, 1884; *Cardinal Wolsey und die englisch-kaiserliche Allianz, 1522*, Bonn, 1886). Cavendish, Wolsey's gentleman-usher, wrote his master's life in 1557 (*Memoirs of the Life of Cardinal Wolsey containing his Rise and excessive Power*), of which editions appeared in 1641, in 1708, and Singer's edition in 1827, and editions have frequently appeared since (ed. John Holmes, 1872; Keinscott, 1893). Charles Whittingham had reprinted (Chiswick, 1845) one hundred copies of a contemporary satire: *Roy's satire against Wolsey*. A poem by Storer in 1599: *The Life and Death of Th. Wolsey, Cardinall, divided into three parts, his Aspiring, Triumph and Death*, was republished, with an introduction and notes, in 1826 (Oxford, 82 pp.). In the eighteenth century both R. Fiddes (*The Life of Cardinal Wolsey*, 1st ed. 1724, 2nd ed. 1726, with the Cardinal's portrait and six engravings) and J. Grove (*History of the Life and Times of Cardinal Wolsey. . . collected from antient Records, MSS. and Historians*, 4 vols. 1742-44, with portraits and engravings), took a particular interest in the cardinal and his times; E. L. Taunton (*Thomas Wolsey, Legate and Reformer*, London, 1902) has analysed his ecclesiastical and reforming labours. See also *The Chief Minister of England*, by the Hon. Clive Bigham, London, 1923, pp. 207–26. A. F. Pollard, in his *Wolsey* (1929), has explained and defined the great cardinal's role in English history, and Hilaire Belloc (*Wolsey*, London, 1930), in brilliant and lucid prose, has represented the tragedy of his political life in five acts, of which the fatal denouement is supplied by Henry's divorce.

R. S. Deans wrote, for the general public, *The Trials of five Queens: Katherine of Aragon, Anne Boleyn, Mary Queen of Scots, Marie-Antoinette and Caroline of Brunswick* (London, 1909); and in 1932, E. Barrington's *Anne Boleyn* appeared (London).

As regards the king's youth and his marriage with Catherine, Mumby collected together the letters published in various collections: *The Youth of Henry VIII. A Narrative in Contemporary Letters*, London, 1913. Finally, C. D. Powell reviewed the writings concerning the divorce of Catherine and Henry VIII, in the Appendix to his work: *English domestic relations, 1487–1543. A study of matrimony and family life in theory and practice, as revealed by the literature, the law and history of the period*, London, 1917.

C

BIBLIOGRAPHY, CHAPTER IV

In additions to Volumes XIII and XIV of *Letters and Papers*, documents are to be found in Burnet, *op. cit.*, ed. Pocock, Vol. IV, pp. 207–72; in Collier, *op. cit.*, Vol. IV, pp. 287–322; in Dodd, first part, Bk. 3, Art. 5, "Records of Monasteries"; and especially in Wright, *Three chapters of letters relating to the Suppression of the Monasteries*, Camden Society, 1843. The "Instructions of King Henry VIII for the general visitations of the monasteries and nunneries 1538–1539" were reprinted at Edinburgh in 1886, in Vol. XIII of *Historical Reprints*. In 1632 H. Spelman wrote the *History and Fate of Sacrilege*, which appeared only in 1698, after his death; it was republished in 1846, and again in 1888 by S. J. Eales, and in 1895 by the Rev. C. F. Warren. In the middle of the seventeenth century Fuller devoted the sixth book of his *Church History* to "the history of the Abbeys in England: their origin, development, prosperity, decadence and dissolution" (ed. 1845, Vol. III, pp. 241–514); it ends with an Appendix (pp. 519–56) on Waltham Abbey, which fell to the Earl of Carlisle, to whom Fuller was chaplain (1648), and it is dedicated to William Compton, Earl of Northampton, because his ancestors, albeit in favour with Henry VIII, "received not even a shoe-lachet of the monastic lands, when the abbeys were dissolved." But the best work—which has been often republished—on the dissolution of the monasteries is by Cardinal Gasquet: *Henry VIII and the English Monasteries*, London, 2 vols., 1888, an illustrated edition of which appeared in 1902, and the last edition is that of 1906 (cf. *Eng. Hist. Review*, 1906, p. 619); the French translation was made in 1894. No living English historian, save Professor Trevelyan, can pride himself on having produced such a successful "best-seller." *The Last Abbot of Glastonbury and his Companions*, London, 1895, by the same author, completes the previous study. Westlake's *The Life and Times of Abbot John Islip of Westminster Abbey*; *The last days of the Monastery* (1464–1532) is equally useful. J. Gairdner has utilized the documents he published in *Letters and Papers* for the study of the suppression of the religious houses in his *Lollardy and the Reformation in England* (Vol. II), Bk. III, chap. II, "Visitation and Suppression of Monasteries"; chap. III, "Further Proceedings against Monasteries and

and Superstitions." The history of the English monasteries during the Middle Ages, as well as documents relating to their suppression, are to be found in the voluminous work of Sir William Dugdale (author of *The Baronage of England*, 3 vols., London, 1675). This work was republished in London in 1846 (8 vols., in fol.) by Caley, Ellis and Bardinel with prints, maps and plans: *Monasticon Anglicanum*. In Collier (*op. cit.*, Vol. IX, pp. 124–31) will be found the oath of obedience given to the bishop by the prior, the ceremonies in use for the installation of an abbess and for the clothing of nuns. On the Franciscan Order in England, Edward Hutton's *The Franciscans in England*, 1224–1538, London, 1926, may be read. Reyner has described the monastic life in his *Apostolatus Benedictorum in Anglia*, Douai, 1626; so, too, has Cardinal Gasquet in *Monastic Life in the Middle Ages* (London, 1922) and in *English Monastic Life* (London, 1924), to which may be added his *Eve of the Reformation* (best edition, London, 1900). The Rev. D. H. S. Cranage has recently written a popular volume on that same monastic life in the Middle Ages: *The home of the monk: an account of English monastic life and buildings in the Middle Ages*, Cambridge, 1926. But a more scientific study will be found in *English Ecclesiastical Studies; Being some essays in research of medieval history*, by Rose Graham, who has also written *The Great Schism and the English Monasteries of the Cistercian Order* (*Eng. Hist. Review*, July, 1929). A Hamilton Thompson, Professor at Leeds University, is one of the foremost English historians in the study of English monasteries in the Middle Ages; in addition to Chapter XX, "The Monastic Orders" of the *Cambridge Medieval History* series (Vol. V, Cambridge, 1926), where a bibliography that leaves nothing to be desired will be found (p. 910 for the English and Irish monasteries), he has written numerous articles or small books and a study on the *English Monasteries* (2nd edition, Cambridge, 1922). He has also edited the *Visitations of religious houses in the diocese of Lincoln*, Vols. I, II, and III, Horncastle and London, 1914–29. The nunneries, with the exceptions of the Gilbertines already considered by Miss R. Graham (*St. Gilbert of Sempringham and the Gilbertines*, 1901), have been studied by Miss Eileen Power (*Medieval English Nunneries, c. 1275 to 1535*, Cambridge, 1922), according to the registers of episcopal visitations, which are scarcely concerned with anything save the breaking of the rules. A jurist, A. Savine, Professor at Moscow University before the war, has studied monastic property under all its aspects at the time of its spoliation by Henry VIII (*English Monasteries on the eve of the Dissolution*, Oxford, 1909). His study may be completed by a more recent one by R. H. Snape (*English Monastic Finances*, Cambridge, 1926) and by No. XI of *English Ecclesiastical Studies*, London, 1929, by Miss Graham, who for more than thirty years has methodically studied English monastic history. Oscar A. Marti, History Professor in the Central Missouri State Teachers' College, has studied the economic political movement from the Middle Ages, which was to result in the suppression of the monasteries, in a work somewhat schematic though scholastic in form, which is too much like a thesis: *Economic Causes of the Reformation in England*, London, 1929. In the short but searching work of J. K. Floyer (*Studies in the history of English Church endowments*, London, 1917), after the Church in England's revenues from the beginning have been considered, the great spoliation of the sixteenth century is examined. For the general public, J. S. Fletcher has set forth, with particular care, the suppression of the religious houses, in his work: *The Cistercians in Yorkshire*, London, 1918. The previous year Miss H. T. Jacka had studied the suppression of the religious orders of women in an unpublished thesis for the London University (*The Dissolution of the English Nunneries*), for a substantial analysis of which the present writer is indebted to the kindness of Mr. H. O. Evennett, Fellow of Trinity College, Cambridge. Burnet, Froude, Dixon, Gairdner, Fisher and Trésal have all devoted a chapter to this subject; some of these writers have at times introduced into their writings things which are irrelevant.

For G. G. Coulton's objections to Cardinal Gasquet's work, see n. 77, chap. IV.

D

BIBLIOGRAPHY, CHAPTER V

(A) FISHER

The oldest complete biography of Fisher that we possess was, until 1891, attributed to Dr. Richard Hall (†1604), who was supposed to have written it in English about 1570. But Father Van Ortroy, in the *Analecta Bollandiana* (Vol. X, 1891, pp. 120–201), has proved that it is not his. The English text, of an elegant simplicity (certain passages are masterpieces of narration), was written, the well-informed Latin translator tells us, by theologians, former students of Christ Church or St. John's, Cambridge; one of them had even been in communication with Gardiner and the Lords of the Council (this must have been Thomas Watson, who was Gardiner's chaplain and devoted friend, and whose collaboration is certain). The Latin translation, which has numerous additions, was by Richard Hall, whence the confusion in attributing the original work to him. Van Ortroy published this English version for the first time, and facing it the Latin translation, taken from a manuscript in the Barberini Library: *Ana. Boll.*, Vol. X, pp. 202-366, and Vol. XII, pp. 97-248 (cf. Rev. R. Bayne's *The Life of Fisher, translated from MS. Harleian 6382*, Early Eng. Text Soc., 1929). This is what we refer to when we speak of the "first biography" or the "first biographers." Thomas Baily, a convert from Anglicanism (1643), after altering the text and making insertions and introducing numerous errors and anachronisms, had the English version printed in 1655 (republished in 1835). The Redemptorist Father T. E. Bridgett, had already made use of this Life o, Fisher and all the material used in compiling it (Arundel MS. 152, British Museum) when he wrote his *Life of Blessed John Fisher, martyr under Henry VIII*, London, 1888, translated into French by the Abbé A. Cardon (Lille, 1890), who added chapter XIX from the author's own notes.

One of Fisher's contemporaries, Richard Hilliard (or Hillyard), priest and secretary to Tunstall, Bishop of Durham (1530-52 and 1553-59), was condemned to death by Parliament in 1543 but took refuge in Scotland and afterwards in Rome, where he became Rector of the English hospice (cf. Bridgett and Knox, *Queen Elizabeth and the Catholic Hierarchy*, p. 214; *Athenae Cantabrigienses*, Vol. I, p. 534). In his Roman retreat he wrote a work on Henry VIII's reign, which has been lost, but of which an extract is preserved in the Arundel MS. 152 in the British Museum, and has been published by Van Ortroy (*Ana. Boll.*, XII, 270-75).

Another of Fisher's contemporaries, who was present at his martyrdom, Mr. Justice William Rastell or Rastall, wrote a Life of More, his uncle, in which many pages illustrate the Bishop of Rochester's life. The manuscript, which was never published, has been lost. But the authors of Fisher's Life consulted it and took from it numerous extracts which are preserved in the Arundel MS. 152 in the British Museum: "Certen breef notes appertaining to B. Fyshere, collected

out of Sr Thomas More's Lyfe written by Mr. Justice Restall."
Van Ortroy has published these extracts (*ibid.*, Vol. XII,
pp. 248–70). A manuscript in the British Museum (Arundel
MS. 152, ff. 91–244) contains an anonymous Life in Latin; its
author, writing in Mary Tudor's time, drew upon almost the
same sources as the authors of Fisher's biography, and at times
completes the latter. It was partly destroyed by fire and only
fragments remain which are sometimes difficult to read
(see *Ana. Boll.*, X, 133 *sq.*). An extract will be found in Van
Ortroy (*ibid.*, XII, 275–78). One of the writers who continued Chacon, A. Vittorelli, has taken from it certain extracts
which were used for Cardinal Fisher's biography, in Vol. III
of *Vitae et res gestae Pontificum romanorum et S.R.E. cardinalium*,
by Chacon and Oldoin, Rome, 1677 (col. 573 *sq.*). "Sic
affatus esse fertur ab Anonymo quodam ejus vitae scriptore,
ut refert Andreas Victorellus in additionibus Ciacconianis."
Vittorelli also knew the English Life of Fisher, as may be
seen from certain episodes recorded in the biography by
Chacon and Oldoin; e.g., the episode telling how Anne
Boleyn had the martyr's head brought to her that she might
insult it (cf. p. 223).

Dr. John Lewis, a Protestant, wrote a Life of Fisher between
1720 and 1740, frankly hostile to the bishop, but with valuable
documents in the appendix. It remained in manuscript for
more than a century till Turner published it in 1855.

In addition to the biographies of Fisher already mentioned,
Kerker wrote in 1860: *John Fisher, der bischof von Rochester,
und Martyrer für den kath. Glauben,* and Dom Bede Camm gave
a summary of his life in 1914, in Vol. I of *The Lives of the
English Martyrs declared Blessed by Pope Leo XIII;* and Fisher
was also mentioned in *The English Martyrs,* fourteen lectures
for the Catholic Summer School (Cambridge, 1929). The
two volumes by Brewer (*Reign of Henry VIII*, London, 1884)
and Volumes IV to VIII of *Letters and Papers,* with prefaces
by Brewer and Gairdner, contain much useful information
and many documents.

(B) THOMAS MORE

In the very year of Sir Thomas More's martyrdom (1535)
one of the witnesses wrote an account of the trial, which
circulated throughout France; Le Laboureur published it in
his *Mémoires de Michel de Castelnau,* Brussels, 1731 (I, 415–19),

and J. Gairdner translated it into English from a manuscript in the *Bibliothèque Nationale* (*Letters and Papers*, VIII, p. 394. For the author of this letter, see Append. III, by R. W. Chambers, in *The Life and Death of Sr Thomas Moore*, by Nicholas Harpsfield, edited by E. V. Hitchcock, 1932). In the following year there appeared at Frankfort a collection which has become very rare, and which contains, together with the biographies of Petrarch, Pius II, Pico Della Mirandola, Œcolampadius, etc., that of Thomas More: *Virorum qui superiori nostroque seculo eruditione et doctrina illustres atque memorabiles fuerunt Vitae; jampridem in hoc volum. collectae*. The *Historia aliquot nostri saeculi martyrum* (1550) by Maurice Chauncy also contains a simple sketch of More (cf. page 135, n. 195). About seven years later (More's *Works*, which he mentions, appeared in 1557) William Roper, in order to enable Nicholas Harpsfield to write a *Life of More*, which remained in manuscript form (Harleian MS. 6253, British Museum), wrote a series of notes (*Life of Sir Thomas More*) from his own personal recollections and those of his wife, Margaret More (†1514), the chancellor's favourite daughter. There was no skill or division in his writing, and scarcely any paragraphs (there are only three in the first three pages, and only three more for the fifty pages which follow), but he took great pains to be accurate. This is certainly the safest, the most direct and living source. Roper had lived fifteen years with his father-in-law under the paternal roof at Chelsea. These notes were published in Paris in 1626 (*The Life, Arraignement and Death of that Mirrour of all true Honour and Vertue, Syr Thomas More*), and in England by Hearne in 1716 (*G. Roperi Vita D. Th. Mori. . . . Accedit Mori Epistola de Scholasticis quibusdam Trojanos sese appelantibus*). Lumby (1st ed., 1879; last, Cambridge, 1908, quoted here) republished Hearne, with a translation of the *Utopia* by Ralph Robynson (1551). Lewis (1729, 1731, 1765 [Dublin]) added a praiseworthy documentary appendix to Roper's *Life of Sir Thomas More*.

The Life of Thomas More written by the Archdeacon of Canterbury, Nicholas Harpsfield, which remained in manuscript form for over three and a half centuries, has been published at last in a most learned manner, with introductions, appendices and historical notes, by Dr. Elsie V. Hitchcock and Professor R. W. Chambers: "*The Life and Death of Sr Thomas Moore, Knight, sometymes Lord High Chancellor of England*, written in the tyme of Queene Marie by Nicholas Harpsfield, L.D., and now edited from eight manuscripts, with collations, textual notes, etc., by Elsie Vaughan Hitchcock . . . London, Milford, for the Early English Text Society, 1932." Dr. Hitchcock's introduction gives the principles of textual induction and the significance of collations. A second Introductory Essay of 130 pages on "The Continuity of English Prose from Alfred to More and his Circle" is due to Professor R. W. Chambers. Both of these have also been published separately. A third Introductory Essay by R. W. Chambers deals with "The Life and Works of Nicholas Harpsfield," who, in many instances, has been confused with his brother John by biographers. In addition to the four appendices there are a hundred pages of textual and historical notes and some very fine illustrations, in particular a beautiful copy of the Basle study by Holbein of the More family, reproductions of the diptych portraits by Quentin Matsys of Erasmus and Peter Giles, and a photograph of the Chelsea tomb.

More's nephew, William Rastall, or Rastell, a printer's son, who published the chancellor's works in 1557 and who knew him well, wrote a notable biography divided into books and chapters, but of which only extracts made from it by Fisher's first biographers were known (see above, D (a), p. 450). The extant fragments, taken from the fifty-eighth and seventy-seventh chapters of Book III (Arundel MSS. 1521) have been published in Appendix I of *The Life and Death of Sʳ Thomas Moore*, by N. Harpsfield, quoted above. For W. Rastall and John Rastall, his father, see A. Wood, *op. cit.*, ed. 1691, I, 38, 114 *sq.*

Ellis Heywood dedicated to Reginald Pole, in 1556 (Florence), a fantastic account of More's relations with his guests at Chelsea, called: *Il Moro*.

Stapleton (1535–98), a prebendary of Chichester under Mary Tudor, and in Elizabeth's time Professor at Louvain University and a controversialist of repute (his complete works in four volumes were published at Paris in 1620; cf. A. Wood, *op. cit.*, I, 253 *sq.*, who calls him the most learned Roman Catholic of his time; L. Ellies Du Pin, *Histoire des auteurs ecclésiastiques du XVIᵉ siècle*, Paris, 1701–1703, V, pp. 566 *sq.*), published in 1558 at Douai his *Tres Thomae*, Lives of St Thomas the Apostle, St Thomas à Becket of Canterbury and Thomas More (re-edition in the 4th Vol. of his works, Paris, 1620). His biography of More was often published in Latin, and translated into French (by Alexandre Martin, with notes by Audin, Paris, 1849); but no English translation appeared before 1928: Mgr. P. E. Hallett's

The Life and Illustrious Martyrdom of Thomas More. Stapleton made use not only of More's works, the letters of Erasmus, and all that had been published about the chancellor, but also collected the testimonies and accounts of more than one witness of Thomas More's life and words: John Clements and his wife Margaret Gigs, the chancellor's adopted daughter who helped Margaret Roper to bury him; John Haywood, writer of epigrams and great friend of Rastall; William Rastall himself; John Harris, More's secretary; and Harris' wife, Dorothy Colley, who had been in Margaret Roper's service. Stapleton says in his preface that Dorothy Colley handed to him several manuscripts and letters written entirely in the illustrious martyr's handwriting.

One of the chancellor's great-grandsons, Cresacre More (John More, the only son of Sir Thomas, had married a Cresacre), wrote between 1615 and 1620 a *Life and Death of Sir Thomas More*, editions of which appeared in 1627, 1726, and 1828 (this last edition had a preface by the Rev. J. Hunter). Inspired by Roper, Stapleton and Harpsfield, it contains very little original matter, although it is well esteemed and often quoted.

A non-Catholic, Sir Henry Spelman (†1641), gathered together, in 1633, the material for a biography of the chancellor, which was edited in 1698 after his death. Anthony Wood, in his *Athenae Oxonienses* (ed. 1691, I, 32, 36), speaks of More as a writer and says that he was one of the greatest prodigies of wit and knowledge that our nation ever produced.

In the nineteenth century G. T. Rudhart published a much documented life of More: *Thomas Morus aus den Quellen bearbeitet*, Nuremberg, 1829. Lord Campbell, in his *Lives of the Chancellors*, considered him chiefly as a barrister. Nisard's essay in *Renaissance et Réforme* (1855) is noteworthy. An American priest, W. J. Walter, wrote a biography of the chancellor (2nd ed. 1840), which was translated into French, with two steel engravings, in 1873: *Thomas Morus et son époque. Traduction . . . suivie d'une analyse de l'Utopie de Thomas Morus.*

Froude (*The Reign of Henry VIII*, chap IX) for the trials of Fisher and More, has been partly inspired by the replies which Henry VIII and Cromwell made to the protests which the execution of these men aroused on the Continent. He tries to justify the king somewhat by insinuating that their attitude might have been dangerous for the peace of the realm. For the chancellor's last days he follows Cresacre More.

J. Gairdner speaks of More and Fisher in *Lollardy and the Reformation*, I, 437–504.

Father T. E. Bridgett, C.SS.R., who had already studied and produced the *Life of Blessed John Fisher* (1888), brought out a *Life of Blessed Thomas More* in 1891, with a reproduction of Holbein's original crayon sketch (More in his fiftieth year) ; the third edition (1904) is the same as the second edition, which had corrected and completed the first, but has an addition of seven appendices: this is the edition we quote.

In his preface (p. xi) Father Bridgett indicates the chief articles on Thomas More, except the one in the *Dictionary of National Biography*, which may not have appeared when the first edition was published. Neither is he aware of J. Spillmann, S.J., who, in the previous year, had spoken of Fisher and More in chapters II to VIII of *Die englischen martyrer unter Heinrich VIII*, a supplement to *Stimmen aus Maria-Laach*, Freiburg, 1887; it was reprinted and continued down to 1654 under the title *Geschichte der Katholikenverfolgung in England 1535–1681*, Freiburg, 1900–1905. O. Meyer (*England und die Katholische Kirche unter Elisabeth*, p. 2, n. 1) thinks that as a study it is not sufficiently critical. Countess J. Grabinski published in Rome, in 1906, *Il B. Tommaso Moro e lo schisma d'Inghilterra*.

(c) REGINALD POLE

Alvise Priuli, brother of the Doge of Venice and Pole's best friend and the executor of his will, would have recounted his life had he not died prematurely. His plan was, however, carried out by another friend, Lodovico Beccadelli, who had been Pole's secretary and afterwards became Archbishop of Ragusa. His *Vita del cardinale Reginaldo Polo*, published at Venice in 1563, translated into Latin (Venice and London, 1690)—a personal rather than a faithful translation—by Dudić de Horehowitz, Bishop of Knin, Csanàd, and Fünfkirchen (Pécs), who afterwards went over to Protestantism (†1589), was republished by A. M. Quirini, O.S.B. (*Epistolae Reginaldi Poli*, 1744–58, Vol. V, pp. 355–91; Dudić's text is in Vol. I, p. 65) and by Morandi (*Monumenti di varia Letteratura tratti dei manoscritti di Monsignor Lodovico Beccadelli, arcivescovo di Ragusa*, Vol. I, Part 2, Bologna, 1799, pp. 277–333), who added an appendix consisting of some unpublished letters (pp. 334–54). Pallavicini (*Istoria del concilio di Trento*, Rome, 1656–57, Bk. XIII, chap. IX, No. 10) made use of this life for his history of the Council of Trent, at which Pole assisted as legate. Maucroix translated it into French (1677) and B. Pye into English (1766). Besides his own personal recollections, Beccadelli obtained those of Pole's servants. He consulted in particular Giambattista Binardi, Pole's secretary in Mary Tudor's time, and Thomas Goldwell, Bishop of St. Asaph (1555-59), who assisted him in his last moments. Graziani also gave a description of the cardinal in his *De casibus virorum illustrium*, as also did Paul Manutius (Paolo Manuzio), the famous Venetian printer, in a very well-written letter to Pius IV. As early as 1556 the Italian Tomitano had praised the cardinal's virtues: *De Reginaldi Poli cardinalis ampliss. laudibus.* But it was Beccadelli's work which inspired the book by G. Lyde, published in London in 1686, during James II's short reign: *Some observations upon the Life of Reginaldus Polus, cardinal of the royal bloud of England, sent in a pacquet out of Wales by G. L., gentleman and servant to the late Majesty of Henrietta Maria of Bourbon, mother to the present king.* Lyde's grandson, T. Philipps, S.J., extracted a good and sufficiently long biography of the cardinal (*The History of the Life of Reginald Pole*, Oxford, 1764, London, 1767, 2 vols.) from Quirini's monumental work in five volumes, already mentioned. His second edition (London and Oxford, 1767, without the author's name) answered Protestant criticisms (*E. Stone, Remarks upon the History and Life of Reg. Pole*, Oxford, 1766). Quirini had already made use of the letters edited by him in recounting Pole's life, under the title *Diatriba* (Vol. I, pp. 193-227; Vol. II, pp. xxvii-cclxiv). Dodd, who wrote in 1737, chiefly followed Beccadelli and a manuscript by H. Pinning, the cardinal's secretary, which was formerly preserved in the English College at Douai but has been lost (letter from the librarian at Douai, October 30th, 1928, *Church History*, Part 3, Bk. II, art. 2 : "Lives of cardinals"). Prior to Dodd, F. Godwin, the Anglican Bishop of Llandaff, gave a biographical notice of Pole (1616) in *De Praesulibus Angliae Commentarius* (pp. 207-17).

In the nineteenth century the following studied Cardinal Pole: In Germany, Kerker (*Reginald Pole, Cardinal der heiligen römischen Kirche und Erzbischof von Canterbury*, Freiburg, 1874), and A. Zimmermann, S.J. (*Kardinal Pole, sein Leben und seine Schriften*, Ratisbon, 1893), and in England, W. F. Hook (*Lives of the Archbishops of Canterbury*, Vol. VIII, London, 1869, a Protestant work; cf. Miss Stewart, *Dr. Gairdner, Dean Hook, Dr. Lee, Mr. Ainsworth*, London, 1901), A. Freeman (*Cardinal*

Pole, a study in the *Saturday Review*, 1869), and F. G. Lee (*Reginald Pole*, London, 1888, an essay on part of the cardinal's life). According to the *Dictionary of National Biography*, Zimmermann's work, although incomplete, is the best modern book on the cardinal; it contains a bibliography.

In the twentieth century Reginald Pole's sympathetic figure drew the attention successively of Dudley Baxter (*Life of Cardinal Pole*, a series of articles in *The Shield*, 1910 and following years); Martin Haile, who made use of the documents collected by the Rev. Ethelred Taunton (*Life of R. Pole*, London, 1910); and Dom R. Biron and J. Barennes (*Un prince anglais cardinal légat au XVIᵉ siècle, Reginald Pole*, Paris [1922]), a very attractive book and full of information. The finding of correspondence written by one of the cardinal's friends, Niccolò Leonico Tomeo, enabled Cardinal Gasquet to throw some light upon the Italian Humanists and to give precision to certain features in Pole's character: *Cardinal Pole and his early friends*, London, 1927. Cf. also Professor Constant's article in *La Révue des Questions historiques*, "*A propos d'une Nouvelle vie de Reginald Pole.*"

Dodd gave a list of Pole's manuscript and published works, in his *Church History*, ed. 1737, pp. 479 *sq.*

The catalogue of the MSS. in the Municipal Library at Douai mentions four volumes, which M. P. Janelle brought to Professor Constant's notice: "Registrum expeditionum in Anglia factarum per Ill. Rᵘᵐ cardinalem Polum legatum. Anno Domini millesimo quingentesimo quinquagesimo quarto." Pinning, Pole's secretary, must have taken them with him to the Continent and deposited them in the College at Douai. Dodd saw them, for he mentions them in his *Church History* (I, pp. xix, 480). Canon Estcourt consulted them, but made little use of them, in *The question of Anglican ordinations discussed*, 1873. In the British Museum there are some extracts "Ex Registro literarum Card. Poli," e.g. in Add. MS. 15,388.

E

BIBLIOGRAPHY, CHAPTER VI

(A) THOMAS CROMWELL

Chapuys' letter to Granvelle dated November 21st, 1535 (*Letters and Papers*, Vol. V, No. 228) gives some details on

Cromwell's origin and early struggles. (For Chapuys, see Garret Mattingley's *A Humanist Ambassador*, in *The Journal of Modern History*, June, 1932, a biography of Chapuys based on the archives of Annecy, his native town.) For the time he spent in Wolsey's service, Cavendish's *Life of Wolsey* (written in 1557, published in 1641, and republished by Singer in 1827) is valuable. From the time he came into power, all the publications of documents relating to the reign, and especially the *Letters and Papers*, speak of him; and nothing that concerns the suppression of the monasteries can be neglected (see chap. IV). Marillac (Kaulek, *op. cit.*) gives us, in the most precise and living manner, first a presentiment and then the knowledge of Cromwell's fall. Foxe, in his *Acts and Monuments* (ed. Pratt, Vol. V, pp. 362-404) gave a *Life of the Lord Cromwell*, in which there are some interesting accounts or documents. At the beginning of the nineteenth century Christopher Wordsworth wrote his *Cromwell, Earl of Essex* (Vol. II of his *Ecclesiastical Biography*, 1818). Cf. also *The Chief Minister of England*, by the Hon. Clive Bigham, London, 1923, pp. 226-243. But Merriman has collected the letters of this all-powerful Minister and has thus given us practically a definite portrait of him: *Life and Letters of Cromwell*, 2 vols., Oxford, 1902, in which the various sources will be found.

(B) THOMAS CRANMER

Not to mention *Letters and Papers*, one of the best authorities for the archbishop's life is the anecdotes of Ralph Morice, Cranmer's secretary, who supplied Foxe with much information. Cranmer's Works were edited by H. Jenkyns (*The Remains of Thomas Cranmer*, Oxford, 1933, 4 vols.) and by Cox (Cambridge, Parker Society, 1844-46), to whom we are indebted for an important preface. Strype was the first to write a Life of Cranmer, in 1694 (*Memorials of the most Reverend Father in God, Thomas Cranmer*). It has been several times republished, particularly at Oxford, 1812-24 and 1848-52 for the Ecclesiastical History Society in three and four volumes, the last of which contains only documents (the last edition is referred to in this book). Strype made use of "documents, registers, letters and other original manuscripts," which are given in great number in an appendix, and which are by far the most useful part of a work which is too much like a compilation. H. J. Todd (*The Life of Archbishop Cranmer*, 2 vols.,

London), in 1831; Le Bas, 2 vols., in 1833 (neither of whom adds much to Strype); W. F. Hook, in his *Lives of the Arch-bishops of Canterbury to A.D. 1663* (12 vols., 1860–76); C. H. Collette (*Life, Times and Writings of Th. Cranmer*, London, 1887); Canon A. J. Mason (in the series *English Leaders of Religion*, 1896 and 1898); J. Gairdner in the *Dictionary of National Biography*; and Theod. Kolde, in the *Realencyclopädie* (3rd ed.) have outlined or rewritten, one after another, Cranmer's Life. Useful indications will also be found in the preface and notes of H. Jenkyns' *The Remains of Thomas Cranmer*. A. F. Pollard also wrote a Life (London, 1904, last ed. 1926) briefly alluding, in his preface, to those already written, and stating the chief sources to which recourse could be made (series: *Heroes of the Reformation*, ed. by S. Macauley Jackson, Professor at New York University). Hilaire Belloc has written the most recent work, *Cranmer* (1931) in which he describes the archbishop as "a hypocrite, a time-server, a coward, a great scholar, timid and suave in manner, courteous also, usually averse from cruelty, a splendid horse-man, a gentleman, in his modest fashion an intriguer, and a quite successful layer of traps for the unfortunate" (pp. 244–245). C. H. Smythe made a study of Cranmer but for a period later than that which concerns us: *Cranmer and the Reformation under Edward VI*, Cambridge, 1926. Canon A. C. Deane recently published (London, 1927) in the series *Great English Churchmen, The Life of Thomas Cranmer, Archbishop of Canterbury*, in which he sets forth the great part played by Cranmer in the translation of the Bible and in composing the Prayer Book, as well as the archbishop's weakness of character, for he was always ready to bow down before the royal despotism and to multiply his recantations. Gerdes (*Historia Reformationis*, IV, 200) gives a portrait of him, as do most of the recent biographies.

F

BIBLIOGRAPHY, CHAPTER VII

In addition to the sources previously indicated (particularly the *Letters and Papers* and *Lollardy and the Reformation*, by Gairdner) and the various works by the Henricians, the following may be consulted: J. Leland, *Principum ac illustrium aliquot et eruditorum in Anglia virorum Encomia, Trophaea,*

Genethliaca et Epithalamia, London, 1589; by the same author, *Antiquarii de rebus britannicis collectanea*, ed. T. Hearn, London, 1770, 6 vols.; Francis Godwin (Bishop of Llandaff and Hereford), *De praesulibus Angliae Commentarius: omnium episcoporum, necnon et cardinalium ejusdem gentis nomina, tempora, seriem atque actiones maxime memorabiles . . . complexus*, London, 1616; by the same author, *Rerum Anglicarum Henrico VIII, Edwardo VI et Maria regnantibus Annales*, London, 1616, 1628, 1630, of which the English translation by Godwin's son, Morgan, has been often published; A. Wood, *Athenae Oxonienses*, London, 1691 or 1721; J. Harington, *Nugae Antiquae: being a miscellaneous collection of original Papers in prose and verse written in the reigns of Henry VIII, Queen Mary, Elizabeth, King James*, etc., London, 2 vols., 1792 (the edition followed in this book), and 1804, 2 vols., ed. T. Parker; *Harleian Miscellany*, ed. W. Oldys and T. Park, 10 vols., London, 1808–13; J. Nichols, *The History and Antiquities of the County of Leicester*, Vol. I, London, 1815; C. H. Cooper, *Annals of Cambridge*, Cambridge, 1842–1908, 5 vols.; by the same author, and continued by G. J. Gray, *Athenae Cantabrigienses*, Cambridge, 1858–1913, 3 vols.; Rev. S. R. Maitland, *Essays on subjects connected with the Reformation*, London, 1849, two editions, the second containing additions; *Documents relating to the University and Colleges of Cambridge*, London, 1852, 3 vols.; J. Le Neve, *Fasti Ecclesiae Anglicanae*, ed. T. D. Hardy, 3 vols., Oxford, 1854; C. Wordsworth, *Scholae Academicae*, Cambridge, 1877; Mullinger, *The University of Cambridge*, Vol. II, Cambridge, 1884; F. W. Maitland, *Roman Canon Law in the Church of England*, 1898; Leach, *A History of Winchester College*, New York, 1899; W. Thompson, *Southwark Cathedral*, London, 1910; G. Evans, *The Principal Secretary of State*, London and New York, 1923.

Three years before his death, in a study on "Stephen Gardiner" (*Typical English Churchmen*, 2nd series, Church Historical Society, London, 1909), J. Gairdner amplified his articles in the *Encyclopaedia Britannica* (11th edition, Cambridge, 1910) and in the *Dictionary of English Church History* (edition Ollard and Cross, London, 1912). Quite recently J. A. Muller, Professor in the Episcopal Theological School at Cambridge (Mass.), published a new biography of the leader of the Henricians, with his portrait from Trinity Hall (Cambridge), because he considered that Gardiner's life had not yet been written: *Stephen Gardiner and the Tudor Reaction*, London, 1926. In France M. P. Janelle intends to adopt the same subject and to bring out a still more perfect biography. In the *Bulletin of the Institute of Historical Research* (June–October, 1928), he gave a long unpublished piece of poetry by a certain William Palmer, a gentleman of the petty nobility attached to the court, greatly addicted to the advanced party of the Reformation, who detested Gardiner and the Henricians: "An unpublished Poem on Bishop Stephen Gardiner." These verses by a contemporary, who wrote them at the beginning of Edward VI's reign (summer, 1547), although they are bad enough, reflect nevertheless the feelings of the partisans of the Reformation towards the moderate party, and confirm, rectify, or complete here and there Foxe's dicta. M. P. Janelle has also published "Gardiner's Answer to Bucer," and re-edited the Latin text, with an English translation, of "Gardiner's Tract on Fisher's Execution" and his "Oration of True Obedience" in *Obedience in Church and State; Three Political Tracts by Stephen Gardiner*, edited with an introduction, translation and notes, Cambridge University Press, 1930. The introduction considers "The Political Thought of Stephen Gardiner." The whole of Gardiner's correspondence, with some accessory documents, will very shortly be published by J. A. Muller.

G

BIBLIOGRAPHY, CHAPTER VIII

There is no recent and comprehensive study on the doctrines of Henry VIII's Church, but the text of the various formularies of faith, in conjunction with the circumstances in which they were elaborated or promulgated, determine for us what that Church was and what it wished to be. The Catholic historian, Charles Butler, was one of the first to consider the Anglican Confessions of Faith: *An historical and literary account of the Formularies*, 1816. Some ten years later (1825) the Anglican Bishop of Oxford, Lloyd, published his *Formularies of Faith put forth by authority during the reign of Henry VIII*. Cardwell republished them at Oxford in 1856 "with the design of putting into the hands of the clergy," as Lloyd said, "treatises valuable for their matter, and of such rare occurrence as to be found only in public libraries or in the private collections of the curious." Charles Hardwick's work (*A History of the Articles of the Church of England*, Cambridge,

1859, 3rd ed. by Procter, 1876 [the last was in 1890]),
contains documents from 1536 to 1615; but, for Henry VIII,
he studies only the articles of 1536 and the Six Articles.
Hardwick also wrote *A History of the Christian Church and
Practice* and Burrow *A Summary of Christian Faith*, which give a
little information. G. G. Perry (*A History of the English Church*,
3 vols., 1861–64, reprinted between 1887 and 1888) goes back
to the origins of Christianity in Great Britain. Makower's
book (*Verfassung der Kirche von England*, 1894, English translation, London, 1895; cf. for Makower, *Seminaire historique de
Louvain*, 1903, pp. 50 *sq.*) is important chiefly for the following
reigns. G. D. Mentz's publication (*Die Wittenberger Artikel
von 1525*, No. 2 of the *Schriften zur Geschichte des Protestantismus*,
Leipzic, 1905) throws light on the attempts at an understanding with the German Protestants and helps us to perceive
the reason for their failure. Dodd had long before noted the
efforts of the advanced party to introduce a reforming leaven
into the Church of England: *Part I, Book I, article* v. Blunt
(*The Reformation of the Church of England*, Vol. I, London, 1892)
reviews the doctrine (chap. VIII) and the worship of the reign
(chap. IX); but he does little more than quote from the
"Erudition of a Christian Man" of 1543; he does not know
the Wittenberg articles, and he neglects the historical circumstances which accompanied the elaboration or the promulga-
tion of the formularies of faith. M. J. Procter, in 1894, studied,
in a general manner, the *Points of difference between the English
Roman and Protestant Churches*, and in *Lollardy and the Reformation
in England* (II, 304–57), J. Gairdner has outlined the history
of the formularies of the reign. Bk. IV, chap. II, "The Making
of Formularies"; see also Bk. III, chap. IV, "German Protestantism and the Act of the Six Articles"; and Bk. IV, chap. IV,
"Results under Henry VIII."

APPENDIX I—NOTES

[1] *History of the Reformation*, London, 1679–1715, 3 vols.; the best edition,
revised and collated with the documents, is Pocock's (Oxford, 1865, 7 vols.).
This edition is quoted here. The most harmful attack that this work had
to suffer was from an English ecclesiastic, Henry Wharton, who had a
personal grudge against Burnet; he wrote, in October, 1692, and published
at the beginning of 1693, under the assumed name of Anthony Harmer,
the *Specimen of some Errors and Defects in the History of the Reformation of the
Church of England* (Harleian MS. 4262, Brit. Mus.). Burnet in turn took
notice of this work (cf. Burnet, *op. cit.*, ed. Pocock, Vol. III, pp. 4, 26 *sq.*,

Vol. VII, pp. 157-65). Two years previously Wharton had published in London (two vols. in fol.), his *Anglia sacra sive Collectio historiarum partim antiquitus, partim recenter scriptarum de archiepiscopis et episcopis Angliae, a prima fidei christianae susceptione ad annum 1540, nunc primum in lucem editarum.*—From the Catholic point of view, in addition to Le Grand (cf. above, pp. 442-43), Varillas, by his *Histoire des Révolutions arrivées dans l'Europe en matière de religion* (Paris, 1686–87, 4 vols.: Italian trans., Venice, 1710), and Bossuet, by his *Exposition de la foi catholique*, translated into English (London, 1685) and especially by his *Histoire des variations des églises protestantes* (Paris, 1690) provoked replies from Burnet (cf. Burnet, *op. cit.*, ed. Pocock, Vol. VII, pp. 133-41 and 154 *sq.*). The criticisms and observations on his book, particularly by Strype, helped Burnet to correct his work. Criticisms and corrections given in an appendix by the author have been given as notes by Pocock to the corresponding passages. The author's touchiness caused relations to be slightly strained between the historian of the English Reformation and the historian of Oxford University, Anthony Wood (see the latter's autobiography, ed. Ph. Blist, Oxford, 1848, p. 215). For Gilbert Burnet, who was chaplain to Charles II when he wrote his History (1679) and afterwards Bishop of Salisbury, see T. E. S. Clarke and Miss H. C. Foxcroft, with Introduction by C. H. Firth, *A Life of Gilbert Burnet Bishop of Salisbury*, London, 1907; by the same, *A Supplement to Burnet's History of my own times*, Oxford, 1902. Ranke had already published a study of Burnet n Vol. VIII, p. 212 of his *Englische Geschichte*.

² *The Church History of Britain, from the birth of Jesus Christ until the year MDCXLVIII*, 1655–56, in-fol. Republished in London in 1837 (3 vols. in 8vo.), this history was again re-edited by J. S. Brewer, in 1845 (Oxford, 6 vols.); the author (G. Constant) follows this last edition of Brewer which is preceded by a biography of 1662 and is the best, although a later edition in three volumes by J. Nichols appeared, with notes, in 1868. Some fifteen years previously Fuller had published *The History of the Holy Warre* (Cambridge, 1639), which quickly passed through five editions: 1640, 1642, 1647, 1651, and 1652. Cf. J. Eg. Bailey, *Fuller's Life*, London, 1874, with portrait.

³ *An ecclesiastical History of Great Britain, chiefly of England, from the first planting of Christianity to the end of the Reign of King Charles the second with a brief account of the Affairs of religion in Ireland*, London, 1708, two vols. in-fol.; Th. Lathbury's edition, London, 1852, consists of nine volumes, of which the last contains the documents and index; this is the edition the author (G. Constant) follows here.

⁴ *Church History of England from the year 1500 to the year 1688*, Brussels, 1737, three vols. in-fol.; Tierney's ed., London, 1839–43, in five vols., goes no further than 1625. Dodd was a Catholic and for a long while professor at Louvain University.

Another eighteenth century Catholic, Thomas Ward, wrote a poem in four cantos on the Reformation in England from Henry VIII's time: *England's Reformation from the time of King Henry VIII, a Poem in four Cantos*, London, 1715.

⁵ *Acts and Monuments*, Latin text, 1st ed., Strasbourg, 1554, and 2nd ed., Basle, 1559; English text, London, 1563. The first Latin edition, afterwards considerably augmented, was entitled: *Commentarii rerum in Ecclesia gestarum, maximarumque persecutionum, a Vivclevi temporibus ad hanc usque aetatem descriptio. liber primus.* This work, known under the popular title of the "Book or Martyrs" has been often published in English; the last and principal editions are those of Cattley and Townsend, eight vols. 1843-49; of R.

Mendham and J. Pratt, also in eight vols., London, 1853-70. This last edition of Pratt (Collection: *The Church Historians of England, Reformation Period*), republished four times, is the best, because it is a re-edition of Townsend and not only are the latter's corrections included but others are also added. Great caution is necessary in consulting Foxe. Cf. S. R. Maitland, *Essays on Subjects connected with the Reformation in England*, 1849, and J. Gairdner, *History of the English Church in the sixteenth century*, pp. 50 *sq.*; J. A. Muller, *Stephen Gardiner*, London, 1926, p. xiii.

The Harleian Manuscripts in the British Museum contain a whole collection of letters and documents relating to the Reformation in England which come from Foxe and have passed through the hands of Strype: thus cod. 418-65th, cod. 590-52nd; MSS. 416-64f. and 417-64f. MS. 2303 has for title: "Ecclesiastical History of England from Henry VIII to Elizabeth."

[6] The complete works of Strype were republished, in twenty-five volumes, at Oxford, between 1812 and 1824. For Henry VIII, the most useful are the *Ecclesiastical Memorials* and the *Memorials of the most Reverend Father in God, Thomas Cranmer*; the author (G. Constant) quotes from the *Ecclesiastical History Society's* edition in 4 vols., Oxford, 1848-52, in which the Appendices contain the most documents.

In the first half of the seventeenth century Francis Godwin, Bishop of Llandaff and of Hereford, studied the first three Tudor reigns after the schism: *Rerum Anglicarum, Henrico VIII, Edwardo VI, Maria regnantibus, Annales*, London, 1628.

[7] Dixon (†1900) himself revised the three editions of the first two volumes and the two editions of Volumes III and IV; the last two, which concern the reign of Elizabeth, were edited, after his death, in 1902, by Henry Gee; twelve years had elapsed between the publication of the fourth and that of the fifth volume. Rector of Warworth and then Canon of Carlisle, Dixon had to wait until he was free to complete, by researches in London, the information required for this or that point in his work; he made a note of them in a book in which he had previously indicated what was lacking. See the Preface to his fifth volume.

[8] *The English Church in the sixteenth century from the accession of Henry VIII to the death of Mary*, London, 1st ed. 1902, 2nd ed. 1903, 3rd ed. 1904, 4th ed. 1912; each successive edition contains corrections.

Besides his works on Richard III, Henry VII, and the seventeenth century, his edition of the *Paston Letters* (3 vols. 1872-75; 2nd ed. 1901; 3rd ed., augmented, 1904), and his seventy-seven biographies in the *Dictionary of National Biography*, while he was editing the *Letters and Papers* of which we shall speak, J. Gairdner also wrote articles on the Reformation in England in *Transactions* or the *English Historical Review*, a Biography of Stephen Gardiner (London, 1909), the fourteenth chapter of the *Cambridge Modern History* (Vol. 11) and *Lollardy and the Reformation in England* (London, 1908-13), the fourth volume of which was published by his friend, W. Hunt, after the author's death (1828-1912). In this last work the first part of the first volume deals with Wiclif's teaching, the struggle conducted by the Church against heresy in the fifteenth century, and the treaties drawn up against the Lollards. Although the sect disappeared after *circa* 1440, a state of mind not very favourable to Rome still continued to exist, a state of mind which favoured the New Learning, to which Gairdner devoted the rest of his work up to the marriage of Mary Tudor (1554).

[9] The first volume contains the king's correspondence with Wolsey until 1530, and with his ministers from 1530 to 1547, and the eighth volume the correspondence with the foreign powers from 1527 to 1537.

[10] Twenty-one volumes in thirty-three parts: I–IV, ed. J. S. Brewer, 1862–76; V–XIII, ed. J. Gairdner, 1880–93; XIV–XXI, ed. J. Gairdner and R. H. Brodie, 1894–1910. Other volumes have recently appeared, *Addenda*, Vol. I, Part 1, 1929, Part 2, 1932. Ch. Johnson has given a concise list of the chief documents in the Record Office in his *The Public Record Office*, and H. Hall has begun *A Repertory of British Archives, Part I, England, 1920*, which is constantly useful. See also the article of M. Bémont on the public archives in England, in Vol. LXVIII of the *Révue Historique*, pp. 97 *sq*.

[11] (a) *Calendar of Letters, Dispatches and State Papers, relating to the negotiations between England and Spain*, edited by G. A. Bergenroth, P. de Gayangos, M. A. S. Hume and R. Tyler, eleven vols., London, 1862–1916.

(b) *Calendar of State Papers and Manuscripts relating to English affairs, preserved in the Archives of Venice*, edited by R. Brown, six vols., London, 1864–84. After 1530 the Venetian documents are resumed in the *Letters and Papers*. (c) *Calendar of State Papers and manuscripts existing in the Archives and Collections of Milan*, edited by A. B. Hinds, London, 1913. The author (G. Constant) quotes here only the Calendars of Henry VIII's reign.

Certain dispatches in French, which are summarized or translated in the *Calendars*, have been published from the text preserved in foreign archives or in the *Bibliothèque Nationale*: J. Kaulek, *Correspondance politique de MM. de Castillon et de Marillac, ambassadeurs de France en Angleterre (1537–42)*, Paris, 1885; W. L. Bourrilly and P. de Vaissière, *Ambassades en Angleterre de Jean du Bellay, La première ambassade, septembre 1527 à fevrier 1529*, Paris, 1905.

A publication similar to the Calendars in which information about England is to be found is the *Nuntiaturberichte aus Deutschland nebst ergänzenden Aktenstücken*, published by the Prussian Institute in Rome and the administration of the Archives of Prussia, 1st section, 1533–59, twelve vols., Gotha, 1892–1900.

[12] (a) Rymer, *Foedera, conventiones litterae et cujuscumque generis acta publica inter reges Angliae et alios quosvis imperatores, pontifices, principes et communitates ab ineunte saeculo duodecimo videlicet ab anno 1101 ad nostra usque tempora habita aut tractata*, 3rd ed., ten vols., The Hague (1739–42), the list of which was published by Hardy between 1869 and 1885. (b) *Statutes of the realm* [Record Commission], Vols. III and IV, ed. Tomlins and E. Taunton, London, 1817–19. (c) R. Steele, *Tudor and Stuart Parliaments*, Vol. I, Oxford, 1910. (d) H. Nicolas, *Proceedings and Ordinances of the Privy Council*, Vol. VII (August 10th, 1540–April 8th, 1542); and J. R. Dasent, *Acts of the Priv Council* (new series, Vols. I–IV, London, 1890–1902; Vol. I covers the period from April 22nd, 1542 to January 26th, 1547).—For the Council's origin and its organization, see F. T. Plucknett, *The King's Council in the Fifteenth Century*, in *Transactions of the Royal Historical Society*, 4th series, Vol. I, 1918; (J. Baldwin had already given *The Beginnings of the King's Council* in *Transactions*); *The King's Council in England during the Medieval Ages*, Oxford, 1913; Pollard's articles (a recension of Dasent and a study on *The Council*) in Vols. XVIII and XXXVII of the *Eng. Hist. Review*, 1903 and 1922; *The sources for the history of the Council in the XVI and XVII Century*, 1924. Ed. R. Turner, History Professor in the John Hopkins University, has dealt with the Privy Council from James I to the end of the eighteenth century: *The Privy Council of England in the seventeenth and eighteenth Century, 1603–1784*, Baltimore, two vols., 1927, etc.; a study of the council under the Tudors is found at the beginning; cf. also Sir Almeric Fitzroy, *The History of the Privy Council*, London, 1928, the first part of which may be usefully consulted.

[13] Wilkins, *Concilia magna Britanniae et Hiberniae a synodo Verulamiens*

A.D. 446 ad Londoniensem, A.D. 1717, London, 1737, four vols.; Gee and Hardy, *Documents Illustrative of English Church History*, London. 1896, re-published in 1910, 1914, 1921, containing one hundred and twenty-four documents from 311 to 1700, taken chiefly from *The Statutes of the realm* (cf. n. 12); E. Cardwell, *Documentary Annals of the Reformed Church of England, being a collection of injunctions, declarations, orders, articles of inquiry, etc., from 1546 to 1716*, two vols., Oxford, 1839 and 1844 (the latter edition is quoted here); *Visitation Articles and Injunctions*, ed. H. Frere and M. C. Kennedy, London, 1910, two vols. (Alcuin Club).

[14] *Journals of the House of Lords*, Vol. I [1509–72], London, undated, in which there are not a few omissions, since for Henry VIII's reign the only reports are from 1509 to 1513 and from 1533 to 1537. The *Journals of the House of Commons* begin only with Edward VI's reign. For Henry VIII's reign use is made of Hall's *Chronicle*, Kaulek's publications (see above, n. 11), and those of Merriman (see Bibliography E (a)).

[15] *Union of the Two Noble and Illustrate Families of Lancaster and York*, 1542, 1548, 1550, 1809, ed. Ellis; the last edition, which contains only Henry VIII's reign, is by Whibley, London and Edinburgh, two vols. 1904, with an interesting preface and two portraits. For Hall's bias, cf. J. Gairdner, *History*, p. 27. A. F. Pollard, in "Edward Hall's Will and Chronicle" (*Institute of Historical Research*, Vol. IX, No. 27, February, 1932), has entirely rewritten the article in the *Dict. Nat. Biog.* on Edward Hall. For the editions of the *Chronicle*, see Graham Pollard's article, *ibid.*, Vol. X, No. 28, June, 1932.

[16] *A Chronicle of England during the reigns of the Tudors from A.D. 1485 to 1559*, ed. D. Hamilton (Camden Society), 1875–77, two vols.

[17] *The Annales or General Chronicle of England*, London, 1615.

[18] *Chronicles of England, Scotland and Ireland*, six vols., London, 1807–1808.

[19] J. G. Nichols published *The Chronicle of Calais* in 1846, *The Chronicle of the Grey friars* in 1859, and especially *Narratives of the days of the Reformation*, a chronicle taken from J. Foxe's manuscripts, with two contemporary biographies of Cranmer, London, 1842. (All Camden Society publications.) See also *Chronicle of Henry VIII, being a contemporary Record of some of the Principal Events of the reigns of Henry VIII and Edward VI*, written in Spanish, translated with notes and Introduction by M. A. S. Hume, 1889.

[20] See particularly the *Calendar of the Marquis of Salisbury*, 1888, published according to the *Reports of the Historical MSS. Commission*, which contain a number of details concerning parliamentary or municipal history (cf. 8th and 9th Reports, 1881, 1883). R. A. Roberts, in 1919, gave the bibliography of the one hundred and fifty-six volumes in this collection (*The Reports of the Historical Manuscripts Commission*). See also what Ch. Bémont has written in Vols. XLVII (p. 103) and L (p. 231) of the *Révue Historique*.— The *Rutland Papers* (ed. W. J. Jerdan, 1842) contain some "Original Documents illust. of the courts and times of Henry VII and Henry VIII."

[21] The Chronicles of the sixteenth century have mostly been published by the Camden Society (in addition to those quoted, Nos. 24, 25, 26, 27, we might mention *The London Chronicle*, ed. C. Hooper, 1859, Vol. IV of the Camden Miscellany). The Seldon Society has made a speciality of legal documents, such as *Select Cases in the Court of Requests* (1898) and *Select Cases before the King's Council in the Star Chamber*, 1477–1544, by Leadam (two vols., 1903 and 1911).

[22] A Catholic society, *The Catholic Record Society*, was established in 1904, and from that date until 1932 has printed thirty-two volumes.

[23] Some writers try to take a general view of the whole Reformation movement (J. H. Blunt, *The Reformation of the Church of England, 1514–1662*,

two vols., 1878–86, 7th ed., the 1st was published in 1869; Perry, *History of the Reformation in England*, London, 1886; Miss Stone, *Renaissance and Reform, 1377–1610*, London, 1904; W. Stubbs' *Lectures in European History* (ed. A. Hassel, London, 1904) may be consulted with advantage; G. V. Jourdan, *The Movement towards Catholic Reform in the early sixteenth century*, London, 1914; P. Smith, *The age of the Reformation*, London, 1922 [a vol. of 861 pp.]; H. Benson, *Anglicanism*, London, 1922; R. H. Murray, *The political consequences of the Reformation. Studies in Sixteenth Century political thought*, London, 1926; F. J. Smithen, *Continental Protestantism and the English Reformation*, London [1927]). Rev. H. A. Moreton, *La Reforme anglicane au XVIe siècle*, with a preface by Lord Halifax, university thesis (Besançon, 1930); G. G. Coulton, *In Defence of the Reformation*, three lectures at the Central Hall, Liverpool, together with discussions, comments and documentary vouchers, London, 1931. After L. von Ranke (*Englische Geschichte*, Vol. XIV of his *Sämmtliche Werke*, 3rd ed., Leipzic, 1870), W. Busch, in Germany, studied Henry VIII's reign, in Vol. II of *England unter den Tudors* (Stuttgart, 1892 *sq.*) and in the *Historisches Taschenbuch* (6th series, Vol. VIII, 1889: *Der Ursprung der Ehescheidung Königs Heinrichs VIII von England;* and Vol. IX, 1890: *Der Sturz des Cardinals Wolsey*). In Bonn, in 1886, he had published *Cardinal Wolsey und die englisch-kaiserlich Allianz, 1522–25*.

At the same time as the *Political History* of W. Hunt and R. Lane Poole appeared in London, in twelve volumes, Oman's *History of England*, in seven volumes, was published in New York. The *Victoria History of the Counties of England*, begun in 1902, contains many facts for the history of the Reformation in the various English counties. See particularly *London* (Vol. I, London, 1909), *Suffolk* (Vol. II, 1907), *Hampshire* (Vol. II, 1903), *Surrey* (Vols. II–IV, 1902–12). Some interesting details will also be found in four of the five volumes published, up to 1930, by the Royal Commission on Historical Monuments (England). *An Inventory of the Historical Monuments in London.* I, Westminster Abbey. II, West London. III, Roman London. IV, London (the City). V, East London (the Tower, Greenwich Hospital, Eltham Palace, etc.). There are about 400 plates in each volume.

The Tudor period attracted the attention of W. Besant (*London in the Time of the Tudors*, London, 1904); of A. D. Innes (*England under the Tudors*, edited by C. W. C. Oman, 1905, latest edition, 1932, revised by J. M Henderson); of W. P. M. Kennedy (*Studies in Tudor History*, London, 1916) who, writing for the general public, gives details of religious history upon which the historian does not generally dwell; of P. van Brunt Jones (*The household of a Tudor noble man*, University of Illinois, 1917); of L. Einstein (*Tudor Ideals*, London, 1921); of R. M. Rayner (*England in Tudor and Stuart Times*, with maps and plans); and of E. Gurney and Salter (*Tudor England through Venetian eyes*, London, 1930, which is a translation of certain passages from the *Relazioni degli ambasciatori Veneti*, known already from other sources). Sir Lewis Dibdin has re-edited various old essays (one dates from 1883) on the relations between Church and State in England and on the establishment of the Royal Supremacy in Henry VIII's time: *Establishment in England. Being Essays on Church and State*, London, 1932.

J. A. Muller published his *Stephen Gardiner and the Tudor reaction*, London, 1926. The author is Professor of Ecclesiastical History in the Episcopal Theological School, Cambridge (Mass.).

A work has recently appeared which, although literary, touches also upon history (it has been quoted occasionally here): G. Ascoli, *La Grande Bretagne devant l'opinion française, depuis la guerre de Cent ans jusqu'a la fin du XVIe siècle*,

Paris, 1927 (*Travaux et Mémoires de l'Université de Lille*, Fasc. 11). In it are found portraits of Anne Boleyn, Thomas More and Mary Tudor.

²⁴ There is also a bibliography at the beginning of the Abbé Trésal's *Origines du schisme anglican*, 1908. The one in Vol. IV of the *Histoire générale* by Lavisse and Rembaud, has been brought up to date by the author (G. Constant) (last ed. 1923, pp. 595 *sq.*). See also the *Annual Bulletin of Historical Literature* (No. XX appeared in 1932).

²⁵ To celebrate his twenty-fifth year as professor in the *École des Hautes Études*, the former pupils of M. Bémont dedicated to him a series of studies on the History of England (*Mélanges d'Histoire*, Paris, 1913); few of them, however, concern the sixteenth century.

²⁶ Kennet republished it in 1706 in the second volume of *The Complete History of England*. Another edition, of 1870, bears this title: *The History of England under Henry VIII*. Cf. *Herbert of Cherbury* (1583–1648), *Autobiography*, with Introduction, Notes, Appendices and a Continuation of the Life, by Sidney Lee. 2nd ed., with portrait and revised; Ed. Feuter, *Geschichte der neueren Historiographie*, Munich, 1911, p. 170.

²⁷ *The reign of Henry VIII* forms part of *The History of England*, in twelve volumes, by Froude, an edition of which was brought out between 1898 and 1901. It was re-edited, in three vols., by E. Rhys, for Everyman's Library (1908). Langlois and Seignobos, in their *Introduction aux études historiques*, mention "Froude's disease," i.e. his incurable tendency to inaccuracy. Recently Waldo H. Dunn (*Froude and Carlyle, a study of the Froude-Carlyle controversy*) tried to vindicate Froude apropos of his Life of Carlyle. Cf. *The Times*, March 6th, 10th, 11th, 1930; and the *Revue Historique*, anuary, 1931, pp. 148 *sq.*

²⁸ J. Gairdner has assembled these prefaces of the *Letters and Papers*, in two volumes, under the title *The reign of Henry VIII from his accession to the death of Wolsey, illustrated from original documents*, London, 1884, with a portrait of Henry VIII.

²⁹ The ordinary edition, quoted here, with only the portrait of Henry VIII by Holbein, is the 1905 edition. It was republished in 1926.

³⁰ However, in the same year as Pollard's *Henry VIII* the fourth volume of J. Gairdner's *Church History* appeared (see above, n. 8) and the author considered its limits too narrow for the vast subject. This English historian, whose impartiality is recognized by all, thought "that religious prejudice had warped the judgment of many who had written on them [matters concerning the Reformation], and that too little account was taken of the wrongs inflicted on Catholics, and of the tyranny, greed and irreverence, the robbery of God and His Church, which in his view disgraced the Reformation in England." *Lollardy and the Reformation in England*, Vol. IV, p. ix (preface by W. Hunt). Cf. Littel, *Historians and the English Reformation*, Mowbray, 1910.

APPENDIX II

The Notes to this Appendix will be found on pages 477-81.

COULD CLEMENT VII ANNUL HENRY VIII's MARRIAGE?

Anglican historians admit that Henry VIII's divorce, which occasioned the English Schism, is not one of the most honourable pages in their history. "It is one of the chapters we should like to omit," says one writer; and indeed if there were good things in the Reformation, there were "many also that were reprehensible and shameful."[1] But they try to mitigate the king's culpability by shifting the responsibility on to the Pope, "who was nothing but a tool in the hands now of this one and now of that, ready to gratify the man upon whom he was dependent at the moment."[2] "Political reasons" were behind the whole business.[3] These alone determined Clement VII, and not his conscience.

Yet one has only to read attentively the numerous documents concerning the royal divorce (they are given in Append. I, B. pp. 441 *sq.*) to be convinced that this was not the case. In perusing them any unbiassed person, who does not attempt to make out a special case *pro domo*, can form an accurate idea both of the events and of the rôle played by the chief characters.

The king's part was very simple: he was eager to have the cause tried in his own country so that he could have judgment given in accordance with his desires. At first he thought he was on the point of succeeding. Wolsey and his agents had taken advantage of Clement VII's isolation at Orvieto, after the sack of Rome, to extract a Decretal from him—which the Pope afterwards regretted—(July, 1528) and also permission for the case to be tried in England by Cardinals Campeggio and Wolsey. The queen's attitude, her rejection of the suspect judges and her appeal to the Roman court having wrecked this scheme, Henry in turn pleaded, as Catherine had done, that the place of trial was suspect—the imperialists were powerful in Rome—and again demanded, insistently at first and then menacingly, that the cause should be sent back for trial in England.[4] A series of schismatic measures were passed by Parliament (1531–33) in order to bring pressure to bear on the Pope.[5] As the latter would not yield, the king regarded the proceedings pending before the Roman court as invalid and submitted the case to his clergy, whose sentence he knew in advance. Delighted with the result of this, he afterwards made use of the same simple method on two occasions to dissolve marriages which were distasteful to him. The marriage with Anne Boleyn, which had just been declared valid with all solemnity, was to be proclaimed invalid with no less solemnity on May 17th, 1536, and Anne of Cleves' marriage was treated in the same way on July 9th, 1540.

This proves better than any lawyers' arguments the wisdom of the old law reserving the matrimonial causes of all sovereigns to the Holy See: *Consuetudo Sedis Apostolicae et Romanae curiae, a tempore cujus initu memoria fuit et est ut causae hujusmodi matrimoniales et aliae spirituales, praesertim inter reges et magnas personas, ac in quibus scandalum facile oriri posse dubitari posset, vel in Romana curia, vel alibi, prout justum aut aequum visum fuerit, committantur, contra quam consuetudinem aut postestatem nostram leges regni tui nihil valent.*[6] "Causes of this importance concern His Holiness and the Holy See, and respecting them neither I nor any others should dare give an opinion," was the reply of Caraffa (afterwards Paul IV) to Henry VIII's envoy, who knowing the Neapolitan's aversion for Spain had sought his opinion.[7] "Hitherto," wrote Cardinal Pacca at the time of Napoleon's divorce, "a constant custom, founded upon very solid reasons, had reserved judgment in affairs of this kind to the Pope, when they concerned sovereigns. It was thought that there were too many disadvantages in that a prince might abuse his authority to extort sentences from his subjects favouring his own desires, and these major causes were reserved to a higher and independent authority. This rule was always observed in the Church, and our history affords more than one example. Several cardinals therefore considered it an infringement of the rights of the Holy See that the officiality of Paris should take upon itself to give a decision in a matter of that importance; and they refrained from assisting at the marriage ceremony between Bonaparte and an Archduchess of Austria."[8]

Clement VII's action was in perfect conformity with the law. The judges of the Rota were unanimously of opinion that he could not refuse the appeal of Catherine of Aragon, who declined to accept the judges in England on account of their partiality,[9] and more especially since the canonical laws removed the defendant from the plaintiff's court if they were not natives of the same country. *Justitiae convenire non videbatur quod regina, quae ex Hispania oriunda et rea conventa erat, cujus forum tu tanquam actor sequi tenebaris, cogeretur, in regno potentissimi actoris causam tuam defendere. Nam secundum canonicas sanctiones, ubi actor et reus civitatum et dioecesum diversarum sunt, in civitate vel dioecesi actoris causa committenda non est.*[10] The Pope acted from the point of view of justice: *Nos enim justitiae deesse non possumus. . . . Decet nos ex pastorali officio nec ad dexteram nec ad sinistram flecti, sed a justitiae tramite non recedendo inviolatam justitiam conservare juxta illud Apocalypsis: Ex ore sedentis in throno procedet gladius bis acutus, quod canones interpretantur intelligi debere de sententia recti judicis, qui contra justitiam nemine debet parcere.*[11] Justice was all he sought in this cause: *quod nobis dignum est quodque justum est, considerare debemus.*[12] On October 6th, 1531, he wrote to two eminent Italian canonists for their opinion *non aliter quam pro mera justitia, veritate, et juris dictamine.* And both men answered: *requisitus et pro veritate et justitia quid mihi videtur consularem, scripsi. . . .*[13] "His Holiness is letting justice take its course,"[14] but is ready to satisfy Henry VIII "in all that does not harm it [justice]."[15]

If Clement VII showed any inclinations, not to say partiality, it was not in favour of Catherine of Aragon and the emperor, but of Henry VIII and the English. *Animi nostri propensionem magis quam juris rigorem secuti commisimus . . .* he said himself when he recalled the delegation given to Cardinals Campeggio and Wolsey in 1528.[16] He subsequently granted the English all that he could *con qualche pretesto di justitia,* as his secretary observed.[17] When Henry asked that Gardiner and Lee should be appointed to the sees of Winchester and York, the Pope forgot the attitude they had adopted in the divorce business, the violence and brutalities of the king, the schismatic acts of Parliament, the harsh language and threats with which Gardiner had displayed his lack of respect for the Holy See at Orvieto,[18] and granted the king's request immediately.[19] All knew Cranmer to be in favour of the divorce, for which he had written a book; he had advised consulting the universities against Rome. If he became primate of England everything was to be feared. But Clement, resolute on the question of justice, was anxious to avoid fresh clashes with the king and on February 21st, 1533 he signed the Bull appointing the royal candidate to the see of Canterbury.

Three months had scarcely elapsed (May 23rd) before Cranmer, caring little for the proceedings then pending in the Roman court, pronounced Catherine of Aragon's marriage invalid and Anne Boleyn's valid.

Although he would not allow partial judges to try the divorce suit, yet Clement VII was very careful not to precipitate the issue. He consulted all the enlightened minds, especially the most distinguished canonists, such as Rinaldo Petrucci,[20] and Filippo Decio (†1535), Leo X's master, whom the universities of Pisa, Padua, Pavia, Siena and Bologna were always anxious to secure and whose teaching was praised on all sides. He was "*uno de' più eccelenti jurisconsulti di quella età*," according to Guichardin, and was consulted both by Henry VIII and the emperor.[21] The Pope sought counsel of Jerome Aleandre and of Cardinal Cajetan, whom Henry himself had asked for an opinion.[22] When the king had obtained a declaration from several universities proclaiming a marriage with a brother's widow to be null *jure divino*, Clement VII wrote to the foremost Hebrew scholar in Italy, Felix de Prato, a converted Jew, who had published the rabbinical Bible at Antwerp in 1518, asking him to give his opinion on the texts in question of Leviticus and Deuteronomy upon the papal power of dispensing from the first degree of affinity.[23] The Dean of the Rota, Giacomo Simonetta— afterwards Bishop of Perugia and cardinal (1535-†39)—was indisputably conversant with all the difficulties of the law; his impartiality and his disinterestedness were beyond suspicion; from the outset he had studied the whole question, and the proceedings as well as the conclusion thereof were placed in his hands.[24]

The long examination of the case and the delays involved were to Henry's advantage in particular. To him they were of consequence in a cause that was against him from a legal point of view; they furthered his game. When he was summoned to Rome and sent an *excusator*, Edward Carne, in lieu of a proctor, instead of being ejected for not having a mandate Carne was heard more than once and brought into the consistory[25]; and the debate arising out of his mission was indefinitely prolonged.[26] He was allowed to demand for the king any defenders he wished. One of them, Girolamo Previdello, decided to come, and spoke in presence of the Pope and cardinals on April 17th, 1532; later he even demanded that Henry's marriage with Anne Boleyn should be justified.[27]

If any had reason to complain of the Roman proceedings, it was Charles V; and he did not fail to do so. He observed that such numerous delays prejudiced his aunt's cause and abetted the king's obduracy and rebellion. "S. M^tas non solum aegre sed aegerimme tulit hoc; it seems to him that all this is detrimental to his honour and is calculated to make his aunt despair."[28] "A letter received this morning from Catherine has broken his heart," wrote Aleandre,[29] it "reveals all that she suffers, the affronts she endures, her tears. . . . So the emperor has requested me to beg His Holiness to pronounce sentence." "Is it not a strange and abominable thing," he added, "that a madman and a mad woman can thus suspend justice and perpetrate such an outrage and cause such a good and holy queen so much evil?" Charles told Cardinal Campeggio that if the proceedings went on at the same rate, they would never see the end of them.[30] "He complains because the cause proceeds so slowly and also of the queen's situation; he says he often receives from her letters which rouse his pity; he has begged me to request His Holiness to expedite the business."[31] "I earnestly beg Your holiness," wrote the emperor himself,[32] "to give orders without delay for judgment to be given according to justice; for to delay the cause might cause serious dangers; to terminate it, on the contrary, will be for Your Holiness the fulfilment of your duty to God and to yourself, and will place me under a deep debt of gratitude." "I beseech Your Holiness with all my strength," again he repeats,[33] "to decide and to finish the cause of England, because there can be no reason for delaying any longer; it is no small disadvantage for what is happening over yonder and for the whole of Christendom to see that in so just a cause there has been so much delay in rendering justice. If sentence had been pronounced the King of England would probably have behaved quite differently." Granvelle and the imperial counsellors were of the same mind, they were "certain that immediately the sentence was pronounced against him, Henry would relent and take his wife back again; several times the emperor's representatives have made use of strong words in this business, and the king suddenly became like a lamb."[34]

This was not the Pope's view. He thought that in dealing with a character such as Henry VIII's any sentence which thwarted his passion would but make him more obstinate; Catherine of Aragon's position would not be made better and the schism would become imminent. "His Holiness," wrote Aleandre to the emperor,[35] "is doing his best, and is letting time bring the matter to a head; already it is noticed that the rival's [Anne Boleyn's] authority is on the wane.[36] It is still possible for sentence to be pronounced; but once it is given the trouble which will ensue will not be easily allayed. . . . If the S^{me} Queen can be patient a little longer, hoping in the Divine goodness and prudence, she will be rewarded by God and praised by men for having prevented by her martyrdom a serious schism in the Church of God, a schism from which the emperor would be the first to suffer, both as regards the public weal and his own honour." "To pronounce sentence," Campeggio in turn wrote to Charles V,[37] "would be to give the King of England an opportunity of shaking off obedience to the Holy See; the consequence would be serious: in order to defend his authority and the liberty of the Church, His Holiness would have to proceed against Henry and his realm; but the effect would be null if the sentence were not executed, and this execution concerns His Majesty as the first-born of the Church." But Charles V had no desire— and men thought as much—to be drawn into such a ticklish business.[83] Any prospect of political complications made him at once less impatient over the issue of the proceedings.[39] Clement VII was therefore not wrong in not precipitating matters. When, at the emperor's insistence, he ordered the king to take back Catherine and to send Anne Boleyn away until sentence had been given,[40] he delayed sending the letter when he heard that an envoy had arrived from the king, who might possibly be the bearer of better news from England.[41] Being a keen psychologist, he suspected that the king's passion would last only for a while: he compared it to fruit which has only to be left to ripen for it to fall from the tree: *Sperando che la benignità et prudentia divina maturi questa durezza col tempo.*[42] Had it not been for Anne's pregnancy and the imminent birth of a male heir, events would have proved him to be right.[43] For nearly seven years already the cause had been protracted.

All the Pope did during those critical years was to prevent Henry from taking to the courts in his own country the proceedings then pending before the Roman court. Hence the first admonition of March 7th, 1530, forbidding him to contract another marriage under pain of excommunication so long as the cause was not ended.[44] Hence also the second admonition of January 5th, 1531 prohibiting Parliament, the universities, the law-courts and the Archbishop of Canterbury

from interfering in the matter.[45]   Hence again the third
admonition of November 15th, 1532, following on the meeting
at Boulogne between Henry VIII and Francis I, when Anne
Boleyn was present, and which forebodes a denouement.[46]
Henry himself provoked them on each occasion; and by his
shameless behaviour he determined the final sentence.   He
married Anne Boleyn (January, 1533), Archbishop Cranmer
pronounced the marriage valid and the former union invalid
(May 23rd, 1533), and eight days later Anne was crowned as
queen. It was nothing less than open defiance of the Pope's
authority.   So, on July 11th, 1533, at the request of the
emperor and of the queen, sentence of excommunication was
pronounced against Henry, and his marriage with Anne was
declared invalid.[47]   Even in this stern action, which his office
demanded, Clement's forbearance and his regret at having to
take severe measures against Henry were clearly to be seen.
The penalty was held in abeyance until September; it was to
take effect only if by that date Henry had not separated from
Anne Boleyn; and in September a further prorogation was
granted at the request of Francis I. It was a residue of hope.

Until the end the Pope showed extreme condescension
and patience towards England and the English king, and was
rewarded only with insults; by Henry's orders all the English
bishops, save Fisher, taught the people to "despise the naughty
acts of this bishop of Rome," who had been unjust to the
king, and who "in his bulls, usurps the name of pope, and
arrogates to himself the principality."[48] Certain people might
call this forbearance of Clement mere weakness. But to go so
far as to write that he acted only "through fear," and that he
refused to annul Catherine's marriage because "Charles V
had greater power over him,"[49] is to ignore the truth. The
Pope could not annul this marriage.

Indeed, the invalidity of Julius II's dispensation on account
of juridical defects was the reason first put forward in the
Roman court against the royal marriage.   Not a single
historian or canonist would admit it at the present day.

In the second phase of the divorce, when the king, at
Cranmer's instigation, gradually resolved to take the case
out of the Pope's hands and have it tried at home, he requested the English and foreign universities to decide that
the divine law forbids marriage with a brother's widow; the
Pope then had not dispensed from anything, since he could
not do so. It is certain that upon this point ancient discipline
was extremely strict. The 61st canon of the Council of Elvira

(306) excommunicated all who continued to live in such a union. And Innocent III (†1216), in a letter to the Bishop of Livonia incorporated in the *Corpus juris canonici* (*Decretal.* IV, xix, ix), admitted the exception given in Deuteronomy (xxv, 5)[50] only for those who had married before receiving baptism. Gradually it was applied to Christians themselves: and Cochlaeus, the famous controversialist, based his arguments upon Deuteronomy to declare Henry VIII's first marriage indissoluble: *De matrimonio serenissimi regis Angliae Henrici octavi congratulatio disputatoria* (dedicated to Paul III, 1535). In England Tyndale, as well versed in Scripture as he was inclined towards the New Learning, decided against Henry: "If it was lawful under the Mosaic law to marry a brother's wife, it must be lawful still, though it may no longer be a duty" (*The Practice of Prelates*, 1530). Duns Scotus (†1305?), professor at Oxford, had long taught that this invalidating impediment was of human origin. Accordingly Martin V (†1431) investigated the case of John, Count of Foix, who asked that he might marry his sister-in-law, Blanche of Navarre.[51] In 1500 Emmanuel of Portugal, with a dispensation from Alexander VI, married his siter-in-law, Mary, daughter of the Most Catholic King Ferdinand and his wife Isabella, who considered it quite a matter of course to ask Julius II for a similar dispensation for their fourth and last daughter, Catherine of Aragon. After objecting somewhat, Julius II granted it,[52] and none in England, including Henry, questioned the Pope's power to dispense in this case.[53]

For centuries now in the Latin Church a dispensation from affinity in the first degree, in the collateral line, no longer presents the same insurmountable difficulties as formerly, and there is no need to invoke State reasons, as did the Count of Foix.[54] The Eastern Church, albeit somewhat lax in certain matrimonial questions, yet until recently remained quite strict on the subject of marriage with a brother-in-law or sister-in-law, after the previous partner's death, and considered such unions as incestuous and as implying antecedent adultery.[55] The religious authorities, however, are showing themselves more and more compliant, and at the present day a dispensation could be obtained by means of a donation. As for the reformed churches, for quite a long while they continued to look upon the impediment of affinity in the first degree, in the collateral line, as being of divine law.[56] "Marriage with the sister of a deceased wife or a deceased brother is not allowed, for such marriages are forbidden not only by the laws, but also by the word of God," declared the synod of Poitiers in 1560. Since the Concordat which re-organized worship (April 8th, 1802) the reformed churches of France and Switzerland depend entirely upon the civil laws for matters of consanguinity or affinity. Such is also the practice of the Lutherans.

The prohibition of marriage between a brother-in-law and sister-in-law disappeared then for Continental Protestants at the beginning of the nineteenth century.[57] In the west the Church of England is practically the only church to retain this prohibition, which she still considers a divine law (99th and 100th canons of discipline, 1604).[58] Even so the Act of Parliament passed in 1907 and confirmed, in a particular case, by the Court of Arches [1908] and then by the High Court, the Court of Appeal and the House of Lords (1921), struck a fatal blow at this ancient discipline: marriage between a brother-in-law and a sister-in-law was recognized as being legal.[59] Hitherto the civil law had been that of the statute established by Henry VIII in the thirty-second year of his reign as a justification for his divorce, a statute which was suppressed by Mary Tudor and definitely re-established by Elizabeth.[60]

The development of the matrimonial legislation abundantly proves that no sentence other than that of 1534 could have been pronounced on the marriage of Catherine of Aragon and Henry VIII. Any other sentence would have proclaimed Julius II's dispensation an abuse of power. J. Gairdner admits that "the Church of Rome stood before the world of that day as the real guardian of high principles."[61]

APPENDIX II—NOTES

[1] H. A. Moreton, *La Réforme anglicane au seizième siècle*, Preface by Lord Halifax, thesis, Besançon University, 1930, pp. 2, 50.

[2] *Ibid.*, p. 50.

[3] *Ibid.*, pp. 76, 82. See end of chap. VIII: "The Pope's Dilemma," in A. F. Pollard's *Henry VIII*.

[4] Read Henry's letter to the Pope, dated April 10th, July 13th, December 6th, 1530, and December 28th, 1531, in Pocock, *op. cit.*, I, 429, II, 148, 630; Burnet, *op. cit.*, IV, p. 169 (where the date is wrongly given as 1532 instead of July 13th, 1530), VI, p. 41. Cf. Ehses, *op. cit.*, 154 *sq.*

[5] See above, chap. III.

[6] Clement VII's reply to Henry's letter of December 6th, 1530, as drafted by the Cardinal of Ancona, Pietro di Accolti, in Ehses, *op. cit.*, p. 174.

[7] Caraffa, Bishop of Chieti, to Clement VII, Venice, June 3rd, 1530, Ehses, *op. cit.*, 271. During Leo X's pontificate Caraffa had spent three years in England as nuncio and collector (cf. Maurenbrecher, *Geschichte der*

Katholischen Reformation, Nordlingen, 1880, I, 228). Dr. Richard Croke, who was sent to Italy with a well-filled purse to obtain opinions in favour of the royal divorce, tried to approach him on several occasions, but in vain. He then applied to the Bishop of Verona, the Humanist Matteo Ghiberti (who had also been to England on a diplomatic mission) for a letter of recommendation to Caraffa. The latter sent a friendly reply to Ghiberti, but showed Croke the door (April-May, 1530). Cf. Ehses, 267 *sq.*

[8] *Memoires* of Cardinal Pacca, Queyras' trans., 1845, 1885 ed., I, 289. Cf. Professor Constant's *Église de France sous le Consulat et l'Empire*, Paris, 1928, pp. 289 *sq.* Moreover, the Paris officials pleaded the captivity of Pius VII, and pronounced sentence only "in view of the difficulty in applying to the visible head of the Church, to whom indeed it has always belonged to have cognizance of and to give judgment in these extraordinary cases." Pius VII protested against the "irregularity" of the proceedings, but did not pass sentence upon the validity of the marriage itself.

[9] According to the *Diarium Blasii de Cesena*, the queen had three representatives in Rome: Dr. Pedro Ortiz, Aloys of Aragonia, and Dr. Anguiano. Cf. Ehses, 207, n. 4.

[10] Draft of a reply from the Pope to the royal letter of December 6th, 1530. Ehses, 170, 174. Cf. Decret. Greg. IX, Bk. II, tit. II, c. 1 and c. VIII. The laws of the universal Church, the text adds, count before the English laws: "In causis spiritualibus, etiam in regno tuo Angliae canones quibusvis legibus etiam ejusdem regni praevalere debent."

[11] In his letter of September 27th, 1530 to the bishops and lords of England (Ehses, 163), Clement VII quotes the same interpretation of the text of the Apocalypse.

[12] Same letter (Ehses, 163).

[13] Ehses, 180 *sq.*

[14] Jacopo Salviati, the Pope's secretary, to Campeggio, Rome, October 24th, 1531. *Ibid.*, 185.

[15] Salviati's letter to Campeggio. Clement VII to Henry VIII, October 23rd, 1531. *Ibid.*, 184, 185.

[16] Clement VII to the bishops and lords of England, September 27th, 1530. Ehses, 163. Cf. the letter from the legate in France to Jacopo Salviati, June 20th, 1529. *Ibid.*, 265 *sq.*

[17] J. Salviati to Campeggio, Rome, April 13th, 1532. Ehses, 198.

[18] See above, pp. 59 *sq.*; p. 346, n. 21.

[19] Clement VII to Henry VIII and Gardiner, October 23rd, 1531. Ehses, 183-84.

[20] His two brothers, Frederico and Giovanni, were also jurisconsults. He was an auditor of the Rota in Julius III's time. Cf. G. Tiraboschi, *Storia della Litteratura italiana*, Naples, 1777-86, VII, Part 2, 105 *sq.*

[21] The universities were bidding sums in florins for his services. At twenty-two he was professor first at Pisa and Vienna (1476-1501), then at Padua (1501-1505), at Pavia, whither he was summoned by Louis XII, and at Valenza (1505-15), at Pisa (1517-23) and at Siena, where he remained till his death, although the university of Bologna offered him a professorship and a salary of 1,000 ducats for two lectures a week. Because he took part in the Council of Pisa (1510-12), for which he wrote his *Consilium supra Ecclesiae auctoritate* and a *Sermo* on the same subject, he was excommunicated by Julius II. His works, consisting chiefly of commentaries on the Digest and the Pandects, were published in four vols. at Pavia between 1512 and 1531 with a continuation by his disciple Boeza. His commentaries *in decretales* appeared at Lyons in 1557 and at Venice in 1576. Cf. Tiraboschi, *op. cit.*, VI, Part 1, 435-42; F. Guicciardini, *La Historia*

d'Italia, Florence, 1561, in-fol., Bk. X, 400; G. K. von Savigny, *Geschichte des römischen Rechts im Mittelalter*, Heidelberg, 1839–42, VI, 372–96; J. Fr. von Schulte, *Die Geschichte der Quellen und Literatur des Kanonischen Rechts von Gratian bis auf die Gegenwart*, Stuttgart, 1875–80, II, 361; H. Hurter, *Nomenclator literarius theologiae catholicae*, 3rd ed. Innsbruck, 1903–13, II, col. 1337 *sq.*; A. Renaudet, *Le Concile gallican de Pise-Milan* (1510–12), Paris, 1922; Ehses, 180 *sq.*

[22] See Cajetan's opinion, dated March 13th, 1530, in O. Rineldi, *Annales ecclesiastici, ad ann. 1530*, Nos. 193-201; his answer to Henry VIII, *ibid., ad ann. 1534*, Nos. 1 and 2. Cf. Burnet, I, 104, III, 57.

Aleandre's opinion, which is in the Vatican archives (*Armad.* XI, 38, f. 73-94), appears to emanate rather from a canonist under him than from himself, as the Latin of the text shows.

[23] This opinion is given by Ehses, *op. cit.*, 239-46.

[24] Gardiner says that he had endless arguments with him, on one occasion from 7 a.m. until nightfall. See above, p. 59, n. 80.

Giacomo Simonetta (1475–1539), son of a noble and illustrious family of Milan, was admitted among the jurisconsults of Pavia University in 1498. He took Orders in Rome about the year 1500. A few years later he published his first work on Canon Law: *Tractatus de Reservationibus beneficiorum*. Julius II noted his tact and prudence, his extensive learning and his administrative gifts and appointed him consistorial advocate (1505) and then auditor of the Rota. It was in this capacity that he assisted at the Lateran Council in 1512. Clement VII nominated him to the see of Pesaro (1527) in the very year in which Henry VIII's cause was submitted to him for examination. His report on this cause was read in consistory and the Pope adopted its conclusions (*Acta consistoralia* and Bull of March 23rd, 1534. Ehses, 214 *sq.*). This report, which has never been published, should be in the *Archivio Consistoriale* but up to the present has not been discovered. Cf. Argelatti, *Bibliotheca scriptorum Mediolanensium*, Milan, 1475, col. 1398 *sq.*; E. Sol. *Un canoniste du seizième siècle, Le cardinal Giacomo Simonetta*, in *Annales de Saint-Louis des Français*, Rome, July, 1902.

[25] Thus it was resolved in the consistory of February 7th, 1532 (Ehses, 209 *sq.*): "*ut dictis agentibus pro rege et regina respective auferatur materia justae querelae et deveniri possit ad dictae causae determinationem quod dictae disputationes publicae super praemissis audiantur.*"

[26] Cf. Ehses, 208, 209, 212 *sq.*, 227 *sq.*

[27] Cf. *L. and P.*, V, Nos. 971, 972, VII, No. 368; Pocock, II, 508; Ehses, 227.

[28] Campeggio to J. Salviati, Augsburg, June 26th, 1530. Ehses, 151.

[29] Aleandre and Sanga to J. Salviati, Brussels, November 14th and 19th, 1531. *Ibid.*, 188.

[30] Campeggio to J. Salviati, Ratisbon, June 12th, 1532. *Ibid.*, 200.

[31] Campeggio to J. Salviati, Ratisbon, July 9th, 1532. Ehses, 200.

[32] Letter to the Pope, from Tournai, November 28th, 1531. Ehses, 190.

[33] Charles V to the Pope, Ratisbon, March 22nd, 1532. *Ibid.*, 197.

[34] Aleandre to Sanga, Ratisbon, April 17th, 1532. Ehses, 198.

It should be noticed that the tone of the emperor, in his recriminations, is altogether different from that of Henry VIII and his followers. He never uses threats. And there appears to be no doubt that he would have bowed to the papal sentence, whatever it was: "intervenesse poi quello che se volesse" (Ehses, 188). So it is little in accordance with truth to depict, as some writers have done, Clement VII trembling before an emperor dictating his own will to him. Charles had no doubt about the outcome of the proceedings—for the cause was evident to him—but he never imposed the sentence. This will be clearly perceived on reading the documents again.

[35] Aleandre to J. Salviati, Brussels, November 14th and 19th, 1531. Ehses, 188.

[36] Already, in 1531, it was noticed that the king was somewhat colder towards Anne Boleyn. Cf. *Papiers d'État du cardinal de Granvelle*, II, 33; Friedmann, I, 133; Ehses, 185, 198.

[37] Campeggio to J. Salviati, Enghien (near Brussels), November 25th, 1531. Ehses, 189.

[38] See above, p. 114.

[39] "La Cesarea Maesta non fa tanta furia de la cosa di Anglia, quando gli ne ho parlato, come mi pavea facesse in Brusselle." Aleandre to Sanga, Ratisbon, April 17th, 1532. Ehses, 198.

[40] Clement VII's letter to Henry VIII, January 25th, 1532. Pocock II, 166; Le Grand, III, 560-65; Lord Herbert, 156. It was not delivered to the king until May, 1532.

[41] This envoy, Dr. William Bennet, arrived on February 6th, 1532. Sanga wrote, on behalf of the Pope, to Aleandre on the 25th of the previous month to delay the despatch of the Pope's letter. Ehses, 193.

[42] Ehses, 188.

[43] See above, pp. 83 *sq.* Henry believed that he was about to be presented with the son he so ardently desired; instead, it was Elizabeth.

[44] Brief of March 7th, 1530, in Le Grand, III, 446-53; Dodd, ed. 1737, I, 279; *L. and P.*, IV, No. 6256; Pocock, II, 372.

[45] Brief of January 5th, 1531. Le Grand, III, 531-40; Rinaldi, *ad ann. 1531*, Nos. 79, 80; Dodd, I, 286; Pocock, II, 104; *L. and P.*, V, 27. In the consistory of December 23rd, 1530 (Ehses, 206) the Archbishop of Canterbury had been forbidden to take cognizance of the cause.

[46] Brief delivered on December 23rd, 1532. Le Grand, III, 558-69; Dodd, ed. 1737, I, 288; Pocock, II, 378. Cf. *L. and P.*, V, Nos. 1566, 1567, 1586, 1633, 1642, VI, No. 19, VII, No. 421.

[47] *Diarium Blasii de Cesena*, in Ehses, 228.

[48] Rymer, XIV, 489; Wilkins, III, 772; Burnet, IV, 202. See above, pp. 130 *sq.*

[49] Moreton, *op. cit.*, 50.

[50] "Quando habitaverint fratres simul, et unus ex eis absque liberis mortuus fuerit, uxor defuncti non nubet alteri: sed accipiet eam frater ejus, et suscitabit semen fratris sui." The next verses show that it was a question of a kind of law, as St Bonaventure observes in speaking of the Jews of his day (*In Vum lib. Sentent*, dist. XXXIX, art. 2, quaest. IV). If the brother-in-law refuses, says Deuteronomy, "accedet mulier ad eum coram senioribus, et tollet calceamentum de pede eius, spuetque in faciem illius et dicet: Sic fiet homini qui non aedificat domum fratris sui." As the verse 5, chap. xxv of Deuteronomy was favourable to Catherine of Aragon's marriage, Coverdale, in his translation, substituted "hir kynsman" for "her husband's brother."

[51] For political reasons, the marriage did not take place.

[52] John III of Portugal, who reigned from 1521 to 1557, obtained a dispensation from affinity to marry his aunt, his mother-in-law's sister.

[53] Cf. J. Gairdner, *Lollardy*, I, 377 *sq.*, 382, 385.

[54] Since the Codex of Canon Law was published in 1918, affinity in the collateral line only invalidates marriage up to the second degree.

[55] Two brothers may not even marry two sisters, unless the weddings take place on the same day, for affinity exists only after marriage. Mgr. Ghika, who kindly supplied the author with information concerning the discipline

of the Eastern Church, told Professor Constant that some sixty years ago, when the reigning prince of Walachia's (Gregory Ghika VIII) two daughters married the two brothers Philippesco, two Walachian noblemen, but not on the same day, they were excommunicated, exiled and cursed by their mother.

[56] Yet the Lutherans decided against Henry VIII, considering that in this business passion alone had been responsible for his actions. Croke's letter to the king, July 1st, 1530. Burnet, IV, 134. Cf. I, 162.—Melanchthon, moreover, put forward apropos of this (ibid. I, 162) the opinion which afterwards became the law in the reformed Churches, viz. that the laws of Leviticus are not binding upon Christians and that the Gospel establishes no rule for matrimonial impediments; it remains then for princes and states to decree them.

[57] These details were given to the author by Pastor L. of St André, moderator of the national synod for the reformed evangelical Churches of France.

[58] E. Cardwell, *Synodalia*, Oxford, 1842, I, 222, 226. Where invalidating impediments are concerned, these *Canones ecclesiastici* of 1604 agree with Cranmer s *Reformatio legum ecclesiasticarum*, published in 1571 by John Foxe but without Parliament's approval. They follow Leviticus: *Regulae observandae in jure Levitico* (*De gradibus in matrimonio prohibitus*, cap. 4, 5, ed. Cardwell, Oxford, 1850, 47 *sq.*). Such impediments are declared to be of divine law in these terms: "Nec enim haec illorum capitum praecepta veteris Israelitarum reipublicae propria fuerunt (ut quidam somniant), sed idem authoritatis pondus habent quod religio nostra decalogo tribuit, ut nulla possit humana postestas quicquam in illis ullo modo secus constituere. Itaque pontifex romanus illam impie sibi facultatem arrogat: et conscientias suas graviter consauciant, quicunque vel a pontifice Romano, vel a quocumque alio tales in hac causa dispensationes (ut vocant) conquirunt." It sounds almost like an echo of the sentence of May 23rd, 1533, against Catherine of Aragon.

[59] The Deceased Wife's Sister's Marriage Act, presented to Parliament under the Campbell-Bannerman (†1908) Ministry. Cf. *Encycl. Brit.*, ed. 1929, art. "Law of marriage." See also Vol. XXX, or Supplement of 1922, art. "Church History," p. 678; F. W. Puller, *Marriage with a deceased wife' sister forbidden by the Laws of God and of the Church*, London, 1912.—The 1907 Act does not oblige Anglican ministers to solemnize the marriage.

[60] *Statutes of the realm*, 32 Henry VIII, cap. 38. Elizabeth re-established it (1 Elizabeth, cap. 1) in the modified form fixed by Edward VI (2 and 3 Edward VI, cap. 23).

[61] *Lollardy*, I, 383. Cf. *Revue d'Histoire ecclésiastique*, Louvain, 1931, pp 579–90; *Mélanges*, Albert Dufourcq, 1932, pp. 145–62.

APPENDIX III

Thomas More and Papal Authority

When, on March 6th, 1534, the Bill of Attainder concerning the "Holy Maid of Kent," in which Thomas More's name appeared, was read for the third time, the Lords sent a message to the king asking that the accused men might at least be allowed to defend themselves in the Star Chamber (*cf.* Friedmann, *op. cit.*, I, 297). The outcome of a speech by More was certain, so, although it was restricted to the very minimum of justice, the request of the Upper House was rejected. Henry VIII charged a commission of four, Cranmer, Audeley, Norfolk and Cromwell, to question More in secret and to bring pressure to bear upon him, using both promises and threats in turn, in order to obtain his adherence to the divorce. They "willed him to sit down with them, which he in no wise would." The Lord Chancellor Audeley pressed him to add his consent to the royal marriage "which the parliament, the bishops, and the universities had already passed. The king had showed his love and favour to him in so many ways that More could not refuse any longer." To which More replied: "No man living is there, my lords, that would with better will do the thing that should be acceptable to the king's Highness. Howbeit, I verily hoped I should never have heard of this matter more, considering that I have from time to time always from the beginning so plainly and truly declared my mind unto His Grace; which His Highness ever seemed to me, like a most gracious prince, very well to accept, never minding, as he said, to molest me more therewith." Audeley then tried threats, charged him with ingratitude, "never was there servant to his sovereign so villainous, nor subject to his prince so traitorous as he." He accused him of having incited the king to write his *Assertio septem sacramentorum* and to maintain the Pope's authority therein and so "to put a sword in the Pope's hand to fight against himself." "My lords, these terrors be arguments for children, and not for me," More replied, and he quoted Henry VIII's own words, who desired to "set forth the Pope's authority to the uttermost, for we receive from that See our crown imperial," whereas More himself had reminded the king that he might possibly one day find himself at variance with the Pope. When all this was reported to the king, who knew it to be true, Henry was highly offended and wanted More's name included at all costs in the Bill of Attainder. When it was objected that the Bill would never pass the House of Lords, the king replied that he would go down and be present in person. The Lord Chancellor and the others threw themselves upon their knees before him to restrain him, and begged him not to expose himself in person to a parliamentary defeat, for "it would not only encourage his subjects ever after to contemn him, but also through all Christendom redound to his dishonour for ever." In the case of the nun, Roper concludes (pp. xxxvi-xxxix), More's innocence was so evident, all deeming his conduct to be worthy of praise rather than of blame, that at last the king yielded to the request that had been made to him.

The arguments Margaret Roper used to convince her father, and which had sufficed for her, show, as Bridgett (p. 374) observes, "the enormity of the scandal given to the laity by the prelates and clergy of England . . . and the magnificence of More's loyalty to conscience, that he should be in no ways swayed by that example."

Stapleton summarizes Margaret's arguments and More's replies (Hallett's trans., 163 *sq.*). "These, then, are briefly the objections Margaret urged. First, that one who was under such great obligations to the king and had received so many honours from him was bound beyond all others to conform to the royal will except in matters clearly and obviously contrary to the commandments of God. That in this matter (and this was the second argument) so general was the consent of the whole kingdom, of men of such number and weight, that it was scarcely credible that all should wish to disobey Almighty God. . . . Not only, then, could he, without rashness or danger to salvation, accommodate his conscience to theirs, but indeed he was bound so to do. . . .

"More's answers to these various arguments were on the following lines. First, that certainly no man in the whole kingdom would more willingly take the oath than he . . . if by so doing he should not grievously offend God. That he had not lightly or carelessly dealt with the matter but had given it his close study for seven years [original MS. has "ten," cf. Hallett, p. 38, n.—*Translator*] after the appearance of the king's book against Luther, in reading which book he first realized that the Primacy of the Roman Pontiff was by divine right. That he had read all the Fathers, both Latin and Greek, that he could find upon the subject and—to use his own words—'I have found in effect the substance of all the holy doctors, from St. Ignatius, disciple to St. John the Evangelist, unto our own days, both Latins and Greeks, so consonant and agreeing in that point, and the thing by such General Councils so confirmed also, that in good faith I never neither read nor heard anything of such effect on the other side that ever could lead me to think that my conscience were well discharged, but rather in right great peril, if I should follow the other side, and deny the primacy to be provided by God.' . . . I nothing doubt at all, but that though not in this realm, yet in Christendom about, of those well learned men and virtuous that are yet alive, they be not the fewer part that are of my mind. . . . But go me now to them that are dead before, and that are I trust in heaven, I am sure that it is not the fewer part of them, that all the time while they lived, thought in some of the things the way I think now. I am also . . . of this thing sure enough, that of those holy doctors and saints . . . there thought in some such things as I think now. I say not that they thought all so, but surely such and so many as will well appear by their writings, that I pray God give me the grace that my soul may follow theirs." Stapleton, chap. xvi (Hallett's trans., 163-165, 167), according to Margaret Roper's letter to Lady Alington. Cf. Collier, IV, 279.

CHRONOLOGICAL TABLE OF EVENTS IN THE RELIGIOUS HISTORY OF HENRY VIII'S REIGN

1501 { Arthur, Prince of Wales, married Catherine of Aragon November 14th.

1502 Death of Arthur, April 2nd.

1503 { Agreement between Ferdinand, "the Catholic," and Henry VII for the marriage of the new Prince of Wales, Henry, with Catherine of Aragon. Brief and Bull of dispensation granted by Julius II for this marriage (1504), antedated December 26th, 1503.

1509 { Death of Henry VII and Accession of Henry VIII, April 21st. Henry VIII marries Catherine of Aragon June 11th.

1511 A national council against the Lollards meets in England.

1515 { Accession of Francis I, January 1st. Wolsey created cardinal September 10th.

1516 Mary Tudor born, February 18th.

1517 Luther begins to oppose Rome on Indulgences, October 31st.

1518 Wolsey created legate *a latere* for life.

1519 Charles V elected emperor, June 28th.

1521 { Henry VIII receives the title "Defender of the Faith" from Leo X for his book against Luther.

1522 and 1523 { Wolsey seeks the tiara on the death of Leo X and of Adrian VI.

1525 Battle of Pavia, February 24th.

1527 { The King of England's first attempts to secure a divorce. Sack of Rome, May. Wolsey's mission in France (an alliance against Charles V; independence of the Holy See; divorce), July to September.

1528 { Mission of Stephen Gardiner and Edward Foxe to Clement VII. Clement VII's decretal relating to Julius II's dispensation, July.

1529 { Campeggio and Wolsey, delegated by the Pope, begin and abruptly postpone the divorce proceedings. Wolsey's fall (October 9th). Thomas More takes his place as chancellor. Opening of the Long Parliament (1529-36), November 3rd.

1530 { Cranmer's plan begun: opinions of the universities of England, France and Italy on the question of the divorce. Death of Wolsey, November 29th.

1531
- The clergy recognize the king as "supreme head of the Church of England," with a restrictive clause, February 11th.
- The Protestant Smalcaldic League established (Hesse).

1532
- First Act on the Annates, January.
- Commons' petition against the clergy, January.
- "Submission" of the clergy, May 15th.
- Meeting of Henry VIII, Francis I, and Anne Boleyn, at Boulogne, October.

1533
- Henry VIII's secret marriage with Anne Boleyn, January 25th.
- Cranmer primate of England, February 21st.
- Law forbidding all appeals to the Roman court February-March.
- Cranmer's sentence on the royal divorce, April 23rd.
- Coronation of Anne Boleyn, June 1st.
- Birth of Elizabeth, September 7th.
- The king's appeal to a council, at the meeting between Clement and Francis I at Marseilles, November.

1534
- Jean du Bellay's conciliatory mission, February-March.
- Clement VII's sentence against the royal divorce, March 23rd.
- Abjuration of papal authority by the Convocations of Canterbury (March 31st) and of York (May 5th). Laws (a) depriving the clergy of the right to legislate, (b) forbidding all payments to the Roman Curia and transferring to the king the right of appointing bishops, (c) abolishing papal jurisdiction in England, and establishing the order of succession to the throne, (d) recognizing the king, without any restrictive clause, as "supreme head of the Church of England" (November), (e) declaring any refusal to take the oath against the papal jurisdiction an act of treason.
- Thomas Cromwell, the king's vicar-general, middle f December.

1535
- Schismatic oath imposed by Parliament and taken by the nation.
- Martyrdom of the London Carthusians, of Fisher and More, and of a few other Catholics.
- Dissolution of the lesser monasteries.
- Conference at Wittenberg (January-June).

1536
- The Ten Articles or the First Confession of Faith.
- Anne Boleyn beheaded and Jane Seymour married to Henry VIII, May.
- An œcumenical council summoned at Mantua, June 2nd.
- The first royal Injunctions touching upon tenets, worship, etc.
- The Pilgrimage of Grace: rising in Lincolnshire and Yorkshire, October.

1537
- Union of France and Scotland by James V.
- Marriage with Magdalene of France, January 1st.
- Bloody repression of the Pilgrimage of Grace, January-March.
- Reginald Pole's mission to Francis I and Charles V.
- The Second Confession of Faith: "The godly and pious Institution of a Christian man" or "The Bishops' Book."
- Edward VI born, October 12th.
- Death of Jane Seymour, October 24th.

1538
- Conference with the Lutherans, at London, June-August.
- The Thirteen Articles, outcome of the Conference.
- The Truce of Nice arranged by Paul III between Charles V and Francis I, June 18th.
- Meeting of the two sovereigns at Aiguemortes, July 18th.
- James V of Scotland, widower of Magdalene of France (July 7th) married to Mary de Guise, widow of the Duke of Longueville (June 9th, 1537), August 9th.
- Second royal Injunctions concerning worship drawn up by Cromwell and sent to Cranmer, September 30th.
- The greater monasteries surrendered to the king.
- Profanation of the relics of St Thomas à Becket, September.
- Execution of Lord Montague, Reginald Pole's brother, and of the Marquis of Exeter, December 9th.

1539
- Treaty of Toledo between Charles V and Francis I, partly envisaging England, January 12th.
- Reginald Pole's mission in Spain, January-March.
- Law confirming the surrender of the greater monasteries to the king and abolishing the religious orders in England.
- The three Benedictine Abbots of Reading, Glastonbury and Colchester hanged for refusing to surrender their monasteries.
- Act of the Six Articles, June.

1540
- Demonstrations of friendship between Francis I and Charles V on the latter's entry into Paris, January 1st.
- Marriage of Anne of Cleves and Henry VIII, January 6th.
- Surrender of the last abbey in the realm, Waltham Abbey (Essex), March 23rd.
- Fall of Cromwell (June 10th), and his execution, July 28th.
- Anne of Cleves divorced, July 9th.
- Henry VIII married to Catherine Howard, August 8th.

1541
- The Great Bible ordered to be placed in every parish church, under pain of a severe fine.
- Conspiracy in Yorkshire caused by reprisals against the Pilgrimage of Grace, April.
- The Countess of Salisbury, Reginald Pole's mother, executed, May 28th.

1542
- Catherine Howard beheaded, February 12th.
- The œcumenical council definitely summoned at Trent, May 22nd.
- Death of James V of Scotland (December 14th) after the defeat at Solway Moss, November 25th.
- Mary Stuart born, December 8th.

1543
- Alliance between Henry VIII and Charles V against Francis I.
- The Third Confession: "The Necessary Doctrine and Erudition for any Christian man," or "The King's Book," May 27th.
- Henry VIII marries Katherine Parr, July 12th.
- Three heretics burnt at Windsor, in virtue of the Six Articles, July 28th.
- Plot against Cranmer by the canons of his cathedral.

1544
- The English, the emperor's allies, invade Northern France and capture Boulogne.

1545
- Cranmer accused in Parliament.
- Council of Trent opened, December 13th.

1546
- Death of Luther, February 16th.
- Cardinal Beaton assassinated at St Andrews, May 29th.
- Anne Askew burnt as a heretic, July 16th.

1547
- Death of Henry VIII, January 28th.
- Death of Francis I, March 31st.

POPES AND ARCHBISHOPS OF ENGLAND DURING THE FIRST HALF OF THE SIXTEENTH CENTURY

I. POPES

1492   Alexander VI, elected August 11th, crowned August 26th.

1503   { Pius III, elected September 22nd, crowned October 8th, died October 18th.
       Julius II, elected November 1st, crowned November 26th.

1513   Leo X, elected March 15th, crowned April 10th.

1522   Adrian VI, elected January 9th, crowned August 31st.

1523   Clement VII, elected November 18th, crowned November 26th.

1534   Paul III, elected October 13th, crowned November 1st.

1549   Died November 10th.

II. ARCHBISHOPS OF CANTERBURY AND PRIMATES OF ENGLAND

1486   John Morton, created cardinal on October 6th, 1493.

1501   Henry Deane, Bishop of Winchester, May 26th.

1503   William Warham, Bishop of London, November 29th.

1533   Thomas Cranmer, consecrated March 30th.

1556   Burnt as a heretic, March 22nd.

III. ARCHBISHOPS OF YORK

1501   Thomas Savage, Bishop of London, April 12th.

1508   { Christopher Bainbridge, Bishop of Durham, created cardinal on September 20th, 1511.

1514   { Thomas Wolsey, Bishop of Lincoln, created cardinal on September 15th, 1515.

1531   Edward Lee, December 10th

1545   Robert Holgate or Holdegate, Bishop of Llandaff (†1556).

1554   Deposed under Mary Tudor.

ADDENDA

Page 5, end of note 12.—Rodocanachi (*Académie des sciences morales et politiques*, September 17th, 1932) has shown that the lasquenets—gueux or ardent Lutherans—who captured Rome were most undisciplined, and that once united to the Constable de Bourbon's troops neither Freundsberg nor Bourboules could keep them in hand. After the death of these two leaders the Prince of Orange took part in the sack of Rome.

Page 9, note 30.—Cf. A. Dufourcq, *L'Avenir du Christianisme*, VII, 1924, 85 *sq.*, 331 *sq.*, for works on Ockham.

Page 18, end of note 66.—Cf. Sir J. A. R. Marriott, *The Life of John Colet* (illustrated), 1933.

Page 18, end of note 68.—Cf. A. Hyma, *Erasmus and the Oxford Reformers*, 1493–1503, in "Nederlansch archief voor Kerkgeschiednis," The Hague, 1932.

Page 22, line 3.—Despite the political struggles and troubles of 1459–62 and of 1649–71, these industrial and business classes had developed and grown considerably wealthy during the fifteenth century. They had added oversea-trading and undertakings to their ordinary business pursuits. The churches and guildhalls of that period remain as testimony to their wealth. Cf. *Studies in English Trade in the Fifteenth Century*, edited by Eileen Power and M. M. Postan, 1933.

Page 126, note 163.—Charles VI, who called himself *dominus mundi*, was opposed by the jurists of his father, Charles V. They said that "the king was emperor in his own realm" (Cf. G. Dodu, *Les idées de Charles V*, etc.). Like his predecessors, Henry VIII was certainly indebted to the Gallican jurists for many of his ideas on the royal power, but he improved upon them, admitting no limits, not even spiritual limits, to his immoderately great authority.

Page 136, end of first paragraph.—Thus Henry, who "with the whole Church has recognized the primacy of Rome, Mother of the churches," renewed in himself the contradiction which he had so vigorously criticized in Luther a few years previously, in the second chapter of his *Assertio: pronuntians eos peccare damnabiliter quicumque Papae non obtemperarent.*

Page 198, end of note 262.—Cf. H. Villemann, *Aus anglikanischen Klöstern*, in *Benediktinische Monatschrift*, Beuron, 1932, XIV, 418–25.

Page 209, note 34.—See also Gairdner's *Lollardy* I, pp. 453–56, 461, 472, 541.

Page 230, note 114.—Mgr. P. E. Hallett ("Blessed Thomas More as an English Prose Writer," in the *Dublin Review*, 1932, pp. 117–28) speaks of the masterly qualities of his English prose; with Delcourt (*Essai sur la langue de Thomas More*) he looks upon him as the first master of English prose and in a sense as the founder of modern English literature.

P. 231, note 115.—Cf. Ernst Cassirer, *Die platonische Renaissance in England und die Schule von Cambridge*, Leipzig, 1932.

Page 232, end of note 116.—Cf. C. D. J. Brandt, *Thomas Morus en zijn Utopia*, Utrecht, 1932.

Page 303, note 60.—For the very ancient origin and the custom of offering candles in the sanctuaries of the Saints, see H. Thurston, "Votive Candles," in *The Month*, 1932, pp. 141-51.

Page 306, end of note 68.—Tancred Borenius, after a chapter on the life of Thomas à Becket, has published numerous illustrations representing the martyr, scenes from his life and his death: *St. Thomas Becket in Art*, London, 1932. He has also studied his four murderers: "The Murderers of St. Thomas Becket in Popular Tradition," in *Folk-lore*, 1932, pp. 175-92. On February 9th, 1933, he gave a lecture to the Society of Antiquaries of London (*Further aspects of the Iconography of Thomas of Canterbury*), a summary of which was given in *The Times* on February 11th, 1933, together with a reproduction of the bass-relief at Godmersham Hall, near Canterbury, which is considered to be the most ancient reproduction extant of the martyr.

Page 331, note 152. Cf. Irene Josephine Churchill's *Canterbury Administration*: The administrative Machinery of the Archbishopric of Canterbury; illustrated from original records, S.P.C.K., 1933, 2 vols.

Page 399, note 20.—The *Henrici VIII . . . epistola* mentioned in this note was reprinted from the copy in the *Bibliothèque Nationale* in Paris—which is the only complete copy—in *Concilium Tridentinum*, Vol. XII, Freiburg, 1930, pp. 767-74.

Page 426, note 110.—Certain bishops, however, e.g. Drs. Parsons and Perowne, of Middleton and of Bradford, would like to see women admitted to the priesthood. They are not content with the order of deaconesses, of whom there are two hundred and eighty at present, and which was canonically instituted in 1923-25.

Page 441, line 20.—A. F. Pollard completed his study of *Henry VIII* by publishing his *Wolsey* in 1929.

Page 442, line 40.—The *Love Letters of Henry VIII* (the original Letters are in the Vatican Library, MS. 3731) were published by T. Hearne in *Roberti de Avesbury Historia de mirabilibus gestis Edwardi III* (1720), and also in Vol. III (1745) of *The Harleian Miscellany*, taken from the Earl of Oxford's (†1724) collection. A selection of the Letters given in *The Harleian Miscellany* (pp. 34-63) was published by Henry Savage in 1924. There have been other English editions of these Letters. One of the best editions was published in Paris, in 1826 and 1835, by G. A. Crapelet, who corrected quite a number of the inaccuracies in previous editions. Nine of the seventeen Letters are written in French, but the spelling is very queer.

Page 447, line 34.—The Rev. Francis Aidan Hilbert (†1933) published, n 1910, *The Dissolution of the Monasteries as illustrated by the suppression of the eligious houses of Staffordshire.*

Page 448, line 25.—Winifred D. Coates, in an Oxford thesis (1930), studied *The English Benedictines in the Century preceding the Dissolution, with special reference to their connexion with the University and with learning.*

Page 449, line 7.—Marjorie B. Honeybourne also studied, in a thesis, *The extent and value of the property in London and Southwark occupied by the religious houses.* (Cf. *Bulletin of the Institute of Historical Research*, Vol. VIII, pp. 52-57.)

Page 455. Cf. A. I. Taft, *The Apologye of Sir Thomas More, Knyght*, London, 1930.

Lives of the English Martyrs, by Dom Bede Camm, O.S.B., Vol. I, *Martyrs under King Henry VIII* (1535–45), 1914.

Claude Eustace Shebbeare's monograph, *Sir Thomas More*, 1930, limited to 200 copies for members of the Thomas More Society.

The Fame of Blessed Thomas More : Addresses by Ronald Knox, Hilaire Belloc, G. K. Chesterton and Others. With an Introductory Essay by Professor R. W. Chambers.

Page 460, line 37.—Dr. J. A. Muller has also edited *The Letters of Stephen Gardiner*, Cambridge University Press, 1933.

Page 467, end of note 23.—The continuation of Ascoli's work: *La Grande Bretagne devant l'opinion française au XVIIᵉ siècle*, Paris, 1930, contains (I, pp. 232–42) a short study of the French books that have been published concerning the controversies raised in the seventeenth century on the schism of Henry VIII.

Page 480, note 47.—In 1548 the Privy Council acted in precisely the same way as the Pope and ordered Katherine Parr's brother, the Marquis of Northampton, to live apart from his new wife and not to appear at Court—because he had contracted another marriage with Lord Cobham's daughter—until the Council had decided whether the divorce, which had been declared, gave him the right. *Span. Cal.* IX, p. 253.

INDEX

* An asterisk denotes more than one mention on a page.

n Signifies a note on the page.

Names in italics are those of writers and authors.

All the references to writers and authors are not given here, but simply the first mention or the more important references.

A

Abel, 14

Abell, Thomas, Chaplain to Catherine of Aragon (†1540), 69*n*, 394*n*

Abergavenny (*see* Neville, Lord George)

Achab, 132*n*

Achilles, 41*n*

Acre, Mrs. E. Louie, 426*n*

Acton, Lord, 65*n*

Adrian IV, Pope (*see* Breakspear, Nicholas)

Adrian VI, Pope (1521-22), 6 and *n*

Africa, 198

Agostini (Agostino), Wolsey's physician, 74

Agrippa of Nettesheim (Heinrich Cornelius), philosopher, theologian, jurist, doctor (1486-1535), 320*n*

Aiguesmortes, Meeting at (July, 1538), 273*n**, 275, 276, 309, 412

Ainsty (Yorks), 177

Alane (or Alesius), Alexander, 301 and *n*, 302*n*, 373* and *n*

Albèri, Eug., 7*n*, 31*n*, 38*n*, 41*n*, 42*n**, 43*n**, 44*n**, 46*n*, 47*n*

Alcala de Henares (Spain), 205*n*; Appendices 442

Alcester (Warwick), Priory of, 299*n*

Alcock, Bishop of Ely (1486-1500), 143

Aldermary, Parson of, 212*n*

Aldington (Kent), 209* and *n*, 210, 212*n*

Aldrich, Robert, Bishop of Carlisle (1537-56), 374*n**, 417*n*, 418

Aldridge (Staffs), 345*n*

Aleandre, Jerome, Cardinal (1480-1542), 68, 80 and *n**; Appendices, 472, 473, 474, 479

Alençon, Duchess of, 55*n*

Alexander III, Pope (1159-1181), 1

Alexander VI, Pope (1492-1503), 37*n*, 43*n*, 144*n*; Appendices, 476

Alington, Lady, Sir Thomas More's step-daughter, 244*n*, 245*n*; Appendices, 484

Allen, Dr. John, Chaplain to Wolsey, Archbishop of Dublin (1529-1534), 146, 147 and *n*, 288*n*

Allen, P. S. (and *H. M.*), Editor of Erasmus' Letters, 17*n*, 53*n*, 233*n*

Almedingen, Mrs. Edith, 6*n*

Amann, 9*n*

Amaseo, Romolo, humanist (†1552), 257

Ampthill (Beds), 83*n*, 87*n*, 174

Angelo, Castle St. (Rome), 4, 54*n*, 56*n*, 57*n*, 59

Angers, University of, 77

Angoulême, Duke of, third son of Francis I, 396*n*

Anguiano, Dr., Appendices, 478

Angus, second husband of Margaret, Queen of Scotland, 47*n*

Annates, The, 32*n*, 85*n*, 98, 99 and *n*, 105, 112* and *n**, 121 and *n**, 122*n*, 294

Anne Boleyn (*see* Boleyn)

Anne of Brittany, 43*n*

Anne of Cleves (†1558), Henry VIII's fourth wife, 309, 310 and *n**, 311 and *n**, 312, 314, 315 and *n**, 325, 326*n**, 328, 379, 395, 416, 424; Appendices, 470

Anne of Hungary, wife of Ferdinand I, 48*n*

Annecy, Appendices, 457

Anthony, John, visitor of the English monasteries, 164*n*

Antony, C. M., author's pen-name, 260*n*

Antwerp, 251*n*, 286, 307*n*, 324*n*, 428; Appendices, 472

Ap Rice, John, visitor and agent of Cromwell, 157, 158 and *n*, 163, 164*, 302 and *n*

Aragon, 37*n*

Aragonia, Aloys de, Appendices, 478

Arber, Ed., 335*n*

Ardres, Treaty of (Jan., 1546), 4*n*

Aristotle, 259

Armada, The, 31

Armi, Ludovico dell', condottiere of Bologna (†1547), 278*n*

Arthur, Prince (†1502), Henry VII's eldest son, 35, 36* and *n*, 37 and *n*, 46*n*, 52*n*, 54*n**, 64* and *n*, 87, 257*n*, 349; Appendices, 444

Articles, The Six (1539), 194*n*, 293*n*, 294*n*, 301, 302*n*, 312, 314, 332, 335 and *n*, 336*n*, 340*n*, 369*n*, 374, 379*, 380, 381, 389, 392, 417 and *n*, 418*n**, 419, 421*, 422* and *n**, 423 and *n**, 431, 434; Appendices, 461

Articles, The Ten, 373, 392, 394 and *n**, 402*, 403* and *n*, 404 and *n**, 405*, 407 and *n*, 408, 410

Articles, The Thirteen (1538), 414, 415 and *n**

Arundel, Sir Thomas, 348*n*

Arundell, Humphrey, follower of Henry VIII, 191*n*

Ascham, Roger, humanist, 317

Ascoli, G., 13*n*, 48*n*, 50*n*, 51*n*, 354*n**; Appendices, 467

Ashley, W. J., 192*n*

Aske, Robert, 176*, 177*, 178 and *n*, 179* and *n*, 180*, 181*n**

Askew, Anne, widow of Thomas Kyme; burnt as a heretic; 336*n*, 423 and *n**

Aslacton, 316

Athos, Republic of, 232*n*

Atkinson, 181*n*

Atterbury, F., 96*n*, 353*n*

Audeley (or Audley), Sir Thomas, afterwards Baron, Chancellor, 104*n**, 127, 128*n*, 129, 176, 190, 214*n*, 219, 242, 247, 291, 293, 312, 354*n*, 377*n*, 418; Appendices, 482*

Audin, xv, 254*n*; Appendices, 453

Augsburg, 147*n*, 189*n*, 367, 400*, 401 and *n**, 414, 415 and *n*, 416 and *n*, 421

Augustinians, The, 68, 133, 398*n*

Austin Canons, The, 148*n*, 170*n*, 409

Austria, 45

Austria, Archduchess of, Appendices, 470

Avery, Thomas, Thomas Cromwell's steward, 299*l*

Avignon, 3, 106*, 263 and *n*

Axholme (Lincs), 133, 135*n*

Azequa (Athequa), G., Bishop of Llandaff (1517-37), 208*n*

B

Bacon, Nicholas, 193*n*

Badajoz, Bishop of (*see* Maldonado)

Bailey, E., Appendices, 463

Baily, Thomas, 17th century historian, 220*n*; Appendices, 450

Baker, Thomas, 202*n*

Balan, P., 59*n*

Baldinucci, Filippo, continued Vasari, 253 and *n*

Bale, John, Protestant Bishop of Ossory (Ireland); a partisan of Cromwell (†1556), 161*n*, 187 and *n**, 197*, 317, 355*n**, 357*n*, 371*n*

Balliol College, Oxford, 130*n*

Bancroft, Archbishop of Canterbury (1604-10), 125*n*, 410*n*, 428*n*

Bandello, 285*n*

Bangor, Bishop of, 162*n*, 211, 409, 417*n*

Bangor, See of, 111, 208*n*

Bannister, A. T., 333*n*

Bapst, E., 274*n*

Barbaro, Daniel, Venetian ambassador in London (1547-51), 90*n*, 191, 195

Barbarossa, 115

Barberini Library, Appendices, 450

Barcelona, 278*n*

Barcelona, Treaty of, 71*n*

Barennes, J., Appendices, 457
Barking, cemetery, 222
Barlings, Abbey, 181
Barlow, Friar Jerome, 184n
Barlow, John, chaplain to Anne Boleyn's father, 56n*
Barlow, William, Bishop of St. Asaph and St. Davids (1536-48), of Bath and Wells (1548-53), and of Chichester (1559-69), 56n, 162n, 183n, 184n, 334, 340 and n*, 376n, 408, 409, 417n, 418, 421*, 425n, 427
Barmston (Yorks), 345n*
Barnes, Dr. Robert, burnt as a heretic (1540), 110n, 176n, 306n*, 313*, 318n, 342n, 368 and n*, 369*, 382*, 395n, 398 and n*, 402n*, 422, 423, 432n
Barnes, William, Bishop of London (1504-05), 37n
Barrington, E., Appendices, 446
Barton, Elizabeth, "The Holy Maid of Kent," 118, 209* and *n, 210*, and n, 211* and n*, 212 and n*, 213n*, 240, 241n, 295; Appendices, 482
Baskerville, Geoffrey, 164n, 194n
Basle (Switzerland), 227, 229*, 322n, 374n; Appendices, 453
Basle (Switzerland), Council of, 383, 384 and n
Basset, James, stepson of Lord Lisle; married Thomas More's grand-daughter, Mary Roper; 251n*
Basset, Mary, Thomas More's grand-daughter (see Roper, Mary)
Bath, 157, 299
Bath and Wells, Bishop of, 19n, 20n*, 26, 37n, 103, 207, 208n*, 239n, 240n, 350, 373n, 417n
Battaglia, F., Italian writer, 127n, 261n
Batten, E. C., 39n
Baumbach, 416n
Bautewerk, 326n
Bavaria, 110n, 397n, 416 and n
Baxter, Dudley, Appendices, 456
Baxter, R., 192n
Bayne, Rev. R., Appendices, 450
Bayster, publisher, 306n
Beaton, David, Cardinal (1538); Bishop of St. Andrew's (1539-46); assassinated at the instigation of Henry VIII; 273, 274n*
Beatus, Rhenanus, humanist, 232, 344
Beauvale (Notts), 133, 135n

Beccadelli, Ludovico, O.S.F., secretary to Gasp. Contarini and Reginald Pole, Archbishop of Ragusa (1555-64) (†1572), 222n, 258 and n*, 259* and n, 260*, 263, 264n, 266, 267, 272, 273, 277; Appendices, 455*, 456*
Beck, 19n
Becket, St. Thomas à, Archbishop of Canterbury (1162-70), Martyr, 2n*, 32, 138n, 250 and n, 273, 304, 305* and n*, 306n, 332, 388; Appendices, 453
Bedford, 122n
Bedfordshire, 157, 337
Bednař, Professor Frantíšch, 10n
Bedyll, Thomas, Archdeacon of London; visitor of the English monasteries and agent of Cromwell; 133 and n, 157, 164n, 182, 183n, 218
Bekinson, J., 125n
Bell, John, Bishop of Worcester (1539-43), 380
Bellasys, Richard, visitor of the English monasteries, 164n
Bellay, Jean du (see Du Bellay)
Belleforest, François de, 16th century writer, 254n
Belloc, Hilaire, 22n, 43n, 45n, 48n, 156n*; Appendices, 439, 446, 459
Bembo, Pietro, poet, cardinal (1470-1547), 257, 258, 263, 267n
Bémont, Charles, Appendices, 440, 443, 445, 466, 467
Benedict XIII, Pope (1724-30), 99n
Benedictines, The, 21n, 148n, 387
Benedictine Nuns, 168n
Bengal, 198
Benger, Miss, Appendices, 445
Bennet, Dr. William, Henry VIII's agent in Rome, 82; Appendices, 480
Benoît, Fern., 263n
Benson, last Benedictine abbot of Westminster (†1549), 242
Benson, H., Appendices, 466
Bergenroth, Appendices, 442, 465
Berger, Lina, German writer, 231n
Berkshire, 157, 168n
Bertano, Gurone, papal envoy in France, 419n
Berthelet, 16th century London printer, 362, 399n, 404n, 410, 428n
Berthem-Bontoux, 4n
Berthereau, secretary, 105n

Berwick, 277

Berwick, See of, 122n

Besant, W., Appendices, 467

Beverley (Yorks), 173n, 175n, 180n; Fisher's birthplace, 200

Bigham, Hon. Clive, Appendices, 446, 458

Bigod, Sir Francis, 180n*

Bigongiari, Dino, 127n

Bilney, Thomas, burnt as a heretic, 318n

Binardi, Giambattista, Venetian patrician; Pole's secretary in Mary Tudor's time; Appendices, 455

Birch, T. Bruce, 9n

Bird, John, Bishop of Bangor, and of Chester (1541-53), 417n

Biron, Dom R., O.S.B., 261n; Appendices, 457

Bisham (Berks), Monastery of, 168n, 182

Bisham (Berks), Prior of, 183n, 409

"Black Book," The, 152n*, 153, 165* and n*

Blackfriars Convent, London, 68

Blackfriars Hall, London, 66, 91

Bletchingley, Castle of, 315n

Blount, Elizabeth, Lord Mountjoy's sister, 43, 46

Blount, William (see Mountjoy, Lord)

Bloxham and *Heylin*, 143n

Blunt, Rev. J. H., 7n, 34n, 99n, 122n, 125n, 148n, 153, 155n, 223n, 333n, 376n, 423n; Appendices, 462, 466

Bocking, Dr. Edward, O.S.B., Elizabeth Barton's confessor, 210n, 212n

Bodleian Library, Oxford, 410n

Boehmer, H, 9n

Boeza, disciple of Decio, Appendices, 478

Bohemia, 10n, 22, 45

Boleyn, Anne, 7, 8n, 14n*, 43, 44, 46n, 48 and n*, 48n, 49 and n*, 50n*, 51n, 54n, 55n*, 59n, 61 and n, 62, 68* and n*, 72, 73 and n, 75n, 81n, 83* and n*, 84* and n*, 85n, 88 and n, 89* and n, 90n, 104* and n, 105, 108, 114, 115n, 118 and n, 121 and n, 129, 131, 134n, 138, 207, 208, 210, 211, 214, 222, 223*, 227n, 238, 239, 243 and n, 253*, 256n, 265n, 274, 306n, 321*, 322*, 323* and n*, 324* and n*, 325 and n*, 328, 348n, 349*, 351, 359, 365, 433 and n; Appendices, 444, 445, 451,

467, 470, 472*, 474*, 475*, 480

Boleyn, George, Viscount Rochford, Anne Boleyn's brother, 95, 245, 247, 290n, 322, 349

Boleyn, Mary, sister to Anne Boleyn, 43, 48 and n, 50, 56, 324

Boleyn, Sir Thomas, Viscount Rochford, Earl of Wiltshire, father of Anne Boleyn, 45n, 48, 56n, 70n, 72n, 76n*, 81n, 85n, 134, 247, 318, 319, 348

Bologna, 76n, 81n*, 110n, 278n*, 280, 320n, 350* and n

Bologna, University of, 76 and n; Appendices, 444, 472, 478

Bonifacio, Count Bernardo di San, condottiere of Verona, 278n

Bonner, Edmund, Bishop of Hereford (1538-39), and of London (1539-49), 82, 106 and n, 107n, 125n, 302n, 308, 329n, 341, 343 and n*, 344, 346*, 351* and n*, 354, 358, 359* and n*, 360 and n*, 361 and n*, 364, 369 and n, 370 and n, 371*, 372* and n*, 374*, 377 and n*, 380, 381*, 386, 389, 410n, 425n, 432

Bonner, Edmund, long-sawyer of Hanleyd, 343n

Bonney, Edwin, Appendices, 439

Bonvisi, Antonio, friend of More and Fisher, 251 and n

Borenius, Dr. Tancred, 305n, 491

Borodale, Gawin, Abbot of Holm Cultram, one of Cromwell's tools, 181n

Bossuet, Jacques Bénigne, Bishop of Meaux, 305n, 435; Appendices, 444, 462

Boulogne, 83 and n, 84, 348n, 349, 424; Appendices, 475

Boulter, B. C., 306n

Bourbon, Cardinal, 54n

Bourbon, Constable of, 33n

Bourbon, Duke of, 43, 287n

Bourbon, Mary of, sister to Anthony of Navarre, 274-5n

Bourchier, Thomas, Primate of England, Archbishop of Canterbury (1454-86), and Cardinal (1464), 19 and n

Bourchier, Rev. T., 16th century writer, 135n, 212n

Bourges, University of, Appendices, 444

Bourrilly, W. L., and *Vaissière, P, de.* 45*n*, 77*n*; Appendices, 442, 465

Bowes, Sir Robert, 178*n*

Boxley (Kent), Rood of, 303

Boys, du, Appendices, 445

Boyneburg, George von, 413

Bracton, 13th century lawyer, 126*n*

Bradford, W., 116*n*

Bradsole, near Dover, St. Radegunde's Abbey at, 199*n*

Brady, W. Mazière, 137*n*

Brampton, C. K., 8*n**

Brancetor, Robert, 360*n**

Brandon, Charles, Duke of Suffolk, 47*n*

Brandt, W. J., 127*n*

Breakspear, Nicholas, Adrian IV, Pope (1154-59), 6*n*

Brereton, Sir William, 322

Brewer, J. S., 24*n*, 30, 45*n*, 48*n*, 56*n*, 126*n*, 153, 205*n*; Appendices, 439, 440, 441, 442, 451*, 463*

Brian (or Bryan), Sir Francis, cousin of Anne Boleyn, ambassador in Rome and in France, 55*n*, 66*n**, 72*n*, 78*n*, 106*n*, 347*n*, 360*n*

Bridewell Palace, London, 68 and *n*

Bridgett, Rev. T. E., C.SS.R., 17*n**, 18*n*, 19*n**, 96*n*, 202*n*, 206*n**, 223*n*, 226*n*, 247*n*, 384, 386*n**, Appendices, 450, 455*, 483

Bridgettines, The, 133

Bridgewater, Countess of (*see* Howard, Catherine)

Bridgewater, See of, 122*n*

Bridlington Abbey, 181

Brinklow, 30*n*

Bristol, Bishop of, 162*n*

Bristol, Prior of Dominicans at, 183*n*

Bristol, See of, 122*n*, 193*n*

British Museum, 41*n*, 85*n*, 88*n*, 103*n*, 107*n*, 109*n*, 161*n*, 219*n*, 319*n*, 335, 336*n**, 359*n*, 367*n*, 374, 384*n*, 408, 409, 423*n*; Appendices, 451, 457, 463

Brockhaus, H., 232*n*

Brodie, R. H., 255*n*; Appendices, 440, 442

Bromehall, Convent at, 143*n*, 155, 202*n*

Brooke, Z. N., 2*n**

Brownbill, J., 181

Browne, Anne, 53*n**

Browne, Sir Anthony, court steward, 190

Browne, George, Augustinian prior, Protestant Archbishop of Dublin, 84*n*, 131, 137, 184, 186*n*

Bruce, J., 212*n**, 217*n*, 234*n*

Brück, Councillor of John Frederick of Saxony, 298*n*

Bruges, 20*n*, 237*n*

Brunswick-Luneburg, Duke of, 110*n*, 309*n*

Brussels, 274*n*, 307, 344, 345

Bruton, 157

Buccleuch, Duke of, 326*n*

Bucer (or Butzer), Martin, Alsatian reformer (1491-1551), 335, 358, 366 and *n**, 373*n*, 374*n*, 389*n*

Buchanan, E. S., 34*n*

Buchardt (*see* Burchardus)

Bucholtz, 223*n*

Buckden, 412*n*

Buckingham, Duke of, 29*n*, 45 and *n**, 256*n*, 269

Bucklersbury, London, More's residence, 227

Buddensieg, R., 10*n**, 12*n*

Budée, secretary to Francis I; humanist; 227*n*, 228 and *n*, 232 and *n**, 237*n*, 344

Bugenhagen, John (or Pomeranus, from the name of his native country, Pomerania) (1485-1558), 335*, 336*n*, 401

Bullinger, John Henry, Swiss reformer (1504-75), 304*n*, 375, 383, 413 and *n*

Buonamici, Lazzaro, humanist (†1552), 257, 263

Burchardus (or Buchardt), Dr. Franz, Vice-chancellor of Saxony, 375, 379 and *n*, 398*n*, 400*n*, 401, 413

Burgh, 29*n*

Burgio, Nuncio in England, 82, 87;

Burgo, Nicholas de, 77*n*, 349

Burgoyn, visitor of the English monasteries, 163*n*, 164*n*

Burgundy, House of, 55*n*

Burke, Edmund, 162

Burn, R., 196*n*

Burnett, Gilbert, Protestant Bishop of Salisbury (1689-1715), xiii, 3*n*, 4*n*, 6*n*, 38*n**, 42*n*, 46*n*, 49*n*, 113, 152, 168*n**, 169*n*, 183*n*, 185*n*, 186, 193, 204, 231*n*, 263*n*, 270*n*, 284*n*, 321*n*, 368*n*, 375*, 379*n*, 404*n*, 417*n**, 425*n*; Appendices, 439, 444, 449, 462*, 463*

Burrow, 433n; Appendices, 461

Bury St. Edmunds, Abbot and monastery of, 160n

Busch, W., 7n; Appendices, 445, 467

Bush, Paul, Bishop of Bristol (1542-53), 162n

Bush, Thomas, 288n

Busleyden (or Buisleiden), Jerome, Provost of Aire, 232n

Butler, Charles, Catholic historian, 393, 421; Appendices, 461

Butler, F. T., 186n

Butler, James, Irish chieftain, 48, 49n*

Butts, Sir William, physician to Henry VIII, 338n

Buxton (Derby), 304

Bywater, J., 374n

C

Cabrol, Dom, O.S.B., 305n

Caistor (Lincs), 172

Cajetan, Thomas, Cardinal (1469-1534), 80 and n; Appendices, 472

Calais, 107n, 116* and n, 120*, 218, 236n, 237n, 268, 270n, 275n, 277, 380, 396

Calebaut, A., 158n

Caledon, Countess of, 300n

Caligula, 20n

Calshot, 277

Calvin, 325n, 369, 389n

Camber, 277

Cambrai (Treaty of, 1529; Meeting at, 1530), 82, 106, 109 and n, 114, 119, 237n, 268 and n, 346

Cambridge, 143, 155n, 202*, 329, 342 and n, 344, 369n, 370n, 374, 389n, 398n

Cambridge, Michael House, 201*

Cambridge, See of, 122n

Cambridge, University of, 69n, 76 and n, 78n, 130 and n*, 157, 196, 201, 201 and n, 202* and n*, 220n, 301n, 302 and n, 306n, 317*, 318*, 319, 376n, 410n

Cambridgeshire, 157

Camlan, Battle of (537), 304n

Camm, Dom Bede, O.S.B., 132n, 134n, 135n*; Appendices, 451

Campbell, Lord, 213n, 217 and n, 247, 298; Appendices, 454

Campbell, W. E., More's English works edited by, 230n, 231n, 234n, 251n

Campeggio, Lorenzo, Bishop of Salisbury (1524-34), Cardinal (1474-

1539), 7n, 14 and n, 22 and n, 33 and n, 46n, 54n, 59, 60* and n*, 61* and n, 62* and n, 63 and n*, 64 and n*, 65 and n, 66* and n, 67n*, 68, 69 and n, 70 and n*, 72 and n*, 75n, 80n, 84n, 93n, 111, 150, 204, 208n, 273n, 346, 347, 350n; Appendices, 442, 469, 471, 473, 474

Camusat, 83n

Canons Regular, The (*see* The Gilbertines)

Canterbury, 2n, 18, 28n, 32, 84, 97, 104, 111*, 124, 131n, 132n, 209 and n, 210 and n, 212n, 304, 314n, 330, 332, 337n

Canterbury, Archbishop of, 35n, 37n, 39, 53, 75, 79, 81 and n, 82, 84n*, 87n, 88n, 93n*, 95, 98n, 113* and n, 136 and n, 143, 203, 209n, 214, 223, 242*, 285, 293n, 317n, 330, 331n, 338, 345, 426n; Appendices, 474

Canterbury, Archdeacon of, 317, 398

Canterbury, Franciscan House at, 133n

Canterbury, See of, 208n, 338n, 354, 398n; Appendices, 471

Cape, W., 9n

Capharnaum, 366

Capito, Wolfgang, Alsatian reformer (1478-1541), 358

Capon, Dr. John, Bishop of Bangor and of Salisbury (*see* Salcot)

Capranica, residence of the Farnese, 259n

Caraffa, Giovanni Pietro (†1559) (*see also* Paul IV), 76n, 266n, 267n, 273n; Appendices, 470, 477-78*

Cardon, Abbé A., Appendices, 450

Cardwell, Edward, 336n; Appendices, 461, 465

Carini, 113n

Carles, Lancelot de, secretary to Bishop of Tarbes, 48n, 50n, 134n

Carlisle, 180, 277

Carlisle, Bishop of, 97n, 374n, 417n

Carlisle, Earl of, Appendices, 447

Carlyle, R. W. and *A. J.*, 3n

Carmelites, The, 148n*

Carne, Dr. Edward, agent of Henry VIII in Rome, 81n, 82, 83n*, 110n; Appendices, 472*

Carnesecchi, secretary to Clement VII, 105n*, 108n

Carpentras (Italy), 263, 279, 283

Carpi, Pio Rodolpho di, Bishop of Faenza (1528-44), and of Girgenti (1546-64), Cardinal (1536), Papal Nuncio in France (1535-37), 221n, 387n

Carroz (or Caroz), Luis, Spanish ambassador, 41n, 43n

Carter, Thomas, Abbot of Holm Cultram, 181n

Carthusians, The, 127n, 129n, 133, 135 and n*, 136n*, 154n, 197n, 217n, 251, 257, 295, 359, 362, 396

Casale, Sir Gregory, Henry VIII's Italian agent to the Holy See, 46n, 56n, 57n*, 58n*, 75n, 82, 256n*

Castello, Adrian di, Bishop of Bath, 37n*

Castelnau, Anthony de, Bishop of Tarbes (1534-39), Francis I's ambassador in England (1534-37), and in Spain (1538-39), where he died, 281

Castile, 35, 36n, 37n, 345 and n

Castillon, Francis I's ambassador to Henry VIII (1533-34 and 1537-39), 108 and n*, 109, 120n, 139n, 246, 275, 276*, 413n, 414n; Appendices, 445

Castle St. Angelo (see Angelo)

Catesby (Northumberland), Convent of, 163* and n

Catesby (Northumberland), Prioress of, 299n

Catherine of Aragon, 6n, 21n, 32n, 34, 35* and n*, 36* and n*, 37* and n*, 38, 39 and n*, 40n, 42, 43, 44, 45n, 47* and n*, 51n, 52 and n*, 53 and n, 54n, 58n, 61n, 63 and n, 64*, 65, 66, 67* and n, 68n*, 69 and n, 80 and n, 81 and n, 82, 83 and n*, 84, 87*, 88 and n, 89n*, 104n, 108, 109, 110n, 111, 114* and n*, 115n*, 116 and n, 117, 118 and n, 132n*, 150n, 204* and n, 206, 208 and n, 209, 212n, 214* and n, 257n, 261, 264n, 306n, 320n, 321*, 322* and n, 329, 349*, 350, 351*, 394n*, 395*, 396n, 400, 412* and n; Appendices, 442*, 44 3,, 446*, 469, 470, 471, 472, 473* 474, 475, 476, 477, 480, 481

Cavendish, George, Wolsey's gentleman-usher and biographer, 52n, 56n,

66n, 67n, 74, 75n, 289 and n, 290n; Appendices, 446, 457

Cecil, 31n

Cerdagne, 36n

Cervia, 61n

Cervini, Marcello, afterwards Pope Marcellus II (1555), q.v., 284n, 314n, 340n, 421, 434

Chabed, F., Italian writer, 261n

Chabot de Brion, Philip, Admiral of France, 121n, 396n

Chacon - Oldoin, Chacon (Ciaconius), O.P. (†1602), 56n, 223n*; Appendices, 451*

Chalcedon, Bishop of, 137n

Chalcedon, Council of, 404

Chamberlaine, J., Appendices, 441

Chamberlin, Frederick, 40n; Appendices, 441

Chambers, John, Bishop of Peterborough (1541-56), 162n

Chambers, Professor R. W., 230n, 231n*, 234n, 248n; Appendices, 452*, 453*

Chandler, R., 143n

Chandlery, P. S., S.J., 134n

Chapuys, Eustache, Charles V's ambassador in England (from 1529), 14, 25, 32n, 56n, 73n, 74n, 84n, 85n, 86, 93, 96 and n*, 97* and n*, 99n, 104, 111, 112n, 115n, 118 and n, 120* and n, 122n, 123, 125, 150, 151*, 158, 159, 160, 166n, 170, 177n, 207 and n, 208, 213n, 214n, 218n, 219n, 221n, 238*, 239, 262n, 264n, 266n, 285n, 286, 291, 294, 300, 319n, 321, 322, 324n, 350n, 364n, 365, 379n, 396; Appendices, 457*

Charbonnel, J. R., 297n

Charles, Infante, Catherine of Aragon's nephew, 39n

Charles I, King of England, 122n, 186n, 192n

Charles II, King of England (1630-85), 13n; Appendices, 444, 463

Charles V, Emperor, 4*, 5*, 6n, 7, 21n, 32n, 40n, 46n, 47n*, 54n, 58, 61 and n, 80 and n*, 83, 84n, 97, 109, 110 and n, 114* and n, 115* and n*, 116* and n*, 117 and n, 118 and n, 119, 120, 207, 238, 254, 255n, 256, 260, 264n, 268 and n, 273, 274 and n, 275*, 276, 278*, 279, 280*, 281*, 287 and n, 300,

301, 309*, 310n, 311, 312n, 319*, 320 and n*, 321, 326n, 343, 345* and n, 346n, 350n, 358, 360* and n*, 368n, 375, 395*, 396n, 411n, 412*, 413 and n, 424*; Appendices, 473*, 474*, 475, 479

Charles VI, King of France, 126n

Charles VIII, King of France, 36n, 39n

Charterhouse, The—
 Axholme, 135n
 Beauvale, 135n
 Coventry, 135n, 197n
 Hinton, 135n, 183n, 196n
 Hull, 135n
 Kinalkin, 136n
 London, 133, 135n, 183n*, 197n, 225n
 Mountgrace, 136n, 196n
 Perth, 136n
 Sheen, 136n, 197n, 209n, 257, 260, 261
 Witham, 135n, 197n

Chartres, Duchess of, 55n

Chauncy, Maurice, Carthusian, 129n, 135n*, 220n; Appendices, 452

Cheke, Sir John, Professor at Cambridge, tutor to Edward VI, and his secretary of State, 374n*

Chelsea, More's residence, 227, 228 233, 237, 239 and n*, 244, 246; Appendices, 452

Chelsea Parish Church, 226

Chelsea, More's tomb at, Appendices, 453

Cheney, A. D., 209n

Cheney, C. R., 154n*

Chertsey (Surrey), Benedictine Abbot of, 182

Cheshire, 178n

Chester, 345

Chester, Bishop of, 137n

Chester, Earldom of, 36n

Chester, See of, 193n

Chester, J. L., 388n

Chesterton, G. K., 156n*

Chetham, Thomas, Bishop of Sidon, 137n

Cheyne, Baron, 29n

Cheyney, Sir Thomas, Treasurer of the Royal Household and Governor of the Cinque Ports, 190n

Chichele (or Chicheley), Henry, Archbishop of Canterbury (1414-43), 3 and n, 93n, 143

Chichester, 304, 352*, 363, 387n; Appendices, 453·

Chichester, Bishop of, 19n*, 38n, 86n, 111, 264n, 313, 363, 373n, 379, 380

Chieregato, Francesco, nuncio, 42 (quotation).

Chièvres, Lord of (see Croy, William of)

Child, G. W., 298n

Chitty, Herbert, 22n, 194n

Christchurch (Hants), 272

Christ Church College, Oxford (see also Oxford, Wolsey's College at), 74n, 144n, 348

Christian III, King of Denmark (†1559), 274n

Christie, Donald Benedict, 135n

Christina of Denmark, Duchess of Milan, widow of Francis Sforza (1535), niece of Charles V (1523-90), 274* and n*, 310-11, 412

Christ's College, Cambridge, 202 and n*, 205n

Cibo, Cardinal, 34n

Cifuentes, 107n, 190

Cinque Ports, The, 109n

Cirencester (Glos), 157

Cistercians, The, 168n; Appendices, 449

Cistercian Monasteries, The, 155n

Cistercian Nuns, 170n

Clarence, George, Duke of, brother to Edward IV (†1478), 44n, 257n

Clarendon Constitutions, 2 and n*

Clarke, T. E. S., Appendices 463

Claude, Queen of France, Francis I's first wife, 48 and n*

Clement V, Pope (1305-14), 142n

Clement VII, Pope (1523-34), 4, 5* and n, 6 and n*, 8n, 33n, 34, 53n, 54n, 55n, 56n*, 57, 58n, 59 and n*, 60, 61n*, 62n, 63, 64, 65 and n, 66n, 70 and n, 71 and n, 78 and n*, 79*, 81n*, 83n, 84, 85, 89 and n, 92n, 94n, 98, 105*, 106*, 107 and n, 109 and n, 116, 118, 144n, 145, 168n, 205, 214, 320n, 324, 329n, 342, 346* and n, 347, 350, 351, 354, 385n, 396, 398; Appendices, 442, 444, 469*, 470, 471*, 472*, 474, 475*, 478*, 479*

Clements, John, married Sir Thomas More's adopted daughter, Margaret Gigey or Gigs (for this Margaret see Gigey), 228n; Appendices, 454*

Cleopatra, 20n

Clerk, John, ambassador to Rome, Bishop of Bath and Wells (1523-41), 103, 144n, 208n, 240n, 350, 373n, 399n, 417n

Cleveland (Yorks), 177

Cleves, Anne of (see Anne)

Cleves, Duke of, 310n*, 311n, 312n, 326

Clifford, H., 135n

Clinton, Lord, 190

"Cloth of Gold, Field of," 40 and n, 41n, 237n, 343

Cluniac Order, The, 142n

Cobb, Thomas, estate agent to Archbishop Warham, 209

Cobham, Lord, 89n, 149

Cochlæus (real name, Dobneck), John, humanist and Catholic controversialist, 42n, 222n, 232, 254n; Appendices, 476

Cockerel, James, Prior of Gisborough, 181n

Cockermouth (Cumb.), 175n

Cocks (or Cox), Dr. Richard, 425n, 429n

Colchester, Benedictine Abbot of, 185, 296

Colchester, Bishop of, 162n, 183n

Colchester, See of, 122n

Colet, Dr. John, Dean of St. Paul's, humanist (1466-1519), 17, 18n*, 223n, 226 and n, 230n, 232, 260n*, 344

Collette, C. H., Appendices, 458

Collier, Jeremy, dissenting minister (1650-1726), 34n, 38n*, 402n; Appendices, 439, 448

Collins, burnt as a heretic (1540), 422n

Cologne, 345, 397n

Colt, Jane, Sir Thomas More's wife (see More, Jane)

Colt, Thomas More's father-in-law, 226

Commons (See House of Commons)

Como, Cardinal of, 4n

Compiègne, 55n, 56n

Compton, Sir William, Earl of Northampton, 291; Appendices, 447

Constable, Sir John, 179n

Constable, Sir Robert, 177, 178n, 179 and n, 180*, 181n

Constable, Sir William, 179n

Constance, Council of, 353, 383

Constant, G., 10n, 16n, 19n, 35n, 366n; Appendices, 441, 457*

Constantine, Emperor, 98n

Constantinople, Council of, 404

Contarini, Gasparo, Cardinal (1483-1542), 263, 264n, 265n*, 266n, 267n, 273 and n, 283, 362-3, 419n, 432n, 435n

Convocation, 22, 23, 24, 26, 31n, 32* and n, 82, 86, 88, 94*, 95 and n, 97*, 99n, 100* and n, 101, 102, 103 and n, 122, 124n, 128*, 130* and n, 136n, 204, 207 and n*, 208, 212, 238, 263n, 297, 301, 302n, 306*, 314n, 325, 326 and n, 332, 333*, 335*, 339, 349 and n, 350, 353 and n*, 361, 375, 376n, 382, 391*, 392, 407 and n, 409, 410 and n, 421, 428, 431*, 432

Conyers, Lord, 179n

Cook, Hugh (also called Faringdon), last abbot of Reading, 387

Cooper, C. H., Appendices, 460

Copland, Robert, 16th century writer, 195

Corcoran, T., 22n

Corneto, 60

Cornwall, 36n

Cornwallis, Mrs., 190 n

Corpus Christi College, Cambridge, 389n, 410n

Corsini Library, Rome, Appendices, 444

Cortese, Gregorio, O.S.B., native of Modena, Abbot of San Giorgio Maggiore in Venice (†1547), 263, 266n

Costanzi, V. A., 263n

Cotton Library, 162n

Coulton, G. G., 19n, 155n*, 156n*; Appendices, 449, 467

Courayer, Le, 42n

Courtenay, Catherine, mother of Henry Courtenay, Edward IV's daughter, 269n

Courtenay, Sir Edward, Earl of Devonshire, son of Henry Courtenay 270n

Courtenay, Lord Henry (see Exeter, Marquis of)

Courtenay, Hugh de, married Edward I's grand-daughter, 269n

Courtney, Archbishop, 13n

"Court of Augmentation," The, 168, 169 and n, 173, 185n, 186, 190n, 194n

Coventry, Bishop of, 215, 308*n*

Coventry, Charterhouse of, 135*n*, 197*n*

Coventry, See of, 111, 161*n*, 208*n*

Coverdale, Miles, Bishop of Exeter (1551-53), 306* and *n**, 307*n**, 318*n*, 382; Appendices, 480

Cox, Dr. Richard (*see* Cocks)

Cox, editor of "Remains of Cranmer," 134*n*; Appendices, 458

Coxford, Priory of, 299*n*

Cram, P. P. (*see Witney* and *Cram*)

Cranage, Rev. D. H. S., Appendices, 448

Cranmer, Edmund, youngest brother of Thomas Cranmer, 317*

Cranmer, Thomas, Archbishop of Canterbury (1533-56), 7, 11, 50 and *n*, 75* and *n*, 76*n**, 77*n*, 81*n*, 84*n*, 85* and *n**, 86, 87* and *n**, 88 and *n**, 89 and *n*, 93*n*, 104, 111*n**, 123, 124 and *n*, 129, 130 and *n*, 131*n*, 134*n*, 137*n*, 138*n*, 160*n*, 167*n*, 208, 210*n**, 214*n*, 215*, 242, 243, 262*n**, 285, 286, 301*, 306, 308 and *n**, 312, 313, 316*, 316, 317* and *n*, 318*, 319*, 320* and *n**, 321* and *n*, 324* and *n*, 325* and *n**, 326 and *n*, 328, 329* and *n**, 330 and *n*, 331*, 332* and *n*, 333*, 334* and *n**, 335* and *n**, 336 and *n**, 337*, 338* and *n**, 339*, 340*, 341* and *n*, 349* and *n*, 351, 354, 366*n*, 373*n*, 374*, 375*, 376*n*, 377* and *n*, 379, 380, 399*n*, 404, 408* and *n*, 409*n*, 410*n**, 417*n**, 418, 421*, 422, 425, 426*, 427* and *n*, 431, 435; Appendices, 458*, 459*, 466, 471, 472, 475*, 482

Crapelet, G. A., 48*n**, 49*n*, 50*n*

Creighton, 5*n*, 20*n*, 155*n*, 287*n*

Croke, Dr. Richard, 76* and *n*, 319; Appendices, 478*

Cresacre, Anne, daughter-in-law of Sir Thomas More (*see* More, Anne)

Cressy of Waltham, 75, 318*

Crome, Dr. Edward, preacher, said to be of the advanced party, 98*n**, 318*n*, 382, 422*n*

Cromwell, Gregory, son of Thomas Cromwell, 286

Cromwell, Mrs., wife of Gregory Cromwell, 299

Cromwell, Oliver, the Protector, 190, 286

Cromwell, Richard, Thos. Cromwell's nephew (*see* Williams, Richard)

Cromwell, Robert, cousin of Thomas Cromwell, 287*n*

Cromwell, Thomas, 1, 27 and *n**, 28 and *n**, 31*n*, 73 and *n*, 75*n**, 85, 90 and *n*, 92*n*, 96*n*, 99, 100*n*, 101*n**, 102*n*, 110, 111*n*, 121*n*, 124*n*, 126, 127*n*, 130*n*, 133* and *n*, 134*n*, 135*n*, 136 and *n**, 139 and *n**, 141, 147*, 150* and *n*, 152, 153, 155, 156* and *n*, 157* and *n**, 158, 159* and *n*, 160* and *n**, 161*n*, 163* and *n*, 164*, 165 and *n**, 166*n*, 170, 172, 173 and *n*, 176 and *n*, 177*n*, 181 and *n*, 183 and *n**, 184*n**, 185*n**, 186*n*, 188*, 190 and *n*, 192 and *n*, 203*n*, 210*n**, 211*n*, 212* and *n**, 213* and *n**, 215, 217, 218*n*, 219, 222, 240 and *n**, 242*, 243*, 245, 246* and *n*, 247, 254*n*, 260*, 261*n**, 266 and *n*, 267, 270*, 271, 272 and *n*, 285*, 286*, 287 and *n*, 288* and *n*, 289* and *n*, 290* and *n**, 291*, 292*, 293* and *n*, 294*, 295* and *n**, 296* and *n*, 297 and *n**, 298* and *n*, 299* and *n**, 300 and *n*, 301* and *n*, 302* and *n**, 303, 305*n*, 306* and *n*, 307 and *n**, 308* and *n**, 309* and *n**, 310 and *n**, 311* and *n**, 312* and *n**, 313*, 314 and *n**, 315, 316* and *n**, 317*n*, 319, 323, 325, 329*n*, 331*, 332*, 333, 334, 335 and *n*, 336 and *n**, 338*, 339 and *n*, 340 and *n*, 343*n*, 344, 352 and *n*, 353, 354 and *n*, 360*n**, 361*n*, 363, 364, 365, 368*n**, 373, 374, 375*, 377* and *n**, 378* and *n**, 379*, 380*, 381* and *n**, 384*n*, 392, 397* and *n*, 401*n*, 403, 407*n*, 409*n**, 412, 417 and *n**, 418, 422 and *n**, 424* and *n*, 432*; Appendices, 454, 457*, 458*, 482

Cromwell, Walter, father of Thomas Cromwell, 285 and *n**

Cronin, H. S., 9*n*

Crosby Place, London, More's residence, 227

Crowland (or Croyland) (Lincs), 299

Crowley, 30*n*

Croy, Robert de, Bishop of Cambria (†1556), 268

Croy, William of, Lord of Chièvres, 54*n*

Croydon, Vicar of, 242*

Cruse, H., 231n

Cruziger (Creuciger or Creutzinger), Gaspar, humanist and Lutheran Reformer (1504-48), 401

Cumberland, 28n, 175 and n*, 180

Cumberland, Duke of, 181n

Cunningham, 151n

Curia, The Roman, 58n, 67, 78n, 87 and n, 99, 112, 294, 351

Curwen, Richard, court chaplain, 132n*

Cuthbert, Father, O.S.F.C., 133n

D

Darcy of Templehurst, Lord Thomas, Baron, 29n, 118, 171, 176, 177* and n*, 179* and n, 180*, 181n

Dark, Sidney, 305n

Darvel Gadarn (or Gathern), wooden statue, 303, 304n

Dasent, J. R., Appendices, 465

Daubeny, Giles, first Baron, Governor of Calais, 29n

Daunce (or Daunsey), William, Sir Thomas More's son-in-law, 227

Dauphin of France, 45n*, 46n*, 51 and n, 52n, 345 and n, 396

Davanzati, Bernardo, Appendices, 444

Davenham (Cheshire), 343n

Davey, R., 423n

Davidson, Archbishop, 129n

Davies, G. S., 135n

Day, Dr. George, Bishop of Chichester (1543-56), 425n, 429n

Deane, Canon A. C., Appendices, 459

Deans, R. Story, Appendices, 446

Decio, Filippo (†1535), Appendices, 472

"Defender of the Faith," 33, 89, 126, 385 and n

Delaruelle, French writer, 232n*

Deley, Miss A., 2n

Demaus, Rev. R., 307n

Denmark, 116n, 335, 359, 360n

Denmark, King of, 274n, 377n

Denonville, C., Bishop of Macon and ambassador to Paul III, 108n, 218n

Derby, Countess of (Lady Edward Stanley), 212

Derbyshire, 178n

Dering, John, O.S.B., 212n

Dermenghem, E., French writer, 231n

Devonshire, Earl of, Edward IV's grandson, 45n

Dibdin, Sir Lewis, 96n, 126n; Appendices, 467

Dietz, C., 189n

Dinteville, John de, Sieur of Polizi, Bailly of Troyes, Francis I's ambassador to Henry VIII, 105n, 396n

Dixon, Richard Watson, Canon of Carlisle, 98n, 99n, 123n, 125n, 148n, 153, 155n, 158n, 162n, 168n*, 368n, 402n, 414n, 422n; Appendices, 439, 449, 464*

Dixon, W. H., Appendices, 445

Dodd, Charles, Catholic historian, 4n, 18n, 38n, 40n, 49n, 167 and n; Appendices, 439, 445, 456*, 457*, 462, 463

Dodds, M. H. and R., 171n

Dodieu, Claude, Lord of Vely, Bishop of Rennes (1672-1743); afterwards ambassador to Charles V, 52n

Dodu, G., 126n

Dolman, 251n

Dominicans, The, 19, 131n, 148n; (German) 154n; 181n, 183n

Doncaster (Yorks), 177, 179

Doreau, V. M., 135n

Dorpius (or Dorp), Martin van, Dutch humanist, Professor at Louvain, 224 and n*, 230n, 233n

Dorset (Thomas Grey, Lord Ferrers), first Marquis of, 29n

Douai, 253n; Appendices, 439, 453, 457*

Douai, English college at, Appendices, 456*

Dover, 2n, 199n, 277*

Dover, See of, 122n

Dover, Suffragan Bishop of, 164n, 184

Doyle-Davidson, 230n

Drake, xi

Dreux, A., 52n

Du Bellay, Jean, Bishop of Paris (1532-†1560), Cardinal (1536), 13, 52n, 53n*, 71n*, 72 and n, 75 and n, 91, 108* and n*, 109* and n*, 110n*, 114n, 117n, 119, 204n, 256n; Appendices, 442

Dublin, Archbishop of, 147 and n, 186n

Dubois, Peter, Norman legist in the time of Philip the Handsome, 127n*

Duchesne, André, 17th century historian, 400n, 402n, 421n, 434n

Dudley, John, Lord Lisle, 191n

Dugdale, Sir William, 142*n*, 148*n*, 183*n*; Appendices, 448

Dunn, Waldo H., Appendices, 468

Dunstable (Bucks), 87 and *n*, 351

Dupuys, Pierre, 126*n*

Durham, 97, 111, 175*n*, 180, 304 and *n*, 350, 351

Durham, Bishop of, 20*n**, 21*n*, 88*n*, 97, 233*n*, 239*n*, 240*n*, 265*n*, 267*n*, 341, 417*n*, 425*n*; Appendices, 450

Durham, Chapter Library, 197*n*

Durham, Monastery of, 185*n*

Durham, Prior of, 299*n*

Durham, See of, 208*n*

Dykes, D. Oswald, 134*n*

Dynham, Baron, 29*n*

Dziewicki, 10*n**

E

East Durham (Norfolk), 351

Eck, John, 414*n*

Eden, Richard, 342*n**

Edward I, King of England (1272-1307), 2*n*, 47, 142 and *n*

Edward II, King of England (1307-27), 96*n*, 142 and *n**

Edward III, King of England (1327-77), 3, 4*n*, 44*n**, 45 and *n*, 93*n*, 142* and *n**, 325 and *n*

Edward IV, King of England (1461-83), 45*n**, 212*n*, 257*n*, 269 and *n*, 270*n*

Edward VI, King of England (1547-53), 13*n*, (birth of) 46*n*, 47*n*, 112*n*, 124*n**, 189 and *n*, 194*n*, 228*n*, 261*n*, 267*n*, 270*n*, 271*n*, 294*n*, 306*n*, 325 and *n**, 328, 335, 336*n*, 340, 342*n*, 358*n*, 362*n*, 366*n*, 389*, 390*n*, 393, 394, 398*n*, 415, 416 and *n*, 423 and *n*, 431, 433*, 434*n*; Appendices, 461, 466

Ehses, Mgr. Stephen, 5*n*, 14*n*, 22*n*, 33*n*, 58*n*; Appendices, 442

Einstein, L., Appendices, 467

Elizabeth, Henry VIII's daughter, Queen of England (1558-1603), 13*n*, 50*n*, 88, 111*n*, 112*n*, 113*n*, 118, 122*n**, 124*n*, 125*n**, 128, 132, 134*n**, 138, 165 and *n*, 195 and *n*, 198, 228*n*, 270*n*, 271*n*, 325 and *n*, 328, 346, 351, 366*n*, 370*n*, 371 and *n**, 372*n**, 389, 393, 396, 407, 416, 433, 435; Appendices, 443, 444*, 453, 477

Elizabeth of Bavaria, mother of Philip of Bavaria, 416*n*

Elizabeth of York, daughter of Edward IV, first wife of Henry VII (†1503), 45*n*, 269*n*

Ellerker, Sir Ralph, 178*n*, 179*n*, 180 and *n*

Ellerkar, William, 176*n*

Ellis, Henry, Editor of "Original Letters," 36*n*, 50*n*, 287*n*

Ellis, John Tracy, 3*n*

Elstow, Henry, guardian of the Franciscan House at Greenwich, 132 and *n*, 133*n*

Elvira, Council of, Appendices, 475

Ely, 320*n*

Ely, Bishop of, 143, 154, 207, 271, 317, 334, 373*n*, 417*n*

Ely, See of, 111, 208*n*

Elyot, Sir Thomas, ambassador in Germany (†1546), 255*n**, 317, 319, 320*n*

Emerton, 233*n*

England, 27, 31*, 32, 35, 36*n**, 37*n*, 38*n**, 42*n*, 44, 51*n*, 54*n**, 55*n**, 56*n*, 57, 58*, 60* and *n*, 61*n**, 62, 65*n*, 66*n*, 67*n*, 68*, 70, 71*n**, 72, 75*n**, 78, 81 and *n*, 82 and *n*, 89 and *n*, 91, 93*n**, 94*n*, 95, 98, 104*n*, 105* and *n*, 106*n*, 108, 109, 110*n*, 111*n*, 112*n*, 113 and *n**, 114*, 115 and *n**, 116*n*, 118 and *n*, 119, 120 and *n*, 130* and *n**, 131, 133, 135*n*, 139, 141, 143*, 144, 147*, 154*n*, 160 and *n*, 169, 171, 172, 176, 177, 182, 184, 186 and *n*, 192, 195*, 196*, 198*, 200, 201, 205 and *n*, 206*n*, 218, 222*n*, 229, 232, 233, 237* and *n*, 238*n*, 249, 252*n*, 253, 255* and *n*, 256, 258, 259*n*, 260, 261, 262, 264*, 265 and *n*, 266*, 267*, 268*, 269, 271 and *n*, 272, 273*, 274 and *n*, 275* and *n*, 276, 277, 278*, 280*, 281*, 282*n*, 283*, 287*n*, 290, 291, 292*, 293 and *n*, 301, 307, 308, 309*, 310, 315, 318*n*, 319, 320*n*, 322, 325, 333, 334, 335, 340*n*, 342, 344, 345 and *n*, 346*n*, 348, and *n*, 350, 351, 352, 354*, 363*n*, 367*, 368 and *n*, 372 and *n*, 375*, 377, 380, 383, 384, 388 and *n*, 393, 395*, 396*, 397, 398, 399, 401 and *n*, 412, 413, 419*n*, 421, 424*n*, 435 and *n*; Appendices, 443, 469, 470, 471*, 473, 474, 475, 476*

Enthoven, Marion, 261*n*

Ephesus, Council of, 404

Erasmus, 15 and *n*, 16 and *n*, 17 and *n**, 18 and *n*, 42 and *n**, 73*n*, 202, 203*, 224* and *n**, 225 and *n**, 226*, 227* and *n*, 228* and *n*, 229*, 230*n*, 232* and *n**, 233* and *n**, 234 and *n**, 235, 237*n**, 251, 252*n*, 254, 257, 258*n*, 305*n*, 317, 342 and *n**, 343*, 344*; 365, 385; Appendices, 453, 454

Ercole, F., French writer, 261*n**

Erfurt, 398 and *n*

Erlangen, University of, 231*n*

Ermland, Bishop of, 257

Esher, 289, 353

Essex, County of, 157, 185

Essex, Cromwell, Earl of, 298, 313, 380

Essex, Earl of, 132*n*

Estcourt, Canon, Appendices, 457

Este, Hercule II d', Duke of Ferrara (†1559), 55*n*

Estrada, Duke of, Spanish ambassador, 37*n**, 38*n*

Evans, G., Appendices, 460

Evenwett, H. O., Appendices, 449

Evers, Sir Ralph, 180*n*

Exeter, 131, 360

Exeter, Bishop of, 20*n*, 151*n*, 239*n*, 306*n*, 321*n*, 410*n*

Exeter, Marquis of, 29*n*, 118 and *n*, 177, 212* and *n*, 269*, 270* and *n**

Exeter, Reginald Pole, Dean of, 260, 262, 263*n*

Exeter, Marchioness of, 270

Exmew, William, Carthusian, 154*n*

Eyre, Ch., 304*n*

F

Fairfax, Sir Nicholas, 179*n*

Fairfax, Sir William, 179*n*, 181

Fairon, E., 268*n*

Falieri, Venetian ambassador in London (1528-31), 7*n*, 21*n*, 37*n*, 40, 43*n*, 44 (quotation), 46*n*, 68*n*, 82*n*

Fano (Italy), Bishop of, 263

Farnese, Alessandro, nephew of Paul III and his secretary of state; Cardinal (1520-89), 281, 413*n*, 421

Faversham, Abbot of, 184*n*

Fawell, William, Bishop of Hippo, 137*n*

Ferdinand I, brother of Charles V,

King of the Romans, afterwards Emperor, 80*n*, 109*n*

Ferdinand V, the Catholic (1479-1516), 35*, 36 and *n**, 37*n**, 38 and *n**, 39 and *n*, 41*n**, 43*n*, 44*n*, 47*n**; Appendices, 476

Fernandez, Diego, Confessor to Catherine of Aragon, 42, 43*n*

Feron, Robert, Vicar of Teddington, 134*n*

Ferrajoli, Al, 263*n*

Ferrara, 269

Ferrara, Duchess of, 55

Ferrara, Duke of, 55*n*

Ferrara, University of, 77

Fetherstone (or Featherstone), Richard, chaplain to Catherine of Aragon and tutor to Princess Mary (†1540), 394*n*

Feuter, Ed., 42*n*; Appendices, 468

Fiddes, R., 143*n*, 146; Appendices, 446

Fiedler, 116*n*

Field of Cloth of Gold (*see* Cloth of Gold)

Fink, C., German writer, 231*n*

Firth, C. H., Appendices, 463

Fish, Simon, 149 and *n**, 234, 365, 369

Fisher, John, Cardinal, and Bishop of Rochester, 20*n*, 22, 69 and *n**, 92, 97*n*, 111, 118, 129, 136*n*, 138, 143 and *n**, 155*n*, 157*n**, 175 and *n*, 200* and *n**, 201* and *n**, 202* and *n**, 203*, 204* and *n**, 205* and *n*, 206* and *n**, 207 and *n**, 208 and *n**, 209 and *n**, 212* and *n*, 213, 214* and *n**, 215* and *n*, 216*, 217* and *n**, 218* and *n**, 219* and *n**, 220, 221*n**, 222 and *n**, 223 and *n**, 242, 245, 246 and *n*, 248*, 251*n**, 253* and *n*, 254 and *n*, 255 and *n**, 256*, 264*n*, 284, 295, 296, 302 and *n*, 329*n*, 361, 363, 387, 396; Appendices, 442, 449, 450*, 451*, 454, 455*, 475

Fisher, H. A. L., 6*n*, 13*n*, 25*n*, 31*n*, 48*n*, 148*n*, 168*n*, 402*n*; Appendices, 440, 449

Fisher, Robert, brother to Cardinal Fisher, 215*n*

Fitzgerald, Thomas, son of Earl of Kildare, 115*n**

Fitzjames, Richard, Bishop of London (1506-22), 18*n*

Fitzroy, Sir Almeric, Appendices, 465

Fitzwilliam, William, Earl of Southampton; Admiral of England; Lord Privy Seal; cousin of Anne Boleyn, 55*n*, 68, 271*, 314*n*

Flach, F., French writer, 231*n*

Flaminio, Marcantonio, humanist (†1550), 257, 263

Flanders, 114, 115, 116, 119* and *n*, 120* and *n*, 204, 236, 268* and *n*, 271*n*, 273*n*, 282 and *n**, 301*n*, 307*n*, 309, 311, 355*n*

Fletcher, J. S., 171*n*; Appendices, 449

Flodden Field, Battle of, 344*n*

Florence, 279

Florence, Council of (1439), 383, 384*n**

Floud, Sir Francis L. C., 192*n*

Floyer, J. K., Appendices, 449

Foix, John, Count of, Appendices 476*

Foley, editor of English Jesuits' *Records*, 269*n*

Foligno, 56*n*

Forest, John, Franciscan; Confessor to Catherine of Aragon; executed for denying royal supremacy, 132 and *n**, 136*n*, 304, 387

Fortescue, 44*n*

Fountains Abbey (Yorks), 181*n*

Fourier, 231*n*

Fowler, R. C., 154*n*

Fox, Richard, secretary to Henry VII (1485-87); Keeper of the Privy Seal, Bishop of Bath and Wells (1492-94), of Durham (1494-1501), and of Winchester (1501-28), 37*n*, 39 and *n*, 53*n*, 151*n*, 155*n*, 348*n*

Foxcroft, Miss H. C., Appendices, 463

Foxe (or Fox), Edward, King's Chaplain; Provost of King's College, Cambridge; Bishop of Hereford (1535-38), 58, 59*n*, 63*n*, 71*n*, 75*, 76 and *n*, 77*n*, 256*n*, 261* and *n*, 318*, 334, 347 and *n*, 348*n*, 349, 355*n*, 373*n*, 398, 399 and *n*, 402 and *n*, 404, 427*n*

Foxe, John, martyrologist (1517-87), 12*n*, 28*n*, 102*n*, 252*n*, 301, 328*n**, 335*n*, 336*n*, 337*n*, 338*n*, 342, 359*n**, 365, 367*n*, 369, 370* and *n**, 371*n**, 372* and *n**, 377*n*, 378*n*, 380*n*, 382*n*, 410*n*, 418*n*, 422*n*, 423*n*; Appendices, 439, 458*, 461, 463, 464, 466

Fraikin, J., 33*n*, 45*n*

France, 21*n**, 29*n*, 33*n*, 39*n**, 43, 47*n**, 48 and *n**, 49, 51*n*, 54*n**, 55*n*, 60, 61*n*, 68, 71*n*, 75*n*, 76*, 77, 78, 105, 110*n*, 116*n**, 117*n**, 119, 133, 142*n**, 189, 237 and *n*, 249, 254 and *n*, 263, 268* and *n*, 273 and *n*, 274*n**, 275*, 278, 279, 287 and *n**, 298, 309, 312 and *n*, 342 and *n*, 345 and *n**, 346, 348 and *n**, 349 and *n*, 354, 361, 375, 377 and *n**, 378, 386, 387*n*, 396*, 397 and *n*, 398, 412*, 413*n*, 424 and *n*; Appendices, 477

Francis I, King of France, 6 and *n*, 21*n**, 33*n*, 40*n**, 41*n*, 47*, 48 and *n*, 52*n*, 53*n*, 55*n**, 57*n*, 74, 76, 82*n**, 83* and *n*, 89 and *n*, 105* and *n**, 106* and *n**, 107 and *n*, 108 and *n**, 109 and *n*, 110 and *n*, 115*, 116 and *n**, 117* and *n**, 118* and *n**, 186, 237*n*, 254 and *n*, 255 and *n*, 256*n**, 261, 268* and *n*, 272*n*, 273 and *n**, 274* and *n*, 275* and *n*, 276*, 278, 279*, 280*, 281*, 292, 301 and *n*, 307*n*, 309*, 310 and *n**, 312*n**, 324, 326*n*, 327*n*, 329*n*, 346, 348 and *n*, 349*, 350*n*, 351, 354*, 360* and *n**, 361*n*, 367*n*, 387*n*, 395*, 396* and *n*, 397 and *n*, 412, 413, 417*n*, 418, 424*, 427*n*, 431; Appendices, 475*

Franciscan Friars, The, 132 and *n**, 133 and *n**, 136*n*, 148*n*, 212*n*, 279; Appendices, 448

Franciscan Houses, 133*n*, 279

Frankfort, 421*n*; Appendices, 452

Frederick II, Holy Roman Emperor, King of Naples and Sicily (1194-1250), 127*n*

Freeman, A., Appendices, 456

Freeman, John, royal inspector of Lincolnshire, 171*n**, 187 and *n*

Freund, M., German writer, 231*n*

Friedensburg, 80*n*

Friedmann, Paul, 20*n*, 43*n*, 48*n**, 96*n**, 114*n*, 316*n*, 324*n*, 377*n*, 402*n*; Appendices, 445

Frith, John, burnt as a heretic (1533), 234, 369* and *n**, 382

Frodsham, Elizabeth, 343*n*

Froude, J. A., 2*n*, 48*n*, 135*n*, 137*n*, 152*n*, 216, 324*n*; Appendices, 441, 445, 449, 454, 468*

Fry, F., 306*n*, 307*n*

Fuensalida, Spanish extraordinary ambassador to Henry VII, 43*n*

Fuggers, Augsburg, bankers, 189*n*

Fuller, *Thomas*, prebendary of Salisbury (1608-61), 18*n*, 141, 143, 147*n*, 158*n*, 163*n*, 165, 167 and *n**, 177*n*, 182*n*, 190 and *n*, 191*n*, 192 and *n*, 194, 197, 198*n*, 334*n*, 372 and *n**, 375, 402*n*; Appendices, 439, 447*, 463

Furlong, *P.*, 8*n*

Furness Abbey (Lancs), 181 and *n**, 182*n*

Furness Abbey, Abbot of, 181*n*

Furnivall's Inn, London, 224

Furstenau, *H.*, 11*n*

G

Gabel, *Miss Leona G.*, 2*n*

Gairdner, *James*, historian, 4*n**, 8*n*, 12*n**, 13*n**, 14*n**, 16*n*, 19*n*, 24*n*, 31*n*, 36*n*, 37*n*, 42*n*, 48*n**, 56*n*, 126*n*, 144*n*, 148*n*, 153*, 155*n*, 159, 162*, 166*n*, 168*n**, 185*n**, 209*n**, 218, 238*n*, 248*n*, 284, 287*n*, 306*n*, 337*n*, 402*n*; Appendices, 439, 440*, 441, 442*, 445, 447, 449, 451, 452, 455, 458, 459, 460, 462, 464*, 466, 468*, 477

Galt, *J.*, 6*n*

Gambara, Uberto, Nuncio in England; Bishop of Tortona (1528), Cardinal (1539), Legate in Lombardy (†1549), 56*n*, 57*n*

Ganz, *P.*, 300*n*, 310*n*, 326*n*

Gardiner, *Mrs. D.*, 129*n*

Gardiner, Germain, the Bishop of Winchester's nephew and secretary, executed for denying the royal supremacy (March 7th, 1544), 136*n*, 337 and *n*, 381*n*

Gardiner, Stephen, Bishop of Winchester (1531-51 and 1553-55); Lord Chancellor (1553-55), xii; 26, 28*n**, 58, 59* and *n**, 61, 63 and *n*, 65 and *n*, 66*n**, 67*n*, 69*n**, 71*n*, 73*n*, 74*n*, 75*, 76 and *n*, 78*n*, 85*n*, 93*n**, 99, 101, 102*n*, 104*, 106* and *n**, 124*n*, 125*n*, 127, 128*n**, 139*n*, 208*n*, 216, 238, 240*n*, 251*n*, 255 and *n**, 260*n*, 264*n*, 298* and *n*, 312, 313*, 314*n*, 318*, 326*n**, 328 and *n*, 331 and *n*, 332, 333, 335, 341, 342* and *n**, 343, 346*, 347* and *n**, 348* and *n**, 349 and *n**, 351*n*, 352, 353* and *n**, 354* and *n**, 355 and *n*, 357*n*, 358* and *n**, 359*n**, 360 and *n**, 362*n*, 364*, 365*n*, 366 and *n**, 367*n**, 368 and *n**, 369* and *n*, 370* and *n**, 371* and *n**, 373 and *n*, 374*, 375* and *n*, 376* and *n**, 377* and *n*, 378 and *n**, 379, 380*, 381* and *n*, 382*n**, 386*, 387 and *n*, 388 and *n**, 389 and *n*, 390*n*, 397, 399*n*, 417*n*, 418, 419*n**, 424, 425*n*, 429 and *n**, 432, 434*n**; Appendices, 449*, 460*, 461*, 471*, 479

Gardiner, *R. B.*, 18*n*

Gardiner, William, Canon of Canterbury, 337*n**

Garigliano, Battle of (1530), 286

Garrard (or Garret), Thomas, burnt as a heretic (1540), 368*n*, 382, 395*n*, 422, 432*n*

Garter, *Bernard*, 359*n*

Gascoigne, Thomas, Chancellor o Oxford, 4*n*, 19*n*

Gasquet, *Francis Adrian*, *O.S.B.*, Cardinal, xiii; 19*n*, 20*n*, 132*n*, 148*n**, 153, 155*n*, 156*n**, 168*n*, 206*n**, 233*n*, 251*n*, 258*n*, 289*n*; Appendices, 445, 447, 448, 449, 457

Gay, *E. F.*, 147*n*

Gayangos, *Don Pascual de*, Appendices, 442, 465

Gee, *Henry*, Appendices, 464

Gee and *Hardy*, 2*n**, 10*n*, 11*n**, 12*n*, 13*n**, 19*n*, 24*n*; Appendices, 465

Gelderland, Duchy of, 312*n*

Gerdes, *Daniel* (1698-1765), 131*n*; Appendices, 459

Germain, St., heretic, 176*n*

Germany, 4*n*, 31, 62, 77*n*, 110*n**, 115, 150, 254, 255*n*, 260*n*, 269, 284*n*, 307*n*, 309, 310*n**, 312*n*, 319*n*, 358*, 360, 365, 367*, 368, 369, 377, 379*n*, 388, 397*n*, 399, 400*n*, 402 and *n*, 413, 419*n*, 422, 424, 431, 432

Gerona, 269

Gerson (derived from the name of his native village), or Charlier, John, Chancellor of Paris University (1363-1428), 384

Gherio, Cosimo, Bishop of Fano (1528-37), 222*n*, 263

Ghiberti, Matteo, Bishop of Verona (1524-43), 76*n*, 257, 266*n*, 268*n*, 269*n*, 361; Appendices, 478*

Ghika, Mgr., Appendices, 480

Ghinucci, Girolamo, Bishop of Worcester (1523-34), Cardinal (1534); (†1541), 56*n**, 61*n*, 65, 76 and *n*, 82, 111, 154, 208*n*, 273*n*

Gigey (or Gigs), Margaret, adopted by Sir Thomas More, married John Clements, 228*n*, 252, 253; Appendices, 454.

Gigliis, Silvestro de, Bishop of Worcester (1499-1521), 33*n*, 37*n*, 38*n**

Gilbert de Tournai, O.F.M., 17*n*

Gilbertines, The, or Canons Regular, 148*n*, 168*n*

Gilbertine Nuns, 168*n*; Appendices, 448

Gilby, Anthony, controversialist in the time of Elizabeth, 366*n*

Giles (or Egidius), Peter, employed by the Antwerp printer, Thierry Martens, and secretary to the town of Antwerp (1487-1533), 232*n*; Appendices, 453

Gisborough, 181*n*

Giustiniani, Marino, (1489-1542) son of Sebastiano ; ambassador in France (1532-36), to Ferdinand I (1537-40), and to Charles V (1541-†1542), 117*n*

Giustiniani, Sebastiano, Venetian ambassador in London, 20*n**, 40*n*, 41*n**, 45*n*

Gladstone, W. E., 208*n*

Glastonbury (Somerset), 157, 295

Glastonbury, Benedictine Abbot of, 185 and *n*, 295

Gloucester, Bishop of, 366*n*

Gloucester, County of, 100*n*, 157

Gloucester, Duke of, 29*n*

Gloucester, See of, 122*n*, 193*n*, 429*n*

Godstow (Oxon), 359

Godstow, Benedictine Abbess of, 165*n*, 184*n*

Godwin, Francis, Bishop of Llandaff (1601-17), 344*n*, 346, 371, 372; Appendices 456, 459, 460, 464

Goldast, 8*n*

Golde, George, servant to the Lieutenant of the Tower of London, 246*n*

Goldwell, Thomas, Bishop of St. Asaph (1555-59); expelled under Elizabeth; died in Rome (1581), Appendices, 455

Gontier, Palamedes, secretary to Admiral Chabot, 121*n*, 130*n*, 139*n*, 396*n*

Goodrich, Thomas, Bishop of Ely (1534-54); Lord Chancellor (1552-53), 271, 317, 334, 373*n*, 376*n*, 399, 408, 417*n*, 418

Gorham, G. C., 304*n*

Gostwick, Sir John, 337*

Gotha, 413, 414*n*

Goudge, H. L., 426*n*

Goupil, Appendices, 441

Gourmont, Gilles, 17*n*

Grabinski, Countess J., Appendices, 455

Grafton, Richard, 16th century London printer, 307 and *n**, 308*n*, 333*n*, 382, 423*n*

Graham, Miss Rose, 142*n*; Appendices, 448*, 449

Grammont, Gabriel de, Bishop of Tarbes (1524-30); Cardinal (1530), 52*n**, 350*n*

Grantham (Lincs), 316

Grantham, See of, 122*n*

Granville, Anthony Perrenot de, Cardinal (1517-86), 97, 273*n*, 278, 285*n*, 292, 320*n*, 368*n*, 419 and *n*; Appendices, 457, 473

Gratianus Pullus, 18

Grauert, 17*n*

Gray, G. J., Appendices, 460

Graziani (or *Gratiani*), *Antonio-Maria*, secretary to Cardinal Commendone during his legations in Poland (1571, 1572-73); Bishop of Amelia (1592-1611); Nuncio at Venice (1596-98); Appendices, 456

Green, author of "History of England," 152*n*

Greenwich, 39*n*, 51*n*, 88, 132 and *n*, 133*n*, 348*n*, 353*n*, 378*n*

Greenwich, Franciscan House at, 133*n*

Gresham, Richard, member of House of Commons, 152*n*

Grillanderus, Appendices, 443

Grocyn, William, humanist (1442-1522), 224 and *n*, 225*n*, 232

Gross, 9*n*

Grove, J., Appendices, 446

Guicciardi, F., 7*n*

Guichardin, Appendices, 472

Guienne, 142, 279

Guildford, Comptroller, 69

Guildford (Surrey), 122*n*

Guise, 115*n*

Guise, Duke of, 274n
Guizot, 20n
Gumbley, W., O.P., 137n
Gunnell, William, tutor to Sir Thomas More's family, 228n
Gurney, E., Appendices, 467
Gyffard, George, visitor of the English monasteries, 163, 164n

H

Hackett, Francis, Appendices, 441
Hackforth (Yorks), 344n
Haddon, William, 336n
Hadley, a penitentiary of Canterbury, 210n
Haggar, A. C. P., 118n
Haile, Martin, Appendices, 439, 457
Haines, C. Reginald, 156n
Hale, John, Vicar of Isleworth, 134 and n
Halifax, Lord, Appendices, 467
Halifax (Yorks), 173n
Halkin, L., 268n
Hall, Edward, chronicler, 36n, 95n, 146*, 167, 206n, 337, 369n*; Appendices, 440, 445, 466*
Hall, Richard (†1604), John Fisher's biographer, 435n; Appendices, 449, 450
Hallam, Thomas, Bishop of Philadelphia (Austra Canon), 137n
Hallam, historian, 28n, 186
Hallett, Mgr. P. E., xv; Appendices, 453
Hallom, John, 180n
Hamburg, 116n, 307n, 358, 359, 377n
Hampshire, 157
Hampton Court, 40n
Hamy, 83n
Hanleyd (Worcs), 343n
Hapsburgs, The, 110n, 115n, 116n
Harding, Dr. Thomas, Catholic priest; Chaplain to Stephen Gardiner; took refuge at Louvain in Elizabeth's time (†1572); Appendices, 443
Hardwick, Charles, 125n, 199n, 403n, 414n, 415n; Appendices, 461*
Hardy (see Gee and Hardy)
Hargrave, Francis, 324n
Harington, Sir John, 343n, 370n*, 371, 378n, 390n; Appendices, 460
Harmer, Anthony, pen-name for Henry Wharton, Appendices, v462

Harold II, King of England (†1066), founded Waltham Abbey, 197
Harpsfield, John, brother to Nicholas Harpsfield, Appendices, 453
Harpsfield, Nicholas, Archdeacon of Canterbury (1554); imprisoned in the Tower by Elizabeth (†1575), xv; 35n, 52n, 104n, 123n, 131, 133n*, 180 and n, 189n, 196n, 205n, 248n, 252; Appendices, 442-43, 452*, 453, 454
Harris, Dorothy (née Colley), 253 and n*; Appendices, 454*
Harris, John, Sir Thomas More's secretary, 228n; Appendices, 454
Harris, C. R. S., 158n
Harrow-on-the-Hill (Mddx), 164, 299, 345n
Hartfelder, 18n
Harvel, Edmund, Henry VIII's representative at Venice (1526-47), 278n
Hasenclever, A., 424n
Hauser, 51n
Havercamp, 374n
Hawkyns, Nicholas, Archdeacon of Ely, 50n, 88n*, 320n
Hayles, Holy Blood of, 303
Haynes, Dr. Simon, Dean of Exeter, 360
Haywood, John, 16th century epigrammatist, Appendices, 454
Hearne, Appendices, 452*
Heath, Dr. Nicholas, Bishop of Rochester (1540-43), of Worcester 1543-51), and Archbishop of York (1555-58), 380, 397n, 398 and n, 402n, 425n, 429n, 435 and n
Hector, 41n
Hedio, Gaspar, a Baden reformer (1494-1552), 358
Heilig, K. J., 158n
Hendle, William, visitor of the English monasteries, 164n
Hendriks, 135n
Henley, agent of Cromwell, 304n
Henricians, The, 341 and n, 346, 351, 359, 361, 363, 364*, 365, 369, 370, 372, 374, 375, 377*, 379*, 380, 383*, 388* and n, 389*, 390, 398n 404, 408, 409, 418, 424n, 429, 432* Appendices, 460
Henrietta of France, 435
Henriquez, Crisostomo, 305n
Henry I, King of England (1100-35), 3u, 197

Henry II, King of England (1154-89), 1, 2 and n*, 3, 197, 305n

Henry IV, King of England (1399-1413), 3, 4n, 11, 13n, 33, 44n, 93n, 142, 143, 405n

Henry V, King of England (1413-22), 13n, 143*, 149

Henry VI, King of England (1422-71), 384

Henry VII, King of England (1485-1509), 13n, 29n, 31n, 35*, 36 and n*, 37n, 38* and n*, 39* and n*, 45n*, 46n*, 64n, 65n, 69n, 132n, 144, 201*, 225n, 257n*, 269n; Appendices, 464

Henry VIII, King of England, 2, 3, 5n, 6, 7* and n, 8*, 11*, 13n*, 15, 15, 20, 21n*, 25, 26n, 27 and n, 29 and n*, 30 and n*, 31, 32n, 33* and n*, 34* and n*, 35 and n, 36n, 37 and n, 38*, 39, 40n*, 41*, 42 and n*, 42n, 43, 44* and n, 45 and n*, 46* and n*, 47* and n*, 48, 49n, 50*, 51*, 52n, 53* and n*, 54n*, 55n*, 56 and n*, 57n*, 59n, 60, 61* and n*, 62* and n, 63 and n, 64, 65* and n, 67* and n, 68n, 69 and n, 71n*, 72 and n, 73*, 74* and n, 74n, 75* and n*, 76n, 77 and n, 78 and n*, 79n, 80 and n*, 81 and n*, 83* and n*, 84* and n*, 85*, 87, 88*, 89* and n*, 90* and n, 91*, 92 and n*, 93n, 94*, 96 and n*, 97, 98*, 99*, 100n, 101, 102*, 104 and n, 105* and n, 106* and n*, 107* and n, 108* and n*, 109*, 110 and n, 11 and n*, 112n*, 113, 114* and n, 115* and n*, 116* and n*, 117* and n*, 118 and n, 119*, 120* and n*, 121 and n, 12, 123* and n*, 124 and n, 125 and n, 126n*, 127*, 128, 129*, 130n*, 131, 132n*, 133, 134n*, 135n*, 136*, 138, 139* and n*, 141* and n, 143 and n, 144, 145n*, 146 and n, 147n, 148 and n*, 149n, 151, 153, 154, 156, 162, 166*, 169, 170n, 174* and n, 177n, 178*, 179, 180 and n, 182, 186 and n, 189*, 190 and n, 191 and n*, 192 and n, 193, 194n, 195, 198, 200, 201n, 202 203 and n, 204, 205n, 206, 207, 208n, 211, 212n*, 213n, 214* and n*, 215, 216*, 218*, 222 and n, 223, 225n, 229, 233 and n, 234n,

236* and n*, 238*, 241 and n*, 243, 245, 253n, 254n*, 255 and n, 256 and n*, 257 and n*, 258, 260, 261* and n, 262* and n, 264*, 265* and n*, 266 and n, 267 and n*, 268*, 269, 271, 272, 273*, 274* and n*, 275* and n, 276*, 277*, 278 and n*, 280*, 281*, 282 and n, 285*, 289, 290*, 292, 293, 294*, 298, 305n, 307n, 309, 310 and n*, 311*, 312 and n*, 314*, 315 and n*, 316n, 318, 319*, 320* and n, 321* and n, 322, 324, 325* and n*, 326 and n*, 327* and n, 328*, 329n*, 331*, 332, 334 and n, 335 and n, 336 and n, 337*, 338* and n*, 339, 340*, 341* and n, 342n, 343*, 345n*, 346* and n, 347*, 348n*, 349*, 350, 351*, 354 and n, 355, 358, 359, 360n, 361 and n, 362, 263n, 364*, 365, 367, 370, 374, 375, 376, 377*, 378*, 379 and n*, 380n, 382 and n, 383, 384, 385n, 386n, 387n, 388*, 389*, 390* and n, 391, 392 and n, 383* and n, 394*, 395*, 396* and n*, 397* and n*, 398, 399 and n, 400* and n, 401n, 402, 403 and n, 404, 406 and n, 407, 409, 411, 412*, 413* and n*, 414*, 415, 417, 419 and n*, 420n*, 423 and n, 424* and n, 427, 429n, 430, 431 and n, 432* and n, 433* and n, 434* and n*, 435*; Appendices, 440, 441*, 442*, 445, 446*, 447, 449, 454, 461*, 466*, 469*, 470, 471*, 472*, 473*, 474*, 475*, 476*, 477*, 479*, 481, 482*

Henry II, King of France, Dauphin until 1547 (see Dauphin)

Henson, H., Bishop of Hereford, 153n

Herbert (Ch. Somerset), Earl of Worcester, 29n

Herbert of Cherbury, Lord (Edward, first Baron), 39n, 42n, 141, 145* and n, 156n, 325, 337, 355n, 410n, 432; Appendices, 441*

Hercourt, R., French writer, 231n

Hereford, Bishop of, 19n, 20n*, 77n, 256n, 261, 308, 334, 349, 373n, 398 and n, 425n

Hereford, Diocese of, 167n, 333, 360n, 361, 380

Herkless, J., 274n

Herod Antipas, 205

Heron, Giles, Sir Thomas More's son-in-law, 227n, 237n

Hertford (Edward Seymour), Earl of, Jane Seymour's brother, 191n, 325n

Herzog-Hauck, 9n

Hesse, 397n, 423

Hesse, Philip, Landgrave of (*see* Philip the Magnanimous)

Hexham (Northumberland), 170n

Heylin (*see* Bloxham and *Heylin*)

Heylin, 325n

Heywood, Sir Richard, 249

Heywood, B. A., translated Gardiner's *De Vere Obedientia*, 355n

Heywood, Ellis, Appendices, 453

Highgate, 372n

Hilles, Richard, 383n

Hilliard (or Hillyard, Richard, secretary to Tunstall, 207n, 208n*, 379n*; Appendices, 450

Hilsey, Dr. John, Dominican provincial, Bishop of Rochester (1535-39), 131, 162n, 183n, 184, 303*, 334, 380, 399n, 408, 417n, 418, 421

Hinton (Somerset), Charterhouse of, 135n, 183n, 197n

Hippo, Bishop of, 137n

Hitchcock, Dr. Elsie Vaughan, 248n; Appendices, 452*, 453*

Hobby, Sir Philip, 190n

Hochstetter, Joachim, 147n

Hockley (near Birmingham), 359n

Hoker, John, 304n

Holbeach, Henry, Bishop of Rochester (1544-47), and of Lincoln (1547-51), 162n, 183n

Holbein, 32n, 40n, 41, 48n*, 200n, 205 and n, 223, 227, 228n, 229*, 233n, 253, 274n, 300*, 310 and n*, 322n, 326n, 355, 378n; Appendices, 441, 453, 455, 468

Holcroft, Thomas, 183n

Holderness (Yorkshire), 177

Holgate (or Holdegate), Robert, Bishop of Llandaff (1537-45) and Archbishop of York (1545-54; †1556), 162n, 183n

Holinshed, R., chronicler, 84n; Appendices, 440

Holloway, H., 186n

Holm Cultram Abbey (Cumberland), 181 and n

Holm Cultram Abbey (Cumberland), Abbot of, 181n

Holt, Nicholas, humanist, 223n

"Holy Maid of Kent," The (*see* Barton, Elizabeth)

Holy See, The, 56n, 57 and n, 59n, 60, 67, 86, 89, 93n, 98, 99n, 105 and n, 106, 107, 109n*, 110n, 112n, 113n, 115n, 124, 134n, 136, 137, 140, 205, 207, 221n, 255n, 256, 273n, 278, 330n, 368n, 384, 413n, 434n; Appendices, 470*, 471, 474

Hook, Dean W. F., historian, 75n, 261n, 296; Appendices, 456, 458

Hooper, John, Bishop of Gloucester (1550-54), and Worcester (1552-54); burnt under Mary Tudor (1555), 366n, 367n

Hope, Mrs., Appendices, 445

Horde, Edward, Prior of Hinton, 183n

Horehowitz (Andrew Sbardelato), Dudić de, Bishop of Knin (1562-63), of Csanád (1563), and of Fünf-Kirchen (1563-67) (†1589), Appendices, 455

Hornby (Lancs), Appendices, 439

Horncastle (Lincs), 172, 174

Horsey, Dr., Chancellor to Fitzjames, the Bishop of London, 14n

Hosius (or Hosz), Stanislaus (1504-79), Bishop of Culm (1549-51), of Ermland (1551-70); Cardinal (1561); Legate at the Council of Trent (1561-63), 257

Houghton, John, Prior of London Charterhouse, 133*, 135n*, 183n

House of Commons, 21, 24 and n, 25, 26 and n*, 27n*, 29*, 32n*, 86*, 92* and n*, 99*, 100 and n*, 101* and n*, 102, 104n, 113n, 119, 121 and n, 122, 128n, 136n, 152n, 166*, 236, 287 and n, 289, 293n, 353*; Appendices, 466

House of Lords, 26, 29, 92n*, 97, 99, 104, 111 and n, 112n, 113n, 121, 122, 136n, 145, 153n, 166, 167 and n, 211, 212n, 213 and n, 238, 241 and n, 350, 353, 362n, 363, 388, 417; Appendices, 465, 477, 482

Howard, Catherine, niece of Duke of Norfolk, fifth wife of Henry VIII, 315, 325, 326* and n*, 327, 328 and n, 340n

Howard, Catherine, sister of third Duke of Norfolk, Countess of Bridgewater, 327

Howard, Elizabeth, mother of Anne Boleyn, 47

Howard, Thomas, Duke of Norfolk (*see* Norfolk, third Duke of)

Howard of Effingham, Lord William, brother of third Duke of Norfolk; ambassador to James V of Scotland and Francis I, 327

Hueffer, Madox, 328*n*

Huillard-Bréholles, 127*n*

Hull (Yorks), 177, 180* and *n*

Hull (Yorks), Charterhouse of, 135*n*

Hull (Yorks), See of, 122*n*

Hume, David, Historian (1711-76), 294

Hume, M. A. S., Appendices, 465, 466

Humphrey, Dr. Laurence, 369*n*, 372*n*

Hungary, 45

Hunne, Richard, London tailor, 14*n*

Hunt, W., Appendices, 439, 467

Huntingdon, 173*n*

Huntingdon, Earl of, 177, 247

Huntingdon, See of, 122*n*

Hurry, J., 185*n*

Hurst Castle (Hants), on the Solent, 277

Hurtado, J. Piernas, 35*n*

Hurter, 9*n*

Husee, John, 14 and *n*

Huss, John (1369-1415), 10 and *n*, 176*n*

Hussey, Lady, 212

Hussey, Lord (John), Baron, 171 and *n*, 212

Hutten, Ulrich von, humanist (1488-1523), 224*n*, 234, 236*n*

Hutton, Edward, 133*n*; Appendices, 448

Hutton, V. H., 305*n*

Hyma, Alb., 233*n*

Hymens, Dr., Dean of St. John's College, Cambridge, 202*n*

I

India, 198

Ingworth, Richard, Suffragan Bishop of Dover (1535-47), 164*n*, 184*n*

Innes, A. D., 321*n*; Appendices, 467

Innocent III, Pope (1198-1216), 1 and *n*, 78*n*; Appendices 476

Innocent IV, Pope (1243-54), 78*n*

Innocent VIII, Pope (1484-92), 143*n*,

Ipswich (Suffolk), 73*n*, 122*n*, 144, 288*, 290*n*, 304, 342, 348 and *n*

Ireland, 2, 7, 136*n*, 147*n*, 186 and *n*, 189

Ireland, King of, 46*n*

Ireland, Lord Deputy of, 115*n*

Isabella, sister of Charles V; married to Christian II, deposed King (1523) of Denmark, 274*n*

Isabella d'Este, 42

Isabella of Portugal, wife of Charles V (†May, 1539), 47*n*

Isabella of Spain, "The Catholic," 35, 36 and *n**, 37*n*, 38, 64; Appendices 476

Isleworth, 134 and *n*

Isocrates, 317

Italian States, The, 61*n*

Italy, 4, 57*n*, 61, 76* and *n*, 78, 85*n*, 107, 117*n*, 224, 254, 257 and *n*,258 and *n*, 260, 266, 270*n*, 286, 320, 345, 350; Appendices, 440, 472, 478

Iung, Nicolas, 9*n*

Ivychurch (Kent), 343*n*

J

Jacka, Miss H. T., 159*n*; Appendices, 449

Jacob, E. F., 4*n*

Jacobs, H. E., 13*n*

James I, King of England (1566-1625), 194*n*; Appendices, 465

James II, King of England (1685-88), Appendices, 456

James IV, King of Scotland (1488-1513), 15

James V of Scotland (1567-1603), became James I of England (1603-25), 45*n*, 115 and *n**, 273 and *n*, 274*n**

Janelle, M. P., 69*n*, 255*n*, 355*n**, 388*n*, 389*n*; Appendices, 457, 460, 461

Janni, Ettore, 261*n*

Jay (or Joye) (*see* Joye)

Jeanne de Valois (†1505), daughter of Louis XI, 43*n*, 63*, 64*n*

Jenkinson, W., 129*n*

Jenkyns, H., 138*n*, 317*n*, 334, 402*n*, 403*n*, 414*n*, 415*n*, 416*n*; Appendices, 458, 459

Jerome, William, Rector of Stepney, burnt as a heretic (1540), 368*n*, 382, 395*n*, 422, 432*n*

Jervaulx Abbey (Yorks,) 181

Jervaulx Abbey (Yorks), Abbot of, 181*n**

Jesus College, Cambridge, 317

Joan, sister to Catherine of Aragon (†1554), 37*n*

John Frederick (*see* Saxony, Elector of)

John (Lackland), King of England (1199-1216), 2* and *n*, 142*n*

John of Gaunt, Duke of Lancaster, third son of Edward III, 44*n*

John XXII, Pope (1316-34), 9*n*

Joliffe, Henry, 367*n*

Jonas (Justus) (real name, Jodukus Koch), reformer (1493-1555), 401

Jones, P. van Brunt, Appendices, 467

Jordan, G. J., 4*n*

Jourdan, G. V., Appendices, 466

Joye (or Jay), George, Tyndale's secretary, 234, 342*n*, 367*n*, 368*n*, 369, 382

Judges, A. V., 195*n*

Julius II, Pope (1503-13), 4, 37 and *n*, 38 and *n*, 43 and *n*, 57*n*, 60, 64 and *n*, 77; Appendices, 444, 475, 476, 477, 478, 479

Julius III, Pope (1550-55), 267*n*, 284*n*; Appendices, 478

Jusserand, 305*n*

K

Kalkoff, Paul, German writer, 233*n*

Kaulek, 28*n*; Appendices, 465, 466

Kautsky, 231*n*

Kennedy, W. P. M., Appendices, 467

Kennett, 39*n*

Kenninghall, 298

Kent, 28*n*, 119, 157, 182, 335, 337 "Kent, Holy Maid of" (*see* "Holy Maid of Kent")

Kerker, 203*n*; Appendices, 451, 456

Kildare (Gerald Fitzgerald), eighth Earl of, Lord Deputy of Ireland, 115*n*

Kimbolton, 412*n*

Kinalkin (Ireland), Charterhouse of, 136*n*

King, Robert, Bishop of Rheon (1535), of Osney (1542), and of Oxford (1545), 137*n*

King's College, Cambridge, 318

King's Langley (name derived from Edmund Langley, son of Edward III, Duke of York, whose tomb is in the parish church, †1402), (Hertfordshire), 299

Kingston, Sir William, Lieutenant of the Tower, 220*, 250*n**

Kirkby (Yorks), 177

Kirkham Abbey, 199*n*

Kirkstead Abbey (Lincs), 181

Kitchin (or Dunstan), Anthony, Bishop of Llandaff (1545-63), 162*n*

Kleinwächter, German writer, 231*n*

Knight, 18*n**

Knight, Dr. William, secretary to Henry VIII, and his envoy to Rome, 46*n*, 49, 56* and *n**, 57 and *n**, 58 and *n**

Knights of Malta, 136*n*, 148*n*, 185, 185-86*n*

Knights Hospitallers, 142*n**

Knights of St. John of Jerusalem, 136*n**, 186*n*, 313

Knights Templar, 142

Knyghtley, E., visitor of the English monasteries, 163*n*, 164*n*

Knyvet, Sir Henry, envoy to Charles V's court, 419*n**

Kolde, T. 320*n*, 401*n*; Appendices, 459

Korea, 198

Korzeniowski, J., 110*n*

Koszul, A., 184*n*

Kullnick, M., German writer, 230*n*

Kyte, John, Bishop of Carlisle (1521-37), 97*n*

L

Lachmore, Nicholas, Baron of the Exchequer, 343*n*

Lackland (*see* John, King of England)

Lacy, Henry, 288*n*

Laemmer, 89*n*

Lafforgue, 52*n*

Lambert (or Nicholson), John, burnt as a heretic, in 1538, 318*n*, 334*n*, 369, 434

Lambeth Palace, 129 and *n*, 214, 241*, 243*n*, 362*n*, 409 and *n*, 410*n*, 426*n*, 428*n*

Lämmer, H., Appendices, 442

Lancashire, 178*n*, 181

Lancaster, House of, 47*n*, 269*n*, 344*n*

Lancaster, Duke of, 44*n* (John of Gaunt).

Landerfield (Wales), 304*n*

Landry, B., 158*n*

Lane, visitor of the English monasteries, 163*n*, 164*n*

Langdon (Kent), 182 and *n*

Langley (Norfolk), Prior of, 184

Lanz, 84*n*

Lark, 21*n*

Lark, Miss, 22*n*

Lateran, Fifth Council of (1512-17), 20n; Appendices, 479

Latimer, Hugh, Bishop of Worcester (1535-39), 152n, 160n, 179n, 194n, 196, 223n, 242, 302n, 308n, 313, 318n, 334 and n, 336 and n, 340, 355n, 373n, 376, 380 and n*, 382, 399n, 409, 417n, 418, 421, 422

Latimer, Lord John, third baron, Katherine Parr's second husband, 177, 178n, 179n, 328

Latimer, William, humanist (†1545), 257n

Laun, J. Ford, 31n

Lautrec (Odet de Foix), Viscount de, last French Governor of the Duchy of Milan (1516-21), 58n

Lavisse and Rembaud, 16n

Lawrence, Robert, Carthusian, Prior of Beauvale, 133

Layton, Dr. Richard, visitor of the English monasteries, 156, 157* and n, 160, 162, 163, 164, 165n, 176, 218

Leach, Appendices, 460

Leadam, 195n

Leader, a priest, contemporary of Sir Thomas More, 245n*

Le Bas, Appendices, 458

Lee, Dr., 270n

Lee, F. G., Appendices, 456

Lee, John Edward, Archbishop of York (1531-44), 19, 65, 81n, 85n, 88n, 133n, 177, 179, 319, 363n, 373n, 374n*, 417n, 418; Appendices, 471

Lee, Roland (or Rowland), Bishop of Chester, Coventry and Lichfield (1534-43), 84n, 133, 137n, 215

Legbourne (Lincs), Convent of, 170 and , n172

Le Grand, Joachim, Oratorian Father (1653-1738), 5n, 6n, 21n, 26n. 34n, 38n, 45n, 47n, 49n, 50n, 52n, 339; Appendices, 442, 443, 444, 462

Leicester, 348, 351, 359n, 360n

Leicester, Abbey of, 74

Leicester, Abbot of, 299n

Leicester, See of, 122n

Leigh (or Legh), Dr. Thomas, visitor of English monasteries, 157* and n, 160, 162, 163, 164*, 165n, 173n, 176, 184, 302 and n

Le Laboureur, 17th century writer, 248 Appendices, 451

Leland, John, Chaplain and Court Librarian under Henry VIII (1506-62), 51n, 198* and n*; Appendices, 459

Lemon, The Brothers, editors of State Papers, 52n; Appendices, 440, 442

Le Neve, J., 347n; Appendices, 460

Lenton (Notts), Prior of, 184n

Leo X, Pope (1513-21), 6n*, 34n, 56n; Appendices, 472

Leo XIII, Pope (1878-1903), 284

Lewes (Sussex), Priory of, 299n

Lewis, David, translator of Sander, xv; 5n; Appendices, 444

Lewis, John, 306n

Lewis-Turner, 201n*, 223n; Appendices, 451

Lichfield, 111

Lichfield, Bishop of, 19n, 84n, 133, 215, 308n

Lichfield, Diocese of, 161n, 208n

Liége, 268

Liége, Bishop of, 271n

Liljegren, S. B., 192n

Lille, 40n

Lillechurch (Kent), 143n, 202n

Lilly, William, humanist (†1522), 229n, 230n, 232

Linacre, Thomas, humanist (†1524), 224 and n, 232, 257n, 344

Lincoln, 73, 173, 174 and n*, 175, 176n, 345n

Lincoln, Auxiliary Bishop of, 137n

Lincoln, Bishop of, 19n, 26, 103n, 143, 173n, 183n, 208n, 321n, 326, 373n, 422n

Lincoln, County of, 168 and n, 179n, 171*, 172, 175* and n*, 176n, 178*, 179, 181n, 359, 423

Lincoln, Wiclif, Canon of, 9n

Lincoln's Inn, London, 224

Lingard, John, Catholic historian (1771-1851), 48n, 324n, 393, 417; Appendices, 439*

Linz, 320

Lipson, E., 192n

Lisle, Lord (Arthur Plantagenet (†1542), 14n, 106n, 251n, 270n

Lisle, Lord (John Dudley), 191n

Little Hales, 138n, 329n

Livonia, Bishop of, Appendices, 476

Llandaff, Bishop of, 20n, 111, 162n*, 183n, 208n, 297n, 417n; Appendices, 456

Llantwit Major (Glamorganshire), 304n

Lloyd, Charles, Bishop of Oxford (1827-29), 433 and n; Appendices, 461*

Loches, 309

Lodge, 343

Lodge, E., Appendices, 441

Löhe, W., 336n

Lohr, G., O.P., 154n

Lollards, The, 11 and n, 12n*, 13 and n, 18, 148, 149; Appendices, 464

London, 2n, 28, 38n, 52n, 65n, 66, 72, 73, 74, 77n, 79, 91, 92, 106n, 108 and n, 111, 113n, 118n, 133, 135n, 136n, 149n, 159, 176n, 183n, 187, 188, 197n, 201, 208n, 210, 213, 214*, 223 and n, 225n, 230n, 249, 251n*, 255, 272, 276, 277, 285, 286, 288, 296, 298n, 303, 304 306n, 307n, 308, 309 and n, 320, 332n, 342n, 345, 347 and n*, 349, 350n, 351, 354n, 355n*, 358, 359n, 362n, 366, 372n, 374n, 378 and n, 379 and n, 409n, 413, 414n, 415, 418, 422, 423, 425n

London, Archdeacon of, 53n

London, Bishop of, 19n, 26, 37n, 76, 77n, 103n, 133n, 203, 267n, 341*, 345, 349, 350*, 359, 369, 373, 380, 387

London Bridge, 134, 222, 253

London, Guildhall, 369

London, See of, 208n, 361

London, Tower of, 40n, 74, 88n, 133*, 134, 135, 157n*, 179n, 180, 181n, 200n, 202 and n, 205, 215 and n, 219 and n, 220*, 222 and n, 225n, 228n, 243*, 245n, 246, 250 and n, 251 and n, 253n, 269, 270 and n*, 271 and n, 272, 295, 302n, 304, 313, 314, 315n, 322, 323, 324n, 327, 328n, 338*, 370n, 380, 394n

London, Tower Hill, 220

London, Dr. John, Dean of Christ Church, Oxford; Dean of Wallingford; visitor of English monasteries, 157, 163, 164, 165n*, 184 and n, 187, 188, 304n, 337

Long, Sir Richard, 190n

Longland, John, Bishop of Lincoln (1520-47), and Confessor to Henry VIII, 52n, 103n, 208n, 321, 373n, 408

Longolius (de Lognueil), Christopher, humanist (†1522), 257, 258n

Longré, E., 158n

Longueville, Duke of, 274n

Longueville, Duchess of (see Lorraine, Mary of)

Lordington (Sussex), 271n*

Lords (see House of Lords)

Loreto, 269

Lorraine, Duke of, 311n

Lorraine, Duke of, daughter of, 412

Lorraine, John of, Cardinal, Archbishop of Rheims (1533-38; †1550), 54n, 82n*, 384n

Lorraine, Louisa of (1520-42), second daughter of Claud of Lorraine, first Duke of Guise, 274n

Lorraine, Mary of, elder sister of Louisa of Lorraine, Duchess of Longueville, afterwards Queen of Scotland (1538-60), 115n, 274n*

Loserth, J., 9n*, 10n*, 11n*, 12n

Louis IV, of Bavaria, Emperor (1328-47), 9n, 127n

Louis VII, King of France (1137-80), 305

Louis XI, King of France (†1383), 43n

Louis XII, King of France (†1515), 39n, 43n, 44n, 47n, 48n, 55 and n, 57n, 63; Appendices, 478

Louisa of Savoy (†1531), Francis I's mother, 5n, 55n

Lound (Leicestershire), Priory of, 299n

Louth (Lincs), 172, 174

Louth Park, 172

Louvain, 231, 283n, 363n; Appendices, 443, 453, 463

Louvre, The, 32n, 253, 310 and n

Low Countries, 45, 48, 84n, 86, 312n, 344

Lucca, 278n

Lucian, 233 and n*

Luebeck, 116n

Luffield, 144

Lumby, Rawson, 1n, 17n, 224n, 232n; Appendices, 452

Lumley, Lord John, Baron, 177, 179n

Luneburg (see Brunswick-Luneburg)

Lunn, J. R., 340n

Lupset, Thomas, secretary to Richard Pace, 258n

Lupton, J. H., 18n*, 232n

Luther, Martin, 8, 9n, 12n, 15, 17n*, 34n*, 56 and n, 102 and n, 110n, 129, 149n, 176n, 177n, 203*, 233* and *n*, 234*n*, 309*n*, 334, 353, 365, 368, 369, 385, 386*n*, 398*n*, 399*n*, 400 and *n*, 401*, 403*n*, 406*n*, 413, 415, 432*, 434; Appendices, 483

Lutherans, The, 77*n*, 108*n*, 115, 116*n*, 125*n*, 278, 309*n*, 325*n*, 365, 366*n*, 368, 373, 376, 393, 395*, 397* and *n*, 398, 399, 400* and *n*, 403, 404, 405*, 413 and *n*, 415, 421*n*, 424 and *n*, 430, 433

Lutterworth, Wiclif, Vicar of, 9*n*

Luze, Albert de, 41*n*

Lyde, G., Appendices, 456*

Lyons, 351*n*, 360*n*

M

Macaulay, Lord, 10*n*, 218

MacColl, 331*n*

Machiavelli, Niccolo (†1527), 33, 261 and *n**, 292*, 295*n*, 297*n*, 300

Mackarell, Matthew, Bishop of Chalcedon and auxiliary Bishop of Lincoln, 137*n*

Maclean, 191*n*

Madge, T., 22*n*

Madrid, Appendices, 443

Magdalen, daughter of Francis I (†1537), 273-4*n**, 324

Magdalen College, Oxford, 143, 257, 343*, 378*n*

"Magna Charta," 33*n*, 124*n*,* 249

Mai, Miguel, imperial ambassador in Rome, 66*n**

Maidstone (Kent), 303

Mainz, 397*n*

Maitland, F. W., Appendices, 460

Maitland, Rev. S. R., historian, 1, 8*n*, 24*n*, 355*n**, 359*n*, 370*n*, 372*n*; Appendices, 460, 463

Makower, F., 122*n*, 394, 404*n*, 428*n*; Appendices, 462*

Maldonado, J. Suarez, Bishop of Badajoz (1532-45), 248*n*

Manchester, 394

Manning, Cardinal, 384

Manning, H. B. L., 12*n*, 26*n*

Mantua, 266*n*, 320, 398, 399*n**, 400

Manutius, Paul (Paolo Manuzio), humanist, 252*n**; Appendices, 456

Marbeck, John, accused of heresy, 376*n*

Marcel, L. E., 83*n*

Marcellus II, Pope (1555) (*see also* Cervini, Marcello), 284*n*, 434

March, Earl of, 29*n*

Marck (or Mark), Ehrard van der Bishop of Liége (1506-38), 254*n*, 268 and *n**

Margaret, Osiander's niece and Cranmer's wife, 85, 320

Margaret of Austria (or of Savoy) (†1530), daughter to Maximilian I, aunt to Charles V, widow of Philip the Handsome of Savoy (1504), and Regent of the Low Countries (1507), 39*n*, 40*n*, 48, 117*n*

Margaret Beaufort, Lady, Countess of Richmond, mother of Henry VII, 201* and *n**, 202 and *n*, 257*n*

Margaret, Queen of Scotland, daughter of Henry VII, mother of James V of Scotland, 45*n*, 47*n*, 225*n*, 233*n*

Marguerite of Navarre (*see* Navarre, Marguerite of)

Marignan, 4*n*

Marillac, 127*n**, 135*n*, 150*n*, 275*n*, 277, 301*n*, 312*n*, 313*, 315*n*, 326*n*, 326*n**, 336*n*, 381 and *n*, 417*n*, 418*n**, 420*n*, 421, 427*n*, 430*n*, 431; Appendices, 445, 458

Marlborough, 122*n*

Marlow, Little, 159*n*

Marseilles, 105 and *n**, 106*n*, 108 and *n*, 109, 116, 137, 329*n*, 351 and *n*, 354, 396, 412

Marshall, Dorothy, 196*n*

Marsilius of Padua (1280-1343), 127*n**, 128*n*

Marti, Oscar A., 11*n*, 14*n*, 196*n*; Appendices, 449

Martin V., Pope (1417-31), 3, 93*n*, 378; Appendices, 476

Martin, Alexander, Appendices, 453

Martindale, Rev. C. C., S.J., 6*n*

Martyr Vermigli, Peter, of Florence (1500-62), Reformer in Strasbourg (1542-47 and 1553-56), in England (1547-53), and in Zurich (1556-62), 47*n*, 336, 366, and *n*

Mary of Lorraine (*see* Lorraine, Mary of)

Mary Tudor, Henry VIII's daughter, Queen of England (1553-58), 13*n**, 39*n* (Princess), 44*, 45*n**, 46*n**, 51 and *n*, 52*n*, 68*n*, 88, 111*n*, 112*n**, 113*n*, 115 and *n**, 122*n**, 224*n*, 132*n*, 133 and *n*, 137*n*, 138*n*, 165*n*, 169, 171*n**, 175*n*, 189, 198, 212*n*, 251*n*, 257*n*, 263, 364*n*, 270*n**, 271, 272*n*, 275, 300, 305*n*, 307*n*, 310*n*,

315n, 317, 322, 325 and n, 334n, 345 and n, 346n, 370n, 371, 380, 386, 388n, 389, 396 and n, 398n, 423n, 429; Appendices, 443*, 451, 453, 455, 467, 477

Mary, sister to Henry VIII, Queen of France, afterwards Duchess of Suffolk, 45n, 47n, 48n*, 53n, 233n

Mary, sister of Charles V, 84n

Mary, daughter of King Ferdinand of Spain, Appendices, 476

Masham (Yorks), 177

Mason, Canon A. J., 305n*, Appendices, 458

Massie, Robert, 347n

Masters, Richard, Vicar of Aldington, 210 and n, 212n

Matilda, disputed Queen of England (1126-48), 44, 45n

Matsys, Quentin, Appendices, 453

Matthew, F. D., 9n

Matthews, Thomas (pseudonym of John Rogers), 306, 307n

Mattingley, Garret, Appendices, 457

Maucroix, Francis de, Canon of Rheims translator of Sander (†1709), Appendices, 444*, 455

Maximilian I, Emperor (1493-1519), 40n*, 47n, 117n, 345 and n

Mayo, Rev. T., 330n

Mayor, J. E. B., 202n*

McCaffrey, Rev. P. R., 148n

McKisack, Miss, 29n

Medow, William, Stephen Gardiner's chaplain, 359n

Meinecke, German writer, 261n

Mekins, Richard, burnt as a heretic (1541), 369, 422n

Melanchthon, Philip (known as Schwarzerd) (1497-1560), 176n, 301, 356 and n, 374n, 379, 380n, 401* and n*, 403 and n, 405, 406n, 413, 416* and n, 423 and n, 433; Appendices, 481

Melton Mowbray (Leics), Cluniac Priory of, 299n

Memo, Dionisio, organist of St. Mark's, Venice, 41n

Mendoza y Zuñiga (Iñigo Lopez de), Bishop of Burgos (1529-39), Charles V's ambassador in England (1526-29), 58n

Mentz, G. D., 394, 401, 402 and n*, 414n, 415n; Appendices, 462

Merriman, R. B., 25n, 27n, 28n, 96n, 101n, 381n, 397n*; Appendices, 458, 466

Mestwerdt, P., 17n

Meyer, A., 17n

Meyer, Oskar, 131n; Appendices, 455

Micheas, 132n*

Michel, André, 74n, 310n

Michelangelo, 272

Michelet, 393

Micheli (or Michiel), Giovanni (†1596), Venetian Ambassador in England (1554-57), and in France (1557-60, 1572, 1575, 1578), 139n

Mickleham (Sussex), Priory of (Canons Regular), 299n

Middlemore, Humphrey, London Carthusian, 133, 154n

Middleton, Alice, Sir Thomas More's second wife (see More, Alice)

Mignet, 118n

Milan, 279, 348, 396

Milan, Duchy of, 116 and n, 275, 311

Milan, Duchess of (see Christina of Denmark)

Milles, John, Canon of Canterbury, 337n

Mirandella, Pico Della, Appendices, 452

Mocenigo, Alvise, 116n*

Mocenigo, Pietro, Venetian ambassador to Charles V (1538-40), 281

Modenham (Kent), Priory of, 299n

Molini, 56n

Möller, W., 141n

Molton, See of, 122n

Mombert, J. I., 307n

Montague, Lord (Henry Pole), brother to Cardinal Pole, 247, 256n, 262 and n, 266n*, 269, 270* and n*

Monte, Giovanni Ciocchi dal (see also Julius III), 267n, 284n

Montmorency, Anne, first Duke of, Grand Master, afterwards Constable of France, 72n, 275 and n, 276, 280, 360

Morandi, Giambattista, Canon of Bologna, Appendices, 455

More, Alice, Sir Thomas More's second wife, 227 and n, 243, 245, 363

More, Anne, daughter-in-law of Sir Thomas More, 227n

More, Cecily, third daughter of

Sir Thomas More, married Giles Heron, 227n

More, Cresacre, great-grandson of Sir Thomas More, 225n, 252n; Appendices 454*

More, Elizabeth, sister to Sir Thomas More, married John Rastall, 240n

More, Elizabeth, second daughter of Sir Thomas More, married William Daunce (or Daunsey), 227n

More, Jane, Thomas More's first wife, 227* and n

More, Sir John, father of Thomas More, 223n, 225n

More, John, only son of Sir Thomas More, 227n, 228n; Appendices, 454

More, Margaret ("Meg"), eldest daughter to Thomas More, married William Roper, 129, 226n*, 228, 229n, 244 and n, 245n*, 246n*, 249, 251, 253* and n*, Appendices, 452, 454*, 483*, 484

More, Sir Thomas, 1, 15*, 17* and n*, 19, 34n*, 68, 73, 104*, 129 and n, 136n, 138, 139 and n, 149 and n, 155n, 157n, 175 and n, 200*, 206, 209n, 212, 214, 215* and n, 216*, 217 and n*, 218*, 219n, 221n, 223* and n, 224* and n*, 225 and n*, 226* and n*, 227* and n*, 228* and n*, 229*, 230* and n*, 231n*, 232 and n*, 233* and n*, 234 and n*, 236* and n*, 237* and n*, 238* and n*, 239 and n*, 241* and n*, 242* and n, 243* and n, 244*, 245* and n*, 246* and n*, 247* and n, 248* and n*, 250* and n, 251n*, 252, 253*, and n 254* and n*, 255 and n*, 264n, 265n, 266n, 270, 284, 287n, 295*, 296, 307n*, 317, 329n, 333, 344*, 345n, 353, 354n, 361, 363, 365, 384n*, 385*, and n*, 386n, 387, 396; Appendices, 451, 452*, 453*, 454*, 455*, 467, 482*, 483*

More, William, Bishop of Colchester (1536-41), 162n, 183n

More (Herts), 83n

Mores, John, a Sion monk, 354n*

Moreton, Rev. H. A., 393n; Appendices, 440, 466

Morice, Ralph, Cranmer's secretary, 335* and n, 337n, 338n*; Appendices, 458

Morison, Sir Richard, ambassador to

Charles V in Edward VI's reign (1553-54), 210n, 222n*, 255n

Morlaix, 117n

Morone, Giovanni, Bishop of Modena (1529-50), Cardinal (1542; †1580), Nuncio to the Emperor (1536-38; 1539-41), 284n, 399n

Morone-Laton, Appendices, 441

"Mors, Roderick, Complaynt of," 30n, 149 and n

Mortimer, Margaret, Lady Suffolk, 53n

Morton, John, Bishop of Ely (1479-86), Archbishop of Canterbury (1486-†1500), Cardinal (1493), Chancellor of England, 14, 223, 224n

Mottisfont (Hants), Priory of, (Canons Regular), 144

Mountgrace (Yorks), Charterhouse of, 136n, 197n

Mountjoy, Lord (William Blount), 42 and n, 232 and n, 233n

Mouti, G. M., 269n

Muller, J. A., historian, 66n, 255n, 348n, 359n, 370n, 389n; Appendices, 460, 461, 463

Müller, K., 9n

Mullinger, J. B., historian, 202n; Appendices, 460

Mumby, F. A., 36n, 37n, 89n; Appendices, 446

Mundt, Christopher, agent of Henry VIII in Germany, 110n*, 397n

Murray, R. H., 17n; Appendices, 466

Mussolini, Preface by, 261n

Muxetula, J. A., Spanish ambassador in Rome, 96n

Myconius, Friedrich, fellow citizen and collaborator of Luther, 413 and n, 433

N

Naples, 8n, 116n

Napoleon, Appendices, 470*

National Portrait Gallery, 49, 274n

Navarre, Anthony of, 275n

Navarre, Blanche of, Appendices, 476

Navarre, Marguerite of, sister to Francis I, 83n

Neale, J. E., 26n, 29n

Netherdale (Yorks), 177

Netter, Thomas, of Walden, Carmelite, theologian (1380-1430), 384

Neville, Lord George, third Baron of Abergavenny, 118, 269*, 270

Neville, Lord Ralph, 177, 179n

Newark (Notts), Franciscan House at, 133n

Newcastle, Franciscan House at, 133n

New College, Oxford, 158n, 337

Newgate Prison, 183n

Newsholme, Sir Arthur, 196n

Newton Abbot (Devon), St. Augustine's Priory, 226

Nice, 273 and n, 274n, 275*, 276, 278, 280, 309, 360n, 412

Nicea, Council of, 404

Nichols, F. N., 16n, 17n, 24n, 28, 42n, 338n

Nichols, J., Appendices, 460, 463, 466

Nicolas, H., Appendices, 465

"Night Crow," The, (Anne Boleyn) 69 and n

Nisard, Appendices, 454

Norfolk, 347 and n

Norfolk, County of, 119, 157

Norfolk (John Howard), first Duke of (†1485), 45n

Norfolk, Duchess of, wife of Thomas Howard, second Duke of Norfolk, 327

Norfolk (Thomas Howard), Earl of Surrey, second Duke of Norfolk (1521), son of John Howard, Lord of the Treasury under Henry VII and Henry VIII, grandfather of Anne Boleyn, 23, 29n*, 45n

Norfolk (Thomas Howard), Earl of Surrey and third Duke of Norfolk (†1554), eldest son of Thos. Howard the second Duke, and uncle of Anne Boleyn, 56n, 7 and n, 73, 74, 81n, 85n, 134, 177* and n, 178 and n, 179*, 180 and n, 181, 190, 191n, 212n, 214n, 226*, 237 and n, 239, 241 and n*, 247, 262, 289, 293, 298 and n, 302, 313, 315, 322, 327n, 328, 338, 342, 348 and n, 350n, 377n, 381*, 417 and n; Appendices, 482

Norris, Sir Henry, 245, 322

North, Sir E., 190n

Northampton, 388

Northampton, Earl of, Appendices, 447

Northern Council, The, 181 and n

Northumberland, Earl of, 29n, 49n, 324

Norway, 335

Norwich, Bishop of, 86n, 111, 162n, 373n

Norwich, Diocese of, 161n, 193n, 352

Norwich, Monastery of, 185n

Norwich Castle, 47

Nottingham, 173n, 179, 316

Nottingham, See of, 122n

Nuremberg, 320 and n

O

Oatlands, 326

O'Brien, G., 192n

Ockham, William of, disciple of Duns Scotus (1280-1347), 8, 9n*

O'Donovan, Louis, 34n*

Œcolampadius (or Hausschein), John (real name Heusgen), a reformer (1482-1531), 203 and n, 367n; Appendices, 452

Offer, Clifford J., 154n

Offor, George, 307n

Oglethorpe, Dr. Owen, 425n

Okeham, Baron Cromwell of, 298

Oldham, Hugh, Bishop of Exeter (1504-19), 151n

Oldoin (see Chacoin-Oldoin)

Oman, 12n; Appendices, 467

Orleans, Duke of, 396

Orleans, University of, 77, 81; Appendices, 444

Ormanetto, Niccolo, Reginald Pole's secretary in England (1554-57), Bishop of Padua (1570-77), 113n

Ormonde, Earl of, 47, 49n

Ortiz, Dr. Pedro, Charles V's ambassador in Rome, 118n, 159n; Appendices, 478

Orvieto, 56n, 57n*, 58n*, 59, 346n, 349n; Appendices, 469, 471

Osiander (or Osiandre), Andrew, Nuremberg Reformer (1498-1552) 85, 320* and n

Osler, W., 224n

Osney, Bishop of, 137n

Owst, G. R., 12n

Oxford, 73n, 74n, 75n, 143, 144 and n*, 150, 157*, 158n, 233, 257 and n, 333n, 343*, 344, 428n

Oxford, Bishop of, 137n

Oxford, See of, 193n

Oxford, University of, 76 and n, 78n, 130 and n, 157*, 196, 197n, 202, 224*, 228n, 302, 342n, 376n; Appendices, 476

Oxford, Wolsey's College at, 21n, 73n, 74n, 144 and n, 288*, 290, 318, 342, 348

P

Pacca, Cardinal, Appendices, 470

Pace, Richard, Dean of St. Paul's, Henry VIII's ambassador at Venice, 4 and *n**, 23, 51*n*, 53*n*, 258*n*

Paciulo, Luca, O.S.F., mathematician (†1514), 344*n*

Padua, 257 and *n*, 258*n*, 263, 350

Padua, University of, 76*n*, 77, 344; Appendices, 444, 472, 478

Paget, Sir William, 189*n*, 320*n*, 397*n*

Pallavicini, Sforza, S.F., Cardinal (1659), historian of the Council of Trent, 283 and *n*; Appendices, 455

Palmer, William, 355*n*, 388*n*; Appendices, 460

Parfew, Robert, Bishop of St. Asaph (1536-54), and of Hereford (1554-58), 162*n*

Paris, Philip, visitor of the English monasteries, 164*n*

Paris, 51*n*, 117*n*, 232, 252*n*, 261, 276, 307, 309, 310, 342*n*, 360; Appendices, 452, 470, 478*

Paris, Bishop of, 108 and *n*, 109*n**

Paris, University of, 77, 81; Appendices, 444

Parisio, Pierpaulo, jurisconsult, afterwards Cardinal (1534) (†1545), 283*n*

Parker, Matthew, Archbishop of Canterbury (1559-75), 336*n*

Parker, Dr., Vicar-General to Bishop of Worcester, 100*n**

Parkinson, 132*n*

Parr, Katherine, Henry VIII's sixth wife (†1548), 191*n*, 328* and *n**, 371 and *n*, 434

Parr, William, visitor of the English monasteries, 164*n*

Paschini, P., 264*n*

Paslew, Abbot of Whalley, 171*n*

Pasquet, 29*n*

Pate, Richard, ambassador in Germany (†1565), 255*n**

Patenson, Henry, Sir Thomas More's fool, 228*n*

Patterson, L. K., 130*n*

Paul III, Pope (†1549), 56*n*, 110*n*, 218, 256 and *n*, 263*n*, 266* and *n*, 267, 269, 273 and *n*, 274*n*, 278, 281, 283, 292, 324, 368*n*, 396, 397, 398*, 400, 412, 413*n*, 419*n*; Appendices, 476

Paul IV (Caraffa), Pope (†1559), 76*n*, 132*n*, 259, 267*n*

Pavia, Battle of (1525), 47*n*, 117*n*, 345

Pavia, University of, 77; Appendices, 472, 478

Peasant War, The, 12*n*

Pemberton, W. S. C., 43*n*

Pembroke, Marquis of (Anne Boleyn), 50, 83 and *n*, 348*n*

Penizzoni, Girolamo, 106

Penrith (Cumberland), See of, 122*n*

Percy, Sir Henry Algernon, sixth Earl of Northumberland, 49 and *n**, 287*n*, 324

Percy, Sir Thomas, 177, 180*n*

Perpaglia, Vincenzo, Abbot of San Salvatore, 279* and *n*

Perrat, Charles, 39*n*

Perry, G. G., Appendices, 461

Perth, Charterhouse of, 136*n*

Perth, See of, 122*n*

Perugia, Bishop of, Appendices, 472

Pesaro, See of, Appendices, 479

Peter and Poulet, 187*n*

Peterborough, Bishop of, 162*n*

Peterborough, See of, 193*n*

"Peter's Pence," 32*n*, 42*n*, 112 and *n*, 113 and *n**, 140*n*, 294

Petit, John, 24*n*

Peto, William, Franciscan, Cardinal (1557), 132 and *n**, 133*n*, 155

Petrarch, 343*n*; Appendices, 452

Petre, Dr. William, visitor of the English monasteries and Secretary of State, 26*n*, 31*n*, 164*n*

Petrucci, Frederico, Appendices, 478

Petrucci, Giovanni, Appendices, 478

Petrucci, Rinaldo, Appendices, 472, 478

Philadelphia, Bishop of, 137*n*

Philip II, King of Spain (1556-98), Appendices, 441

Philip of Bavaria (1503-48), son of the Palatine Robert (†1504), 416 and *n*

Philip the Fair, 127*n*

Philip the Handsome, 37*n*, 345*n*

Philip the Magnanimous, Landgrave of Hesse (1519-67), 110*n**, 116*n*, 309*n*, 413, 416

Philippa, daughter of Duke of Clarence, 44*n*

Philipps, Rev. T., S.J., 256*n*, 257*n*; Appendices, 456

Picardy, 117n*

Pickering, Dr. John, Dominican, 181n

Picus, John, Earl of Mirandula (†1494), life written by Sir Thomas More, 230n

"Piers Plowman, Vision of," 9h

"Pilgrimage of Grace," The, 124n, 137n, 163, 171n*, 176* and n, 177, 181, 183n, 267, 271, 293n, 295 and n, 328, 332, 377n, 408

Pin, Ellies du, 18th century writer, 201n

Pineau, J. B., French writer, 233n

Pini, Filippo, condottiere of Lucca, 278n

Pinning, H., secretary to Cardinal Pole, Appendices, 456, 457

Pipwell (Northumberland), Cistercian Abbot of, 299n

Pisa, Council of, Appendices, 478

Pisa, University of, Appendices, 472, 478*

Pisani, Francesco, Cardinal (1517), 56n, 110n

Pius II, Pope (1458-1464), Appendices, 452

Pius III, Pope (1503), 37n

Pius IV, Pope (1559-65), Appendices, 456

Pius VII, Pope (1800-23), Appendices, 478

Plantagenet, Arthur (see Lisle, Lord)

Plantagenet, George (†1478) (see Clarence, Duke of)

Plato, 231, 259, 292

Plattard, J., French writer, 232n

Plovézet (Finistere), 304n

Plucknett, F. T., Appendices, 465

Plutarch, 317

Pocock, Nicholas, Editor of "Records of the Reformation," 37n; Appendices, 442

Poggio, Giovanni, prothonotary, afterwards Bishop of Tropea (1541-56), Nuncio in Spain (1529-51), Cardinal Legate in Spain (1551-53), 281

Poissy, 58n

Poitiers, Synod of, Appendices, 477

Poland, 397n

Pole, Geoffrey, youngest brother of Cardinal Pole, 256n, 269, 270

Pole, Geoffrey, son of Geoffrey Pole, 271

Pole, Margaret, Countess of Salisbury, mother of Cardinal Pole (1473-1541), 136n, 212, 257 and n, 271

Pole, Reginald, Cardinal (†1558), 15, 76 and n, 90, 113n, 119n, 127n*, 200, 201n, 214n, 219n*, 248n, 254n, 255 and n, 256*, 257* and n*, 258 and n*, 259, 260* and n*, 261* and n*, 262* and n*, 263* and n*, 264* and n*, 265* and n*, 266* and n*, 267* and n*, 268* and n, 269, 270 and n*, 271 and n*, 272, 273* and n*, 277, 278* and n*, 279*, 280, 281*, 282 and n, 283* and n*, 284, 286, 288*, 290, 292, 300, 305n, 310n, 315, 316n, 321, 352 and n, 354, 357, 358, 359 and n*, 361, 362* and n*, 363n*, 387, 410n, 413n, 429 and n, 432 and n, 435n; Appendices, 453, 455*, 456*, 457*

Pole, Sir Richard, father of Cardinal Pole (†1505), 256, 257n*

Pole, Ursula, only sister of Cardinal Pole, 256n

Pole, Rev. Herbert, 195n, 431n, 433n

Politian (born at Montepulciano) (Angélo del Ambroginis, known as Poliziano), humanist (1454-94), 224

Pollard, A. F., historian, xii, xiii; 2n, 7n*, 11n, 13n, 14n, 15n, 18n, 19n, 21n, 22n*, 24n*, 25n, 29n*, 30n, 32n*, 33n, 36n*, 37n*, 38n*, 41n, 43n*, 118n, 126n, 148n; Appendices, 441, 446, 459, 466

Pollard, A. W., 10n, 11n

Pollard, Richard, visitor of the English monasteries, 164n

Pollen, J. H., S.J., 305n

Pollini, Girolamo, O.P., 186n, 234n; Appendices, 444

Polsted, Henry, visitor of the English monasteries, 164n

Pomerania, 335

Pomerania, Dukes of, 397n

Pomfret or Pontefract (Yorks), 175n*, 176n, 177*, 178, 179n*

Pommeraye, Gilles de la, Francis I's ambassador to Henry VIII (1532), 99n, 348n

Poole, Reginald Lane, 9n*, 10n; Appendices, 466

Pope, Sir Thomas, 190n, 250, 252

Porrit, E. and A., 29n, 293n

Porsenna, 372

Porter, John (†1541), 369, 370

Portsmouth, 277

Portugal, Emmanuel of (†1521), Appendices, 476

Portugal, Infante of, 275

Portugal, Queen of, 46n

Potter, E. S. G., 9n

Powell, C. D., Appendices, 446

Powell, Edward, executed for denying the royal supremacy (†1540), 69n, 394n

Powell, F. York, 394

Power, Miss Eileen, 146n, 154 and n, 155n; Appendices, 448

Powicke, F. W., 2n

"Praemunire," 23, 72* and n, 92 and n*, 93n*, 94* and n, 94, 97, 124n, 289, 335n

Prat, Cardinal Anthony du, Archbishop of Sens (1525-35), Cardinal (1527), negotiated the Concordat of 1515, 54n

Prato, Felix de, Augustinian, a converted Rabbi, canonist (1559), 78n*; Appendices, 472

Pre, Convent of, 146n

Premonstratensians, The, 168n, 182

Prentout, H., French writer, 305n

Preston, Thomas, 371

Previdello, Girolamo, Appendices, 472

Previté-Orton, 127n

"Prideaux, Mr." (pen-name), 370n

Priuli, Alvise, friend of Cardinal Pole, 260n, 263, 264n*, 265n, 268n, 277; Appendices, 455

Privy Council, 26, 97 and n, 101n, 211, 217, 218, 233n, 236*, 291*, 313*; Appendices, 440, 465*

Procter, M. J., Appendices, 462

Prussia, 397n

Pucci, Antonio, Cardinal (1531), 57, 58n, 59n, 144n

Pusey, E. B., 125n

Putney, 285

Pye, B., translator, Appendices, 455

Q

Queen's College, Cambridge, 16n, 200n, 201, 205n

Quiñones, Francisco, O.S.F., General of his Order (1523), Cardinal (1528; †1540), 58n, 336n

Quirini (or Querini), Angelo Maria, O.S.B. (1680-1755), Cardinal and Bishop of Brescia (1727-55), 248n, 283n, 358n; Appendices, 455, 456*

R

Rabelais, 109n, 273n

Ragusa, Archbishop of, 263; Appendices, 455

Raince, Nicholas, secretary to Roman Embassy, 89n

Ramsey (Huntingdon), Benedictine Abbey of, 190, 197n

Ranke, Leopold von, 6n, 141, 152, 230n, 394; Appendices, 463, 467

Rastall (or Rastell), John, brother-in-law to Sir Thomas More, 240n; Appendices, 453

Rastall (or Rastell), William, nephew of Sir Thomas More, 206n, 207n, 222n, 230n, 240 and n; Appendices, 450, 453*, 454*

Ratisbon, 320, 373n, 419 and n

Ravenna, 61n, 269

Rayner, R. M., Appendices, 467

Reading (Berks), 295, 359, 387n

Reading (Berks), Benedictine Abbot of, 185, 295, 287n

Rebitté, French writer, 232n

Record Office, The, 27n*, 101n, 161n*, 162n, 205n, 247n, 367n; Appendices, 464

Redman (or Redmayn), Dr. John, 428*, 429n*, 430n

Reed, Professor A. W., 230n, 231n

Regnault, 16th century Parisian printer, 308

Reid, R. R., 181n

Rembaud (see Lavisse and Rembaud)

Renaudet, A., 17n*, 18n, 233n*

Renée, daughter of Louis XII, Duchess of Ferrara (1510-75), 55 and n

Reusch, H., German writer, 233n, 369n

Revers, Earl of, 29n

Revetta, 109n

Rewley (Oxfordshire), Abbot of, 159n, 299n

Reyner, 191 and n; Appendices, 448

Reynolds, Richard, Carthusian, 134 and n, 136n, 154n, 329n

Rezneck, Samuel, 135n

Rheon, Bishop of, 137n

Rhodes, 230n

Rhys, E., Appendices, 468

Ribadeneira, Pedro de, S.J. (†1611), Appendices, 443, 444

Rich, Franciscan, executed with Elizabeth Barton, 212n

Rich, Sir Richard, solicitor-general, afterwards Lord Rich (1541), and Chancellor of England (1550), 175n, 176, 190n, 217, 247*

Richard II, King of England (1377-99), 3, 4n*, 13n, 93n, 142, 378

Richard III, King of England (1483-85), 36n, 118; Appendices, 464

Richardson and Sayles, 32n

Richmond (Surrey), 37n

Richmond (Surrey), Franciscan House at, 133n

Richmond (Yorks), 177

Richmond Castle, 315n

Richmond, Duke of, (Elizabeth Blount's son), 43, 46n*, 76n, 325n

Richter, 122n

Ridolfi, Niccoló, Bishop of Vicenza (1525-50), Archbishop of Florence (1543-47), Cardinal (1517; †1550), 110n

Rievaulx Abbey, 199n

Rinaldi (Raynaldus), Oderico, oratorian (1595-1671), 9n, 89n, 434n

Rinzio, Bernardo, 51n

Ripon (Yorks), 175n, 177

Risby, Richard, Franciscan, executed with Elizabeth Barton, 212n

Rishton, Edward, edited and continued Sander, 208n, 379n; Appendices, 443

Ritter, S., 263n

Rivius, J. (†1533), 254

Robert, The Palatine (†1504), father of Philip of Bavaria, 416n

Roberts, R. A., Appendices, 466

Robespierre, 312

Robinson (or Robertson), Dr. Thomas, 425n, 429n

Robynson, Ralph, translator of Utopia, 17n, 232n*; Appendices, 452

Rocaberti, J. Th., O.P., 265n

Roche Abbey (Yorks), 187

Rochester, 310, 378n

Rochester, Bishop of, 19n, 20n, 162n*, 183n*, 201, 207, 208*, 213n, 215, 218, 221n*, 222n*, 251n, 255n, 266n, 303, 334, 398n, 417n, 425n

Rochester, Bishop's Palace at, 222n

Rochester, Diocese of, 143n, 202n, 217, 380

Rochester, John, Carthusian, executed for denying royal supremacy (1537), 183n

Rochford, Viscount, Anne Boleyn's father, 48, 72n

Rochford, Viscount, Anne Boleyn's brother, 95

Rochford, Lady, wife of George Boleyn, 328

Rockingham, 388

Rodocanachi, 55n

Roerich, Ed., 399n, 401n

Rogers, John, first reformer burnt in Mary Tudor's time (1555), 306, 307n*

Rogers, P., 186n

Rome, 4 and n, 5n, 20, 24, 31, 32*, 33 and n, 34 and n, 49, 53, 54n*, 56 and n, 57n*, 58 and n, 60 and n, 61n*, 62 and n, 63*, 64n, 65, 66* and n*, 67* and n*, 69n, 71n, 72n, 75n, 76n*, 78, 79, 82* and n*, 83 and n, 84 and n, 86, 89, 90*, 91, 92, 96n, 98*, 99*, 102, 104, 105*, 106*, 107, 108*, 110 and n, 112* and n, 113, 115n, 117n, 118n, 124*, 130n*, 136*, 137 and n, 140, 141, 149, 150, 153, 154, 176, 205n, 208n, 215, 218, 222n, 230n, 233n, 249*, 252n, 266 and n*, 267, 269, 271n, 273 and n*, 279*, 283, 284, 291, 292, 309, 318, 319, 320n, 321*, 328n, 329n, 331 and n, 347n, 351*, 358, 365, 379n, 386, 388*, 389n, 390*, 398, 399n*, 419 and n*, 434, 435; Appendices, 450, 469*, 471, 472

Ronan, Rev. M. V., 186n

Roos, J. F., 400n*, 402n

Roper, Margaret, Sir Thomas More's eldest daughter (see More, Margaret)

Roper, Mary, Thomas More's grand-daughter, married to James Basset, 251n

Roper, William, son-in-law of Sir Thomas More, 1n, 6n, 224n, 226 and n*, 226n, 227n, 232n, 236, 237, 238n*, 239n*, 240 and n*, 241*, 242, 243n, 247, 250n*, 255n; Appendices, 452*, 454, 483

Roses, Wars of the, 29, 44, 45, 119, 214n, 223

Ross, William, pen-name of Sir Thomas More, 233, 234n

Rota, The Roman, 57n, 70, 84n, 89n; Appendices, 470, 472, 478, 479

Roussillon, 36n

Rovere, Giuliano della, Cardinal and Bishop of Urbino (1548-51; †1578), 264n

Rovezzano, Bernardo da, 74n

Roye, William, secretary to Tyndale, 369, 382

Rudhart, G. T., Appendices, 454

Ruding, 189n

Rugg, John, Prebendary of Chichester, retired to Reading, executed for denying the royal supremacy (1539), 129, 387 and n

Rugg (or Repps), William, Bishop of Norwich (1536-50), 162n, 373n, 408, 418

Russell, Sir John, Baron, first Earl of Bedford, 191n

Russelli, G., 34n

Russo, L., Italian writer, 261n

Ruth, 190

Ruthal, Thomas, Dean of Salisbury and secretary to Henry VII, Bishop of Durham (1509-29), 233n

Rutland, Thomas Manners, first Earl of, 29n, 177, 191n

Rye, R. A., London University Librarian, 197n

Rymer, Thomas (1641-1713), 36n*, 37n*, 38n, 39n, 182n*; Appendices, 465

S

Sadler (or Sadleir), Sir Ralph, secretary to Henry VIII, 190n, 313

Sadolet, Jacopo (1477-1547), Bishop of Carpentras (1517-40; †1547), Cardinal (1536), 260n, 263 and n*, 267n, 273, 279, 283

Saint-Simon, 231n

St. Albans (Herts), Abbey of, 21n, 146n, 290n

St. Andrews, 301n

St. Andrews, Archbishop of, 274n

St. Anselm, 388

St. Asaph, Bishop of, 23, 26, 69n, 85n, 103n, 162n, 183n, 204n, 321n, 350; Appendices, 455

St. Asaph, Diocese of, 304n

St. Athanasius, 240n

St. Bartholomew's Hospice, London, 197n

St. Cyprian, 251, 420n

St. David's, Bishop of, 19n, 162n, 183n, 334, 409, 417n, 425n

St. Faith, Priory of, 299n

St. Frideswede's Monastery, Oxford, 144n

St. Germain's (Cornwall), See of, 122n

St. Jerome, 385

St. John (William Paulet), Lord, afterwards Lord Treasurer, Earl of Wiltshire (1550), and Marquis of Winchester (1551), 191n

St. John the Baptist, 69, 204, 222*, 223 and n

St. John's College, Cambridge, 143 and n, 155n, 202* and n*, 205n, 306n; Appendices, 450

St. Lawrence, Church of, London, 225, 232

St. Michael's Mount, Abbey of, 191n

St. Osithe's (Essex), Priory of, (Canons Regular), 299n

St. Paul, 249, 393*

St. Paul's, London, 201, 232, 303, 307n, 313*, 332*, 361n, 369*, 378n;

St. Paul's Churchyard, London, 203

St. Paul's Cross, 68, 113n, 211, 213n, 303, 336n, 355n, 368

St. Peter ad Vincula (Tower of London Chapel), 222 and n, 253n

St. Radegunde's Abbey, Bradsole, near Dover, 199n

St. Stephen, 249

St. Thomas à Becket (*see* Becket)

St. Thomas of Villanova, 260n

Salcot (or Capon), Dr. John, Bishop of Bangor (1534-39), and of Salisbury (1539-57), 162n, 211, 380, 399n, 409

Salisbury, 257n, 345

Salisbury, Bishop of, 19n, 20n*, 60, 143n, 154, 308n, 334, 336n, 373n, 382, 417n, 422; Appendices, 463

Salisbury, Cathedral of, 164

Salisbury, Countess of (*see* Pole, Margaret)

Salisbury, Diocese of, 143n, 202n, 208n, 380

Salter, Appendices, 467

Salviati, Giovanni, Leo X's nephew, Bishop of Fermo (1518-23), Cardinal (1517), 5n, 7n, 14n, 22n, 33n, 54n*, 62n, 84n

Sampson, Richard, Dean of the Chapel Royal and Bishop of Chichester (1536-43), 264n, 313, 352*, 353, 373n, 379 and n, 380, 418

Sander (or Sanders), Nicholas, theologian and historian (1527-81), xv; 36*n*, 40*n*, 49 and *n*, 50*n**, 52*n**, 54*n*, 68*n*, 72*n*, 89*n*, 132*n*, 168*n*, 169, 201*n*, 207*n*, 208*n**, 334, 341 and *n*, 387*n*, 394, 420*n*, 432*n*, 434 and *n**, 435 and *n*; Appendices, 443*, 444*

Sanga, Giambattista, secretary to Clement VII, 61*n*

Sarpi, Paolo (†1623), 42*n**

Savage, George, Rector of Davenham (Cheshire), 343*n*

Savine, Dr. Alexander, 148*n**, 152*n*, 169*n*, 190*n*; Appendices, 448

Saxony, 397*n*, 423

Saxony, Duchess of, 310*n*

Saxon, Duke of, 233*n*, 319*n*

Saxony, John Frederick, Elector of, 110*, 309 and *n*, 398 and *n*, 400*n*, 402 and *n*, 413, 414 and *n*, 416, 424*n*

Saxony, Vice-Chancellor of, 374*n*, 379*n*, 401, 413

Saxy, priest, arrested for heresy (1540), 422*n*

Sayle, C., 10*n*

Sayles, 32*n*

Scarborough (Yorks), 180 and *n**

Schanz, G., 295*n*

Scheffer, J. C. de Hoop, Dutch writer, 307*n*

Schelhorn, 267*n*

Schleswig-Holstein, 335

Schmalkalden, 398, 400*n*, 401*n*, 402*n*

Schulten-Rechberg, G. von, 263*n*

Scotland, 115*n**, 133, 136*n*, 181 and *n*, 189, 273, 274*n**, 277*, 349*n*, 379*n*; Appendices, 450

Scotland, King of, 109*n*, 225*n*, 274, 278, 283*n*

Scott, Rev. Herbert, 358*n*

Scotus, John Duns, O.S.F. (1274-1308), 158*n**, 302; Appendices, 476

Scrope, Lord, 177, 179*n*

Searle, 200*n*

Seckendorf, Lutheran 17th century writer, 255*n*, 400*n**, 401, 402*n**, 414*n*

Sedbar (or Sedbergh), Adam, Cistercian Abbot of Jervaulx, 181*n*

Seebohm, F., 17*n*, 18*n**, 226*n*, 231*n*

"Segnatura, The Roman," 71*n*

Segovia, 37*n*

Selborne (Hants), Augustinian Priory of, 143*n*

Sele, Priory of, 143*n*

Sempringham (Lincs), Prior of, 183*n*

Seripando, Girolamo, O. S. Aug., general of this order (1539), Archbishop of Salerno (1554-63), Cardinal (1561), 260*n*

Seville, 36*n*

Seymour, Edward, Jane Seymour's brother (*see* Hertford, Earl of)

Seymour, Jane, Henry VIII's third wife, 46*n*, 286, 306*n*, 322 and *n*, 324, 325 and *n**, 407, 412

Seymour, Sir John, father of Jane Seymour, 325*n*

Seymour, Thomas, High Admiral, Jane Seymour's brother, 191*n*

Sforza, Francis, 274*n*

Sforza, Christina (*see* Christina of Denmark)

Shaftesbury (Dorset), 122*n*

Shakespeare, 337, 338*n*

Shaxton, Nicholas, Bishop of Salisbury (1535-39), 334, 336 and *n* 340, 373*n*, 380 and *n*, 382, 399*n* 417*n*, 418, 421, 422 and *n*.

Sheen (Surrey), Charterhouse of, 136*n*, 197*n*, 209*n*, 257, 260, 261

Sherborne, Robert, secretary to Henry VII (1496), Dean of St. Paul's (1499), Bishop of Chichester (1508-†36), 38*n**, 364*n*

Sherburn, Hospital of, 164

Shether, Edmund, preacher, 337*n*

Shirley, W. Waddington, 9*n*

Shrewsbury (Shropshire), See of, 122*n*

Shrewsbury (Francis Talbot), fifth Earl of, son of Geo. Talbot, fourth Earl, 191*n*

Shrewsbury (George Talbot), fourth Earl of, 49*n*, 173*n*, 177, 178, 191*n*

Sicily, 8*n*, 116*n*

Sidon, Bishop of, 137*n*

Siena, 56*n*

Siena, University of, Appendices, 472, 478

Silva, Mendez, 296

Simancas, 35 and *n*; Appendices, 442

Simar, T., French writer, 258*n*

Simonetta, Giacomo, Dean of the Rota, Bishop of Perusa (1535-†1539), Cardinal (1535), 58*n*, 59*n*, 79, 109; Appendices, 472, 479

Simpson, 18*n*

Singer, S. W., editor of *Life of Wolsey,* 287*n*

Sion Abbey (Middlesex), 133, 134 and *n,* 191*n,* 240, 354*n*

Sion Nuns, 209*n,* 327

Sittingbourne (Kent), 378*n*

Skip (or Skipp), John, Bishop of Hereford (1539-52), 380, 425*n*

Slimbridge (Glos.), 343*n*

Smalcadic League, The, 110, 309*n,* 311, 319, 367, 397, 413 and *n,* 416

Smeton (or Smeaton), Mark, 322, 323

Smith, John, visitor of the English monasteries, 164*n*

Smith, Sir Thomas, Professor at Cambridge and Secretary of State and Privy Councillor under Edward VI and Elizabeth, 374*n**

Smith, Walter, *alias* for Thomas Cromwell's father, 285*n*

Smith, William, Bishop of Lincoln (1495-1514), 143

Smith, Lucy Toulmin, 198*n*

Smith, P., 34*n;* Appendices, 466

Smithen, F. J., Appendices, 466

Smithfield, 298*n,* 423, 432*n*

Smythe, C. H., Appendices, 459

Snape, R. H., Appendices, 449

Sockman, R. W., 198*n*

Sodom, 167*n*

Soliman II (1520-66), 281

Solway Firth, 181

Somerset, Duke of, 29*n,* 190

Somerset, Duke of, Elizabeth Blount's son, 46*n*

Somerset, Protector, 29*n,* 93*n,* 127 128*n**, 216*n,* 294*n,* 364, 381

Soranzo, Giacomo, Venetian ambassador in England (1551-54), and to the Emperor (May, 1559-December, 1561), 47*n*

Sorbonne, The, 53*n,* 76, 77*n,* 233*n,* 261

Southampton, 122*n*

Southampton, Earl of, 174*n,* 314 and *n*

Southampton, Franciscan House at, 133*n*

Southwell (Lincs), 73 and *n,* 79

Southwell, Sir Richard, member of the Royal Council under Henry VIII Edward VI and Mary Tudor, 190*n*

Southwell, Sir Robert, brother of Sir Richard, Master of the Rolls under Henry VIII, 190*n*

Spain, 35, 36*n,* 37*n**, 38*n,* 39* and *n**, 44 and *n,* 45, 47, 56*n,* 64, 65* and *n,* 67, 105, 114, 119*n,* 177*n,* 254, 273*n,* 277, 278, 282, 320*n,* 397*n,* 412; Appendices, 440, 470

Speaker of House of Commons, The, 36*n,* 27*n,* 101, 102, 104*n*

Speed, John, 17th century historian, 148*n**, 161*n,* 163*n*

Spelman, Clement, son of Sir Henry Spelman, 191*n*

Spelman, Sir Henry (†1641), 166 and *n,* 191 and *n;* Appendices, 447, 454

Spencer, L., 4*n*

Spillman, Rev. J., S.J., 131*n,* 231*n;* Appendices, 455

Stafford, Edward, Duke of Buckingham, 45*n*

Stafileo, Giovanni, Dean of the Rota, 57*n**

Stamford (Lincs), 174*n*

Standish, Henry, Guardian of London Franciscans, Bishop of St. Asaph (1518-35), 23*, 69*n,* 103*n,* 204*n,* 321*n,* 350

Stanhope (Co. Durham), 345*n*

Stapleton, Thomas, theologian and controversialist (1535-98), Canon of Chichester (1558), took refuge at Louvain under Elizabeth, xv; 225*n,* 226 and *n**, 228*n**, 231, 234*, 238 and *n**, 239*n**, 243*n,* 252*n**, 253 and *n**, 254*n**, 255*; Appendices, 453, 454*, 483, 484

Starkey, Thomas, Court Chaplain, 264, 265

Steele, R., 29*n;* Appendices, 465

Steelyard, The, London, 68*n*

Steeple-Langford (Wilts), 345*n*

Stephen, nephew of Henry I, 45*n*

Stephens, Mr., *alias* for Stephen Gardiner, 347

Stephens, W., Appendices, 439

Stern, 116*n*

Stevens, William, translator of Gardiner's *De Vera Obedientia,* 355*n*

Stevenson, 11*n*

Stewart, Miss, Appendices, 456

Stixwold (Lincs), Nunnery of, 168*n*

Stokes, F. G., 15*n*

Stokesley, John, Bishop of London (1530-39), 76* and *n,* 77*n,* 81*n,* 87*n,* 133*n,* 216, 238*n,* 267*n,* 319, 331, 341*, 343*, 346, 349* and *n,* 350* and *n**, 359, 361, 365, 369* and *n**, 372*n,* 373*, 375, 377*, 378, 380, 387, 399*n,* 408 and *n,* 418, 432

Stone, J., Augustinian, 136n

Stone, author of *History of Mary*, 46n, 47n

Stone, *Miss*, 16n; Appendices, 466

Storer, Appendices, 446

Stowe (or Stow), John, the Chronicler, 132n*, 158n, 159n; Appendices, 440 445

Strafford (Thomas Wentworth), Earl of (†1641), 192n

Strasbourg, 358

Strickland, *Agnes*, 325n, 326n, 328n; Appendices, 445

Stroick, *P. A.*, 17n

Strype, *John* (1643-1737), 15n, 50n, 99n*, 137n, 146, 148n, 316, 319n, 332 and n*, 338n*, 343n, 365, 370, 375, 382n, 402n, 414n, 417, 425n; Appendices, 439, 458, 463, 464*

Stuarts, The, 192, 331n

Stubbs, *W.*, 4n, 95n, 290n; Appendices, 466

"Submission of the Clergy" Act, 103, 111, 126n, 238, 263n, 353

Suffolk, County of, 157

Suffolk, Duke of, 29n, 41n, 45n, 47n, 53 and n, 57n, 70, 72 and n, 117n, 129, 173 and n*, 174, 190, 214n, 247, 291, 348n

Sumtleger, Sir Anthony, 249n

"Supplication Against the Ordinaries," 100, 349n, 353

"Supplication of Beggars," The, 149 and n*, 369n

"Supplication of Poor Souls," The, 149 and n

Surrey, 157*, 182

Surrey, Duke of, 328

Surrey, Earl of, 47, 117n, 241n

Sussex, County of, 143n, 157

Sussex, Robert Ratcliff, first Earl of, 191n

Swadale (Yorks), 177

Switzerland, 4n, 31; Appendices, 477

T

Talbot, George (Shrewsbury), 29n

Tanner, *J. R.*, 29n, 134n, 148n*, 193n

Tarbes, Bishop of, 48n, 51*, 52n*, 53n; Appendices, 445

Taunton (Somerset), 122n, 290n, 319, 342

Taunton, *Ethelred L.*, 22n, 43n; Appendices, 446, 457

Tawney, *R. H.*, 175n, 192n

Taylor, John, Bishop of Lincoln (1552-53), 22, 422n

Taylor, Roland, a Suffolk rector, 390n

Taylor, *Rev. T.*, 191n

Taylor, *W. F.*, 135n

Teddington (Middx.), 134n

Templier, 51n

Temse, member of House of Commons, 26 and n, 101n

Tewkesbury (Glos), 299

Tewkesbury (Glos), Benedictine Monastery of, 183n, 194n, 196

Thames, The, 132n, 222n, 227, 239n, 277, 282, 283, 324, 335

Theiner, 70n; Appendices, 442

Thetford (Norfolk), 122n

Thévenot, Appendices, 445

Thirlby, Dr. Thomas, Bishop of Westminster (1540-50), of Norwich (1550-54), and of Ely (1554-58), 193n, 360n, 364 and n, 374n, 378n*, 388, 425n, 49n

Thirsk, William, quondam abbot of Fountains, 181n

Thompson, *Prof. A. Hamilton*, Appendices, 448

Thompson, *Miss E. Margaret*, 136n, 197n

Thompson, *W.*, Appendices, 460

Thomson, *S. Harrison*, 10n*

Thornley, *Miss I. D.*, 134n

Throckmorton, Michael, in Reginald Pole's service, 265 and n

Thuringia, 413n

Thurland Castle (Lancs), 344n*

Thwaites, Edward, compromised in the Elizabeth Barton affair, 213n

Tiepolo, Nicolò (†1551), member of Grand Council of the Venetian Republic (1495), sent to the Pope (1534), to the Emperor (1536), and to the meeting at Nice (1538), 80n

Tillotson, John, Archbishop of Canterbury (1691-†1694), 317n

Tiraboschi, *Girolamo, S.J.*, Professor at Modena University and Historian of Italian Literature (1731-94), 263n

Tittenhanger Park (Herts), 300n

Todd, *H. J.*, 308n, 317, 33n; Appendices, 458

Toledo, 36n, 274, 278, 279, 280, 345

Tomeo, Niccolò Leonico, humanist and friend of Cardinal Pole, 257, 258n; Appendices, 457

Tomita:to, Bernardino, physician, philosopher, poet, grammarian (1506-76), Appendices, 456

Torrigiano, Pietro, Florentine sculptor, 74*n*, 272

Toulouse, University of, 77; Appendices, 444

Tour, Imbarte de la, 17*n*

Tournai, See of, 20*n*

Tournon, Francis de (1489-1562), Cardinal (1530), Archbishop of Lyons (1551-62), 89*n*, 256

Tout, Professor F. T., 155*n*, 394 and *n*

Tower Hill (*see* London, Tower Hill)

Townsend, edited John Foxe, 370*n*

Tracy, Richard, Gloucestershire gentleman, suspected of heresy, 382

Trafford, William, new Prior of London Charterhouse, 183*n*

Treasons Bill of 1534, The, 27*n*, 175*n*

Tree, H. B., 43*n*

Tregunwell, John, chief judge of the Admiralty, 133*n*

Trent, 269, 283*n*

Trent, Council of, 153*n*, 209*n*, 283, 384*n*, 398, 430; Appendices, 455

Trent, River (Notts and Yorks), 178*n*

Trésal, Abbé, 117*n*; Appendices, 449, 467

Trevelyan, George Macaulay, 12*n*; Appendices, 447

Treves, 397*n*

Treville, Priuli's villa near Verona, 264*n*

Trinity College, Cambridge, 205*n*

Trinity Hall, 318, 342*; Appendices, 460

Trivulzio, Agostino (†1548), Cardinal (1517), Legate in France (1536), 110*n*

Tudors, The, 24*n*, 118, 192, 302*n*, 331*n*; Appendices, 465

Tunis, 397

Tunstall, Brian, brother of Bishop Tunstall, 344*n*

Tunstall, Cuthbert, Bishop of London (1522-30) and of Durham (1530-52; 1553-59), 51*n*, 88*n*, 97 and *n**, 207*n*, 216, 240*n*, 265 and *n*, 266*n**, 267*n*, 307*n*, 313, 333, 341, 344* and *n*, 345 and *n**, 346* and *n**, 350, 351*, 359 and *n*, 361*, 362 and *n**, 363* and *n**, 364, 365, 369, 373*, 374 and *n*, 375*, 377, 278*, 379*n*, 380, 384, 386*n*, 389, 399*n*, 408 and

n, 415, 417*n*, 418, 420*n*, 425*n*, 432; Appendices, 450

Tunstall, Marmaduke, son of Brian Tunstall, 344*n*

Tunstall, Sir Richard, grandfather of Bishop Tunstall, 344*n*

Tunstall, Thomas, father of Bishop Tunstall, 344*n*

Tupling, G. H., 192*n*

Turin, 270*n*

Turner, R., Appendices, 465

Turner, William, adversary of Stephen Gardiner, 374*n*, 382

Tuscany, Appendices, 444

Tyburn, 134, 212*n*, 227*n*

Tyler, R., Appendices, 465

Tyms, William, Rector of Hockley, accused of heresy, 359*n**

Tyndale (or Huchyns), William, burnt in Flanders as a heretic (1536), 15, 16 and *n*, 20 (quotation), 149*n*, 176*n*, 234 and *n*, 306*, 307*n**, 308, 318*n*, 365, 366, 369 and *n*, 376, 382; Appendices, 476

Tytler, B. F., 31*n*

U

Ughtred, Sir Anthony, 286

Uhlirz, M., 9*n*

Ulysses, 31

Urban VI, Pope (1378-89), 10*n*

Urbino, 42*n*

Urbino, Cardinal of (*see* Rovere, Giuliano della)

"Uses and Wills," Act of, 25 and *n*, 172 and *n*, 175*n*, 295

Ushaw College, Appendices, 439

Usherwood, R. C., 364*n*

"Utopia" of Sir Thomas More (1515-16), 17 and *n**, 224*n**, 231* and *n**, 232*n*, 234*n**, 345 and *n*

V

Vaissière (*see Bourrilly* and *Vaissière*)

Vale Royal (Cheshire), Abbey of, 183*n*

Valenza, Appendices, 478

Vannes, Peter, Latin Secretary and agent of Henry VIII, 347*n*

Van Ortroy, 96*n*, 200*n**, 204*n*, 206*n*, 223*n*, 289*n*; Appendices, 449, 450*, 451*

Varillas, Anthony, historian (1624-96), 105*n*; Appendices, 462

Vasari, Giorgio, painter, architect and biographer (1512-74), 253n
Vatican Council, 383
Vaughan, Stephen, friend of Cromwell, 110n*, 288n, 309n
Ven. English College, Rome, 205n
Venice, 4n, 41n, 76n*, 252n, 263*, 265n, 278n, 280, 281*, 286, 319, 350; Appendices, 455
Venice, St. Mark's, organist of, 41n
Venice, Abbot of San Giorgio Maggiore in, 263
Vergerio, Pier Paulo (†1565), Nuncio to Ferdinand, King of the Romans (1533-36), 105n*, 254n, 265n, 282n, 298n, 400n*
Vergil, Polydore, 42n, 45n, 52n, 204n, 305n
Verona, 264n, 266n, 278n
Verona, Bishop of, Appendices, 478
Verzosa, Juan de, Director of the Spanish Archives in Rome, Appendices, 441
Vicenza, 360
Victoria, Queen of England, 205n
Vida, Ottenello, secretary to Vergerio, 282n
Vienna, 97n, 320, 322n, 398n, 416n; Appendices, 478
Vigne, Pierre de la, Chancellor to Frederick II (†1246), 127n
Vilenus, 203
Villa, Antonio Rodriguez, 5n
Villach (Austria), 320
Villanova, St. Thomas of, 260n
Vilvorde, near Brussels, 306
Viterbo, 259n, 283
Vittorelli, Andrea, editor of the second edition of Vitae . . . R. Pontificum et S.R.E. cardinalium, 221n; Appendices, 451*
Vives, Juan Luis, humanist and Spanish theologian (1492-1540),
Vocht, H. de, 261n
Voigt, 78n
Volusenus (or Wilson), F., Scotch philosopher (†1546), 374
Volz, H., 356n

W

Wadding, 9n
Wake, 103n
Wakefield, Robert, Hebrew Professor at Oxford, 75n, 197n

Walachia, Appendices, 481
Walachia, Gregory Ghika VIII of, Appendices, 481
Walberg, E., 306n
Walden (Essex), 384
Walden, Prior of, 183n
Wales, 36n, 160n
Wales, Prince of, 36n*, 38, 51n
Wallingford (Berks), Dean of, 164
Wallis, J. E. W., 199n
Wallop, Sir John, ambassador in France, 106n, 108n, 254 and n, 256n, 361, 396
Walsingham (Norfolk), 304 and n*
Walsingham, Thomas, chronicler, 143
Walter, Rev. W. J., Appendices, 454
Waltham (Essex), 75, 318*
Waltham Abbey, 185, 197, 198n; Appendices, 447
Walther, W., 34n, 40n
Walworth, James, Carthusian executed for denying royal supremacy, 183n
Warblington (Hants), 271
Ward, Thomas, Appendices, 463
Warham, William, Bishop of London (1502-03), Archbishop of Canterbury (1503-32), xii; 2, 18n, 32 and n*, 37n, 39*, 53 and n, 79, 85 and n*, 95, 96n, 100 and n, 104 and n, 144n, 209, 286, 321n, 344, 354, 361
Wars of the Roses (see Roses)
Warwick, County of, 343n
Warwick, Earl of, 36n, 45n, 257n
Watkyns, Richard, visitor of the English monasteries, 164n
Watson, Thomas, Chaplain to Stephen Gardiner, Appendices, 450
Watt, Joachim von, Zwinglian (†1551), 334n
Waugh, W. T., 93n
Waynflete, William of, Bishop of Winchester (1447-86), 143 and n*
Webb, John, 249n
Webb, C. J., 306n
Webb, S. and B., 196n
Webster, Augustine, Carthusian, Prior of Axholme, 133, 134n, 329n
Weekes, W. Self, 171n
Weever, 142n
Weg, Jervis, 4n
Weimar, 401, 414n, 415n
Weiss, 109n
Welland, River, 174n
Wells (see Bath and Wells)

Wensleydale (Yorks), 177

West, Nicholas, Bishop of Ely (1515-33), 154

Westlake, Appendices, 447

Westminster, 31, 39n, 88, 94, 100, 122, 130n, 149n, 219*, 249, 314, 326n, 349n, 369, 409n

Westminster, Abbey of, surrender of, 182n

Westminster, Abbot of, 242*, 243

Westminster, Bishop of, 374n

Westminster Hall, 248

Westminster, See of, 193n*, 364n

Westmorland, 175 and n*, 180

Weston, Sir Francis, 322

Whalley Abbey (Lancs), Cistercian, 181, 199n

Wharton, Henry, Appendices, 462*

Wharton, Sir Thomas, 191n

Whitechurch, Edward, 16th century London printer, 307n, 333n

Whitehall, 73, 74n

Whiting, Richard, Abbot of Glastonbury, 185n*

Whitney, J. P., 125n

Whittingham, Charles, Appendices, 446

Wickham Legg, J., 335n, 336n*

Wiclif (or Wycliffe), 9 and n*, 10n*, 11* and n*, 12n*, 13 and n*, 14n, 33, 143, 148, 149n, 150, 333 and n*, 382, 384 and n; Appendices, 464

Wiclif Society, 9n

Wight, Isle of, See of, 122n

Wilkins, 19n, 95n

Wilkins' formula recognising "supreme head," 96n; Appendices, 465

William the Conqueror, King of England (1066-†1087), 2n, 3, 269n

Williams, Sir J., 190n

Williams, John, visitor of the English monasteries, 164n

Williams, Joshua, 25n

Williams, Richard, Thomas Cromwell's nephew, 190n, 286 and n

Willoughby (Warwick), 343n

Willoughby, Dr., King's chaplain, 337n

Willoughby, Sir Robert, first Baron Willoughby de Broke, 29n

Willoughby, Thomas, 269n

Wilson, Dr. Nicholas, 425n

Wilson, servant to Bishop Fisher, 246n

Wilson, Rev. R. Mercer, 156n

Wilton (Wilts), Abbess of, 146n

Wiltshire, 119, 157, 325n

Wiltshire, Earl of, 45n, 48, 76n, 81n, 134, 319, 348n, 477n

Wimborne (Dorset), 257n

Winbolt, S. E., 199n

Winchcombe, Abbot of, 23

Winchelsey, 32 and n*

Winchester, 53n, 73*, 85n, 104, 111, 290n, 304, 378 and n

Winchester, Bishop of, 20n*, 22n, 37n, 39, 73*, 93n, 101, 143, 208 and n, 238, 240n, 251n, 337n, 341, 360n, 370n*, 374, 375, 378n, 380, 386, 417n, 425n

Winchester College, 355

Winchester House, Stephen Gardiner's London residence, 208n

Winchester, See of, 194n, 208n, 261 348, 354n; Appendices, 471

Windsor, 78n, 83n, 144, 178, 325n, 337, 346n, 348n, 369, 370, 378n

Windsor Castle, 326n

Windsor, St. George's Chapel, 74n

Wingfield, Sir Richard, 346n

Witham (Somerset), Charterhouse of, 135n, 197n

Witney, E. A., and *Cram, P. P.*, 42n

Wittenberg and the Wittenberg Articles (1536), 17n, 233, 309, 368n, 395, 400, 401* and n, 402* and n*, 403* and n, 404, 414 and n; Appendices, 462

Woburn (Beds), Abbot of, 160

Wobun (Beds), Cistercian Abbey of, 184n

Wolf, G., 9n, 10n, 232n, 233n

Wolf, Reginald, 16th century editor, 362n

Wolman, Dr. Richard, 53n

Wolsey, Thomas, Bishop of Lincoln (1514), Archbishop of York (1514-30), Cardinal (1515), 5* and n*, 6* and n*, 7n*, 14 and n, 20 and n*, 21n*, 22 and n*, 23, 24n, 25 and n*, 33n*, 40n, 42n, 45n*, 46n*, 49n*, 51 and n, 52 and n*, 53 and n*, 54* and n*, 55 and n*, 56 and n*, 57* and n*, 58* and n*, 59 and n*, 60* and n*, 62* and n, 63, 64 and n, 65 and n*, 66, 67n* 69 and n, 70 and n*, 71* and n*, 72 and n*, 73* and n*, 74 and n*, 75 and n*, 78n, 79, 90, 91, 92n, 93n, 94*, 97n, 111, 119*, 143n,

144* and *n**, 145* and *n**, 146* and *n**, 147 and *n*, 149, 163, 168*n*, 177*n*, 193*n*, 203, 204* and *n**, 205, 206, 108*n*, 210, 237* and *n*, 26€, 286, 287*n**, 288* and *n*, 289**, 290* and *n**, 292, 293, 306*n*, 309, 317, 335*n*, 338, 341, 342* and *n**, 343*, 344, 345*n**, 346* and *n*, 347* and *n*, 348 and *n*, 351, 395, 398*n*; Appendices, 442, 457, 464, 469**, 471

Wolsey, a spy, 173*n*

Wood, John, servant to Sir Thomas More, 243*n*, 246*n*

Wood, Michael (*pseudonym*), 355*n*

Wood, Anthony, 4*n*, 18*n*, 21*n**, 257*n*, 260*n*, 344, 355*n*; Appendices, 454, 460, 463

Wood, Clement, Appendices, 441

Wood, Miss Everett, 326*n*

Woodstock (Oxfordshire), 371*n*

Worcester, 28*n*, 296, 347 and *n*

Worcester, Bishop of, 20*n**, 37*n*, 38*n*, 56*n**, 61*n*, 76, 154, 196, 242*n*, 304, 308*n*, 334, 366*n*, 373*n*, 382, 398*n*, 417*n*, 422

Worcester, Chapter of, 130*n*

Worcester, County of, 157, 343*n*

Worcester, Earl of, 29*n*

Worcester, Prior of, 183*n*

Worcester, See of, 208*n*, 380

Wordsworth, Christopher, 34*n*; Appendices, 458, 460

Wordsworth and *Littlehales*, 138*n*

Workman, H. B., 9*n*, 12*n*

Worms, 365

Worms, Diet of (1540), 345

Wotton, Nicholas, Dean of Canterbury and of York (†1566), 310*n*

Woysey, John, Bishop of Exeter (1519-51; and 1553-54), 321*n*, 410*n*

Wright, A., 223*n*

Wright, editor of letters relating to

"Suppression of the Monasteries," 161*n*; Appendices, 447

Wriothesley, Sir Thomas, secretary to Thomas Cromwell, Chancellor of England (1544-47), Earl of Southampton on accession of Edward VI (1547), 69*n*, 189*n*, 191*n*, 255*n*, 312, 313, 378*n**, 380

Wriothesley, Sir Thomas, chronicler, Appendices, 440, 445

Wurm, C. F., 116*n*

Wyatt, Sir Henry, 47

Wyatt, Sir Thomas, ambassador at the court of Charles V, 278, 360*n**

Wyatt, Thomas, poet, 49

Wykys, Elizabeth, wife of Thomas Cromwell, 286

Wynter, Thomas, son of Wolsey, Archdeacon of Norfolk, 21*n*, 347*n*

Y

Yarmouth (Norfolk), Priory of, 299*n*

York, 20*n*, 21*n**, 73, 74, 85*n*, 97**, 111, 122, 179, 180**, 183*n*, 314*n*, 344, 361

York, Archbishop of, 76*n*, 83*n*, 88*n*, 93*n*, 140*n**, 133*n*, 155, 308*n*, 319, 331, 359, 373*n*, 374*n*, 398

York, Cardinal of, 292

York, Dean of, 164

York, Diocese of, 161*n*, 162, 208*n*, 261-62; Appendices, 471

York, Duke of, 29*n*, 54*n*

York, House of, 47*n*, 269 and *n*

York Palace, London, 73, 74*n*, 262

Yorkshire, 152*n*, 160, 162, 168, 171, 173*n*, 175, 176*n**, 179, 200, 272, 298

Z

Zimmermann, A., S.F., 264*n*; Appendices, 456*

Zoar, 167*n**